ELEMENTS OF NUCLEAR ENGINEERING

ELEMENTS OF NUCLEAR ENGINEERING

By Jacques P. Ligou

École Polytechnique Fédérale de Lausanne (Switzerland)

Revised edition translated from the French by
Sara Mitter
with the assistance of P. K. Mitter,
Directeur de Recherche,
Centre National de la Recherche Scientifique,
Université Pierre et Marie Curie, Paris

Routledge
Taylor & Francis Group
LONDON AND NEW YORK

First published 1986 by Harwood Academic Publishers

Published 2020 by Routledge
2 Park Square, Milton Park, Abingdon, Oxon OX14 4RN
52 Vanderbilt Avenue, New York, NY 10017

First issued in paperback 2020

Routledge is an imprint of the Taylor & Francis Group, an informa business

We also thank these companies for granting us permission to use the following figures:
Combustion Engineering Inc: Fig. 5.19a; General Atomic; Figs. 2.11, 5.31, 5.32, and 5.33; General Electric Co: Figs. 5.19b, 5.21 and 5.23; Novatome: Figs. 5.34 and 5.35; Westinghouse Electric Corp: Fig. 5.24.

Library of Congress Cataloging-in-Publication Data

Ligou, Jacques, 1930–
Elements of nuclear engineering.

Translation of: Installations nucléaires.
Bibliography: p.
Includes index.
1. Nuclear engineering. I. Title.
TK9145.L5313 1986 621.48 86-19401

ISBN 13: 978-0-367-58035-3 (pbk)
ISBN 13: 978-3-7186-0363-3 (hbk)

To Helyett

Contents

Acknowledgements

Unfortunately, it is not possible for us to cite all the nuclear engineers who provided firsthand information. We would however like to thank particularly Professor W. Paskievici, Director of the Institute of Nuclear Engineering of the École Polytechnique of Montreal, thanks to whom we were able to present the latest characteristics of CANDU reactors. Numerous figures and tables come from documents which he most kindly sent to us.

We wish also to thank Dr J. Rognon, sub-director of the "Forces Motrices" of Berne who was kind enough to give an attentive reading to the first draft. His comments were highly useful, especially with regard to the nuclear fuel cycle in which he is a specialist. On the didactic level we are very grateful for the pertinent remarks of Dr A. S. Tai of the "Office Fédéral de la Propriété Intellectuelle" at Berne. Because it was of interest to have the point of view of a "client", we asked M. F. Gabela of the Mechanics section to make a critical examination of the course. We have taken his remarks very much into consideration.

Finally, we wish to render thanks to our former colleagues J. Panossian, Director of Studies at Framatome, and J.-P. Crette, Director of Studies at Novatome, to whom we owe much professionally.

This introduction could not conclude without a word of thanks to all those who participated in the material realization of this book: Denise Besson for the typing of the manuscript; François Gabela, Jacques Rognon, and Ai Siang Tai for their comments and criticisms; Claude Jacquat for the illustrations, and Tran Trach Minh for correcting the proofs, as well as the Institute of Atomic Engineering of the EPFL, without which this work could not have appeared.

Introduction

Type of teaching concerned

This work should be considered as a simple introduction to nuclear engineering. It covers and somewhat enlarges upon a set of courses that we currently give at the École Polytechnique Fédérale of Lausanne, Switzerland.

The first of these courses is meant for students of mechanics and electricity. These students, without claiming to become accomplished nuclear engineers, must nonetheless acquire the basic notions of nuclear energy. This form of energy, whose contribution to electricity production exceeds 30% in many countries, has attained sufficient maturity so that today's young engineer must have a minimum knowledge in this domain, comparable to that demanded of him in other disciplines.

The second course given in this domain is meant for working engineers who come to the EPFL to follow a continuing education course on energy, which includes a nuclear component. Although more qualitative, this teaching is analogous to the preceding.

In both cases, these courses are intended for people with a good technical and scientific background who nonetheless are fairly ignorant of the subject. This necessitates a first chapter which presents a few indispensable concepts of nuclear physics. Finally, in order to finish with the "rules of the game" that were imposed during the writing, we should note that we were asked to cover as large a domain as possible; this accounts for the title adopted. Thus the reader will find that we have treated questions ranging from thermonuclear fusion to wastes, from fission reactors to uranium enrichment, etc. For these reasons, we have only been able to touch upon these varied subjects.

It is in this spirit that the first seven chapters were written; initially, we had planned to restrict ourselves to this. Nonetheless, from the outset certain appendices were envisaged to respond to the desire for rigor of some readers. It appeared that these appendices corresponded more or less to the course entitled "Neutron Physics" (optional course of the physics department), so that we have decided to give them a certain importance. As a result, all the courses of the EPFL in the domain of nuclear engineering were covered. This does not put into question the initial project, since in spite of their extent, these appendices are not necessary for the understanding of the other chapters.

General organization

By virtue of the preceding, this work can be used in different ways.

The hurried, nonspecialist reader might limit himself to Chapters 1 and 3, with a quick overview of Chapters 4 and 5. This elementary approach should enable him qualitatively to understand the working of nuclear power plants and to approach Chapters 6 and 7 concerning the environment and the fuel cycle. This material can serve as a basis for a one-semester course.

A more thorough reading of the first seven chapters will evidently lead to a better understanding of the subject, the more so in that the subdivision of the text has been conceived in this light. In particular, the assimilation of elementary notions of reactor physics (Chapter 4) and of thermohydraulics (Chapter 5) will enable the reader to understand the reasons for certain choices concerning the design or the mode of operation of installations described elsewhere. Naturally, as we have ourselves discovered, it is difficult to teach this much material in one semester.

A course in neutronics meant for physics students (who are supposed to know nuclear physics) would be based essentially on Chapters 3 and 4 and Appendices 8 and 9, which form a unit, with Chapter 5 concerning nuclear power plants serving an illustrative role. Despite their theoretical aspect, these appendices have been written with a utilitarian goal and neutronic questions which are of little or no interest for nuclear reactors have been systematically put aside, even if they often lead to very beautiful problems of mathematical physics (these problems can be reserved for exercise sessions). Thus, contrary to usage, we do not present the "two-group" formalism which is unnecessarily complicated for the understanding of the functioning of thermal reactors and much too schematic for making thermal reactor calculations. We have thus preferred to present in Chapter 9 the currently utilized methods without claiming to treat in depth a subject which is clearly at a post-graduate level.

Finally, thermonuclear fusion has been treated in an independent fashion in Chapter 2. Given the state of the art, we have restricted ourselves to describing the principles on which current researches are based, so this chapter is at the same level as the first. This is the reason why it follows the first, but this does not imply any preference. Moreover, one can see that the problems posed at the end of Chapter 1 concerning fusion and fission naturally lead to Chapters 2 and 3.

In conclusion, we are conscious of having taken certain risks in pursuing several goals at the same time. It would clearly have been easier to focus on one particular type of reader (physicists, for example), but we nevertheless hope that this choice will not detract from the clarity of the work, even if sometimes certain repetitions could not be avoided.

Conventions

Each of the ten chapters of this book is identified by an arabic numeral (Chapter 3). Each chapter is divided into sections identified by two arabic numerals (7.6). Each section is subdivided into subsections identified by three arabic numerals (5.3.7).

The bibliographic references are numbered continuously and indicated by a single arabic numeral in brackets [3]; the page numbers concerned are placed in parentheses (pp. 313–317).

Technical terms are underlined the first time they appear. Underlining is also used to emphasize important points.

The figures and tables are numbered continuously by chapter and identified by two arabic numerals (Table 5.18), (Figure 5.23). To the extent that they represent a step in a demonstration, the equations are numbered in the same fashion, by two arabic numerals in parentheses without any other particular mention (4.50).

FOUNDATIONS OF NUCLEAR PHYSICS

1.1 COMPOSITION OF THE ATOM

1.1.1 Rutherford's Atom

At the beginning of the nineteenth century, Dalton set out to reconsider on a more solid basis the atomic hypothesis of the Greek philosophers. How fruitful this hypothesis was for chemistry is well known. The atom, the smallest quantity of matter associated to a simple chemical type, must possess all the properties necessary for the understanding of macroscopic phenomena. In particular, the atom must be electrically neutral, as is the matter of which it is a part.

It was not until the beginning of the twentieth century that there emerged a preliminary notion of the composition of the atom. First, the discovery of the electron, the particle carrying the smallest negative electric charge that one can find in nature (experiments of Millikan and Perrin), provided a crucial piece of information. Experiments in which X-rays were scattered off simple bodies showed that the number of electrons per atom was independent of the density of the irradiated samples. This number, Z, was thus a characteristic of the atom, and, more importantly, it was none other than the atomic number of Mendeleyev's classification. This was confirmed in a more precise fashion by Moseley in his interpretations of the spectra of X-ray emission of atoms.

The condition of neutrality evidently made it necessary to postulate the existence of positive charges equal in number to that of the electrons. This was not surprising. The idea that matter, although neutral, was made up of charges of two signs was supported by numerous previous experiments: electrification by the rubbing of insulators (electrostatics), ionization of chemical substances in solution, etc. At first it was supposed that the positive charges (of unknown nature) and the negative charges (electrons) were uniformly distributed in the atom (Thompson), but this hypothesis was rapidly discarded.

α-particle scattering experiments (§1.2.1), interpreted by Rutherford, indicated that the positive charges were necessarily localized at the center of the atom. In addition, these experiments furnished the value of these charges, and thus a new determination of the atomic number Z.

The first valid atomic model is that shown in Figure 1.1. It is known nowadays as Rutherford's atom.

Z electrons of charge $(-e)(e = 1.602\ 10^{-19} C)$ revolve around the nucleus of charge +Z e insuring the neutrality of the atom. The analogy with the solar system is evident ($1/r^2$ interactions in both cases), but this analogy should not be pushed too far, because quantum mechanics teaches us that one can speak at most of a "cloud of electrons" associated to the nucleus.

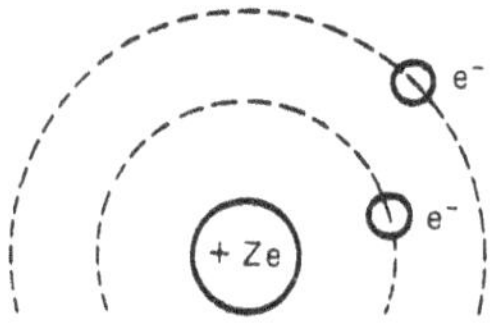

FIGURE 1.1.

The first measurements of the mass of the electron showed that it is much smaller than that of the lightest nucleus, the proton, which is nothing other than the nucleus of hydrogen (Z = 1).

$$\frac{m_H}{m_e} = 1837$$

It follows that practically all the mass of an atom is contained in its nucleus.

An atom can easily lose or gain some electrons, in which case its neutrality is no longer assured. One obtains thus a positive or a negative ion. In particular, an atomic nucleus or nuclide can be considered as an atom which has been ionized Z times (having lost its Z electrons).

It is important to note in the preceding that the charge of the nucleus remains the same, whether the atom is neutral or has been ionized. Only nuclear processes (intervening in the heart of the nucleus) can change the charge of the nucleus.

1.1.2 Comments

For the sake of precision, we shall say a few words about the quantum nature of atoms. What corresponds to each electron is not one trajectory (Rutherford's model) but various quantum numbers: the first roughly determines the energy, the second the orbital angular momentum, etc. Thus the peripheral layer contains electrons which are on the average at a large distance from the nucleus, with large quantum numbers and in particular, small binding energies. On the other hand, for the innermost layers, the average distances to the nucleus are minimal, the quantum numbers close to one, and there are large binding energies. Keeping all this in mind, one can continue to use the language of classical physics.

In particular, it can be shown that the dimensions of the atom and of its nucleus are respectively of the order of 10^{-8}cm and 10^{-13}cm, although the notion of distance makes little sense in quantum physics. This shows the extent to which the structure of the atom is heterogeneous.

Nonetheless, the interaction of electromagnetic waves (light, X-rays) with matter can only be understood in the framework of the quantum model of atoms. These waves must also be quantized. In other words, there exists a quantum of energy, the photon, which represents a "grain of light" just as the atom represented a "grain of matter" (Planck). The photon is a particle of zero rest-mass, electrically neutral, travelling in vacuum with the speed of light. When an electron jumps from one level to a deeper one, a photon is emitted (Bohr). In the same way, the opposite transition requires the absorption of a photon. From the macroscopic point of view, this implies that matter emits radiation in the first case, and absorbs it in the second. In the limiting case, a very energetic photon can eject a weakly-bound atomic electron. This is the photo-electric effect which was interpreted for the first time by Einstein.

1.1.3 Units of Energy

In atomic and nuclear physics we introduce the electron-volt (eV), which represents the energy acquired by an electron having traversed a potential difference of 1 V:

$$1 \text{ eV} = 1.602\ 10^{-19}\text{C} \times 1 \text{ V} = 1.602\ 10^{-19}\text{J}$$

A multiple of the electron-volt, the MeV (10^6 eV), is frequently used.

The energy necessary to tear off the outermost electrons is of the order of a few eV. The energies associated to chemical reactions (corresponding to the rearrangements of the outermost layers) are of the same order. The extraction of the innermost electrons requires a few keV (absorption of X-rays). We will see that the phenomena which take place in the heart of the nucleus involve energies of the order of a MeV.

This latter unit has a practical interest. When one speaks of a proton accelerator of 1 MeV, it is clear that this refers to the energy of each of the protons, whereas if one speaks of a megajoule, one thinks rather of a burst (ensemble) of protons produced by the accelerator in the course of one impulse.

In summary, the microscopic unit is the electron-volt and the macroscopic unit the joule. Because electromagnetic radiation also has a corpuscular nature, the energy of its constituent photons will be given in eV (light), keV (X-rays) or in MeV. The passage from the classical concept to the quantum concept is made with the help of the celebrated formula $E = h\nu$ (Einstein), which enables one to calculate the energy E of a photon from the frequency ν of the corresponding radiation. Planck's constant h is a fundamental constant of contemporary physics.

$$h = 6.625\ 10^{-34}\ \text{J.s (joule x second)}$$

Or, $\quad = 4.14\ \ 10^{-15}$ eV/Hz (electron-volt/Hertz)

The above numbers indicate how small is the energy associated to a photon. Classical physics corresponds to the approximation $h = 0$.

1.2 STRUCTURE OF THE NUCLEUS

1.2.1 First Experimental Results

The preceding model does not teach us anything about the structure of the nucleus; at most we know that the nucleus contains practically all the mass of the atom. The very first data were furnished by the radioactivity of uranium. Uranium was discovered by Becquerel at the beginning of this century. Interested by electromagnetic emissions (atomic or molecular) of certain salts (fluorescence), Becquerel observed that uranium always emitted the same rays irrespective of the chemical form in which it was being studied. Moreover, these rays were of a new type, which he called α, β, and γ. In electric or magnetic fields, α and β rays deviated, whereas γ rays did not. Detailed studies led to the following conclusions:

- α rays are composed of helium nuclei of charge + 2e;
- β rays represent electrons (negative) analogous to cathode rays; these electrons have energies much higher than those of atomic electrons;

• γ rays are equivalent to X-rays, but much harder (more energetic).

The importance of the energies brought into play (MeV and not keV or eV, as in atomic processes) and especially the emission of helium nuclei led to the conclusion that these rays came from the decay of nuclei. This explains at the same time why chemical structures had no influence on these emissions, as Becquerel had already noted.

1.2.2 Atomic Masses

We know that chemistry is based on the atomic hypothesis (18th century). Long before the elementary atoms had been isolated (by mass spectrography) chemists had been able to determine the atomic mass ratios m(X) of various elements (but not the absolute masses) by reflecting on the weighable quantities of matter M(X) also called gram atoms. These ratios can be written:

$$\frac{m(X)}{m(O)} = \frac{M(X)}{M(O)}$$

where X stands for an arbitrary element and O stands for oxygen taken as a reference. By arbitrarily taking 16 g for the gram atom of oxygen, and using the above ratios furnished by the study of typical chemical reactions, it was possible to set up the first table of atomic masses. It was found, for example:

$$M(H) \cong 1$$
$$M(C) \cong 12$$
$$M(O) = 16 \text{ (by definition)}$$
$$M(S) \cong 32$$

The proportionality relation given above implies that all gram atoms contain the same number N_A (very large) of elementary atoms:

$$\frac{M(X)}{m(X)} = \frac{M(O) = 16}{m(O)} = N_A = 6.023\ 10^{23}$$

N_A is called Avogadro's number.

It was only with the advent of modern physics that this number could be determined, but such knowledge was not necessary at the time chemistry was being developed. At that stage, it was quickly seen that most of the masses of gram atoms could be expressed by a whole number if one took 16 grams for oxygen (see the above example). In particular, one found approximately 1 for hydrogen (the lightest atom). There were some anomalies (for example chlorine M(Cl) = 35.5), but the discovery of isotopes put everything into order (two isotopes have the same atomic number Z, but different atomic masses). Provided one considers various isotopes and not chemical elements which are mixtures of isotopes, one finds that atomic masses are without exception very close to integer multiples of the atomic mass of hydrogen. The slight deviation from this law was attributed to the lack of precision of atomic mass measurements, but we shall see that in fact this deviation has a profound physical significance (§1.3.4).

1.2.3 Conclusion

Given these results, it was tempting to conclude that all nuclei could be constructed with the help of A nucleons, each having the mass of a proton (nucleus of hydrogen), with $A \cong M(X)/M(H)$. There remained two possibilities:

- All nucleons are protons. The mass condition is thus satisfied without respecting neutrality because the nucleus has charge + A e, whereas the external electronic cloud has charge -Z e (Z is known independently thanks to spectroscopy). It suffices to admit the existence of numerous "nuclear electrons" (A - Z), to reestablish the neutrality of the atom without affecting the mass balances. At the same time, β radioactivity was explained.

- The A nucleons have the mass of the proton but among them only Z are really protons, whereas the others (A - Z) are neutrons, which are neutral as their name indicates. In this case, the β radioactivity is explained by saying that the nucleus is unstable, a neutron decaying by the reaction: $n \rightarrow p + \beta^-$ (proton + electron). In a free state the neutron decays spontaneously in the same way, which explains why the free neutron is never seen in nature.

Of these two hypotheses, evidently the second is correct. Theoretical considerations on the parity of the number of particles which comprise the nucleus led to the rejection of the first hypothesis (existence of nuclear electrons), but it was of course the experimental discovery of the neutron which was decisive.

1.2.4 Discovery of the Neutron

The preceding hypothesis was verified only in 1931-32. Nuclear physics at that time dealt with transmutations (nuclear reactions) resulting from the interaction of beams of charged particles with matter. The ancient dream of alchemists was being realized. The available sources of ions were of two types:

- α sources (helium nuclei) coming from the natural radioactivity of uranium, of which we have already spoken; more exactly, one used two "descendants" of uranium, radium and polonium, which exist in equilibrium with it (§1.4.2);
- accelerators producing light ions, protons, deuterons, etc., having the desired energy (a few MeV).

It was relatively easy to identify the reaction products when they were charged particles. But in bombarding beryllium with α rays emitted by radium, the appearance of electrically neutral radiation was noted. One thought of course of γ rays, which had already been discovered (cf. the natural radioactivity of uranium cited earlier). Subsequently, Joliot-Curie observed that this radiation induced emissions of protons in hydrogen media. To explain this phenomenon he invoked the Compton effect, that is, the collision of a γ photon with a proton. The Compton effect, which results from the interaction of the γ photons with atomic electrons, takes place all the time (it plays an important role in studies of the penetration of matter by γ rays). In contrast, the "proton" Compton effect only takes place for extremely high energy γs ($\cong$ 1000 MeV). This was in contradiction with what was known of the energy balance of this reaction, which could already be produced at that time (measurement of the stopping distance of charged particles).

It was thus necessary to abandon the hypothesis of a γ radiation. It was Chadwick who had the idea of invoking the neutron, an idea which was, moreover, already "in the air" (see the preceding theoretical considerations).

Events followed rapidly, and Fermi discovered the first properties of the neutron, in particular, its ability to activate a large number of materials; and all the more so, if it had been initially slowed down. In other words, a nucleus can transform itself into an unstable nucleus by neutron capture, and hence become radioactive (generally β plus γ). Because it is neutral, the neutron does not have to overcome the "potential barrier" which nuclei set up against charged particles (Coulomb repulsion). We shall come back to this property of neutrons.

1.3 NUCLEAR REACTIONS AND NOTATIONS

1.3.1 Symbols

In accordance with the preceding, the nucleus is composed of A nucleons, made up of Z protons and (A-Z) neutrons. The nucleus X will be denoted as follows:

$$_{Z}X^{A}$$

Other notations will be used often, but A will always figure as an upper index and Z as a lower index:

$$X_{Z}^{A}\ ,\ {}_{Z}^{A}X\ ,\ \text{etc.}$$

Two different isotopes have the same value of Z and hence identical chemical properties.

Very often, we will not distinguish nuclei from atoms because in nuclear physics the energies brought into play are such that the external electronic cloud (which is essential in chemistry) has practically no influence on processes.

The mass number, A, and the atomic number, Z, are integers. With these notations, nuclear reactions are written for example as:

$$_{2}He^{4} + {}_{4}Be^{9} \rightarrow {}_{6}C^{12} + {}_{0}n^{1} \quad \text{(discovery of the neutron)}$$

We see that in contrast to chemical elements, atomic nuclei are characterized by two integers. Except for heavy nuclei, such as uranium, the numbers of protons and neutrons are approximately the same (A is of the order of 2 Z). This explains why Mendeleyev's idea of classifying chemical elements by order of increasing atomic masses was fruitful, whereas we know today that the atomic number Z is the appropriate parameter.

An unstable nucleus will be denoted $_{Z}X^{A\,*}$ and radioactivity is given by the equations:

a) $_{Z}X^{A\,*} \rightarrow {}_{Z-2}X^{A-4} + {}_{2}He^{4}$ (α radioactivity)

b) $_{Z}X^{A\,*} \rightarrow {}_{Z+1}X^{A} + \beta^{-}$ (β radioactivity)

c) $_{Z}X^{A\,*} \rightarrow {}_{Z}X^{A} + \gamma$ (γ radioactivity)

In the last case we have a simple rearrangement of nucleons which gives rise to the emission of a γ photon (zero mass and zero charge).

β and γ radioactivities are often associated, because the nucleus ${}_{Z+1}X^A$ (b) is almost always excited and leads to the emission of a γ (c).

In order to balance a nuclear reaction, it suffices to apply the following two laws:

- The number of nucleons remains fixed, in other words, the sum of the mass numbers is an invariant with the convention A = 0 for β^- particles (an electron is not a nucleon).
- Electric charge is conserved, or if one prefers, the sum of the atomic numbers is invariant, with the convention Z = -1 for β^- particles and Z = 0 for the neutron.

It is customary for electrons of nuclear origin to be denoted β^- to distinguish them from "usual" electrons (atomic electrons, cathode beams, etc.)

At this stage we have introduced four elementary particles: the proton (${}_1H^1$), the neutron (${}_0n^1$), the β^- particle (${}_{-1}e^0$) and the photon γ (A = Z = 0).

1.3.2 Other Elementary Particles

There exists also a β^+ radioactivity which corresponds to the emission of positive electrons (positrons). As soon as positrons are emitted, they are annihilated by the ordinary electrons (negative). Because of this, the positron, the antiparticle of the electron, does not exist in a free state. Besides, the radioactive bodies that we shall consider will rarely be β^+ emitters. For these reasons, in the following we will disregard this particle. Our purpose in mentioning it now is only to explain why the electron emitted in β radioactivity described in the preceding paragraphs was noted β^-. For the sake of completeness, we must also mention that during β^- and β^+ decays, a neutrino is emitted simultaneously. This neutral particle, of negligible mass, interacts so little with matter that we can ignore it, although it is produced in large quantities in nuclear reactors. Discovered in 1956, its existence had been predicted much earlier by Fermi in the context of his explanation as to why, during β decay, the emitted electron carried only a fraction of the available energy.

1.3.3 Calculation of Nuclide Masses

In practice, we will keep the masses of gram atoms, and the (true) masses will be obtained from them easily with the help of Avogadro's number.

$$m(X) = \frac{M(X)}{N_A} \quad (\S 1.2.2)$$

We obtain for example for carbon ${}_6C^{12}$:

$$m \cong 2 \times 10^{-23}\ g \qquad \text{taking } M \cong 12 \text{ and } N_A = 6.023\ 10^{23}$$

The masses thus defined are so small that we introduce a new unit.

The atomic mass unit (a.m.u.) represents by definition one-twelfth of the mass of the isotope ${}_6C^{12}$ of carbon:

$$1 \text{ a.m.u.} = \frac{1}{12}\ m\ (C)$$

or $$\frac{1}{12}\frac{12g}{N_A} = \frac{1g}{N_A} = 1.66\ 10^{-24}\ g$$

It is thus the mass of a hypothetical atom of which the corresponding gram atom would represent exactly 1 g, that is, approximately the mass of hydrogen. With this unit, one can express the masses of nucleons:

proton: $m_p = 1.007277$ a.m.u. $= 1.6725\ 10^{-24}$ g

neutron: $m_n = 1.008665$ a.m.u. $= 1.6748\ 10^{-24}$ g

with: $\frac{m_p}{m_e} = 1836 \quad m(C) = 12$ a.m.u. (by definition)

Let us note that today, in contrast to past usage, carbon and no longer oxygen constitutes the reference.

For practical calculations, we will always use the a.m.u., and the approximate mass of a nucleus will be:

$$m(X) \cong Z\, m_p + (A-Z)\, m_n \qquad (1.1)$$

In other words, if one supposes $m_p \cong m_n \cong 1$ a.m.u., we get the important result:

$$\left.\begin{aligned} m(X) \text{ (in a.m.u.)} &\cong A \\ m(X) \text{ (in g)} &\cong \frac{A}{N_A} \end{aligned}\right\} \qquad (1.2)$$

which is in accord with the conclusions of subsec. 1.2.3.

With the exception of the considerations below, the preceding approximation is always used in reactor physics.

1.3.4 Energy of Reactions and Mass Defect

Taking a closer look at things, we find that Einstein's law $E = \Delta mC^2$ (where C is the speed of light) implies that the mass of an assembly of bound nucleons (in other words, the mass of the nucleus) must be smaller than the sum of the masses of isolated nucleons (well-separated so that they do not interact), whence:

$$\Delta m(X) = (Z\,m_p + (A - Z)\,m_n) - m(X) = \frac{E_\ell}{C^2} \neq 0 \qquad (1.3)$$

The quantity Δm is called the mass defect and E_ℓ represents the binding energy which is necessarily non-zero.

An analogous mass defect exists for a molecule and its constituent atoms, but the binding energies E_ℓ are so small (a few eV) that the mass defect is hardly perceptible. Lavoisier's law (conservation of mass) is found to be verified with an extraordinary precision ($\Delta m/m \cong 10^{-8}$) even if it is not true rigorously.

On the other hand, for nuclei, the binding energies are much stronger (at least a few MeV), and in spite of the size of the denominator C^2, the mass defect becomes significant ($\Delta m/m$ can attain 1%).

To obtain the energy E_ℓ, or more generally the energy Q of a nuclear reaction, it is necessary to know the atomic masses to 4 or 5 decimal places, in order to get the mass defect within 2 or 3 digits. Nowadays mass spectrography enables us to obtain these accuracies and hence the desired energies. For certain reactions, these energies can be measured directly; this has enabled the verification of Einstein's law with high precision, one of the most striking successes of the theory of special relativity.

Langevin was the first to make the following remark: the fact that the masses of nucleons expressed in a.m.u. are not one, and that the masses of nuclei (always in a.m.u.) are not integers, results from the preceding. In fact, if nuclear masses were truly integers, then mass defects would vanish, and so also the binding energies, which would be absurd. For the same reason, the neutron and the proton have slightly different masses. The β decay of the neutron $n \rightarrow p + \beta^-$ implies that $m_n > m_p + m_e$, since the electron is emitted with an energy of 0.78 MeV.

Thus we have found the explanation as to why the atomic masses of different isotopes are not exactly integers when one takes 16 for oxygen (§1.2.2.).

Because of the mass-energy equivalence, masses are often expressed in energy units. Taking $C = 2.998\ 10^8\ m\ s^{-1}$ for the velocity of light, one is led to:

$$1 \text{ a.m.u.} \rightarrow 1.66\ 10^{-27}\ \text{kg}\ (2.998\ 10^8\ \text{m s}^{-1})^2$$

$$\rightarrow 1.492\ 10^{-10}\ \text{J}$$

$$1 \text{ a.m.u.} \rightarrow 931 \text{ MeV}$$

With these units, the mass defects directly furnish the desired energies. One can thus calculate the binding energy per nucleon

$$\frac{E_\ell}{A} (\text{MeV}) = 931 \left(\frac{Zm_p + (A - Z)\ m_n - m(X)}{A} \right) \text{ a.m.u.}$$

as a function of the mass number. We see in Figure 1.2 that the corresponding curve has a maximum for $A \cong 50$.

The <u>fusion</u> of light nuclei and the <u>fission</u> of heavy nuclei lead to tighter bound nucleons, and hence to <u>energy liberation</u>, because the total number of nucleons is conserved.

As an example, let us consider nuclear fission, which will be analyzed later in detail. Let us suppose here only that a <u>uranium</u> nucleus $_{92}U^{235}$ is divided into two equal parts. We will have:

- for $_{92}U^{235}$: $\frac{E_\ell}{A} \cong 7.5$ MeV/nucleon
- for $_{46}X^{A \cong 235/2}$: $\frac{E_\ell}{A} \cong 8.4$ MeV/nucleon

The increase E_ℓ/A is thus of the order of 0.9 MeV/nucleon, and thus for the assembly of nucleons $235 \times 0.9 \cong 212$ MeV. This last value represents the energy emanating from a fission. This is a very good order of magnitude in spite of the crude nature of the calculation.

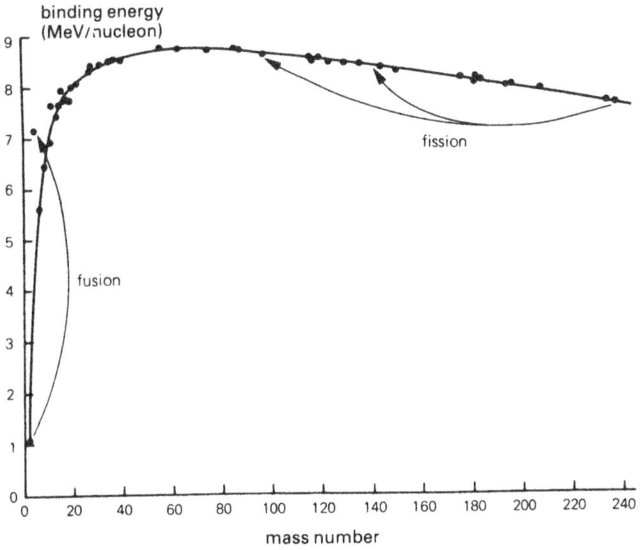

FIGURE 1.2.

In fact, in order to obtain the energy of a nuclear reaction, we will not use Fig. 1.2, but Einstein's law applied directly to the case at hand. Given two nuclei of masses m_1 and m_2 giving, after reaction, two new nuclides of masses m_3 and m_4, the energy of the reaction will be:

$$Q \text{ (MeV)} = 931 \ (m_1 + m_2 - m_3 - m_4) \text{ a.m.u.} \qquad (1.4)$$

This formula applied to one of the fusion reactions gives for example:

$${}_1H^2 + {}_1H^2 \rightarrow {}_1H^3 + {}_1H^1 + 4.03 \text{ MeV}$$

taking the following masses (in a.m.u.)

1.007277 for ${}_1H^1$

2.0141018 for ${}_1H^2$

3.016599 for ${}_1H^3$

In this example, three isotopes of hydrogen intervene: normal hydrogen ($_1H^1$), deuterium ($_1H^2$) and tritium ($_1H^3$). We note that the masses in a.m.u. are very close to the mass numbers A, but it is the small deviations which enable us to calculate Q.

1.4 RADIOACTIVITY

1.4.1 Fundamental Laws

A substance is said to be radioactive when its nuclei decay spontaneously emitting radiation (§1.2.1) It is thus a matter of a particular nuclear reaction analogous to chemical reactions of dissociation. Such unstable nuclei are generally called radio-isotopes or radionuclides.

The rate of decay of a radioactive substance is called its activity A_c, in other words, the number of nuclei destroyed in a unit of time. In the case where a single particle is emitted by an event, A_c represents the emission rate or the source of radiation expressed in number of particles emitted per unit time.

The fundamental law of radioactivity is given by:

$$A_c = \lambda N \tag{1.5}$$

where N is the number of nuclei at the considered instant (this refers to the parent nuclei and not its descendants).

The decay constant λ (in s^{-1}) is independent of the quantities of matter considered, and is a function only of the characteristics of the nuclei. In case of several competing decay modes, one defines partial activities A_{ci} which represent the sources of radiation of each type. Each mode is defined by a probability p_i such that:

$$A_{ci} = p_i A_c \tag{1.6}$$

with summation $\Sigma p_i = 1$, because the sum of partial activities is equal to a total activity A_c, the latter always representing the decay rate. Like λ, the probabilities p_i are nuclear data.

For historic reasons (§1.4.3), one often expresses activities in curies:

$$1 \text{ Ci} = 3.7 \times 10^{10} \text{ decays per second}$$

Let us consider a single isolated radioactive substance characterized by the number of nuclei N(t). Following the decay, this number can only decrease, such that:

$$\frac{dN}{dt} = - A_c = - \lambda N \tag{1.7}$$

This equation can be immediately integrated:

$$\begin{aligned} N(t) &= N(0) \exp (- \lambda t) \\ A_c(t) &= A_c(0) \exp (- \lambda t) \end{aligned} \tag{1.8}$$

Looking for the time T at the end of which the number of nuclei have diminished by half, one finds:

$$\frac{N(T)}{N(0)} = \frac{1}{2} = \exp (- \lambda T)$$

whence:

$$T = \frac{\ln 2}{\lambda} \cong \frac{0.693}{\lambda} \tag{1.9}$$

T is called the period, or more correctly, the half-life, of the radio-isotope.

The preceding is valid for all types of radioactivity (α, β, γ), whether the bodies be natural (uranium) or artificial. We note in this context that artificial radioactivity was discovered by Joliot-Curie who, in bombarding aluminum with α rays, obtained radioactive phosphorous ($_{15}P^{30}$)* which is not found in nature because its half-life is 2.5 minutes. Today, the most abundant artificial radio-isotopes are fission products which accumulate in nuclear reactors.

1.4.2 Decay Chains

The decay of a nucleus can lead in its turn to an unstable nucleus satisfying the same laws as the original one. A decay chain is thus established. This applies not only to the "natural" radioactivity of uranium U^{238} (Table 1.3), but also to most fission products, such as, for example, iodine I^{139}:

$$_{53}I^{139} \xrightarrow[2.7s]{\beta^-} {}_{54}Xe^{139} \xrightarrow[41s]{\beta^-} {}_{55}Cs^{139} \xrightarrow[9mn]{\beta^-} {}_{56}Ba^{139} \xrightarrow[83mn]{\beta^-} {}_{57}La^{139}$$

We note that the half-lives vary greatly in the two cases (particularly the first). Evidently a chain ends at a stable element ($T = \infty$, $\lambda = 0$).

In the case of uranium (Table 1.3), this is lead ${}_{82}Pb^{206}$; in the case of radioactive iodine, it is lanthanum ${}_{57}La^{139}$.

By generalizing the preceding, we obtain equations which govern a chain:

$$\begin{aligned} \frac{dN_1}{dt} &= -\lambda_1 N_1 \quad \text{(precursor)} \\ \frac{dN_2}{dt} &= -\lambda_2 N_2 + \lambda_1 N_1 \quad \text{(descendant)} \\ \frac{dN_3}{dt} &= -\lambda_3 N_3 + \lambda_2 N_2, \quad \text{etc.} \end{aligned} \tag{1.10}$$

In the second equation, for example, the isotope (2) appears (the positive term) as a result of the decay of the isotope (1), but in its turn decays (the negative term), giving rise to the third isotope, and so on. We see that, apart from the first isotope, whose law of evolution is given by equation (1.8), the others are characterized by functions of time which are much more complicated (combination of exponential functions). All the same, there is a simple, important case.

Suppose that the first isotope has a very long half-life ($\lambda_1 << \lambda_2$), and that all the others, its descendants, have short half-lives (large λ_2). Then we arrive at equilibrium at the end of a certain time which is small compared to the period of the precursor, but large compared to the periods of its descendants. We will have $N_1(t) \cong$ constant and $\lambda_1 N_1 = \lambda_2 N_2 = \lambda_3 N_3 = \ldots$ since at equilibrium

$$\frac{dN_2}{dt} = \frac{dN_3}{dt} = \ldots = 0$$

These conditions are often realized for the uranium U^{238} chain (Table 1.3).

By virtue of the preceding, the activities of the descendants are identical (although of different types: α, β, γ), but the number of nuclei (or the total masses of different isotopes) are of course different. Thus one has for the isotope (i)

$$N_i = \frac{\lambda_1}{\lambda_i} N_1 = \frac{T_i}{T_1} N_1$$

At radioactive equilibrium, the shorter the half-life of the isotope, the weaker is its concentration.

TABLE 1.3. Decay chain of uranium $_{92}U^{238}$.

Usual name or symbol	Isotope's symbol	Period (half-life)	Type of radiation emitted
Uranium I	$_{92}U^{238}$	$4{,}5 \cdot 10^9$ a	α
Uranium X_1	$_{90}Th^{234}$	24 j	β
Uranium X_2	$_{91}Pa^{234}$	1,17 mn	β
Uranium II	$_{92}U^{234}$	$2{,}5 \cdot 10^5$ a	α
Ionium	$_{90}Th^{230}$	$8 \cdot 10^4$ a	α
Radium	$_{88}Ra^{226}$	$1{,}62 \cdot 10^3$ a	α
Radon	$_{86}Rn^{222}$	3,82 j	α
Radium A	$_{84}Po^{218}$	3 mn	α
Radium B	$_{82}Pb^{214}$	26 mn	$\beta + \gamma$
Radium C	$_{83}Bi^{214}$	20 mn	$\beta + \gamma$
Radium C′	$_{84}Po^{214}$	164 μ s	α
Radium D	$_{82}Pb^{210}$	22 a	$\beta + \gamma$
Radium E	$_{83}Bi^{210}$	5 j	β
Radium F	$_{84}Po^{210}$	138 j	α
Radium G	$_{82}Pb^{206}$	Stable	——

1.4.3 Example: Activity and Composition of a Metric Ton of Uranium

We shall use the data from Table 1.3. Let us consider a metric ton of uranium, the number of nuclei of U^{238} is:

$$N_1 = 10^6/(238/N_A) = 2.53\ 10^{27}$$

The decay constant $\lambda_1 = \dfrac{0.693}{T_1}$ where T_1 must be expressed in seconds, is equal to:

$$\lambda_1 = 4.89\ 10^{-18}\ s^{-1}$$

The activity of uranium and of each of its descendants is thus:

$$A_c = \lambda_1 N_1 = 1.237\ 10^{10} \text{ decays/second}$$

or:

$$A_c = 0.337 \text{ Ci/metric ton}$$

The fifth descendant $_{88}Ra^{226}$ (i = 5) will consist of:

$$N_5 = \frac{T_5}{T_1} N_1 \qquad \text{that is, } 9.107\ 10^{20} \text{ nuclei}$$

the mass of each one being $226/N_A$ g, whence the conclusion: a mass of 0.342 g of Ra^{226} is contained in one metric ton of U^{238} and has an activity of 0.337 Ci, identical to that of uranium.

One can deduce from this also that 1 Ci corresponds approximately to 1 g of Ra^{226} (historical definition of the curie).

If, by whatever means, this quantity of radium is isolated, equilibrium is broken, but the initial activity will be 0.337 Ci, and will subsequently decrease exponentially with a half-life of 1.62×10^3 years. The radiation source thus obtained will have a volume 3×10^6 times smaller than the metric ton of uranium in which the radium was contained.

Analogous calculations apply to the other descendants. All these results of calculations have been verified by experiments.

It should be noted that two other natural chains exist, that of uranium $_{92}U^{235}$ and that of thorium $_{90}Th^{232}$.

1.4.4 Production of Radio-isotopes in a Nuclear Reactor

Let us suppose that at the initial instant the radio-isotope is absent, but that with time, it forms progressively under neutron flux (Sec. 1.5). Its production rate S is clearly independent of its radioactive characteristics. If N(t) represents the number of radioactive nuclei at time t, then the equation of balance is given by:

$$\frac{dN}{dt} = S - A_c$$

The second term of this equation corresponds to the disappearance of nuclei by decay, hence it is the activity defined above. Using the fundamental law of radioactivity (1.5), we are led to the differential equation:

$$\frac{dN}{dt} + \lambda N = S \qquad (1.11)$$

If S is constant (the reactor is functioning at constant power), onc obtains the solution:

$$N(t) = \frac{S}{\lambda}(1 - \exp(-\lambda t))$$
$$A_c(t) = S(1 - \exp(-\lambda t)) \tag{1.12}$$

If the irradiation time t_0 is long compared to the half-life T given by equation (1.9) ($\lambda t_0 >> 1$), the activity attains the saturation value $A_c(t_0) = S$.

Conversely, for radio-isotopes with long half-lives ($\lambda t_0 << 1$) the maximum activity does not exceed:

$$A_c(t_0) = \ln 2 \cdot \frac{t_0}{T} \cdot S$$

When the irradiation stops at time t_0, the activity decreases following the law ($t \geq t_0$):

$$A_c(t) = A_c(t_0) \exp(-\lambda(t - t_0)) \tag{1.13}$$

in accordance with equation (1.8) after changing the origin of time. One should note that if the activity of a radio-isotope of long half-life decreases slowly from the moment that the irradiation ceases, then its maximum activity will remain weak. This is indicated qualitatively by the curves of Fig. 1.4.

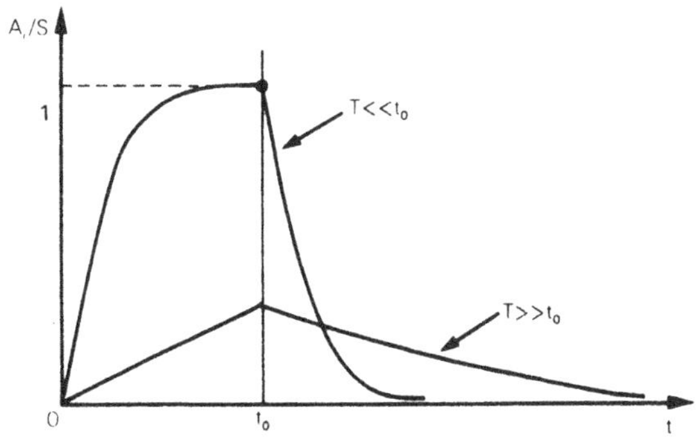

FIGURE 1.4. Formation and decay of artificial radio-isotopes.

1.5 CROSS SECTIONS --REACTION RATES

1.5.1 Introduction

In subsec. 1.3.4 some nuclear reactions were presented. Some of them, such as fission or fusion reactions, are exo-energetic. Unfortunately, it does not suffice for a reaction to be possible. It is necessary that the reaction have a sufficient probability of being realized, otherwise the global energy that one will obtain will be insufficient, or even close to zero, even if the energy balance of the equation is very favorable. Hence it is necessary to bring into play other parameters in order to characterize a nuclear reaction. In an analogous fashion, one refers in chemistry to the notion of affinity.

1.5.2 Definition of Flux and Cross Sections

One can characterize a beam of particles of well-defined velocity $\vec{v}$ by introducing the flux ϕ. By definition, this flux represents the number of particles which traverse per unit time a surface of 1 cm^2 perpendicular to the direction of propagation. We see in Fig. 1.5 that these particles are necessarily contained in a cylinder of height v and of cross section $dS = 1\ cm^2$. If n is the number of particles per unit volume, then the number of particles contained in a cylinder of volume $v \cdot 1$, thus the flux, will be $\phi = n\,v$. The quantities n and ϕ are expressed respectively in cm^{-3} and $cm^{-2}s^{-1}$.

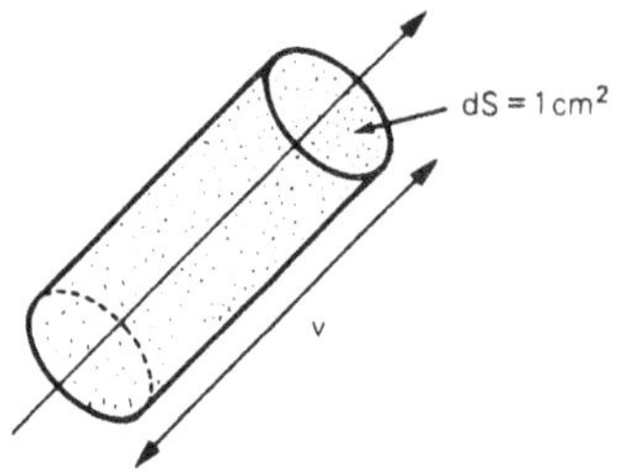

FIGURE 1.5.

Let us consider the interaction of particles of the beam (type 1) with a particular target (type 2) supposed stationary. The number ν_c of processes per unit time can be written:

$$\nu_c = \sigma\phi_1 = \sigma n_1 v_1 \qquad (1.14)$$

This number is evidently proportional to the intensity of the beam, and hence to $\phi_1 = n_1 v_1$.

The coefficient σ which has the dimensions of an area is called the microscopic cross section. It is an intrinsic characteristic of the interaction and is thus independent of the number of particles present. It is called microscopic because it concerns an elementary process: the meeting of two particles; it can only depend on the relative energy of these particles and on the type of interaction being considered.

1.5.3 Different Types of Interactions

Different processes can enter in competition.

- Scattering (Fig. 1.6). The corresponding cross section is noted σ_s. When collision takes place, the incident particles (1) are simply deviated. We say that the scattering is elastic if the target particle 2 remains unchanged (recoil is permitted). The scattering is called inelastic if particle 2 is found in an excited state (A and Z remaining conserved). It de-excites itself by emitting a γ photon.

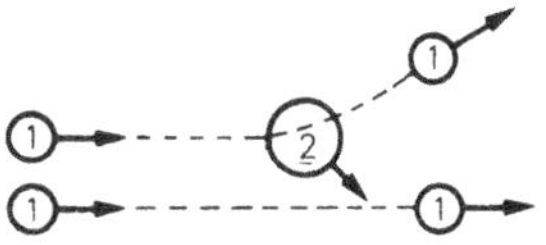

FIGURE 1.6.

- Nuclear reactions (Fig. 1.7). When collision takes place, particles 1 and 2 are destroyed, and two new particles, 3 and 4, are emitted. No particular notations are involved here, except for special cases. We cite for example the case of fission with (1) = ${}_0n^1$, (2) = ${}_{92}U^{235}$, (3) and (4) = fission products, the cross section is noted σ_f, or the case of fusion:

$(1) = {}_1H^2$, $(2) = {}_1H^3$, $(3) = {}_2He^4$, $(4) = {}_0n^1$

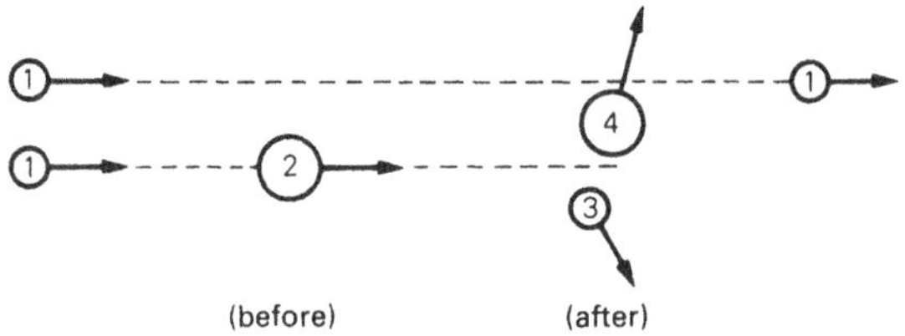

FIGURE 1.7.

• Neutron capture (Fig. 1.8). A standard phenomenon in neutron physics, the incident particle is absorbed by the target nucleus, which then emits a γ photon. The corresponding cross section is noted σ_c. The resulting nucleus can be radioactive and emit delayed γ photons which should not be confused with the γ photon released immediately during the reaction. This remark is of considerable importance in nuclear engineering.

FIGURE 1.8.

When one considers the set of reactions leading to the disappearance of incident particles, one says that absorption has taken place, and the cross section is noted σ_a. For neutrons we will have for example: $\sigma_a = \sigma_f + \sigma_c$.

The sum of the cross sections of all the envisageable processes represents the total or collision microscopic cross section: $\sigma_t = \sigma_s + \sigma_c + \ldots$ When inserted in equation (1.14), this leads to the total number ν_c of collisions per unit time.

If, on the contrary, we introduce only σ_c in this equation, we count only the processes which lead to the disappearance of the incident particle together with the emission of a γ photon.

We can represent the total cross section in the following way. Let us suppose that the target particle is a rigid sphere of radius a. Only the particles of the beam contained in the cylinder of cross section πa^2 can interact, whence $\nu_c = \phi\pi a^2$ and the cross section is nothing but the apparent surface of the target (Fig. 1.9).

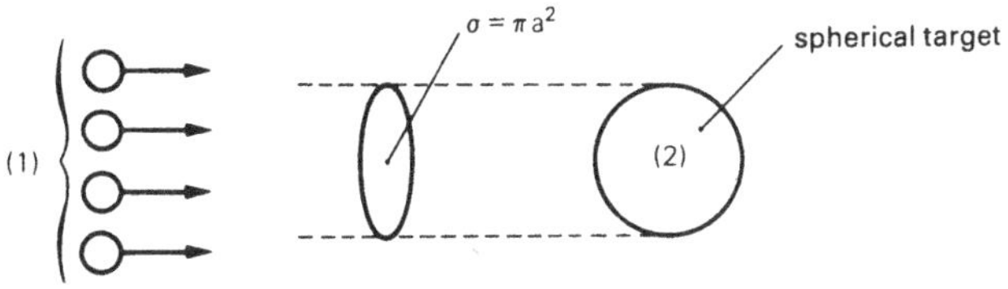

FIGURE 1.9.

This picture, which is, at the very most, valid for molecular collisions, is false at the atomic level, and, a fortiori, at the nuclear level. It simply permits us, however, to understand the choice of the expression "cross section". As predicted by quantum mechanics, the measurements of cross sections show a strong dependence on the energy of incident particles.

1.5.4 Comparison of Fission and Fusion Cross Sections

First let us consider fission reactions (§3.1.1):

$$ {}_0n^1 + {}_{92}U^{235} \rightarrow 2\text{ F.P.} + \bar{\nu}\,{}_0n^1 + 207\text{ MeV} $$

where $\bar{\nu} \cong 2.42$ represents the average number of neutrons created by fission (some reactions create 2, others 3) and F.P. represents fission products (A and Z intermediate).

Fig. 1.10 gives the shape of $\sigma_f(E)$, the fission cross section. We have introduced as usual the barn as a unit for cross sections: one barn $= 10^{-24}$ cm^2. We note that σ_f increases with the decrease of the energy of neutrons. This is an essential characteristic of neutron reactions. The neutrons, in effect, do not "see" the electrostatic field created by the uranium nucleus because they are neutral.

The lowest energy that one can envisage for neutrons is that which corresponds to their thermodynamic equilibrium with the medium in which they propagate. This so-called "thermal" energy is proportional to the absolute temperature of the considered medium, and equals approximately 0.025 eV at 20°C. In these conditions, the cross section σ_f attains 582 b. This is the essential reason for thermal reactors. We shall return to this question in Chapter 3.

Figure 1.10 furnishes a second interesting example with reference to fusion reactions. We consider deuterium nuclei ($d = {}_1H^2$) in interaction with a nuclear target of tritium ($d = {}_1H^3$). The incident energy given in the abscissa represents this time the kinetic energy of the ions ${}_1H^2$. We observe that the cross section noted $\sigma(d,t)$ is practically zero below 8 keV. We call this a threshhold reaction. This is a characteristic of charged particle reactions, the electrostatic potential of the nuclear target creating a "potential barrier" which can only be crossed at the cost of a sufficient amount of incident energy.

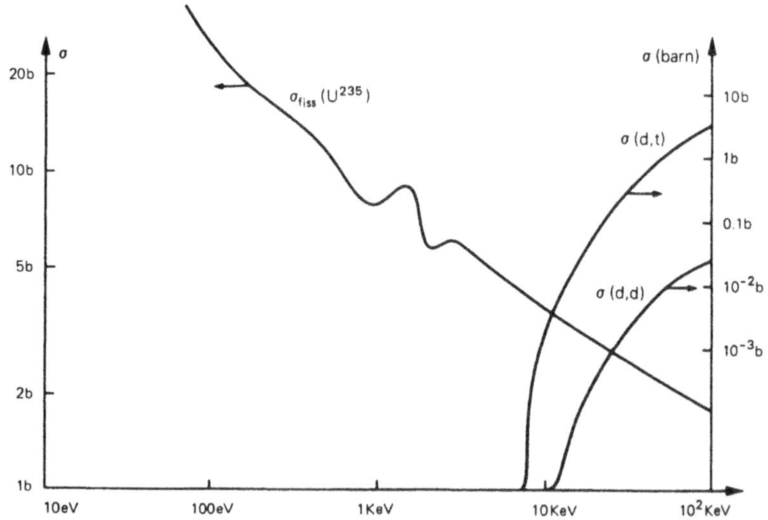

FIGURE 1.10. Microscopic cross sections of fission and fusion reactions.

In the case of each of the phenomena we have just studied, we must add the process of scattering. Rapid incident particles, which are neutrons in the first case and deuterons in the second, lose energy each time they encounter a nuclear target, and each such encounter is of the scattering type. The scattering cross section in the case of charged particles is much higher than the cross sections of the reactions which interest us. As a result, the incident particles very rapidly lose all their energy before giving rise to nuclear reactions in a significant way. The residual energy is of the order of the thermal energy mentioned earlier, in other words around 0.025 eV at the ambiant temperature (20°C). This is advantageous for fission because σ_f is very big, but it is unacceptable for fusion because the thermal energy is much lower than the threshholds of these reactions.

The only way to avoid this obstacle in the second case is to raise the thermal energy higher than the threshhold (8 keV). This leads to the realization of temperatures of at least the order of 10^8 °K. In these conditions, matter is completely ionized, and one obtains a plasma: the nuclei are mixed with the electrons which were initially bound to them. The reactions which take place in this medium are called thermonuclear, because of the great amount of heat necessary to bring them about. This procedure concerns all threshhold reactions, and not just fusion reactions.

1.5.5 Reaction or Collision Rates

We consider two populations of moving particles which interact. The particles of type (1) have a relative velocity v_r with respect to the target particles (2). The latter can now be considered stationary and equation (1.14) applies: $\nu_c = \sigma(E_r)n_1v_r$ where the relative energy E_r is given by (§4.4.2):

$$E_r = \frac{1}{2}\,\frac{m_1m_2}{m_1 + m_2}\,v_r^2$$

Since ν_c represents the collision rate for a nuclear target, the global collision rate per unit volume can be written:

$$R = n_2\nu_c = n_2n_1v_r\sigma\,(E_r) \tag{1.15}$$

where n_2 is equal to the density of nuclear targets (in cm^{-3}), the other quantities keeping their earlier meaning.

Equation (1.15) is perfectly symmetric, as is normal: the exchange of indices (1) and (2) should not change the result, as the distinction between target and incident particles is arbitrary. This permutation of indices does not affect the relative velocity $v_r = |\vec{v}_1 - \vec{v}_2|$. We note that the microscopic cross section σ depends in general on the relative energy. For fusion reactions, this dependence appears in Figure 1.10 (where the incident energy must be replaced by the relative energy).

In most problems of neutron physics, one can suppose on the contrary that the nuclei are at rest and the neutrons in motion. It is thus natural to consider the former as targets. The relative velocity of neutrons is then equal to their absolute velocity, in other words, $v_r = v_1 = v$, $v_2 = 0$.

Adopting the usual notation: $n_2 = N$ (nuclear density), $n_1 = n$ (neutron density), one can express the collision rate R in the following way (1.15):

$$\left.\begin{aligned} R &= \Sigma(E)\phi \\ \Sigma(E) &= N\sigma(E) \\ \phi &= nv \text{ (neutron flux)} \end{aligned}\right\} \tag{1.16}$$

The quantity Σ is called the macroscopic cross section of collision, absorption, etc. according to the process envisaged. It depends on the nuclear density N, and thus on the problem considered, whence the appellation "macroscopic". It is expressed in cm^{-1}.

The notations are those used for microscopic cross sections:

$$\left.\begin{aligned} \Sigma_t &= N\sigma_t & R_t &= \Sigma_t\phi & &\text{(collision rate)} \\ \Sigma_f &= N\sigma_f & R_f &= \Sigma_f\phi & &\text{(fission rate)} \\ \Sigma_c &= N\sigma_c & R_c &= \Sigma_c\phi & &\text{(capture rate)} \end{aligned}\right\} \text{ etc.} \tag{1.17}$$

If the neutrons interact with a mixture of isotopes, we generalize the preceding by giving the macroscopic cross section by:

$$\Sigma = \sum_i N_i\sigma_i \tag{1.18}$$

where σ_i represents the microscopic cross section characterizing the interaction of neutrons with nuclei of type (i) in number N_i (per unit volume).

We note as an example that the production rate S of a radio-isotope (§1.4.4) can be calculated by multiplying one of the reaction rates given by equations (1.17) by the volume of irradiated matter.

THERMONUCLEAR FUSION

2.1 GENERAL CHARACTERISTICS

2.1.1 Introduction

All thermonuclear reactions between light nuclei have cross sections which vanish below an energy threshhold of the order of at least 10 keV (Fig. 1.10). Among these reactions, the most important are:

$$(d,t) \quad {}_1H^2 + {}_1H^3 \rightarrow {}_2He^4 + {}_0n^1 + 17.6 \text{ MeV}$$

$$(d,d) \quad {}_1H^2 + {}_1H^2 \begin{cases} \xrightarrow{50\%} {}_2H^3 + {}_0n^1 + 3.2 \text{ MeV} \\ \rightarrow {}_1H^3 + {}_1H^1 + 4.0 \text{ MeV} \end{cases}$$

$$(d,He) \quad {}_1H^2 + {}_2He^3 \rightarrow {}_2He^4 + {}_1H^1 + 18.3 \text{ MeV}$$

$$(p,B) \quad {}_1H^1 + {}_5B^{11} \rightarrow 3\ {}_2He^4 + 8.7 \text{ MeV}$$

We have already mentioned the first two reactions. In fact, the reaction (d,d) consists of two equally probable branches. The third reaction only involves charged particles; it is called "clean" in the sense that its reaction products are not activating agents like neutrons.

As for the last, it is rather a fission reaction whose cross section has a fairly high threshhold (>20 keV). This reaction is thus of the same type as the others.

The general considerations of subsec. 1.5.4 indicate that these reactions can only take place at very high temperature. In these conditions matter is completely ionized, because the necessary thermal energy is much greater than the binding energy of atomic electrons.

2.1.2 Calculation of Reaction Rates

Let us calculate the reaction rates corresponding to these conditions.

In an ionized gas, or plasma, particles which are in thermodynamic equilibrium do not have a well-defined "thermal" energy, as the previous reasoning shows. These particles are distributed, on the contrary, according to the Maxwell distribution as shown by statistical physics [1]. This means, on the one hand, that the particles move in all directions with the same probability (isotropic distribution), on the other hand, they have a probability:

$$p(E,T)dE = \frac{2}{\sqrt{\pi}}\sqrt{\frac{E}{kT}}\left[\exp\left(-\frac{E}{kT}\right)\right]\frac{dE}{kT} \qquad (2.1)$$

of moving with kinetic energy between E and E + dE.

In equation (2.1) T represents the absolute temperature and k Boltzmann's constant. By definition this quantity is equal to R/N_A, where R is the perfect gas constant (R = 8.31 J/°K). In other words:

$$k = 8.62\ 10^{-5}\ \text{eV/°K}$$

In the kinetic theory of gases this law is often given as a function of velocities [1]. Changing to the variable energy ($E = 1/2\ m\ v^2$) and employing the normalization condition of probabilities:

$$\int_0^\infty p(E,T)dE = 1$$

leads effectively to equation (2.1).

What has just been said applies also to the different components of a plasma. Let us return to equation (1.15). The reaction rate corresponded to particles in (1) and (2), each having the same relative velocity v_r. If, on the contrary, all energies are possible, then (1.15) can only apply to pairs of particles having relative energies comprised between E_r and $E_r + dE_r$. The number of pairs enjoying this property is equal to the total number n_1n_2 multiplied by the probability $p(E_r,T)dE_r$ of finding a particle of type 1 and a particle of type 2 having a relative energy E_r. The differential reaction rate is then given by:

$$dR = [n_1n_2p\ (E_r,T)\ dE_r]\ v_r\ \sigma\ (E_r)$$

where $p(E_r,T)$ is always given by (2.1). Summing over all possible energies we find the desired reaction rate:

$$R_f(cm^{-3}\ s^{-1}) = n_1 n_2 <\sigma v> \tag{2.2}$$

with :

$$<\sigma v> = \int_0^\infty v_r \sigma\ (E_r)\ p\ (E_r, T)\ dE_r \tag{2.3}$$

Equation (2.2) thus furnishes the number of fusion reactions per unit volume and unit time.

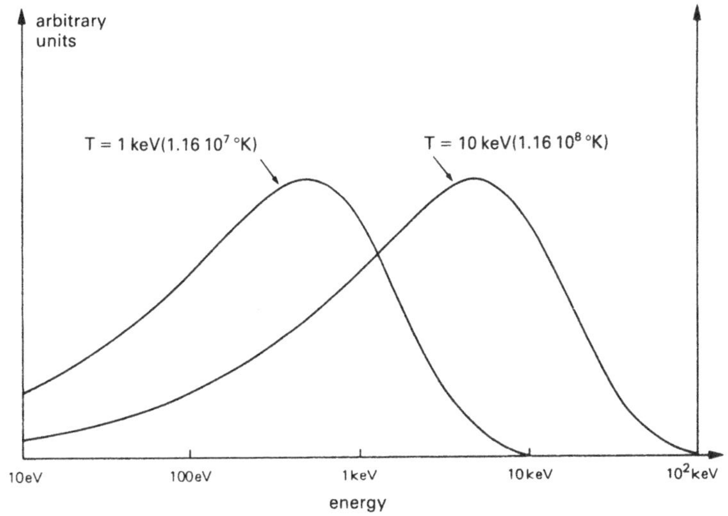

FIGURE 2.1. Maxwell distributions.

The microscopic cross section $\sigma(E_r)$ is a characteristic of the reaction and does not depend at all on the variables of the state of the plasma: n, T, etc. Equation (2.2) generalizes equation (1.15) in which the product $v_r\ \sigma(E_r)$ has simply been replaced by its average value, taken with the help of the Maxwell distribution (2.1). In Fig. 2.1 this distribution is represented for two temperatures, the variable carried in the abscissa representing this time the relative energy. In order to obtain significant values of the reaction parameter $<\sigma v>$ the curves $\sigma(E_r)$ and $p(E_r, T)$ must have a certain overlap as indicated by (2.3). Comparing Figures 1.10 and 2.1, we see that it is not necessary that the maximum of the distribution

($E_r = kT/2$) be situated above the energy threshhold. The values of $<\sigma v>$ are represented in Fig. 2.2 as a function of the temperature T.[2] As is customary, temperatures are expressed in energy units (eV or keV), Boltzmann's constant enabling us to make this conversion ($E_t = kT$). We see, for example, that for a temperature of 10 keV the parameter of the reaction (d,t) attains a significant value, whereas the maximum of the distribution (5 keV) is situated below the threshhold (8 keV). In other words, the ions belonging to the "tail of the thermal spectrum" play a preponderant role.

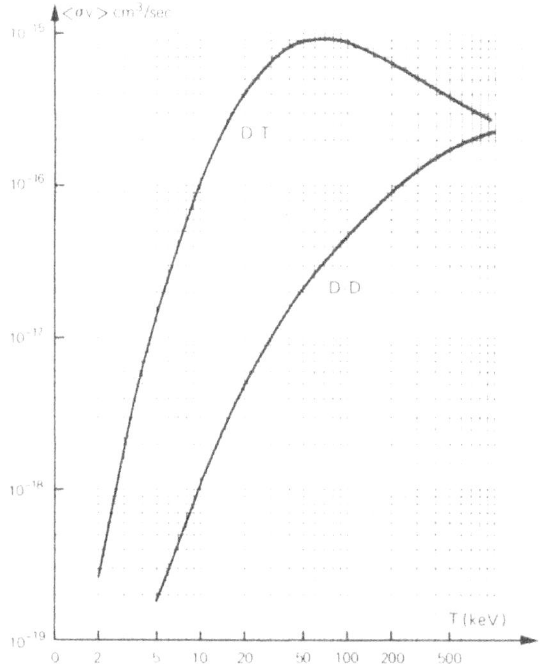

FIGURE 2.2. The reaction parameter $<\sigma v>$ as a function of the plasma temperature [2](p.76).

2.1.3 Fusion Reaction Products

We observe thus that temperatures of several keV are necessary and that the reaction (d,t) is easier to put into operation than the others. This reaction leads unfortunately to a neutron, and necessitates tritium $_1H^3$. The neutron is an activating agent and tritium is a hydrogen isotope which is extremely rare in nature. It has a half-life of 12.3 years and is a β^- emitter, which poses serious technological problems (manipulation, contamination, etc.) Tritium production has been envisaged in a blanket external to the plasma. This always uses lithium in one form or another. The two isotopes of lithium contribute to the regeneration of tritium according to the following neutron reactions:

$$_0n^1 \text{ (slow)} + {_3Li^6} \rightarrow {_2He^4} + \underline{_1H^3} + 4.8 \text{ MeV}$$

$$_0n^1 \text{ (fast)} + {_3Li^7} \rightarrow {_2He^4} + \underline{_1H^3} + {_0n^1} \text{ (slow)} - 2.5 \text{ MeV}$$

The second reaction requires neutrons having more than 2.5 MeV of kinetic energy, which is the case for fusion neutrons, as one can see below.

The (d,t) reaction liberates an energy Q = 17.6 MeV in the form of kinetic energy carried by the particles resulting from the fusion,that is to say, a helium nucleus (α) and a neutron. The α particles rapidly lose their energy in the plasma and thus contribute to heating it. The neutrons on the other hand leave the plasma and are only slowed down in the blanket. Their energy is thus recovered at this level in a calorific form and evacuated by the coolant.

As a consequence, it is important to know how much of the energy Q is divided between the neutron and the α particle. For this, we will use the conservation laws of momentum and energy during a collision.

$$\vec{p}_3 + \vec{p}_4 = \vec{p}_1 + \vec{p}_2$$

$$E_3 + E_4 = E_1 + E_2 + Q$$

where, for example, the indices 1,2,3,4 are relative to the particles $_1H^2$, $_1H^3$, $_2He^4$, $_0n^1$.

Particles (3) and (4) are emitted in all directions with energies much greater (because of Q) than the energies of particles (1) and (2), which have fused. We can thus write approximately $E_1 \cong 0$, $E_2 \cong 0$ in the preceding relations (and also $p_1 \cong 0$, $p_2 \cong 0$). The system of equations thus reduces to:

$$p_3 = p_4 \text{ and } E_3 + E_4 = Q$$

But since the momentum p is related to the energy E by the relation $p^2 = 2\,mE$ one finally finds:

$$\left.\begin{aligned} E_3 &= \frac{m_4}{m_3 + m_4}\,Q \\ E_4 &= \frac{m_3}{m_3 + m_4}\,Q \end{aligned}\right\} \qquad (2.4)$$

These results applied to the reaction (d,t) furnish the desired energies:

$$E_3 = E\,({}_2He^4) = \frac{1}{5}\,Q = 3.52 \text{ MeV}$$

$$E_4 = E\,({}_0n^1) = \frac{4}{5}\,Q = 14.08 \text{ MeV}$$

Since only ratios intervene, masses have been replaced by mass numbers (1.2): $m_3 \cong 4$ for ${}_2He^4$ and $m_4 \cong 1$ for the neutron.

These results have been experimentally verified. In summary, for each reaction we find the following kinetic energies:

3.52 MeV in the form of α
14.08 MeV in the form of neutrons
4.80 MeV in the lithium of the blanket

22.40 MeV total

The reaction rate being small, we have neglected the reaction involving lithium ${}_3Li^7$.

2.2 ENERGY BALANCES

2.2.1 Introduction

In a fusion reactor, the confinement of a hot plasma (10^8 °K at least) must be achieved for a sufficiently long time to permit the fusion reactions to develop. The plasma must not be in contact with the inner wall of the combustion chamber. One fears not only the destruction of the wall, but also the deterioration of the properties of the plasma, due to impurities torn off from the inner wall, and causing a rapid fall of temperature below the operating threshhold. The modes of confinement will be described in the following sections. We propose here to define the criteria that a plasma must satisfy in order that a positive energy balance may be expected. A certain energy investment is necessary in order to raise the gas from its ambiant temperature to the functioning temperature T. It is also necessary to take account of energy losses due to radiation and to particles which escape confinement. In everything which follows, the temperatures will be expressed in energy units, which permits us to ignore Boltzmann's constant (k = 1).

2.2.2 Energy Balance of a Plasma

In thermodynamic equilibrium a plasma must be viewed as a mixture of two extremely hot gases consisting of n_e electrons and n_i ions per unit volume. Each of these particles has an average energy 3/2 T [1], so that the internal energy density of the plasma can be expressed as:

$$U = \frac{3}{2}(n_e + n_i)\,T \tag{2.5}$$

If P_i is the power injected into the plasma (of internal or external origin), P_r the radiated power and P_L the kinetic energy per unit time carried by the particles escaping the system, then the variation of internal energy can be expressed as:

$$\frac{dU}{dt} = P_i - (P_r + P_L) \tag{2.6}$$

All the foregoing quantities depend in general on time and are relative to the unit of volume. The losses P_r and P_L never vanish, so that an insufficient power P_i will entail the cooling of the plasma ($dU/dt < 0$), thus rendering it unsuitable for thermonuclear fusion.

Let us now evaluate the losses. The power dissipated by bremsstrahlung radiation is due to the thermal agitation of the electrons (whether there is thermonuclear fusion or not). This radiation is analogous to that emitted by stars. We shall say a few words about it.

We know that an accelerated particle radiates electromagnetic waves (e.g., production of X-rays by a beam of electrons falling on a target). In a plasma, during collision the electrons are accelerated (and then decelerated) in the electrostatic field created by the ions which they encounter. Classical electromagnetism permits us to calculate the radiated energy per unit volume and unit time. We find that the power density is proportional to [3] (pp.23-25):

$$Z_i^2 \, n_e n_i v_r$$

where n_i and n_e are the densities of ions and of electrons [cm^{-3}] and v_r their relative velocity. If the ions of atomic number Z_i and the electrons constitute a plasma in thermodynamic equilibrium then one must replace v_r by the average velocity of thermal agitation. The latter is proportional to $\sqrt{T}$, since the thermal energy varies like T.

We finally obtain for the desired power density:

$$\left.\begin{array}{l} P_r \; (\text{keV cm}^{-3}\ \text{s}^{-1}) = KZ_i^2 \, n_i n_e \, \sqrt{T(\text{keV})} \\ \text{with } K = 3.344 \; 10^{-15} \; \text{keV}^{1/2} \; \text{cm}^3 \; \text{s}^{-1} \end{array}\right\} \qquad (2.7)$$

Let us now consider the particles which escape the system. Their escape rate is proportional to the number of ions and electrons present in the plasma ($n_e + n_i$). Since these particles carry a kinetic energy of the order of 3/2 T, it follows that the energy loss per unit time is simply proportional to the internal energy U:

$$P_L = U/\tau \qquad (2.8)$$

where τ is the <u>confinement time</u> which only depends on the means utilized for confining the plasma.

The evolution equation (2.6) can now be rendered more explicit by using equations (2.5), (2.7), (2.8), and remarking that the neutrality of the plasma demands $n_e = n_i Z_i$. We have thus:

$$\frac{d}{dt}\left(\frac{3nT}{2} \; (Z + 1)\right) = P_i - \left[KZ^3 n^2 \sqrt{T} + \frac{3nT}{2} \, \frac{(Z + 1)}{\tau}\right] \qquad (2.9)$$

where n characterizes the ionic density and Z the mean atomic number (for a mixture consisting only of hydrogen isotopes, Z = 1). To understand the meaning of τ, let us consider a hot plasma left to itself without bringing any energy to it ($P_i = 0$). If in addition one neglects the radiation (K = 0), then equation (2.9) can be integrated and one finds that the temperature behaves like $\exp(- t/\tau)$. The confinement time thus represents the time at the end of which the plasma has cooled significantly due to the fact that particles have escaped.

To solve equation (2.9) in the general case, it is necessary to specify the mode of heating characterized by P_i.

2.2.3 External Heating and Steady State

We shall suppose that all the fusion energy has been recovered outside the plasma. The injected power P_i then comes from an external machine (subsec. 2.5.4). As the system is in steady state, the derivative figuring in equation (2.9) vanishes. One must thus satisfy the condition:

$$P_i = KZ^3n^2 \sqrt{T} + \frac{3nT}{2} \frac{Z+1}{\tau} \qquad (2.10)$$

The power P_i is taken from the power furnished by the fusion reactor whence the loop represented in Fig. 2.3.

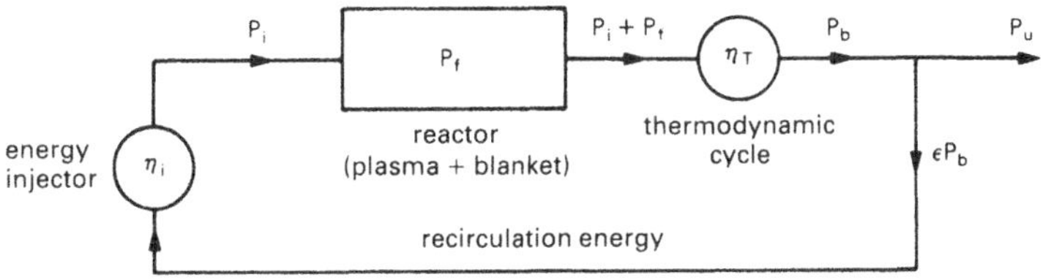

FIGURE 2.3

The power associated to the thermonuclear fusion can be written simply as $P_f = Q\, R_f$, where R_f is given by equation (2.2) and Q represents the energy of the reaction. For an equimolecular mixture of two ionic populations ($n_1 = n_2 = n/2$), this power can be expressed as:

$$P_f \ (\text{keV cm}^{-3}\ \text{s}^{-1}) = \frac{n^2}{4} <\sigma v> Q \ (\text{keV}) \qquad (2.11)$$

where the parameter $<\sigma v>$ is the function of the temperature represented in Fig. 2.2 in the case of the reactions (d,t) and (d,d).

From these two expressions one deduces the expression of the <u>gain</u>, defined as a ratio of the fusion energy to the injected energy:

$$G = \frac{P_f}{P_i} = \frac{<\sigma v> Qn\tau}{4\ KZ^3 \sqrt{T}\ n\tau + 6(Z+1)T} \qquad (2.12)$$

Let us analyze Fig. 2.3. The fusion reactor furnishes to the external medium (blankets) the thermal power $P_f + P_i$, since the injected energy P_i has not been lost but simply degraded (heat). The gross electric power obtained is thus:

$$P_b = \eta_T(P_i + P_f)$$

if η_T is the output of the thermodynamic cycle utilized.

The effective electric power P_u will be smaller than P_b since the fraction εP_b, the recirculation power, is necessary to produce P_i.

If η_i is the output of the energy injector, we then have:

$$P_i = \eta_i \varepsilon P_b = \eta_i \varepsilon \eta_T (P_f + P_i)$$

or:

$$G = \frac{1}{\eta_i \varepsilon \eta_T} - 1 \qquad (2.13)$$

The gain of the plasma must attain a certain value imposed by the characteristics of the external loop. This implies that the product $n\tau$ no longer depends on anything but the temperature when the gain G has been fixed (2.12). One arrives thus at the important relation:

$$n\tau = \frac{6(Z + 1)T}{\frac{1}{G} <\sigma v>Q - 4KZ^3 \sqrt{T}} \qquad (2.14)$$

The product $n\tau$ measures the performances of a plasma, and the values to be attained for different gains and temperatures are represented in Figure 2.4. The name Lawson's criterion is usually used to designate the value of $n\tau$ obtained by putting: $\eta_T = 1/3$ (reasonable value for a standard thermodynamic cycle), $\eta_i = 1$ and $\varepsilon = 1$. The latter value which implies that $P_u = 0$ signifies that the reactor produces just the energy necessary for its operation. It is thus necessary in practice to realize at least this value of $n\tau$, which corresponds to G = 2 (2.13).

For the reactions (d,t) or (d,d) one must put in principle Z = 1, which is assumed in Figure 2.4. All the same, the pollution of the plasma by erosion of the inner wall of the combustion chamber (subsec. 2.5.3) leads to a value $Z_{eff} > 1$, which is highly undesirable, since the energy losses by radiation increase very rapidly with Z (the term in Z^3 of equation (2.14)).

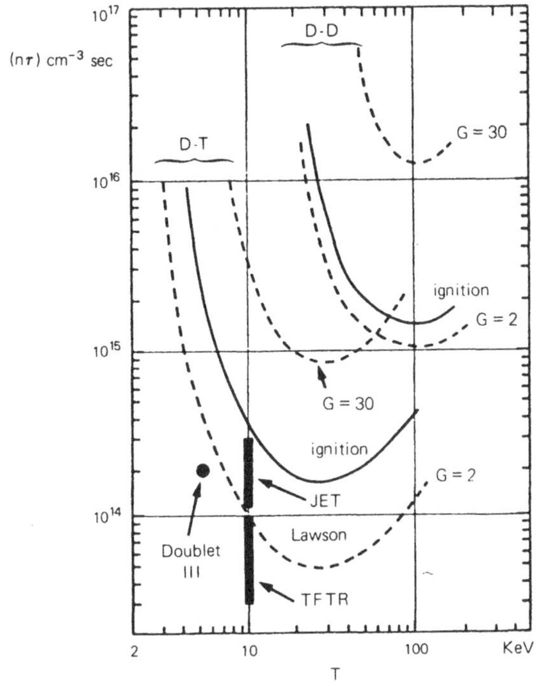

FIGURE 2.4. Performance parameter nτ to attain for different temperatures.

2.2.4 External Pulsed Heating

Certain machines by their very nature are pulsed. The energy is injected in a quasi-instantaneous fashion at the beginning of each impulse. After attaining its maximum temperature, the plasma cools in a time of the order of τ and one must in principle return to equation (2.9). Let us integrate this equation with respect to time in an interval covering one impulse. The initial and final conditions being the same, the integral of the term on the left gives zero contribution. Hence:

$$E_i = \int_0^\infty P_i dt = K \int_0^\infty Z^3 n^2 \sqrt{T}\, dt + \frac{3}{2\tau} \int_0^\infty nT(Z + 1)\, dt$$

where E_i is the energy injected per impulse.

Since the characteristic magnitudes of the plasma only take significant values over the time interval τ, one can write:

$$E_i \cong KZ^3 n^2 \sqrt{\bar{T}}\,\tau + \frac{3}{2} n \bar{T} (Z + 1) = \tau P_i\ (\bar{T}) \tag{2.15}$$

where P_i is always defined by equation (2.10). Equation (2.15) indicates that the energy of the injector must compensate radiation losses during time τ and permit the plasma to attain the temperature T.

If the energy is furnished by the reactor, then one must consider afresh Fig. 2.3, where the powers which appear are the average values per cycle $\bar{P}$. If f is the frequency of injection, we have simply (2.15):

$$\overline{P_i} = fE_i = f\ \tau P_i\ (\bar{T})$$

and in the same way $\overline{P_f} = f\ \tau P_f\ (\bar{T})$. The gain G which is defined here as $\overline{P_f}/\overline{P_i}$ in fact has its previous value, and equation (2.14) is always valid provided we consider average temperatures $\bar{T}$ per impulse. All the same, it is necessary to note that the energy E_i injected per impulse must satisfy equation (2.15), independently of the criterion (2.14).

2.2.5 Internal Heating in the Plasma

Let us return to the steady state and consider heat sources inside the plasma. For these sources to exist, it suffices that a fraction of the fusion energy remain in the plasma. In the previous considerations, we have supposed that the fusion power was carried outside of the system and recovered only in the blankets. This hypothesis is only partially correct: in effect, charged particles created in the plasma have little chance of leaving it, since they are confined in the same way as the initial ions.

The corresponding fusion power can be written:

$$P_{fc} = \frac{n^2}{4} \langle\sigma v\rangle\ Q_c \tag{2.16}$$

an expression analogous to (2.11) where the fraction Q_c replaces the total energy Q of the reaction. For certain reactions, only charged particles are emitted (subsec. 2.1.1) and in this case $Q_c \cong Q$.

If the power P_{fc} suffices to maintain the temperature aimed for, then it plays the same role as P_i in the preceding subsections. Thus, putting $P_i = P_{fc}$ in equation (2.10), one arrives at the desired criterion:

$$n\tau = \frac{6\,(Z+1)\,T}{\langle\sigma v\rangle\, Q_c - 4KZ^3\sqrt{T}} \qquad (2.17)$$

This criterion is analogous to the preceding one (2.14), except that this time characteristics external to the plasma no longer intervene. We have represented these results by solid lines in Fig. 2.4. If the preceding condition is realized, we say that there is ignition and it is no longer necessary to supply energy in order to maintain the plasma in the conditions required by thermonuclear fusion. The system is self-maintained.

One sometimes calls ignition temperature T_{ig} [4] that value of T which makes the denominator of equation (2.17) vanish. This nomenclature is open to question, since in order to achieve ignition with a product $n\tau$ which is reasonable, it is in fact necessary that $T > T_{ig}$ (Fig. 2.4). Nonetheless, the interest of this definition is due to the fact that T_{ig} only depends on the microscopic characteristics of the plasma $\langle\sigma v\rangle$ (Fig. 2.2). For each type of reaction T_{ig} can be determined independently of the ionic densities n and the confinement times τ. It is of course necessary that we know in advance the fraction Q_c of the fusion energy which remains confined. This is practically equal to the kinetic energy of the charged particles emitted during fusion reactions. For example, we have for the mixture D - T: Q_c = 3.5 MeV (subsec. 2.1.3) and $T_{ig} \cong 4$ keV.

2.2.6 Recovery of the Fusion Energy

In all cases, energy produced in the plasma is recovered outside it in the form of heat. In order to know the source of this heat generation, one needs to know the types of radiation which assure the transfer of energy.

Let us consider as an example the reactions (d,t) which lead to the emission of an α particle supposed perfectly confined (Q_c = 3.5 MeV and Q = 17.6 MeV). From the point of view of recovering the energy outside the plasma, one gathers together the different components:

- $P_{fn} = \frac{n^2}{4} \langle\sigma v\rangle Q_n$ neutrons (Q_n = 14.1 MeV)
- $P_r = Kn^2 \sqrt{T}$ bremsstrahlung radiation (X photons)
- $\frac{3nT}{\tau}$ energy associated to ions which leave the plasma

thus the total:

$$P_{tot} = P_{fn} + Kn^2 \sqrt{T} + \frac{3nT}{\tau}$$

But according to the condition of thermal equilibrium of the plasma (2.10, Z = 1) we have $P_{tot} = P_{fn} + P_{fc} = P_f$; we always recover the total energy of the reaction as expected, but in various forms. We have assumed the hypothesis of ignition, since we have taken $P_i = P_{fc}$. Analogous reasonings lead to similar results for different types of functioning. The energy P_{fn} is only dissipated in the blanket in lithium (subsec. 2.1.3), whereas the two other components are to a large extent stopped by the first inner wall (subsec. 2.5.3). In the limiting case, for fusion reactions not emitting any neutrons (d, He) and for perfect confinement ($\tau = \infty$) all the energy would be recovered in the form of radiation ($P_f = P_r$).

2.3 MAGNETIC CONFINEMENT

2.3.1 Introduction

Let us consider a uniform magnetic field $\vec{B}$. A charged particle moving in a plane perpendicular to the field will describe a circular trajectory. In effect, the laws of mechanics give:

$$\left.\begin{aligned} m \frac{dv}{dt} &= 0 \\ m \frac{v^2}{\rho} &= e \frac{vB}{c} = f \text{ (Gauss units)} \end{aligned}\right\}$$

since the Lorentz force $\vec{f}$ is perpendicular to the trajectory (Fig. 2.5). One obtains:

$$v = \text{const.} \qquad \text{and } \rho = \frac{mc}{eB} \cdot v = \text{const.}$$

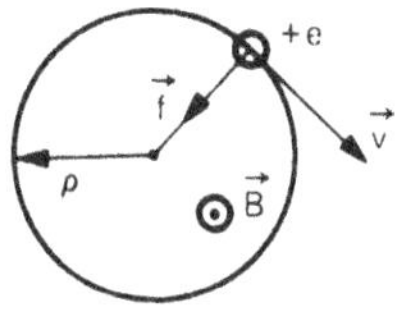

FIGURE 2.5 .

The trajectory is thus circular and the motion uniform.

For a velocity in any direction whatever, the preceding law applies to the component normal to the field.

$$\rho = \frac{v_\perp}{\omega_c} \quad \text{with} \quad \omega_c = \frac{eB}{mc} \quad \text{(cyclotron frequency)}$$

To this uniform circular motion we must add the uniform rectilinear motion of velocity $v_{/\!/}$ parallel to the field (no axial forces). The trajectory is thus a helix (Fig. 2.6). In principle, the particles are confined radially but not axially (following $\vec{B}$).

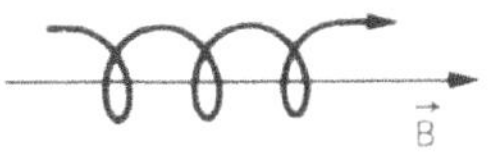

FIGURE 2.6 .

2.3.2 Machines with Magnetic Mirrors

Let us consider for the lines of force of the field the configuration indicated in Fig. 2.7. The magnetic flux being conserved, the field $\vec{B}$ will be more intense at the two extremities than at the center. One can realize such a configuration with the help of a coil whose turns are localized at the extremities of the machine. The field remains approximately uniform locally and hence the trajectories keep the form indicated above. The kinetic energy w of the particles is always constant but its radial and axial components are slowly varying, because of the nonuniformity of the field. One can write: $w = w_\perp + w_{/\!/} = \text{constant}$.

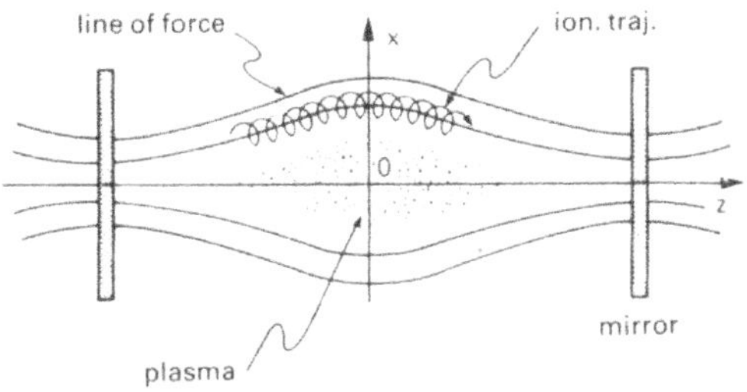

FIGURE 2.7.

On the scale of one step of the helix, the field $\vec{B}$ varies very little so that the adiabatic approximation is valid:

$$\frac{w_\perp}{B} \cong \mu = \text{constant}$$

where μ is the magnetic moment of the particle corresponding to its circular motion around $\vec{B}$. It follows from this that:

$$w_{/\!/}(z) \cong w - \mu B(z) \qquad (2.18)$$

Since B increases when one moves away from the center, $w_{/\!/}$ can very well vanish at the extremities of the device. Hence there will be "reflection": we have thus realized a magnetic mirror. The particles are then confined in most directions. In reality we are dealing with a plasma and hence a very large number of ions and electrons which create their own magnetic field, so that the phenomena are more complex. Magneto-hydrodynamic studies (the plasma is treated as a fluid) show that one obtains an equilibrium but this equilibrium is unstable: any perturbation gets rapidly amplified and the confinement is destroyed. One can stabilize the plasma by creating an additional magnetic field whose lines of force in the plane perpendicular to $\vec{B}$ have the form indicated in Fig. 2.8. This stabilizing field $\vec{b}$ is created by currents parallel to the principal field $\vec{B}$. [3] (p.14). Other modes of stabilization are possible.

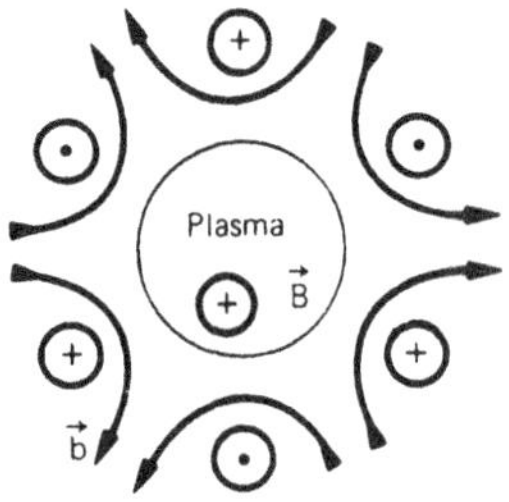

FIGURE 2.8.

When this type of instability has been corrected, there remain micro-instabilities which permit the diffusion of particles across the lines of force. There is no question here of studying these phenomena, which constitute at present one of the major obstacles to the realization of a fusion reactor. These considerations are pertinent to all machines utilizing magnetic confinement.

Let us return to the magnetic mirrors. We know for certain that the reflection is not perfect, if only because of the phenomena cited above. Some of the ions (and their associated kinetic energy) escape from the system at the extremities. It thus appears difficult to realize a permanent regime by ignition in such a machine. In order to suppress these losses, one has thought of joining the two ends of the plasma. This has led to toroidal machines.

2.3.3 Tokamaks

An external coil (poloidal current) creates in the torus occupied by the plasma a longitudinal magnetic field, B_{tor}, which creates the principal confinement (Fig. 2.9). Here, too, the plasma is unstable. This is corrected by circulating a longitudinal current I_p (a plasma is a conductor) which creates the stabilizing poloidal field B_{pol} [3](p.11). The current is induced in the plasma by constructing the system in such a way that the plasma appears as the secondary of a transformer. By this method one heats the plasma as well (ohmic heating) but this heating is insufficient for obtaining the necessary temperatures.

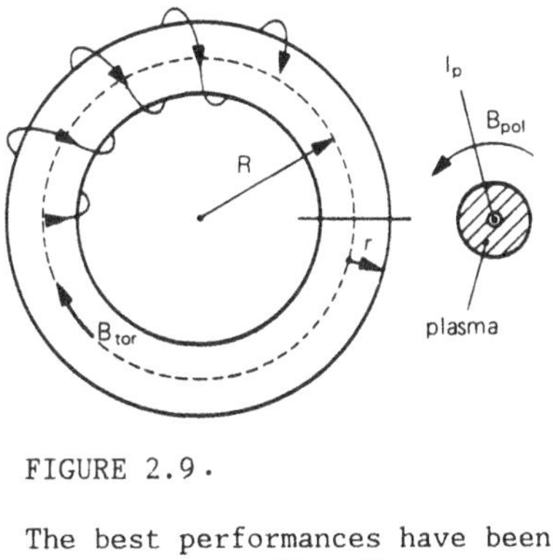

FIGURE 2.9.

The best performances have been obtained with this type of machine ($T > 1$ keV, $n\tau > 10^{13}$ cm^{-3} s), with the result that great hopes have been placed in this approach. In Table 2.10 we find the characteristics of some Tokamaks already built or under construction. In the last case, the characteristics of the plasma result from theoretical calculations (or those extrapolated from known machines)[5]. The first two Tokamaks have already functioned. The second has permitted the attainment of the value

10^{13} for $n\tau$ (a factor of 10 below Lawson's criterion), but the temperature remained too low (1 KeV). More recently, temperatures of 6 keV have been realized in the Princeton Tokamak.

TABLE 2.10. Characteristics of some Tokamaks functioning or under construction [5].

	ORMAK	ALCATOR	DOUBLET-III	JET	TFTR	JT-60
Major radius of the torus R (m)	0.8	0.54	1.4	2.98	2.65	3
Minor radius of the plasma r_p(m)	0.23	0.10	0.45 × 1.5	1.25	0.85	0.95
Magnetic field B_{tor} (T)	2.5	7.5	2.6	2.7to3.5	5.2	4.5
Current in the plasma I_p (MA)	0.275	0.1	< 5	3.8to4.8	2.8	2.7
Mean temperature T (keV)	0.5	1	4	10	10	10
Performances $n.\tau(10^{14}\,cm^{-3}\,s)$	0.002	0.1	1 to 2	1.1to3	0.37to1	0.27to0.73

Considering that in the 1960's the performances were around $n\tau \cong 10^{10}$ and T = 100 eV, one can measure the progress made. The DOUBLET-III (USA) experiment should have permitted Lawson's criteria to be satisfied (Fig. 2.4) but difficulties have delayed the realization of this objective originally projected for 1979. There is still no question of producing fusion energy in a significant way, since the use of tritium is not envisaged.

In Fig. 2.11 we see a schematic representation of DOUBLET-III. We note that the plasma has an elongated cross section (whence the two numbers given in Table 2.10 for the minor radius of the torus), which should improve its performances. In the same way, a vertical magnetic field of weak intensity increases the stability even further. This is created by a coil perpendicular to the principal coil.

The last three Tokamaks (Table 2.10) achieve even higher temperatures (10 keV) and should attain or surpass Lawson's values (Fig. 2.4). The European project JET could even lead to ignition. It is envisaged that these machines will eventually use tritium.

2.3.4 Other Machines

There exist a large number of types of magnetic confinement other than that of the mirror machines and the Tokamaks. We can mention the Stellarator, a toroidal machine which only differs from the Tokamak by its method of stabilization. It no longer calls upon a current circulating in the plasma, but upon special external coils which create the necessary stabilizing fields. The confinement is unfortunately extremely sensitive to the least perturbation affecting these fields. The advantages from the point of view of a reactor are accessibility and the possibility of continuous operation.

Based on another principle are the so-called "pinch" machines which are inherently-pulsed systems. A strong current is induced in the plasma during the discharge of a set of condensers in the primary circuit. The contraction ("pinch") thus created in the plasma leads to both heating and confinement.

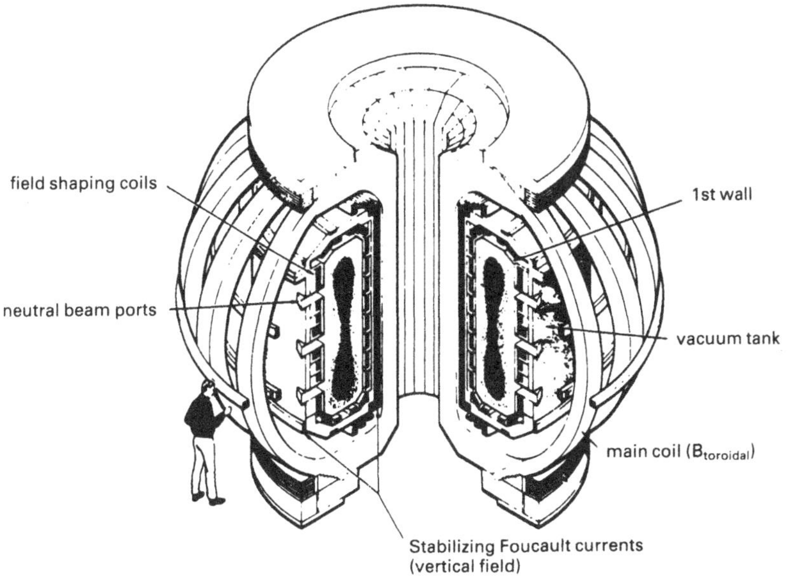

FIGURE 2.11. Schematization of DOUBLET-III.

2.3.5 Remark

The energy balances of Sec. 2.2 are somewhat optimistic in the case of magnetic confinement. In effect, the centripetal acceleration of an electron on its helicoidal trajectory entails a "cyclotron emission" proportional to n^2T^2 that has been ignored in equation (2.7). This additional loss of energy becomes important only at high temperature.

2.4 INERTIAL CONFINEMENT

2.4.1 Principle of Inertial Fusion

In this approach, we do not appeal to external magnetic fields. We consider instead a small sphere of hydrogen (D-T or D-D) that is compressed by being submitted to intense laser (or electron) beams. This being done, the plasma created will have an expansion phase during the course of which its density and its temperature will diminish significantly in time τ. This time, which can be obtained from hydrodynamic calculations, is called the inertial confinement time, since it is related to the inertia of a system which has not been submitted to any external action (the beam no longer acts at this stage). The time is given approximately by the expression: $\tau \cong r/v_s$ where v_s is the speed of sound in the compressed plasma and r is its radius. τ is no longer a quantity with which one can play for a given type of target. It is important that the fusion reactions develop in a time which is smaller than the disaggregation time τ of the compressed system, because beyond this time the densities and temperatures decrease dramatically.

If we wish to obtain by thermonuclear fusion more energy than was necessary to invest in the beams, detailed hydrodynamic calcuations show that the attained densities must be at least 10^2g cm^{-3} at the center, and that the confinement times must be of the order of a nanosecond (10^{-9} s) for a target of 60 μ in diameter after compression. This implies an average ionic density of 10^{23} to 10^{24} cm^{-3}. One gets back Lawson's criterion $n\tau \cong 10^{14}$ cm^{-3} s.

These results should be compared with what one hopes to obtain with magnetic confinement: $\tau \cong 0.1$ s to 1 s and $n \cong 10^{14}$ to 10^{16} cm^{-3}. In the latter case the ionic densities are smaller than that of a solid ($\cong 10^{22}$ to 10^{23} cm^{-3}), whereas they are higher for inertial confinement.

2.4.2 Necessity of Compression

We can explain the concept in the following way. Whatever may be the mode of confinement, we know that the product $n\tau$ must attain a certain value or, which is the same thing, that the performances are related to the product n.r (since τ is proportional to r). On the other hand, if one wants to profit from ignition, the charged particles emitted during fusion reactions which develop in the central part must have a stopping distance smaller than the radius of the microsphere. This implies that the product n.r should be quite large. Hence, for several reasons, the product n.r is the essential parameter of inertial fusion.

Let us now consider the energy W_i injected per impulse (with the help of beams). It must attain at least the value (2.15):

$$W_i = E_i V = nV \, [KZ^3 \, (n\tau) \, \sqrt{T} + \frac{3}{2} \, (Z + 1) \, T]$$

where V is the volume of the spherical pellet. Hence, for the performances imposed ($n\tau$ and T fixed), the energy W_i behaves like nV. We can thus write

$$W_i = \text{constant } nr^3 = \text{constant } \frac{(nr)^3}{n^2}$$

Since the choice of $n\tau$ implies that of nr, we deduce that the energy demanded of the beams will be smaller the higher are the densities.

2.4.3 Compression by Beams

We should now say a few words about compression. If a set of beams hits a target without strongly penetrating it, the external layer is volatilized, which leads to the compression (action-reaction) of the central part. This compression is accompanied by an increase of temperature (we simultaneously increase n and T, which is beneficial). One has thus brought about an implosion. The ulterior phase is that described above. The fusion reactions are going to develop in time τ. There results a micro-explosion similar to that which takes place in an "H-bomb" except that the ignition is assured by the initial compression and not by the fission of a detonator of uranium U^{235}. In Fig. 2.12 we have represented six laser beams heating the external (shaded) part of the target. The number of beams must be sufficient, otherwise the sphere would be deformed, rather than compressed.

With laser beams the difficulty comes from focalization and bad coupling. The energy is deposited in the form of heat in the least dense part (the furthest away) of the system, after which it is transported by thermal conduction towards the solid part, bringing about the ablation necessary for its implosion. A number of uncertainties remain concerning this energy transfer.

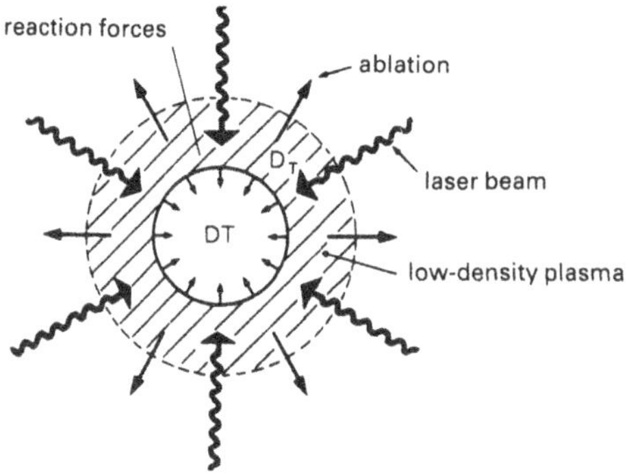

FIGURE 2.12.

With electron beams, the opposite takes place. They are too penetrating, and liable to heat the target in a homogeneous fashion, suppressing the desired effect. This situation can be remedied by introducing an external envelope of high Z, of gold, for example. The thickness of gold is chosen so as to stop completely the electron flux. One part is ejected (ablation) and the other part (pusher) directs itself toward the center, thus compressing the mixture D-T (Fig. 2.13).

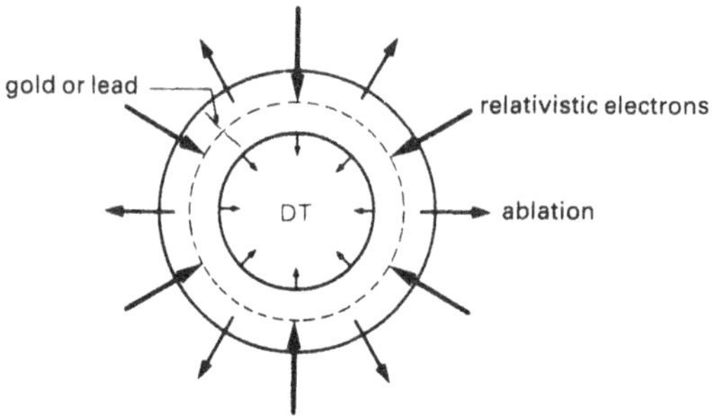

FIGURE 2.13.

More recently, it has been proposed to utilize beams of light ions (protons of a few MeV) which present better coupling characteristics with the targets than relativistic electrons. The devices producing relativistic electrons can be transformed into generators of ion beams, whence the current tendency to abandon the approach based on electron beams.

Finally, the recourse to beams of heavy ions (Xe, U of several hundreds of MeV) appears promising, since the corresponding technology already exists (powerful accelerators of particles built for other purposes).

In the last two approaches,the spherical targets are of the type indicated in Fig. 2.13.

The essential problem of inertial fusion is evidently to obtain beams of sufficient energy with the help of mechanisms of acceptable efficiency:

- the laser output hardly surpasses 5% and the best from this point of view unfortunately offer the worst beam-target coupling.
- the generators of particle beams (electrons or ions) have much higher outputs (20% to 30%) but the problems of focalization are more difficult, whence the use of thicker targets (Ø 1 mm).

2.4.4 Characteristics of Reactors Based on Inertial Fusion

Since one counts on having 200 MJ per micro-explosion for a commercial reactor, an injection of 10 pellets per second would lead to a power of 2000 MW. One of the great advantages of these reactors is the absence of instability of the type described earlier for magnetic confinement. In order to attain this goal, it is necessary to have beams of at least 100 kJ per impulse (case of lasers), for "peak powers" of 200 TW (1 TW = 10^{12} W). These evaluations rely on numerical simulations, and it is interesting to note that the last number depends very little on the type of beam.

The first experiments were carried out with laser beams (2 to 4 TW) and the validity of the concept has been proved. The first thermonuclear neutrons have even been obtained, but the gains (2.12) barely went beyond 10^{-4}. We see thus that these first experiments were at a level four orders of magnitude below the desired goal, which places them far behind the magnetic fusion experiments. All the same, research in inertial fusion is much more recent and developments have been so rapid that it is difficult to furnish up-to-date information.

Research in laser fusion is being pursued in the United States in two directions [6]:

- The first relies on glass-neodymium lasers. The SHIVA experiment has permitted the exploration of two extreme domains. In one case, strong compression (densities 100 times that of a liquid) has been obtained thanks to beams of 10 to 25 TW for impulse times of 0.2 to 2 ns, the temperatures remaining much below 1 keV. In the other case temperatures have been obtained of from 1 to 6 keV, but at the cost of diminished compression, with the help of beams of 4 to 10 kJ. The following stage relative to the NOVA experiments should permit the attainment of the Lawson threshhold in 1984-86 for injected energies of the order of 100 kJ/3 ns. or 150 TW/0.1 ns.

- The second approach involves a CO_2 laser of better efficiency but leading to a worse beam-target coupling. These experiments have resulted in densities 20 times higher than that of a liquid, and the next stage (ANTARES) is comparable to NOVA since it anticipates beams of 100 kJ/1 ns.

All these experiments have had the merit of confirming the validity of numerical simulations so well that the values indicated at the beginning of the subsection appear reasonable.

Concerning ionic fusion, which tends to supplant fusion by electron beams, there are fewer experimental results, and the decisive stage will without doubt be the starting up of PBFA, a device producing proton beams of 3.5 MJ per impulse. This machine will in principle permit ignition and the envisaged timetable is more or less that of laser fusion. All the same, serious doubts remain as to the transport of beams towards the target (defocalization) so that this latter problem is being studied in priority.

2.5 TECHNOLOGY OF FUSION REACTORS

2.5.1 Introduction

Whatever the mode of confinement, the fusion energy, as we have seen, is generated in a plasma and recovered in the form of heat in the external blankets. Thus all the energy that is produced traverses in one form or another the first inner wall (§2.2.6), that is, the envelope of the combustion chamber in which the plasma is confined. From this point of view, fusion reactors compare badly with fission reactors because, for the latter, energy is recovered from the very place where it is produced (Ch. 5).

In particular the neutron flux through the first inner wall will be able to reach 10^{15} n $cm^{-2}s^{-1}$, that is, 100 to 1000 times more than what one observes in fission reactor vessels. Let us add that fusion neutrons cause much more damage to materials than fission neutrons, since they are more energetic (14 MeV compared to 2 MeV).

For all these reasons, the technological problems posed by thermonuclear fusion are at present the object of in-depth studies. It would be of no use for physicists to achieve in laboratories their objective of satisfying Lawson's criteria if certain technological constraints rendered impossible the realization of commercial fusion reactors.

In what follows, we shall consider essentially toroidal machines, and in particular, Tokamaks, for which some results are available. All the same, most of the problems touched upon are common to all concepts of reactors. It goes without saying that technological studies are at their beginning, and thus there is nothing comparable to what is known of fission reactors.

2.5.2 Design

We will suppose that the plasma is in stable equilibrium and is made up of an equimolecular mixture of deuterium and tritium. The first generation of reactors will in fact be based on the (d,t) reactions, which are easier to start up. Although the energy source is situated in the plasma, it is possible to define the minimal dimensions of a power reactor without much reference to the plasma. There are two essential factors [3](pp. 313-17):

- The efficiency of the blanket from the point of view of thermo-hydraulics and regeneration of the tritium which leads to the fixing of its thickness.

- The possibility of lodging superconducting coils which create the necessary magnetic fields without spending additional energy.

A toroidal machine can be schematized as indicated in Fig. 2.14. One of the most important points (if not the most important) is related to the thermal loading which can be supported by the first inner wall encountered by the radiation emanating from the plasma. Everything is done so that the plasma never meets this inner wall ($r_p < r_w$); there is thus no thermal exchange (by conduction) between these two milieus. In contrast, we have to consider various energy fluxes corresponding to rapid particles:

- the neutrons of 14 MeV, most of which traverse the inner wall
- the ions which have escaped confinement
- the bremsstrahlung radiations (X photons)

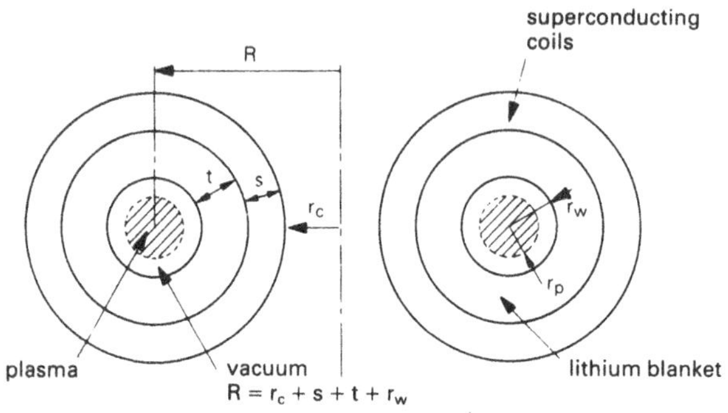

FIGURE 2.14.

Although each of these components acts differently, the global energetic flux is an essential datum; it constitutes the " thermal loading," an expression which is not quite suitable, since it is not a matter of thermal flux in the strict sense of the term. The temperature of the inner wall does not exceed 800 to 1000°C. For molybdenum (which is interesting for its small neutron capture cross section) the permissible thermal loading would be of the order of 1300 W cm^{-2}[7]. Other values have been proposed, but we will have to wait for the projected irradiation experiments (§2.5.3) in order to get the precise limits of this energy flux P_w.

For economic reasons it is desirable to operate the reactor in the neighborhood of this limit.

The average power density P_D corresponding to the volume V of the machine (blanket and coils included) can be written (Fig. 2.14):

$$P_D = \frac{2\pi r_w P_w}{\pi(r_w + s + t)^2} = \frac{P_t}{V}$$

This quantity must be as large as possible, since for a given total power P_t the volume V of the installation (and hence its cost) will be minimum. As s and t are fixed (see above), one chooses r_w in such a way as to maximize P_D. We thus find:

$$P_D = \frac{P_w}{2r_w} \quad \text{with: } r_w = s + t \qquad (2.19)$$

Different projects lead to the choice: t = 125 cm and s = 50 cm, whence r_w = 175 cm. Moreover, the major radius of the torus must be significantly larger than $(r_w + t + s)$ for reasons of accessibility (Fig. 2.14). On the other hand, the thermal power of the reactor can be written simply as:

$$P_t = 2\pi R \times 2\pi r_w P_w \qquad (2.20)$$

For a radius R = 500 cm of the torus and the preceding values of r_w and P_w one is led to:

$$P_t = 4490 \text{ MW and } P_D = 3.7 \text{ W cm}^{-3}$$

The power density of a Tokamak is thus quite low compared to the power densities of existing nuclear power stations (50 to 100 W cm^{-3}). Besides, one can hope for a thermodynamic output of the order of 40% if liquid lithium is used as a heat carrier. One thus arrives at a gross electric power $P_b \cong 1800$ MWe. This figure is comparable with the powers envisaged for commercial fast breeder reactors (§5.4.5). Large-size installations seem to be indicated in both cases. Naturally, if the chosen materials demand weaker energy fluxes, we might be led to increase the radius R of the torus, since r_w is fixed by the thickness of the blankets.

It is now necessary to define the plasma so that the desired power can be achieved. The fusion power can be written (2.11):

$$P_f \text{ (W cm}^{-3}) = 1.6\ 10^{-13} \frac{n^2}{4} <\sigma v> Q \text{ (MeV)}$$

with Q = 22.4 MeV,an energy which includes neutron capture in lithium (§2.1.3). The linear power density can be written in two different ways:

$$\pi r_p^2 P_f = 2\pi r_w P_w \qquad \text{(in W cm}^{-1})$$

whence:

$$nr_p = 1.494\ 10^6 \sqrt{\frac{r_w P_w}{<\sigma v>}} \qquad \text{(in cm}^{-2}) \qquad (2.21)$$

In the preceding, r_p designates the radius of the plasma. For a given thermal power P_t and a given radius R of the torus, equation (2.20) leads to fixing the product ($r_w P_w$). Thus the parameter $n\ r_p$ to be realized depends only on the temperature through the reaction parameter $<\sigma v>$ (Fig. 2.2). Its value is indicated in Table 2.15 for some operating temperatures T and thermal loading $P_w = 1300\ W\ cm^{-2}$.

TABLE 2.15. Determination of the operating point of a fusion reactor $P_t = 4490\ MW_t$, $R = 500$ cm, $r_p = 125$ cm, $B_{tor} = 10$ T, $\eta_T = 0.4$.

T (keV)	5	10	20	30	70
nr_p (cm^{-2})	2.10^{17}	$6.8 \cdot 10^{16}$	$3.5 \cdot 10^{16}$	$2.8 \cdot 10^{16}$	$2.4 \cdot 10^{16}$
$n\tau$ (cm^{-3} s)	2.10^{16}	$2.3 \cdot 10^{15}$	$6.0 \cdot 10^{14}$	$3.9 \cdot 10^{14}$	$2.8 \cdot 10^{14}$
G	8.8	26.1	20.6	14.6	6.5
$\eta_i \varepsilon$ (%)	25.5	9.2	11.5	16	33.3
f (%)	11.2	11.2	11.2	11.2	11.2
n (cm^{-3})	$1.6 \cdot 10^{15}$	$5.4 \cdot 10^{14}$	$2.8 \cdot 10^{14}$	$2.2 \cdot 10^{14}$	$1.9 \cdot 10^{14}$

It is only at this stage that plasma physics intervenes. Various extrapolations based on results furnished by operational Tokamaks have led to the scaling law [5]:

$$n\tau\ (cm^{-3}\ s) = 5\ 10^{-19}\ (n\ r_p)^2 \qquad (2.22)$$

where $n\ r_p$ is expressed in cm^{-2}.

Naturally, equation (2.22) is open to question and the goal of the projected experiments (JET, TFTR, cf. Table 2.10) is precisely to verify such a law. If we accept this law, we observe that the product $n\tau$ to be obtained is proportional to $(n\ r_p)^2$ hence, to the number of ions per unit length, or even to the "fuel load" if we use an expression often applied to current nuclear reactors. But this last parameter $(n\ r_p)^2$ only depends as we have seen on the temperature, and hence the same is true of $n\tau$ (always for a given product $r_w P_w$). The expected "$n\tau$ performances" are indicated in Table 2.15. They are represented by a decreasing curve which furnishes by intersection with the lattice of curves of Fig.2.4 a set of operating points (T, G). More simply equation 2.12 furnishes in virtue of the preceding values ($n\tau$) the gain G as a function of the temperature.

Supposing the energy injected in the plasma to be of external origin, then equation (2.13) gives the fraction of the gross power which must be "recirculated" (§2.2.3). Among the possible operating points, the most advantageous is evidently that which corresponds to the minimum recirculation power. Table 2.15 indicates that the plasma characterized by the second column is optimum. The temperature corresponding to it is 10 keV.

If on the contrary we consider the case of ignition, then we must seek the intersection of the corresponding curve of Fig. 2.4 with the curve that is represented by the third line of Table 2.15. This procedure is equivalent to solving simultaneously equations (2.17), (2.21) and (2.22). We find $T = 70$ keV and $n\tau = 2.82\ 10^{14}\ cm^{-3}\ s$, in other words, the plasma defined by the last column. In order to attain this operating point it is not necessary to carry the plasma to 70 keV, which would be problematic. It suffices to consider a plasma having a good product $n\ r_p$ (in other words, the necessary quantity of fuel) and to heat it at a temperature such that the operating point is situated above the ignition curve (Fig. 2.4). The system will evolve by itself in such a way as to attain the envisaged regime. Because of "cyclotron emissions" (§2.3.5), the operating temperature will be closer to 50 keV than to 70 keV.

The last aspect that we have to consider is that of fuel consumption. Up until now we have supposed without saying so that S atoms of hydrogen per unit volume and unit time were being introduced in the plasma in order to compensate for losses. We can thus write:

$$S = 2 \times R_f + \frac{n}{\tau}$$

where R_f is the reaction rate given by equation (2.2) ($n_1 = n_2 = \frac{n}{2}$) and n/τ the leakage rate. The factor 2 before R_f indicates that two hydrogen ions are destroyed per reaction. The consumption rate can be written by definition as:

$$f = \frac{2 \times R_f}{S} = \frac{1}{1 + \frac{n}{2R_f\ \tau}} = \frac{1}{1 + \frac{2}{n\tau\ \langle\sigma v\rangle}} \qquad (2.23)$$

The preceding method of calculation is based on equations (2.21) and (2.22) which implies that the product $(n\tau)\ \langle\sigma v\rangle$ is constant. The same is true of the consumption rate which gets established at 11%.

The last line of Table 2.15 corresponds to a choice of the radius of the plasma. Taking $r_p = 125$ cm, one leaves a sufficient interval between the plasma and the first wall ($r_w = 175$ cm), but it remains to be seen if this value is attainable. We can repeat the previous reasoning for various thermal charges P_w and look for the operating points on the ignition curve (Fig. 2.4). We find that there exists a minimum thermal loading

$P_w \cong 200$ W cm^{-2}, in other words, a power of 680 MW (with the preceding values of R and r_w), below which the reaction cannot function by ignition. This operating point corresponds to $n\tau = 3.5\ 10^{14}$ cm^{-3} s and T = 10 keV. The last Tokamaks (Tab. 2.10) should have performances quite close to the above values.

2.5.3 Radiation Damage

The preceding dimensioning is based on a limit of the incident energy flux falling on the first wall. It remains to know why. The study of the interaction of various radiations with the external medium and more particularly with the first wall, which is the most exposed, furnishes in principle the answer to this question. Although all the phenomena have not been completely elucidated, we class them under the term "erosion". The erosion of a solid wall bombarded by fast particles is due essentially to three processes:

- Tearing off of atoms (sputtering). This phenomenon takes place at low temperatures. The particles which penetrate the wall give rise to collisions (scattering) with atoms which were at rest. At each shock they communicate to the atoms a part of their energy. It is by this procedure that the coolant (liquid lithium) heats itself, carrying away in the form of heat the energy which it receives from the plasma. In the solid wall this phenomenon can have a negative effect, since the atoms situated near the inner surface can be ejected towards the plasma, contaminating it. These atoms of high Z mixed with the plasma will increase the radiation losses, rendering ignition more difficult. This process leads to a progressive disappearance of the wall. Although representing less than 10% of the total thermal charge, the ions (α, d or t) which succeed in escaping confinement play a preponderant role in the erosion phenomenon. Theoretical calculations cross-checked with some experimental results lead to erosion rates which can surpass 10^{15} atoms/cm^{2}s for a wall of niobium 5 mm thick (density 8.57g cm^{-3}, A = 93). One deduces from this that in less than one year the entire wall could disappear.

- Evaporation. When the first wall is subjected to a sudden major thermal charge, a large number of atoms acquire sufficient thermal energy to leave it. The evaporation rate is proportional to the sublimation vapor pressure well known for various metals. The phenomenon becomes important above 1500° C.

- Formation of gaseous bubbles (blistering). After recoil, the atoms which have been submitted to shocks from incident particles leave gaps in the solid. These gaps can trap the incident particles, especially if the latter are not very soluble (inert gases in metals). In the extreme case, gaseous bubbles can be formed. This phenomenon can damage the wall. Among the envisaged metals, the elements V, Nb, Ta, Ti, Zr have a high solubility for hydrogen, which is not the case for Mo, W, Cu and Be. The latter will thus suffer from the presence of hydrogen. As for helium, all metals can trap it. Recent results have shown that helium bubbles of Ø 400 μm were formed in niobium irradiated by a beam of α particles. Moreover, numerous threshhold neutron reactions (n,p) (n,α) will produce deep in the wall gaseous hydrogen and helium, the most critical for this type of phenomenon.

A major experimental program is needed for a detailed study of the erosion of the first wall. For this, major radiation sources must be developed. (We cannot wait for the realization of fusion reactors). A neutron source of 14 MeV (10^{14} n/s) is in construction in the US, as are intense ion sources. With what we already know, we can predict that the firstinner wall will have to be replaced every two or three years, whence reactor concepts permitting easy replacement, the leakproofness being assured by an enclosure outside the blanket.

2.5.4 Energy Injection

We have seen that in most cases it is necessary to inject energy into the plasma so as to raise it to a high temperature (> 5 keV). Even when ignition has been achieved for a continuous operation, energy must be injected at least once at the beginning. A number of heating methods exist:

- Neutral beams. Let us consider a beam of ions which have been initially accelerated (100 to 200 keV). It is indispensable to neutralize them so that they can penetrate the plasma. If the plasma is magnetically well confined, it by definition impedes its ions from escaping and at the same time prevents ions from penetrating it. When the neutral particles have traversed the "magnetic barrier" they ionize instantaneously in contact with the hot plasma. Finally, by successive collisions, they depose their energy, just like the α particles created in the heart of the plasma. This mode of heating is especially envisaged for the Tokamaks, and current experiments have led to efficiencies η_i = 10% (one hopes to pass to 60%).

• Relativistic electron beams. They are specially envisaged for inertial fusion (Sec. 2.4). Beams have already been obtained of 1.5 MV and 6 MA (9 TW) for a duration of 24 n s.

• Waves. Electromagnetic waves propagate in plasmas following particular laws which depend on certain characteristic frequencies. One should cite in the first place the plasma frequency ω_p proportional to $\sqrt{n}$ where n is the electronic density, and also the cyclotron frequencies ω_{ci}, ω_{ce} (see §2.3.1) which play a fundamental role in the case of magnetic confinement. Other characteristic frequencies, called hybrid since they are a function of the preceding and of the magnetic field, also intervene. It is not possible here to give more details. Let us simply say that when the frequency of the EM waves is close to that of one of these characteristic frequencies (resonance), a significant transfer of energy can take place. It is evidently the ionic component of the plasma that one seeks to heat. This can result from a direct or an indirect interaction. In the latter case, the electrons transmit by collision with the ions the energy which they have received from the EM waves. In practice, certain radio frequency generators can furnish up to 1 MW of power for frequencies not exceeding 10 to 20 GHz (2×10^{10} Hz).

• Adiabatic compression. None of the preceding methods permits attainment of the ignition temperature. Thus at a second stage, one envisages adiabatic compression as the ultimate means. Taking the case of the Tokamak, let us increase the small vertical field which stabilizes it. Given the presence of a toroidal current, a force will displace the plasma towards the axis of the torus, and hence into a domain where the toroidal field is stronger. There results an adiabatic compression which heats the plasma. We recall that in certain machines (Tokamaks) the stabilizing current furnishes by ohmic means the greater part of the heating energy.

2.6 CONCLUSIONS

Concerning the physics of plasmas we have seen that there is good hope of obtaining controlled fusion in the laboratory in the near future. In other words, a sufficient product ($n\tau$) should be obtained with machines now in the course of construction. Once this is achieved, the passage to an industrial prototype will require the solution of technological problems analyzed in the last section. There exist other problems, such as perfecting superconducting coils. The latter have not so far been envisaged in the machines under construction. However, it will be necessary to call upon them to attain the necessary magnetic fields (10 T) while avoiding all the same unacceptable ohmic losses.

We have not taken up the question of the cooling of the blankets and of the thermodynamic cycle, since the problems involved are similar to those which must be solved in the case of breeder fission reactors (§5.4.5). The lithium envisaged for fusion reactors should be quite similar to sodium from the point of view of thermal hydraulics. The same temperatures (600° C) are envisaged but two new problems appear:

- It is necessary at one point of the circuit to remove a part of the lithium in order to extract from it the tritium that has been formed;
- When the velocity of the lithium flow is perpendicular to the magnetic field, transversal currents are induced. An additional pressure drop results.

The use of molten salts (2 LiF, BeF_2) in place of liquid lithium should suppress the last problem. Unfortunately, the conversion factor (into tritium) diminishes.

The maintenance of a vacuum is assured by a special circuit consisting of pumps. This system must permit the reinjection of deuterium and tritium which have not reacted. Refuelling, finally, consists of introducing into the plasma pellets of deuterium/tritium.

Fig. 2.16 is a rough schematization of a reactor based on laser fusion. An intermediate circuit (not represented) is inserted between the primary exchangers and the steam generators in order to avoid all risk of contact between the water and the lithium of the blanket (this is true for all fusion reactors). Fusion by inertial confinement permits original technological solutions. Thus the reactor represented in Fig. 2.16 uses

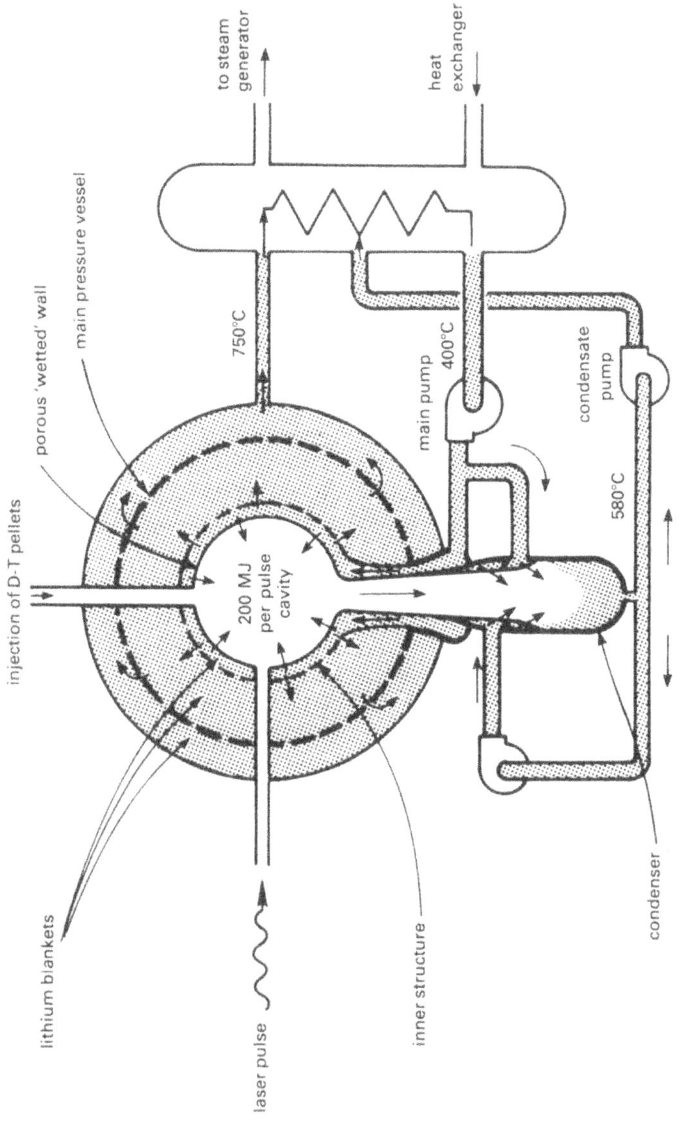

FIGURE 2.16. Inertial fusion reactor: "wetted wall" concept.

for its first wall a porous material which permits a small fraction of the liquid lithium to penetrate to the interior of the cavity, forming a protective film on its surface. The problem of erosion is in part resolved [3].

NUCLEAR FISSION

3.1 GENERAL CHARACTERISTICS

3.1.1 Introduction

From this chapter onwards, we will only be concerned with nuclear fission and its applications. Here we will confine ourselves to general considerations related on the one hand to the nuclear fuel and on the other hand to the various modes of energy recovery. This chapter will thus give the basis for more detailed studies which will be the object of subsequent chapters: reactor physics, nuclear power plants, safety, etc. We will begin with a brief historical review.

Soon after the discovery of the neutron (§1.2.4), it was observed that the neutron was very easily captured by atomic nuclei. The nuclei thus formed were very often β^- radioactive, giving schemes of the type:

$$ {}_0n^1 + {}_ZX^A \rightarrow {}_ZX^{A+1} \overset{\beta^-}{\rightarrow} {}_{Z+1}X^{A+1} \rightarrow \text{ etc.} $$

The irradiation of uranium (Z = 92) by neutrons should thus lead to nuclei of higher atomic numbers (Z = 93, 94, etc.) corresponding to <u>trans-uranic</u> elements. Although this process exists (§3.2.3), it could not be immediately shown. What was observed on the contrary was the unexpected appearance of nuclei of intermediate Z, such as barium (Z = 56). This could only be explained by admitting that uranium nuclei could split into two fragments of comparable masses (Hahn and Strassman 1939).

This important phenomenon is known by the name of <u>induced nuclear fission</u> (by one neutron). We have already invoked this process in subsec. 1.5.4 when treating cross sections of fission and fusion reactions. If one analyzes this phenomenon more closely, one observes that for a given <u>fissile</u> nucleus (${}_{92}U^{235}$ for example), a large number of reactions are possible. We can still write globally:

$$ {}_0n^1 + {}_{92}U^{235} \longrightarrow 2FP + \bar{\nu}\,{}_0n^1 + 207 \text{ MeV} $$

with $\bar{\nu} \cong 2.42$.

One should note here that heavy nuclei such as ${}_{92}U^{238}$ which are not fissionable in the sense of the preceding reaction are nevertheless subject to spontaneous fission. These nuclei like all unstable nuclei are characterized by a decay constant (§1.4.1). This phenomenon being negligible in nuclear reactors (except perhaps in the course of the first start-up), the term fission will always be employed in the following in the sense of induced fission.

3.1.2 Fission Products (or Fission Fragments)

Each fission leads to two well-defined fission products (FP) as well as to two or three fission neutrons. The fission rarely corresponds to a half and half sharing of the original fissionable nucleus, contrary to the simple schematization of the first chapter.

Given 100 fissions, if we call $y(A_i)$ the number of fission products of mass number A_i corresponding to a particular type of fission, we observe that the points thus obtained are distributed on a curve in the shape of a "camel's humps" (Fig. 3.1). We will of course have $\sum_i y(A_i) = 200$, because we are considering 100 fissions.

The most probable fissions thus lead to fission products of atomic masses 94 and 140 respectively. We have for example:

$$ {}_0n^1 + {}_{92}U^{235} \longrightarrow {}_{38}Sr^{94} + {}_{54}Xe^{140} + 2\,{}_0n^1 $$

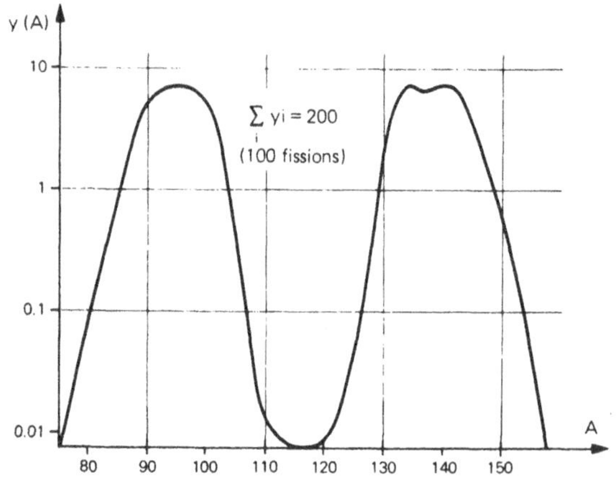

FIGURE 3.1. Distribution of fission products as a function of mass numbers.

Uranium U^{235} possesses an excess of neutrons with respect to protons, and these neutrons will thus be found in the fission products. For intermediate atomic masses this configuration is unstable and the fission products will disintegrate following chains analogous to those mentioned in the context of the natural radioactivity of uranium. There is no difference in nature except that α radioactivity will be absent. Let us cite as an example the following chain:

$$_{54}Xe^{140} \xrightarrow[16s]{\beta-} {}_{55}Cs^{140} \xrightarrow[66s]{\beta-} {}_{56}Ba^{140} \xrightarrow[12.8d]{\beta-} {}_{57}La^{140} \xrightarrow[40h]{\beta-} {}_{58}Ce^{140} \text{ (stable)}$$

We note as usual a great variety of half-lives going from 16s to 12.8d.

In spite of the great complexity of fission (numerous $y(A_i)$ and long chains), there is at present very little uncertainty about the detailed inventory of fission products. The fission products accumulate in the fuel and pose problems of protection against radiation during the handling of irradiated fuel elements. These absorb a considerable portion of the radiated energy (β: 100%, γ: 30 to 60% depending on the geometry of the rods). There results a source of heat intrinsically linked to the fission products and to their descendants. We must thus cool the fuel even after the reactor stops (except of course during the first loading before the power rises). We will return to this question in the context of safety studies.

3.1.3 Fission Neutrons and Chain Reactions

On the average $\bar{\nu}$ neutrons are created by fission. Here too there are a large number of possibilities. Depending on the type of fission (characterized by y(A)) the emitted neutrons will be more or less energetic. From a global point of view we can speak of a fission spectrum having the aspect indicated in Fig. 3.2. The most probable emission energy is about 0.75 MeV, and the average energy of fission neutrons is about 2 MeV. This last number should be kept in mind. The fission neutrons play a major role in the functioning of a nuclear reactor. In effect, the neutron does not exist in a free state in nature (because of its instability) and the envisageable sources (α + Be, cf. §1.2.4) have intensities which are much too weak. The mechanism of fission thus permits the creation "on-site" of the neutrons necessary for new fission. Because $\bar{\nu}$ is of the order of 2.4 to 2.9 depending on the fissile matter under consideration, a chain reaction is possible. It is called divergent when the neutron population increases due to an excess of emissions over disappearances. We will see in Sec. 4.6 that this increase has an exponential character. We have schematized in Fig. 3.3 a chain reaction which is particularly divergent because every absorption of neutrons is "useful." We have only taken account of the phenomenon of fission in this diagram. In reality, many neutrons are lost through radiative capture or leakage from the system.

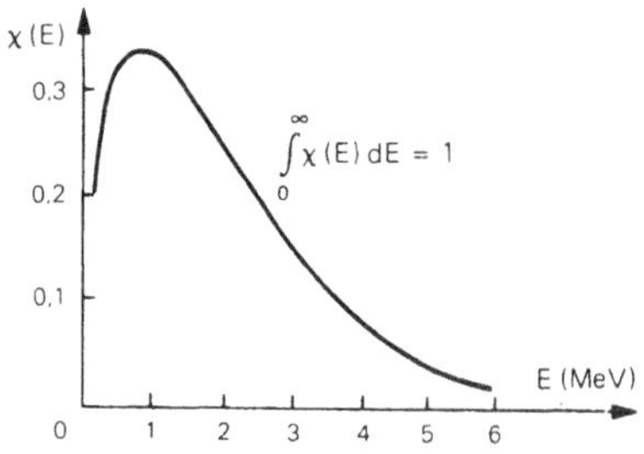

FIGURE 3.2. Fission neutron spectrum.

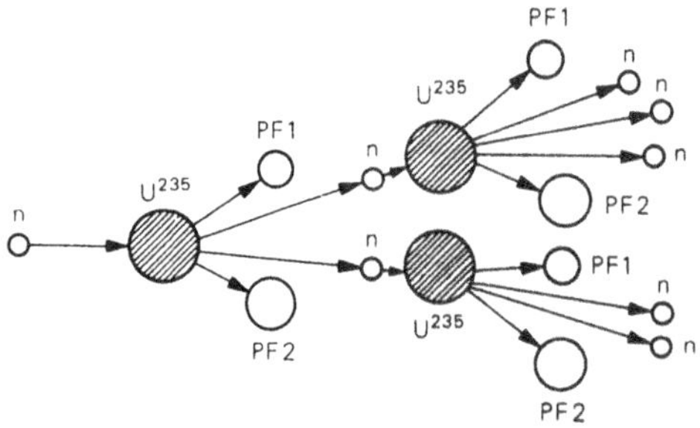

FIGURE 3.3.

A last characteristic of the fission resides in the fact that a very small proportion β of neutrons is emitted in a delayed fashion. Some chains of fission products decay in the following way:

$$_{35}Br^{87} \xrightarrow[55s]{\beta^-} {}_{36}Kr^{87} \xrightarrow{\beta^-} {}_{37}Rb^{87} \xrightarrow{\beta^-} {}_{38}Sr^{87} \text{ (stable)}$$

$$_{36}Kr^{87} \xrightarrow{{}_0n^1} {}_{36}Kr^{86} \text{ (stable)}$$

In this example one "branch" leads to a neutron, but this can only appear after the formation of krypton $_{36}Kr^{87}$, and thus after a certain time.

The delayed (or retarded) neutrons, although not numerous, play a fundamental role in reactor kinetics (Sec. 4.6). For uranium U^{235} the characteristics of delayed neutrons appear in Table 3.4. The decay constants λ_i (or the half-lives) are defined for each of the six groups of delayed neutrons in the usual way (Sec. 1.4). Each appearance of a delayed neutron expresses the decay (β^-) of a precursor fission product.

TABLE 3.4. Characteristics of delayed neutrons.

Group	Half-life [s] T_i	Decay const. [s^{-1}] λ_i	Energy [MeV]	Proportions β_i
1	55.72	0.0124	0.25	0.000215
2	22.72	0.0305	0.56	0.001424
3	6.22	0.111	0.40–45	0.001274
4	2.30	0.301	0.450	0.002568
5	0.610	1.14	0.42	0.000748
6	0.23	3.01	—	0.000273
Total				$\beta = \Sigma \beta i = 0.0065$

Whether they are prompt or delayed, fission neutrons have a high energy (on the average 2 MeV in the first case and 0.4 MeV in the second) with respect to the thermal energy (0.025 eV) for which they are the most efficient (Fig. 1.10) We can directly conclude that it is necessary to slow them unless the contrary is indicated. We achieve this result by using a moderator which will necessarily be a material of small atomic weight, as shown by reactor physics (Sec. 4.4). We will thus speak of reactors moderated by water, graphite, etc. We call thermal neutrons those neutrons which have attained the minimum energy or which are in thermodynamic equilibrium with the matter in which they are slowed down.

3.1.4 Detailed Energy Balance

The energy of a fission reaction, about 207 MeV, is distributed in the following way ($_{92}U^{235}$):

• Fission products (kinetic energy)	168 MeV
• Fission neutrons (kinetic energy)	5 ($\bar{\nu}$ x 2 MeV)
• Prompt radiation γ	7
• Radioactivity of fission products:	
β radiation	8
γ radiation	7
Neutrinos	12
Total	207 MeV

We see that the largest fraction of energy is carried away in the form of kinetic energy by fission products (168 MeV). These are heavy ions and are thus rapidly slowed down in the fuel. The same is true of the β rays in spite of the long distance they travel. The γ photons on the contrary have the possibility of leaving the fuel and only part of them are absorbed in it.

The neutrons depose their energy (by slowing down) for the most part outside of the fuel. To the kinetic energy of 5 MeV that they carry we must add an energy γ relative to additional neutron captures. This greatly depends on the constitution of the reactor. It is of the order of 5 to 10 MeV and does not appear in the preceding breakdown because primary fission energy is not involved.

Finally, the neutrinos associated to the β radioactivity of the fission products leave the reactor entirely (§1.3.2).

From the preceding we conclude that in normal operation an energy of 180 to 190 MeV per fission will be released in the form of heat in the fuel and will be recovered by the coolant which is nearly in contact with it (Ch. 5). In contrast to fusion reactors, almost all the energy of the reaction (92%) is recovered at the very place where it is produced. If one considers the totality of the reactor, the preceding numbers become 200 - 205 MeV, because one is taking into account the energy of the neutrons (including that of γ photons from capture).

At reactor shutdown, only the contribution of the radioactivity of the fission products ($\beta + \gamma$) must be taken into account, that is to say 15 MeV per fission, which is about 7% of the rated thermal power. From the moment the chain reaction stops, the radioactive equilibrium of the fission products is broken; the preceding numbers thus concern the initial value of the residual power. The latter decreases slowly with time, and still represents 0.8% of the rated power one day after shutdown. After 10 seconds this decrease is well represented by the curves in Fig. 3.5 which furnish the residual calorific power of the fuel after reactor shutdown for various cooling times t and irradiation times T. A long time after reactor shutdown, only the fission products of long life-time remain. It is for this reason that the results depend strongly on the irradiation time (§1.4.4). The isotopes which decay very slowly are in effect those which demand the longest time to form in the functioning reactor (under neutron flux). The afterheat plays an important role in the study of safety of nuclear power plants as well as in the designing of equipment for the transport of the irradiated fuel.

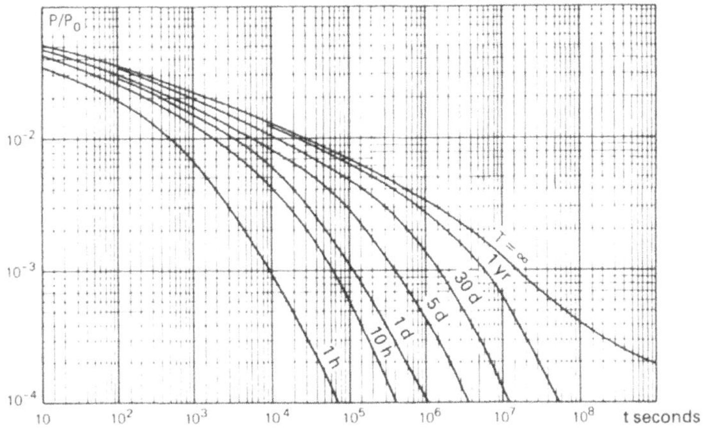

FIGURE 3.5. Residual power; cooling time t; irradiation time T; rated power P_o of the reactor.

3.2 NUCLEAR FUEL

3.2.1 Definition

A material which is capable of furnishing energy (in the form of heat) from nuclear reactions is called nuclear fuel. Under present conditions, only the fission of heavy nuclei is involved, since the thermonuclear fusion of light nuclei has not yet been mastered. The word nuclear will henceforth be employed only in the sense of nuclear fission.

3.2.2 Comparisons between Nuclear and Fossil Fuels

If we employ the expression "nuclear fuel" it is of course by analogy with fossil fuels: coal and fuel-oil. In both cases "heat" is produced in the heart of the combustibles, but the analogy stops there.

First, the only two natural nuclear fuels, uranium and thorium, contain very little or no fissile matter. In the first case, the fissionable fraction (U^{235}) represents only 0.7%; in the second case, it is absent and only appears in the course of the cycle by neutron irradiation of the fuel (§3.2.3).

Another difference resides in the mode of combustion. The fossil fuel burns instantaneously in the furnace in the presence of air. In the case of nuclear fission, by contrast, the reaction rates are very low. Let us consider a certain quantity of fissile matter corresponding to N nuclei per unit volume and submitted to a neutron flux ϕ . The absorption rate can be written (§1.5.5):

$$R_a = N\sigma_a\phi \ (cm^{-3}s^{-1})$$

To each absorbed neutron corresponds the destruction of a nucleus. Hence, R_a represents the consumption rate of the fissile matter. We have thus:

$$\frac{dN}{dt} = - N\sigma_a\phi$$

an equation which is easily integrated when the flux is constant:

$$N(t) = N(0) \exp(-\sigma_a \phi t) \tag{3.1}$$

Let us take the case of uranium ${}_{92}U^{235}$ for which $\sigma_a = 680b = 6.810^{-22}$ cm^2 (thermal neutrons) and let us consider a flux of $10^{13} n\ cm^{-2}s^{-1}$.

At the end of a year, only 20% of the initial fissile matter will have been consumed. This is the consequence of the fact that the energy emitted by fission is so high that in order to arrive at reasonable power densities (evacuable) the neutron flux in a reactor must be limited to the value indicated above, whence a low annual consumption rate.

Thus, a fission liberates an energy of about 200 MeV, whereas (chemical) combustion of a carbon atom only buys us 4.25 eV (1 eV = $1.6\ 10^{-19}$ joules). We deduce that the fission of a gram of uranium U^{235} furnishes (§1.2):

$$\left(\frac{6.023 \cdot 10^{23}}{235}\right)(200 \cdot 10^{6})\ 1.6\ 10^{-19} = 8.2 \cdot 10^{10}\ \text{J} = 82\ \text{GJ}$$

whereas we only obtain:

$$\left(\frac{6.023 \cdot 10^{23}}{12}\right) 4.25 \cdot 1.6\ 10^{-19} = 3.4 \cdot 10^{4}\ \text{J} = 34\ \text{kJ}$$

from a gram of coal. The ratio is thus more than 2×10^6 in favor of nuclear fission. If we consider natural uranium which only contains 0.7% of fissionable uranium (U^{235}), this ratio, although lower, remains considerable. The energy content of a gram of natural uranium represents $0.7 \times 10^{-2} \times 82 \times 10^{6} = 57 \cdot 10^{4}$ kjoules, in other words, more than 10,000 times that of a gram of coal. We will keep in mind the equivalence:

1 kg of natural uranium → 16.7 metric tons of coal

We are only at the stage of rough considerations, since the effective thermal energy that is extracted is in both cases inferior to the above values because of incomplete burning. Moreover, under neutron flux, new isotopes appear and the composition of the fuel becomes very complex (see the following subsection and Sec. 5.3). We can all the same deduce from the preceding that the stockage capacities to envisage <u>at the entry and at the exit (waste)</u> of power plants are <u>much more modest</u> in the case of nuclear power plants. In nuclear engineering the megawatt-day is often introduced as the unit of energy. Its value follows from its name:

$$1\ \text{MWd} = 10^{6} \cdot 24 \cdot 3600 = 8.64 \cdot 10^{10}\ \text{J}$$

Hence, following the preceding:

<u>One gram of fissioned uranium ${}_{92}U^{235}$ furnishes 1 MWd</u>. This very simple result permits a rough evaluation of the performances of a nuclear reactor.

3.2.3 Fissile Matter and Fertile Matter

Other than fissions, neutrons present in a nuclear reactor can give rise to various nuclear reactions. Radiative capture (§1.5.3) is by far the most important.

We have already seen that this contributes to a small extent to the improvement of the energy balance of a reactor. All the same, it has the inconvenience of rendering more difficult the establishment of a sustained chain reaction (a captured neutron is no longer available for a new fission). This aspect will be analyzed quantitatively in the following section. What interests us here is the property of certain isotopes called fertile of giving artificial fissionable isotopes by neutron capture. The consequences for the fuel cycle are considerable. The two natural fertile materials are uranium ${}_{92}U^{238}$ and thorium ${}_{90}Th^{232}$. They give rise by neutron capture to the following reactions:

$$ {}_0n^1 + {}_{92}U^{238} \rightarrow {}_{94}Pu^{239} + 2\beta^- $$

$$ {}_0n^1 + {}_{90}Th^{232} \rightarrow {}_{92}U^{233} + 2\beta^- $$

The two negative electrons which appear result from the β radioactivity of intermediate isotopes which have been omitted in the preceding equations for reasons of simplicity. The second reaction permits us to understand why thorium is considered a nuclear fuel, even though in contrast to natural uranium it does not have any fissionable isotopes at the outset.

Plutonium ${}_{94}Pu^{239}$ and uranium ${}_{92}U^{233}$ are not found in nature. They give rise, especially the first, to α emissions similar to those of natural uranium. Of much shorter half-life (25,000 years), the specific activity per gram (§1.4.3) of plutonium is much higher. The fertile materials have another interesting characteristic. They give rise to non-negligible fission cross sections for fast neutrons. This is shown in Fig. 3.6. As we have seen for fusion reactions, threshhold reactions are difficult to put into operation under normal temperature conditions. Fission neutrons emitted with an energy of 2 MeV are in effect rapidly slowed down below the threshhold without having given rise to new fissions in a significant way. Thus we cannot hope to realize a nuclear reactor only by using fertile materials in spite of the "fast fission" to which they give rise. The presence of fissile matter, in other words, of isotopes which can be fissioned by neutrons of all energies, is always necessary, even in the case of reactors using fast neutrons.

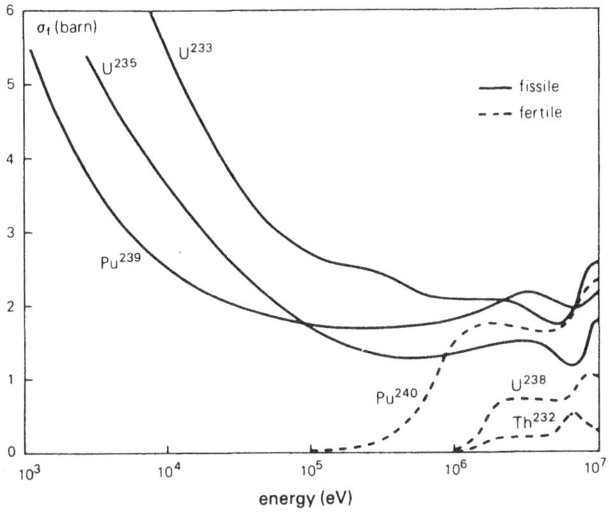

FIGURE 3.6. Microscopic fission cross sections for various fissionable or fertile isotopes.

For it to be otherwise, the energy of fission neutrons would have to be much higher than the energy threshholds (Fig. 3.6). All the same, for plutonium Pu^{240}, an artificial fertile material, this condition is satisfied. In certain very special assemblies, a chain reaction can be born by basing itself on this isotope, which is however not fissionable in the strict sense of the term.

TABLE 3.7. Nuclear properties of the most important heavy isotopes.

Nuclear reactions \ Isotopes		$_{92}U^{235}$, $_{92}U^{233}$, $_{94}Pu^{239}$ Fissile	$_{92}U^{238}$, $_{90}Th^{232}$, $_{94}Pu^{240}$ Fertile
Fission	thermal	significant	none
	fast	insignificant	insignificant
Capture		parasite	useful

The neutron captures occasioned by the not-fertile isotopes are called parasitic because they degrade the neutron balance without any compensation.

Table 3.7 summarizes the nuclear characteristics of the most important fissile and fertile materials.

3.3 NEUTRONIC CHARACTERISTICS OF THE FUEL

3.3.1 Multiplication Factor of Fissile Materials

Given the preceding, we can set up at least qualitatively a first neutron balance sheet. Let us consider a homogeneous core consisting of fissile and fertile materials, as well as of structural materials indispensable for the realization of any reactor. The latter are very often neutron absorbers, so that they should be employed in as limited a way as possible. A compromise must always be made between neutronic and technological imperatives. Given N (cm^{-3}) the density of fissionable nuclei and ϕ the neutron flux, at any point of the system the fission rate can be written $R_f = N\,\sigma_f\phi$. To this corresponds a production of fission neutrons equal to $\bar{\nu}R_f = \bar{\nu}N\sigma_f\phi$ ($cm^{-3}s^{-1}$). The neutron absorption rate for the fissile matter can be written $R_a = N\sigma_a\phi$ whence one deduces the multiplication factor for the fissionable isotope under consideration:

$$\eta = \frac{\bar{\nu}R_f}{R_a} = \frac{\bar{\nu}\sigma_f}{\sigma_a} = \bar{\nu}\,\frac{\sigma_f}{\sigma_f + \sigma_c} \qquad (3.2)$$

η represents the number of fission neutrons produced by each neutron absorbed in the fissile matter. The result depends neither on the flux ϕ nor on the number of fissionable nuclei N. The parameter η is thus a characteristic of the fissionable nucleus under consideration in the same way as the microscopic cross section. As radiative capture is always in competition with fission ($\sigma_c \neq 0$), η is always smaller than $\bar{\nu}$ but greater than one, as shown in Table 3.8.

These characteristics, valid for thermal neutrons, show that uranium U^{233} gives the best multiplication factor η although giving rise to fissions which are less rich in neutrons ($\bar{\nu}$) than those of plutonium. We also note the low value of the rate of delayed neutrons β which characterizes plutonium. Other than these differences, which appear in the table, the fission process is virtually the same for all three fissionable isotopes, whether these fissions are induced by fast or slow neutrons.

TABLE 3.8 . Nuclear data relative to the 3 fissionable isotopes bombarded by thermal neutrons.

	σ_a [b]	σ_f [b]	η	$\bar{\nu}$	β
$_{92}U^{233}$	579	531	2.287	2.49	0.0026
$_{92}U^{235}$	681	582	2.068	2.42	0.0065
$_{94}Pu^{239}$	1011	742	2.108	2.87	0.0021

3.3.2 Breeding

Taking the preceding homogeneous core, let us this time make up a global neutron balance sheet. If S_f and A represent respectively the fission and absorption rates relative to the system as a whole, the condition that a sustained chain reaction (stationary flux) be possible can be written:

$$\bar{\nu}_1 S_{f1} + \bar{\nu}_2 S_{f2} = A_1 + A_2 + A_p + F \tag{3.3}$$

where the indices 1, 2, p characterize respectively fissionable isotopes, fertile isotopes, and structure materials responsible for parasite captures, and where F represents the leakage of neutrons from the system. Equation (3.3) only expresses the fact that at equilibrium the production of neutrons (due exclusively to fissions) exactly compensates absorption and leakage losses.

By definition the fission rates in fertile materials are small. We can thus neglect S_{f2} and take for the absorption rate A_2 the capture rate ($\sigma_{a2} = \sigma_{c2}$, $\sigma_{f2} = 0$). Dividing equation (3.3) by A_1 we thus obtain:

$$\eta = 1 + C + \frac{A_p + F}{A_1} \tag{3.4}$$

with:

$$C = \frac{A_2}{A_1} \tag{3.5}$$

The factor $\eta = \bar{\nu}_1 S_{f1}/A_1$ is identical to the multiplication factor already introduced for fissionable isotopes (3.2). To be sure of this, it suffices to remark that for a homogeneous system the quantities S_f and A are proportional to the usual reaction rates R_f and R_a taken for an average value of the flux.

Equation (3.4) gives an expected result. Among the η neutrons produced by each fissionable nucleus destroyed, one neutron must be available for a new absorption by the fissile matter, whence an excess (η - 1) of fission neutrons (per fissionable nucleus destroyed). At equilibrium, when the reactor is critical, this excess exactly compensates neutron losses by capture in other materials or by leakage from the reactor.

In the absence of fertile materials and for judiciously chosen structural materials ($A_2 \cong 0$, $A_p \cong 0$), this neutron excess uniquely serves to compensate the escapes. Taking account of the value of η - 1 (Table 3.8), we see that these escapes are significant. This means that the systems using almost exclusively fissile matter will be small in size. The reactors on board nuclear submarines are an example, or, even smaller, those which equip certain satellites.

If on the other hand we add fertile materials ($A_2 \neq 0$), the neutron balance will be "tighter", hence the reactor dimensions are much larger, but one benefits from the advantages provided by fertile isotopes. The ratio of the production of fissile matter to its consumption is called the conversion factor C.

As each new fissionable nucleus created corresponds to a neutron capture by a fertile nucleus, it follows that C is given by equation (3.5). The quantity (η - 1 - C) now represents the neutron excess necessary to compensate both parasite captures in the structural materials and leakage, as indicated by equation (3.4). In order to obtain a good conversion, leakage and parasite absorption must be minimized, which is not always possible. We are thus led to large-size reactors and to a very restricted choice of structural materials.

If C is greater than 1, we say that the reactor is a breeder, but the neutron excess is at most η - 2. If the condition that a reactor is critical is written $\eta > 1$, the condition of breeding demands $\eta > 2$. This second condition is much more difficult to achieve, especially as it must be so with a large margin, since the compensation of parasite capture and leakage (which can never be 0) must be assured.

In fact, only uranium $_{92}U^{233}$ permits breeding with thermal neutrons.

For the other two isotopes the value of (η - 2) is too small, as is indicated by Table 3.8.

If we consider fast neutrons (Fig. 3.9), we see in contrast that plutonium ${}_{94}Pu^{239}$ has the highest η factor. This factor is of the order of 2.4 to 2.5 in current fast reactors (average energy of neutrons 0.1 to 0.2 MeV). The margins become comfortable in as much as the effective value of η is higher if one takes account of fast fissions (§3.2.3). Unfortunately the microscopic cross sections are smaller at high energy (Fig. 3.6), thus a greater investment in fissile materials is called for.

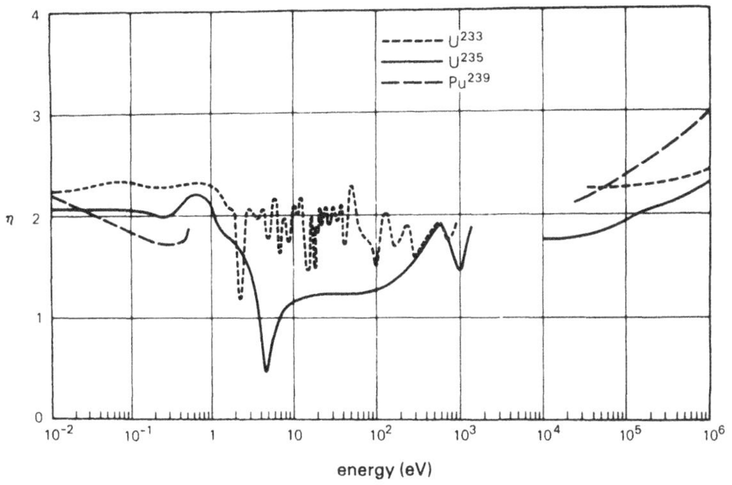

FIGURE 3.9. Multiplication factor η of three fissionable isotopes as a function of neutron energy.

When the breeding condition cannot be achieved, as is the case for current thermal reactors burning uranium ${}_{92}U^{235}$, it is always advantageous to use fertile materials.

The conversion factor C, this time smaller than one, will still play an important role. In any case, the absence of fertile materials leading, as we have seen, to reduced critical sizes, it would be impossible to have the kinds of powerful reactors that exist today. The power density is in fact limited by thermohydraulic considerations (Sec. 5.2); hence reducing the size of a reactor amounts to reducing its power.

3.3.3 Fuel Multiplication Factor

Since in practice, fertile materials are most often intimately associated with fissile materials, the nuclear fuel will correspond to a mixture of fissionable and fertile isotopes in well defined proportions. The multiplication factor η can be defined for the fuel just as it was for each fissionable isotope. Attributing the same value of $\bar{\nu}$ to all types of fission, we will write:

$$\eta_c = \bar{\nu} \frac{R_f}{R_a}$$

But now with (§1.5.5):

$$R_f = (N_1\sigma_{f1} + N_2\sigma_{f2})\ \phi = \Sigma_f\ \phi$$

$$R_a = (N_1\sigma_{a1} + N_2\sigma_{a2})\ \phi = \Sigma_a\ \phi$$

whence:

$$\eta_c = \bar{\nu} \frac{N_1\sigma_{f1} + N_2\sigma_{f2}}{N_1\sigma_{a1} + N_2\sigma_{a2}}$$

The indices 1 and 2 refer respectively to the fissionable and fertile isotopes. Introducing x, the isotopic fraction of the fissile matter, η_c can be written:

$$\eta_c = \bar{\nu} \frac{x\sigma_{f1} + (1 - x)\ \sigma_{f2}}{x\sigma_{a1} + (1 - x)\ \sigma_{a2}} = \left(\frac{\bar{\nu}\Sigma_f}{\Sigma_a}\right)_c \qquad (3.6)$$

with $x = N_1/(N_1 + N_2)$.

In the case where the fissionable and fertile nuclei are isotopes of the same chemical element (U^{235} and U^{238} for example), x also represents the enrichment.

As in the preceding, η_c - 1 represents the neutron excess available for a neutron absorbed in the fuel (and no longer only in the fissile material). At equilibrium, with the reactor critical, this excess must compensate parasite capture and escape since we have already taken account of the fertile captures in the definition of η_c. Up to a multiplicative coefficient, $(\eta_c - 1)$ has the same sense as $(\eta - 1 - C)$ in the preceding.

The multiplication factor η_c plays a preponderant role in the search for the critical condition which assures the operation of a fission reactor in steady state. The search for this condition constitutes the essential object of reactor physics (Ch. 4). At our present qualitative stage, it is not possible to calculate the neutron leakage F but it is evident that the higher the factor η_c the easier it is to achieve the critical condition.

Let us consider the important case of enriched uranium ((1) → U^{235}; (2) → U^{238}). Table 3.8 furnishes the nuclear characteristics ($\bar{\nu}$, σ_a, σ_f) of fissionable uranium. By taking for the fertile component (U^{238}): σ_{a2} = 2.73 b and $\sigma_{f2} \cong 0$, we can calculate η_c for different values of the enrichment x. The results which appear in Table 3.10, valid for thermal neutrons, lead to important conclusions.

Starting from the natural isotopic fraction x = 0.72%, we observe that η_c increases very rapidly. For an enrichment of only 1.5% (twice the natural concentration) η_c attains 1.64, the median value between the two extremes: 1.33 for natural uranium and 2.068 for pure uranium U^{235}. If one accepts a small enrichment of the uranium, the neutron multiplication is greatly improved, to such a point that one must change the reactor assembly, so important and numerous are the consequences at a technological level (Sec. 5.1).

TABLE 3.10. The multiplication factor η_c of uranium fuel for various enrichments and thermal neutrons.

x	0.0072 (Natural)	0.010	0.015	0.020	0.030	0.20	0.93	1
η_c	1.33	1.48	1.64	1.73	1.83	2.035	2.067	2.068

3.3.4 Fuel Cycles

We see from the preceding that the cycles envisageable from the viewpoint of nuclear fission can call upon the three following fissionable isotopes:

$${}_{92}U^{235},\ {}_{94}Pu^{239},\ {}_{92}U^{233}.$$

Only the first is present in nature. As to the two others, they are produced by neutronic transmutations of fertile isotopes, uranium ${}_{92}U^{238}$

and thorium $_{90}Th^{232}$ (§3.2.3).

A reactor will aways burn a mixture of fissile and fertile materials, whether this mixture pre-exists in nature (natural uranium) or whether artificial fissionable isotopes ($_{94}Pu^{239}$ and $_{92}U^{233}$) must be created. By simplifying, we are led to the four basic cycles shown in Fig. 3.11.

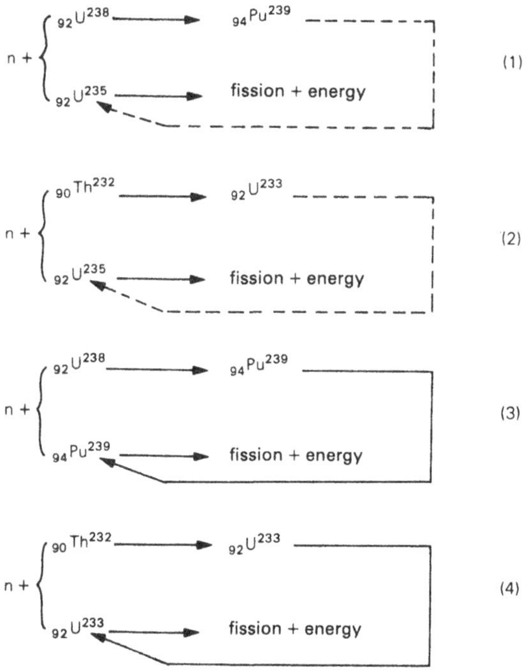

FIGURE 3.11. Flow diagram of four possible fuel cycles.

Nuclear energy was able to develop initially only on the basis of the first two cycles, since the only natural fissionable isotope is uranium U^{235}. Moreover, since natural uranium is already a mixture (fissile + fertile), all existing nuclear power plants (first generation) are based on the first cycle (§5.1.3):

- Natural uranium reactors moderated by graphite or heavy water
- Slightly enriched uranium reactors moderated by ordinary water.

The latter are by far the most common. The second cycle is that envisaged for high temperature reactors moderated by graphite. This too can start off on the basis of what nature has to offer, but it requires more or less pure uranium U^{235} (otherwise one obtains a more complex cycle).

The last two cycles rely on artificial fissile materials (Pu^{239}, U^{233}). In order for the corresponding reactors to operate autonomously, their production of fissile material must exceed their consumption. The surplus is thus used to start off other reactors of the same type. One says that in this case there is breeding since the conversion coefficient C must be greater than one (§3.3.2). Naturally, such reactors can function without being breeder reactors but then a supplement of fissile material must be furnished either by other reactors producing the necessary isotopes (Pu^{239} or U^{233}) or by nature itself in the form of uranium U^{235}. In the latter case we get back the first two cycles (Fig. 3.11) with the recycling of fissionable isotopic products.

For the third cycle as we have seen, breeding can only be realized for a *spectrum of fast neutrons* (hence no moderator); to abbreviate, we speak of *fast reactors*, which can cause some confusion. Prototype reactors are already in operation (France, Great Britain, USSR).

The condition of breeding for the fourth cycle (Th^{232} + U^{233}) demands on the contrary a *spectrum of thermal neutrons* analogous to that of existing reactors. One speaks of *thermal reactors*, once again an unfortunate expression which could imply that a thermal reactor is "hotter" than the others. As we have already said, this means simply that the neutrons are in thermodynamic equilibrium with the milieu and hence have minimum kinetic energy.

The advantage of breeding is evident, since it all takes place as if one were burning fertile materials (U^{238} or Th^{232}) which are much more abundant than the single natural fissionable isotope U^{235}. In this case plutonium Pu^{239} or uranium U^{233} are only intermediary agents.

Even if the condition of breeding is satisfied at the beginning, a certain quantity of Pu^{239} or U^{233} is necessary to feed the first core of the breeder reactor. In other words it is necessary to "set off" the cycle and hence to have recourse to first generation reactors based on the first cycle. Thus even if we had had the necessary technology, breeder reactors could not have been constructed before reactors of the first type.

In the absence of a program of breeder reactors, the question is raised: what should be done with the plutonium produced in existing reactors?

- It can be considered as waste in the same way as fission products. In this case the fuel does not have to be reprocessed (Fig.3.12). This is not a very reasonable attitude either from the long-term economic or the environmental point of view, since plutonium, without being the most dangerous nuclide, nevertheless presents significant radiotoxicity.

- The plutonium produced in existing reactors can be recycled. We then arrive at ternary fuels: $U^{238} + Pu^{239} + U^{235}$. The last isotope is always necessary because the reactors not being breeders (for neutronic reasons), nature must furnish the complementary fissile matter (in a lesser quantity than during the first loading).

All existing nuclear power stations are based on the first cycle, and so uranium will occupy a large place in what follows. All the same, we attempt to give as much information as we can on the thorium cycle. Concerning the latter it should be noted that the possibilities of breeding at the practical level have not been demonstrated. In the high-temperature power plants (§5.1.3) proposed until now (second cycle), the goal has not been breeding but thermodynamic performances. From the neutronic point of view, it seems that reactors with molten salts lead to a higher rate of breeding, but this remains to be proved.

3.3.5 Setting Up the Fuel Cycle

We have schematized in Fig. 3.12 the transformations undergone by the fuel, all the way from its extraction until the definitive storage of the wastes, including the eventual recycling of recovered fissile materials.

Operations which already take place on an industrial scale are indicated by arrows in solid lines. They correspond to the operation of the existing reactor assembly without plutonium recycling.

Impoverished or depleted uranium produced by isotopic separation plants could eventually be used as fertile material in the blankets of fast breeder reactors. It could also be used as protective material against γ rays.

For a thorium cycle the enrichment stage disappears in part; it is

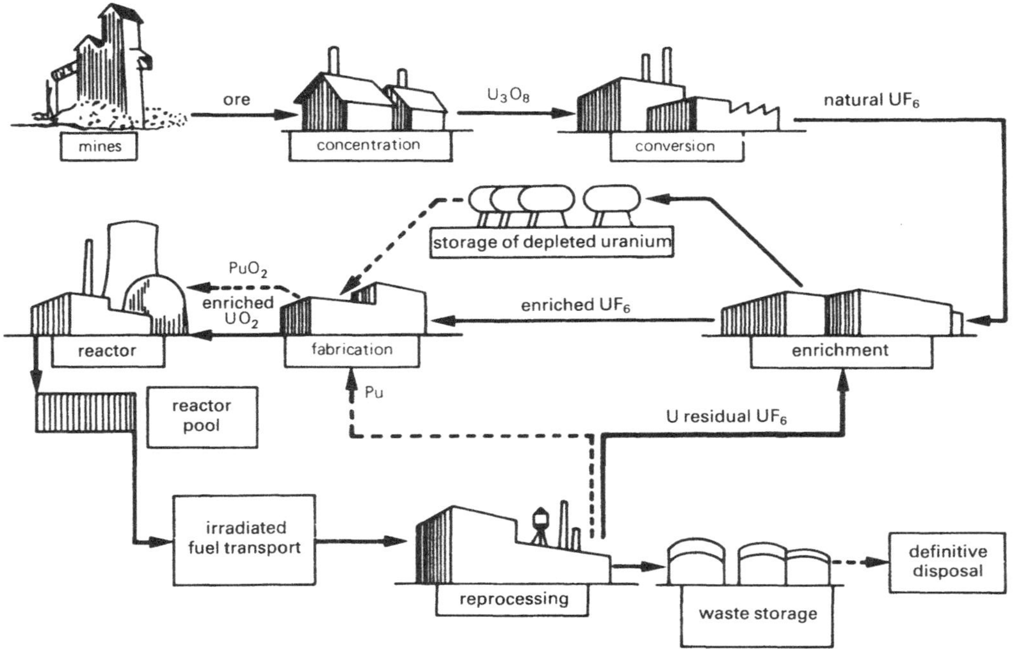

FIGURE 3.12. Operations carried out on the fuel in the course of the cycle.

the reprocessing plant which supplies the uranium U^{233} necessary for this cycle.

The behavior of the nuclear fuel in the actual reactor will be the subject of Ch. 5, in which several types of power plants are presented. The processes which take place pre- and post- reactor operation will be described in Ch. 7.

3.4 UTILIZATION OF FISSION ENERGY

3.4.1 Introduction

We have seen (Sec. 3.1) that fission energy, always associated to neutron emission, appears in the form of heat in the core of a nuclear reactor (essentially in the fuel). A fission reactor can thus be viewed either as a neutron source or as a heat source, which leads to a first classification.

3.4.2 Zero Power Reactors

The level of neutron flux is so low (10^6 to 10^8 n/cm^2 s) that the thermal power output does not exceed a few watts. This energy is easily evacuated by natural convection. Reactors of zero power or critical assemblies permit the study of reactor physics (Ch. 4), in other words, the determination of the neutron characteristics of a power reactor of the same type.

The construction of these assemblies poses few technological problems. The different materials are at the ambiant temperature. The combustion rate being insignificant, few of the fission products accumulate in the fuel, so that the activities are negligible. An example is the critical assembly CROCUS of the Institute of Atomic Engineering of the Ecole Polytechnique Fédérale of Lausanne (Switzerland). This device permits the study of lattices of slightly enriched uranium rods moderated by ordinary water.

3.4.3 Cold Power Reactors

The power densities attained (thermal power per unit volume) require cooling by forced convection. In crossing the reactor core the coolant heats itself, carrying away the thermal energy produced in the fuel, and thus maintaining the temperature of the fuel at an admissible value (Sec. 5.2). It then passes into a heat exchanger where it is cooled.

Barring leakage, the thermal power of the reactor is then transmitted to the secondary of the exchanger and gets dissipated in the environment. In Fig. 3.13 we have schematized an experimental reactor cooled by river water. The exchanger permits the coolant, which is always more or less active, to be insulated (Ch. 6), and avoids cooling by water which may not be appropriate for the type of reactor chosen.

Although the power density may attain that of electricity-generating reactors, the outlet temperatures of the coolant remain low (≦ 100°C) and the conversion thermal energy/electric energy is excluded (the calories are "too cold"). These temperature conditions make it much easier to build these reactors than to build today's nuclear power stations. Industrial nations thus started off their nuclear programs by constructing reactors of this type.

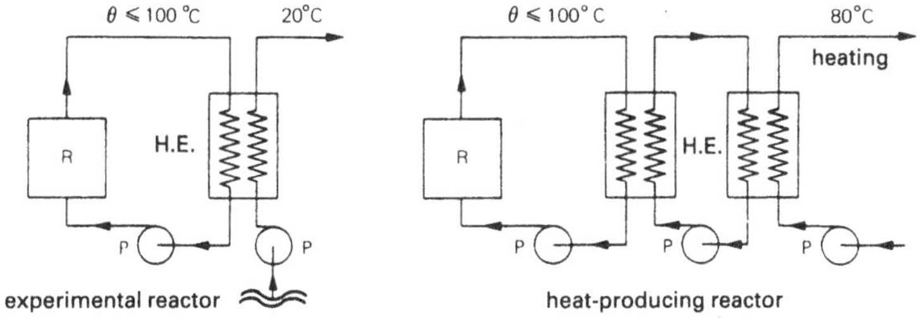

FIGURE 3.13. "Cold" power reactors: R reactor; P pumps; HE heat exchangers.

The neutron fluxes (10^{13} to 10^{14} n/cm^2 s) and the burnup rates are such that the problems of protection against radiation and the handling of irradiated fuel are practically the same as those that one meets in electricity-generating power plants. This type of reactor has found diverse applications.

- Neutron physics. The reactor is used as an intense source of neutrons for experiments in solid state physics (neutron diffraction). Quite often, natural uranium reactors moderated by heavy water have been chosen (EL 3 at Saclay (France) or DIORIT at Würenlingen (Switzerland) as well as "swimming pool" reactors using highly enriched uranium and light water as moderator (SAPHIR at Würenlingen).

- Fabrication of isotopes. The neutrons give rise to a very large number of nuclear reactions, essentially radiative captures (Sec.1.5). Very often the nuclei resulting from these reactions are unstable. Thus with the help of a reactor of the preceding type (high neutronic flux but "cold" calories), one can produce appreciable quantities of artificial radioactive isotopes which are used in particular in medicine (cobalt $_{27}Co^{60}$).

- Military applications. Obtaining a plutonium (§3.2.3) of good quality for the manufacture of nuclear explosives (A-bombs) calls for reactors which are much closer to the preceding ones than to nuclear power stations. "Military quality" plutonium demands low combustion rates in order to avoid the appearance of the isotope $_{94}Pu^{240}$ coming from fissionable plutonium $_{94}Pu^{239}$. It is the latter which is of interest (in the same way as pure uranium $_{92}U^{235}$) for manufacturing A-bombs. A low burnup rate calls for flexible installations, permitting a frequent unloading of the reactor, sometimes even in the course of operation. The plutonium producing reactors belong thus to the above category (the Marcoule reactors: graphite/natural uranium; Savannah River: heavy water reactors, etc.) Commercial nuclear power plants are not suitable for this type of production. To want to use them at any price for this goal would be to choose the most costly and complicated route.

- Remote heating. Since the outlet temperature of the coolant can attain a value in the vicinity of 100°C, one can think of using these calories for remote heating. In this case we sometimes speak of a heat-producing reactor. For safety reasons, two exchangers are generally envisaged, the hot water produced having to be used without danger by consumers (Fig. 3.13). A small reactor has already been used in Sweden in this manner, and various projects are under study: the swimming pool reactor "THERMOS" for heating the nuclear research center of Saclay and its surroundings (France), an analogous project at Grenoble, adaptation of the already existing experimental heavy water reactor MZFR (West Germany), etc. In general the use of nuclear energy for urban heating is in the reach of most industrial nations because it relies on a relatively rustic technology. Any experimental pile (from 20 to 200 MW) conceived for another goal can likely be adapted to this task. At the same time one makes use of the excess neutrons (for manufacturing radioactive isotopes, for example) as well as the heat produced, instead of rejecting it into the environment, as is usually done. The absence of distribution networks of hot water has without doubt discouraged the promoters of this direct use of fission energy.

Reactors of the same type can be used for the desalination of sea water. Numerous proposals have been made.

3.4.4 Hot Power Reactors

The existence in industrial nations of largescale electric networks has led to the conception of nuclear reactors almost exclusively in function of the production of electrical energy. In this way one makes the most of the calories produced. The outlet temperature of the coolant is chosen as high as possible within technological limits (Sec. 5.2). It is this type of reactor that we have in mind when speaking of nuclear power plants. The conversion of thermal energy into electric energy takes place in accordance with the first diagram of Fig. 3.14. The implementation of such reactors calls for a more "sophisticated" technology than in the preceding cases. The description of the different assemblies either existing or projected will be the object of Ch. 5. In that chapter, we will propose a new classification based on the operating principles of nuclear reactors. Here we only call attention to the fact that other applications can be envisaged.

If existing nuclear power plants employing light water and slightly enriched uranium have modest thermodynamic outputs (30 to 33%), a new type of reactor now in the course of development permits much higher outlet temperatures of the coolant, about 700°C compared to 300°C for existing reactors. This brings about outputs of at least 40%. These high temperature reactors (graphite-moderated) already mentioned in the context of the thorium cycle (§3.3.4), permit in principle the combined production of electrical energy and hot water by drawing off water vapor at the entry of certain levels of the turbine or by increasing the temperature of the condenser (30°C to 100°C). In the latter case the cooling water of the condenser becomes usable, which in principle eliminates the problem of waste heat (Sec. 6.5).

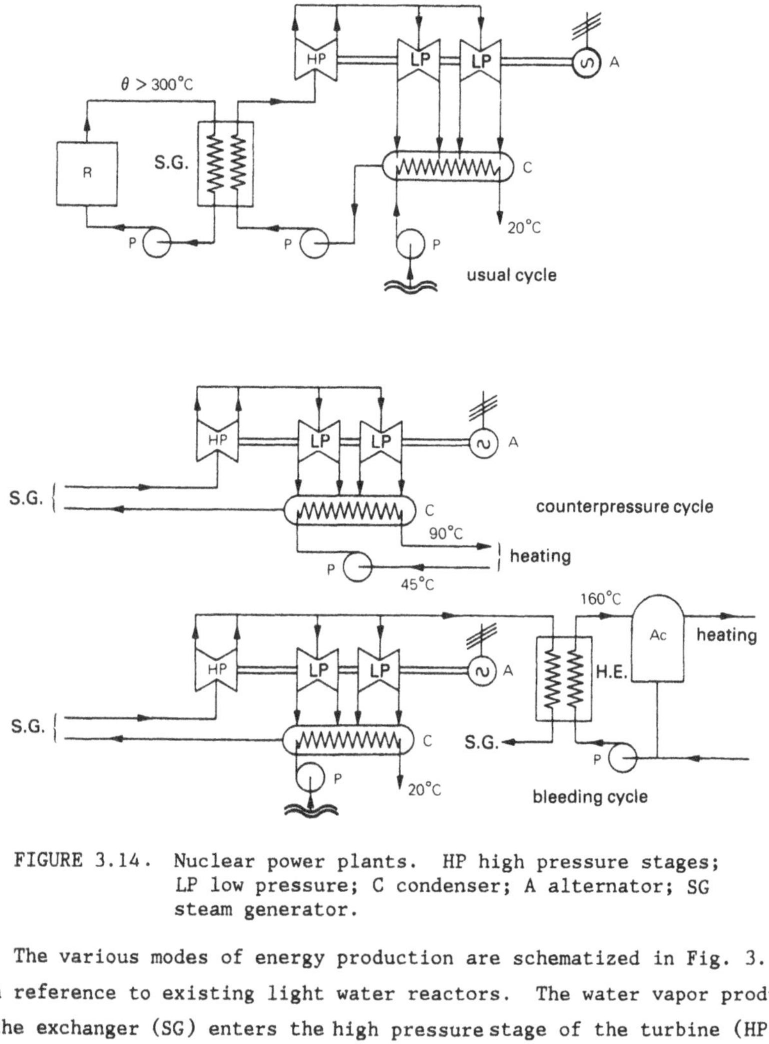

FIGURE 3.14. Nuclear power plants. HP high pressure stages; LP low pressure; C condenser; A alternator; SG steam generator.

The various modes of energy production are schematized in Fig. 3.14 with reference to existing light water reactors. The water vapor produced in the exchanger (SG) enters the high pressure stage of the turbine (HP), then the low pressure stage (LP) and at last reduces to a temperature of about 30°C. The condenser cooling water which barely exceeds 20°C is not usable. It is thus rejected into the environment. This is the usual cycle of an electricity-producing power plant (fossil or nuclear). In the so-called counterpressure system, increasing the temperature of the condenser permits the use of the cooling water with the advantage cited earlier. Unfortunately this system is not flexible because there exists a constant ratio between electricity production and heat production.

In the last system, a partial bleeding of the steam to an intermediate pressure permits a certain flexibility, but the heat pollution remains, since the condenser stays cold. In charging a heat accumulator (Ac), one can bleed steam only at night when electricity demand is low.

Both these methods present advantages and disadvantages, making mixed solutions advisable for the present. Naturally, in all these cases the thermodynamic output diminishes and the cost price per KWhe increases. The increased expense must be compensated by the sale of hot water. The initial output being quite small, light water power plants do not lend themselves to this hybrid production. Nevertheless, in Switzerland there exist several projects involving the first generation reactors of Beznau and Mühlberg. Just as for the calogenic "cold" reactors, a distribution network for hot water (at about 90°C) must be available, or else additional investments must be anticipated.

In certain very high temperature (950°C) reactor projects, production of hydrogen or methane is envisaged starting from steam and coal (gasification), as can be seen in Fig. 3.15. Very hot helium which leaves the reactor permits the preheating of the gasification agent necessary for obtaining methane from lignite. After this, the helium enthalpy is still sufficient to assure the production of steam in a standard generator. The latter feeds not only a group turbo-alternator but also the gasification system which consumes the steam. In this installation the nuclear reactor furnishes the energy necessary for the synthesis of methane, while assuring at the same time a certain production of electrical energy (small in this case). In other words, nuclear energy has been transformed into chemical and electrical energy.

The temperatures given in this subsection are only indicative. They can change significantly from one installation to another.

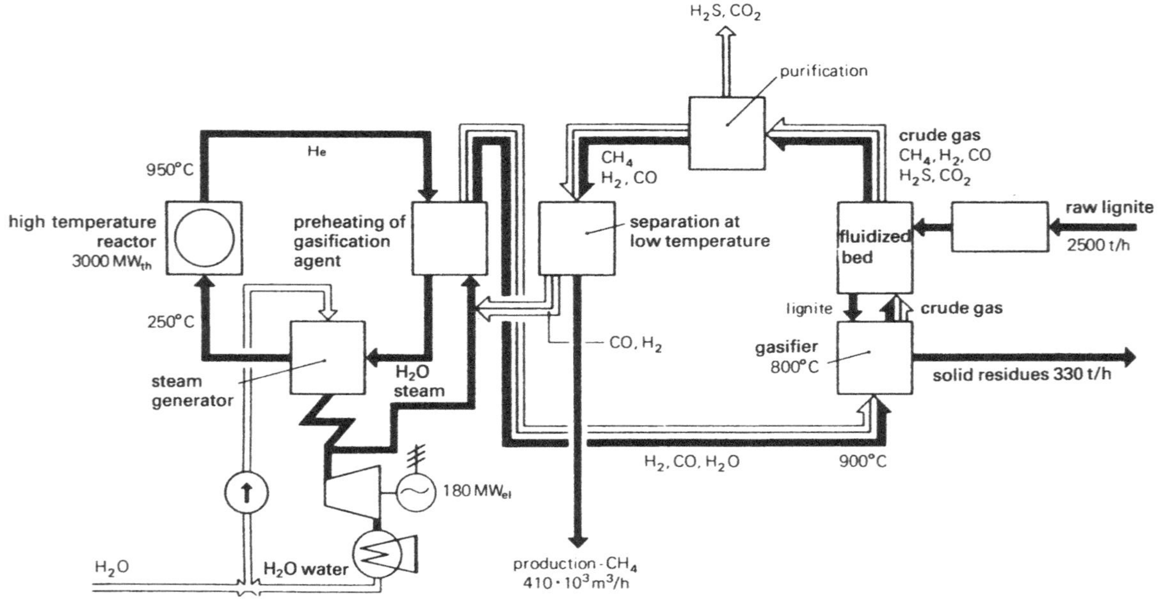

FIGURE 3.15. Gasification of lignite by nuclear preheating.

Chapter 4

FISSION REACTOR PHYSICS

4.1 GENERAL REMARKS

4.1.1 The Object of Reactor Physics

At the heart of neutron physics (the study of the propagation of neutrons in matter), reactor physics holds a special place because of its numerous practical applications. It permits us to determine not only the "critical condition" to which every reactor is submitted, but also the distributions of neutron flux indispensable for the evaluation of specific powers, burnup rates, etc. It is not our intention here to give a detailed account, which would need a course of many semesters, but rather to approach certain essential points which will permit a better understanding of reactor operation, and to define their structure qualitatively. The conception of operational or projected reactors has necessitated highly advanced neutron studies as well as other investigations, both technological and economic. The different reactor assemblies which have resulted will be the subject of Ch. 5.

4.1.2 Nuclear Data

The data of a problem of neutron physics are naturally the already-defined microscopic cross sections (Sec. 1.5) which characterize, as we have seen, the possible interactions of one neutron with one atomic nucleus. They are furnished by nuclear physics either theoretically or experimentally. Neutron physics (and hence reactor physics) constitutes in some sense the bridge between the microscopic level (elementary interactions) and the macroscopic level (such questions, for example, as how much heat is liberated at a point of the reactor). In the following, we will always suppose the neutron to be a stable particle. Its halflife (12 min) is in effect quite large compared to its "lifetime" in a material medium (§4.6.2). In other words, it is infinitely more probable that a neutron will be absorbed by an atomic nucleus than that it will disappear spontaneously by virtue of its radioactivity. We must distinguish two sorts of media:

- media which are passive or non-multiplying (of neutrons) are characterized by the scattering cross sections σ_s and capture cross sections σ_c of the various isotopes of which they are composed.
- media which multiply (neutrons) contain at least one fissionable isotope (Table 3.7). Apart from the preceding cross sections they are distinguished by fission cross sections σ_f and the number $\bar{\nu}$ of neutrons created by fission.

For nonfissionable isotopes the notions of absorption and of capture are the same ($\sigma_a = \sigma_c$). In contrast, for the fissionable isotopes, absorption includes fission (Sec. 3.3) whence $\sigma_a = \sigma_c + \sigma_f$.

Once the isotopic compositions of the various media are known, we can determine their macroscopic cross sections according to the considerations of subsec. 1.5.5. The cross sections being by definition additive quantities, at least in the energy domain which interests us, we will have, for example:

$$\Sigma_s = \sum_i N_i \sigma_{si}, \quad \bar{\nu}\,\Sigma_f = \sum_i N_i\, \bar{\nu}_i \sigma_{fi} \tag{4.1}$$

where N_i represents the atomic density of the isotope (i) (in cm^{-3}). In the last sum, only the terms corresponding to the fissionable isotopes intervene.

The totality of macroscopic cross sections on the one hand and the definition of the geometry of the problem treated on the other, permit us to obtain the distributions of neutron flux as well as all useful quantities connected with it. If all the media are passive, it will evidently be necessary to introduce a neutron source somewhere in the system.

4.1.3 Problems to be Treated

Because of the successive shocks they receive, the neutrons are slowed down in the materials in which they propagate. We must therefore determine at every point their "energy spectrum" even if they all had the same energy at the outset. In other words, the neutron flux depends on space and on energy. Provided that we have available suitably weighted cross sections, we can treat numerous problems by supposing that the neutrons are monoenergetic. Much more complicated problems can be reduced to this simple case, which will be the subject of the following two sections. The theory of the slowing down of neutrons is sketched in Sec. 4.4, whence we will see how to use the earlier results.

The passage from passive media to multiplying media will take place without difficulty in Sec. 4.5. The particular case of mono-energetic neutrons permits us to introduce the notion of critical size, which is in fact very general. With the exception of the last section, we will only consider steady states (time-independent neutron flux).

The behavior of non-steady state reactors will be analyzed in Sec. 4.6. A global reasoning will lead to the equations of point kinetics often used in the studies of the control and safety of nuclear power plants.

The appendices contain certain additional details (justifications or mathematical proofs) which are not strictly necessary for the understanding of this chapter, provided we accept two or three formulae following from more general theories.

4.2 PROPAGATION OF MONO-ENERGETIC NEUTRONS

4.2.1 Collimated Beams and Mean Free Paths

Let us consider a collimated neutron beam hitting perpendicularly the boundary (entry face) ($x = 0$) of a semi-infinite homogeneous medium. These neutrons having the same direction and velocity constitute a flux in the usual sense (§1.5.2). Let $\phi(0)$ be the entering flux, which takes at depth x a smaller value $\phi(x)$. The flux $\phi(x)$ is composed of neutrons which have escaped collisions of all sorts, after crossing a distance x. The calculation of the distribution $\phi(x)$ is based on the neutron balance of an infinitely thin slice dx represented in Fig. 4.1. The difference between the entering and exit fluxes can be written:

$$\phi(x) - \phi(x + dx) = - \frac{d\phi}{dx} dx$$

since dx is an infinitesimal. This difference corresponds to neutrons which have left the beam in the slice dx following an absorption or a scattering. It is also obtained by multiplying the collision rate R_t ($cm^{-3}s^{-1}$) by the thickness dx. We can thus write:

$$\phi(x) - \phi(x + dx) = - \frac{d\phi}{dx} dx = R_t dx$$

whence:

$$\frac{d\phi}{dx} = - R_t$$

We have seen (§1.5.5) that this collision rate was written, by the definition of cross sections, $R_t = \Sigma_t\phi = N\sigma_t\phi$ where the flux ϕ must be taken at the depth x (dx being small, ϕ varies very little between x and x + dx). We deduce from the preceding the differential equation:

$$\frac{d\phi}{dx} = - \Sigma_t\phi \qquad (4.2)$$

and after integration:

$$\phi(x) = \phi(0) \exp(- \Sigma_t x) \qquad (4.3)$$

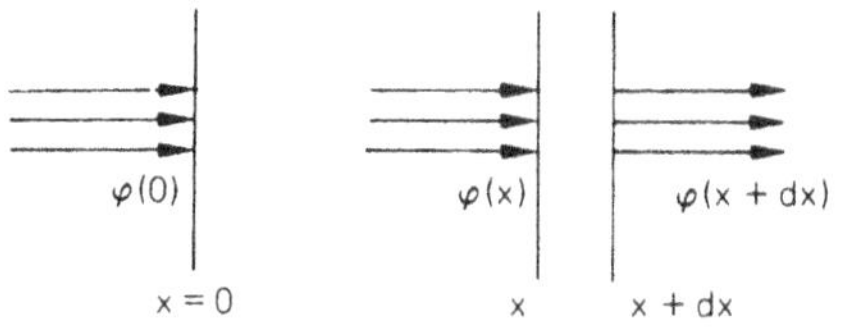

FIGURE 4.1.

Equation (4.3) represents the attenuation of a neutron beam collimated in a material of total macroscopic cross section Σ_t. The exponential law is characteristic of neutron and photon attenuation. We can interpret the last two equations in terms of probabilities.

$$p_1(x)dx = - \frac{d\phi}{\phi} = \Sigma_t dx$$

$$p_2(x) = \frac{\phi(x)}{\phi(0)} = \exp(- \Sigma_t x)$$

where $p_1(x)dx$ represents the probability that a neutron <u>which has already arrived at x</u> suffers a collision between x and x + dx, and $p_2(x)$ the probability that a neutron <u>entering through the face x = 0</u> travels at least the distance x without collision. From these two probabilities we deduce a third which is much more important:

$$P(x)dx = p_2(x) \cdot p_1(x)dx$$

whose physical meaning is evident. It is the probability that a neutron penetrating the system at x = 0 suffers its first collision between x and x + dx or, if one prefers, that it traverses a distance x in a straight line.

Replacing p_1 and p_2 by their value, we get:

$$P(x)dx = \exp(-\Sigma_t x)\Sigma_t dx \qquad (4.4)$$

We see that in principle a neutron can travel no matter what distance x in contrast to charged particles (α or β) which have a well-defined stopping distance. Nevertheless, equation (4.4) indicates that deep penetrations ($x \gg 1/\Sigma_t$) are very improbable.

In order to characterize a medium we introduce the notion of the <u>total mean free path</u> λ_t. By the definition of the mean we can write:

$$\lambda_t = \langle x \rangle = \int_0^\infty xP(x)dx = \int_0^\infty \exp(-\Sigma_t x)x\Sigma_t dx$$

and an integration by parts leads to:

$$\lambda_t = \frac{1}{\Sigma_t} \qquad (4.5)$$

The smaller is λ_t, the more opaque is the material to neutrons.

In an analogous fashion we can treat the problem of the propagation of neutrons emitted by a pointlike source S (Fig. 4.2).

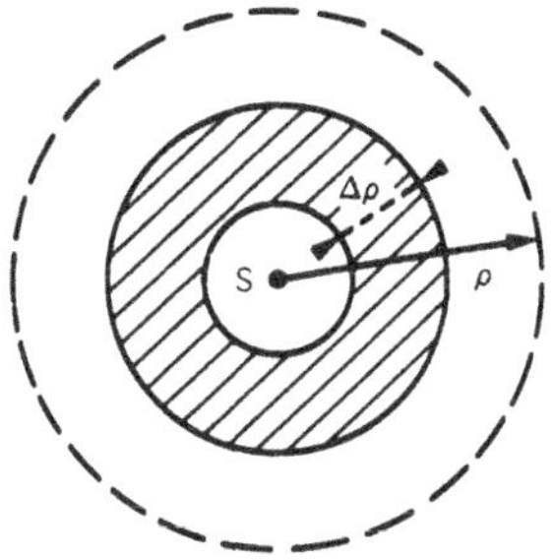

FIGURE 4.2 .

For reasons of symmetry the flux can only depend on the distance ρ from the source, so that $4\pi\rho^2\phi(\rho)$ represents the number of neutrons traversing the sphere of radius ρ per unit time. In the absence of any material the last quantity must be equal to the intensity of the source S (s^{-1}), whence the flux:

$$\phi(\rho) = \frac{S}{4\pi\rho^2}$$

If one now places a material of thickness $\Delta\rho$ between the source S and the point considered, the preceding flux becomes:

$$\phi(\rho) = \frac{S}{4\pi\rho^2} \exp\left(-\Sigma_t \Delta\rho\right) \quad (4.6)$$

We recognize in this expression the earlier exponential attenuation factor (4.3).

Let us return to the problem of the neutron beam falling on a plate (Fig. 4.3). If every collision corresponded to a real disappearance (capture) the flux at point B would effectively be given by equation (4.3).

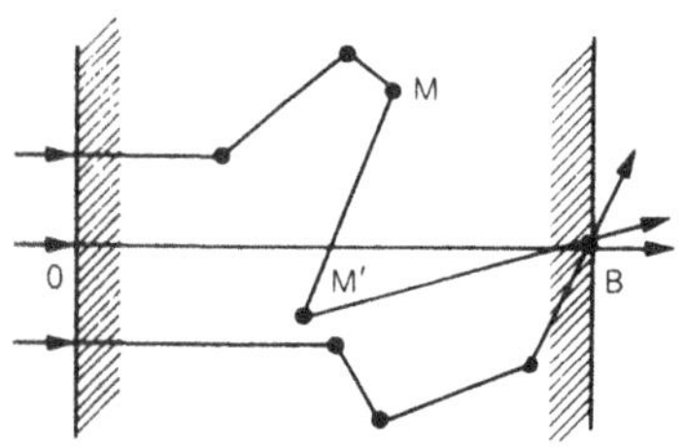

FIGURE 4.3.

In fact, thanks to the process of successive scattering, a neutron can arrive at point B without having been propagated along OB. The global flux observed at B will thus be greater than that given by equation (4.3). This last equation only characterizes those neutrons which have not left the initial direction (virgin neutrons). The same remark is also valid for equation (4.6).

From the preceding, one thing remains: a neutron travels between two successive scatterings a distance $x = MM'$ with probability $\exp(-\Sigma_t x)$, and the segments MM' have the average value $\lambda_t = 1/\Sigma_t$.

In order to solve this problem completely, we are inevitably led to introduce the notion of angular flux. In all practical cases and in this example in particular, the neutrons move in all directions (like molecules of a gas) because of the scattering process.

4.2.2 Angular Flux, Scalar Flux, Currents

In the general case, we can keep all that has been said with respect to fluxes and cross sections, provided these definitions are restricted to neutrons which travel in a well-specified direction $\vec{\Omega}$. We are thus led to define the angular flux $\phi(\vec{\Omega})$ such that the quantity $\phi(\vec{\Omega})d\Omega$ plays the same role as ϕ did in the preceding (§1.5.2). In other words, one isolates in the angular space (Fig. 4.4) a "cone" of neutrons defined by the infinitesimal solid angle $d\Omega$ surrounding the direction $\vec{\Omega}$. Since these neutrons are monodirectional we can apply the preceding formalism to them. We will thus have $\phi(\vec{\Omega}) = n(\vec{\Omega})v$ where $n(\vec{\Omega})$ represents the angular neutron density in the direction $\vec{\Omega}$. The corresponding reaction rates are always given by equation (1.17):

$$dR = \Sigma\phi(\vec{\Omega})d\Omega$$

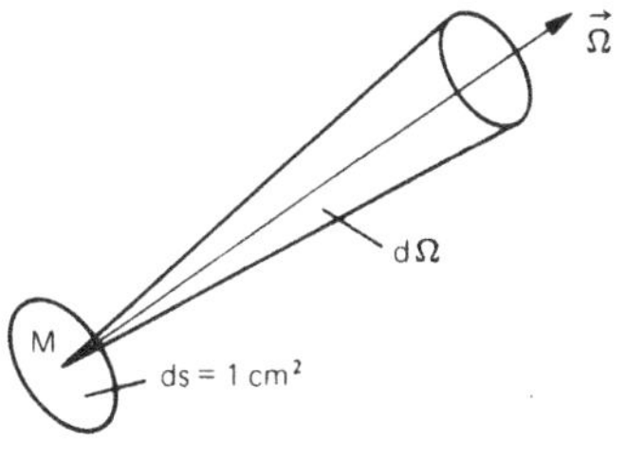

FIGURE 4.4 .

Since in practice we are only interested in global rates, we must integrate the above expression over all the possible directions $\vec{\Omega}$, keeping in mind that the cross sections Σ do not depend on the direction of the incident neutrons, whence:

$$R = \Sigma\Phi = N\sigma\Phi \tag{4.7}$$

$$\Phi = \int \phi(\vec{\Omega})d\Omega = v\int n(\vec{\Omega})d\Omega = nv \tag{4.8}$$

We get back equation (1.17) but the scalar flux Φ replaces the directional flux ϕ. The scalar flux properly speaking is not a flux, although it has the same dimensions. It is also expressed in the form of the product of the neutron density by the velocity of neutrons, but the density now corresponds to all possible directions.

Depending on the process envisaged, equation (4.7) will give fission rates, absorption rates, etc. starting from the macroscopic cross sections Σ_f, Σ_a, etc. We can calculate in particular the specific power $\bar{\omega}_{sp}$ liberated in a fuel of density ρ_c:

$$\bar{\omega}_{sp}(W/g) = [E_f(J)/\rho_c(g\ cm^{-3})]\ R_f(cm^{-3}\ s^{-1}) \tag{4.9}$$

where E_f is the energy liberated by fission and R_f is the fission rate. We have thus:

$$\bar{\omega}_{sp} = \frac{E_f}{\rho_c} N_c \sigma_f \Phi$$

It follows from the preceding that in practice only the scalar fluxes Φ are necessary. Unfortunately, the determination of these fluxes depends on the solution of a fairly complicated equation called the "transport equation" which gives the angular fluxes and in consequence the scalar fluxes (4.8). The study of this equation is beyond the scope of this chapter but some useful elements are given in an appendix (Sec. 8.1).

Luckily, one can very often make nuclear reactor calculations by appealing to an approximate equation which only depends on the scalar fluxes, which as we have seen are the only useful quantities. This "diffusion equation" will be the subject of Sec. 4.3. To arrive at this equation, it is necessary to introduce one more notion.

Let us consider once more neutrons which propagate along the direction $\vec{\Omega}$ and traverse a surface dS = 1 cm^2 not necessarily perpendicular to $\vec{\Omega}$ (Fig. 4.5). The number of neutrons which traverse this surface per unit time (along the direction $\vec{\Omega}$) is called the angular current. It is written:

$$J_x(\vec{\Omega}) = n(\vec{\Omega})v\cos\theta = \phi(\vec{\Omega})\cos\theta \quad (cm^{-2}\ s^{-1})$$

The subscript x specifies that the surface dS is perpendicular to the axis Ox fixed in space. The angular current corresponds to neutrons contained in the "oblique" cylinder of height v cos θ represented in Fig. 4.5 (analogous reasoning to that of subsec. 1.5.2).

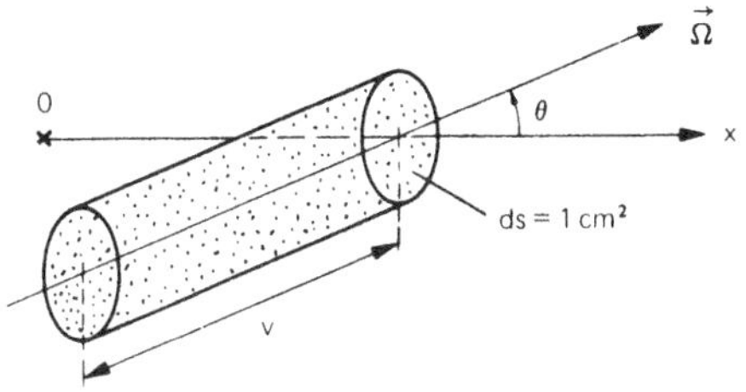

FIGURE 4.5.

The total current J_x^+ corresponding to neutrons going from left to right without reference to their direction is obtained by integrating the preceding angular current in the space $\vec{\Omega}$ with the restriction $\Omega_x > 0$, where $\Omega_x = \cos\theta$ represents the component along Ox of the unit vector $\vec{\Omega}$ (Fig. 4.6).

In the same way, the total current J_x^- for neutrons going from right to left implies the restriction $\Omega_x < 0$. We have thus:

$$\left.\begin{aligned} J_x^+ &= \int_{\Omega_x > 0} J_x(\vec{\Omega})d\Omega = \int_{\Omega_x > 0} \phi(\vec{\Omega})\Omega_x d\Omega \\ J_x^- &= -\int_{\Omega_x < 0} J_x(\vec{\Omega})d\Omega = -\int_{\Omega_x < 0} \phi(\vec{\Omega})\Omega_x d\Omega \end{aligned}\right\}$$

With these definitions the currents J_x^- are positive quantities. Finally the difference $J_x = J_x^+ - J_x^-$ represents the net current of neutrons traversing the surface dS per unit time. By virtue of the preceding one can write:

$$J_x = \int_{4\pi} \phi(\vec{\Omega})\Omega_x d\Omega$$

where the integral is now taken over the entire angular space without restriction.

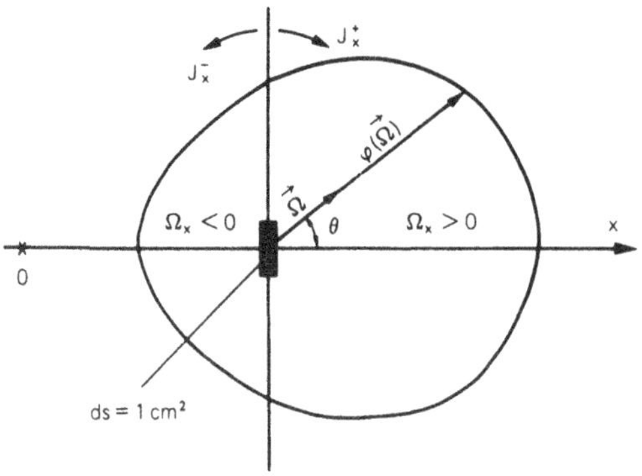

FIGURE 4.6. Polar diagram of angular fluxes.

The net current J_x thus expresses the neutron balance at the crossing of the surface. Like the scalar fluxes Φ, the net currents are integral quantities which no longer depend on directions. They have the same dimensions ($cm^{-2}\ s^{-1}$) but can be positive or negative. One could define in the same way currents J_y or J_z for surfaces perpendicular to Oy or Oz. The net current is thus a vector which we will denote $\vec{J}$ with the definition:

$$\vec{J} = \int_{4\pi} \vec{\Omega}\phi(\vec{\Omega})d\Omega \tag{4.10}$$

In an infinite homogeneous system fed by a uniform distribution of sources, the angular fluxes are isotropic such that ϕ is independent of $\vec{\Omega}$. It follows that the net current $\vec{J}$ vanishes, as is shown by equation (4.10). We also have: $J_x^+ = J_x^-$, $J_y^+ = J_y^-$, etc. (the polar diagram of Fig. 4.6 becomes spherical).

In contrast, for a system of finite dimensions, the net current, which is different from zero, plays a fundamental role.

4.2.3 Equation of Neutron Balance

A first equation can be obtained by basing ourselves on the preceding definitions. Let us isolate in a material medium an infinitesimal volume element $\Delta V = \Delta x\Delta y\Delta z$ (cf. Fig. 4.7).

Starting from the net currents defined above, we can obtain the neutron balance of this elementary volume. Let us take for example the direction Ox perpendicular to the faces ABCD and A'B'C'D' of area $\Delta y\Delta z$.

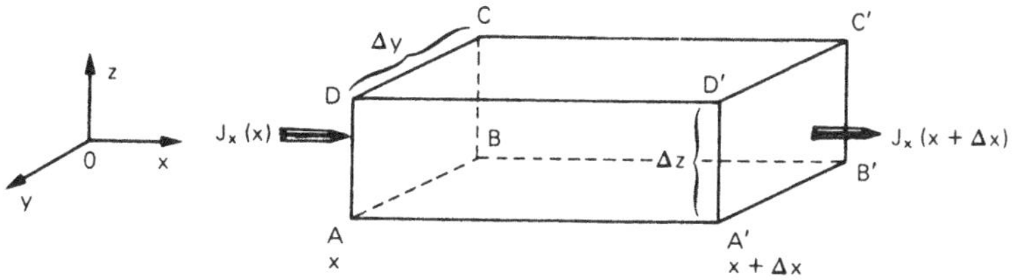

FIGURE 4.7.

The net number of neutrons entering through the face ABCD will be $J_x(x)\Delta y\Delta z$ (this number includes the neutrons traversing the surface from right to left, if they dominate $J_x < 0$). In the same way the neutrons which leave ΔV through the face A'B'C'D' are in number $J_x(x + \Delta x)\Delta y\Delta z$. The net loss along Ox can be written:

$$[J_x(x + \Delta x) - J_x(x)]\ \Delta y\Delta z = \frac{\partial J_x}{\partial x}\ \Delta x\Delta y\Delta z = \frac{\partial J_x}{\partial x}\ \Delta V$$

The last expression follows from the fact that Δx is infinitesimal.

The same reasoning for the other two directions leads to losses of the type $(\partial J_y/\partial y)\Delta V$ and $(\partial J_z/\partial z)\Delta V$. The total leakage of neutrons ΔF through the six faces of the volume element ΔV is thus:

$$\Delta F = (\text{div}\ \vec{J})\ \Delta V \tag{4.11}$$

with:

$$\text{div}\ \vec{J} = \frac{\partial J_x}{\partial x} + \frac{\partial J_y}{\partial y} + \frac{\partial J_z}{\partial z} \qquad (\text{in cm}^{-3}\ \text{s}^{-1})$$

For the steady states envisaged here, it is easy to calculate the neutron balance of such a volume element by writing that the disappearances of neutrons, by leakage or absorptions, are compensated by the creations characterized by the source density Q (in neutrons/cm^3 s):

$$\Delta F + R_a\Delta V = Q\Delta V$$

Using for ΔF expression (4.11) and replacing the absorption rate by its value (4.7) one is led to the desired equation:

$$\text{div}\ \vec{J} + \Sigma_a\ \Phi = Q \tag{4.12}$$

where $\vec{J}$, Q, Φ are functions of the coordinates x, y. z.

It should be noted that here Σ_a represents the absorption cross section, and not the total cross section. The scatterings do not correspond to the destruction of neutrons but only to their slowing down. However, the mono-energetic theory that we have exposed here cannot take this slowing down into account, so that, after a collision the neutron always belongs to the "same family". It is thus normal that the scattering rate does not intervene explicitly in the equation of balance (4.12).

For the passive milieus considered here, the source densities Q are data of the problem. They cannot vanish at every point, otherwise the flux would also vanish. Equation (4.12) is rigorous. It could be proved from the transport equation mentioned earlier (Sec. 8.1). Unfortunately it contains two unknowns $\vec{J}$ and Φ so that a second equation is necessary (4.3.1).

In what follows, as angular fluxes are no longer the question, for simplicity the term flux will be employed in the sense of "scalar flux."

4.2.4 Numerical Applications

a) Mean free path of thermal neutrons in graphite. We are given:

- the mass density $\rho = 1.6\ \text{g cm}^{-3}$
- the microscopic cross sections of scattering and of absorption $\sigma_s = 4.8$ b; $\sigma_a = 0.0048$ b.

The number of carbon nuclei per unit volume can be calculated by the formula: $N = \rho(N_A/12)$ where N_A is Avogadro's number (§1.3.3). We thus obtain:

$$N = 8 \cdot 10^{22}\ \text{cm}^{-3} \text{ and } \sigma_t = \sigma_s + \sigma_a \cong \sigma_s = 4.8 \text{ b}$$

whence the macroscopic cross sections: $\Sigma_a = N\sigma_a = 3.84\ 10^{-4}\ \text{cm}^{-1}$, $\Sigma_t \cong N\sigma_s = 0.384\ \text{cm}^{-1}$ and the total mean free path: $\lambda_t = 1/\Sigma_t = 2.60$ cm.

b) In the same way we can calculate Σ_t and λ_t for uranium oxide UO_2 enriched at 3% and of mass density $\rho(UO_2) = 10\ \text{g cm}^{-3}$. We must consider this time a mixture of the molecules of type $U^{235}O_2$ and $U^{238}O_2$. Let N_1 and N_2 be the corresponding molecular densities (cm^{-3}). We can write:

$$\rho(UO_2) = (N_1m_1 + N_2m_2) = \frac{N}{N_A}[xM_1 + (1 - x)M_2]$$

where the masses of the elementary molecules are denoted m_1 and m_2, the molar masses M_1, M_2 and the enrichment $x = N_1/N$ (§3.3.3). The molecular density (molecules of two types) is then obtained explicitly:

$$N = N_1 + N_2 = \frac{\rho(UO_2)N_A}{xM_1 + (1 - x)M_2}$$

and the various atomic densities follow from it:

$$N_U235 = N_1 = xN \qquad = 6.691\ 10^{20}\ cm^{-3}$$

$$N_U238 = N_2 = (1 - x)N \qquad = 2.163\ 10^{22}\ cm^{-3}$$

$$N_O = 2N \qquad = 4.46\ 10^{22}\ cm^{-3}$$

(since one molecule UO_2 contains two atoms of oxygen).
Taking as nuclear data (thermal neutrons):

$$U^{235}\begin{cases}\sigma_c = 108\ b\\ \sigma_f = 580\ b\\ \sigma_s = 8.3\ b\end{cases} \qquad U^{238}\begin{cases}\sigma_c = 2.75\ b\\ \sigma_f = 0\\ \sigma_s = 8.3\ b\end{cases} \qquad O^{16}\begin{cases}\sigma_c = \sigma_f = 0\\ \sigma_s = 4.2\ b\end{cases}$$

we find by applying equation (4.1):

$\Sigma_a = 0.520\ cm^{-1}$, $\Sigma_s = 0.372\ cm^{-1}$ whence $\Sigma_t = 0.892\ cm^{-1}$ and $\lambda_t = 1.12$ cm.

The mean free paths will thus be of the order of 1 to 2 cm and hence much smaller than the dimensions of the nuclear reactors (several meters).

c) For the oxide defined above we can determine in addition the fission rates and the specific power (4.9) with the additional data:

- scalar flux $\Phi = 3 \cdot 10^{13}$ thermal neutrons/cm^2 s
- energy per fission $E_f = 185$ MeV (§3.1.4)

We find respectively:

- $\Sigma_f = (N\sigma_f)U^{235} = 0.3888\ cm^{-1}$ for the fission cross section
- $R_f = 1.164 \cdot 10^{13}$ fissions/cm^3 s for the fission rate
- $\bar{\omega}_{sp} = 34.5$ W/g for the specific power

It is evidently the last quantity that interests the nuclear engineer. It is at this level that the thermal and neutron calculations are connected.

4.3 THE ELEMENTARY THEORY OF NEUTRON DIFFUSION

4.3.1 Fick's Law

This law states that at each point $\vec{r}$ of a material medium the net currents are proportional to the gradients of the neutron densities $n(\vec{r})$ or the scalar fluxes $\Phi(\vec{r}) = n(\vec{r})v$. In addition, the currents are such that the "neutron flow" takes place from high density to low density zones, whence:

$$J_x(x) = -D\frac{\partial\Phi}{\partial x} = -Dv\frac{\partial n}{\partial x}$$

or more generally:

$$\vec{J}(\vec{r}) = -D\,\vec{\text{grad}}\,\Phi \tag{4.13}$$

The diffusion coefficient D is characteristic of the medium in which the neutrons propagate.

This type of law is frequent in physics. We recall the law of conduction which states that the heat flux is proportional to the temperature gradient as well as the properties of inhomogeneous solutions which show a migration of the dissolved substance towards zones of weak concentration.

In neutron physics, the diffusion coefficient is necessarily related to the cross sections. Transport theory shows that Fick's law is approximate and that the diffusion coefficient is given by the expression (§8.1.3):

$$D \cong \frac{\lambda_t}{3} = \frac{1}{3\Sigma_t} \tag{4.14}$$

where the mean free path λ_t has already been introduced (§4.2.1).

A very simple reasoning permits us to get back qualitatively equations (4.13) and (4.14). Let us give ourselves a unit surface perpendicular to Ox and situated at height x (Fig. 4.8). The current $J_x^+(x)$ which traverses it from left to right is composed of neutrons which on the average have undergone their last scattering in a zone centered at point $x - \lambda_t$ of the abscissa, by the very definition of the mean free path λ_t. The current $J_x^+(x)$ is thus proportional to the flux in this zone, hence roughly to the quantity $\Phi(x - \lambda_t)$.

We will thus write $J_x^+(x) \cong k\Phi(x - \lambda_t)$ where k is an unknown numerical constant. Applying the same reasoning to the neutrons coming from the right, we obtain: $J_x^-(x) \cong k\Phi(x + \lambda_t)$ whence a net current $J_x(x) \cong k[\Phi(x - \lambda_t) - \Phi(x + \lambda_t)]$.

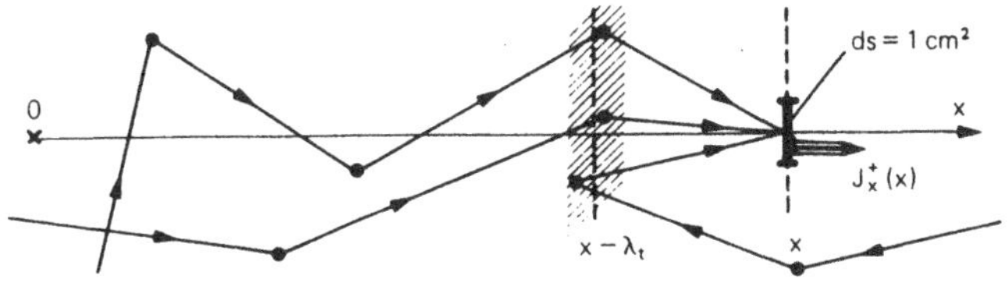

FIGURE 4.8.

A Taylor expansion to the first order leads to:

$$J_x(x) \cong -2k\lambda_t \frac{\partial\Phi}{\partial x}$$

Thus we get back Fick's law including the proportionality of the diffusion coefficient to the mean free path λ_t. To arrive at this result it was necessary to suppose λ_t to be infinitely small. However, this parameter is given by the characteristics of the considered material and one cannot make it tend to zero as one did for an arbitrary increment Δx (§4.2.3).

The preceding reasoning, which does not claim to be a proof of Fick's law, permits us to draw an important conclusion. We have just seen that the mean free path must be small for this law to be valid, but small with respect to what? The only characteristic length apart from λ_t is represented by the "scale of variations" of the flux, and this is fixed by the size of the material system being studied, whence the following conclusion:

Diffusion theory (or Fick's law) implicitly supposes that the mean free path λ_t is much smaller than all typical dimensions of the problem under study (diameter of the reactor core, thickness of the protection screen, etc.). This condition is very often achieved, since λ_t is of the order of a few centimeters (cf. the numerical examples in subsec. 4.2.4). We will find in an appendix (§8.1.3) a much more detailed study of the conditions of validity of Fick's law. To the preceding condition we must add another one, often satisfied in practice: the considered media must be more diffusive than absorbing ($\Sigma_s > \Sigma_a$) which justifies the term "diffusion" given to the equation which follows.

4.3.2 The Diffusion Equation

By combining the equation of neutron balance (4.12) and Fick's law (4.13) we obtain the diffusion equation:

$$\operatorname{div}\left(D(\vec{r})\,\vec{\operatorname{grad}}\,\Phi(\vec{r})\right) - \Sigma_a(\vec{r})\Phi(\vec{r}) + Q(\vec{r}) = 0 \tag{4.15}$$

We have shown that the macroscopic cross sections Σ_a and Σ_t depend in general on the point considered ($\vec{r}$) through the atomic densities (4.1).

In practice, a material system is composed of large homogeneous zones (Σ_a and D constants) for which the preceding equation becomes:

$$D\nabla^2\Phi - \Sigma_a\Phi + Q = 0 \tag{4.16}$$

where $\nabla^2\Phi$ represents the Laplacian of Φ, in other words [8]:

$$\nabla^2\Phi = \operatorname{div}\left(\vec{\operatorname{grad}}\,\Phi\right) = \frac{\partial^2\Phi}{\partial x^2} \quad \frac{\partial^2\Phi}{\partial y^2} \quad \frac{\partial^2\Phi}{\partial z^2}$$

The last expression assumes that one has chosen Cartesian coordinates (x,y,z) for $\vec{r}$. In unidimensional problems (the flux only depends on one space variable), the Laplacian has a particularly simple expression (Fig. 4.9):

- Plane geometry

$$\nabla^2\Phi = \frac{d^2\Phi}{dz^2} \tag{4.17}$$

The flux at point M is presumed independent of the two other coordinates x and y.

- Cylindrical geometry

$$\nabla^2\Phi = \frac{1}{r}\frac{d}{dr}\left(r\,\frac{d\Phi}{dr}\right) \tag{4.18}$$

The flux at M depends only on the distance r from an axis of symmetry.

- Spherical geometry

$$\nabla^2\Phi = \frac{1}{\rho^2}\frac{d}{d\rho}\left(\rho^2\,\frac{d\Phi}{d\rho}\right) \tag{4.19}$$

The flux depends only on the distance ρ from a center of symmetry.

We recall that equation (4.16) governs the behavior of mono-energetic neutrons in steady state. In contrast to equation (4.2) relevant for collimated neutron beams, the diffusion equation applies to neutrons moving in all directions. It thus has a much wider field of application. Apart from the term $\Sigma_a\Phi$, this equation is of the "Poisson type" well-known in electrostatics, and the numerical methods of solving it are analogous.

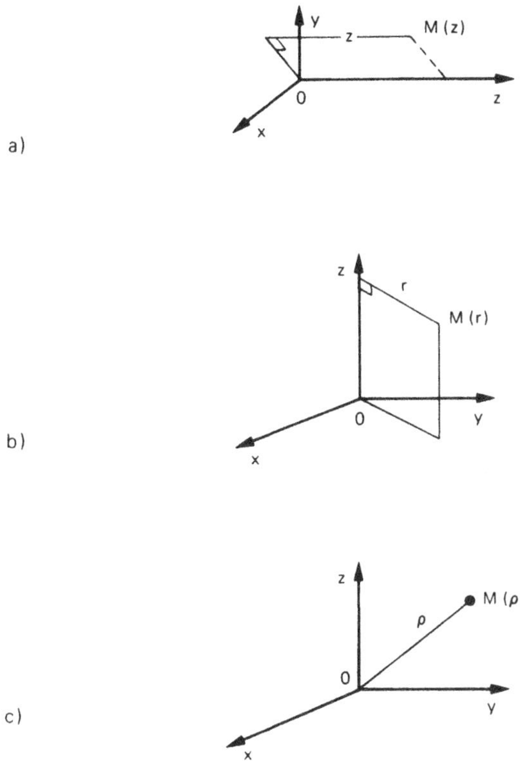

FIGURE 4.9. One-dimensional geometries: a) plane, b) cylindrical, c) spherical.

In order to solve an equation with partial derivatives of the second order (elliptic type), one shows in mathematics that it is necessary to give an additional condition on the external boundary of the system under study. From the physical point of view this means that it must be stipulated whether neutrons penetrate the system or not.

For isolated systems this condition can be written: $\Phi(S_e) = 0$.

The flux vanishes on the extrapolated surface obtained by displacing an arbitrary point of the external surface by a small amount d in the direction of the normal (Fig. 4.10).

Transport theory shows that the extrapolation distance d is given by the expression (§8.1.4):

$$d = 0.71\ \lambda_t$$

In nuclear reactors we will very often be able to identify the extrapolated surface with the true surface (d = 0).

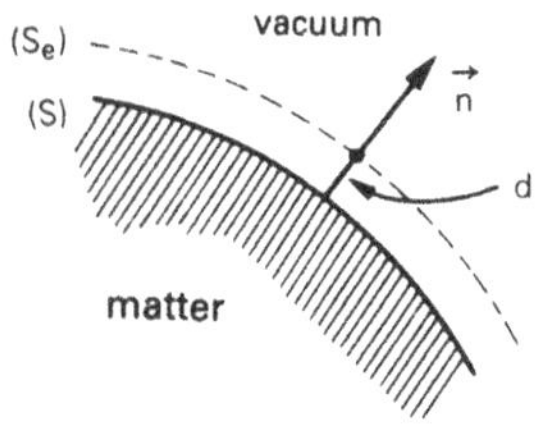

FIGURE 4.10.

When one considers an ensemble of contiguous homogeneous zones, the solutions obtained by solving (4.16) in each of them must be matched by writing the continuity of the flux and of the net currents when crossing the surfaces of separation.

It is clear that the continuity of the flux $\Phi = n\ v$ results from the continuity of the neutron density n. On the other hand, the discontinuity of the net currents would imply an accumulation of neutrons at the interfaces, which would be absurd.

Finally, by definition, the flux Φ is positive, just as the neutron density n (4.8); the net current in contrast can have an arbitrary sign.

4.3.3 Pointlike Source in an Infinite Medium

Let us consider a pointlike source in an infinite homogeneous medium characterized by cross sections Σ_t and Σ_a. The entire neutron emission is concentrated at the origin of the coordinates, the intensity of the source being denoted S(n/s). The diffusion problem to be solved has spherical symmetry. Thus we will take the expression (4.19) of the Laplacian given above. In these conditions, the diffusion equation (4.16) can be written (note that $Q = 0$ for $\rho \neq 0$):

$$\frac{1}{\rho^2}\frac{d}{d\rho}\left(\rho^2\frac{d\Phi}{d\rho}\right) - \frac{\Phi}{L^2} = 0 \qquad (4.21)$$

with:

$$L^2 = \frac{D}{\Sigma_a} = \frac{1}{3\Sigma_t\Sigma_a} \qquad (4.22)$$

The physical sense of the <u>diffusion area</u> L^2 or of the <u>diffusion length</u> L will be clearer later on.

We transform the preceding expression by putting $\Phi(\rho) = X(\rho)/\rho$, which leads to the new equation:

$$\frac{d^2X}{d\rho^2} - \frac{X}{L^2} = 0$$

The general solution of this equation is well known:

$$X(\rho) = A \exp\left(-\frac{\rho}{L}\right) + B \exp\left(+\frac{\rho}{L}\right)$$

whence the flux:

$$\Phi(\rho) = \frac{1}{\rho}\left[A \exp\left(-\frac{\rho}{L}\right) + B \exp\left(+\frac{\rho}{L}\right)\right]$$

The integration constants A and B depend on the boundary conditions. The external surface which limits the system reduces to spheres of radii $\rho \to \infty$ and $\rho \to 0$.

Since the flux cannot diverge at infinity, $B = 0$. As for the constant A, it depends necessarily on the intensity S of the pointlike source.

By definition of the net currents, neutron leakage across a sphere of infinitely small radius ρ can be written (Fig. 4.11):

$$\left| 4\pi\rho^2 J(\rho) \right|_{\rho\to 0} = S$$

since such a sphere contains the entire source. By using Fick's law the preceding condition becomes:

$$-4\pi D \left| \rho^2 \frac{\partial\Phi}{\partial\rho} \right|_{\rho\to 0} = S$$

Replacing the flux by its expression:

$$\Phi = \frac{A}{\rho} \exp\left(-\frac{\rho}{L}\right)$$

we obtain:

$$- 4\pi DA \left\{ \rho^2 \left[-\frac{1}{\rho^2} \exp\left(-\frac{\rho}{L}\right) - \frac{1}{\rho L} \exp\left(-\frac{\rho}{L}\right) \right] \right\}_{\rho \to 0} = S$$

and after passing to the limit: $A = S/4\pi D$.

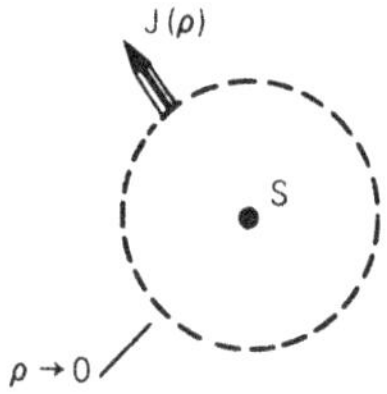

FIGURE 4.11.

The solution of the problem is thus:

$$\Phi(\rho) = \frac{S}{4\pi D\rho} \exp\left(-\frac{\rho}{L}\right) \quad (4.23)$$

The flux $\Phi(\rho)$ has the shape represented in Fig. 4.12. The divergence at the origin may be surprising. In fact, a source is never pointlike, but occupies a small region of space, let us say, a sphere of radius r_o. The solution of the diffusion equation in the two zones $\rho < r_o$ and $\rho > r_o$ would furnish the curve in dotted lines. The two curves rapidly approach each other for $\rho > r_o$.

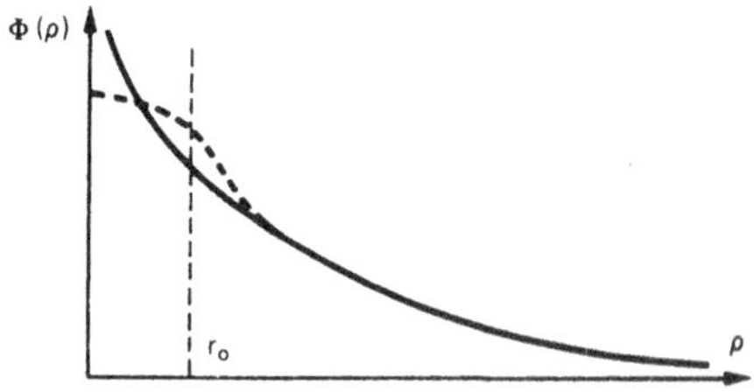

FIGURE 4.12. Distribution of the induced flux by a pointlike source in an infinite medium.

4.3.4 The Physical Meaning of Diffusion Length

The absorption rate at a distance ρ is always given by $\Sigma_a\Phi(\rho)$ where now $\Phi(\rho)$ is known (4.23). The number of neutrons absorbed in a spherical shell of radii ρ and $\rho + d\rho$ is thus given by: $\Sigma_a\Phi(\rho) \cdot 4\pi\rho^2 d\rho(s^{-1})$.

At the same time the number of neutrons emitted by the pointlike source is S, whence the probability of absorption at distance ρ is given by:

$$P(\rho)\ d\rho = \frac{\Sigma_a\Phi(\rho)4\pi\rho^2 d\rho}{S} = \frac{\rho}{L^2}\ \exp\left(-\frac{\rho}{L}\right)\ d\rho \qquad (4.24)$$

One checks that $\int_0^\infty P(\rho)d\rho = 1$, in other words, every neutron emitted in an infinite system is necessarily absorbed somewhere.

$P(\rho)$ represents the probability of absorption taking account of a certain number of scatterings which have already taken place, as indicated in Fig. 4.13. From this we see a big difference with respect to the probability $P(x)$ introduced in subsec. 4.2.1 (4.4) which only concerned motion in a straight line of the type MM'.

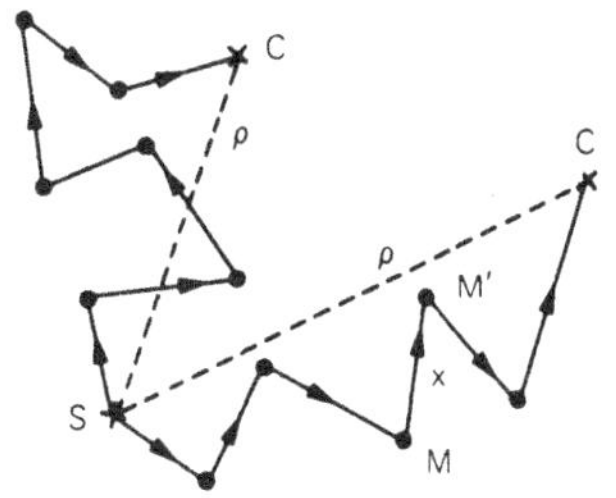

FIGURE 4.13.

The mean of ρ^2, denoted $<\rho^2>$ can be written by definition:

$$<\rho^2> = \int_0^\infty \rho^2 P(\rho)d\rho = \frac{1}{L^2}\int_0^\infty \rho^3\ \exp\left(-\frac{\rho}{L}\right)d\rho$$

Several integrations by parts then give:

$$<\rho^2> = 6L^2 \quad \text{or} \quad L = \frac{1}{\sqrt{6}}\sqrt{<\rho^2>}$$

The mean square distance at which a neutron is absorbed taking account of successive scatterings is proportional to the diffusion length L.

Clearly we should not confuse L with λ_t, since the latter corresponds only to the mean free path between two collisions (MM'). The straight line SC is not necessarily a trajectory followed by a neutron (Fig. 4.13).

In practice, especially in moderating media, the absorption cross sections are small compared to the total cross sections. It follows that $L \gg \lambda_t$ (4.22), which is, as we have already seen, a condition of validity of the diffusion equation. The diffusion length will play a much more important role than the mean free path in nuclear reactor calculations.

4.3.5 Comments

To understand well the meaning and the limits of diffusion theory, we return to the problem of a pointlike source emitting isotropically in an infinite homogeneous medium. The considerations of subsec. 4.2.1 led us to predict the flux distribution:

$$\phi(\rho) = \frac{S}{4\pi\rho^2} \exp\left(-\frac{\rho}{\lambda_t}\right) \tag{4.25}$$

To arrive at this result, it suffices to put $\Delta\rho = \rho$ in (4.6), since the material medium extends from the source to the receptor point considered (Fig. 4.2).

This result appears in contradiction with expression (4.23). In fact that is not the case, as indicated by the following observations:

- Let us at first suppose that the medium is weakly absorbing ($\lambda_t \ll L$) and let us consider increasing values of ρ. Very rapidly the results stemming from diffusion theory (4.23) greatly exceed those furnished by (4.25). The two exponential functions are in effect very different. This is not surprising if one remembers that expression (4.25) only represents the flux of virgin neutrons. These fluxes are calculated exactly, but do not have much interest. Equation (4.23) on the other hand gives the total fluxes (corresponding essentially to neutrons which have scattered a great many times). These fluxes are much more useful, since they permit us to calculate the true reaction rates.

- On the other hand, very close to the source, diffusion theory is inexact. In this zone of a few mean free paths λ_t, it is equation (4.25) which furnishes realistic results.

• Finally, for absorbing media ($\lambda_t >> L$ or $\Sigma_a >> \Sigma_s$) diffusion theory becomes false in the whole system. In the limiting case, when $\Sigma_s = 0$, equation (4.25) gives at each point the right value of the flux. In the intermediate cases ($\Sigma_a \cong \Sigma_s$), neither of these two approaches gives good results. At that point we cannot avoid solving the transport equation (Sec. 8.1).

• We will make a last remark with respect to equations (4.23) and (4.25). In the first equation, Φ represents the scalar flux but the neutrons arrive at the point C considered following all possible directions. In the second equation on the other hand, ϕ represents the scalar flux as well as the angular flux since the neutrons propagate only along SC (Fig. 4.13).

4.3.6 Absorbing Media Immersed in a Diffusing Medium

Let us consider at first a homogeneous and infinite diffusing medium, fed by neutrons from a uniform source Q. In these conditions, the scalar flux Φ is itself uniform and has the value:

$$\Phi_\infty = \frac{Q}{\Sigma_a} \tag{4.26}$$

This result is obtained without appealing to the diffusion equation. It suffices to remark that the net currents vanish (§4.2.2) and to utilize (4.12). We see that if $\Sigma_a = 0$, the flux becomes infinite, which is normal, since in the absence of leakage (infinite system) and of absorptions a continuous supply of neutrons ($Q \neq 0$) can only lead to a progressive increase of the flux in the course of time. In this limiting case, a stable state is not possible. In fact, this is a completely unrealistic case, since there does not exist any material whose absorption cross section strictly vanishes.

Let us now immerse in this system of small Σ_a a material which does not differ much from the preceding except for its large absorption cross section: $\Sigma'_a > \Sigma_a$. In order to realize this configuration, it suffices to add to the initial material a small quantity of a powerful absorber (boron for example) in a limited region of space. Having realized a system with two zones, the flux will no longer be uniform.

Let us consider a planar geometry, that is, an absorbing plate of infinite lateral dimensions and thickness 2h, placed in the infinite diffusing medium described above. For reasons of symmetry we can restrict ourselves to positive values of z (Fig. 4.14). We will suppose that the inequality $\Sigma_a < \Sigma'_a < \Sigma_s$ is satisfied so that diffusion theory applies to the two zones. Taking expression (4.17) of the Laplacian, the diffusion equations (4.16) can be written:

$$\left.\begin{array}{ll} -D\dfrac{d^2\Phi}{dz^2} + \Sigma'_a\,\Phi = Q & z \leq h \\ -D\dfrac{d^2\Phi}{dz^2} + \Sigma_a\,\Phi = Q & z \geq h \end{array}\right\}$$

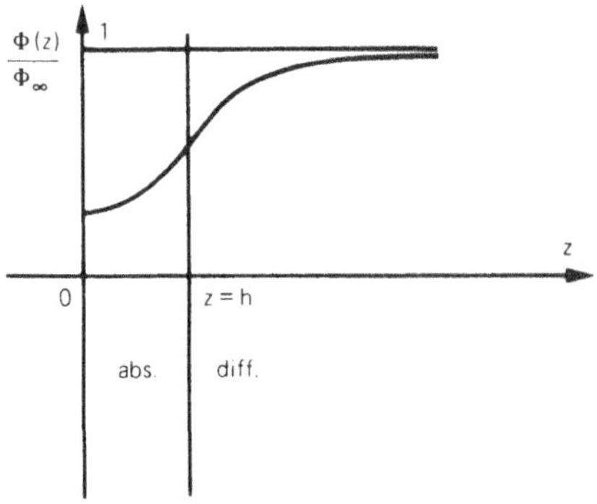

FIGURE 4.14. Diminution of flux in an absorber.

The diffusion coefficients of the two zones have been taken to be the same. Such a hypothesis is often justified in practice. The absorptions being small compared to diffusions (even in relatively absorbing materials), we have approximately (4.14):

$$D = \frac{1}{3\Sigma_t} \cong \frac{1}{3\Sigma_s}$$

where Σ_s is here by hypothesis independent of the zone considered.

The preceding equations can be easily integrated. It suffices to add to the general solution of the equations without the source term the particular solutions Q/Σ'_a or Q/Σ_a depending on the case. We thus arrive at the expressions:

$$\left.\begin{aligned}\Phi(z) &= \frac{Q}{\Sigma'_a} + A' \exp\left(-\frac{z}{L'}\right) + B' \exp\left(+\frac{z}{L'}\right) \qquad z \leqq h \\ \Phi(z) &= \frac{Q}{\Sigma_a} + A \exp\left(-\frac{z}{L}\right) + B \exp\left(+\frac{z}{L}\right) \qquad z \geqq h\end{aligned}\right\}$$

where we have put (4.22):

$$L^2 = \frac{D}{\Sigma_a} \quad \text{and } L'^2 = \frac{D}{\Sigma'_a}$$

Since the solution has to be symmetric with respect to $z = 0$, the net current at this point must vanish. Thus we obtain from Fick's law:

$$\left(\frac{d\Phi}{dz}\right)_0 = 0, \quad \text{or } A' = B'$$

In the second zone ($z \geqq h$) the flux cannot diverge at infinity and hence $B = 0$. The preceding solution can then be put in the form:

$$\left.\begin{aligned}\Phi(z) &= \frac{\Sigma_a}{\Sigma'_a}\Phi_\infty + 2A' \cosh\left(\frac{z}{L'}\right) \qquad z \leqq h \\ \Phi(z) &= \Phi_\infty + A \exp\left(-\frac{z}{L}\right) \qquad z \geqq h\end{aligned}\right\}$$

where we have exhibited the flux Φ_∞ (4.26) which existed at every point before the absorbing plate had been placed. One sees that far from the plate $\Phi(z)$ tends to Φ_∞.

In order to determine the constants A' and A we must apply the procedure indicated in subsec. 4.3.2. We write the continuity of the flux and of the currents at $z = h$. Since the diffusion constants D are the same on both sides of the frontier, this is equivalent to writing the continuity of the derivatives (4.13). We finally obtain:

$$z \leqq h \qquad \frac{\Phi(z)}{\Phi_\infty} = \frac{\Sigma_a}{\Sigma'_a} + \frac{\Sigma'_a - \Sigma_a}{\Sigma'_a} \; \frac{\cosh\left(\frac{z}{L'}\right)}{\cosh\left(\frac{h}{L'}\right) + \frac{L}{L'}\sinh\left(\frac{h}{L'}\right)}$$

$$z \geqq h \qquad \frac{\Phi(z)}{\Phi_\infty} = 1 - \frac{\Sigma'_a - \Sigma_a}{\Sigma'_a} \; \frac{\frac{L}{L'}\sinh\left(\frac{h}{L'}\right)\exp\left(-\frac{z-h}{L}\right)}{\cosh\left(\frac{h}{L'}\right) + \frac{L}{L'}\sinh\left(\frac{h}{L'}\right)} \tag{4.27}$$

These expressions tend to unity when $\Sigma'_a \to \Sigma_a$, in other words, when the perturbation disappears. We obtain the same result when $h \to 0$. In this case we say that there is infinite dilution and the absorbing region is submitted to the pre-existing flux. In all other cases the flux gets more or less depressed (Fig. 4.14).

The absorption in the first zone can be written:

$$\int_0^h \Sigma'_a \Phi(z)dz = \Sigma'_a \bar{\Phi}\, h$$

where $\bar{\Phi}$ represents the mean flux that one can deduce from the first equation (4.27). This absorption is thus smaller than the value $\Sigma'_a \Phi_\infty h$, to which a hasty reasoning might have led. We call this a self-shielding property. The absorbing plate partially protects its central part by attenuating the neutron flux coming from the external zone. This property remains qualitatively true, even when diffusion theory is no longer applicable. It plays an important role in practice, and that is why we have chosen this example to illustrate diffusion theory.

4.3.7 Numerical Applications

We will restrict ourselves to thermal neutrons. Let us again take the case of graphite. We have already obtained (§4.2.4):

$$\Sigma_t = 0.384\ \text{cm}^{-1},\ \Sigma_a = 3.84\ 10^{-4}\ \text{cm}^{-1}\ \text{and}\ \lambda_t = 2.60\ \text{cm}$$

We deduce that D = 0.866 cm according to equation (4.14), $L^2 = 2257\ \text{cm}^2$ whence L = 47.5 cm (4.22). We can find in the same way for various moderating materials the characteristics indicated in Table 4.15.

TABLE 4.15. Diffusion lengths of several moderators (thermal neutrons).

	ϱ [g/cm^3]	λ_t [cm]	D [cm]	L [cm]
H_2O	1	0.43	0.14	2.76
D_2O	1.1	2.41	0.80	107
Beryllium	1.85	1.48	0.49	21

Because of its relatively large absorption cross section, light water has a small diffusion length. After thermalization, the neutrons emitted by the fuel are rapidly absorbed by the water (parasitic capture), whence the closely spaced lattices observed in light water reactors. This inconvenience of light water is largely compensated by its excellent slowing-down power (Sec. 4.4).

If we now consider the characteristics of uranium oxide UO_2, Σ_a = 0.520 cm^{-1} and Σ_t = 0.892 cm^{-1} (§4.2.4), we find:

$$D = 0.373 \text{ cm}, \; L^2 = 0.72 \text{ cm}^2, \; L = 0.85 \text{ cm}$$

whereas the mean free path λ_t equals 1.12 cm. Diffusion theory is thus not valid in a fuel but this does not mean that we cannot apply it to a nuclear reactor. In effect, the moderator/fuel mixture is such that in most cases the diffusion length is much greater than the mean free path.

4.4 SLOWING DOWN OF NEUTRONS

4.4.1 Introduction

In the preceding subsections we have restricted ourselves to the mono-energetic neutrons. Thermal neutrons and very fast neutrons can be analyzed in this way. All the same, in a thermal reactor, most of the neutrons have by definition a minimal energy (0.025 eV), whereas they were created by fission at a much higher energy (around 2 MeV, cf. §3.1.3). It is thus necessary to study the phenomenon of slowing down in order to know how neutrons pass from fission energy to thermal energy.

Fast neutron reactor calculations also demand studies of this type. In spite of all the precautions taken to avoid their moderation, neutrons in this type of reactor have energies which go roughly from 10 keV to 2 MeV, in other words a mean value much smaller than the energy they had during their emission by fission. Since we do not know a priori their distribution in this energy range, it is difficult to assign to them accurate cross sections and thus to treat them as a family of mono-energetic particles.

4.4.2 Study of a Collision

Here we shall only consider elastic scattering, which is the most important for thermal reactors.

Consider a neutron of mass m and velocity $\vec{v}'$, entering into elastic collision with a nucleus of mass M and velocity $\vec{V}'$. After collision, their velocities will be respectively $\vec{v}$ and $\vec{V}$. The law of conservation of momentum gives:

$$m\vec{v}' + M\vec{V}' = m\vec{v} + M\vec{V} = (m + M)\,\vec{V}_g$$

The velocity of the center of gravity (or center of mass) $\vec{V}_g$ remains unchanged during collision (no external forces).

It is convenient to introduce the relative velocities:

$$\vec{v}'_r = \vec{v}' - \vec{V}' \quad \text{and} \quad \vec{v}_r = \vec{v} - \vec{V}$$

whence we deduce:

$$\left.\begin{aligned} \vec{v}' &= \vec{V}_g + \frac{M}{m+M}\vec{v}'_r \\ \vec{V}' &= \vec{V}_g - \frac{m}{m+M}\vec{v}'_r \end{aligned}\right\} \tag{4.28}$$

Analogous expressions relate $\vec{v}$ and $\vec{V}$ to $\vec{v}_r$. The conservation of momentum is then automatically realized. One can show with the help of equations (4.28) that the kinetic energy of the system can be written:

$$m\frac{v'^2}{2} + \frac{MV'^2}{2} = \frac{m+M}{2}V_g^2 + \frac{1}{2}\frac{Mm}{M+m}v_r'^2$$

where v', V', V_g, v'_r are magnitudes of the vectors $\vec{v}'$, $\vec{V}'$, $\vec{V}_g$, $\vec{v}'_r$. The last term represents the relative kinetic energy of the neutron with respect to the nucleus. It is this which fixes the microscopic cross sections of interaction when they depend on energy (§1.5.5).

After having expressed the conservation of momentum, we must assure the conservation of energy, since the collisions are elastic. Taking the second form of the kinetic energy of the pair (neutron + nucleus) and noting that V_g is unchanged during the collision, one is led to:

$$v'_r = v_r \tag{4.29}$$

In the course of a collision the relative velocity is thus conserved in magnitude, only its direction changing. A diffusion is thus characterized by a single parameter, the deflection angle θ_c, in the center of mass system. θ_c is given by:

$$\vec{v}'_r \cdot \vec{v}_r = v_r^2 \cos\theta_c$$

When we study the slowing down of neutrons of intermediate energies ($E \gg E_t$) we can consider the nuclei of mass M as being initially at rest. Putting $\vec{V}' = 0$ in equations (4.28), we find that:

$$\vec{v}' = \vec{v}'_r$$

$$\vec{V}_g = \frac{m}{m + M} \vec{v}'$$

Using the first equation (4.28) in the conditions which prevail after the collision, and taking account of the preceding value of $\vec{V}_g$, we get:

$$\vec{v} = \vec{V}_g + \frac{M}{m + M} \vec{v}_r$$

or:

$$\vec{v} = \frac{m}{m + M} \vec{v}' + \frac{M}{m + M} \vec{v}_r$$

Taking the scalar square of the last vectorial equation (cf. Fig. 4.16), we arrive at the relation:

$$v^2 = \left(\frac{mv'}{M + m} \right)^2 + \left(\frac{Mv_r}{M + m} \right)^2 + \frac{2mv' . Mv_r}{(M + m)^2} \cos \theta_c$$

where we have noted that $\vec{v}'$ and $\vec{v}_r$ form an angle equal to the angle θ_c defined earlier (since $\vec{v}' = \vec{v}'_r$).

While the relative velocity after the collision $\vec{v}_r$ is different from $\vec{v}'_r$, and hence from $\vec{v}'$, the same is not true for the magnitude of these vectors (4.29). Replacing v_r by v' and designating by E' and E the energies of the neutron before and after the collision, one is led to the important relation:

$$\frac{E}{E'} = \frac{v^2}{v'^2} = \frac{A^2 + 2A \cos \theta_c + 1}{(A + 1)^2} \tag{4.30}$$

where we have put $A = M/m$, a parameter which can be identified with excellent precision with the mass number of the nucleus (§1.3.3). We thus note that:

- for $\theta_c = 0$, $E = E'$, the neutron does not lose energy
- for $\theta_c = \pi$, on the contrary, this loss is maximum, and one has $E = \alpha E'$ with:

$$\alpha = \left(\frac{A - 1}{A + 1} \right)^2 < 1 \tag{4.31}$$

The parameter α plays a major role in the theory of slowing down.

Equation (4.30) indicates that there is a correlation between the deflection angle θ_c and the energy E. More precisely, for a given incident energy E' all the diffused neutrons inside a cone with vertex angle θ_c will have the same energy E; the results do not depend on the azimuthal angle ω, as can be seen in Fig. 4.16.

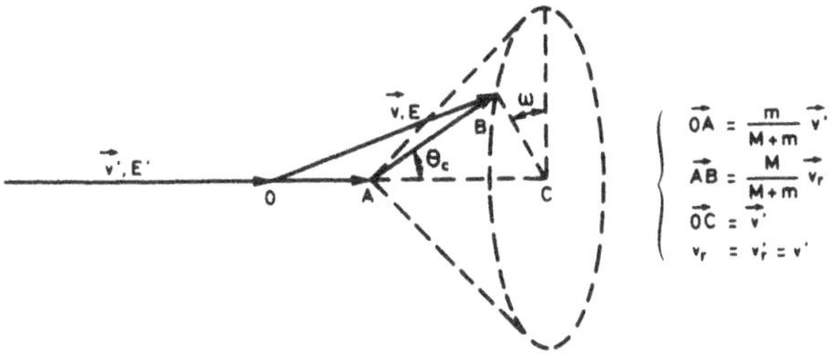

FIGURE 4.16.

Except for heavy nuclei and very fast neutrons (E > 100 keV), the diffusion process is always isotropic in the center of mass coordinate system. We place ourselves henceforth in the framework of this hypothesis and put $\mu = \cos\theta_c$. The preceding property means that the number of neutrons scattered in the directions included between μ and $\mu + d\mu$ is simply proportional to the width $d\mu$ of this interval. In other words, all the intervals are equivalent provided they have the same width. The maximum envisageable interval (-1, +1) of width $\Delta\mu = 2$ corresponds to all possible deflections. It follows that the fraction of neutrons scattered in $d\mu$ is simply equal to $d\mu/2$. Let us differentiate equation (4.30) and express $d\mu/2$ as a function of dE (with E' constant). We get:

$$d\mu/2 = \frac{(A+1)^2}{4A}\frac{dE}{E'}$$

or introducing α (4.31):

$$\frac{d\mu}{2} = \frac{dE}{(1-\alpha)E'}$$

Given the preceding meaning of $d\mu/2$, the righthand side of the last relation can be interpreted as the probability $P_1(E' \to E)dE$ that a neutron of energy E' appears after an elastic collision with an energy between E and E + dE. We will thus put:

$$P_1(E' \to E) = \begin{cases} \dfrac{1}{(1-\alpha)E'} & \text{for } \alpha E' < E < E' \\ 0 & \text{otherwise} \end{cases} \tag{4.32}$$

This probability density necessarily vanishes for $E < \alpha E'$, since $\alpha E'$ represents, as we have seen, the smallest energy that a neutron can have after collision ($\theta_c = \pi$). Moreover, it satisfies the expected normalization condition:

$$\int_0^\infty P_1\ (E' \to E)dE = \int_{\alpha E'}^{E'} \frac{dE}{(1-\alpha)E'} = 1$$

It follows from all this that the materials of high atomic weight ($A >> 1$) will have a weaker slowing down power. Equation (4.31) shows in effect that α is in the neighborhood of unity and hence that the minimum energy after shock ($\alpha E'$) is close to the initial energy E'.

On the other hand, for hydrogen ($A = 1$) the parameter α vanishes. Hence the neutron can lose all its energy in a single collision, whence the interest of hydrogenic materials for the moderation of neutrons.

Starting from the probability density $P_1\ (E' \to E)$ one can introduce a new probability which will often be used henceforth and which represents the fraction of neutrons having after collision an energy smaller than the prescribed value E. These neutrons are thus confined in the energy band $(\alpha E', E)$ as indicated in Fig. 4.17, whence:

$$P_2\ (E' \to E) = \int_{\alpha E'}^{E} P_1\ (E' \to E'')dE''$$

or:

$$P_2\ (E' \to E) = \begin{cases} \dfrac{E - \alpha E'}{(1-\alpha)E'} & \text{for } \alpha E' \leqq E \leqq E' \\ 0 & \text{otherwise} \end{cases} \tag{4.33}$$

Like $P_1(E' \to E)$, this new probability is different from 0 only in the interval $(\alpha E', E')$. It attains the value 1 for $E = E'$; the appearance of a scattered neutron of energy inferior to its initial energy is equivalent to certainty. As E diminishes, the chances that a neutron attain this energy dwindle, and they vanish completely for $E = \alpha E'$.

According to the preceding, the energy loss of a neutron in the course of a collision is a random variable just like the deflection angle θ_c to which it is related. Thus the mean values that one can attach to certain quantities are more interesting.

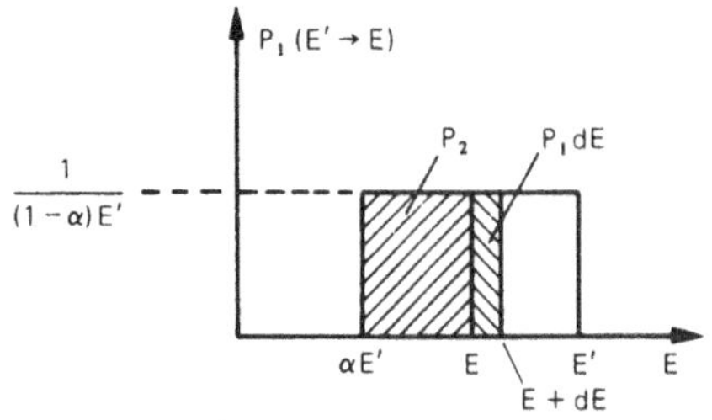

FIGURE 4.17.

The mean energy loss per collision can be written:

$$<\Delta E> = \int_0^\infty (E' - E)\, P_1(E' \to E)dE = \int_{\alpha E'}^{E'} \frac{E' - E}{(1 - \alpha)E'}\, dE$$

whence:

$$<\Delta E> = \frac{1 - \alpha}{2}\, E' \tag{4.34}$$

This result depends on the initial energy E' of the neutron. Let us now consider the average logarithmic energy loss per collision. This is usually denoted ξ and by definition:

$$\xi = <\ln\left(\frac{E'}{E}\right)> = \int_0^\infty \ln\left(\frac{E'}{E}\right)P_1\ (E' \to E)dE = \int_{\alpha E'}^{E'} \ln\left(\frac{E'}{E}\right) \frac{dE}{(1-\alpha)E'}$$

The last integral can easily be calculated by putting $x = E/E'$. We get:

$$\xi = -\int_\alpha^1 \ln x\, \frac{dx}{1-\alpha} = -\frac{1}{1-\alpha}\ \left|x \ln x - x\right|_\alpha^1$$

and finally:

$$\xi = 1 - \frac{\alpha}{1-\alpha}\ \ln\left(\frac{1}{\alpha}\right) \tag{4.35}$$

The interest of this parameter comes from the fact that it does not depend on the initial energy E' but only on the mass number A of the target nucleus (4.31). Its introduction may appear arbitrary, but its justification resides in the developments of subsec. 4.4.4. We can all the same deduce from its value a first characteristic of moderating media. In a thermal reactor the energy of neutrons passes from about 2 MeV (fission neutrons) to 0.025 eV (thermal energy), in other words, a logarithmic energy loss of $\ln (2\ 10^6/0.025) = 18.2$. Since the corresponding loss per collision is represented by ξ (4.35), the <u>average</u> number of collisions necessary amounts to:

$$N = \frac{18.2}{\xi} \tag{4.36}$$

One finds that this number is minimum for hydrogen, which has the largest value of ξ ($\alpha = 0$, $\xi = 1$) and becomes bigger and bigger as one considers heavier and heavier nuclei ($A \nearrow \xi \searrow$). To say that N is equal to 18 for hydrogen means that on the average neutrons will suffer 18 collisions in order to arrive at thermal energy, but some of them will undergo more and others less, like those which are scattered in the angle θ_c for which a single collision suffices (4.30).

4.4.3 Fundamental Equations of Slowing Down

Let us consider neutrons with energy between E and E + dE. At each point of space we can introduce the preceding notions of flux, current, etc., for this energy band. These quantities being proportional to dE, we will denote them $\Phi(\vec{r},E)dE$, $\vec{J}(\vec{r},E)dE$. The quantities $\Phi(\vec{r},E)$ and $\vec{J}(\vec{r},E)$ are called <u>spectral densities</u> or more simply, <u>densities</u>, of flux, current (with respect to energy). The flux densities are expressed in $cm^{-2}\ s^{-1}\ MeV^{-1}$, if the neutron energies are measured in MeV; the same is true for the current densities.

To solve a slowing down problem amounts to determining the flux densities $\Phi(\vec{r},E)$ from which one can calculate all useful quantities. The fission rate for example can be written:

$$dR_f = \Sigma_f(E)(\Phi(\vec{r},E)dE)$$

for neutrons situated in the band dE, or:

$$R_f(\vec{r}) = \int_0^\infty \Sigma_f(E)\Phi(\vec{r},E)dE \qquad (\text{in } cm^{-3}\ s^{-1}) \tag{4.37}$$

for all the neutrons situated at the point $\vec{r}$. Clearly it is the last rate which is interesting, since it permits us to calculate the source of heat $(E_f/\rho_c)R_f$ associated to fissions (4.9).

To arrive at the equation which governs flux and current densities, it suffices to reemploy the reasoning of subsec. 4.2.3, applied this time to neutrons confined in the energy band (E, E + dE). We thus obtain (4.12):

$$\text{div}\,(\vec{J}dE) + \Sigma_a(\Phi dE) = (QdE) \tag{4.38}$$

Recall that for mono-energetic neutrons, Q represented a source in the strict sense (creation of neutrons following nuclear reactions). Now this is no longer completely true, since we must add to the "true" sources QdE an additional term corresponding to higher energy neutrons which after an elastic collision appear with an energy between E and E + dE (4.3.2).

Let us consider energies E' greater than E. The number of neutrons undergoing elastic collisions in the band (E', E' + dE') is equal to the elementary scattering rate:

$$dR_s = \Sigma_s(E')(\Phi(\vec{r},E')dE')$$

Among these neutrons, some are scattered with energies smaller than E. They represent the fraction $P_2(E' \rightarrow E)$ defined earlier (4.33). If one now considers all the possible energies E', then the number of neutrons slowed down below E, per unit time and unit volume, can be written:

$$q(\vec{r},E) = \int_E^{\infty} P_2(E' \rightarrow E)\Sigma_s(E')\Phi(\vec{r},E')dE'$$

or (4.33):

$$q(\vec{r},E) = \int_E^{E/\alpha} \frac{E - \alpha E'}{(1-\alpha)E'}\,\Sigma_s(E')\Phi(\vec{r},E')dE' \tag{4.39}$$

This last quantity will be called the <u>slowing down source</u>. It is better known by the name <u>slowing down density</u>, but this terminology is unsuitable since q has the dimensions of a source ($cm^{-3}\ s^{-1}$) and not that of a source density ($cm^{-3}\ s^{-1}\ MeV^{-1}$). The upper limit E/α of the integral (4.39) results from the definition of $P_2(E' \rightarrow E)$ (4.33). It means in particular that neutrons of too high an energy E' cannot arrive by a single collision at the energy E.

Let us form the difference q(E + dE) - q(E). We obtain the number of neutrons scattered in the slice dE. They thus constitute a source for the neutrons of energy (E, E + dE) which propagate in space obeying equation (4.38). In this equation, the second term QdE must then be replaced by QdE + q(E + dE) - q(E), whence after division by dE and passage to the limit (dE → 0) we obtain:

$$\operatorname{div} \vec{J}(\vec{r},E) + \Sigma_a \Phi(\vec{r},E) = \frac{\partial}{\partial E} q(\vec{r},E) + Q(\vec{r},E) \tag{4.40}$$

This equation generalizes the equation of balance (4.12) pertaining to mono-energetic neutrons to the more general case of neutrons in the course of slowing down. The elimination of q between equations (4.39) and (4.40) gives us a relation between $\vec{J}$ and Φ. Differentiating (4.39) with respect to E we find:

$$\frac{\partial q}{\partial E} = \int_E^{E/\alpha} \frac{\Sigma_s(E')\Phi(\vec{r},E')}{(1-\alpha)E'} dE' + \frac{1}{\alpha}\left[\frac{E-\alpha E'}{(1-\alpha)E'}\, \Sigma_s(E')\Phi(\vec{r},E')\right]_{E'=E/\alpha}$$

$$- \left[\frac{E-\alpha E'}{(1-\alpha)E'}\, \Sigma_s(E')\,\Phi(\vec{r},E')\right]_{E'=E}$$

or:

$$\frac{\partial q}{\partial E} = \int_E^{E/\alpha} \frac{\Sigma_s(E')\,\Phi(\vec{r},E')}{(1-\alpha)E'} dE' - \Sigma_s(E)\,\Phi(\vec{r},E) \tag{4.41}$$

In order to eliminate $\vec{J}$ we can appeal to Fick's law (4.13). We then arrive at the desired equation:

$$\operatorname{div}[D(\vec{r},E)\operatorname{grad}\Phi(\vec{r},E)] - [\Sigma_a(\vec{r},E) + \Sigma_s(\vec{r},E)]\Phi(\vec{r},E)$$

$$+ \int_E^{E/\alpha} \frac{\Sigma_s(\vec{r},E')\,\Phi(\vec{r},E')}{(1-\alpha)E'} dE' + Q(\vec{r},E) = 0 \tag{4.42}$$

analogous to the diffusion equation established for mono-energetic neutrons (4.15).

We have written the last equation only to show that the fluxes $\Phi(\vec{r},E)$ are perfectly defined when the sources $Q(\vec{r},E)$ are known. In fact, in practice it is more convenient to work with the pair of equations (4.39) and (4.40), whose physical sense is clearer and which involve the use of Fick's law only when necessary (§4.5.8).

4.4.4 Neutron Spectra in Infinite Homogeneous Media

This case is not as academic as one might think. In a large-size nuclear reactor, one can locally define homogeneous zones of large enough dimensions so that the neutrons have time to slow down before leaving them.

In an infinite homogeneous medium fed by a uniform distribution of neutron sources the angular fluxes are isotropic and the net currents vanish (§4.2.2) We arrive at the same conclusion by noting that the scalar fluxes are the same at each point of space (put $\vec{\text{grad}}\Phi = 0$ in Fick's law (4.13)). Equation (4.40) becomes in this case:

$$\Sigma_a(E)\Phi(E) = \frac{dq}{dE} + Q(E) \tag{4.43}$$

where the slowing down source q is always given by (4.39), the fluxes and cross sections depending this time only on energy E.

We first study the case $\Sigma_a = 0$ which corresponds quite well to moderating materials used in nuclear reactors. We then have the simple relation:

$$\frac{dq}{dE} + Q(E) = 0 \tag{4.44}$$

In practice Q will represent the source of fission neutrons (or rather its density). This function is practically zero below an energy $E_s \cong 0.2$ MeV and attains its maximum near 0.75 MeV decreasing slowly thereafter (Fig. 3.2).

Integrating (4.44) from $E \leqq E_s$ to infinity we get:

$$q(\infty) - q(E) + \int_E^\infty Q(E')dE' = 0$$

For energies $E \to \infty$, the sources and hence the fluxes tend to zero. We can thus put $q(\infty) = 0$. On the other hand there is no emission below $E_s (Q(E)=0)$. Hence:

$$q(E) = \int_{E_s}^\infty Q(E)dE = Q_f \tag{4.45}$$

for $E \leqq E_s$.

We see thus that the slowing down source q(E), which is a priori a function of energy, is in fact constant and equal to the total source Q_f. This result is evident, since in the absence of absorption ($\Sigma_a = 0$) and of leaks ($\vec{J} = 0$), the number of neutrons which cross any energy E is necessarily equal to the number of neutrons Q_f created by fission (otherwise there would be accumulation and variation of fluxes in time).

We must now find a solution $\Phi(E')$ which, once we have taken account of (4.39), assures that q(E) has a constant value. This condition is satisfied if we put:

$$\Phi(E') = \frac{C}{E'\Sigma_s(E')}$$

where C is a constant. In fact, substituting this expression into (4.39) we get:

$$q(E) = C \int_E^{E/\alpha} \frac{E - \alpha E'}{(1 - \alpha)E'^2} dE' = C \left[1 - \frac{\alpha}{1 - \alpha} \ln\left(\frac{1}{\alpha}\right)\right]$$

The last integral is energy-independent and its value is none other than ξ, the average logarithmic energy loss per collision (4.35). We thus obtain:

$$\Phi(E) = \frac{q(E)}{E\,\xi\,\Sigma_s(E)} \tag{4.46}$$

with $q(E) = Q_f$ = const. and $E \leq E_s$ (the lower limit of the fission spectrum). The scattering cross sections depend very little on energy. We thus arrive at the conclusion that the energy distribution of neutrons in the process of slowing down varies like 1/E (this result was obtained for the first time by Fermi).

When the considered medium is a mixture of isotopes characterized by N_i, σ_{si}, α_i the slowing down source is obtained by generalizing (4.39):

$$q(E) = \sum_i \int_E^{E/\alpha_i} \frac{E - \alpha_i E'}{(1 - \alpha_i)E'} \Sigma_{si}(E')\Phi(E')dE' \tag{4.47}$$

Assuming that the scattering cross sections are energy-independent, one verifies that a solution of the type $\Phi(E') = K/E'$ assures that q is constant, whence the result:

$$\Phi(E) = \frac{q}{E \sum_i \xi_i \Sigma_{si}} \tag{4.48}$$

which is an expression identical to (4.46) if we put:

$$\xi\,\Sigma_s = \sum_i \xi_i \Sigma_{si}$$

with by definition: $\Sigma_s = \Sigma_i \; \Sigma_{si}$. The last results show us how to define correctly the parameter ξ of a mixture of isotopes.

The method used for arriving at (4.46) does not permit us to affirm that we have obtained the general solution of the problem. In fact a more complete study to be found in the appendix (§8.3.2) shows that for a mono-energetic source (the fission neutrons are all emitted at $E = E_0$) the expression (4.46) only represents the asymptotic solution, in other words, it is only valid for energies much lower than E_0. In fact, the change observed near E_0 is not very important in practice since it totally disappears for hydrogen and is significantly attenuated when we consider realistic sources (fission neutrons, as we have seen, are emitted in a large energy band above E_s). Hence, in all practical cases equations (4.46) or (4.48) furnish a good estimate of the flux in nonabsorbing media.

Let us now pass to the more realistic case where neutrons may be absorbed in the course of slowing down. This is what happens in a nuclear reactor composed of a fuel (essentially absorbing) and of a moderator (which,above all, slows down neutrons).

We must now solve simultaneously (4.43) and (4.39) without putting $\Sigma_a = 0$. There does not exist an analytic solution to this problem in the general case. All the same, we shall establish an expression whose domain of validity is much larger than the hypotheses made would lead us to suppose.

Let us suppose at first that absorption is small compared with scattering. We can admit that in the first order (in Σ_a) the law (4.46) remains valid. Of course the slowing down source q is no longer constant and obeys the relation (4.43). For $E < E_s$ (for energies smaller than that of fission neutrons) this relation can be written:

$$\Sigma_a(E)\Phi(E) = \frac{dq}{dE} \tag{4.49}$$

whence by eliminating Φ between (4.46) and (4.49):

$$\frac{E_a(E)}{E\,\xi\Sigma_s(E)}\,q(E) = \frac{dq}{dE}$$

and after integration:

$$q(E) = q(E_s) \exp\left[- \int_E^{E_s} \frac{\Sigma_a(E')}{\xi\Sigma_s(E')} \frac{dE'}{E'} \right] \tag{4.50}$$

If we accept that above E_s there is no absorption, then $q(E_s) = Q_f$ (4.45) and the flux can be written (4.46):

$$\Phi(E) = \frac{Q_f}{E\xi\Sigma_s(E)} \exp\left[- \int_E^{E_s} \frac{\Sigma_a(E')}{\xi\Sigma_s(E')} \frac{dE'}{E'} \right] \tag{4.51}$$

In the absence of absorption (4.51) reduces to equation (4.46) written for $q = Q_f$. Hence:

$$p(E) = \exp\left[- \int_E^{E_s} \frac{\Sigma_a(E')}{\xi\Sigma_s(E')} \frac{dE'}{E'} \right] \tag{4.52}$$

represents the probability that a neutron has to escape absorptions during its slowing down from the emission energy ($>E_s$) to the energy E considered.

In the preceding reasoning we have assumed that the absorptions are small compared to scattering. We can thus replace Σ_s by Σ_t in the expression for p. Whence the important result:

$$p(E) = \exp\left[- \int_E^{E_s} \frac{\Sigma_a(E')}{\xi\Sigma_t(E')} \frac{dE'}{E'} \right] \tag{4.53}$$

The preceding equation is valid in cases which are very different form the one just treated. For example, for hydrogenic materials, if one accepts that hydrogen alone is responsible for the slowing down, this equation is correct even for large values of Σ_a (§8.3.3). It also constitutes a very good approximation when the cross sections have very large values for certain <u>resonance</u> energies. These resonances play an important role in nuclear physics since they give information on the structure of nuclei, and also in reactor physics since the absorption in the course of slowing down takes place in the fuel essentially by resonance in fertile isotopes.

This last case is thus very important and it may appear curious that equation (4.53) remains valid given the extremely high values of the absorption cross sections at the level of resonances. This can be explained by the fact that these resonances are very narrow, whence the justification given in the appendix (§8.3.4).

4.4.5 Application to the Core of a Nuclear Reactor

The core of a nuclear reactor can be seen in a first approximation as a homogeneous mixture of fuel and moderator. We shall see in Sec. 5.1 that other materials are present for technological reasons, but they contribute very little to the slowing down and absorption of neutrons. In the fuel we will only take account of fertile isotopes (§3.2.3).

The fissile isotopes give rise also to the resonance phenomenon, but here the absorptions and fissions are epithermal and can generally be neglected in simple studies (these resonances have a much weaker influence on neutron balances since they correspond simultaneously to the creation and the destruction of neutrons).

We shall apply to the macroscopic cross sections the mixture rule (4.1), assigning the index (c) to the fuel and (m) to the moderator. We can thus write by definition:

$$\left.\begin{aligned} \Sigma_a(E) &= N_c\,\sigma_{a,c}(E) \\ \Sigma_t(E) &= N_c\,[\sigma_{a,c}(E) + \sigma_{s,c}(E) + \sigma^*_{s,c}] + N_m\sigma_m \end{aligned}\right\} \tag{4.54}$$

The moderator does not contribute to the absorption of neutrons in the slowing down domain. Hence we have put $\sigma_{s,m} = \sigma_{t,m} = \sigma_m$. In addition we have decomposed the scattering cross section of the fuel into two parts: one $\sigma_{s,c}(E)$ has resonance contributions like $\sigma_{a,c}(E)$, the other $\sigma^*_{s,c}$ has a non-vanishing value (small and constant) outside the region of resonances.

Substituting expressions (4.54) into (4.53) we are led to the definitive expression for p:

$$p = p(E^*_t) = \exp\left[-\frac{N_c I_{eff}(\sigma_e)}{\xi(N_m\sigma_m + N_c\sigma^*_{s,c})}\right] \tag{4.55}$$

where we have put:

$$I_{eff}(\sigma_e) = \int_{E_t^*}^{E_s} \frac{\sigma_{a,c}(E)}{1 + \dfrac{\sigma_{a,c}(E) + \sigma_{s,c}(E)}{\sigma^*_{s,c} + \sigma_e}} \frac{dE}{E} \qquad (4.56)$$

and

$$\sigma_e = \frac{N_m}{N_c} \sigma_m = \frac{\Sigma_m}{N_c} \qquad (4.57)$$

with the following definitions:

- p has been given the name of <u>resonance escape probability</u> which recalls the resonant nature of absorptions. In order to arrive at this definition, we have put $E = E_t^*$, in such a way as to take account of all resonances encountered by the neutron in the course of its slowing down. We see in Fig. 4.18 that E_t^* is quite arbitrary. This value must only be smaller than the energy of the last resonance, but greater than the energy of thermal neutrons which will be treated differently (§4.5.4).

- $I_{eff}(\sigma_e)$ is called the <u>effective resonance integral</u>. For a fuel it only depends on the parameter σ_e. In the limit $\sigma_e \to \infty$, this quantity is perfectly determined. It is designated by the name <u>resonance integral</u>, which is noted:

$$I = \int_{E_t^*}^{E_s} \sigma_{a,c}(E) \frac{dE}{E}$$

- σ_e is called the <u>microscopic dilution cross section</u>. It only depends on the ratio N_m/N_c (hence on the dilution) for a given moderator.

If one considers a large quantity of moderator ($N_m >> N_c$), the effective resonance integral tends to the resonance integral I. We say that there is <u>infinite dilution</u> ($\sigma_e \to \infty$). In the opposite case I_{eff} can be much smaller and a self-shielding phenomenon appears, somewhat analogous to that of subsec. 4.3.6. The flux which exists at the level of resonances is depressed with respect to that which one observes just above (Fig. 4.18). When the quantity of moderator is increased ($N_m \nearrow$), the resonance escape probability p approaches unity (4.55). The moderator permits the neutrons to "jump over the traps" because of the fact that the energy loss per collision in the moderator is on the average higher than the width of the resonances. All the same, p does not increase as rapidly as we would have been led to suppose by a simple examination of the slowing down power $\xi(N_m\sigma_m + N_c\sigma^*_{s,c})$ since simultaneously the effective integral $I_{eff}(\sigma_e)$ increases (4.56).

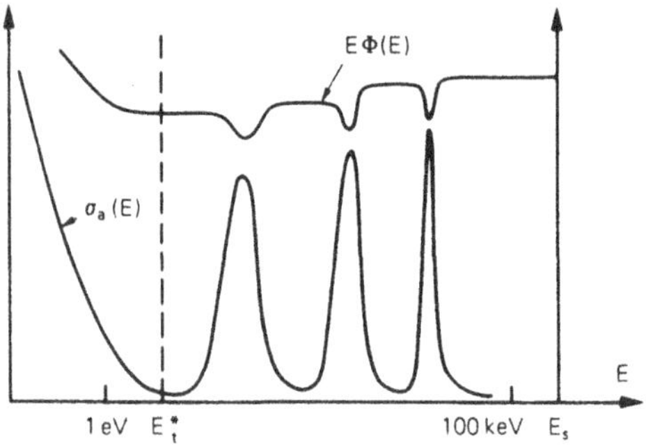

FIGURE 4.18. Effects of resonances on neutron spectra (This figure is purely schematic since cross sections can have several hundreds of resonances).

In practice a reactor core is not homogeneous and the fuel is present in the form of rods regularly distributed in the moderator (Sec. 5.1). All the same, one can show (§8.4.1) that the whole of the preceding formalism can be kept provided we introduce atomic densities per unit volume of the core $\overline{N}_c$ and $\overline{N}_m$ and we put [9](p.301):

$$\sigma_e = \frac{b}{N_c \ell} \qquad (4.58)$$

where ℓ is a dimension characteristic of the rods (their diameter $\emptyset$ if they are cylindrical), N_c the number of resonant nuclei (U^{238} or Th^{232}) per unit volume of the fuel (usual atomic density) and b a numerical factor which can sometimes depend on the lattice spacing (§8.4.2).

The dilution cross section is now independent of the moderator, hence the same is true of the effective integral I_{eff}. We thus see that for a given moderating ratio ($\overline{N}_m/\overline{N}_c$) we obtain a better value of p than in the preceding, provided we use quite thick rods ($\sigma_e \to 0$). Conversely, very thin rods lead to infinite dilution as was defined above. Thus from the point of view of neutron physics, and independently of technological questions, a limited fractionation of the fuel is called for (Ch. 5).

The parameter ℓ which figures in expression (4.58) can be generally evaluated from the approximate formula:

$$\ell = 4\ V_c/S_c$$

where V_c and S_c are respectively the volumes and peripheral surfaces of the fuel element considered. Since N_c is proportional to the mass density of the latter, σ_e and hence I_{eff} (4.56) only depend on the relation S_c/M_c. Starting from these theoretical foundations experimental results have been obtained in the form [10]:

$$\left.\begin{aligned} I_{eff} &= 4.15 + 25.8\sqrt{\frac{S_c}{M_c}} && \text{for metallic uranium} \\ I_{eff} &= 5.35 + 26.6\sqrt{\frac{S_c}{M_c}}, && \text{for uranium oxide } UO_2 \end{aligned}\right\}$$

where I_{eff}, S_c and M_c are expressed respectively in barns, cm^2 and grams.

4.5 MULTIPLYING MEDIA (REACTORS)

4.5.1 Introduction

The preceding studies had to do with passive media characterized only by the macroscopic cross sections Σ_a and Σ_t (or Σ_s) of the materials employed. If we add to these a certain quantity of fissionable nuclei, a source density of neutrons $Q_f(\vec{r})$ will automatically be induced by the neutron flux $\Phi(\vec{r})$ thanks to the phenomenon of fission (§3.1.3). In the absence of external sources (other than Q_f), the neutron problem to solve is such that all the sources (which heretofore constituted the data) now depend on the flux and thus on the solution sought for. Mathematically one is led to consider one or several homogeneous equations in Φ whatever the theory considered, and in general, no stationary solution exists, except if the ensemble of geometric and nuclear data satisfy a special condition called the critical condition.

We have already indicated (§3.3.2) that a sustained chain reaction was only possible if the emissions of fission neutrons compensated exactly the various absorptions and escapes of neutrons. If the intensity of these emissions is insufficient, we cannot play with the flux to reestablish equilibrium, since the fission, absorption, and escape rates vary in the same proportions. The critical condition is thus independent of the flux (up to some nonlinear effects) and depends only on the data of the problem, at least one of which cannot be chosen arbitrarily.

To understand better this particularity of multiplying systems, we shall limit ourselves in the first subsections to homogeneous bare reactors (that is to say, isolated in space). We will see afterwards how to generalize the results obtained to the calculation of standard reactors comprised of several zones. All these demonstrations will be carried out in the framework of the one-group theory of neutrons, basing ourselves on the results of the preceding sections. This assumes that most of the neutrons are found in an energy band such that it is possible to assign to them unique values of cross sections, whereas the latter depend essentially on the energy. Everything happens as if the neutrons were mono-energetic. We will see in the last subsections how to get rid of this restriction by introducing the multigroup theory which currently serves as the basis of reactor calculations (thermal or fast).

4.5.2 Neutron Multiplication Factors

In the absence of neutron leaks, that is, for an infinite homogeneous system of the same characteristics as the system under study, the multiplication factor, by definition, will be equal to:

$$k_\infty = \frac{\bar{\nu} S_f}{A}$$

where S_f and A represent respectively the total number of fissions and absorptions (per unit time) while $\bar{\nu}$ neutrons are emitted by fission.

In such a system the scalar fluxes and the reaction rates related to them are independent of the considered point. We have thus:

$$S_f = R_f V = \Sigma_f \Phi V \quad \text{and} \quad A = R_a V = \Sigma_a \Phi V$$

where V is the volume of the system (arbitrarily large). The multiplication factor can thus be simply written:

$$k_\infty = \frac{\bar{\nu}\Sigma_f}{\Sigma_a} \tag{4.59}$$

It is very useful in practice to highlight in the expression above the contribution of the fuel. Letting c and p characterize respectively the absorptions in the fuel and the absorptions (parasite) in other materials, we can make explicit the macroscopic cross sections as follows:

$$\bar{\nu}\Sigma_f = (\bar{\nu}\Sigma_f)_c$$

$$\Sigma_a = (\Sigma_a)_c + (\Sigma_a)_p$$

since the fission can only take place in the fuel. Substituting these expressions in equation (4.59) we obtain:

$$k_\infty = \eta_c \cdot f \tag{4.60}$$

where we have:

$$\left.\begin{aligned} \eta_c &= \left(\frac{\bar{\nu}\Sigma_f}{\Sigma_a}\right)_c > 1 \\ f &= \frac{(\Sigma_a)_c}{(\Sigma_a)_c + (\Sigma_a)_p} < 1 \end{aligned}\right\}$$

We get back the multiplication factor η_c of the fuel alone. This only depends on the enrichment and on the microscopic cross sections of fissile and fertile isotopes (3.6).

The utilization factor f depends especially on the presence of structural materials but also on the moderator and the coolant. It must be as close as possible to unity if we wish to have a good neutron multiplication.

We can make f explicit for a reactor consisting of a fuel (c), a moderator (m) and structural materials (g):

$$f = \frac{N_c\sigma_{a,c}}{N_c\sigma_{a,c} + N_m\sigma_{a,m} + N_g\sigma_{a,g}} \tag{4.61}$$

where the quantities N and σ_a are respectively the atomic densities (per unit volume of the mixture) and the microscopic cross sections of absorption for each of the constituents. We obtain a better value of f by multiplying N_m and N_g by coefficients slightly larger than one in order to take account of the diminution of the flux in the fuel (§4.3.6). A precise calculation of f demands the use of transport theory and a method often used is described in the appendix (§.8.2.4)

Let us return to the real case of a homogeneous system of finite dimensions. The neutron multiplication now depends on leaks. The effective multiplication factor k_e is thus smaller than the preceding (4.60).

This factor is defined as a ratio of the number of fission neutrons produced ($\bar{\nu}S_f$) to the number of neutrons lost by absorption (A) and leakage (F), these quantities being relative to the system as a whole and to the unit of time. We will thus write:

$$k_e = \frac{\bar{\nu}S_f}{A + F} = \frac{\bar{\nu}S_f}{A} \frac{A}{A + F} = k_\infty P_{NF} \tag{4.62}$$

The first factor is none other than k_∞, while the second represents the non-leakage probability $P_{NF} = A/(A + F)$ which will be calculated further on.

There are three cases to consider:

- $k_e = 1$ The reactor is critical, the chain reaction is self-maintained, the fluxes are stationary (in these conditions (4.62) and (3.3) are identical).
- $k_e > 1$ The reactor is supercritical, the chain reaction is divergent, and the flux increases with time.
- $k_e < 1$ The reactor is subcritical, the chain reaction is convergent, the flux decreases with time.
All the same, in the last case, a steady state can be realized thanks to the addition of an independent source.

Of all the multiplication factors introduced until now, k_e is clearly the most important because it is this which establishes the operating regime of the reactor. We note the following important inequalities:

$$k_e < k_\infty < \eta_c < \bar{\nu} \tag{4.63}$$

4.5.3 Critical Condition

We will place ourselves in the framework of the one-group diffusion theory. For a homogeneous medium the fluxes are governed by equation (4.16), but in contrast with examples treated in section 4.3, the source density Q must be identified with the source density of fission neutrons Q_f:

$$Q = Q_f = \bar{\nu}R_f = \bar{\nu}\Sigma_f \Phi$$

where R_f is the fission rate (in $cm^{-3}\ s^{-1}$). Substituting this expression into (4.16), we obtain:

$$D\nabla^2\Phi + (\bar{\nu}\Sigma_f - \Sigma_a)\Phi = 0$$

Using expression (4.59)for k_∞ and dividing by D, the preceding equation takes the form:

$$\nabla^2\Phi + \left(\frac{k_\infty - 1}{L^2}\right)\Phi = 0 \qquad (4.64)$$

where the diffusion area $L^2 = D/\Sigma_a$ has already been introduced (§4.3.3).

The reasoning which led to the diffusion equation assumed a steady state. Equation (4.64) thus corresponds (in the absence of supplementary sources) to the critical state ($k_e = 1$). We observe, as was stated in the introduction, that this equation is homogeneous.

We are naturally led to define the quantity:

$$B_m^2 = \frac{k_\infty - 1}{L^2} \qquad (4.65)$$

This quantity is called the material buckling. It contains all the nuclear information (k_∞ is calculated with the help of expressions (4.59) or (4.60) and L^2 with (4.22)).

Since k_e (=1) is smaller than k_∞ the material buckling of a critical system is necessarily positive. We finally rewrite equation (4.64) in the form:

$$\nabla^2\Phi + B_m^2\Phi = 0 \qquad (4.66)$$

To go further, it is necessary to choose a geometry. The simplest unidimensional closed system corresponds to a homogeneous spherical reactor. Following steps parallel to those of §4.3.3, we start from equation (4.66) expressed in spherical geometry:

$$\frac{1}{\rho^2}\frac{d}{d\rho}\left(\rho^2\frac{d\Phi}{d\rho}\right) + B_m^2\,\Phi = 0$$

and we put $\Phi(\rho) = X(\rho)/\rho$, whence:

$$\frac{d^2X}{d\rho^2} + B_m^2\,X = 0$$

We note the presence of the + sign in the second term. The general solution can be written:

$$X(\rho) = A \sin B_m\rho + C \cos B_m\rho$$

or:

$$\Phi(\rho) = A \frac{\sin B_m\rho}{\rho} + C \frac{\cos B_m\rho}{\rho}$$

We must consider here a finite system $\rho \leq R$ where R represents the radius of the reactor. The flux should not diverge for $\rho = 0$ (here there is no source localized at the center). We therefore deduce that the constant C must vanish, whence:

$$\Phi(\rho) = A \frac{\text{Sin } B_m\rho}{\rho} \tag{4.67}$$

When ρ tends to zero, the expression remains well bounded. A second condition must be satisfied: the flux must vanish on the extrapolated surface of the reactor (§4.3.2), which leads to:

$$\Phi(R + d) = 0, \text{ or: } \sin [B_m(R + d)] = 0$$

This last condition is not generally satisfied, since B_m and R are part of the data. To satisfy this condition, it is necessary to identify B_m to one of the roots B_i of the equation $\sin [B(R + d)] = 0$, in other words:

$$B_i = i \frac{\pi}{R + d}$$

where i is an arbitrary integer. One is led to an infinity of solutions, but in fact only one is physically acceptable. By replacing B_m by $i\ \pi/(R + d)$ in equation (4.67), one is led to the distributions of Fig. 4.19.

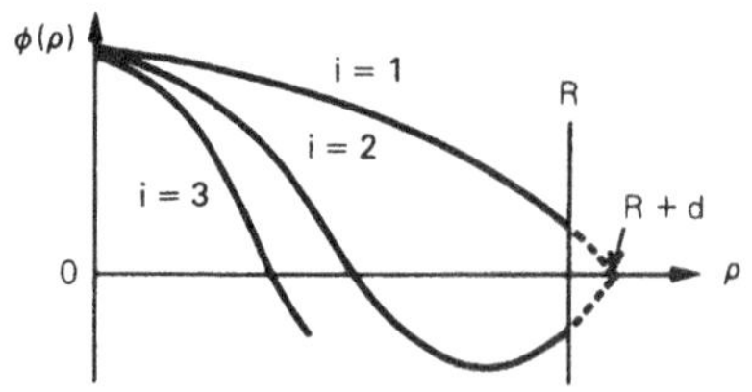

FIGURE 4.19. Flux distribution in a spherical reactor.

The fluxes corresponding to values $i > 1$ take negative values in the interval (O,R). We must reject the value $i = 0$, since B_m cannot vanish in general. There remains the solution $i = 1$, whence the critical condition:

$$B_m^2 = B^2 \tag{4.68}$$

with:

$$B^2 = \left(\frac{\pi}{R + d}\right)^2 \tag{4.69}$$

and the flux distribution

$$\Phi(\rho) = \frac{A}{\rho} \operatorname{Sin} \left(\frac{\pi\rho}{R + d}\right) \tag{4.70}$$

Since B_m and d follow from the nuclear properties of the multiplying medium considered, we find that R is determined.

In order to realize a self-sustained chain reaction, the reactor must have a so-called "critical" radius R_c compatible with the materials of which it is made. The associated critical mass can be easily calculated:

$$M_c = \frac{4}{3} \pi R_c^3 \rho_c$$

where ρ_c is the mass density of the homogeneous medium being considered.

Whatever the form of the bare homogeneous reactor, we are always led to the critical equation (4.68). For that, we must first look for the eigen values of the equation [11]:

$$\nabla^2\Phi + B^2\Phi = 0 \tag{4.71}$$

specifying only that the eigen functions Φ must vanish on the extrapolated contour of the reactor (§4.3.2). We will only take the smallest eigen value B^2, called geometric buckling. It is this last quantity which appears in equation (4.68). For spherical reactors the value is given by (4.69). Finally we have to choose a multiplying medium whose material buckling B_m^2 (4.65) equals the geometric buckling B^2 which we have just determined. We can play for example with the enrichment x (3.6) and hence with η_c and k_∞ (4.60). If on the other hand the multiplying medium is defined in advance (B_m^2 imposed), the size of the reactor will have to be modified in such a way as to give the geometric buckling B^2 the best value. This last procedure was adopted in the foregoing example.

In every case, when the critical condition (4.68) is satisfied, the flux distribution $\Phi(\vec{r})$ is simply proportional to the eigen function of (4.71), associated with the smallest eigen value B^2. The fluxes are thus known up to a multiplicative constant. Thus in the preceding example, the constant A which figures in the expression of the flux (4.70) remains undetermined, which is a particularity of critical systems. Neutron calculations will furnish the spatial distributions of the flux, the energy distributions, etc., but never the true magnitude of the flux. This is related to the power level which is itself determined by technological considerations (Ch.5).

The case of a "slab reactor" of height H constitutes another interesting example. The lateral dimensions are supposed to be infinite, so that the flux is independent of x and y (Fig. 4.20) Following the procedure indicated above, we are led to seek the eigen values of (4.71) which can be simply written here (4.17):

$$\frac{d^2\Phi}{dz^2} + B^2\Phi = 0$$

This equation must be solved in the interval $- H/2 < z < H/2$. The general solution is of the type:

$$\Phi(z) = A \cos Bz + C \sin Bz$$

As the flux distributions are symmetric with respect to the median plane $z = 0$, the second term disappears ($C = 0$) whence:

$$\Phi(z) = A \cos Bz$$

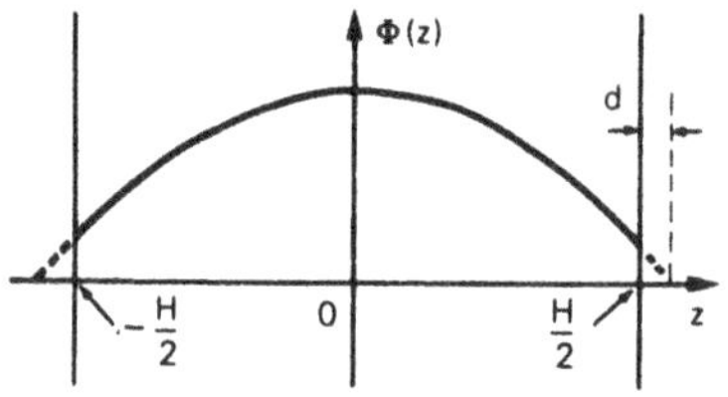

FIGURE 4.20. Flux distribution in a slab reactor.

It remains to express the fact that the flux must vanish on the extrapolated surface of the reactor, which amounts to imposing the condition:

$\Phi(z = \frac{H}{2} + d) = \Phi(z = -\frac{H}{2} - d) = 0$, or, by replacing Φ by its value:

$$\cos B\,(\frac{H}{2} + d) = 0$$

whence:

$$B_i = (2i + 1)\frac{\pi}{H + 2d} \qquad \text{with } i = 0,1,2, \ldots$$

For reasons invoked above, only the first root must be kept (here $i = 0$), whence the geometric buckling

$$B^2 = \left(\frac{\pi}{H + 2d}\right)^2 \tag{4.72}$$

to which corresponds the flux distribution (4.20):

$$\Phi(z) = A \cos\left(\frac{\pi z}{H + 2d}\right) \tag{4.73}$$

In reality, reactors have a more or less cylindrical form (Ch. 5), but the axial flux distributions are quite well represented by the expression (4.73), despite the finite lateral dimensions and especially the great complexity of the loads (cores with several radial zones). In the planes perpendicular to the axis the reactors are not homogeneous. Of course one cannot appply to them the procedures proposed above and the radial distributions of flux are much more complicated. We will nevertheless see (§4.5.7) that much more complicated problems can be treated, if necessary on the computer. We always arrive at a critical condition (more or less buried in the formalism) which in some way relates the geometry to the nuclear properties of the reactor. If the size and the composition of the reactor are fixed, we can play with the depth of the control rods (geometrical parameter). If, on the contrary, the entire geometry is fixed (in all its details), we can modify the quantity of fissile material in order to achieve the critical state.

Let us return to homogeneous reactors. We can summarize the preceding by writing the critical condition in the form (cf. equations (4.65) and (4.68)):

$$\frac{k_\infty - 1}{L^2} = B^2$$

where the geometric buckling B^2 depends on the problem treated. We have for example for the spherical reactor

$$B^2 = \left(\frac{\pi}{R + d}\right)^2$$

and for the "slab reactor":

$$B^2 = \left(\frac{\pi}{H + 2d}\right)^2$$

In other words, the multiplication factor k_∞ <u>must attain</u> a certain value:

$$k_\infty = (1 + L^2B^2) \qquad (4.74)$$

Comparing this expression to equation (4.62) written for $k_e = 1$, we deduce the nonleakage probability:

$$P_{NF} = \frac{1}{1 + L^2B^2} \qquad (4.75)$$

In the more general case of noncritical reactors, we will keep this value, so that the effective multiplication factor (4.62) will be given by the expression:

$$k_e = \frac{k_\infty}{1 + L^2B^2} \qquad (4.76)$$

We conclude this section with two important remarks.

- We can interpret (4.76) as a critical condition (4.74) characterizing a fictitious medium which only differs from the real medium by the number of neutrons produced by fission $\bar{\nu}/k_e$ in place of $\bar{\nu}$. The material buckling for such a medium can be written:

$$B_m^{2*}(k_e) = \frac{\dfrac{k_\infty}{k_e} - 1}{L^2}$$

and the critical condition $B_m^{2*}(k_e) = B^2$ (4.68) leads to the preceding value of k_e (4.76). Thanks to this artifice, we can calculate noncritical systems by using a formalism which is in principle reserved for stationary cases. We can then fix at the same time all the nuclear and geometrical characteristics and k_e appears as an adjustable parameter permitting us to satisfy the critical condition.

Naturally we will find in general that $k_e \neq 1$. If we want to render the real system critical at a later stage, we will have to modify one of the data in order to satisfy the condition $k_e = 1$. The intermediate values of k_e, depending on whether they are greater or less than one, guide us in this search. For the homogeneous reactor studied here, we have at first placed ourselves in the critical conditions ($k_e = 1$ or $B_m^{2*} = B_m^2$), but in the general case we will be obliged to follow the latter procedure, since it is not convenient to introduce variable geometric parameters into a numerical code (§4.5.7).

· Replacing k_∞ and L^2 by their definitions (4.59) and (4.22), the expression of the effective multiplication factor (4.76) can be put in the form:

$$k_e = \frac{\bar{\nu}\Sigma_f}{\Sigma_a + DB^2}$$

By analogy with the definition of k_∞ (4.59) it appears that the quantity DB^2 expressed in cm^{-1} plays the role of a macroscopic capture cross section (parasite). In other words, we can replace a finite reactor by an infinite reactor provided we include in it a fictitious poison of macroscopic cross section $\Sigma_a' = DB^2$. Of course this is an artifice which does not enable us to avoid the solution of the diffusion equation, since knowledge of the geometric buckling is indispensable. The preceding result will be used in the following subsection.

4.5.4 Application to Thermal Reactors

In a thermal reactor, most of the neutrons are to be found, by definition, in thermodynamic equilibrium with the multiplying matter. These "thermal" neutrons have energies in a relatively narrow band (0, 0.4 eV). They thus constitute a group of slow neutrons approximately mono-energetic and governed by the diffusion equation (4.16). The source Q in this equation represents those neutrons, coming from the fission neutron source Q_f, which appear at each point in the thermal state. We can thus identify Q with the slowing down source $q(\vec{r}, E_t^*)$ taken at an energy E_t^* situated below the last resonance (Fig. 4.18). This quantity represents the number of neutrons (per unit volume and unit time) slowed down from their energy of emission (fission) to the zone of thermal energy considered here (§4.4.5).

We have seen that for homogeneous infinite media this slowing-down source q was equal to the fission neutron source Q_f multiplied by the resonance escape probability p. For systems of finite dimensions, we must in addition take account of leakage in the course of slowing down. According to the last remark of the preceding subsection (§4.5.3), this is equivalent to introducing fictitious absorption $D(E)B^2$, depending this time on energy. For this fictitious absorption, generally weak, we can appeal to equation (4.52) to calculate the probability a neutron has of evading this phenomenon. We have thus:

$$P_{NF,r} = \exp(- B^2\tau) \tag{4.77}$$

with:

$$\tau = \int_{E_t^*}^{E_s} \frac{D(E')}{\xi\Sigma_s(E')} \frac{dE'}{E'} \tag{4.78}$$

We note that:

- $P_{NF,r}$ is the non-leakage probability of the neutrons in the course of slowing down, analogous to the probability P_{NF} defined for mono-energetic neutrons (4.75).
- τ is the <u>slowing down area</u> (or Fermi age) which plays the same role as the diffusion area L^2 for mono-energetic neutrons.

Finally, the slowing down source to the thermal level can be written:

$$q(\vec{r}, E_t^*) = p \exp(-B^2\tau)Q_f(\vec{r})$$

or if one accepts that only thermal neutrons can induce fission:

$$q(\vec{r},E^*_t) = (\bar{\nu}\Sigma_f)_t \; p \exp (-B^2\tau)\Phi_t(\vec{r})$$

Substituting this last expression into (4.16), we arrive at the diffusion equation which governs thermal neutrons:

$$D_t\nabla^2\Phi_t + [(\bar{\nu}\Sigma_f)_t \; p \exp (-B^2\tau) - (\Sigma_a)_t]\Phi_t = 0$$

or dividing by D_t:

$$\nabla^2\Phi_t + \left[\frac{k_\infty \exp (-B^2\tau) - 1}{L_t^2}\right] \Phi_t = 0 \tag{4.79}$$

The index t recalls that the flux Φ_t is relative to the thermal neutrons and the factor k_∞ takes the new value:

$$k_\infty = \left(\frac{\nu\Sigma_f}{\Sigma_a}\right)_t \cdot p = (\eta_c f)_t \, p$$

in which the contribution of the fuel has been made explicit as in subsec. 4.5.2.

In order to take account of phenomena which take place at high energies (inelastic scattering, fast fissions, etc.), one completes the preceding expression by writing:

$$k_\infty = (\eta_c f)_t \, p\varepsilon \tag{4.80}$$

where the <u>fast fission factor</u> ε is very slightly greater than unity (§8.4.4).

The expression (4.80) is known as the four factors formula. It plays a certain role in reactor project studies.

Equation (4.79) generalizes equation (4.64) and can be solved in the same way by noting that the quantity in square brackets must be identical to the geometrical buckling B^2 (defined as the smallest eigen value of (4.71)). We are thus led to the new critical equation:

$$k_\infty = (1 + L_t^2 B^2) \exp (B^2 \tau) \tag{4.81}$$

For $p = 1$ and $\tau = 0$, that is to say, when there is no loss of neutrons in the course of slowing down, this last expression reduces to (4.74). As to the distributions of thermal flux Φ_t, they will be, as in the preceding, proportional to the first eigen function of (4.71). As a consequence, the fission neutron sources $Q_f(\vec{r})$ and the neutron fluxes at any energy (4.51) will have the same structure.

For a noncritical reactor, we apply (4.81) to a medium of characteristic k_∞/k_e (cf. the end of subsec. 4.5.3), whence the expression of the effective multiplication factor:

$$k_e = \frac{k_\infty}{(1 + L_t^2 B^2)} \exp (- B^2 \tau) \tag{4.82}$$

This equation replaces (4.76).

Although in a thermal reactor the neutrons are far from being mono-energetic (energies going from 0 to 2 MeV), we have been able to make use of the one-group formalism of the preceding subsection. This has only been possible because important phenomena take place at thermal energies (fissions and absorptions) whereas the disappearance of neutrons in the course of slowing down has been accounted for just by introducing the two parameters p (4.55) and τ (4.78).

We note that η_c and f are now relative to the thermal neutrons; f is thus called the thermal utilization factor (given by (4.61)), while the multiplication factor η_c of the fuel only depends in the case of uranium on the enrichment x (3.6) and on the microscopic cross section of fissile and fertile isotopes. This leads for thermal neutrons to Table 3.10.

If we want to know the critical size of a reactor of fixed composition (k_∞, L_t^2, τ known), we must solve equation (4.81) for B^2. In practice, $B^2\tau$ and $B^2L_t^2$ are sufficiently small for us to write:

$$k_\infty \cong (1 + L_t^2B^2)(1 + \tau B^2)$$

$$\cong 1 + (L_t^2 + \tau)B^2$$

whence the explicit value:

$$B^2 \cong \frac{k_\infty - 1}{M^2} = B_m^2 \tag{4.83}$$

The migration area M^2 (cm^2) is equal to the diffusion area L_t^2 for thermal neutrons augmented by the slowing down area τ. The latter is virtually fixed by the moderator, since the fuel has practically no influence on the slowing down of the neutrons. The diffusion area L_t^2 depends, on the contrary, on the detailed composition of the reactor, especially through its macroscopic cross section Σ_a (4.22). The latter as well as Σ_t is obtained by applying the mixture rule (4.1).

Comparing equations (4.65) and (4.83) we see that the entire formalism of subsec. 4.5.3 can be kept, provided we adopt the new expression of k_∞ in (4.80) and replace L^2 by $M^2 = L_t^2 + \tau$.

We can show that the migration length M is proportional to the mean square distance at which a neutron disappears on account of successive diffusions, at first in the course of slowing down, and subsequently at the thermal level.

Apart from the fundamental "thermal constants", η_c, f, L_t^2, the "slowing down constants" p and τ depend essentially on the performances of the moderator.

Formulae (4.55) and (4.78) show the importance of the parameter ξ, for which a few values are given in Table 4.21. A large value of ξ will simultaneously diminish the effect of the resonances ($p \cong 1$) and the magnitude of leakage (small τ, hence $P_{NF,r} \cong 1$).

In the table, the parameters α and ξ have been calculated starting from expressions (4.31) and (4.35). The slowing down area τ has been experimentally obtained. It includes effects of which the theoretical expression (4.78) does not take account, but still this gives a good order of magnitude.

TABLE 4.21. Moderating power of some materials.

	A	α	ξ	τ [cm²]
H	1	0	1	
H_2O	-	-	0.920	≅ 27
D	2	0.111	0.725	
D_2O	-	-	0.509	131
Be	9	0.640	0.207	102
C	12	0.716	0.158	368
Na	23	0.840	0.0844	-
U	238	0.983333	0.00840	-

We see that as predicted, the materials of small atomic mass have the best slowing down power (large ξ and small τ). This is the reason why it is necessary to add a moderator to the fuel (which has a very bad ξ), if one wants to realize a thermal reactor. Otherwise, the factors p and $P_{NF,r}$ are so small that the neutrons disappear (by absorption or leakage) before they have been thermalized.

Light water is the best for slowing down. It has a large value of ξ as well as a large scattering cross section Σ_s (it is the product $\xi\Sigma_s$ which intervenes in the expressions for p and $P_{NF,r}$). But as we have already seen, it is a significant absorber of thermal neutrons. Heavy water and graphite which have a very small capture cross section, afford a better compromise. They alone permit the use of natural uranium (Ch. 5).

4.5.5 Schematization of a Chain Reaction and Neutron Spectra

For thermal reactors we can picture the sequence of important processes by considering the diagram of Fig. 4.22. We start at bottom left with a thermal neutron absorbed in the reactor. After allowing for parasite thermal captures, f neutrons are absorbed in the fuel. A fraction of these produce thermal fissions, whence the creation of $\eta_c f$ fission neutrons. Subsequent fast fissions lead to $\eta_c f\varepsilon$ available neutrons. Then one starts the slowing down process in the course of which a fraction P_r of neutrons avoid leakage and a fraction p avoid resonances (these two phenomena take place simultaneously). In these conditions $\eta_c f\varepsilon pP_r$ neutrons arrive at thermal energy. In the course of their diffusion at this energy, some of them leave the system before being utilized. Finally, $\eta_c f\varepsilon pP_rP_t$ neutrons are effectively available in the reactor. By hypothesis, a single thermal neutron has been absorbed, whence, to avoid a contradiction:

$$\eta_c f\varepsilon pP_rP_t = 1$$

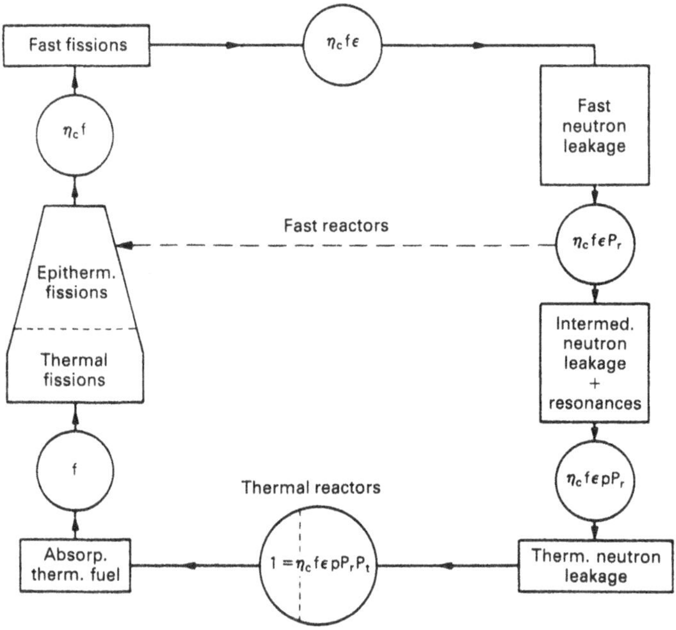

FIGURE 4.22. Flow diagram of a chain reaction.

Putting:

$P_r = P_{NF,r}$ (4.77) and $P_t = P_{NF,t}$ (4.75)

we get back the critical condition (4.81).

The shapes of the spectra are given in Fig. 4.23. Let us first consider a thermal reactor.

- In zone I, thermal neutrons (the most numerous) are distributed according to a slightly deformed Maxwell distribution (because of the large absorptions at very small energy). It is in this zone that the most important processes take place (95% of the fissions). In order to have more detailed knowledge of the neutron distribution in this zone, we will use the normalized expression of a Maxwell distribution as we have already done for plasmas (2.1). The neutron density in the slice dE is thus of the form $\sqrt{E}\exp(-E/kT)dE$. As the fluxes are given at each energy by the product vn(E), it suffices to multiply the preceding result by $\sqrt{E}$ to obtain the shape of a thermal spectrum in this zone:

  $$\Phi(E) = C\ E \exp\left(-\frac{E}{kT}\right)$$

  This expression leads to the curve in solid lines of the thermal zone of Fig. 4.23. The real spectrum is obtained by replacing the true temperature T by a higher temperature T_n (temperature of the neutrons) which takes account of the deformation of the distribution mentioned above (§9.1.4).

- In zone II, the neutrons in the course of slowing down are distributed according to the law 1/E demonstrated in subsec. 4.4.4. Certain "accidents" due to resonances have not been represented in this figure, which remains schematic.

- In zone III, which plays a marginal role, the distribution of fast neutrons takes the form of the fission spectrum (Fig. 3.2), very "flattened out" because of the presence of a moderator.

For a fast reactor, the energy distributions are totally different, since the moderation of neutrons is rendered as weak as possible. The distributions have the form of a fission spectrum shifted towards intermediate energies (Fig. 4.23) because of a certain slowing down which subsists.

One sees to it that the neutrons conserve an energy higher than 1 keV, otherwise the resonances would intervene unfavorably, and the multiplication factor η would decrease. As represented in Fig. 4.22, the chain reaction now "loops" at a relatively higher energy. At this energy the fission cross sections are small and thus a greater quantity of fissile matter is needed than in the preceding. This is the price to pay for a spectrum of fast neutrons for which the η factor is high and breeding possible (§3.3.2).

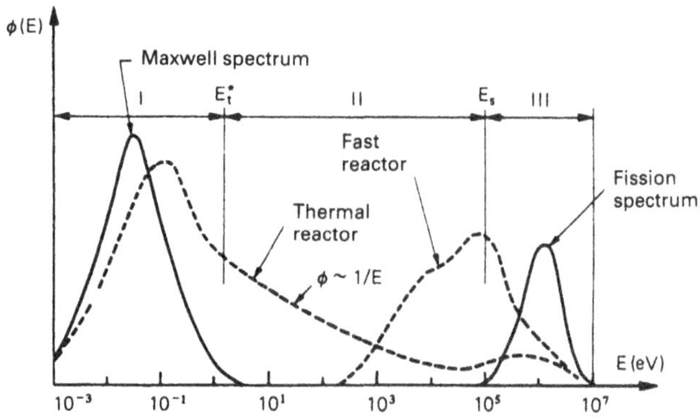

FIGURE 4.23. Typical neutron energy distributions.

4.5.6 Numerical Applications

a) Calculation of the critical mass of a sphere of plutonium (A-bomb). The one-group theory (§4.5.3) is applicable to this case. There is no moderator, and hence the neutrons remain fast (energy near to that of neutrons emitted during each fission) and constitute a well-defined "energy group". For an isotopic mixture Pu^{239} (95%) and Pu^{240} (5%), a good set of microscopic cross sections is the following:

$$\left.\begin{aligned} \sigma_t &= 5.87 \text{ b} \\ \bar{\nu}\sigma_f &= 5.52 \text{ b} \\ \sigma_a &= 1.81 \text{ b} \end{aligned}\right\}$$

Both isotopes are included in these data. The plutonium considered is found in metallic state ($\rho_c = 19$ g cm^{-3}). Its atomic density is thus:

$$N_{Pu} \cong \frac{\rho_c N_A}{239} = 4.786\ 10^{22}\ \text{nuclei/cm}^3$$

whence:

$$\Sigma_t = 0.281\ \text{cm}^{-1},\quad \bar{\nu}\Sigma_f = 0.2642\ \text{cm}^{-1},\quad \Sigma_a = 0.0866\ \text{cm}^{-1}$$

Formula (4.59) permits us to calculate k_∞:

$$k_\infty = \eta_c = \frac{0.2642}{0.0866} = 3.051$$

(the utilization factor f = 1, since in this sphere there is no parasite material, the fuel being pure.) This value is a record for multiplying systems. We know in effect that plutonium has a very high η factor, above 1 MeV (Fig. 3.9). In the same way, one calculates starting from Σ_t the quantities λ_t = 3.56 cm and D = 1.186 cm, whence the diffusion area L^2 = 13.70 cm^2 (4.22) and the material buckling B_m^2 = 0.1497 cm^{-2} (4.65).

The critical condition for a spherical reactor (4.68) and (4.69) enables us to write:

$$R_c + d = \frac{\pi}{B_m} = 8.12\ \text{cm}$$

Finally, using for the extrapolation distance d the expression 0.71 λ_t (§4.3.2), we find the critical radius: $\underline{R_c = 5.59\ \text{cm}}$, that is, a critical mass of about 13.9 kg.

Although the critical radius is not very large compared to λ_t (condition of validity of the diffusion equation, cf. §4.3.1), this result is not too far from the exact value (5.20 cm) given by transport theory or by experiment (JEZEBEL experiment of Los Alamos) [12].

The preceding theory applies even better to homogeneous thermal reactors of large dimensions ($R \gg \lambda_t$) provided we include in the formalism a few modifications which take account of the slowing down process (§4.5.4).

b) Calculation of a homogeneous spherical reactor moderated by graphite. Let us consider a graphite reactor (ρ = 1.6 g/cm^3) in which is diluted a very small quantity of pure uranium U^{235} in the proportion of 0.0035% ($N_c/N_M = 3.5\ 10^{-5}$). We want to calculate the critical radius of such a device. The medium is sufficiently moderated so that the reactor is thermal. The data for graphite are those of subsec. 4.2.4(a). Since it is industrial graphite, its absorption is far greater than that of pure carbon; the cross sections take account of certain impurities.

We will also refer to subsec. 4.2.4(b) for the characteristics of uranium U^{235}. Since there is no fertile matter in the envisaged reactor, we have simply: $\eta_c = \eta(U^{235})$ and $p = \varepsilon = 1$.

We first calculate the macroscopic cross sections of this mixture starting from the atomic densities $N_m = 8\ 10^{22}$ and $N_c = 2.8\ 10^{18}$ where the subscript (m) characterizes the moderator (graphite) and (c) the fuel (pure U^{235}). We have thus (4.1):

$$\Sigma_a = N_c(\sigma_a)_c + N_m(\sigma_a)_m = 2.8\ 10^{18} \times 688\ 10^{-24} + 8\ 10^{22} \times 0.0048\ 10^{-24}$$

$$\Sigma_a = 2.310\ 10^{-3}\ \text{cm}^{-1}$$

and:

$$f = \frac{N_c(\sigma_a)_c}{\Sigma_a} = 0.8339 \qquad \text{(cf. equation (4.61))}$$

In the same way we calculate the scattering cross section of this mixture:

$$\Sigma_s = N_c(\sigma_s)_c + N_m(\sigma_s)_m = 2.8\ 10^{18} \times 8.3\ 10^{-24} + 8\ 10^{22} \times 4.8\ 10^{-24}$$

$$\Sigma_s = 0.384\ \text{cm}^{-1}$$

whence the total cross section:

$$\Sigma_t = \Sigma_s + \Sigma_a = 0.386\ \text{cm}^{-1}$$

We can now calculate the nuclear parameters of this reactor (equations (4.14) and(4.22)):

$$D = \frac{1}{3\Sigma_t} = 0.8635\ \text{cm},\ L^2 = \frac{D}{\Sigma_a} = 373.8\ \text{cm}^2,\ M^2 = L^2 + \tau = 741.8\ \text{cm}^2$$

by taking for the slowing down area τ that of graphite (Table 4.21) and the multiplication factor k_∞ (4.80) is simply equal to (Table 3.8):

$$k_\infty = \eta(U^{235})f = 2.068 \times 0.8339 = 1.7245\ (p = \varepsilon = 1)$$

Finally, the geometrical buckling to attain for criticality is:

$$B^2 = \frac{k_\infty - 1}{M^2} = \frac{0.7245}{741.8} = 9.766\ 10^{-4}\ \text{cm}^{-2}$$

whence, using expression (4.69) relative to spherical reactors:

$$R_c + d = \frac{\pi}{B} = 100.53 \text{ cm}$$

The extrapolation distance $d = 0.71/\Sigma_t$ here attains only 1.8 cm. It is thus small compared to the sought-for critical radius $\underline{R_c = 98.68 \text{ cm}}$.

These calculations show that the absorption cross sections are small compared to the total cross sections ($2.31\ 10^{-3}\ \text{cm}^{-1}$ as against 0.386) and that the mean free path $1/\Sigma_t$ is negligible compared with the size of the reactor. The two conditions of validity of the elementary theory of diffusion are thus fulfilled. Finally we note that the fuel plays practically no role in the calculation of total cross sections.

4.5.7 Inhomogeneous Reactors

In reality, reactors are never homogeneous. In the simplest cases they are constituted of zones of different compositions (Ch.5). Moreover, the irradiation of the fuel modifies its composition in the course of time; as the irradiation is fixed by the fluxes (Sec. 5.3), depending on the point considered, a reactor which is initially homogeneous progressively loses this property. Finally, a reactor is never bare, but always surrounded by a reflector whose role is to send back towards the multiplying zones a part of the neutrons which have escaped them.

We can nevertheless in the framework of the one-group theory define a quite simple analytic method which in the past has often been used for optimizing thermal reactors (roughing-out studies).

Let us return to subsec. 4.5.3. In order to arrive at equation (4.64) we based ourselves on the diffusion equation (4.16) valid for homogeneous media. In the same way we shall now start from the more general form (4.15) by always putting:

$$Q(\vec{r}) = \bar{\nu}\Sigma_f(\vec{r})\Phi(\vec{r})$$

It is generally accepted that the diffusion coefficient D is not very sensitive to the composition of the system (it depends especially on the moderator), so that (4.15) becomes:

$$D\nabla^2\Phi(\vec{r}) + [\,\bar{\nu}\Sigma_f(\vec{r}) - \Sigma_a(\vec{r})]\,\Phi(\vec{r}) = 0$$

the cross sections Σ_f and Σ_a now depending on $\vec{r}$. By dividing by D and introducing the parameters k_∞, L^2, one is finally led to the equation:

$$\nabla^2\Phi(\vec{r}) + B_m^2(\vec{r})\Phi(\vec{r}) = 0 \tag{4.84}$$

This equation is identical to (4.66) and B_m^2 is always given by expression (4.65). All the same, the material buckling is in general a function of $\vec{r}$ by the intermediary of $k_\infty(\vec{r})$ and of $L^2(\vec{r})$. For thermal reactors L^2 will simply be replaced by $M^2 = L_t{}^2 + \tau$ (4.83).

In practice, we will have to consider homogeneous zones in which B_m^2 takes a constant value. For example, in zone (i) the one-group equation can be written:

$$\nabla^2\Phi(\vec{r}) + B_{m,i}^2\Phi(\vec{r}) = 0 \tag{4.85}$$

The flux Φ does not vanish at the extrapolated frontier of such a zone which in general is not isolated but exchanges neutrons with contiguous zones. Thus we cannot identify (4.85) with equation (4.71) which implies this boundary condition. It is not possible to define a geometric buckling per zone (the critical condition (4.68) no longer has any sense). Moreover, the notion of geometric buckling is little used nowadays, as it is too restrictive. We will thus directly solve equation (4.85) since the notion of the material buckling B_m^2 continues to have sense in each zone.

In a homogeneous critical reactor we necessarily have $k_\infty > 1$ and hence $B_m^2 > 0$ (§4.5.3). Here, in contrast, we can at most affirm that a certain mean value of k_∞ (taken over the ensemble of zones) must be greater than unity, which does not exclude the existence of zones in which $k_{\infty,i} < 1$ and $B_{m,i}^2 < 0$. In the latter case we will put: $K_i^2 = -B_{m,i}^2 > 0$.

As an example, let us put ourselves in the framework of one-dimensional plane geometry, that is, let us consider a "slab reactor" (§4.5.3) consisting of several zones (Fig. 4.24) numbered i = 1, 2, ...I. We can then integrate (4.85) by noting that $\nabla^2\Phi = d^2\Phi/dz^2$ (4.17), whence solutions of the type:

$$\Phi(z) = A_i \cos(B_{m,i}a) + C_i \sin(B_{m,i}z) \qquad B_{m,i}^2 > 0$$

or: (4.86)

$$\Phi(z) = A_i \exp(-K_i z) + C_i \exp(+K_i z) \qquad B_{m,i}^2 < 0$$

At this stage we cannot eliminate either of the constants A_i or C_i as was the case for a homogeneous slab reactor (§4.5.3). We must on the contrary match the solutions obtained in each zone by writing at the interfaces the continuity of the flux and of its derivative. In effect, the hypothesis of a constant diffusion coefficient D transforms the continuity condition of currents to that of the derivatives of the flux as indicated by Fick's law (4.13). Finally on the extrapolated surfaces of the system ($z = -d$ and $z = H + d$) the flux must vanish (Fig. 4.24).

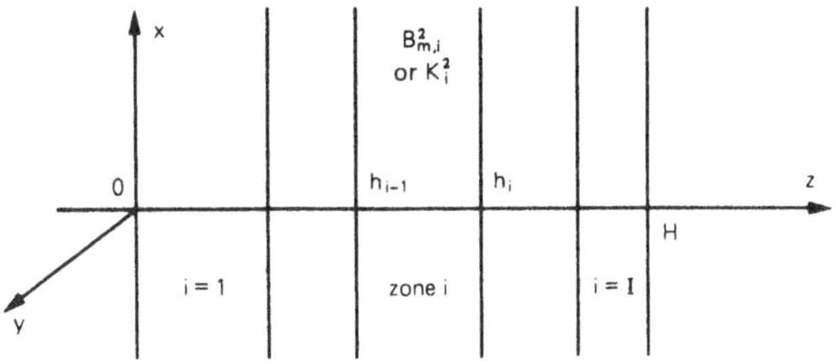

FIGURE 4.24. Slab reactor of several zones.

For I zones and hence 2 I unknowns A_i and C_i, one arrives at:

- 2 (I - 1) conditions on the (I - 1) internal boundaries,
- one condition on each of the extrapolated boundaries,

that is, a total of 2 I equations in A_i, C_i. To obtain a solution different from zero, the determinant of this system of homogeneous equations must vanish, which constitutes the sought-for critical condition. The elements of this determinant only depend on the positions of the boundaries (h_i, H) and the material bucklings $B^2_{m,i}$. Thus, as foreseen (§4.5.1), at least one of these parameters must be adjusted. We can for example iterate on the width of the richest zone ($B^2_{m,i}$ maximum) to determine its critical thickness. This dimension has a great influence on the results. In contrast, the choice of the thickness of a passive medium ($k_\infty = 0$) to realize the critical condition may lead to an impossibility (beyond a certain value the thickness of a reflector has no further influence).

We can also fix all the geometrical and nuclear characteristics and iterate on the parameter k_e which divides all the $k_{\infty,i}$. In consequence the material bucklings are modified and the value of k_e which assures the vanishing of the determinant is exactly the effective multiplication factor (cf. the end of subsec 4.5.3).

When the critical condition is satisfied, we can, by returning to the system of equations in A_i, C_i, calculate all these constants as a function of one of them, and subsequently the flux distributions $\Phi(z)$ by utilizing (4.86).

The present approach is only conceivable for a limited number of zones. Instead of evaluating a determinant, it is more convenient in practice to proceed to the progressive elimination of unknowns by taking account of the particularities of the problem.

If the system schematized in Fig. 4.24 has finite transversal dimensions (x, y), we can very simply adapt the preceding formalism to the new situation. In this case equation (4.84) takes the form:

$$\frac{\partial^2\Phi}{\partial x^2} + \frac{\partial^2\Phi}{\partial y^2} + \frac{\partial^2\Phi}{\partial z^2} + B_m^2(z)\Phi(x,y,z) = 0$$

which expresses the fact that the zones are transversally homogeneous, and which suggests a solution of the type:

$$\Phi(x,y,z) = \cos(B_x x)\cos(B_y y)\Phi^*(z)$$

This form permits the flux to vanish on the extrapolated lateral surface, no matter what z, by putting:

$$B_x = \frac{\pi}{H_x} \quad \text{and} \quad B_y = \frac{\pi}{H_y}$$

where H_x and H_y are the extrapolated heights corresponding to the directions x and y (cf. equation (4.73)). Substituting this factorized form of the flux into the preceding differential equation, we find:

$$\frac{d^2\Phi^*}{dz^2} + b_m^2(z)\Phi^*(z) = 0$$

where we have put: $b_m^2(z) = B_m^2(z) - (B_x^2 + B_y^2)$.

Everything takes place as if the slab reactor (inhomogeneous in direction z) had infinite lateral dimensions with the indicated reduction of the material buckling.

In the general case where one must consider a very large number of zones (the material buckling varies almost continuously with $\vec{r}$), we have to have recourse to numerical methods. Obtaining criticality or the calculation of k_e needs a more fundamental approach which will be described in the course of the discussion of multigroup theory.

4.5.8 Multigroup Theory

It is sometimes impossible to apply a one-group model. If we have no information on neutron energy distributions, we do not see how to determine a set of average cross sections applicable to a neutron population whose energies go from zero to a few MeV. We must in principle calculate the neutron flux as a function of space, as we have done in the preceding subsections, as well as a function of energy. Among all the possible approaches, the multigroup theory is the most popular and practically all current numerical codes are based on this formalism.

Let us consider the energy domain $(0, E_0)$ where E_0 is an energy above which no neutron is emitted (10 to 15 MeV), and let us divide this domain into G intervals by introducing a sequence of values E_g with $g = 1, 2\ldots, G$. We say that the neutrons situated in the energy band $E_g \leqq E \leqq E_{g-1}$ belong to group g.

Let us place ourselves in the slowing down domain (§4.4.3) and integrate the general equation (4.40) from E_g to E_{g-1}. We obtain the equation for group g:

$$\text{div}\,(\vec{J}_g) + \Sigma_{a,g}\Phi_g(\vec{r}) = q(\vec{r},E_{g-1}) - q(\vec{r},E_g) + Q_g(\vec{r}) \qquad (4.87)$$

where we have put:

$$\begin{Bmatrix} \vec{J}_g(\vec{r}) \\ \Phi_g(\vec{r}) \\ Q_g(\vec{r}) \end{Bmatrix} = \int_{E_g}^{E_{g-1}} \begin{Bmatrix} \vec{J}(\vec{r},E) \\ \Phi(\vec{r},E) \\ Q(\vec{r},E) \end{Bmatrix} dE \qquad (4.88)$$

as well as:

$$\Sigma_{a,g}(\vec{r}) = \int_{E_g}^{E_{g-1}} \Sigma_a(\vec{r},E)\Phi(\vec{r},E)dE/\Phi_g(\vec{r}) \qquad (4.89)$$

The quantities J_g, Φ_g, Q_g have the usual meanings: currents, flux, source densities, but only apply to the neutrons of group g. As to the macroscopic absorption cross section $\Sigma_{a,g}$, it depends on the spectrum $\Phi(\vec{r},E)$ in the interval (E_g, E_{g-1}) but the dependence is very weak if the latter is narrow.

In order to go further, we will assume that the energy distributions vary like 1/E (§4.4.4) in each group but not in the whole interval ($0,E_0$) which is much less restrictive. We shall thus put:

$$\Phi(\vec{r},E) = K_g(\vec{r})/E \quad \text{for } E_g \leqq E \leqq E_{g-1} \tag{4.90}$$

with, following (4.88):

$$K_g(\vec{r}) = \Phi_g(\vec{r})/\ln\left(\frac{E_{g-1}}{E_g}\right) \tag{4.91}$$

Using this structure, we can make explicit $\Sigma_{a,g}$ (4.89) and bring out the atomic density N:

$$\Sigma_{a,g}(\vec{r}) = N(\vec{r})\ \sigma_{a,g}$$

with:

$$\sigma_{a,g} = \frac{1}{\ln\left(\frac{E_{g-1}}{E_g}\right)} \int_{E_g}^{E_{g-1}} \sigma_a(E)\ \frac{dE}{E} \tag{4.92}$$

For a mixture, we apply the usual rule (4.1) relative to microscopic cross sections thus defined. When resonances are present in group g, the integral which appears in (4.92) is nothing but a partial resonance integral and a better value can be obtained with the help of equation (4.56) in which the dilution parameter is present (see also appendix §9.1.3).

We now pass to the calculation of the slowing down sources which figure in the right hand side of (4.87). According to expression (4.39) we have for elastic collisions:

$$q(\vec{r},E_g) = \int_{E_g}^{E_g/\alpha} \frac{E_g - \alpha E'}{(1-\alpha)E'}\ \Sigma_s(\vec{r},E')\Phi(\vec{r},E')dE'$$

This integral can be expressed in general as a function of the fluxes Φ_g

with lower indices (§9.1.2), but we will restrict ourselves here to the case which appears very often in practice where the groups are so large compared to the average loss of energy per collision that we have: $E_g < E_g/\alpha < E_{g-1}$. We are thus authorized to use expression (4.90) to calculate this integral, whence:

$$q(\vec{r},E_g) = \xi K_g(\vec{r})\Sigma_{s,g}(\vec{r})$$

and by considering (4.91):

$$q(\vec{r},E_g) = \Sigma_{R,g}(\vec{r})\Phi_g(\vec{r}) \tag{4.93}$$

with:

$$\Sigma_{R,g}(\vec{r}) = \frac{\xi\Sigma_{s,g}(\vec{r})}{\ln\left(\frac{E_{g-1}}{E_g}\right)} \tag{4.94}$$

The parameter ξ (4.35) appears naturally as in subsec. 4.4.4 and the ratio $(1/\xi)\ln(E_{g-1}/E_g)$ represents the average number of collisions necessary for a neutron to leave group g. We have in addition assumed in the preceding that the scattering cross sections do not vary much with energy, and we have put $\Sigma_s(\vec{r},E) = \Sigma_{s,g}(\vec{r})$. This approximation is justified, at least within a group.

Finally, the current $\vec{J}_g$ can be calculated with the help of Fick's law (4.13):

$$\vec{J}_g(\vec{r}) = -D_g(\vec{r})\,\vec{\text{grad}}\,\Phi_g(\vec{r}) \tag{4.95}$$

where the diffusion coefficient D_g is well defined. According to (4.14), the diffusion coefficient D(E) depends on the scattering cross section $\Sigma_s(E)$ which, as we have just seen, is practically constant. We shall say nothing about the case where the presence of empty cavities in a reactor core renders this question extremely delicate[9](p.339).

Substituting expressions (4.93) and (4.95) into equation (4.87) we finally obtain:

$$\begin{aligned} &\text{div}\,[D_g(\vec{r})\,\vec{\text{grad}}\,\Phi_g(\vec{r})] - [\Sigma_{a,g}(\vec{r}) + \Sigma_{R,g}(\vec{r})]\,\Phi_g(\vec{r}) + \\ &[\Sigma_{R,g-1}(\vec{r})\Phi_{g-1}(\vec{r}) + Q_g(\vec{r})] = 0 \end{aligned} \tag{4.96}$$

This diffusion equation for group g generalizes the mono-energetic equation (4.15). From a numerical point of view, it is not much more complicated. In effect, if we solve the system of equations (4.96) for g = 1,2,..G, that is to say, for decreasing energies, the term $\Sigma_{R,g-1}\Phi_{g-1}$ which represents the transfer of neutrons from group (g - 1) to group g can be considered as a known source (which is added to Q_g). <u>We thus have to solve a succession of one-group problems</u>. For g = 1, the term $\Sigma_{R,0}\Phi_0$ evidently vanishes since it corresponds to energies higher than E_0, a domain in which by hypothesis there is no neutron.

The cross section $\Sigma_{R,g}$ given by expression (4.94) is called a <u>macroscopic removal cross section</u>; it has the expected dimensions (cm^{-1}) but it does not constitute a fundamental nuclear datum since it depends strongly on the arbitrary subdivision (E_g) that we have adopted. For group g it represents a pseudo-absorption since it is added to the true absorption ($\Sigma_{a,g}$), but this disappearance of neutrons corresponds to an appearance (source term) in the following group (g + 1). If the last group (g = G) is relative to thermal neutrons, then we will put $\Sigma_{R,G} = 0$, since in this group the neutrons can no longer be slowed down. In effect, this group being characterized by a lower bound $E_G = 0$, the slowing down source $q(\vec{r},E_G)$ vanishes (4.39), which leads according to (4.93) to $\Sigma_{R,G} = 0$. We also note that the expression (4.92) is no longer valid for this group, since the thermal neutrons are distributed according to a particular spectrum (§9.1.4).

The multigroup equations (4.96) apply to passive systems characterized in each group by nuclear parameters D_g, $\Sigma_{a,g}$, $\Sigma_{R,g}$ and source densities Q_g. In multiplying systems the fission process permits us to relate these sources to the flux. We will thus take the general expression for the fission rate R_f (4.37) and multiply it by $\bar{\nu}$ to obtain the source density Q_f of fission neutrons. In the multigroup formalism this source can be written:

$$Q_f(\vec{r}) = \sum_{g=1}^{G} \bar{\nu}_g \Sigma_{f,g}(\vec{r})\Phi_g(\vec{r}) \tag{4.97}$$

where the macroscopic fission cross sections for group g are obtained by the same procedure as $\Sigma_{a,g}$. Expression (4.97) enables us to take account of all the fissions and not only those due to thermal neutrons (last group). Moreover, without complicating the formalism, we can affix the index g to $\bar{\nu}$ to express the fact that rigorously speaking the number of neutrons emitted by fission depends on the energy of incident neutrons.

If the spectrum of fission neutrons is spread over several groups, then we must multiply the source Q_f by χ_g in order to know the sources in each group (χ_g can be obtained by integrating $\chi(E)$ (Fig. 3.2) over the energy interval (E_g , E_{g-1})). Finally, the source densities Q_g to be employed in (4.96) are given by the expression:

$$Q_g(\vec{r}) = \chi_g \sum_{h=1}^{G} (\bar{\nu}\Sigma_f(\vec{r}))_h \Phi_h(\vec{r}) \tag{4.98}$$

with:

$$\sum_{g=1}^{G} \chi_g = 1$$

Because of the characteristics of the fission spectrum (high energies) the sources Q_g are only different from zero in the very first groups, and very often one identifies the first group with the fission spectrum ($\chi_1 = 1$ and $\chi_g = 0$ for $g > 1$).

Replacing Q_g by its expression (4.98), equation (4.96) leads to a homogeneous system of equations in Φ_g which in general does not have a solution unless one of the data is judiciously chosen. The critical condition can no longer be explicitly given, which is hardly surprising considering the large number of data. The trick which consists in dividing $\bar{\nu}$ by k_e (§4.5.3) and hence introducing in (4.96) the sources Q_g/k_e in place of Q_g is without interest here. In effect, right from the first diffusion equation, the fluxes $\Phi_g (g > 1)$, which are not yet known at this stage, would intervene in the source term Q_1 (4.98). We would lose the benefit of the procedure described earlier, which consists in solving the diffusion equations successively starting from $g = 1$.

The following method is used for calculating the effective multiplication factor k_e. We give ourselves a priori a distribution $Q_f^*(\vec{r})$(for example a constant) to which corresponds $Q_g^* = \chi_g Q_f^*$. We solve (4.96) group by group and when all the $\Phi_g(\vec{r})$ have been obtained, expression (4.97) gives a new value of Q_f. Let us form the ratio:

$$k = \frac{\int_V Q_f(\vec{r})\, dV}{\int_V Q_f^*(\vec{r})\, dV} \tag{4.99}$$

where V represents the volume of the whole system.

The numerator represents the total number of neutrons emitted by fission for flux distributions $\Phi_g(\vec{r})$ obtained starting from a given choice of Q_f^*. The denominator corresponds to the total number of neutrons arbitrarily injected into the system. It is also equal to the sum of all the absorptions and leaks, since (4.96) is a stationary equation; this can be demonstrated (§9.1.3). We can thus identify k with the multiplication factor k_e by referring to the general definition (4.62), or rather to a first estimation, since the results are based on an arbitrary distribution of sources Q_f^*. The calculations are repeated for the successive groups with a new distribution Q_f, and so on. We obtain the sought-for effective multiplication factor by the convergence of this procedure. These iterations are called <u>outer</u> in order to distinguish them from <u>inner</u> iterations to which one is sometimes led by numerical methods employed for solving equation (4.96) with g fixed. We can subsequently modify the system by trial and error in order to render it critical ($k_e = 1$). At this stage, the last values of $\Phi_g(\vec{r})$ must be kept, since they enable us to calculate all the useful physical quantities (§9.1.5), like, for example, the fission rates $R_f(\vec{r})$ and the specific powers which follow from them (§5.2.5). We can also get an idea of neutron spectra by calculating the flux densities at the center of each group; we thus have according to equations (4.90) and (4.91):

$$\Phi(\vec{r},E_{g-1/2}) \cong \frac{\Phi_g(\vec{r})}{E_{g-1/2}\ln\left(\frac{E_{g-1}}{E_g}\right)}$$

A good knowledge of the spectra thus necessitates a large number of groups, and we note that the numerator and the denominator of the preceding expression tend to zero when $E_g \to E_{g-1}$ $(G \to \infty)$.

4.5.9 Particularities of the Multigroup Formalism

The preceding theory leads us to make the following remarks:

- The multigroup theory has supplanted all the approaches, more or less analytic, used in the past. The four factors formula (4.80) has only a didactic interest; at best it can orient project studies of a thermal reactor, but it takes nuclear phenomena into account in too schematic a fashion, whereas a set of multigroup cross sections has a much richer physical content. If the number of groups is sufficient then we make virtually no restrictive hypothesis on the structure of the spectra; on the contrary, these result from the solution of equations (4.96) and can differ from point to point in the system. Clearly, it would not have been possible to approach the problems of neutron physics in this way, without the appearance of large computers.

- The choice of groups depends on the problems treated. For thermal reactors, the last group (the most important) will of course correspond to thermal neutrons, but only two to three groups will suffice to describe the phenomena in the slowing down domain. For fast reactors, the lower bound E_G is taken quite high in order to avoid useless calculations (we know in advance that there are very few neutrons below 1 keV). Finally, if a cross section varies greatly in a given energy domain, then this domain can be covered by several groups in order to display the influence of this variation.

- If there intervenes inelastic scattering (§1.5.3) or elastic scattering by very light nuclei (hydrogenic with $\alpha = 0$), group g is no longer connected only to group (g - 1) but also to all the groups of lower indices. This in no way changes the method of solution described earlier, as one can see in the appendix (§9.1.2).

- We have claimed that the absorption cross sections depended very little on the choice of a spectrum in the interior of each group. This is the justification of the multigroup theory. All the same, this assertion is open to discussion, when resonances are present, and a special treatment is inevitable (§9.1.3). This being so, one can show (§9.3.4) that the multigroup formalism leads to the expected results in the case of bare homogeneous thermal reactors (§4.5.4).

- In all cases, an equation of the type (4.96) can be seen as a diffusion equation for mono-energetic neutrons where the only unknown is the flux $\Phi_g(\vec{r})$. The third term of this equation constitutes at each point a known source term starting from the solutions obtained in the preceding groups. Hence, even if the system can be divided into homogeneous zones, searching for an analytical solution is excluded. On the contrary, this equation can only be solved by numerical methods. We will find some information relative to this subject in the appendix (Sec. 9.2).

From a practical point of view, the numerical calculations take place in the following way. The basic nuclear data are collected in a program library comprising all the microscopic cross sections as functions of the energy (0 to 15 MeV) as well as certain parameters characterizing the resonances (§9.4.1). In current libraries [13], this can represent thousands of data per isotope! Subsequently a data processing code furnishes condensed information, that is to say, the multigroup sections defined earlier. At this stage, the reactor type does not play much of a role, except for the choice of the structure of the groups and for the approximate composition of the media studied [14]. One thus has available multigroup libraries (50 to 200 groups) which should not be confused with the preceding more fundamental ones. This preparatory work is generally accomplished in nuclear research centers because it requires large-scale capacities. The second phase, which interests the nuclear engineer, consists in solving the multigroup equations (4.96) with the help of the above libraries. At this stage, the entire geometry of the problem must intervene, and one has recourse to standard codes for one, two, or three dimensions [15]. The multidimensional diffusion calculations are very costly. One generally passes by an intermediate stage which makes it possible to condense the basic multigroup program library to a library of a few groups (3 to 4 for thermal reactors, about 10 for fast reactors). This condensation takes place in a simplified geometric framework (§9.3.3).

4.6 REACTOR KINETICS

4.6.1 Introduction

The study of the behavior of reactors in non-steady state demands in principle a knowledge of neutron flux distributions in the course of time, in other words, the determination of a function $\Phi(\vec{r},E,t)$. By generalizing the formalism of the previous sections, we can obtain a time-dependent diffusion equation which can only be solved numerically in real cases. Usually, one deduces from this equation the so-called equations of "point kinetics" which govern the global behavior of the reactor or, if one prefers, its total neutron population P(t) given by the expression:

$$P(t) = \int_{React.} n(\vec{r},t)\, dV \qquad (4.100)$$

where $n(\vec{r},t)$ represents the neutron density (§4.2.2) at point $\vec{r}$ and instant t.

In fact, we can obtain the point kinetic equations in a much more direct way. We have chosen this route because it offers two advantages: the demonstrations are very simple, and the restrictive hypotheses of diffusion theory are no longer required. This feature attests to the general character of these equations, which is not evident from the usual demonstrations. Very complex reactors subject to intimately related variations of flux in space and time can demand a more detailed knowledge of these phenomena. The point kinetic equations remain useful in this case, even if they do not furnish all the necessary information.

4.6.2 The Point Kinetic Equation

Let us recall the previous notations (§4.5.2):

- $\bar{\nu}S_f(t)$ the number of fission neutrons created (per unit time)
- $A(t)$ the number of neutrons absorbed (per unit time)
- $F(t)$ the number of neutrons escaping the reactor (per unit time)

Since we are considering non-steady states, the variable t must figure in these notations. The quantity $[\bar{\nu}S_f(t) - (A(t) + F(t))]$ represents the excess of neutrons per unit time; it must hence be identical to the increase per unit time dP/dt of the neutron population, whence the identity:

$$\frac{dP}{dt} = \bar{\nu}\, S_f(t) - [A(t) + F(t)] \qquad (4.101)$$

We can write by definition the effective multiplication factor:

$$k_e(t) = \frac{\bar{\nu}\, S_f(t)}{A(t) + F(t)} \qquad \text{(cf. equation (4.62))}$$

The factor k_e only depends on the cross sections of the various materials and not on the true magnitude of the fluxes (as we have seen, the cross sections only fix the flux distributions). It is thus independent of P(t) or of the power level. Its determination does not necessarily imply the use of the theories that we have presented until now. By using this definition of k_e the preceding equation becomes:

$$\frac{dP}{dt} = (k_e(t) - 1)[A(t) + F(t)]$$

The absorptions and leaks are evidently proportional to the total number of neutrons present in the system. We will thus put:

$$A(t) + F(t) = \frac{P(t)}{\ell(t)} \tag{4.102}$$

where ℓ is called the neutron lifetime. We thus arrive at the desired equation:

$$\frac{dP}{dt} = \frac{k_e(t) - 1}{\ell(t)} P(t) \tag{4.103}$$

In order to understand the physical meaning of the lifetime ℓ, let us consider a passive medium ($k_e = 0$) having the same cross sections as the multiplying medium studied (and hence the same value of ℓ.)

Equation (4.103) can be written:

$$\frac{dP}{dt} = - \frac{P(t)}{\ell}$$

Supposing ℓ independent of time, this equation can be integrated:

$$P(t) = P(0) \exp\left(- \frac{t}{\ell}\right)$$

For times which are large compared to ℓ, the neutrons disappear ($P \to 0$); ℓ thus measures their lifetime in the system given their absorptions and escapes. This law is identical to that given for radioactivity (cf. equation (1.8)) and $1/\ell$ plays the role of the decay constant. Another analogy is useful: one can speak of the confinement time, as we have for fusion reactors (in the latter case $A \cong 0$ and ℓ is uniquely fixed by the leakage).

4.6.3 Application to Bare Homogeneous Reactors

The lifetime ℓ is, in the same way as k_e, a neutronic parameter that can be measured or calculated starting from more elaborate theories. Still, it is interesting to evaluate it in the particularly simple case of a homogeneous reactor by using mono-energetic diffusion theory (§4.5.3, §4.5.4).

The number A of neutrons absorbed per unit time can be calculated from the absorption rate (equat. 4.7) and by using the definition of P (4.100):

$$A(t) = \int \Sigma_a \Phi(\vec{r},t)dV = \Sigma_a v \int n(\vec{r},t)\, dV = \Sigma_a vP(t)$$

We note the proportionality to P(t). One can calculate in the same way the leakage term F by recalling that it suffices to introduce a fictitious absorption cross section DB^2 (last remark of §4.5.3), whence: $F(t) = DB^2\, vP(t)$. We thus have: $A(t) + F(t) = (\Sigma_a + DB^2)vP(t)$ and comparing with the definition of ℓ (4.102), we get:

$$\ell = \frac{1}{v(\Sigma_a + DB^2)} = \frac{1}{v\Sigma_a(1 + L^2B^2)} \qquad (4.104)$$

We recall that we have obtained in the same conditions for the multiplication factor (4.82):

$$k_e = \frac{k_\infty \exp(-B^2\tau)}{1 + L^2B^2}$$

In contrast to k_e, the lifetime depends on the velocity of the neutrons. For thermal reactors, this is the velocity of the thermal neutrons ($v \cong 2.5\ 10^5\ \text{cm s}^{-1}$). This example shows that the lifetime ℓ (like k_e) is independent of P, which justifies the defining relation (4.102). This result can be demonstrated in the framework of much more elaborate theories (the transport equation); the lifetime will no longer be given by expression (4.104), especially if the system is inhomogeneous, but it will remain independent of the flux levels or of the power, and will thus keep its meaning intact. All the same, because the macroscopic cross sections depend on the thermodynamic state of the system (temperatures, mass densities, etc.), a modification of the power (or of P) will have an influence on parameters k_e and ℓ of a reactor, but this is a completely different matter, since in this case the nuclear data are no longer fixed (Sec. 5.3).

4.6.4 Point Kinetics of Delayed Neutrons

Let us return to the kinetic equation (4.103) and suppose that the characteristics of the reactor are time-independent (k_e and ℓ constant). This equation can be immediately integrated:

$$P(t) = P(0) \exp \left(\frac{k_e - 1}{\ell} t\right) \qquad (4.105)$$

We see that if $k_e > 1$, the neutron population grows, whereas it decreases if $k_e < 1$ (supercritical and subcritical states §4.5.2)).

For thermal reactors the lifetimes are of the order of 10^{-3}s (they are much smaller for fast reactors). Thus, if the reactor is supercritical by only 0.5% (k_e = 1.0005), the neutron population grows at least like exp(5t). At the end of one second its initial value is multiplied by a factor 148, which is enormous. If the preceding theory was exact, nuclear reactors would be difficult to control. Happily, this is not the case, since an important aspect of fission has been overlooked.

In the preceding chapter (§3.1.3), it was indicated that a small fraction β of fission neutrons were emitted in delayed fashion. These neutrons are governed by the decay of precursor fission products, and hence must be counted separately. We rewrite equation (4.101) in the following way:

$$\frac{dP}{dt} = S_p(t) + S_d(t) - [A(t) + F(t)] \qquad (4.106)$$

where S_p and S_d are respectively the sources of prompt and delayed neutrons. If $\bar{\nu} S_f$ represents as in the preceding the source of fission neutrons (without distinguishing the two types) we have simply $S_p(t) = (1 - \beta)\bar{\nu} S_f(t)$. The delayed neutron source S_d is on the contrary not related directly to S_f but rather to the number $C_i(t)$ of precursors of each type (i) to which corresponds a decay rate $\lambda_i C_i$ (law of radioactivity (§1.4.1)). To every disappearance of a precursor corresponds the emission of a neutron (for example bromine $_{35}Br^{87}$ (§3.1.3)), and hence $\lambda_i C_i(t)$ constitutes a delayed neutron source (in s^{-1}). By considering all types of precursors, we get:

$$S_d(t) = \sum_i \lambda_i C_i(t)$$

Using these expressions for S_p and S_d in equation (4.106), we are led to the relation:

$$\frac{dP}{dt} = (1 - \beta)\bar{\nu}\, S_f(t) - [A(t) + F(t)] + \sum_i \lambda_i C_i(t)$$

Taking up the previous reasoning (we first introduce the multiplication factor k_e and then the lifetime ℓ (4.102)), we then obtain the new kinetic equation:

$$\frac{dP}{dt} = \frac{(1-\beta)k_e(t) - 1}{\ell(t)} P(t) + \sum_i \lambda_i C_i(t) \qquad (4.107)$$

The neutronic parameters k_e and ℓ are the same as in the preceding. This is why ℓ is called the prompt neutron lifetime in order to emphasize that it is independent of the presence of delayed neutrons.

As the functions $C_i(t)$ are not known, we must add to the previous neutron equation the equations of the precursors. Of the $\bar{\nu}\, S_f$ fission neutrons emitted, β_i are in an indirect fashion through the intermediary of a precursor. The quantity $\beta_i \bar{\nu} S_f$ thus represents the number of precursor nuclei of type (i) created per unit time. In a parallel way, the disappearance rate by decay amounts to $\lambda_i C_i$, whence the equation of balance:

$$\frac{dC_i}{dt} = \beta_i \bar{\nu} S_f - \lambda_i C_i$$

This equation is identical to equation (1.11) except that the source term is not explicitly known. After introducing k_e and then ℓ, we get:

$$\frac{dC_i}{dt} + \lambda_i C_i = \beta_i k_e\ [A(t) + F(t)] = \beta_i \frac{k_e}{\ell} P(t) \qquad (4.108)$$

It is customary to introduce the generation time Λ as well as the reactivity ρ with the definitions:

$$\rho = \frac{k_e - 1}{k_e} \quad \text{and } \Lambda = \frac{\ell}{k_e} \qquad (4.109)$$

In practice, the multiplication factor k_e is in the neighborhood of unity, so that the lifetime and the generation time are approximately the same ($\Lambda \cong \ell$). On the other hand, the reactivity ρ is small, and is thus a good measure of the departure from criticality. We deduce from its definition the following properties: for supercritical reactors the reactivity is positive, and in the opposite case, negative.

With the help of these two definitions, the point kinetic equations can be written (cf. equations (4.107) and (4.108)):

$$\left.\begin{aligned} \frac{dP}{dt} &= \frac{\rho(t) - \beta}{\Lambda(t)} P(t) + \sum_i \lambda_i C_i(t) \\ \frac{dC_i}{dt} + \lambda_i C_i(t) &= \frac{\beta_i}{\Lambda(t)} P(t) \end{aligned}\right\} \tag{4.110}$$

This system of linear equations is complete; it is at the base of numerous studies of reactor stability and safety.

Let us consider a steady state: $P(t) = P(0)$ and $C_i(t) = C_i(0)$. The preceding system becomes:

$$0 = \frac{\rho-\beta}{\Lambda} P(0) + \sum_i \lambda_i C_i(0)$$

$$\lambda_i C_i(0) = \frac{\beta_i}{\Lambda} P(0)$$

Substituting this value of $\lambda_i C_i(0)$ in the first equation and noting that by definition

$$\beta = \sum_i \beta_i$$

we get the identity:

$$\frac{\rho}{\Lambda} P(0) = 0$$

The only interesting solution is:

$$\left.\begin{aligned} &\rho = 0, \quad P(0) \text{ arbitrary} \\ &\lambda_i C_i(0) = \frac{\beta_i}{\Lambda} P(0) \end{aligned}\right\}$$

The steady states thus correspond to zero reactivities ($k_e = 1$) and the delayed neutrons have no influence on the results. Because of this we have not taken account of them in the preceding sections. In non-steady states, on the contrary, they play a fundamental role, as shown by the example which follows.

4.6.5 Constant Reactivities

Let us consider at instant $t = 0$ the sudden introduction of a reactivity ρ which will subsequently remain constant (the sudden movement of a control rod, for example). The generation time Λ also being independent of time, equations (4.110) can be rigorously solved by a Laplace transform. Denoting the transforms of P(t) and $C_i(t)$ respectively by $\tilde{P}(s)$ and $\tilde{C}_i(s)$, we obtain the transformed system of equations [16]:

$$s\tilde{P}(s) - P(0) = \frac{\rho - \beta}{\Lambda} \tilde{P}(s) + \sum_i \lambda_i \tilde{C}_i(s)$$

$$s\tilde{C}_i(s) - C_i(0) + \lambda_i \tilde{C}_i(s) = \frac{\beta_i}{\Lambda} \tilde{P}(s)$$

whence, after elimination of $\tilde{C}_i(s)$:

$$\tilde{P}(s) = \Lambda \frac{P(0) + \sum_i \frac{\lambda_i C_i(0)}{\lambda_i + s}}{\beta - \sum_i \beta_i \frac{\lambda_i}{\lambda_i + s} + \Lambda s - \rho}$$

Let us suppose that the reactor was critical at the instants before the introduction of the reactivity ρ. In these conditions, the number of precursors and neutrons are related, as we have just seen, by the relation $\lambda_i C_i(0) = \beta_i P(0)/\Lambda$. Substituting this last value into the expression for $\tilde{P}(s)$, we get:

$$\frac{\tilde{P}(s)}{P(0)} = \frac{\Lambda + \sum_i \frac{\beta_i}{\lambda_i + s}}{\beta - \sum_i \beta_i \frac{\lambda_i}{\lambda_i + s} + \Lambda s - \rho} \qquad (4.111)$$

This rational fraction can be developed into a sum of simple fractions:

$$\frac{\tilde{P}(s)}{P(0)} = \sum_j \frac{B_j}{s - \omega_j}$$

the quantities ω_j being the roots of the denominator of equation (4.111). We are thus led to the important characteristic equation:

$$\rho - \Lambda\omega = \beta - \sum_i \frac{\beta_i \lambda_i}{\lambda_i + \omega} = \sum_i \frac{\beta_i \omega}{\lambda_i + \omega} \qquad (4.112)$$

and to the desired solution:

$$\frac{P(t)}{P(0)} = \sum_j B_j \exp(\omega_j t) \qquad (4.113)$$

Let us consider I groups of precursors (in general I = 6, cf. Table 3.4). We can represent on the same graph the straight line $y_1(\omega)$ corresponding to the lefthand side of equation (4.112) and the function $y_2(\omega)$ corresponding to the righthand side. The desired roots are then found at the intersection of these two curves.

For a given reactor Λ is more or less fixed, whence the array of parallel straight lines shown in Fig.4.25, each of which corresponds to a given reactivity ρ.

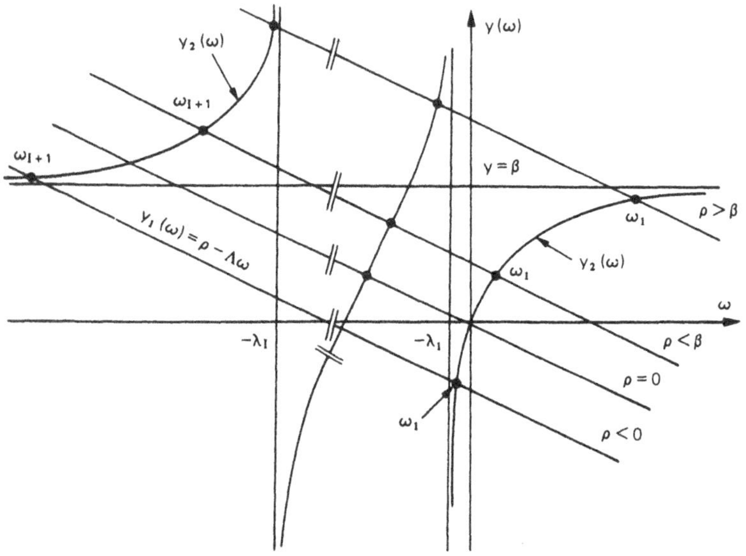

FIGURE 4.25. Graphical solution of the characteristic equation (4.112).

The function $y_2(\omega)$ has I asymptotes ($\omega = -\lambda_i$) and only depends on the characteristics β_i, λ_i of the fissionable isotope considered. The straight lines $y_1(\omega)$, on the contrary, depend on the entire structure of the reactor through ρ and Λ. A significant modification of the reactor will affect $y_1(\omega)$ strongly but $y_2(\omega)$ very little (insofar as we keep the same fissile matter). Therein lies the interest of this method of solving.

Figure 4.25 shows that one always obtains (I + 1) roots ω_j. When the reactivities are negative, so are all the roots, so that the neutron population decreases as shown by (4.113). In the opposite case (supercritical reactors, $\rho > 0$), one and only one positive root appears, all the others remaining negative. It follows that after a certain time only the term $B_1 \exp(\omega_1 t)$ remains, since the other functions $\exp(\omega_j t)$ have arguments which are more and more negative.

Let us make a closer analysis of this important case. The quantity

$$T = \frac{1}{\omega_1} \qquad (4.114)$$

is called the stable period of the reactor. As shown by Fig. 4.26 (lower curve), the neutron population behaves very quickly like exp(t/T) and hence the period T is the fundamental time constant of a supercritical reactor. The sharp jump at the beginning comes from the hypothesis of an instantaneous introduction of reactivity at time t = 0, which is not very realistic. A detailed analysis of the transform P(s) would give all the amplitudes B_j and hence the complete solution P(t) in this first time interval. This having very little interest, it suffices to note that this transition is very brief for reactivities envisaged in practice.

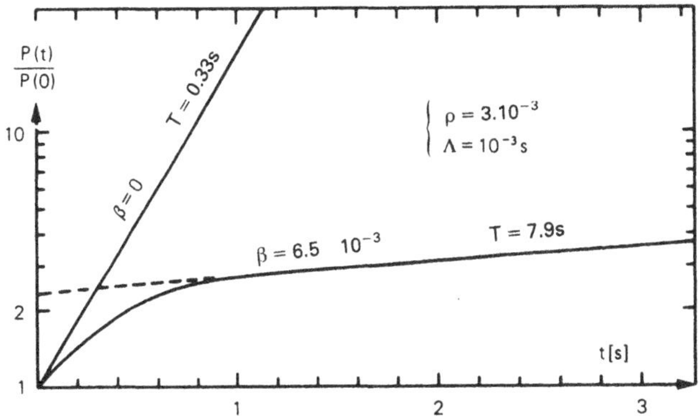

FIGURE 4.26. Divergence with and without delayed neutrons.

The graphical solution of the characteristic equation (4.112) (cf. Fig. 4.25) enables us to establish a correlation between periods and reactivities. Thus for uranium U^{235} the various curves of Fig. 4.27 give the correspondance between each reactivity ρ and the positive root ω which fixes the period ($T = 1/\omega$). We observe that for reactivities smaller than 3.5 10^{-3} ($\beta/2$) the results depend very little on the generation time Λ, whereas in the absence of delayed neutrons ($\beta_i = 0$), equation (4.112) leads to the law $\omega = \rho/\Lambda$ in accordance with the conclusion of subsec. 4.6.2 (Fig. 4.27, curves in dotted lines). Since the generation times are very small, the behaviors of a reactor with or without delayed neutrons are radically different. If we insert a reactivity of 3 10^{-3}, for example, then the stable period is 7.9 s (ω= 0.127 s^{-1}) in the first case and at most 0.33 s (ω= 3 s^{-1}) in the second. A factor of 24 in the time constants has, to be sure, a considerable importance. The fission reactors thus become controllable. More significant, perhaps, are the curves of Fig. 4.26 relative to the time variations of the neutron population corresponding to the preceding numerical example.

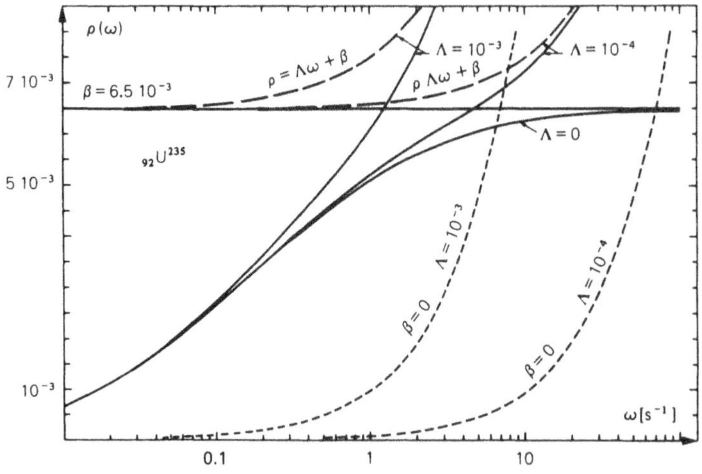

FIGURE 4.27. Stable periods and reactivities.

For more significant reactivities, the influence of the generation time Λ is felt progressively. The improvement brought by the delayed neutrons nevertheless remains important, especially for small values of Λ.

When the reactivity sufficiently exceeds the rate β of delayed neutrons, the curves $\rho(\omega)$ rapidly become asymptotic to the straight line $\Lambda\omega + \beta$, whence the simple expression of the period: $T = \Lambda/(\rho - \beta)$. The law of increase of the fluxes resembles more and more what happens in the absence of delayed neutrons. The latter have no more influence for very large reactivities $\rho >> \beta$; the divergences are, as in subsec. 4.6.2, exptremely rapid and one of the necessary conditions for a nuclear explosion is satisfied (additional conditions must be satisfied to arrive at an outright explosion).

Returning to reactors, we deduce from the preceding that two cases are to be considered: $\rho < \beta$ and $\rho > \beta$. In the first case, one says that the reactor is delayed supercritical because its behavior is governed by delayed neutrons, and in the second case it is said to be prompt supercritical. During the elaboration of a reactor project, one insures that untimely introductions of reactivity remain much smaller than β. Locking systems, for example, will prevent an operator from withdrawing too many control rods simultaneously (Ch. 6).

The foregoing numerical study was relative to uranium U^{235}. One arrives at similar results with the two other fissionable isotopes, but the delayed neutron rates β are significantly lower (Table 3.8). Thus, from the point of view of neutronics, the current breeder reactors have more sensitive responses to the introduction of reactivity, not, as one often thinks, because they are characterized by a spectrum of fast neutrons, but because they use plutonium as fissile matter, with a value of β smaller by half than that of the β of uranium U^{235}. All the same, one must pay careful attention when comparing thermal reactors (with U^{235}) with fast reactors (with Pu^{239}). The introductions of reactivity in the latter are generally weaker and it is in fact the ratio ρ/β (often expressed in dollars, \$1 corresponds to $\rho = \beta$) which is important.

4.6.6 Conclusions

The foregoing study has shown the influence of the delayed neutron rate β on the kinetic behavior of a reactor. This influence remains qualitatively the same in all cases.

Studies of kinetics in a more realistic framework depend on the numerical solutions of equations (4.110). The reactivity ρ is no longer constant for two reasons:

- Changes in reactivity due to external causes are never extreme. The most rapid variation that one might envisage corresponds probably to the fall of safety rods, an event that would take place in about one second.

· Variations of the neutron population entail proportional modifications of the power, and then with a certain delay, changes in the temperatures and densities of the various materials which make up the reactor. The latter parameters have an influence on the macroscopic cross sections and hence on the reactivities. We speak of <u>response</u> or <u>feedback</u>, and generally these effects act as a brake (see the safety studies). In this case the reactivity is not known a priori and equations of thermohydraulics must be coupled with those of kinetics. These phenomena will be described in the context of reactor control (Sec. 5.3).

Chapter 5

NUCLEAR POWER PLANTS

5.1 CONCEPTION

5.1.1 Introduction

In the last twenty years, technical-economic as well as neutronic studies have led to about a dozen concepts of reactors as well as numerous variants. Although most of these concepts have resulted in "neutronic mock-ups" (§3.4.2), and sometimes even industrial prototypes, it is out of the question to analyze them separately. We shall only study in some detail, in Sec. 5.4, those reactor types which have been commercially viable (reactors moderated by light water or heavy water) or those which have benefited from sufficiently sophisticated studies and realizations so that a new generation of more performing reactors is in sight (breeder reactors and high temperature reactors).

All the same, a large number of features are common to all types of nuclear power plants. They will be the subject of the first three sections, which treat, respectively, the structure of reactors, problems of thermo-hydraulics, and problems of control.

5.1.2 Structure of a Nuclear Reactor

The structure of every reactor, going from the center to the periphery, consists of: an approximately cylindrical active core in which the chain reaction takes place, reflectors, means of control, a tank containing all the foregoing, and various thermal and biological shields (Fig. 5.1).

When the tank must contain a certain pressure, we use the term vessel. If the vessel is made of steel (water-cooled reactors), this plays at least a partial role of thermal protection. It attenuates various radiations emanating from the core and protects the biological screens, always in concrete, which complete the shielding of the reactor. "Biological" here means that the operating personnel can approach the reactor block without danger, or, if one prefers, that the biological doses to which they are submitted remain admissible (Sec. 6.2).

In the same way, when the vessel is of prestressed concrete (gas-cooled reactors), it assures biological protection. But in this case a thermal protection (of steel) must cover its inner surface.

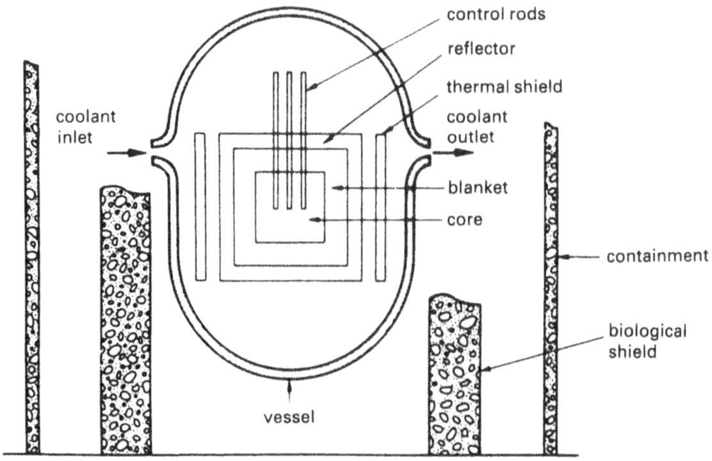

FIGURE 5.1. Schematic structure of a reactor.

As its name indicates, the reflector makes it possible to economize on neutrons (§4.5.7). In the case of breeder reactors, it assures in addition a conversion of fertile matter into fissile matter which adds to the (insufficient) conversion taking place in the core. In this case, the term blanket replaces the term reflector. The reactor (vessel and shielding) is situated in a containment enclosure whose role will be discussed in detail in another chapter (Sec. 6.3).

5.1.3 Composition of the Core

With the exception of very special cases (molten salt reactors), the fuel is always in a solid state in the form of cylindrical rods. The extraction of the heat energy liberated in the fuel (§3.1.4) demands the presence of a coolant. The reactor core is thus heterogeneous in contrast to the multiplying media studied in the preceding chapter. The fuel rods as well as the portions of the moderator and the coolant connected to them are regularly distributed and constitute a lattice. The repetitive pattern or elementary cell thus consists of all the elements necessary to the neutronic and thermohydraulic functioning of the reactor. The distance between the axes of two contiguous cells is called the lattice pitch. Some typical cells are displayed in Fig. 5.2. For reasons of safety (Sec. 6.3), the fuel is separated from the other materials by a sheath or cladding. As for the moderator, if it is liquid, it can play the role of coolant.

The cell of the first type (Fig. 5.2) is characteristic of today's light-water reactor (LWR) assemblies. The water serves both as coolant and as moderator. Fast breeders (LMFBR) use a similar scheme. The coolant however is now liquid sodium (weak moderation) and the fuel a mixture of uranium and plutonium oxides.

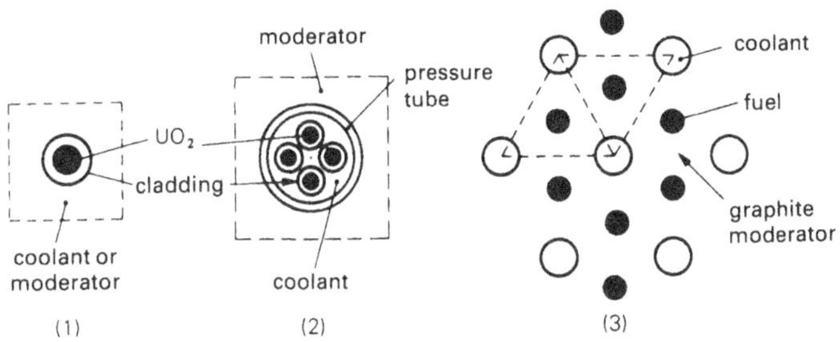

FIGURE 5.2. Characteristic cells of principal assemblies (repetitive pattern in dotted lines).

The cell of the second type corresponds to reactors moderated by heavy water (HWR). The moderator and the coolant are now separated by a pressure tube even when they are of the same nature. A greater splitting up of the fuel is now necessary, and therefore a bundle of fuel pencils is used instead of a single rod.

The last cell concerns high-temperature reactors moderated by graphite and cooled by helium. Here the coolant is not in contact with the fuel, so that the heat flows (by conduction) through the graphite before it is evacuated by the helium.

TABLE 5.3. Principal types of reactors.

Thermal reactors

Type	Fuel	Moderator	Coolant
LWR (Light Water Reactor)	UO_2 enriched in U^{235} (2 to 3%)	H_2O	
HWR (Heavy Water Reactor) CANDU	natural UO_2 (0.72% U^{235})	D_2O	D_2O
HTGR (High Temperature Gas cooled Reactor)	highly enriched UO_2 (93%) + Th 0_2 (fertile)	graphite	helium
MSR (Molten Salt Reactor)	uranium and thorium fluorides (molten salts)	graphite	fuel

Fast reactor (breeders)

Type	Fuel	Coolant
LMFBR (Liquid Metal Fast Breeder Reactor)	$PuO_2 + UO_2$	liquid sodium
GCFR (Gas Cooled Fast Reactor)	$PuO_2 + UO_2$	helium

We shall return later in more detail to these various types of reactors which, for the moment, we simply catalogue (Tab. 5.3).

Among currently operating reactors, light water reactors are very much at the head of the list. They are of two categories, depending on whether the water is maintained in a liquid state thanks to sufficient pressurization (PWR = Pressurized Water Reactor) or whether boiling is permitted (BWR = Boiling Water Reactor). In the latter case, the reactor becomes a steam generator. Some heavy water reactors (HWR) have been built (especially in Canada). LMFBR and HTGR reactors are in the prototype stage, and all the others only represent more or less advanced projects. We recall that the first generation of nuclear reactors developed in France and Great Britain made use of natural uranium and graphite. Although they attained commercial status, these types of reactors have been abandoned.

5.1.4 Neutronic Aspects

In spite of its restrictive hypotheses, the entire formalism of the preceding chapter can be kept provided we make the following modifications. Consider a cell of volume V and the three media of which it is formed: the fuel, the cladding and the moderator, of respective volumes V_c, V_g and V_m. If N_i is the atomic density of an element belonging to a medium (i) of volume V_i, the number of atoms per unit volume of the core will be $\bar{N}_i = N_i V_i / V$ and the corresponding macroscopic cross sections:

$$\left.\begin{aligned} \bar{\Sigma}_i &= \bar{N}_i \sigma_i = N_i \frac{V_i}{V} \sigma_i = \frac{V_i}{V} \Sigma_i \\ \bar{\Sigma} &= \sum_i \bar{N}_i \sigma_i = \sum_i \frac{V_i}{V} \Sigma_i \end{aligned}\right\} \qquad (5.1)$$

where Σ_i represents the usual macroscopic cross section for the material (i) (§1.5.5).

We thus obtain by weighting in volume the macroscopic cross sections $\bar{\Sigma}$ of the core for each of the envisaged processes (scattering, fission, etc.) In fact this procedure is not completely correct for thermal reactors, since in each cell the fluxes are low at the level of the fuel (cf. §4.3.6 or §8.2.4). With this reservation, the technique of homogenization (5.1) is applicable to all reactors.

Let us consider in this framework the simple case of a bare homogeneous thermal reactor. We have seen in subsec. 4.5.4 that a few parameters alone enable us to completely define such a system, that is: η_t, f_t, ε, p, L_t^2 and τ. In particular, f_t and p are given by equations (4.61) and (4.55), which we shall rewrite in the form:

$$\left.\begin{aligned} f_t &= \frac{\sigma_{a,c}}{\sigma_{a,c} + \frac{\bar{N}_g}{\bar{N}_c} \sigma_{a,g} + \frac{\bar{N}_m}{\bar{N}_c} \sigma_{a,m}} \\ p &= \exp\left[- \frac{I_{eff}(\sigma_e)}{\bar{\xi} \left(\sigma^*_{s,c} + \frac{\bar{N}_m}{\bar{N}_c} \sigma_m\right)} \right] \end{aligned}\right\} \qquad (5.2)$$

For given fuel rods (Ø and N_c known), the effective resonance integral

I_{eff} is completely determined by expressions (4.56) and (4.58). The resonance escape probability p is thus an increasing function of the moderating ratio:

$$\frac{\bar{N}_m}{\bar{N}_c} = \frac{N_m}{N_c}\frac{V_m}{V_c} \tag{5.3}$$

even if the integral I_{eff} increases slightly with the latter for very closely spaced lattices (§8.4.2).

On the other hand, the thermal utilization factor f_t, which is a function of absorption cross sections for thermal neutrons (5.2), decreases when the moderating ratio increases. The product p f_t then passes through a maximum. The same is true for the multiplication factors k_∞ (4.80) and k_e (4.82) with, however, a displacement of the maximum due to the fact that the diffusion and slowing down areas (L_t^2 and τ) depend also on the moderating ratio (cf. equations (4.22) and (4.78) to which are applied the homogenization rules (5.1)). Finally, for closely spaced lattices, the variation of the fast fission factor ε has a tendency to displace the maximum slightly towards smaller values of the moderating ratio, but whatever the case, the effective multiplication factor of thermal reactors will always have the form indicated in Fig. 5.4. The moderating ratio is thus the essential parameter (from the neutronic point of view) of this type of reactor. It is very sensitive to the lattice spacing (through V_m) and to the moderator density (through N_m) as is shown by its definition (5.3).

The conversion factor C can also be determined in the same framework (§3.3.2). According to the definitions of subsec. 3.3.3, we can write for thermal neutrons:

$$(\eta_c)_t = \bar{\nu}\left(\frac{N_1\sigma_{f,1}}{N_1\sigma_{a,1} + N_2\sigma_{a,2}}\right)_t = \eta_t\left(\frac{N_1\sigma_{a,1}}{N_1\sigma_{a,1} + N_2\sigma_{a,2}}\right)_t$$

where $(\eta_c)_t$ and η_t are the multiplication factors for the fuel and the fissile isotope considered (Tab. 3.8). We can deduce from this equality the quantity:

$$C_t = \left(\frac{N_2\sigma_{a,2}}{N_1\sigma_{a,1}}\right)_t = \left(\frac{\eta}{\eta_c}\right)_t - 1$$

which represents, since the two components of a fuel are submitted to the same fluxes, the ratio of neutron capture in the fertile matter to the absorption of neutrons in the fissile matter, or the number of artificial fissionable nuclei produced in the first for each nucleus destroyed in the second. The quantity C_t can thus be identified with the conversion factor relative to the phenomena which take place at thermal energy.

In the course of their slowing down, certain neutrons may also be absorbed by fertile nuclei (§4.4.5), whence a new contribution to the conversion. For each thermal neutron absorbed in the fissile matter, η_t fission neutrons are emitted (Tab. 3.8) and, after taking into account the fast fissions and escapes, $\eta_t \varepsilon P_r$ neutrons penetrate the zone of resonances (Fig. 4.22). By definition of the resonance escape probability p (4.55), a fraction (1 − p) disappears by capture in this zone, so that:

$$C_r = \eta_t \ \varepsilon P_r \ (1 - p)$$

represents the resonance contribution to the conversion factor, which can finally be written:

$$C = C_t + C_r = \left[\left(\frac{\eta}{\eta_c} \right)_t - 1 \right] + \eta_t \varepsilon \ (1 - p) \ \exp\ (- B^2 \tau) \qquad (5.4)$$

As can be seen in the appendix (§9.3.4), this result is identical to that which can be deduced by multigroup theory applied to this case.

The conversion factor only depends on the moderating ratio through the second term of (5.4). For a given enrichment (η_c fixed) we will always have to make a compromise between the highest possible conversion and an acceptable multiplication factor k_e (Fig. 5.4). In thermal reactors burning more or less enriched uranium, breeding cannot be attained, as we have already seen. All the same, for heavy water natural uranium reactors (maximum η/η_c), C can be of the order of 0.8, and the plutonium produced will have a considerable impact on the cost of the cycle. For light water reactors enriched at 3%, the conversion factor will never surpass 0.6, and from this point of view, these reactors are among the least satisfactory.

Let us return to Fig. 5.4. The multiplication factor k_e attains its maximum value for a moderating ratio which in turn depends on the moderator in question. The optimum volume ratio V_m/V_c is of the order of 4 for light water reactors, and of at least 10 for heavy water reactors, since the latter have a weaker slowing down power ($\xi\Sigma_s$). Light water lattices are thus very closely spaced and their corresponding cores are among the smallest.

For the same fuel, the maximum value of k_e is higher for heavy water lattices, these being not very absorbant, or, to put it another way, heavy water reactors allow for weaker enrichment (small η_c, Tab. 3.10), or even simply natural uranium.

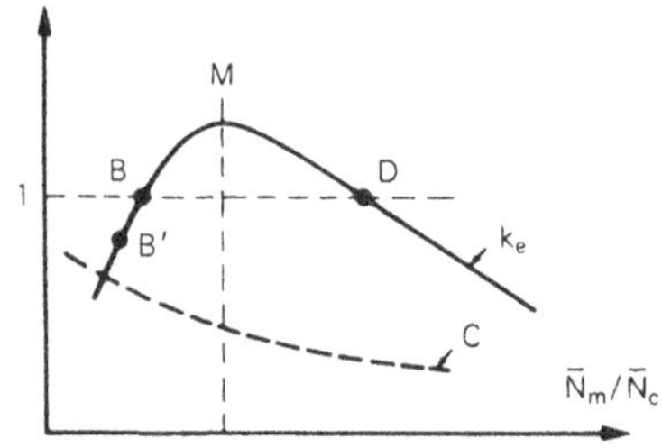

FIGURE 5.4. Influence of the moderating ratio on neutronic parameters.

In normal conditions, a reactor is in the critical state. In Fig. 5.4, the straight line $k_e = 1$ determines two operating points B and D. The first corresponds to an under-moderated lattice and the second to an over-moderated one. In the first case, useful resonance captures in the fuel overtake parasite captures in the moderator (small p, large f). In the second case, it is the opposite which occurs. The operating point B is thus preferable, since for the same neutron balance ($k_e = 1$) a better conversion factor is obtained (Fig. 5.4).

When the moderator acts in addition as coolant, a second reason works in favor of this choice. In fact, when a power excursion takes place, it causes the moderator density to drop (temperature increase or partial boiling), which is equivalent to a decrease of the moderating ratio ($N_m \searrow$ in expression (5.3)), the operating point passing from B to B' (Fig. 5.4). The reactor then becomes subcritical ($k_e < 1$), which is likely to bring the power back to its initial value. This stabilizing effect plays an important role from the safety point of view (Chap. 6). The same reasoning would show that point D corresponds to an unstable critical state. Point M, which is optimal from the point of view of neutronics, leads to the minimum critical mass (economy of fissile matter). In order to bring back the factor k_e to unity, it is necessary to diminish η_c and hence the enrichment. This economic advantage is not sufficient reason to give up the highly stabilizing effect just described. In any case, light water reactors always have an operating point of the B type, which corresponds in addition to a high power density. At this point B, the ratio of the moderating volume to the fuel volume (V_m/V_c) is of the order of 2 as against 4 at the optimum point M.

For fast reactors, the factor k_e decreases greatly if the moderating ratio increases. A decrease in the average energy of the neutrons entails a drop in the factor η (Fig. 3.9). Here f and p intervene only marginally.

5.1.5 Thermal Reactor Reflectors

Let us conclude this analysis with some considerations on reflectors. To be efficient, a reflector should absorb little and scatter a lot. In effect it is only the scattering process which permits a neutron to return to its starting point as long as it has not been absorbed during its journey. In addition, if neutrons are slowed by the reflector and return to the core in the thermal state, the reactivity is automatically improved. One thus demands the same qualities of reflectors as of moderators, and the same materials are often used. In light water reactors, for example, the peripheral cells (close to the vessel) are not provided with fuel, so that a radial water reflector appears automatically. In the same way axial reflectors result if the length of the fuel rods (active height) is less than the height of the water in the tank.

As an example, we shall return to the homogeneous spherical reactor (§4.5.3) this time surrounded by a reflector. One can show by applying mono-energetic diffusion theory to this system composed of two zones (see the method explained in subsec. 4.5.7)that the critical condition (4.68) remains approximately valid. For a given material buckling B_m^2 the quantity (R_c + d) is thus the same. The main difference comes from the fact that d is no longer the extrapolation distance (1 to 2 cm) but the reflector gain which is of the order of the diffusion length L (thick reflectors). It follows that the critical radius R_c of the core is smaller, and thus fissile matter is economized.

Finally we note that a reflector plays the role of a shield vis-a-vis fast neutrons coming from the core, not because it absorbs them, but rather that it slows them, thus rendering them less penetrating for the surrounding materials (vessel, concrete, etc.)

5.1.6 Advantages and Drawbacks of Enriched Uranium in Thermal Reactors

During the 1950's this question was paramount in the controversy over choice of reactor types, between supporters and opponents of enriched uranium. We will note the following significant points:

- A reactor can be operated with natural uranium in spite of the relatively low value of η_c (Tab. 3.10). One thus avoids having recourse to uranium enrichment techniques which are not within the reach of all countries. To succeed, it is necessary to use minimally absorbing materials (they are very few), which leads to the choice of graphite as moderator (the first Anglo-French assembly) or heavy water (the present Canadian assembly), and of magnesium or zirconium alloys as structural materials. Neutronic considerations are fundamental in this type of reactor.
- A very weak enrichment (2 to 3% instead of 0.72%) on the other hand purchases great flexibility in technological choices. Light water can be used as moderator and materials such as steel for cladding. Naturally, even with enriched uranium, it is highly desirable, though not imperative, to avoid parasite captures, and thus "zircalloy" is preferable to steel as a structural material in light water reactors.
- Another advantage of enriched uranium resides in the availability of strong initial reactivities, thanks to the high value of η_c (Tab. 3.10, for $x = 3\%$, $\eta_c = 1.83$ rather than 1.33 for natural uranium). There result higher radiation rates (three to four times that of natural uranium reactors), which make possible less frequent loading-unloading operations and a better use of the fuel. Reactors which burn natural uranium have, on the contrary, such small reactivity margins that they need to be continuously unloaded. This makes it necessary to have machines capable of intervening while the reactor is in operation.
- Enriched uranium allows less weight to be given to neutronic aspects. Since a good value of η_c is assured, certain sacrifices can

be allowed, for example, with regard to resonances (small p, (5.2)). The cell geometry (rod diameters, lattice spacing, etc.) is essentially fixed by thermohydraulic criteria (cf. the following section), whence a greater admissible power density (kW/1).

We see that enriched uranium has numerous advantages, at least on the technical side. The only drawback is the need for enrichment equipment (Chap. 7). The problem is much more a political than economic one, since the cost of isotopic separation is altogether reasonable when compared to the total cost of the fuel element. Political reasons which may lead certain countries to prefer the natural uranium option are evident. In effect, only a few major industrial powers today are equipped with isotopic separation plants, and in case of world crisis, third party countries which possess enriched uranium nuclear power plants may justly have some fear about receiving their fuel supply.

Manufacturing fuel elements based on natural uranium is on the other hand within the reach of most industrial countries. All these considerations explain in part why countries like France and Great Britain have in the past shown a certain reticence regarding light water reactors. For the same reasons, several third world countries are interested in the Canadian option, the only commercial assembly using natural uranium with heavy water as moderator.

5.2 THERMOHYDRAULICS OF THE CORE

5.2.1 Introduction

We know that reactor physics (Sec. 4.5) does not enable us to fix the flux levels and thus the power of a nuclear power plant. Technological limits (melting temperatures, thermal constraints, etc.) determine these levels and hence in particular the power density at the hot spot, that is, the point at which the materials are most in demand. Determining the thermohydraulic characteristics of the most charged cell (the one whose heat emission is the strongest) thus has considerable importance. Once the safety coefficient has been chosen, the specific power at the hot spot is fixed. Neutron calculations then enable us to know the true magnitude of all the distributions of interest: neutron fluxes, specific powers, etc.

5.2.2 Radial Distribution of Temperatures in the Fuel

The temperatures in the fuel are governed by the equation of thermal conduction. This equation follows, as we know, on the one hand from Fourier's law

$$\vec{\Psi}(\vec{r}) = -\lambda\ \vec{\text{grad}}\ T(\vec{r})$$

which gives the proportionality of the heat flux $\vec{\Psi}$ to the temperature gradient, on the other hand from the equation of thermal balance:

$$\text{div}\ \vec{\Psi} = \bar{\omega}_c$$

where $\bar{\omega}_c$ is the source density of heat in the considered medium (here the fuel) which is customarily expressed in W cm^{-3}.

Formally, the first equation is identical to Fick's law characterizing neutron diffusion (4.13), and the second to the equation of neutron conservation (4.12) which is shown in the same way ($\vec{J} \to \vec{\Psi}, \Phi \to T$, $D \to \lambda$ and $\Sigma_a = 0$). We have already mentioned this analogy (§4.3.1). However that may be, the combination of the preceding equations leads to the well-known equation of thermal conduction:

$$\lambda\ \nabla^2 T + \bar{\omega}_c = 0 \qquad (5.5)$$

valid for steady states.

In what follows, we shall limit ourselves to the most frequent case where the fuel elements are made up of cylindrical rods. These rods are sufficiently thin for the axial conduction to be negligible ($\partial T/\partial z = 0$). The heat thus flows radially. For this cylindrical geometry, the Laplacian takes the simple form (4.18), whence the equation:

$$\lambda \left[\frac{1}{r} \frac{d}{dr} \left(r \frac{dT}{dr} \right) \right] + \bar{\omega}_c = 0$$

Let us place ourselves at a point with cylindrical height z. The heat source density $\bar{\omega}_c$ is radially constant. The preceding equation is easily integrated:

$$\frac{d}{dr}\left(r \frac{dT}{dr} \right) = - \frac{\bar{\omega}_c r}{\lambda} \quad \text{whence:} \quad r \frac{dT}{dr} = - \frac{\bar{\omega}_c r^2}{2\lambda} + A$$

and finally:

$$T(r) = -\frac{\bar{\omega}_c r^2}{4\lambda} + A \ln r + B$$

For the full rods considered here, one cannot exclude the point $r = 0$ whence, in order to avoid a divergence on the axis, $A = 0$. Taking account of the temperature at the periphery of the rods (of radius $r = a$), we obtain the parabolic distribution:

$$\lambda[T(r) - T(a)] = \frac{\bar{\omega}_c}{4}(a^2 - r^2)$$

represented in Fig. 5.5. On the axis of the rod, the temperature will reach the maximum value T_0. Thus:

$$T_0 - T_g = \frac{\bar{\omega}_c a^2}{4\lambda} = \frac{\bar{\omega}_1}{4\pi\lambda} \tag{5.6}$$

where T_g, the cladding temperature, has been identified with the peripheral temperature $T(a)$. The power emitted per unit length, or <u>linear heat rate</u> $\bar{\omega}_1$, is expressed in W cm^{-1} and the <u>thermal conductivity</u> λ in W cm^{-1} $°C^{-1}$.

In fact, at the fuel-cladding interface the temperature drops, because the thermal contact is not perfect. Moreover, the cladding is not infinitely conducting, so that the approximation $T(a) = T_g$ is optimistic. In addition, because of the decrease of the neutron flux (§4.3.6), the heat sources $\bar{\omega}_c$ are not uniform in a section of a rod. They are slightly stronger at the periphery, which improves the exchanges for the same linear heat rate $\bar{\omega}_1$.

Let us pursue our study leaving aside these two fine points. In the adjacent coolant, we must use an entirely different law. For reasonable heat fluxes the law of convection can be written:

$$\Psi(a) = h(T_g - T_c) \tag{5.7}$$

where T_c represents the temperature of the coolant and h the convection (or transfer) coefficient expressed in W cm^{-2} $°C^{-1}$. For the envisaged powers one appeals to <u>forced convection</u>. The heat exchange coefficient h increases considerably if the fluid circulates parallel to the fuel elements. Pumps situated outside the reactor assure the necessary rate of flow (Sec. 5.4).

In steady state, the heat exchanged in a cell is equal to the heat produced. The energy balance per unit length of the rod can then be written:

$$2\pi \; a \; \Psi \; (a) = \bar{\omega}_1$$

whence, by considering equation (5.7):

$$T_g - T_c = \frac{\bar{\omega}_1}{2\pi \; a \; h} \tag{5.8}$$

For a well defined flow the preceding equations (5.8) and (5.6) furnish the temperatures of the cladding and the fuel starting from the coolant temperature (this should not be confused with the temperature of the film, cf. Fig. 5.5).

The coefficients of $\bar{\omega}_1$ in equations (5.6) and (5.8) are often called thermal resistances by analogy with Ohm's law (T → potential and $\bar{\omega}_1$ → current).

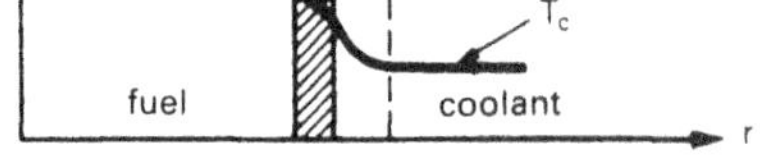

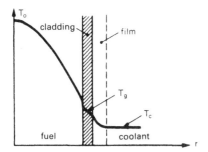

FIGURE 5.5. Radial distribution of temperatures in a fuel rod.

The preceding results depend of course on the height z through the linear heat rate, itself governed by neutron fluxes. Still, we can draw certain conclusions about the fuel without too much reference to the coolant in noting that the temperature of the former (at the center) is high compared with that of the latter. Thus equation (5.6) will be serving as a base for what follows. For greater accuracy, we should take note of the fact that the conductivities depend in general on the temperatures. One can show that equation (5.6) takes the new form:

$$I\,(T_0) = \int_{T_g}^{T_0} \lambda\,(T)\; d\,T = \frac{\bar{\omega}_1}{4\pi} \tag{5.9}$$

The lefthand side of this equation, the integral conductivity, only depends on the characteristics of the fuel and the temperature T_0 at the center of the rod. Each type of fuel has a corresponding temperature that should not be exceeded (its melting temperature, for example). This imposes a limit on the integral conductivity, since the temperature of the cladding T_g is approximately known and is small compared to T_0. Such a limit can also result from taking into account the thermal stresses which are functions of temperature gradients. For all these reasons, we are led, after choosing a safety coefficient, to fix the acceptable limit of the integral conductivity. The latter, much more than the temperatures, measures the performances of a fuel, since it gives directly the maximum authorized linear heat rate $\bar{\omega}_1$ at the hot spot and thus the power level of the reactor. Here we have a first technological constraint which is very simply expressed since the geometry of the fuel rod does not intervene (5.9).

We note that two fuels which differ in melting temperature and thermal conductivity can have the same permissible integral conductivity I_M; they are thus equivalent for the nuclear engineer.

For a given type of rod, the specific power (§4.2.2, equation (4.9)) is directly related to the integral conductivity :

$$\bar{\omega}_{sp}\;(W/g) = \frac{\bar{\omega}_c}{\rho_c} = \frac{\bar{\omega}_1}{\pi a^2\;\rho_c} = \frac{4\;I}{a^2\rho_c} \tag{5.10}$$

where ρ_c is the mass density of the fuel. This specific power often crops up in nuclear reactor catalogues. In fact it only characterizes the fuel. It should not be confused with the power density (kW/l) where the unit of volume is related to the core. It provides a first indication of the minimum quantity of fuel to be envisaged to achieve a total power P_t, taking account of the preceding limitations (§5.2.5).

Let us give as an example the characteristics of mixed fuels (uranium plus plutonium) envisaged for breeder reactors. Tab. 5.6 gives the data enabling us to evaluate the limiting integral conductivity $I_M = \bar{\lambda}(T_f - T_g)$ corresponding to fuel melting on the rod axis ($T_0 = T_f$). The indicated values are relative to an arbitrary cladding temperature, $T_g = 480°C$. All the same, for the sake of safety it is best to choose the maximum value envisageable for this temperature. Taking $T_g = 620°C$, a reasonable limiting value for stainless steel cladding (§5.4.5), the conductivity integrals I_M decrease by only 7%, which shows their intrinsic nature. This decrease is in any case negligible compared with the uncertainties which lead us to choose much wider safety margins. Thus the linear heat rate corresponding to the limit I_M (5.9) is established at 690 W cm^{-1} for uranium oxide (last col. of Tab. 5.6), whereas the authorized value in most reactors hardly exceeds 450 W cm^{-1}.

TABLE 5.6. Thermal characteristics of uranium oxides and carbides.

Fuels	T_f (°C)	$\bar{\lambda}$ (Wcm^{-1} $°C^{-1}$)	I_M (Wcm^{-1})	$\bar{\omega}_l = 4\pi I_M$
Oxides	2700	0.025	55	690
Carbides	2400	0.17	330	4100

Thanks to their greater conductivity and a melting temperature of the same order, the carbides permit much higher linear heat rates (Tab. 5.6), but they cannot be considered for water reactors for reasons of chemical compatibility. Great hopes, however, are placed on them for breeder reactors.

Metallic uranium possesses a very high conductivity, but in spite of it, the acceptable integral conductivity is quite small. It is in fact fixed not by the melting temperature, but by a phase transition which takes place in the vicinity of 660 °C.

At the present time, all reactor assemblies use uranium oxide UO_2, by itself in thermal reactors, and mixed with plutonium oxide PuO_2 in breeders.

5.2.3 Axial Temperature Distributions

Limits on power levels may also be placed by the cladding materials. Thus it is important to know the axial distributions of the temperatures, first in the coolant, and then in the cladding. Let us again consider the most charged cell; the coolant which laps the exchange surface evacuates the thermal energy liberated in the fuel.

Given a slice dz at height z, the transmitted thermal power $\bar{\omega}_1(z)dz$, in a steady state, brings about the increase of the enthalpy $d\mathcal{H}$ of the coolant. The first law of thermodynamics can then be written:

$$\mathcal{W}\, d\mathcal{H} = \bar{\omega}_1 (z)\, dz$$

where $\mathcal{W}$ represents the mass flow rate. The preceding equality is based on the hypothesis that the kinetic energy per unit mass of the fluid is a constant of the flow. This supposes, since the passage cross section is generally the same on the entire active height of the core, that the mass density of the coolant does not vary too much.

We restrict ourselves to the simple case of one-phase flows (gas or pressurized water reactors). The enthalpy variation can be simply written:

$$d\mathcal{H} = C_p\, d\, T_c$$

where C_p is the specific heat at constant pressure and $T_c(z)$ the temperature of the coolant at the height z.

This last equation is only strictly valid for perfect gases. Nonetheless, in real cases it constitutes a good approximation, since the pressure variations are small compared to the temperature variations (one can put dp = 0 in the general expression of the enthalpy differential). However, when it comes to designing the circulation pumps, it becomes essential to take into account the pressure drop in the core. Our hypotheses thus amount to decoupling the problems of heat exchange from the classical problems of hydraulics.

To remain consistent with the previous subsection, we shall express the flow rates $\mathcal{W}$ in g s^{-1}, the enthalpies in J g^{-1}, linear heat rates $\bar{\omega}_1$ in W cm^{-1} and the lengths z in cm.

We are thus led to solve the equation:

$$\mathcal{W}\, C_p \frac{d\, T_c}{dz} = \bar{\omega}_1 (z) \qquad (5.11)$$

In what follows we shall assume that the thermodynamic characteristics of the coolant (C_p, ρ, etc.) do not depend on the temperature; in this way the problem posed can be solved by analytical methods. (More precise calculations, necessarily of a numerical nature, enable us to free ourselves of this restriction as well as the simplifying hypotheses adopted at the beginning of this section.) Very frequently the axial distributions of the neutron flux are well represented by a cosine (§4.5.3). For a given fuel element, the same is true of the linear heat rate, which can be written:

$$\bar{\omega}_1(z) = \bar{\omega}_1(0) \cos \left(\frac{\pi z}{H + 2d} \right) \tag{5.12}$$

where the height z = 0 is taken in the median plane of the reactor and d designates the extrapolation distance (d<< H).

The coolant enters the core at height z = −(H/2) with temperature T_e and goes out at height z = +(H/2) with temperature T_s. Taking account of (5.12), the integration of equation (5.11) furnishes the distribution:

$$T_c(z) = T_c(0) + \frac{\bar{\omega}_1(0)}{\mathscr{W} C_p} \frac{H + 2d}{\pi} \sin \left(\frac{\pi z}{H + 2d} \right) \tag{5.13}$$

The coolant temperature is highest at its outlet from the core as indicated in Fig. 5.7. This temperature is obtained by integrating equation (5.11) over the entire active height:

$$\mathscr{W} C_p (T_s - T_e) = \int_{-\frac{H}{2}}^{+\frac{H}{2}} \bar{\omega}_1(z)\, dz = P_t \tag{5.14}$$

where P_t is the thermal power liberated in the cell.

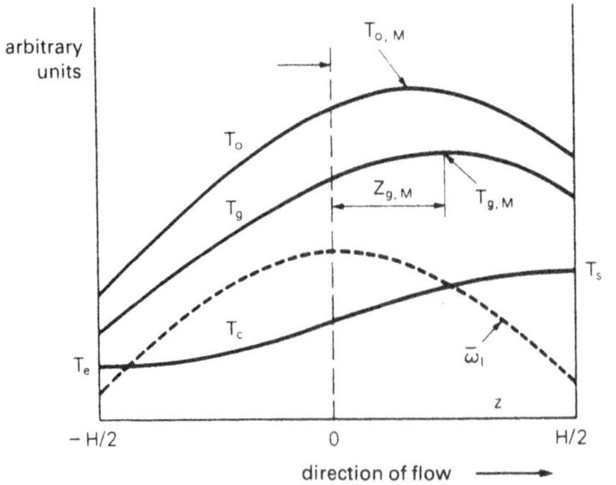

FIGURE 5.7. Axial distributions: $\bar{\omega}_1$ linear heat rate; T_c,T_g,T_0 temperatures of the coolant, cladding and fuel on the axis of the rod.

Provided we consider the total flow rate traversing the core, the preceding equation also furnishes the global thermal power of the reactor. The thermodynamic measure of the power is based on this important relation.

Knowing the function $T_c(z)$ (5.13), we can easily pass to the temperatures of the cladding and the fuel by using equations (5.6) and (5.8) and replacing $\bar{\omega}_1(z)$ by its value (5.12):

$$\left.\begin{aligned} T_g(z) &= \frac{\bar{\omega}_1(0)}{2\pi\ a\ h} \cos\left(\frac{\pi z}{H + 2d}\right) + T_c(z) \\ T_0(z) &= \left[\frac{1}{4\pi\ \bar{\lambda}} + \frac{1}{2\pi\ a\ h}\right] \bar{\omega}_1(0) \cos\left(\frac{\pi z}{H + 2d}\right) + T_c(z) \end{aligned}\right\} \qquad (5.15)$$

The corresponding axial distributions are shown in Fig. 5.7. They show a maximum not far from the median plane ($z = 0$). It is at this point, which corresponds to the hot point, that we must analyze the behavior of the various materials. We have already considered the fuel, and now it remains to consider the cladding. The temperatures are much lower than those of the fuel, but so are the permitted limits. Zircalloy, an alloy of zirconium containing at most 1.7% tin and 0.2% iron, used in water-cooled reactors, has a high melting temperature (≅ 1850 °C), but starting at around 400 °C, one can begin to fear a chemical reaction with uranium oxide. This, and such other considerations as the loss of coolant accident (§6.4.4), lead to the choice of maximum temperature of the order of 350 °C.

The foregoing results show that, for a given flow rate $\mathscr{W}$ and inlet temperature T_e, and thus for an approximately known heat exchange coefficient h, the temperature distributions only depend on the maximum linear heat rate $\bar{\omega}_1(0)$. This latter is thus fixed, as is the outlet temperature T_s of the coolant, as soon as one has given a maximum cladding temperature $T_{g,M}$. We have thus arrived at the second technological constraint capable of limiting the power of a reactor.

It is possible to pursue analytical calculations in this framework, and find an explicit relation connecting $T_{g,M}$, T_e and $\bar{\omega}_1(0)$. In practice, in order to take account more accurately of the physical phenomena (nonlinearity of the equations) and of the axial power distributions which are not exactly of the type (5.12), we have to make use of a purely numerical approach to obtain the temperature distributions of Fig. 5.7. In this case, we can only satisfy the condition $T_g(z_M) = T_{g,M}$ by iterating on $\bar{\omega}_1(0)$ for each value of $\mathscr{W}$ or of T_e, which is essentially the preceding method.

This new technological constraint nevertheless offers more flexibility for making choices than the preceding one (§5.2.2). At fixed $T_{g,M}$ we can for example increase to some extent $\bar{\omega}_1(0)$ provided we reduce the inlet temperature T_e. This amounts to increasing the reactor power but at the same time diminishing its thermodynamic output. The optimal choice can only result from technico-economic considerations related to the power station as a whole.

In order to give a few details, let us see how the principal thermohydraulic parameters intervene in an optimization study. From the economic point of view, it is necessary to have a power density $\bar{\omega}_d$(kW/l) as high as possible, since for a given thermal power of the reactor, the volume of the core will then be smaller, which is cost favorable. By definition, the power density can be written:

$$\bar{\omega}_d(\text{kW/l}) = \frac{\bar{\omega}_1(\text{W/cm})}{V(\text{cm}^2)}$$

where V is the cross section of a fuel cell (§5.1.4).

Let us again take up the simple formalism of the beginning of this section. Applied at the hot spot of the cladding, equation (5.15) becomes:

$$T_{g,M} = T_g(z_M) \cong \frac{\bar{\omega}_1(0)}{2\pi\ a\ h} + T_s$$

since at this height we have approximately $T_c(z_M) \cong T_s$. By combining the last two relations we obtain:

$$T_{g,M} \cong \frac{V}{2\pi\ a\ h} \cdot \bar{\omega}_d + T_s \qquad (5.16)$$

Since the maximum cladding temperature $T_{g,M}$ is fixed (second technological constraint), we see that the coefficient $V/2\pi a\ h$ must be as small as possible in order to permit a large power density $\bar{\omega}_d$ assuring at the same time a sufficiently high outlet temperature. The outlet temperature is in effect the most important parameter in the evaluation of the output of the thermodynamic cycle.

For one-phase flows, various empirical formulae enable us to evaluate the forced convection coefficient h. For water, Colburn's formula is often used:

$$h = 0.02 \frac{\lambda}{D_H} \left(\frac{G\,D_H}{\mu} \right)^{0.8} \left(\frac{C_p \mu}{\lambda} \right)^{0.4}$$

where the two dimensionless quantities which appear in this formula are respectively the Reynolds and Prandtl numbers.

For a given fluid, the conductivity λ, the viscosity μ, and the specific heat C_p are known. Hence the exchange coefficient only depends on the unit mass flow rate G and on the hydraulic diameter D_H. Let us consider a PWR reactor. For a square cell $D_H = 4\ V_m/2\pi a$, since the passage cross section of the fluid is the same as that of the moderator (§5.1.4) and the wetted perimeter is $2\pi a$. Introducing the massive flow rate, $\mathscr{W} = V_m \cdot G$, we see that h behaves like: $a^{0.2}\mathscr{W}^{0.8}/V_m$ and the coefficient $V/2\pi ah$ of equation (5.16) behaves like:

$$\frac{V_m\,(V_m + \pi a^2)}{a^{1.2}\mathscr{W}^{0.8}}$$

We see the advantage of choosing a small passage cross section V_m, but various restrictions appear. First of all, significant under-moderation (§5.1.4) leads to a loss of reactivity. This is not too serious. In fact, the purpose of enriched uranium is to allow for such an under-moderation. Next, a decrease of the passage cross section and hence of the hydraulic diameter D_H brings about much greater pressure drops. Thus, what is gained in power density or in the outlet temperature risks being lost in pumping power. We arrive at the same conclusions when we consider an increase in the flow rate $\mathscr{W}$. The coefficient of equation (5.16) decreases as desired and moreover, for the same power, the inlet temperature T_e approaches the outlet temperature T_s (5.14) thus improving the thermodynamic output of the installation. But here the pumping power increases very rapidly (like $\mathscr{W}^3$). We cannot define the optimum without taking account of economic considerations as well as reactor safety.

When we have defined all the parameters for a chosen cladding temperature, we must then verify that the maximum linear heat rate $\bar{\omega}_1(0)$ does not exceed the value $4\pi I_M$ (5.9) fixed by the fuel; this condition is generally satisfied. If it is not, then the entire optimization must be redone by taking I_M as a given and not $T_{g,M}$.

In fact, certain phenomena which take place in the film give rise to a better exchange coefficient (see the following section). In spite of that, the outlet temperatures of light water reactors barely exceed 320 °C for power densities of the order of 50 to 100 kW/l depending on the reactor type.

For fast breeder reactors, the use of liquid metals as coolants, and especially the adoption of stainless steel as cladding material, leads to better performances: $T_S \cong 560°C$, $\bar{\omega}_d \cong 580$ kW/l.

5.2.4 Critical Heat Flux

In the previous section we saw that the heat exchanges at the cladding-coolant interface followed the law of convection (5.7); in other words, the heat flux Ψ was a linear function of the cladding temperature T_g for a well-defined temperature T_c of the cooling fluid (outside the film). For liquid coolants and high cladding temperatures, this law ceases to be valid and the heat flux becomes a complicated function of the cladding temperature as shown in Fig. 5.8. Even if the cooling fluid remains liquid ($T_c < T_{sat}$), complex phenomena take place in the film [17]. If the cladding attains a high enough temperature, vapor bubbles form on its surface and, helped by the turbulence of the flow, they migrate toward the coolant. Then there are two possibilities. Either these bubbles recondense when the coolant temperature T_c is lower than the saturation temperature T_{Sat} (PWR reactors) or, in the opposite case, they take part in the production of steam (BWR reactors). In both cases, this phenomenon of nucleate boiling considerably improves the heat exchanges, since the heat flux Ψ varies like $(T_g - T_{sat})^4$.

Let us analyze Fig. 5.8, which represents the variation of Ψ as a function of the temperature difference $\Delta T = T_g - T_{sat}$ in the domain $T_g \geqq T_{sat}$. The first region corresponds to classical convection without change of phase in the film, although the cladding temperature exceeds T_{sat}. The convection coefficient h is well defined (§5.2.3) but depends on the flow rate, which gives rise to the set of curves represented (AB). We note that for $\Delta T = 0$ the heat flux takes the value $h(T_{sat} - T_c) \neq 0$.

The second region (segment BC) is related to the nucleate boiling described above and is characterized by a very rapid increase of Ψ . Beyond the point C which corresponds to the critical heat flux, we see the progressive formation of a vapor film. Vapor, like gases, has a low thermal conductivity resulting in poor heat exchanges. When the vapor film has been completely formed (point D), its heat transfer coefficient attains its minimum value and subsequently the heat flux increases with the cladding temperature. The heat is now only evacuated by conduction and thermal radiation via the vapor, which leads to the observed high temperatures.

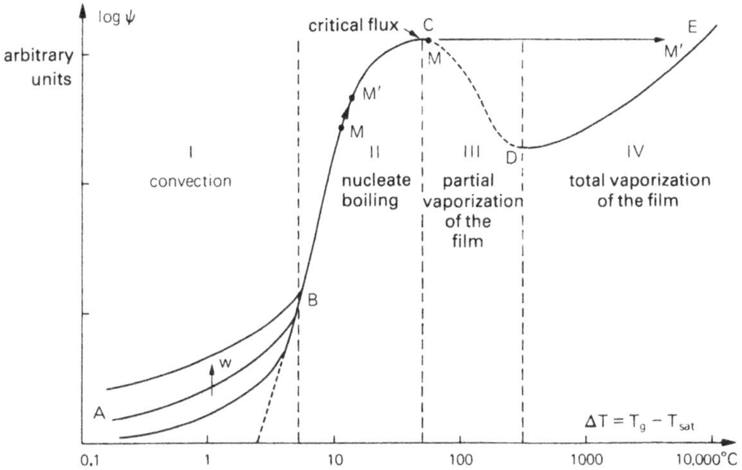

FIGURE 5.8. Variations of the heat flux Ψ as a function of cladding temperatures T_g.

A careful examination of this diagram reveals a problem of stability. Let us consider an operating point M situated to the left of point C. An increase of the linear heat rate of the rod from $\bar{\omega}_1$ to $\bar{\omega}'_1$ entails an increase of the fuel temperature and then, via conduction, that of the cladding. According to Fig. 5.8 there results an increase in the heat flux from Ψ to Ψ' which leads to a new equilibrium state (M') characterized by the relation: $\bar{\omega}'_1 = 2\pi a \Psi'$. If we employ the same reasoning at a point situated slightly to the right of C, the increase of the cladding temperature now entails a decrease of the heat flux and the distance between $\bar{\omega}_1$ and $2\pi a\Psi$ increases more and more rapidly. No stable equilibrium point is possible between C and D (the third zone). The system evolves towards the point E, but the latter corresponds to such high temperatures that fuel and cladding will have melted before this point is reached.

At no point of the reactor should the critical heat flux be exceeded and this constitutes the third technological constraint. Reactors are designed in such a way that the maximum heat flux remains well below the critical heat flux, so that power fluctuations will cause no damage. The phenomena that appear at point C are sometimes termed "boiling crises". We also designate the critical flux as calefaction flux. This expression evokes the phenomenon which occurs when water droplets are thrown on a very hot plate. They remain liquid for some time, since they are thermally isolated by a small cushion of vapor which carries them and assures them a certain mobility.

The determination of the critical heat flux is crucial in planning studies. Unfortunately, precise formulae for calculating it do not exist. Hence the choice of a safety coefficient becomes necessary. On the other hand, one should not deviate too far from the critical heat flux, at the risk of losing the benefits of nucleate boiling. Among the favorable parameters we should mention the flow rate, and, when the coolant remains liquid, the temperature difference $T_{sat} - T_c$. It should be noted that a boiling crisis may occur even in the absence of large-scale boiling of the coolant. PWR reactors can thus also become victims of this phenomenon.

To conclude, we have represented in Fig. 5.9 the different types of flows that can be encountered in an externally heated channel [18]. This simulates very well what happens in a LWR reactor cell. In the lower part, the cooling fluid is liquid, this being the condition of PWR reactors and partially that of BWR reactors at the coolant inlet. The fluid gets progressively heated and when it has reached its saturation temperature T_{sat}, large-scale boiling begins with homogeneous distribution of vapor bubbles. When the proportion of steam becomes large an annular flow is formed. These three states, although different with regard to the coolant, display the same type of heat transfer based on nucleate boiling. At all levels the cladding temperature is higher than the saturation temperature, but the boiling crisis never takes place since the heat flux is always less than its critical value.

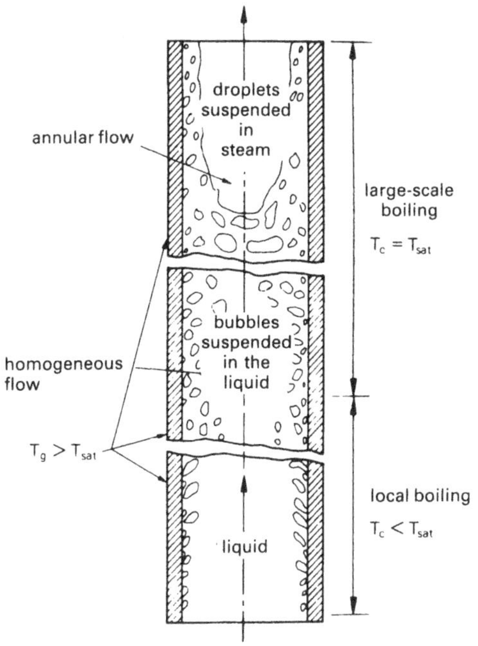

FIGURE 5.9. Various flow states in an externally heated channel.

5.2.5 Reactor Performances

In brief, the conductivity integral of the fuel, the maximum cladding temperature, and the critical heat flux determine the power levels which must not be exceeded. For a reactor to be well designed, these three technological constraints must be taken into account as far as possible, otherwise one might have, for example, poor cladding along with excellent fuel.

Having chosen a permissible linear heat rate according to the previous criteria, as well as the diameter of the fuel elements, the allowed maximum specific power $\bar{\omega}_M$ is then defined by equation (5.10). Starting from this, one can determine all the characteristics of the reactor by making use of the results of neutronic studies. For example, let us give ourselves $\bar{\omega}_{sp}(\vec{r})$, the specific power at a point of the reactor. If the fuel elements only differ from one another by their isotopic composition (ρ_c = const.), this quantity is simply proportional to the fission rate $R_f(\vec{r})$ at this point (4.9). It can thus be written:

$$\bar{\omega}_{sp}(\vec{r}) = \bar{\omega}_M \, f_p(\vec{r}) \tag{5.17}$$

with

$$f_p(\vec{r}) = \frac{R_f(\vec{r})}{R_f(\vec{r}_M)} \tag{5.18}$$

where r_M determines the position of the maximum of $R_f(\vec{r})$ to which corresponds the specific power $\bar{\omega}_M$ defined above. Neutronic calculations only furnish the flux and hence the fission rates up to a multiplicative factor, but they enable us to determine without ambiguity $\vec{r}_M$ as well as the <u>form factor</u> $f_p(\vec{r})$.

If thermohydraulic calculations are performed at each point of the core, we can then determine starting from (5.17) the cladding temperature of each fuel element as well as the corresponding coolant temperature (§5.2.3). Since by definition $f_p(\vec{r}) < 1$, these temperatures are lower than those that prevail in the most highly charged cell ($\vec{r} = \vec{r}_M$).

When the fuel elements are hydraulically independent (reactors with pressure tubes (§5.1.3)), the flow rates per channel can be regulated in such a way as to render uniform the outlet temperatures of the coolant. By using diaphragms one can thus diminish the flow rates in the least-charged cells ($\bar{\omega}_{sp} < \bar{\omega}_M$) which otherwise would have unnecessarily low temperatures.

In thermal reactors the fissions are essentially induced by thermal neutrons, and hence the form factor can be written:

$$f_p(\vec{r}) = \frac{\Sigma_{f,c}(\vec{r})\Phi_t(\vec{r})}{\Sigma_{f,c}(\vec{r}_M)\Phi_t(\vec{r}_M)} \tag{5.19}$$

where the macroscopic fission cross section $\Sigma_{f,c}$ can depend on the considered point through the isotopic composition of the fuel (reactors with several zones).

In the framework of more elaborate theories, such as the multigroup theory (§4.5.8), the form factors as well as the true values of the neutron spectra (necessary for shielding calculations) are obtained by an analogous procedure(§9.1.5).

In particular one can deduce from the preceding the thermal power of the reactor, given the technological constraints. Let $\bar{\rho}_c(\vec{r})$ be the <u>fuel</u>

mass per unit volume of the core, the reactor power can be obtained by integrating the specific powers:

$$P_t = \int_{core} \bar{\omega}_{sp}(\vec{r})\bar{\rho}_c(\vec{r})\ dV$$

while the total mass of the fuel can be simply written:

$$M_c = \int_{core} \bar{\rho}_c(\vec{r})\ dV$$

It is of interest to display in the expression for the power the permitted value $\bar{\omega}_M$ of the specific power. Following (5.17), let:

$$P_t = \bar{\omega}_M\ M_c\ \alpha_p \qquad (5.20)$$

with:

$$\alpha_p = \frac{\int_{core} \bar{\rho}_c(\vec{r})f_p(\vec{r})\ dV}{\int_{core} \bar{\rho}_c(\vec{r})\ dV} \qquad (5.21)$$

All the neutronic information is concentrated in the flattening coefficient α_p, but it is tacitly assumed in the preceding that the distribution and the composition of the fuel as well as all the geometrical characteristics of the reactor satisfy the critical condition.

When the fuel is uniformly distributed (regular lattices) the coefficient α_p can be identified with the volume average of the form factor $f_p(\vec{r})$ as indicated by expression (5.21) in which $\bar{\rho}_c$ is constant.

Equation (5.20) clearly shows how to increase the reactor power for a given fuel mass, or, in other words, how to increase the average specific power: $\langle\bar{\omega}_{sp}\rangle = P_t/M_c$. There are only two possible solutions: either we increase the maximum specific power $\bar{\omega}_M$ or we improve the flattening coefficient α_p.

For a fixed conductivity integral, we can only increase $\bar{\omega}_M$ by decreasing the diameter of the fuel rods (5.10), but these become fragile if they are too thin (not to mention the neutronic aspects relative to resonance integrals (§4.4.5)). Only the fast reactors use the thinnest rods (in this case called pins) and their diameter is never much smaller than 6 mm (§5.4.5). Short of finding new materials, which at present seems improbable, there is no question of increasing the linear power $\bar{\omega}_1$, a fundamental technological constraint, as we know.

We shall spend more time on the flattening coefficient α_p. Here the possibilities are greater, but because of its very definition this coefficient cannot be greatly increased. It can attain unity (its maximum value) only if the form factor $f_p(\vec{r})$ does the same (5.21), which is impossible in practice.

Let us consider the case of thermal reactors to which expression (5.19) can be applied. We see that the variations of the form factor are at first related to those of the thermal flux $\Phi_t(\vec{r})$.

In a homogeneous reactor equipped with a reflector, the radial distribution of the flux has the shape indicated in Fig. 5.10 (curve #1), where R is the radius of the core and d the reflector gain (§5.1.5) (or the extrapolation distance when there is no reflector). For a spherical reactor, expression (4.70) leads effectively to a curve of this type. Whatever the geometry considered, the hot spot is situated at the center and the neutronic flux decreases rapidly with r as does the form factor f_p which is proportional to it. It follows that the flattening coefficient is quite small, especially for spherical and cylindrical geometries, for which the volume elements dV ($2\pi r\ dr$ and $4\pi r^2\ dr$) give greater importance to the peripheral zones where the form factor is minimum (5.21). One can show for example, with the help of expressions (4.70) and (4.73) that in the absence of a reflector ($d \cong 0$), the flattening coefficient α_p takes the values $3/\pi^2$ or $2/\pi$, depending on whether a spherical or a slab reactor is being considered.

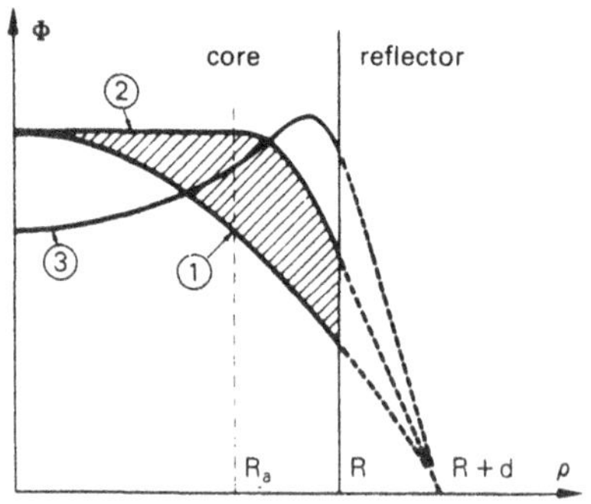

FIGURE 5.10. Neutron flux flattening.

We can thus understand the interest of "flattening" flux distributions. In the physics of thermal reactors, the material buckling B_m^2 plays as we know a major role (§4.5.7). If this parameter increases with the distance to the center in a reasonable way (the reactor is no longer homogeneous), we can achieve much more favorable flux distributions. This is indicated in curve #2 of Fig. 5.10, which corresponds to an ideal flattening of the flux in the zone $\rho \leqq R_a$. Too large an increase of the material buckling would lead to curve #3, which is less favorable. We can achieve ideal flattening in a two-zone system by making the material buckling vanish in the central zone of radius R_a (Fig. 5.10), that is, by making its multiplication factor k_∞ (4.83) equal to unity.

In order to understand this procedure, let us consider a spherical reactor whose central and peripheral zones are characterized respectively by the material bucklings $B_{m1}^2 = 0$ and $B_{m2}^2 > 0$. We will leave to the reader the task of showing, by making use of equations (4.85) and the reasoning of section 4.5.3, that the flux distributions are given by the expressions:

$$\left.\begin{array}{lll} \Phi(\rho) = \Phi(0) & & \rho \leqq R_a \\ \Phi(\rho) = \Phi(0)\,\dfrac{R_a \sin B_{m2}(R + d - \rho)}{\rho \sin B_{m2}(R + d - R_a)} & & R_a \leqq \rho \leqq R \end{array}\right\} \quad (5.22)$$

where R_a the flattening radius is the common boundary of the two zones. This distribution is in accordance with curve #2 (Fig. 5.10) and the critical condition would be obtained by making $d\Phi/d\rho$ vanish at the point $\rho = R_a$ (continuity of currents, cf. §4.5.7). One can show that the value of B_{m2}^2 which satisfies this condition is greater than the corresponding value of the homogeneous core of the same radius R, in fact, $B_m^2 = [\pi/(R+d)]^2$ (4.69). This inequality becomes more striking as the flattening radius increases, whence the completely general conclusion: to achieve a uniform flux distribution in a large central zone requires a material buckling in the peripheral zone which is correspondingly higher as the latter zone is narrower.

It remains to see how to achieve the preceding conditions in practice. The three best methods are the following:

- When the fuel composition cannot be changed (natural uranium), we play with the lattice pitch ($\bar{\rho}_c$ variable). In the first-generation graphite-moderated reactors, the peripheral zone had an optimal moderating ratio, whereas the central zone was under-moderated (§5.1.4).

- In light water reactors, the moderating ratio is more or less fixed, but one has the possibility of using different enrichments in different zones, since in any case the uranium must pass through enrichment plants (Ch. 7). The richest fuel occupies the peripheral positions. This method is the most flexible since one is dealing with the most sensitive parameter of the reactor (η_c).
- Finally, one can use certain refuelling modes to advantage. This procedure is similar to the preceding since a highly irradiated enriched element may have the same fissile matter content as a new weakly enriched element (§5.3.7).

We note that in all cases a good flattening pays off in terms of reactivity, that is, in the quantity of fissile matter needed. Only global economic considerations together with the constraints related to the running of a power plant enable us to make the final choices.

5.3 CONTROL

5.3.1 Introduction

Reactor control comprises all the measures which must be taken to keep the reactor critical even though its reactivity in the absence of external intervention is essentially decreasing (§5.3.2/3/4). The standard methods of control make use of poisons which are additional neutron absorbers, as well as particular modes of refuelling (§5.3.7/8).

When it is no longer possible to keep a reactor critical, all the poisons having been withdrawn, all that remains is to renew the fuel which has become too depleted. Conversely, just after a fresh fuel charge and before the power rises, the core has a large reactivity which must necessarily be compensated by the introduction of these poisons. It is this margin of initial reactivity which leads to the design of automatic control mechanisms (absorbing rods, soluble poisons, etc.)

Compensation for variations in reactivity is not the only goal of reactor control. It must also permit the monitoring and regulation of power levels and automatic shutdown in case of accident (§5.3.9).

5.3.2 Reactivity Variations

Variations of the multiplication factor k_e and hence of the reactivity ρ (4.109) can be grouped in two categories depending on whether the causes are external or internal.

External causes. Modification of the position of control rods or of the soluble poison concentration (water-moderated reactors). These actions are set off by the operator (or by electronic systems). Also under this heading are the variations of reactivity due to refuelling during reactor operation (natural uranium reactors).

Internal causes. Modifications intrinsic to the reactor: called reactivity response or feedback. The responsible physical quantities are:

- The various temperatures: fuel, moderator or coolant. In the first case the time constant is a few seconds, and in the second, it can attain several minutes (graphite-moderated reactors, for example).
- Bubble formation in the moderator; this phenomenon particularly concerns BWR reactors, but one may be led to consider it in other reactors in order to analyze certain types of accidents. The time constant is of the order of a second.
- Xenon and samarium poisoning: xenon and samarium are two fission products which are neutron absorbers. They appear during the power buildup and their concentration in the fuel thereafter remains more or less stable. The time constants are of the order of a few hours to a few days.
- The burnup rate (its precise definition is given in §5.3.6): in the course of irradiation, the initial fissile materials partly disappear and others (plutonium) appear in the fertile materials (conversion); the fission products accumulate. The time to consider is of the order of several months.

The time constants mentioned above must be seen as the order of magnitude of time necessary for the effect of the power modification to be felt on the considered quantity. A small variation of the latter, on the other hand, has an instantaneous effect on reactivity. Of the four points above, the last is the most important, since it concerns the residence time of the fuel elements in the reactor and thus the energy to be expected from a metric ton of fuel. Before making a detailed analysis of this long-term evolution of the fuel, we will take up the first three points and give a qualitative description of the physical phenomena which explain these responses.

5.3.3 Short and Intermediate Term Effects

The fuel temperature influences the reactivity essentially through the Doppler effect. The thermal agitation of the nuclei, which was ignored in the study of neutrons slowing down, plays an important role at the level of resonances (§4.4.5). In effect, the relative width of the resonances $\Delta E/E$ is so small that during a collision one can no longer equate the relative and absolute velocities of an incident neutron, although they are extremely close, whence the expression "Doppler effect" by analogy to optics. The appendix provides some information on this effect, which leads to a broadening of the resonances (Doppler broadening) (if one continues to define the neutron energies with respect to a fixed frame). It follows from this mechanism that the effective resonance integrals increase with temperature, and the weaker the dilution the more rapid is this increase (§9.4.1). Finally, since the notion of resonance integrals particularly concerns the fertile isotopes which degrade the neutron balance by their capture, we deduce that the resonance escape probability p (4.55) and hence the reactivity (4.109) decrease as the temperature increases.

The moderator temperature (or that of the coolant if there is no separation of functions) acts in a much more complicated way on the reactivity. First, a temperature increase shifts towards the right the Maxwell distributions representative of thermal neutrons (§4.5.5). Since at low energies the absorption and fission cross sections vary as $1/\sqrt{E}$ (§9.4.1) the decrease of these quantities entails an increase of the diffusion area (4.22) and hence of leakage. From this point of view, the reactivity decreases. According to the same hypotheses the fuel multiplication factor η_c should not be affected, since it only depends on the ratios of cross sections (3.6). In fact, however, there is a slight deviation from the simple law $\sigma_a = K/\sqrt{E}$ and this deviation is not the same for the fission and capture processes. We find for example that η_c decreases with the temperature for natural uranium, but that the appearance of plutonium in the course of irradiation can reverse this tendency, since this fissile nucleus has a broad resonance at 0.3 eV. Heating the moderator amounts to displacing the distribution of thermal neutrons towards this resonance and hence to favorising fissions, and thus to increased reactivity.

Thermal reactors with solid moderator (HTGR) are directly affected by this distribution shift effect. For light-water reactors, the preponderant effect is related to variations of the water density. In contrast to the preceding, this effect is easy to assess, since it results simply from a change of the moderating ratio. If the reactor is well designed, the moderator temperature and reactivity vary in opposite ways. For the same reasons, an increase of the steam rate entails a loss of reactivity.

In the case of sodium-cooled fast reactors, the coolant density works in the other direction. In fact, a rise in the coolant temperature has three consequences:

- the neutrons being less slow (the atomic density of sodium has diminished), their average energy is higher than its rated value, whence a higher multiplication factor η of plutonium (Fig. 3.9);
- sodium being slightly absorbant, even its very partial withdrawal leads to an increase of the utilization factor f (§4.5.2) and hence of the reactivity;
- leakage is favored by a decrease of the density of materials present in the core, therefore of the sodium in particular.

In spite of the latter effect, the reactivity of a fast reactor generally increases with the sodium temperature.

In stability or safety studies, it is customary to linearize short-term effects by writing:

$$\delta\rho = \alpha_c \delta T_c + \alpha_m \delta T_m + \alpha_v \delta v + \ldots \qquad (5.23)$$

with:

$$\alpha_c = \frac{\partial\rho}{\partial T_c}, \quad \alpha_m = \frac{\partial\rho}{\partial T_m}, \quad \text{etc.}$$

where δT_c, δT_m represent respectively the fuel and moderator temperature increases, and δv the increase of the void rate in the liquid coolant (if there is one). These increases, responsible for the change $\delta\rho$ of reactivity, are counted starting from the rated values of the corresponding quantities. The value and especially the sign of the <u>reactivity coefficients</u> α are of considerable importance in the choice of a reactor assembly.

H

If all these coefficients are negative, the reactor will without any doubt be intrinsically stable and able to withstand relatively serious reactivity accidents (Sec. 6.4).

Equation (5.23) enables us to relate the equations which govern the reactor kinetics (4.110) and those which give the thermohydraulic behavior (these may include phenomena taking place outside the core). An example will be given in the framework of safety studies (Sec. 6.4), but for the moment we shall restrict ourselves to qualitative considerations.

As seen in the preceding analysis, the Doppler effect plays a most important role, since it concerns all power reactors and is expressed by a negative fuel temperature coefficient ($\alpha_c < 0$). Moreover, the time constants are of the order of a few seconds because of the small thermal inertia of the fuel. When the power of the reactor increases, it is the fuel temperature which rises before anything else, and hence the Doppler effect represents the first mechanism which works against an accidental divergence (§4.6.5). The effect of the moderator temperature plays a similar role in LWR reactors, for α_m is negative and the time constants remain small. In contrast, in HTGR reactors (graphite moderated), the coefficient α_m may be positive, but the system remains globally stable because of the preponderance of the Doppler effect. Moreover, the high heat capacity of graphite makes for much larger time constants (several minutes), so that the control mechanisms would have time to intervene if that turned out to be necessary after all. The same remarks apply to a positive reactivity coefficient of sodium in a fast breeder reactor.

Calculating reactivity coefficients is in some cases very delicate. We are led to distinguish between two reactivities corresponding to two neighboring states of the reactor (for example, one changes the moderator temperature by 40°C, the other characteristics remaining the same), so that the results can be very sensitive to certain approximations which usually are justified. We have seen in addition that several neutronic parameters can act on the reactivity in opposite ways (see for example sodium), whence an additional lack of precision. For all these reasons, before a power plant becomes operational, a measurement of the reactivity coefficients is always made; in this phase the power station can be viewed as a zero-power reactor (§3.4.2) that can be heated by auxiliary means (pumps, for example).

The temperature coefficients do not only affect safety issues, but also fix (when they are negative) the reactivity margins which are necessary to have at the outset. A strongly negative temperature effect is a penalty from the economic point of view since on the one hand a larger amount of fissile matter is required for a sufficient reserve of reactivity, and on the other hand,there must be more considerable means of control.

To conclude this section, we shall rapidly analyze the effects of two neutron absorbers on reactivity: xenon Xe^{135} and samarium Sm^{149}. These effects are important and easy to assess. Xenon has an extremely high absorption cross section for thermal neutrons ($\alpha_a \cong 3\ 10^6$ b), so that even in small quantities it can significantly affect the utilization factor of a thermal reactor, thus acting as an additional structural material (4.61). It can be formed directly, from fission, or indirectly, from iodine I^{135}, another primary fission product which by β decay leads to xenon. It is interesting to note that xenon and samarium have atomic mass numbers 135 and 149 which situate them in the zone of most probable fissions (Fig. 3.1), whence the importance of these two isotopes.

In contrast to other fission products, xenon Xe^{135} attains its maximum concentration rapidly (2 to 3 days after the start-up of the reactor). This concentration depends on the absolute level of the neutron flux and thus on the power. Depending on the type of reactor, the reactivity loss goes from 2 to 4%, which is far from negligible (especially for natural uranium reactors). From the very first days of operation, the control mechanisms must be able to liberate the necessary reactivity, or the reactor will not be able to attain its full power.

Another particularity appears when the reactor is shut down. Because it is radioactive, xenon itself disappears in a few days, but its concentration first reaches a maximum, since the iodine formed earlier continues for a certain time to produce xenon by β decay. If one wishes to start up the reactor again at any instant, the control methods must also take care of this "hump", or else it will be necessary to wait for a day or two.

Finally, xenon may induce spatial instabilities, especially in large-size reactors (with natural uranium and moderated by graphite). In the appendix can be found a quantitative analysis of the problems posed by xenon (§9.4.2/3/4).

Samarium Sm^{149} has at most a 1% effect on reactivity. It is independent of the flux and its time constant is of the order of a month. It is rather by tradition that this effect is classed under the heading "intermediate term effects", whereas it would be more logical to include it in the long-term evolution of the fuel (§5.3.4). The study of this phenomenon is very simple (§9.4.5).

In contrast to short term effects, xenon and samarium do not pose any safety problems, even if the first can induce spatial oscillations of the neutron flux. The time constants are such that the control methods can easily follow the evolution of these poisons, and the reactor always remains critical. We note that these poisons have practically no bearing on fast reactors; though present, their absorption cross section is too small to have an influence on reactivity.

5.3.4 Long-term Evolution of the Fuel

The initial reactivities must make it possible to cover not only the short term effects, controlled by control rods, but also the long range effects which will concern us here.

For a given initial reactivity margin, these long term effects will fix the fuel burnup rate that one may hope to obtain, and thus the cost of the fuel per kWh produced (this is of course only true if the materials whose properties are altered by irradiation do not impose more stringent constraints).

By simplifying somewhat, we can find four principal causes for long-range variations of reactivity:

- Burnup of the initial fissile matter: that is, uranium U^{235} in most thermal reactors, plutonium Pu^{239} in the case of the fast breeder reactor, and uranium U^{233} in the equilibrium cycle of a HTGR reactor (§3.3.4)
- Formation of fissile matter out of fertile matter (conversion): plutonium Pu^{239} from uranium U^{238}, and at a second stage, plutonium Pu^{241} by transmutation of the isotope Pu^{240}; in the same way, the thorium cycle of HTGR reactors leads us to consider fissile uranium U^{233} resulting from neutron captures in thorium Th^{232} (§3.3.4).
- The appearance of various nonfissile isotopes: U^{236}, Pu^{240}, Pu^{242}, etc., which are neutron absorbers. The first, U^{236}, is a poison

(sterile captures) which accumulates in HTGR reactors with highly enriched uranium. The second, Pu^{240}, leads in its turn to fissile Pu^{241}. For strong irradiations other transuranic elements (§3.1.1) appear: curium, americium, californium, etc.; some of these are fissile.

· Accumulation of fission products: some are neutron absorbers and, with the exception of xenon and samarium, they bring about slow changes in the reactivity.

With the exception of the second, these phenomena all lead to a decrease of reactivity. The problem posed is thus to determine as a function of time the atomic densities of various isotopes belonging to the fuel, after which the usual methods of reactor physics furnish the reactivity and the flux distributions at the instants considered. The problem is not one of kinetics: when we speak of a positive reactivity it is implicitly assumed that control mechanisms intervene to maintain the reactor critical.

The atomic densities are governed by evolution equations which involve at each point of the reactor the microscopic absorption cross sections as well as the neutron flux.

Let us consider the important case of a thermal reactor burning enriched uranium. The variation of the atomic density N_5 of uranium U^{235} is proportional to the absorption rate in this material and in the interval of time dt considered:

$$dN_5 = - R_{a5}(t)dt = - N_5(t)\sigma_{a5}\,\Phi(t)\,dt$$

We have already employed this reasoning in subsec. 3.2.2 to arrive at equation (3.1), but here we will not make any restrictive hypotheses on the temporal variations of the neutron flux. Examination of the preceding equation reveals that the "good variable" of integration is not the time but the integrated flux θ, with:

$$\theta(t) = \int_0^t \Phi\,(t')dt' \tag{5.24}$$

whence the definitive form of the evolution equation:

$$\frac{dN_5}{d\theta} = - \sigma_{a5}\,N_5(\theta) \tag{5.25}$$

whose solution can be written:

$$N_5(\theta) = N_5(0) \exp(-\sigma_{a5}\theta) \tag{5.26}$$

This expression is valid irrespective of whether the flux is constant or varies in time. The similarity of equation (5.25) with the disintegration law (1.7) is striking: the integrated flux θ (in cm^{-2}) plays the role of time and σ_a (in cm^2) that of the decay constant λ. The disappearance of stable nuclei by neutron absorption is analogous to the spontaneous disappearance of radioactive nuclei. The unit of integrated flux (cm^{-2}) is sometimes noted nvt in order to recall the dimensions of this latter quantity (neutron density · velocity · time).

The equations which govern the disappearance of uranium U^{238} and the appearance of various transuranic elements are based on the nuclear reactions (§3.2.3):

$$_0n^1 + {}_{92}U^{238} \rightarrow {}_{94}Pu^{239} + 2\,\beta^- \qquad (\S 3.2.3)$$

$$_0n^1 + {}_{94}Pu^{239} \rightarrow {}_{94}Pu^{240} + \gamma$$

$$_0n^2 + {}_{94}Pu^{240} \rightarrow {}_{94}Pu^{241} + \gamma$$

etc.

Taking account of the creations and destructions of these isotopes, we arrive by a reasoning analogous to the preceding, at a system of equations:

$$\left.\begin{aligned}
\frac{dN_8}{d\theta} &= -\sigma_{a8}N_8(\theta) \\
\frac{dN_9}{d\theta} &= \sigma_{a8}N_8(\theta) - \sigma_{a9}N_9(\theta) \\
\frac{dN_0}{d\theta} &= \sigma_{c9}N_9(\theta) - \sigma_{a0}N_0(\theta) \\
\frac{dN_1}{d\theta} &= \sigma_{a0}N_0(\theta) - \sigma_{a1}N_1(\theta)
\end{aligned}\right\} \tag{5.27}$$

where the indices 8,9,0,1 are relative to the isotopes U^{238}, Pu^{239}, Pu^{240}, Pu^{241}. The preceding system could be extended, but, as we will see

(Fig. 5.11), the concentrations diminish rapidly as we proceed along the chain. We also note here the analogy with the disintegration chains of the radioactive elements, as well as the distinction to be made between absorption (σ_a) and capture (σ_c) when considering fissile nuclei. Thus the term which represents the disappearance of plutonium Pu^{239} in the second equation (5.27) depends on σ_a, since fission or capture leads to the destruction of this nucleus ($\sigma_a = \sigma_f + \sigma_c$), whereas only neutron capture is responsible for the transmutation of plutonium Pu^{239} into plutonium Pu^{240}, as is indicated by the third equation (5.27).

The preceding equations can be integrated analytically and the solutions only depend on the initial atomic density of uranium U^{238}: $N_8(0)$. In effect, except in the case of recycling, the fuel does not contain any transuranic element at the beginning of irradiation ($N_i(0) = 0$ for $i = 9,0,1$).

Lastly, the fission products, with the exception of xenon and samarium which have already been analyzed (§5.3.3), satisfy more complicated equations since, in contrast to the transuranics, one can no longer disregard radioactivity as a mode of disappearance as compared with neutron capture. Even if the calculation of residual power requires taking into account all the fission products (§3.1.4), here we are only interested in the most absorbant ones. In spite of this, a very large number of equations must be solved, but in practice one has recourse to simplifications; it is not reasonable to devote more calculation time to fission products than to transuranics, more important by far.

5.3.5 Comments

Before proceding further, we should make more precise the meaning of intgrated flux. The reasonings that led us to this notion tacitly assumed the one-group formalism, so that the flux Φ in (5.24) is in fact relative to the set of neutrons without reference to their energy. Unfortunately, the cross sections depend on the energy, and the quantities σ_a, which figure in the evolution equations, must be viewed as averages σ_a taken, at time t, over the distribution $\Phi(\vec{r},E,t)$ which depends in addition on the point considered. To be rigorous, the evolution problem can no longer be decoupled from the multigroup calculations (§4.5.8) applied, as many times as necessary, to the reactor as a whole. We can still show (§9.3.3) that in a first approximation the distributions and hence the average cross sections $\bar{\sigma}_a$ only depend on space and on time through the intermediary of the atomic densities N_i. The evolution equations are no longer linear and must be solved numerically, but the essential point remains: we can calculate once and for all the quantities $N_i(\theta)$ and $\sigma_{ai}(\theta)$ independently of the use which will be made of them eventually during multigroup calculations of the reactor. In the case of thermal reactors which concern us here, we can nonetheless make the following remark: most of the phenomena take place at low energy, the integrated flux θ and the cross sections σ_a essentially characterize thermal neutrons; the quantities σ_a are thus more or less known in advance and independent of θ as we have implicitly assumed in subsec. 5.3.4 (this does not apply to uranium U^{238}, since in this case, resonance captures are as important as thermal captures).

Not only does the integrated flux, also called fluence, play an important role in evolution studies, but it also enables us to evaluate the damage that the neutrons inflict on the materials. For completeness, we should add that this damage, like biological doses (§6.2.3), depends in addition on the neutron energies (fast neutrons are the most dangerous). Regarding this problem, one can assume that the neutron spectra do not vary much in time. The efficiency of the neutrons is thus more or less constant, and the behavior of a material depends only on the integrated flux for a given type of reactor. If that is not the case (see the preceding considerations), the ratio of damage to integrated flux is no longer fixed, but depends in its turn on the latter. It increases for example in the course of evolution of the fuel if the fast neutrons become relatively more numerous (spectrum hardening).

5.3.6 Fuel Burnup

The notion of specific integrated power (integrated over time) or fuel burnup rate corresponds very naturally to that of integrated flux. It represents the thermal energy liberated per unit mass. By definition this new quantity can be written:

$$W_{sp}(t) = \int_0^t \bar{\omega}_{sp}(t')dt' \tag{5.28}$$

The specific power $\bar{\omega}_{sp}$ is easily obtained from the fission rates relative to each fissile isotope:

$$\bar{\omega}_{sp}(t) = \frac{E_f}{\rho_c} [N_5(\theta)\,\sigma_{f5} + N_9(\theta)\,\sigma_{f9} + \ldots]\,\Phi(t)$$

This formula generalizes the expression given until now for a single isotope and a steady state (4.9). Taking as a temporal variable the integrated flux θ, the defining equation (5.28) becomes:

$$W_{sp}(\theta) = \frac{E_f}{\rho_c} \int_0^\theta [N_5(\theta')\sigma_{f5} + N_9(\theta')\sigma_{f9} + \ldots]d\theta' \qquad (5.29)$$

since, according to (5.24): $d\theta = \Phi(t)dt$. Here too, considerations based on modifications of neutron energy distributions would lead to a θ dependence of quantities like $\sigma_{f5}(\theta)$, $\sigma_{f9}(\theta)$, etc. (§5.3.5).

Theoretically, W_{sp} could be expressed in J/g or MJ/t, but following the custom, we will use the megawatt-day/ton (1 MWd/t = 86.400 MJ/t) as the unit. The fuel burnup rate W_{sp} is thus an increasing function of the integrated flux θ (for small irradiations these two quantities are proportional). Since the flux is not uniform in a reactor, the integrated flux θ depends simultaneously on the time and on the point considered (5.24). The same holds for the concentrations of various isotopes $N_i(\theta)$ as well as for the burnup rates $W_{sp}(\theta)$. The advantage of the latter quantity rests in the fact that one knows at every instant the thermal power $P_t(t)$ of the reactor starting from thermodynamic measurements (5.14). One easily deduces the mean specific power $\langle\bar{\omega}_{sp}\rangle = P_t/M_c$, as well as the mean fuel burnup rate (5.28):

$$\langle W_{sp}\rangle = \frac{1}{M_c} \int_0^t P_t(t')dt'$$

without appealing to any measurement of a neutronic nature, since M_c represents only the mass of the fuel. The reactivity, isotopic composition, etc., will thus be evaluated as a function of the burnup rate (expressed in MWd/t), even if the atomic density calculations are based on the notion of integrated flux (equations (5.25) to (5.27)), since the identity (5.29) enables us to make the necessary conversion. In these conditions the power plant operators will be able to know approximately the core composition starting from the produced energy, and to predict the moment when unloading will become imperative. If, in addition, more detailed information is available (neutron flux measurements, for example) which enables them to follow the time evolution of the form factor (§5.2.5), they can determine the specific power $\bar{\omega}_{sp}(\vec{r},t)$ at each point of the reactor, and thus the experimental value of the burnup rate at the considered instant (5.28). They can then deduce, as before, the isotopic composition of the fuel, but this time at each point of the reactor.

5.3.7 Consequences for Control

From the preceding considerations we can first of all deduce information on the relative importance of the various isotopes which appear in the fuel in the course of irradiation. We have already seen that 1 gram of uranium U^{235} liberates energy of the order of 1 MWd (§3.2.2). For example, a LWR fuel enriched at 3% and irradiated at 20,000 MWd/t will have lost 20 kg of uranium U^{235} per metric ton. Since it initially consisted of 30 kg U^{235}/ton, we deduce that the enrichment has dropped from 3% to 1%. This is evidently a very rough calculation, since it supposes that the total energy produced comes from uranium U^{235}, and neglects the contribution of the plutonium that has been formed.

This simple reasoning in any case does not enable us to know the core composition for a given irradiation. For that, it would be necessary to solve the evolution equations or measure isotopic concentrations. We have indicated in Fig. 5.11 the evolution of the isotopic concentrations $\xi_i(\theta)$ as a function of the integrated flux. These concentrations can be deduced from the corresponding atomic densities by virtue of the relation (§1.3.3):

$$N_i(\theta) = \frac{N_A}{A_i} \rho_c \xi_i(\theta)$$

where A_i is the atomic mass number of the considered isotope, ρ_c the mass density of the fuel and N_A Avogadro's number. The maximum integrated flux envisaged in this example corresponds to 30,000 MWd/t, in other words, approximately the limiting fuel burnup rate of LWR reactors. Although the curves of Fig. 5.11 are relative to a small-size reactor [19], the final composition of the fuel is very representative of current LWR reactors. By comparing the initial and final compositions, we can draw from Fig. 5.11 the following conclusions.

Of 1 kg of uranium initially enriched at 3.44%, 26 g of U^{235} have been destroyed, of which 22 g by fission (4 g have led to the formation of U^{236}). The fission of 1 g produces 1 MWd and thus the fission of uranium U^{235} represents 22 MWd/kg or 22,000 MWd/t. Since the final state corresponds to 30,000 MWd/t, the difference, 8,000 MWd/t, comes from fissions produced "on the spot" in a portion of the plutonium that has been formed. This explains why the curve Pu^{239} is flattened for strong irradiations: reactors burn part of the plutonium they produce. While 25 to 30% of the energy comes from plutonium in LWR reactors, we obtain better performances with natural uranium heavy - water moderated reactors, since the plutonium contribution then reaches 50% (burnup rate 10,000 MWd/t).

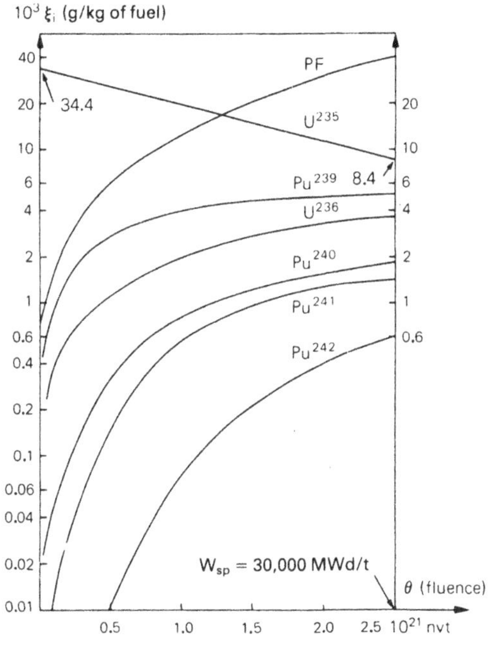

FIGURE 5.11. Evolution of a PWR fuel enriched at 3.44%.

A study of the curves in Fig. 5.11 shows that various plutoniums appear one after the other, which is quite normal since Pu^{240} is formed by neutron capture in Pu^{239}, Pu^{241} from Pu^{240}, etc. For 30,000 MWd/t ($2.5\ 10^{21}$ nvt), the available plutonium (after extraction in a reprocessing plant) has a complicated isotopic composition. The fissile nuclei Pu^{239} and Pu^{241} represent about 73%. Such plutonium is called civil, for the presence of plutonium Pu^{240} makes it a bad nuclear explosive. The plutonium necessary for military applications must contain a much greater proportion of plutonium Pu^{239} and the only way to achieve this is to adopt very low burning rates (< 500 MWd/t), which makes the cost per kWh prohibitively high. For this reason, military plutonium is generally produced in "rustic reactors" which are relatively cold and thus much simpler technologically; there is no question of producing electricity (§3.4.3).

We will now see the effect of fuel irradiation on reactivity. At this stage we must distinguish between natural uranium and enriched uranium reactors (Fig. 5.12). In the first case, the appearance of plutonium leads to an initial increase of reactivity reaching a maximum. This is a characteristic of natural uranium. It may appear curious that initially the reactivity increases in this type of reactor although there is no breeding (the conversion factor C may all the same exceed 0.8). This is due to the fact that plutonium created in insufficient proportions has nevertheless a higher absorption cross section σ_a than uranium U^{235}. For enriched reactors on the contrary the decrease of reactivity is more or less regular and its variation is large if no measure is taken to control it. Note that in the curves of Fig. 5.12 there is a sudden drop in reactivity at the initial instant, associated to intermediate term effects (§5.3.3); the time scale adopted here (in fact, the scale of the fuel burnup rate) does not enable us to represent this decrease in detail.

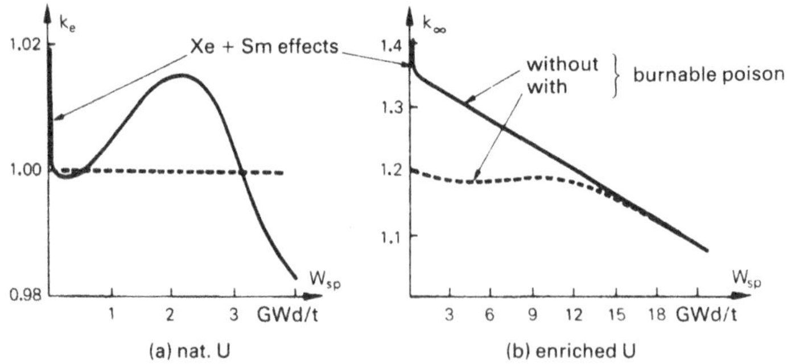

FIGURE 5.12. Multiplication factors as a function of the fuel burnup rate.

To avoid large variations of reactivity which would imply a prohibitive initial investment in fissile matter, partial loadings (unloadings) are always implemented. Let us take the case of loading by thirds when the equilibrium cycle has been attained. The core is divided into three segments, each composed of fuel elements having about the same burnup rate. Let us take as the time origin the instant when the fuel elements of the first segment have just been renewed. Table 5.13 represents the time sequence of loading-unloading operations. The residence time of an element denoted T (in practice, T = 3 years) corresponds to a maximum burnup rate W_M. Rigorously speaking, the last quantity is not completely defined, since the position of the segment in the core plays a certain role, the neutron flux not being spatially constant.

TABLE 5.13. Refuelling by thirds.

Time	Segment n° 1	Segment n° 2	Segment n° 3	Core
0	0	$W_M/3$	$2W_M/3$	$W_M/3$
T/3	$W_M/3$	$2W_M/3$	$W_M \to 0$	$\frac{2W_M}{3} \to W_M/3$
2T/3	$2W_M/3$	$W_M \to 0$	$W_M/3$	$\frac{2W_M}{3} \to W_M/3$
T	$W_M \to 0$	$W_M/3$	$2W_M/3$	$\frac{2W_M}{3} \to W_M/3$

The last column of Table 5.13 gives the average burnup rate for the core as a whole: it is this which roughly fixes the reactivity of a reactor. During refuelling (at instants 0, T/3, 2T/3, etc.), in one of the three segments the burnup rate falls from W_M to 0, whereas from the point of view of reactivity everything goes on as if one was in the presence of a uniform load whose burnup rate fell only from $2W_M/3$ to $W_M/3$ (last column). As represented in Fig. 5.14, the reactivity variations are themselves divided approximately by three with respect to the situation created by a complete unloading. The only difference from a practical viewpoint is that one must intervene more frequently in the reactor if partial refueling is adopted, but the number of unloaded fuel elements remains the same if one considers the period T. This number corresponds evidently to the total number of fuel elements in the core. The main advantage of partial unloadings resides in the economies that can be made in investment in fissile matter, since the necessary initial reactivity is markedly weaker. For LWR reactors, in any case, the annual shutdown for maintenance leads quite naturally to this solution.

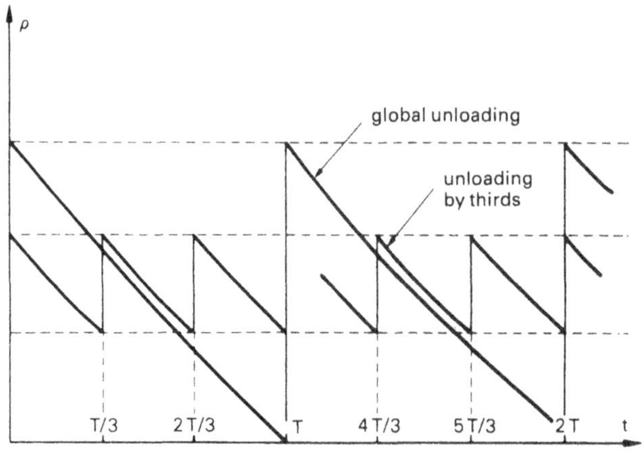

FIGURE 5.14. Influence of unloading by thirds on reactivity.

This amounts to saying that for a given investment in fissile matter (fixed initial reactivity) we will obtain much higher burnup rates thanks to partial refuelings. More fractionated loadings improve the performances even further (refuelling by fourths, sixths, etc.) At the limit, one would be intervening constantly in the reactor, which would require more complicated machinery, the reactor being necessarily in operation (heavy-water moderated reactors).

A final advantage of partial unloadings resides in the "power flattening" to which it leads. We have seen at the end of subsec. 5.2.5 that for a good flattening it is necessary for the most reactive fuel elements to be available at the periphery of the core. Thus one should ensure as much as possible that the <u>most irradiated fuel is always at the center</u>. Taking account of what has been said about partial refuellings, we deduce that the fuel must circulate from the periphery towards the center, and this requires that <u>all</u> the fuel elements be manipulated:

those being loaded, those being unloaded, and those being moved. This refuelling procedure has been adopted for most power reactors. In this way are combined the advantages of flattening and the necessity for partial refuellings.

We will close this subsection with some details about burnup rates. The properties of the materials (fuel and cladding) alter beyond a certain integrated flux (§5.3.5). We are thus led to impose a limit on the burnup rate because these two quantities are related (5.29). The quantity W_M appearing in Tab.5.13 corresponds to this new technological constraint, whose nature is different from the preceding ones (Sec. 5.2).

In LWR reactors, the initial enrichment (about 3%) is so chosen that for a given type of refuelling the permissible burnup rate W_M has been attained in the batch of unloaded fuel elements. There is no advantage in choosing a higher enrichment since in any case one would be obliged to effect unloadings before the reactivity reserve had been exhausted.

For natural uranium reactors the problem is very different. Since one cannot tinker with initial reactivity, once the optimum unloading mode has been adopted (continuous unloading), the burnup rate of the unloaded fuel elements is fixed. In the best case this does not exceed 10,000 MWd/t (heavy water reactors). In this case neutronic considerations and no longer technological criteria fix W_M.

5.3.8 Burnable Poisons and Control Rods

Despite the partial unloadings, reactivity variations may still be considered too strong. To keep the number of classical-type control rods at the minimum, a burnable poison is introduced in the reactor core.

A burnable poison is a neutron absorber which disappears with irradiation, thus tending to offset the natural decrease in reactivity due to the depletion of the fuel. In any case, one can evidently adjust the quantity of poison necessary to compensate the reactivity excess at the start of operation; this being done, it is impossible for the compensation to remain total for the whole cycle. Since the burning of the poison is governed by a law analogous to (5.26):

$$N_p(\theta) = N_p(0) \exp(-\sigma_{ap}\theta)$$

in which $N_p(\theta)$ represents the atomic density of the poison for an integrated flux θ, it is necessary to select an absorber which has a good cross section σ_{ap}. In practice, one can choose only from certain materials (boron, gadolinium, etc.) whose microscopic cross sections are fixed by nature; therefore the compensation can never be perfect. In Fig. 5.12 we saw, for example, how the multiplication factor k_∞ of a light-water reactor changes when a burnable poison is present in the core. This flattening of the function $k_\infty(\theta)$ evidently affects reactivity.

The burnable poison is used in a solid form in the fuel or in soluble form in the moderator if the latter is liquid. This method is prohibited, however, in boiling-water reactors for safety reasons: in the eventuality of a power increase, and thus a rise in the rate of steam, the presence of an absorber in the moderator could lead to the appearance of positive reactivity. More intense boiling brings about a decrease in the quantity of poison present in the core, and the stabilizing effect described in subsec. 5.1.4 disappears. This phenomenon is much less marked in PWR reactors, for the moderator remains liquid; nonetheless, the temperature coefficient α_m (5.23) of the moderator becomes less negative for the same reasons (decrease of the water density with temperature, and thus of the quantity of poison). Even though the reasons are less imperative, solid burnable poisons are used in these reactors as well, the soluble ones being reserved for another use (see below).

Solid poisons have not only the advantage of being insensitive to power fluctuations (they are consumed slowly), but also that of completing the flattening of specific powers when they are judiciously distributed in the core (modification of material buckling, §5.2.5). The power station operator, on the other hand, can only act on them at the moment of refuelling.

Once all the control modes cited above have been put into service, residual fluctuations of reactivity are covered by the control rods. According to their functions, they can be classified as follows:

- Shim or compensating rods. Very effective, and as their name indicates, they offset short-term effects (Xe, Sm, temperature) and later complete the action of the burnable poison (the rods are then almost withdrawn). They are made of such highly absorbant materials (boron carbide B_4C, cadmium, etc.) that the active portions are very thin (layers of 1 to 2 mm at the edge). From a neutronic point of view, they can be likened to black bodies (§8.1.4), at least in thermal reactors: any neutron entering a rod of this type is necessarily absorbed and the consumption of the active material shows as a progressive diminution of its thickness.

Regulating rods. Not very effective, they are permanently present in the core and permit fine adjustments in the power and the automatic regulating of the reactor (§5.3.9). The rapid passage from one power level to another requires only a small introduction of reactivity ($\rho < \beta$, cf. §4.6.5) and as soon as the new level is reached, the regulating rods return to nearly their initial position. The compensating rods (or any other slow control device) then intervene to make up for the variation of the xenon effect resulting from the change in power. The regulating rods, also called fine rods, are most often made of steel, since a high level of efficiency is not required. Like the compensating rods, they are vertically driven by highly reliable motors.

Safety rods. Of similar makeup to the compensating rods (boron carbide), their function is entirely different. In normal functioning, they are in the withdrawn position. In case of an accident, they drop rapidly by gravity and stop the chain reaction in several seconds (see the case $\rho < 0$ of the kinetic studies, §4.6.5). Subsequently, the compensating rods (which move more slowly) are inserted. We will see in connection with safety studies that other devices also make possible the rapid shutdown of a reactor (Sec. 6.4).

While the safety rods have to do only with the kinetics of a reactor, the control rods (compensating and regulating) intervene during normal operation. They alone allow the operator to adjust the reactivity in keeping with the neutron balance, by playing with the insertion level. Unfortunately, there are certain disadvantages. First, a change in the neutron flux distribution causes a more or less predictable shift of the hot spot, which is generally indicated by a performance loss of the reactor (decrease of the flattening coefficient, cf. §5.2.5). Secondly, the depletion of the active material of the rods could require their replacement, which is not a routine type of operation like refuelling. Finally, they must be cooled when they are inserted, because they are a source of heat release due to neutron captures. This poses no particular problem in a light-water reactor, because all the components of the core are simultaneously cooled; but for heavy-water reactors, the control rods being hydraulically independent of the fuel elements situated in pressure tubes, a special cooling circuit must be envisaged.

To offset these disadvantages, a soluble poison (boric acid BO_3H_3, for example) is called upon whenever possible. Being soluble, its concentration is adjustable. The problems to solve are in the domain of chemical engineering: the moderator must be rapidly purified in order to follow the intermediate-term variations in reactivity due to xenon (response time about 1 hour at most); as for long-term variations of reactivity, they are covered without any problem. This procedure makes for a much more limited use of compensating rods (at the limit they serve only to cover the temperature effects) and has no effect on the neutron flux distributions. From another point of view, the presence of a solid burnable poison allows the adjustable soluble poison to be reduced to a minimum amount, as would not be the case if the latter had to play the role of the former. This method is used in reactors with liquid moderators (PWR and HWR), but not in BWR reactors, for reasons already given. In these latter, as well as in graphite-moderated reactors (HTGR), one cannot avoid having recourse to compensating rods and, in this case, the optimization of the solid burnable poison takes on a greater importance.

For the record,we will mention another control method proposed in the past for heavy water reactors; gaseous rods. The injection of an absorbant gas ($_2He^3$) into a tube results in a control rod whose effectiveness varies with the pressure; in this way one eliminates the axial distortions of flux caused by partial insertions of classic control rods, and the mechanical problems are simplified (suppression of driving shafts). All the same, problems of leak-tightness arose to such an extent that this solution was abandoned despite its advantages.

5.3.9 Control of the Power Levels

The purpose of the control devices described above is either to maintain the reactor at the prescribed power level (with the help of regulating rods), or to halt it in case of accident (by dropping the safety rods). To trigger the necessary actions, the power and its variations must be known at every instant. We have seen (5.14) that the power can be obtained from the measurement of the inlet and outlet temperatures of the coolant. This method, which is valid in a steady state, does not make it possible to keep up with rapid variations of power, and even less, to detect a sudden divergence in good time. Thus it is necessary to use neutron flux measurements which call upon the instrumentation described below.

Let us consider two electrodes subjected to a potential difference V and immersed in a chamber containing gas under pressure. An ionizing particle (α, β) penetrating this chamber leads to the formation of N pairs of ions; this number is proportional to the energy of the rapid incident particle, provided that the distance it travels in the gas is less than the dimensions of the apparatus. The corresponding N electrons are collected by the anode and lead to a voltage pulse $\Delta V = eN/C$, where e represents the charge of an electron (§1.1.1) and C the capacity of the two electrodes. We have thus made an ionization chamber. For higher voltages, the secondary electrons in their turn acquire sufficient energy to ionize the gas, whence an increase of the pulse ΔV, which nevertheless remains proportional to N and hence to the energy of the particle that one wants to detect. We thus arrive at a proportional counter. When the detector is placed in a particle flux, the number of pulses received is identical to the number of incident particles. The less sensitive ionization chambers can only detect the most strongly ionizing particles (α, for example), whereas proportional counters have a wider field of application. In both cases, if the flux to be measured is large, the pulses are no longer individually detectable; we then measure an integral quantity, namely an electric current proportional to the flux instead of the absolute number per unit time. Thus, depending on the circumstances, the detectors work on the basis of pulses or of current. In the latter case, we lose information with respect to the energy of incident particles, but this is not important for applications to reactors (this is not true in nuclear physics where one essentially identifies particles and measures their energy).

Reactor control requires neutron detection. Neutrons are weakly ionizing and the distance they travel freely in the gas is much greater than the dimensions of the detectors (§4.2.1). We must thus avail ourselves of nuclear reactions with large cross sections, leading to easily detectable charged particles. We thus get back the conditions which permit the use of the detectors described above. Boron is normally used, either in the form of a solid deposit on one of the electrodes or in the form of a gaseous compound (BF_3) mixed in with the gas filling the detector.

Most control rods use this element. The nuclear reaction to which one is led is the following:

$$_0n^1 + {}_5B^{10} \rightarrow {}_3Li^7 + {}_2He^4$$

One can also use a deposit of uranium U^{235}, fission reactions leading to highly ionizing fission products.

What has just been said about neutrons also applies to γ photons, in the sense that detection is also indirect and involves the secondary electrons (§6.2.2) that the photons tear off from the gas (to which nothing must be added). To check on the power levels, direct measurement of γ ray fluxes could be made, but these give an incorrect impression of the neutron population, since at least one component remains after reactor shutdown (fission products, §3.1.4). One tries instead to eliminate their influence by using compensated chambers. As indicated in Fig. 5.15, one part of the detector is charged with boron and the other is not. The difference in the signals thus represents the neutron flux alone.

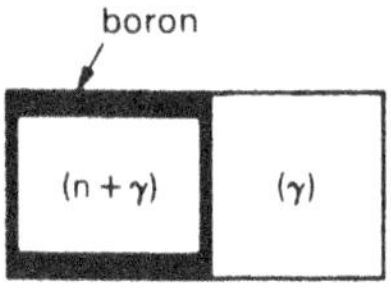

FIGURE 5.15. Compensated ionization chamber.

A measurement system consists of various elements represented symbolically in Fig. 5.16. The detector may be an ion chamber or proportional counter, and the system may employ currents or pulses depending on the flux

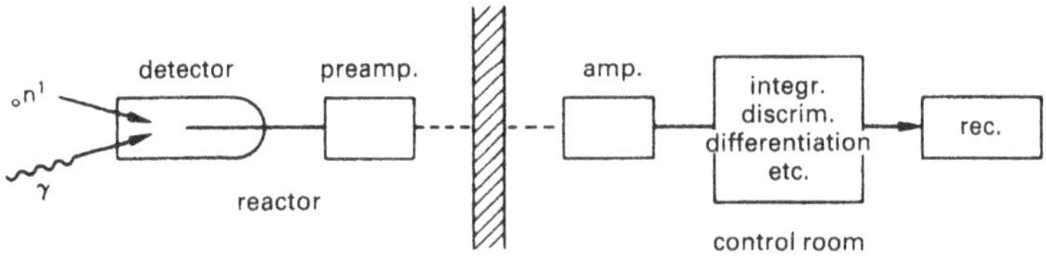

FIGURE 5.16. Flow diagram of a neutronic measurement system.

range and the purpose. The signals are generally so weak that preamplification is necessary before transmission of the information to the control center. The processing of the signal (differentiation, integration, etc.) depends on the function assigned to a given system. Measurement systems can be classified as follows:

- Startup systems. Their range of coverage does not go beyond 10^{-6} P_0, where P_0 represents the rated power. The neutron flux being small, the detectors function as proportional counters and deliver pulses. Fission detectors, although leading to larger pulses, are less sensitive than BF_3 counters. The latter cover the lower end of the range up to 10^{-10} P_0, in other words a flux of the order of 10^4 n/cm^2 s. In fact, during startup, the flux can be even smaller, since in subcritical state it is fixed by other sources of neutrons than those of induced fission. These sources essentially result from spontaneous fission and have a very weak intensity (§3.1.1). This situation is dangerous, for the reactor could become prompt supercritical (§4.6.5) while the operator was "blind". The chain reaction would develop so rapidly that the rated flux level would be quickly attained before the safety rods had time to drop. To correct this situation, a neutron source is added (radium-beryllium (§1.2.4), Am-Be, etc.) so that the minimum flux is within the operating range of the startup system. This source can later be removed.
- Logarithmic systems. These partly cover the preceding range, since they permit measurements from 10^{-7} P_0 up to P_0. The operating conditions correspond to those of the ion chamber; the signal does not depend on the voltage applied to the electrodes and the problem of stabilization of the supply is not as crucial. On the other hand, the loss of sensitivity is tolerable, since the measured flux is higher. These systems work with currents. The logarithm of the power is displayed in the control room. In effect, the rise in power corresponds to delayed supercriticality, and the logarithm of the flux increases linearly with time (§4.6.5).
- Linear systems. These are similar to the preceding but work in a narrow range around the rated power (10^{-2} P_0 to 10 P_0). They permit fine tuning of the power and thus the display is linear. To increase their sensitivity, one gives up γ ray compensation, which is

not necessary at this high level of neutron flux. The tuning can be automatic and in this case a feedback loop makes the connection between the measurement system and the regulating rods by a servomechanism (§5.3.8); in this case we speak of regulating systems.

· Safety systems. Their role is to trigger the fall of safety rods when a neutronic parameter goes beyond the prescribed value. Limits are imposed on the flux as well as on its logarithmic derivative. The latter limit prevents an operator from increasing the power too rapidly, even if the reactor is far from attaining its rated power. During a divergence the flux increases like exp(t/T) (§4.6.5) and its logarithmic derivative is equal to 1/T. This prescription is equivalent to fixing a lower limit on the stable period of the reactor.

The figures given above with respect to the working range of measurement systems are only indicative. Because of the continuous progress being made in electronics, two reactors which are identical in principle can be equipped with quite different measurement systems, depending on the date of their construction.

For reasons of safety, several systems are used (often 3) for each function. There is yet another reason: a good evaluation of the power proceeds by a certain weighting of the information supplied by several detectors, in order to prevent their position from having an influence on the results of the measurements. Furthermore, certain types of reactors are subject to spatial oscillations which can only be detected by comparing the information furnished by several systems. This instability due to xenon (§5.3.3) presents no danger, since its time constant is several hours, but it complicates the job of the operators if an automatic control by sector is not envisaged. If the neutron flux increases in one zone, it diminishes in another; compensating rods are then introduced in the first case and withdrawn in the second. These selective movements are triggered by the regulating systems whose signals are combined in such a way as to detect the position in the core of the maxima and minima of the neutron flux.

The detectors are often placed in the reflectors. Progress in recent years now makes it possible to insert in the core a large number of small ion chambers tolerating high fluxes (10^{13} to 10^{14} $cm^{-2}s^{-1}$). A veritable "flux chart" is thus permanently drawn up, which allows for the optimum functioning of the reactor (§5.2.5).

The measurement systems must be calibrated in power. For this, at the start of operation of a nuclear plant, the power is stabilized at various levels (10^{-2} P_0 to P_0). Each time, data from the measurement systems are recorded, along with the inlet and outlet temperatures of the coolant. This last piece of information directly furnishes the power, and the linear systems are thus calibrated. The calibration of all the other systems follows from the overlapping of the operating ranges.

5.4 DESCRIPTION OF THE PRINCIPAL REACTOR TYPES

5.4.1 Introduction

In this subsection the reader will find the essential features of the most important reactors. These features appear in the form of tables and figures, and in most cases the preceding chapters enable us to understand the functioning of the installations presented. Some additional remarks will, however, round off the general information already given. Naturally, existing reactors with the same assembly may differ significantly, since the constructor must respond to the user's demands and to safety regulations which may vary from country to country. The figures provided are thus only indicative.

5.4.2 Light Water Reactors (LWR)

We know that there are two types of light water reactors (§5.1.3): PWR and BWR. In the first case, the water remains in a liquid phase in the core, while in the second, boiling takes place. We will describe these two types of reactors simultaneously, in order to highlight the differences implied by the above.

The most important differences are related to the mode of energy retrieval as indicated by the sketches of Fig. 5.17. In the boiling-water reactor, the thermodynamic cycle is direct, the reactor itself playing the role of the boiler. In the pressurized water reactor, the latter role is played by the steam generators. There is little to say about these cycles, which are conventional, except that, the outlet temperatures being low ($T_s \cong 300°C$), superheating is not possible (except in certain types of generators, and then in a very limited manner). In both cases we note the reheating of the boiler feed-water by removal of some of the steam

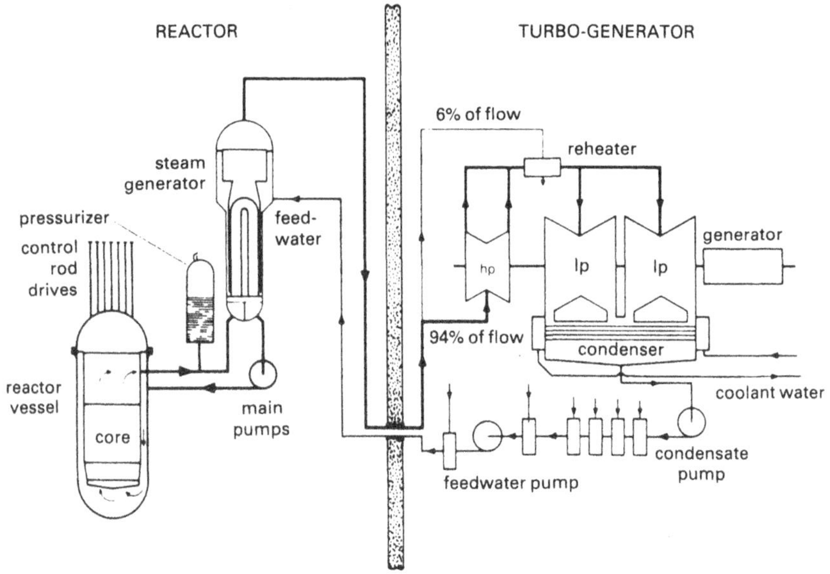

FIGURE 5.17a. Diagram of a PWR power plant.

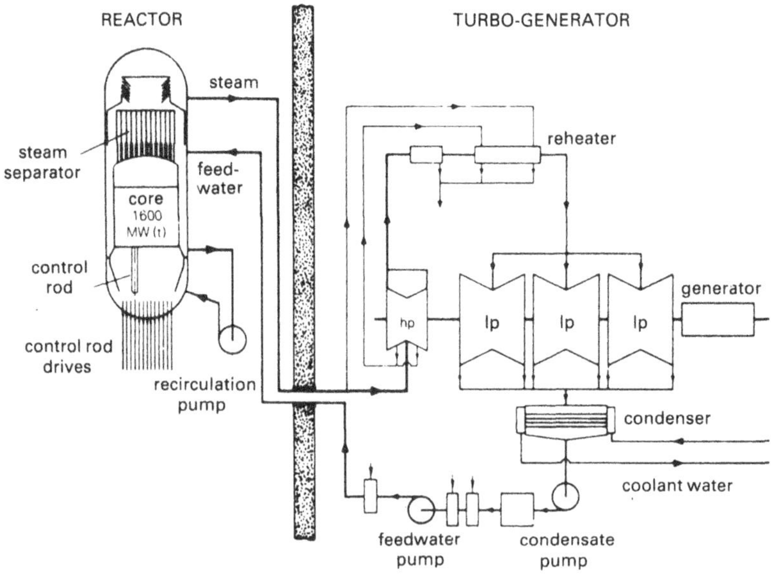

FIGURE 5.17b. Diagram of a BWR power plant.

outflow upstream from the turbines (improvement of the thermodynamic output). The comparative performances of these two types of reactors appear in Tab. 5.18 with reference to power plants of about 1000 MWe [20].

TABLE 5.18. General characteristics of LWR power plants of 1000 MWe.

Characteristics	PWR	BWR
Manufacturer	Westinghouse	General Electric
Type	3000 RR	BWR/6
Power: thermal (MW)	3000	2894
Power: electric (MW)	1000	1000
CORE		
Number of assemblies (cf. Tab. 5.22)	157	592
Active height (m)	4.16	3.76
Equivalent diameter of the core (m)	3.04	4.18
PRIMARY CIRCUIT		
Dimensions of the vessel:		
height (m)	13	21
diameter (m)	4.4	5.5
thickness (cm)	20	14
weight (t)	460	550
Steam generators:		
height (m)	22	—
diameter (m)	5	—
weight (t)	425	—
number	3	—
Number of loops and primary pumps	3	—
Number of loops and recirculation pumps	—	2 + 16 jet pumps
Pressure (bars)	155	72
Outlet temperature of coolant (°C)	~310	~275
Characteristics of the steam:		
pressure (bars)	75.8	72
Dimensions of the containment:		
height (m)	58	50
diameter (m)	42.5	34

One first notes the large differences in the pressures supported by the primary circuits. The BWR reactor in which boiling takes place requires less pressure, thus a thinner vessel.

Other differences appear with regard to the internal configuration (Fig. 5.19). In a PWR reactor, an internal tank isolates (pressurewise) the water entering the vessel from the water leaving it. The external pumps create the overpressure necessary for the circulation of the coolant in the fuel assemblies. In contrast, in BWR reactors the water is sepa-

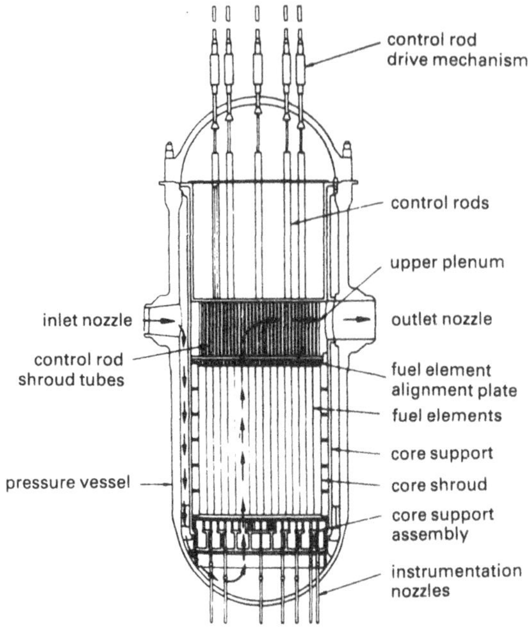

FIGURE 5.19a. Internal configuration of PWR vessels.

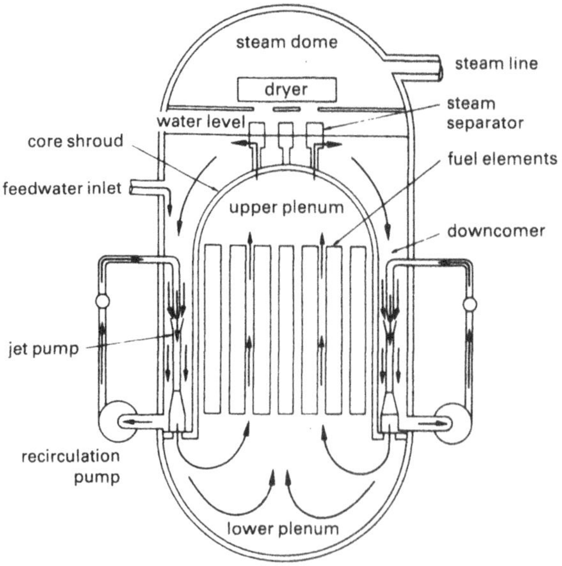

FIGURE 5.19b. Internal configuration of BWR vessels.

rated from the steam at the core outlet in a moisture separator, and mixed with the feed water. In this case, there is a "hydraulic short circuit" and the external pumps serve only to overcome the pressure drops of the primary circuit, exclusive of those which take place in the core. An additional circuit is thus necessary to create an overpressure at the core inlet (Fig. 5.19b). This circuit consists of a recirculation pump and jet pumps,the mechanism operating by suction. To complete the water/steam separation, a dryer is used; it improves the quality of the steam transmitted to the turbine. We find these components (separators and dryers) in PWR power plants at the steam generator outlets. Let us take a rapid look at their operating principle.

The separators are fixed on the dome formed by the internal tank of a BWR. They receive via vertical pipes passing through the head the coolant exiting from the core (Fig. 5.19b). Such devices, though they have no movable parts, induce a separation of the two phases by a centrifuging effect. To achieve this, fixed vanes placed in the entry nozzles impart a helicoidal motion to the fluid. The water received at the periphery of the separators flows downwards and emerges (below the water level) in the intake zone to be recirculated. The steam, on the other hand, is vented upward from the separators and rises into the head of the vessel after having passed through the dryer in which it follows a very winding path between corrugated metal sheets which retain the last traces of moisture.

We see in Tab. 5.18 that in order to increase overall reliability, several circuits, several exchangers, etc. are provided for. As an example, we have given in Fig. 5.20 a primary PWR circuit with four loops. The primary pumps are propelled by direct starting asynchronous motors, whose power is of the order of 8 MW. They are supplied with a heavy flywheel which maintains a certain flow rate, on a temporary basis, in case of loss of electric supply. Some manufacturers make use of several pumps per loop. A large number of variants exist, even for reactors of the same power, and thus the characteristics furnished by Tab. 5.18 here serve only as an example.

In PWR reactors a pressurizer is necessary, since the entire primary circuit is filled with more or less incompressible water (Fig. 5.20). The pressurizer is a small electric boiler containing a water-steam mixture in thermodynamic equilibrium. The use of electric heaters (in the lower part) or of sprinklers (in the upper part) permits the regulation of the fluid temperature and thus of the pressure exerted on the entire primary circuit. In case of overpressure, a valve allows the release of the excess steam into a reserve tank.

Aside from the reactor itself, the steam generators are the most important components of a PWR. Most often the primary water circulates in U-shaped pipes of imposing size (Tab. 5.18 and Fig. 5.20).

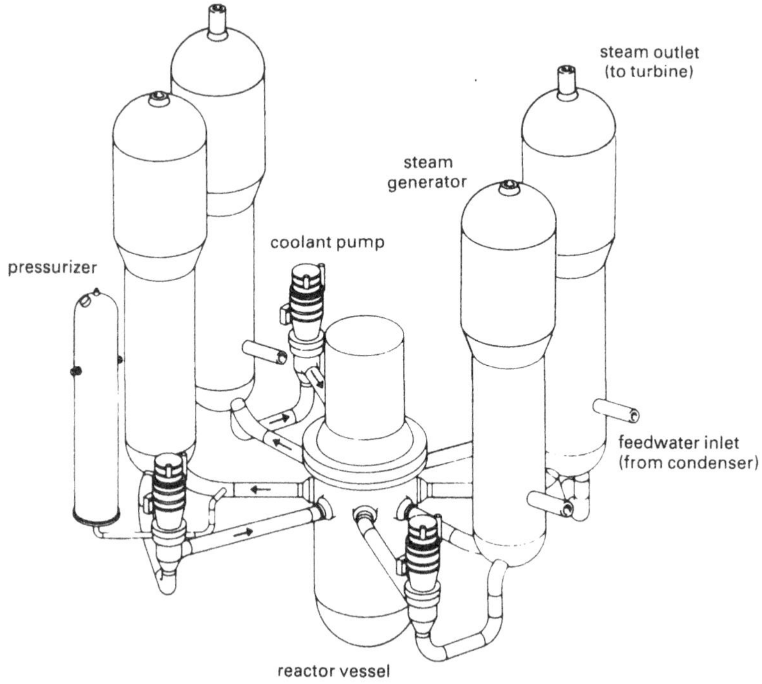

FIGURE 5.20. PWR primary circuit with four loops.

At first sight, one might think that the BWR reactors are less costly than the PWR, since the direct cycle permits in particular the bypassing of steam generators. But this is not at all the case, since complementary circuits are necessary for regulation and safety.

In Fig. 5.21 we have shown a detailed section of a boiling water reactor. Aside from the components already described, various dots appear. They correspond to circuits whose role will be explained in the following chapter. Finally we note that the control rods enter through the bottom, which is a particularity of BWR reactors. The reason for this is purely neutronic: in the lower part the water is in a liquid phase, whence a better moderation and higher material buckling. It follows that the axial distributions of neutron flux (and specific powers) have a maximum located distinctly below the median plane (the cosine distribution of Fig. 5.7 is no longer realized). If the control rods were to enter from the top, they would on the one hand be less efficient and on the other hand would tend to raise this maximum, thus leading to a hot spot problem (§5.2.5).

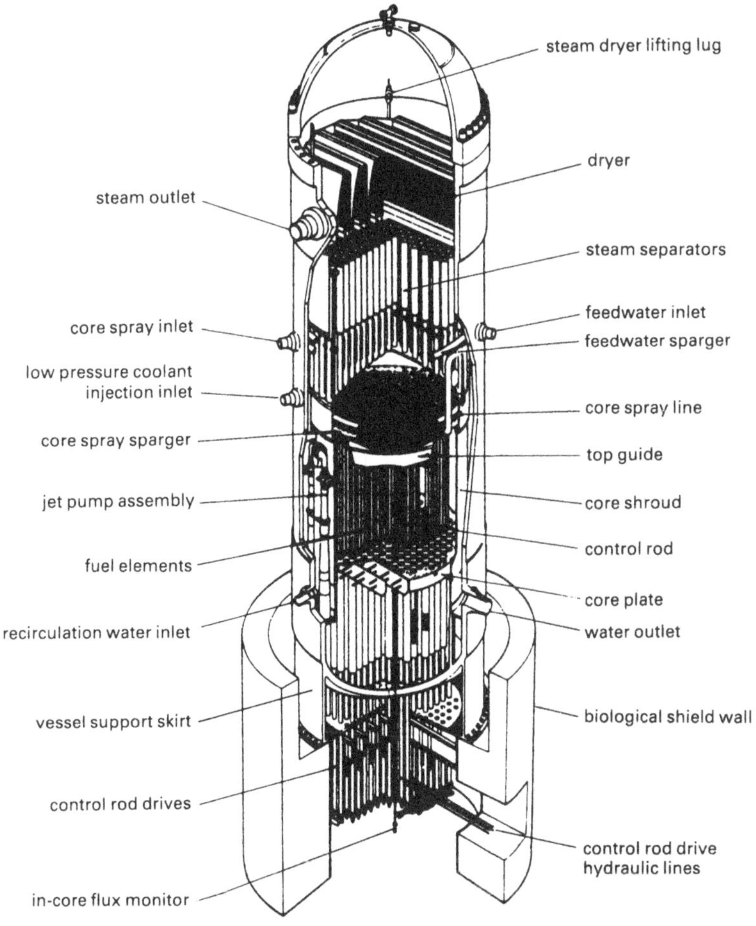

FIGURE 5.21. Boiling water reactor (General Electric).

Let us now look at the characteristics of the fuel used in light water reactors.

The fuel rods are made of UO_2 oxide pellets about 10 mm in diameter and 10 mm long, introduced into a zircalloy sheath (cladding). For reasons of handling, these rods are assembled in bundles or fuel assemblies. Of smaller dimensions, these assemblies are more numerous in BWR reactors and their active length in both cases is of the order of 4 m (Tab. 5.18). Other differences appear in Tab. 5.22. Thus, the volume moderating ratio (§5.1.4) is larger for BWR assemblies, which can be explained by the smaller mean density of the moderator (boiling). In other words, the PWR lattices are more closely spaced, which gives them a higher power density.

The square box surrounding BWR fuel assemblies (Fig. 5.23) is absent in PWR reactors. In the latter, radial mass transfers are allowed, and the control rods are cylindrical as in most reactors. Among the 289 positions (17 x 17) available in a PWR assembly, only 264 are occupied by the fuel rods (Tab. 5.22) and 25 are reserved for guide tubes whose role is to receive control rods, solid poisons, and flux measurement devices. From a mechanical point of view, the control rods which enter a PWR assembly from the top are rigidly bound and constitute a regulating bundle. About 50 bundles are necessary in a PWR reactor of 1000 MWe, each one possessing its driving shaft; hence roughly one assembly in three (Tab. 5.18) will be concerned.

TABLE 5.22. Characteristics of LWR fuel elements.

Characteristics	PWR	BWR
Diameter of rods (cm)	0.95	1.25
Enrichment UO_2 (%) (at equilibrium)	3.2	2.7
Cladding	zircaloy	zircaloy
No. of rods per assembly	264	63
Section of an assembly (cm × cm)	20 x 20	15 x 15
Moderation volume ratio (V_m/V_c)	1.14	1.86
Mean power density (kW/ℓ)	99	56
Mean specific power (MW/t)	36.2	26
Total mass of uranium in the core (t)	82.5	111
Annual refuelling by	1/3	1/4 à 1/5
Initial conversion factor C_0	0.5	0.5
Mean burnup rate (MWd/t)	33,000	26,000

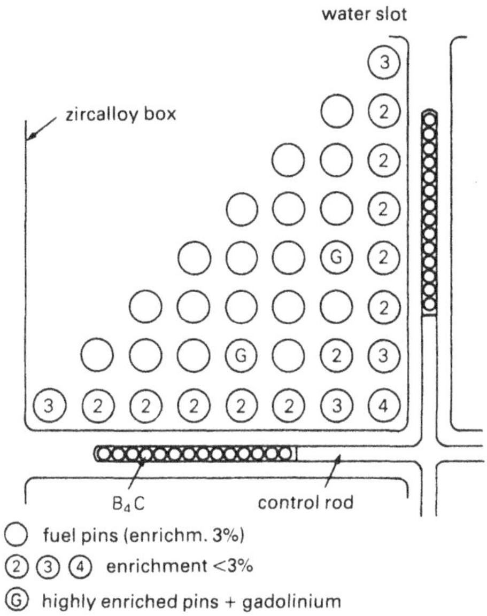

FIGURE 5.23. BWR reactor.

In the case of boiling water reactors, on the other hand, water slots situated between the assemblies assure the passage of various control mechanisms. In particular, cruciform control rods are used, as indicated in Fig. 5.23. We also see in this figure that various enrichments are in fact used to avoid the increase of neutron flux in the vicinity of the water slots (here the problem of flattening also arises (§5.2.5)). Finally, some control rods contain the burnable poison (gadolinium), whereas PWR reactors use a boronized material physically separated from the fuel and hence situated in the guide tubes mentioned earlier in the context of control rods. These tubes create a penalty from the point of view of reactivity, since they are fixed in the core during reactor operation. Their influence is most appreciable at the end of the cycle when the burnable poison has disappeared. In BWR reactors, in contrast, gadolinium oxide Gd_2O_3 does not necessitate any supplementary structural material, since it suffices to add it homogeneously to uranium oxide UO_2 in certain fuel rods; this must be done at the manufacturing stage of the pellets (Sec. 7.4).

The use of an adjustable soluble poison in the moderator is as we know possible in PWR reactors. Boric acid BO_3H_3, which has the advantage of being a weak acid, is introduced in sufficient quantities to cover the effects on reactivity in the intermediate and long term (§5.3.2). One thus keeps to a strict minimum the intervention of the regulating bundles. The concentration to be envisaged at the beginning of the cycle is of the order of 1500 ppm (1 ppm = 10^{-6}); since the water purification system is not perfect, a residual concentration of boric acid remains at the end of the cycle (about 50 ppm), which slightly penalizes the neutron balance.

The refuelling modes are quite similar to the ideal cycle described earlier (§5.3.7). Initially, the flattenings are realized from three enrichments. We have, for example, 2.5% at the center, 2.8% in the intermediate zone and 3.2% at the periphery. An analogous charging is represented in Fig. 5.24. Subsequently, a unique enrichment of 3.2% is adopted

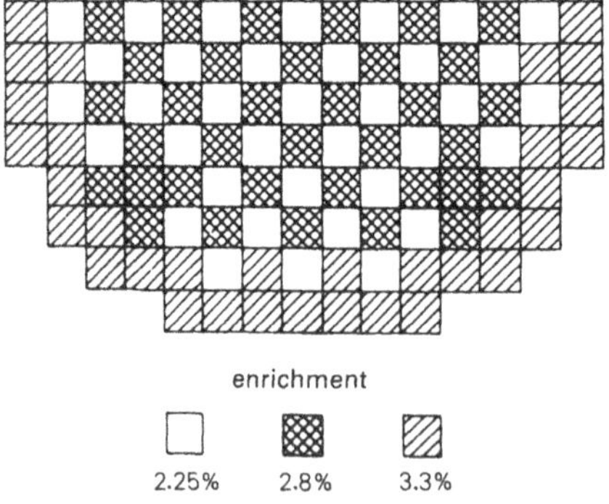

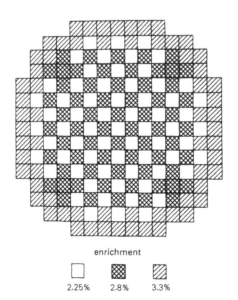

FIGURE 5.24. Initial charging of a PWR core.

and partial refuellings create the desired flattening. A discharging by thirds of the core takes place every year; the annual shutdown of the power station for maintenance reasons is used to advantage. All this is valid for PWR reactors. As for BWR reactors, which originally received one single enrichment for the initial core, current thinking is closer to that for the preceding.

The burnup rates attained in LWR reactors are of the order of 30,000 MWd/t (Tab. 5.22), while the technological limit is in the 50,000 MWd/t range, which makes for a comfortable safety margin.

We shall conclude this section by presenting a control mode peculiar to these reactors, which follows from the importance of temperature effects (§5.3.3).

Let us first consider the case of a PWR reactor running at its rated power. If the power station operator opens the steam intake valve of the turbine just a bit more, the following phenomena will occur:

- the increase of the steam flow not being immediately compensated by an increase of the heat flux from the primary to the secondary circuit, the quantity of steam and thus the pressure will decrease in the steam generators;
- since the steam is at the saturation point in these generators its temperature will diminish and lead to an increase of the heat flux from the primary to the secondary;
- this increase of the heat flux will at first induce a fall in the moderator temperature; since the latter has a negative α_m coefficient, a positive reactivity will spontaneously appear (5.23) and trigger a slow divergence;
- the power increase which results from this tends to bring the temperature of the moderator back to its initial value, whence a lowering of reactivity and, at the end, a return to the critical state.

The new critical state thus obtained corresponds to higher power and steam outflow in the secondary, while the average temperature of the moderator has not varied significantly (if one omits the transient described above). In fact this is only true if the Doppler coefficient α_c is small compared to the coefficient α_m of the moderator, which is the case here. But rigorously speaking, the fuel being hotter, the moderator will be slightly cooler for this second operating point, as is indicated by equation (5.23) where $\delta\rho = 0$ leads to $\delta T_m = -(\alpha_c/\alpha_m)\delta T_c$. Besides, the power having increased, the difference between intake and outlet temperatures of the coolant will have increased in the same proportions, since the primary flowrate has not been changed (5.14). All this is not in contradiction with the fact that the moderator temperature has not varied much on the average.

An analogous reasoning shows that a partial closing of the steam intake valve leads to a reduction of the power. PWR reactors are called power followers, since the production of fission energy follows the demand of the turbine without necessitating the use of control rods. All the same, this type of operation is only possible within certain limits, and in any case, classical control must eventually intervene from the moment that the xenon concentration changes by virtue of the power change.

We will now quickly see what happens with BWR reactors. The cycle being direct, the conclusions are different. Let us once again consider an increase of the steam flow rate. As in the preceding case, the pressure will at first diminish, but here it is a question of the pressure of the steam in the dome (Fig. 5.19b), and hence of the pressure exerted on the moderator whose boiling will increase. The void rate will increase in the core and thus negative reactivity appears ($\alpha_v < 0$, cf. equation (5.23)) and the power decreases. The reactor no longer obeys the turbine and is not a "power follower". One would of course arrive at a new operating point corresponding to lower power and lower steam pressure, but that is not what is sought. We get back a mode of operation similar to that of PWR reactors by playing with the flow rate of the feed pumps (Fig. 5.17b). In fact, an increase of the flow rate entails a decrease of the void rate and hence leads to the appearance of positive reactivity and the desired increase of power. As the effect of voidage on reactivity is preponderant in this type of reactor, the void rate necessarily gets back to its initial value when the new critical state has been attained. This means that the steam flowrate has increased sufficiently to compensate the increased flowrate from the feed pumps. Here too the use of control rods can be avoided, at least in the short term.

5.4.3 Heavy Water Moderated Reactors

This reactor assembly with pressure tubes (§5.1.3) offers in principle a number of possibilities. In particular, the choice of coolant which will circulate in these tubes is fairly open, for, up to a certain point, this fluid has little influence on the neutron balance, its passage cross section being small compared with that of a fuel cell. It is thus possible to come up with original solutions from the thermohydraulic point of view. Likely coolants would be, for example:

- organic liquids which permit operation at low pressure with outlet temperatures higher than those of light water reactors; in addition they are chemically compatible with uranium carbide UC, whose performances are better than those of the oxide (Tab. 5.6);
- inert gases (CO_2): the absence of changes of phase is a safety asset and neutron capture is negligible in these coolants;
- light water, which allows for a direct water-steam cycle analogous to that of BWR reactors;
- heavy water: the best solution from the neutronic point of view, especially if only natural uranium is used, which is the chief advantage of heavy-water-moderated reactors.

The first three variants have been actualized (prototype or test reactors): the first in the Euratom (ESSOR), the second in France (EL 4) and in Switzerland (Lucens), the third in Great Britain (SGHWR) and in Canada (Gentilly-1), but none of these reached industrial maturity; only the fourth variant (heavy water - heavy water) was commercialized by the Canadians under the name CANDU (Canada Deuterium-Uranium). This section will deal only with this type of reactor.

The essential feature is the use of natural uranium oxide (UO_2). Unfortunately, because heavy water has a weaker slowing down power than light water (§5.1.4), the moderator has a considerable volume. The core of a CANDU reactor is thus distinctly larger than that of an LWR reactor without, however, reaching the imposing size of the first generation graphite-moderated reactors. As a result, the power density is lower. As can be seen in Fig. 5.25, the core, and hence the channels which go across it, are horizontal for reasons which will be clearer further on. This prohibits a direct cycle (no boiling in the reactor).

The temperatures of the coolant being comparable with those of the primary circuit of a PWR, the pressures are of the same order. Given its large size, it is not possible to expect the vessel to hold the pressure; the pressure tubes serve this function. At the rate of one per fuel cell

(§5.1.3) these tubes contain the fuel elements and the pressurized coolant. The heavy water in the interstices which assures the neutronic moderation is not subjected to any significant pressure, and thus a thin vessel is allowed. To avoid the heating of the moderator, it is housed in a calandria tube and the space between these two tubes is filled by an insulator. The moderator remains cold (~ 60°C): it is insulated in temperature and in pressure from the coolant. This latter could be, as we have seen, of a different material, but for essentially neutronic reasons, the Canadian assembly uses heavy water for this function.

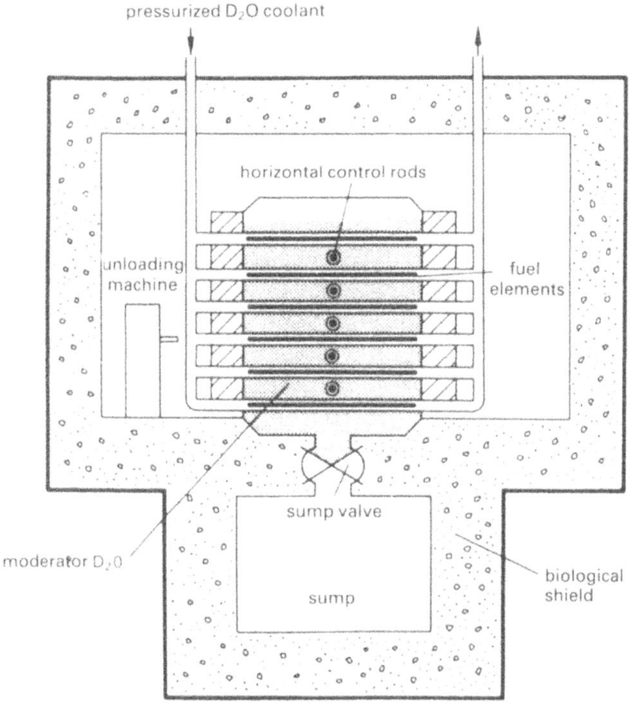

FIGURE 5.25. Sketch of a CANDU reactor.

Reactor concepts using pressure tubes have the advantage of being applicable to installations of variable dimensions and thus of variable power. In principle, there is no size limitation, as there is for reactors in vessels (provided one disregards spatial oscillations of the flux induced by xenon in large-sized cores, §9.4.4).

Apart from the use of heavy water, the primary circuit is similar to that of a PWR reactor, as is the secondary circuit in which a conventional steam cycle is used (ordinary water is of course used in this circuit).

To improve heat transfers, the fuel elements situated in the horizontal pressure tubes are made up of a certain number of "pencils". In contrast to LWR reactors, the active length of a channel corresponds to a set of disconnected bundles of fuel pencils. The annular pressure tubes assure the guidance of this "train" of fuel elements. This arrangement permits an original way of refuelling.

The initial reactivities are small compared to those of LWR reactors, since one can no longer play with the enrichment which is imposed by nature (0.72% instead of 3% in LWR reactors). The use of unloading machines during operation permits a highly fractionated refuelling, namely, one segment = one channel (§5.3.7). The success of this reactor assembly has depended crucially on the creation of machines which are much more complex than those used for operations after reactor shutdown (LWR, HTGR). Such machines are now well mastered.

The use of zircalloy as a structural material and continuous unloading permit burnup rates of about 8000 MWd/t. One cannot hope for better with natural uranium (graphite-gas-natural uranium reactors hardly exceed 4000 MWd/t).

Refuelling is accomplished very simply in CANDU reactors. The "continuous bi-directional axial" method used is in fact applicable to all reactors with annular pressure tubes in which the fuel circulates. Two machines are used. One supplies fresh fuel at one end of the channel. This causes the exit at the other end of the irradiated fuel, which is recieved by the second machine. The reactor-machine coupling must evidently satisfy very strict conditions of leak-tightness. Only when this has been assured can the channel plugs be removed and loading-unloading operations begin. Things are so arranged that the fuel circulates in opposite directions in adjacent channels. Everything takes place as if the fuel was at rest with a burnup rate constant in time and equal to half the rate obtained in the extracted elements. Thus there is practically no reactivity fluctuation associated to refuelling when the equilibrium cycle has been obtained. One sometimes speaks of "ideal refuelling."

The conversion factor of this type of reactor is much better than that of LWR reactors. It can attain 0.8. The plutonium-producing character of these heavy water or graphite moderated natural uranium reactors has been profitably used in installations for the production of military plutonium. For this latter case the burning rates are of course much lower than those of CANDU reactors, for reasons already discussed (beginning of §5.3.7).

CANDU reactors are probably more expensive than LWR reactors in terms of the investments involved (for reasons of size and of the price of heavy water). The fuel cycle is however more advantageous, since one can avoid uranium enrichment and its associated political problems (§5.1.6).

The stabilizing effect mentioned in subsec. 5.1.4 is practically absent, since coolant and moderator are now separated. Since the moderator remains cold, a power excursion and hence an increase of the coolant temperature has very little influence on the reactivity. This is a shortcoming from the safety standpoint; we must not forget however that the effect of the fuel temperature on the reactivity, which is the first to take place during a transient, is here also negative (§5.3.3). In addition, the rapid emptying of the moderator in case of accident buys an enormous anti-reactivity, which reinforces that of the safety rods (§5.3.8). Such an emptying is here envisageable since it does not entail any loss of coolant which continues to circulate in the pressure tubes, assuring the cooling of the fuel even when the reactor has stopped.

We have restricted ourselves so far to the description of the fundamental principles on which this type of reactor rests; this assembly has been continuously improved since going operational in 1962 and we will now indicate its current performances [21]. In what follows, we will try whenever possible to make comparisons with LWR reactors. Table 5.26 gives the essential characteristics of three representative CANDU power plants.

Apart from the neutronic aspects, the need to connect a large number of pressure tubes (600 to 700) to the primary circuit constitutes a first peculiarity. The inlet and outlet coolant <u>collectors</u> appear in Fig. 5.27 for a primary circuit of four loops. This complication is the price to pay for the inherent benefits of this concept; aside from the advantages already cited, the pressure tubes permit the withdrawal of defaulting fuel elements during operation, whereas with LWR reactors one must await the annual shutdown (which can mean several months) or accept an additional shutdown, which might explain their small load factor (60% compared to 80% for CANDU reactors).

TABLE 5.26. Essential characteristics of CANDU reactors.

Characteristics	Pickering	Bruce	Gentilly
Number of reactors	4	4	1
Net electric power per reactor (MWe)	512	732	638
Thermodynamic output (%)	29.1	29.1	29.3
REACTOR DATA			
Number of channels	390	480	380
Max. power of 1 channel (MWt)	5.12	5.74	6.5
N. of bundles per channel	12	13	12
No. of fuel pins per bundle	28	37	37
Min. thickness of pressure tubes (mm)	4.06	4.06	4.19
CONTROL			
Compensating rods	18 (cobalt)	—	21 (stainless steel)
Booster rods (U^{235})	—	16	—
Solid absorbing rods	—	4	4
Liquid absorbing rods	14	14	14
No. of assemblies with detectors	8	20	33
Emergency shutdown no. 1 (rods)	11	30	28
Emergency shutdown no. 2	Moderator dump	Injection of poison	injection of poison
PRIMARY CIRCUIT			
Inlet temperature (°C)	249	252/256	267
Outlet temperature (°C)	293	299	310
Inlet pressure (bars)	95.5	91.1	110
No. of steam generators	12	8	4
No. of pumps	12 + 4 (reserve)	4	4
Pump power (MW)	1,21	6.32	6.6
SECONDARY CIRCUIT			
Steam flow rate (10^6 kg/h)	2.72	4.22	3.72
Steam pressure (bars)	41	43.8	47

The steam generators are situated on both sides of the reactor and the primary circuit is such that in two neighboring channels the coolant flows in opposite directions, but always in the same direction as the fuel pencil bundles. Apart from these features, the primary circuit is quite similar to that of a PWR reactor. Thus in the case of the Gentilly power plant, the four loops are equipped with principal pumps (Fig. 5.27) developing a total of 26.4 MW as against about 32 MW for PWR reactors (§5.4.2) for a weaker thermal power (2000 MWt as against 3000 MWt). Thus, in spite of their complexity, it does not seem that the collectors penalize the installation from the point of view of pressure drops. The primary circuit pressure, here also regulated by a pressurizer, is about 50% lower than that of the PWR reactor (Tab. 5.18 and 5.26) and the thermodynamic outputs are somewhat lower (29% as against 33%).

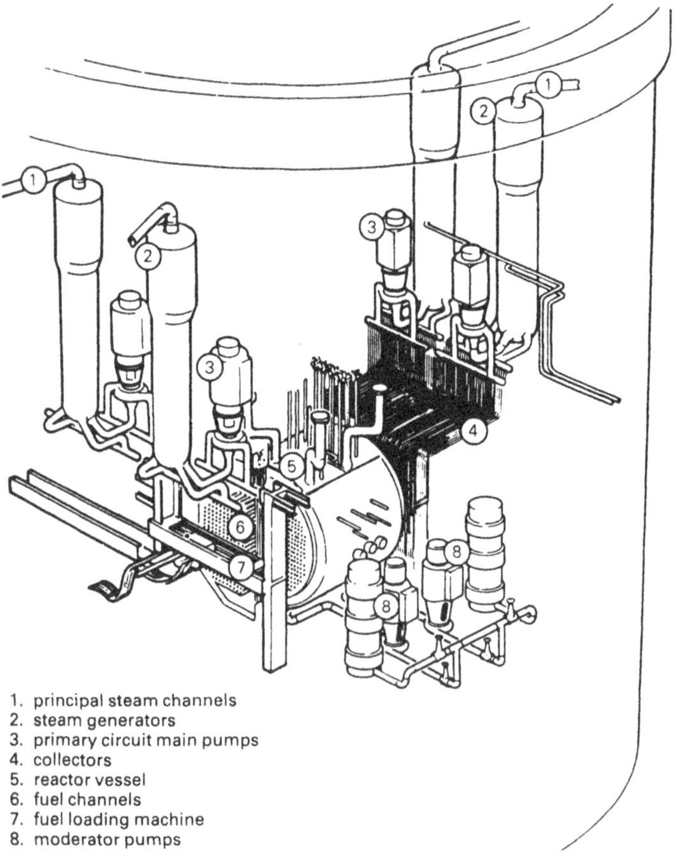

1. principal steam channels
2. steam generators
3. primary circuit main pumps
4. collectors
5. reactor vessel
6. fuel channels
7. fuel loading machine
8. moderator pumps

FIGURE 5.27. CANDU reactor with 4 loops.

Finally, a special circuit must be used for cooling the moderator (Fig. 5.27). Not only is the thermal insulation of the pressure tubes by the calandria tubes imperfect, but also a fraction of the fission energy is dissipated in the moderator (neutrons and γ rays, cf. §3.1.4). We note in passing that the quantities of heavy water used in the Gentilly reactor are respectively 263.3 t for the moderator and 199.1 t for the primary circuit.

We will now consider the fuel (natural UO_2 oxide). In contrast to the sketch in Fig. 5.2, the bundles are now made up of a large number of "pencils". In the first heavy water reactor plans, there were a much smaller number. This evolution can be explained in the following way. Very roughly, neutronic considerations (§5.1.4) impose a moderating volume ratio V_m/V_c of the order of 15, which is distinctly higher than that of LWR reactors (1 to 2). This ratio can be obtained in various ways, but for structural reasons, it is desirable to limit the number of channels (widely spaced lattice), which implies that each channel has a significant fuel cross section, whence the need to fractionate the fuel to improve the heat exchanges (despite the negative effect of this fractionating on the resonance integral, cf. §4.4.5). We thus arrive at bundles comprising up to 37 pencils whose cohesion is assured by two perforated plates (Fig.5.28).

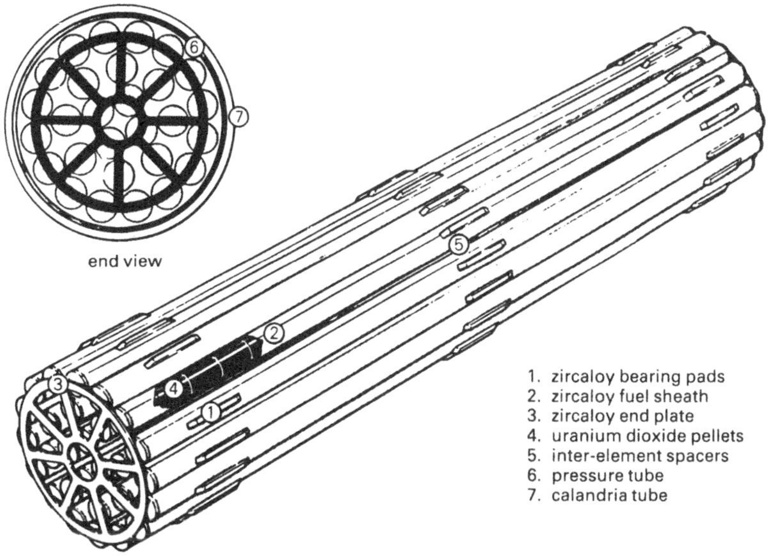

FIGURE 5.28. Bundle of 28 fuel pencils (Pickering).

The principal fuel characteristics of the Gentilly plant as well as the arrangement in the core are given in Tab. 5.29. We observe, as previously noted, that the average power density is much smaller than that of PWR reactors (by a factor of about 10, cf. Tab. 5.22). One should not be too concerned by this last parameter (this is also the case for HTGR reactors), for the heavy water assembly has a number of advantages as we have seen, and a low power density is an undeniable advantage in case of serious accident. From the cross section of a cell (V = 28.57 x 28.57) and from the power density (11.2 kW/l) we can deduce the average linear power of a bundle (end of §5.2.3). Dividing this by the number of pencils (37) and by the flattening coefficient α_p = 0.582 (§5.2.5), we find that the maximum linear power of a pencil can attain 424 W/cm. This value is very close to that deduced from Tab. 5.22 for a PWR reactor, the latter being itself very close to the linear power of a fast breeder reactor, LMFBR. This is not at all surprising, since the three reactors use the same fuel and the linear power follows from the common integral conductivity (§5.2.2), enrichment playing no role in this matter.

TABLE 5.29. Fuel characteristics of the CANDU reactor.

Thermal power (MW)	2062
Quantity of fuel (t)	96
Core: active length (m)	5.944
Core: equivalent diameter (m)	6.285
Mean power density (kW/l)	11.2
Mean specific power (MW/t)	21.5
Global flattening coefficient	0.582
Square lattice pitch (cm)	28.57
Bundles: length (cm)	49.5
Bundles: diameter (cm)	10.2
Bundles: rated power (kW)	830
Pencils: diameter (cm)	1.308
Pencils: number	37
Burnup rate (MWd/t)	7000

Finally, the burnup rate exceeds 7000 MWd/t as compared to 33,000 MWd/t for PWR reactors, but this is not a valid comparison, since in the latter case, uranium enriched at 3.2% is used (Tab. 5.22). To produce 1 kg of enriched uranium of this type, 5.76 kg of natural uranium are required (Tab. 7.11). Thus in terms of natural uranium, the burnup rate of a PWR reactor is 5700 MWd/t, whence: for the same energy production a CANDU reactor consumes 20% less uranium than LWR reactors (not to mention the cost of enrichment).

The control of CANDU reactors conforms to the general philosophy presented in Sec. 5.3. We note the following points:

- Burnable poison is not necessary, since reactivity fluctuations related to fuel consumption are small (continuous unloading: 18 bundles per day).
- Liquid control rods (introduction of ordinary water into 14 compartments) play the role of the classical regulating rods when they act in concert; they also help thwart the spatial instabilities of xenon to which this type of reactor is sensitive (end of §5.3.3).
- A rapid drop in power can be obtained with the help of four cadmium rods (independently of the classical 28 safety rods).
- 21 stainless steel compensating rods permit the flattening of the flux (§5.2.5) and provide for a large reactivity reserve.
- As in PWR reactors, a soluble poison permits the control of slow variations of reactivity.
- All control rods move in tubes perpendicular to the pressure tubes (Fig. 5.27).

5.4.4 High Temperature Reactors (HTGR)

These graphite-moderated (thus thermal) reactors are helium-cooled. These two characteristics (not very effective moderator and coolant) lead to distinctly larger dimensions than those of the LWR cores, and thus to much lower power densities. Although there are several variants with direct cycles, making use of gas turbines (German-Swiss project), most industrial projects are related to indirect cycles. In what follows, we will describe the American concept (General Atomic). Helium circulates in a primary circuit (of several loops) and sets the water boiling in the steam generators. These constitute the boiler of a water-steam cycle whose characteristics are more like those of existing thermal power plants than LWR or CANDU plants. Here, superheating and re-superheating of steam are possible. In fact this type of reactor allows for much higher outlet temperatures of the coolant (700°C as against 320°C)as Tab. 5.30 shows. Even though the pressures are lower (50 bars) than in LWR reactors, the size of the core makes preferable a prestressed concrete vessel, and all the more so since the use of a gas lends itself to this solution. This technology was perfected in France during the 1950's and applied to the plutonium-producing reactors G2-G3 of Marcoule. The high temperatures produced in the core required a special cooling, however (by streams of water), of the inner wall of the vessel.

TABLE 5.30. General characteristics of HTGR power plants.

Characteristics	Prototype	Power reactors	
		4 loops	6 loops
Manufacturer: General Atomic			
Power thermal (MW)	842	2000	3000
Power electric (MW)	330	770	1160
CORE			
Prismatic fuel elements (cf. Fig. 5.33):			
No. of elements per column	6	8	8
No. of columns	247	343	493
Active height (m)	—	6.34	6.34
Equivalent diameter of the core (m)	—	7	8.47
Residence time of fuel in core (yrs)	6	4	4
Power density (kW/ℓ)	6.3	8.4	8.4
Conversion factor C	—	0.8-0.9	0.8-0.9
Maximum burnup rate (MWd/t)	100,000	95,000	95,000
PRIMARY CIRCUIT			
Pressure (bars)	49	49	49
Core inlet/outlet temp. of helium (°C)	404/776	319/727	319/727
Helium circulators			
— power per unit (MW)	3.9	10.5	10.5
— number	4	4	6
STEAM-WATER CYCLE			
— feedwater temperature (°C)	204	187	187
— superheated steam (HP)			
— pressure (bars)	173	173	173
— temperature (°C)	540	513	513
— re-superheated steam (MP)			
— pressure (bars)	41	40.4	40.4
— temperature (°C)	510	539	539

The poor thermohydraulic properties of gases require significant pumping power. Helium circulators or turboblowers driven by turbines which take up the steam from the secondary circuit provide the necessary flow. We see in Fig. 5.31 that the entire primary circuit is immersed in the vessel, which improves the safety of the plant. In particular, the turboblowers and the steam generators are lodged in the same cavities. The same is true of the motor-blowers and auxiliary exchangers which equip the emergency primary circuit.

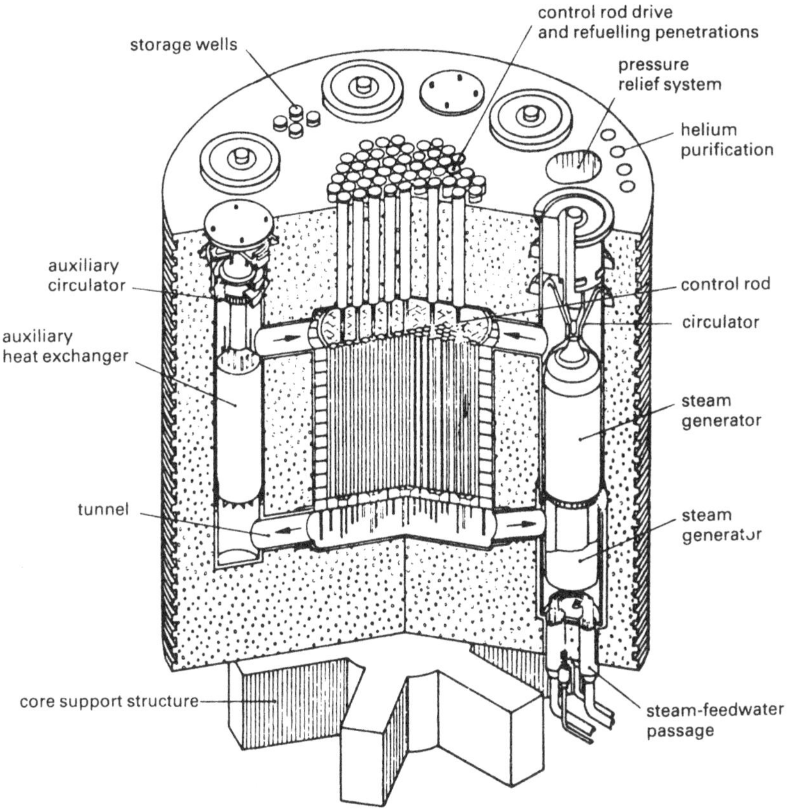

FIGURE 5.31. HTGR power plant - sketch of the reactor block.

The use of an inert gas as coolant makes the technological limits less stringent (Sec. 5.2), and in particular the critical heat flux problem disappears. But it is the development of a very original fuel which has permitted the attainment of the helium temperature indicated earlier.

As we have seen (§3.3.4), HTGR reactors are conceived to function on a thorium-uranium cycle. The fuel is made up of little spheres called <u>coated particles</u> (Fig. 5.32), some of which are composed of highly enriched (at 93%) uranium carbide and the others of thorium oxide. Fissile and fertile materials are thus separated in this type of reactor. The differences in diameter (200 μm and 500 μm) permit the separation of these two types of particles before chemical reprocessing. Uranium U^{233} which is formed from thorium is thus never mixed with the residual U^{235} which remains in the particles of smaller diameter. This is an important point, since reprocessing would not permit the separation of the two uraniums, U^{235} and U^{233}. During recycling, uranium U^{233} appears in particles of intermediate diameter.

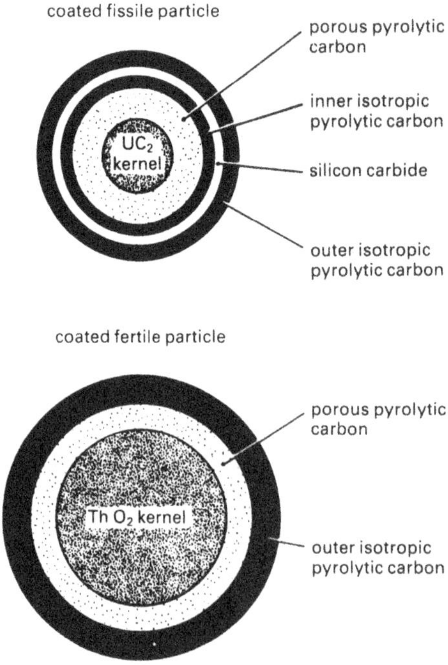

FIGURE 5.32. Coated particles.

The essential characteristic of the fuel lies in the coating of the particles. The role of zircalloy cladding in LWR reactors is here played by several coatings using carbon in various allotropic states as well as silicon carbide. The use of these materials permits much higher operating temperatures, and at the same time assures a good leakproofness with respect to fission products. We note that the coating is much more "sophisticated" in the case of fissile particles, since a much greater generation of fission products is involved (Fig. 5.32).

The fuel particles described above are bound together in graphite matrices to form fuel rods whose diameters are of the order of 1.6 cm. Good moderation ratios as well as equivalent mean enrichment U/(U + Th) are obtained by varying the relative proportions of fissile and fertile particles .

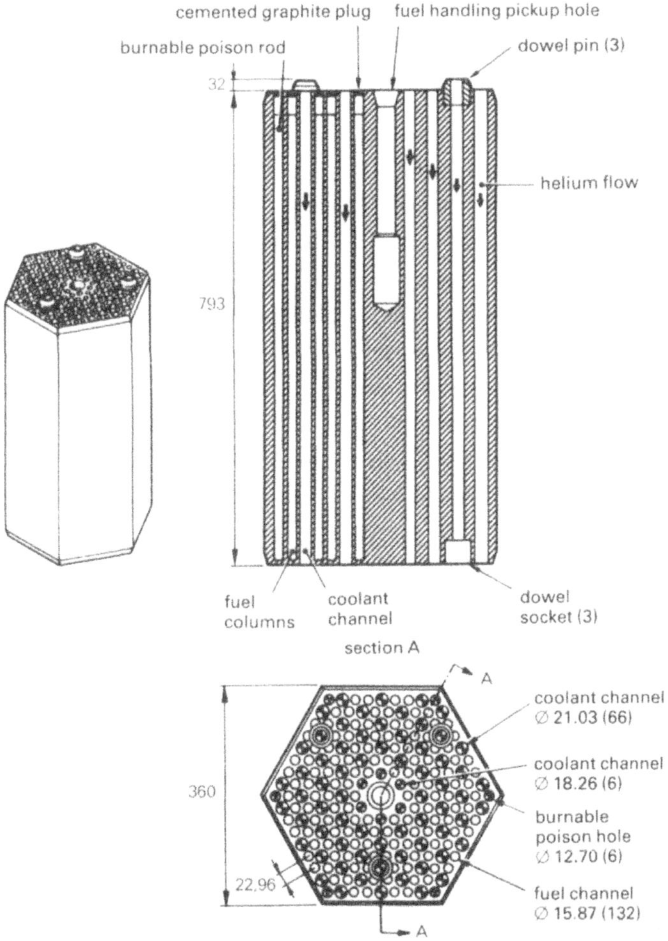

FIGURE 5.33. HTGR fuel elements.

The fuel element or block itself is a graphite prism of hexagonal cross section consisting of two types of channels. One type receives fuel rods and the other, the helium coolant (Fig. 5.33). We note that in contrast to all other reactor assemblies, the coolant (helium) is not in direct contact with the fuel, so that the heat transmission takes place via the graphite.

Refueling (by quarter) takes place after shutdown and on the average once a year. The stacked columns (set of prismatic elements placed one on top of the other) are grouped in loading cells. Each cell consists of seven columns, the central column being equipped with control rods. A set of unloaded (or loaded) cells makes up what we have previously called a segment (§5.3.7). There are four segments, since refueling takes place by quarters. Cells belonging to the same segment have about the same burnup rate, but are uniformly distributed in the core, and are thus not a source of flattening. Two adjacent cells will be of different age and thus belong to different segments. Radial flattening is achieved by dividing the core into five zones whose enrichment increases from the center outward. This type of zoning is used for all loadings in contrast to LWR reactors where it only appears in the initial core. Differentiated enrichments thus continue during the life of the reactor, since one can no longer use the principle of fuel circulation from the periphery to the center, with the new fuel always remaining at the outside. The fuel cells would have to be manipulated too often in such a loading mode.

The conversion factors are quite close to unity during the recycling of uranium U^{233} (Tab. 5.30). We could in principle do better and perhaps attain breeding, but that would not correspond to the goal of these reactors, which is of thermodynamic nature.

Given the large number of available parameters, the HTGR fuel elements make possible almost any type of core. One has even thought of "axial flattening of temperatures" which would necessitate three different enrichments in the same column (since the helium penetrates the core from above, the higher blocs are more enriched).

This type of reactor uses a burnable poison for the long-term control of reactivity. To this end, holes are pierced and rods containing particles of boron carbide (B_4C) are placed in them (Fig. 5.33). In addition, by fine-tuning, the burnable poison permits variations to be made in the relative power liberated in the different segments.

At the present time, there are no commercial HTGR power plants in operation, so that the last two columns of Tab. 5.30 are only the results of detailed planning studies. A prototype exists in the United States, however (Fort St. Vrain, first column of Tab. 5.30) but in particular the irradiations effected in the small reactor of Peach Bottom have shown that the coated particles tolerate high burnup rates (at least 60,000 MWd/t) in the envisaged temperature conditions. A similar concept has been developed in Germany, but this time the coated particles are incorporated in graphite pellets which permit discharging by gravity. The most irradiated pellets are extracted from the bottom of the reactor (coal stove principle).

Finally, we note that the Europeans, who were the promoters of the HTGR assembly (DRAGON project of OECD), have preferred the concept described above to that of a low-enrichment fuel that excluded the thorium cycle. However, since this concept is based on practically pure uranium U^{235} (at least at the start of the cycle) strong criticism has been voiced with regard to the problem of nuclear arms proliferation. It is in fact possible to recuperate the coated fissile particles by simply sifting the ashes obtained by burning the graphite of the fuel elements (Fig. 5.33). This is in fact the normal procedure envisaged for reprocessing. Thus a return to the low-enrichment cycle is not excluded.

5.4.5 Fast Breeder Reactors

Among the breeder reactors, those which have been the most studied are the fast reactors cooled by liquid sodium (LMFBR). These are the only ones to have been industrially implemented at the prototype stage:

- BN 350 (350 MWe) operational in 1972 (USSR)
- Phenix (250 MWe) operational in 1973 (France)
- PFR (250 MWe) operational in 1974 (Great Britain).

These prototypes having been found satisfactory, France and the Soviet Union undertook the second phase of development of this assembly. France went directly into construction of a commercial-sized power plant, Superphenix, of 1200 MWe, situated at Creys-Malville in the Rhone valley, whereas the Soviet Union took up manufacture of the more modest sized (600 MWe) BN 600. The latter achieved full power in 1981, and Superphenix should be operational in 1986.

As we have seen (§3.2.2), breeding is based on the Pu^{239}- U^{238} cycle and requires a conversion of fertile matter not only in the core but also in the blankets. Uranium U^{238} which becomes the true fuel, since plutonium is only an intermediary agent, can be used in the form of natural uranium or in depleted form. Depleted uranium, or "tailings", a waste product of enrichment plants (Sec. 7.3), has so far not found any other use.

In contrast to the preceding reactors, sodium-cooled reactors need three circuits. A secondary circuit using liquid sodium is interposed between the primary circuit and the water-steam circuit. If, following a failure of the steam generator, a violent sodium-water reaction were to take place, it would not affect the integrity of the reactor proper.

The core and its blankets are contained in a vessel filled with liquid sodium and the primary circuit can be conceived in two ways:

- in the so-called loop concept the pumps and the intermediary heat exchangers outside the vessel are connected to it by pipes. This arrangement is analogous to that of PWR reactors (apart from pressure).
- in the pool concept the entire primary circuit is immersed in the reactor tank; one speaks also of an integrated system, but its components (pumps, exchangers, etc.) are the same as in the preceding solution.

Except perhaps for the matter of accessibility of certain components, the second solution seems preferable to the first, especially from the safety point of view: the activity of the primary coolant is confined in the tank and the large quantity of sodium contained in it gives the apparatus a very large thermal inertia. In any case, this is the solution chosen for the BN 600 and Superphenix fast breeders; thus in what follows we will restrict ourselves to this type [22].

For safety reasons, the tank is doubled, as pictured in Fig. 5.34. This permits the retrieval in inert atmosphere of sodium which might have escaped from the principal vessel. The aim of this concept is to avoid all contact of sodium with air, in the presence of which it could ignite ("sodium fire").

Liquid metals have a number of advantages. First, their excellent thermohydraulic properties allow for record power densities (600 kW/ℓ).

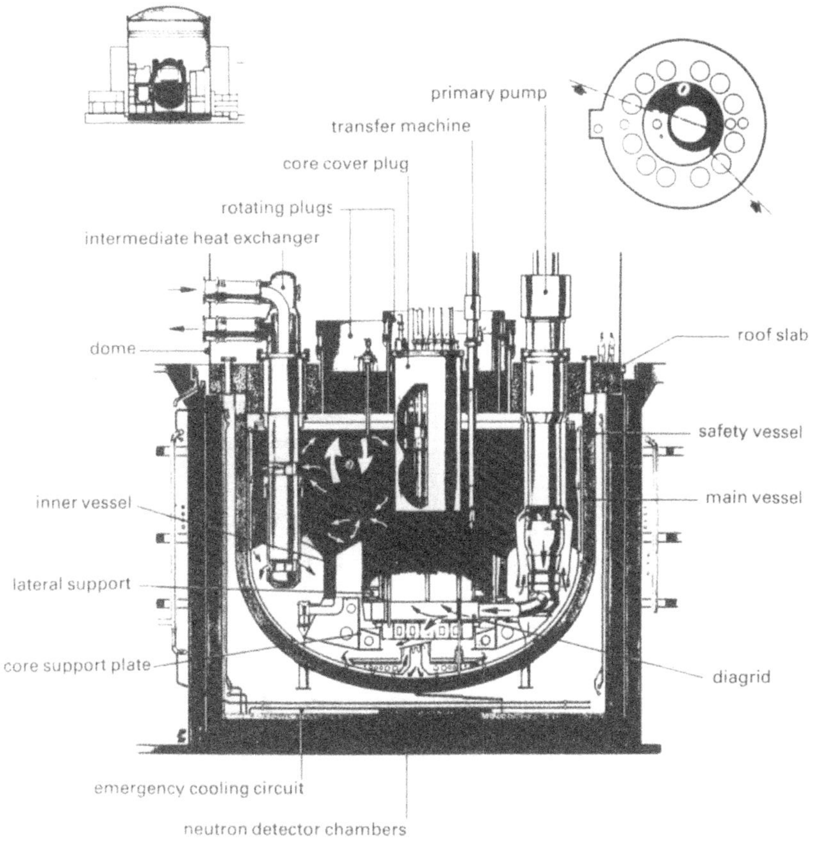

FIGURE 5.34. Superphenix -- internal configuration of the vessel.

Secondly, in the case of sodium, the boiling temperature at atmospheric pressure exceeds 880°C, whereas the maximum envisaged temperature in the primary circuit does not go above 600°C. Thanks to this comfortable margin, there is no need for pressurization, and thus the risk of rupture of the primary circuit is practically eliminated. These thermodynamic performances are quite close to those of HTGR reactors, so that the question has been raised as to whether the latter are still interesting compared to fast breeders. The answer is yes, inasmuch as we are seeking new applications of nuclear energy (chemical industry) demanding even higher temperatures (1000°C), which only HTGR reactors especially conceived for this can attain (cf. end of §3.4.4 and Fig. 3.14).

The Superphenix reactor is equipped with four steam generators and hence with four secondary sodium loops. Each loop possesses its own pump and is connected to two intermediary exchangers which are integrated, as has been seen earlier, into the reactor tank (Fig. 5.34 and Fig. 5.35). The exchangers (straight tubes and counter-current) as well as the primary pumps are suspended from the reactor deck.

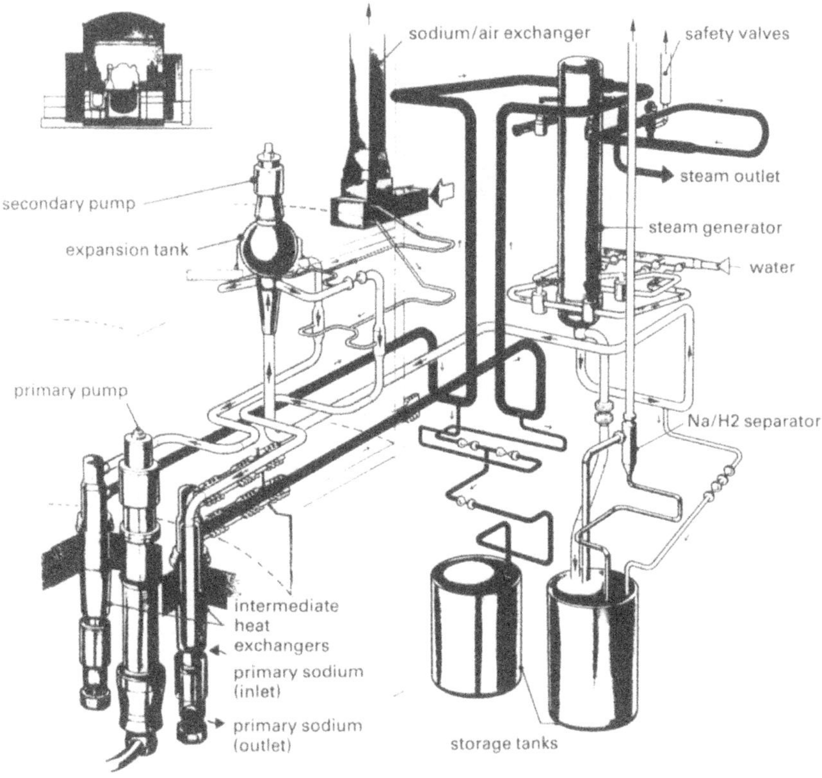

FIGURE 5.35. Superphenix -- diagram of an intermediary secondary circuit.

With the exception, for economic reasons, of steam generators, the solutions adopted are essentially those which proved valid in the Phenix reactor. This reactor which has been working remarkably well since 1974 has furnished valuable information. The principal characteristics of the two reactors appear in Table 5.36 [22]. This type of power plant, like the HTGR plants, allows for the superheating and re-superheating of steam. The outlet temperatures of the primary coolant exceed 580°C, as compared with about 300°C in LWR reactors (Tab. 5.18). We note also that the thermodynamic performances of the Superphenix are lower than those of the Phenix, thus the temperatures are slightly lower, which should enhance its reliability.

TABLE 5.36. Essential characteristics of the Phenix and Superphenix reactors.

Characteristics	Phénix	Superphénix
Manufacturer	EDF/G.A.A.A./CEA	NOVATOME
Power thermal (MW)	563	3000
Power electric (MW)	250	1200
CORE		
Number of assemblies	103	364
Assembly height (m)	4.3	5.4
Fuel PuO + UO^2		
average enrichment (%)	23	15
Plutonium mass (t)	0.85	4.8
Fuel pins ∅ (mm)	5.5	$\gtrsim$5.5
No of pins per assembly	217	271
Conversion factor C	~1.09	~1.19
Burnup rate (MWd/t)	50,000	70,000 to 100,000
PRIMARY CIRCUIT		
Vessel height (m)	8.5	19.5
Vessel diameter (m)	12	21
No of pumps	3	4
No of intermediate exchangers	6	8
Sodium mass (t)	800	3500
Sodium temperature at core inlet/outlet (°C)	400/560	395/545
SECONDARY CIRCUITS		
No of circuits and steam generators	3	4
No of pumps per circuit	1	1
Sodium temp. at intermed. exchanger inlet/outlet (°C)	350/550	395/545
Characteristics of superheated steam:		
— pressure (bars)	168	177
— temperature (°C)	510	487

Let us now consider the fuel (Tab. 5.36): it is composed of thin rods (pins) of mixed uranium and plutonium oxides (UO_2 + PuO_2), which are grouped to form hexagonal assemblies fitted with ducts. These as well as the cladding are of stainless steel.

The enrichment, a concentration of plutonium oxide in the fuel, is on the average lower in Superphenix because of its size (less neutron leakage). For reasons of flattening (§5.2.5), the fuel richest in plutonium is placed at the periphery of the core and the core is surrounded by a radial blanket made up of fertile assemblies (natural or depleted uranium) hexagonal in shape. The last ring of assemblies constitutes a neutron protection screen permitting the reduction of the activity of the secondary sodium of the exchangers as well as the integrated flux in the tank. Moreover, the pins lodged in the core are furnished with fertile materials at their ends, which makes axial blankets possible.

It is of interest to compare the fast breeder fuel with that of LWR reactors by qualitatively analyzing a few essential parameters (a more complete analysis would necessitate multigroup neutronic calculations, cf. §4.5.8). We get a first idea by examining the absorption cross sections σ_{a1} and σ_{a2} of fissile and fertile isotopes. When we pass from a thermal to a fast reactor, all cross sections decrease strongly (Fig. 3.6), but this decrease is greater for fissile isotopes, so that the fertile materials have a more serious effect on the neutron balance (σ_{a2}/σ_{a1} is about 20 times higher) and improving the fissile isotope multiplication factor η_1 is not sufficient to compensate this deterioration of the balance (Fig. 3.9). In order to have a good value of the fuel multiplication factor η_c (3.6), we are thus led to increase the enrichment from 3% (Tab. 5.22) to 15% (Tab. 5.36) in reactors of equivalent power (3000 MWt). We arrive at the same conclusions by considering neutron leakage. Here the absolute value of the cross sections intervenes, and not just their ratio. We know in effect that the leakage increases with the diffusion area (one-group model, §4.5.3), and hence with the neutron energy, since the absorption cross sections diminish (4.22). The only way to avoid this snag is to increase the atomic densities, especially those of the fissile isotopes.

The need for a much greater enrichment here than in LWR reactors (15% as against 3%) implies, for economic reasons, the choice of a much greater specific power for fast breeders. Since the allowed linear powers in the rods are approximately the same (430 W cm^{-1}, the two fuels being thermally similar), the diameters of the pins are necessarily smaller: 5.5 mm as against 9.5 mm for the PWR fuel. We thus arrive at a factor of three between the average specific powers of the two assemblies (5.10). Moreover, the macroscopic fission cross section of the fuel being smaller in fast reactors (in spite of a higher enrichment) the neutron flux will be much higher (4.9). It is of the order of 5 to 7 10^{15} n $cm^{-2}s^{-1}$ and leads to a large integrated flux (5.24) in the structural materials; the proportion of fast neutrons is evidently higher. For all these reasons the behavior of the materials is here more delicate than in thermal reactors without, however, presenting the difficulties that we have already mentioned in regard to fusion reactors (§2.5.3). Fortunately, the structural materials have less of an impact on reactivity when fast neutrons are involved, so that stainless steel can be chosen. Besides, it is this material (as well as the use of sodium as coolant) which permits attainment of the temperatures mentioned earlier (Tab. 5.36). Naturally, to justify this choice, an important experimental program was launched before the construction of the first prototypes (in France the Rapsodie reactor made possible the first irradiations).

Some other particularities arise from the point of view of control. Because breeding is taking place, one might think that the reactivity remains constant throughout one cycle, since there is no depletion of fissile matter, in contrast to what we observe in LWR reactors. This reasoning is in fact incorrect, for the core becomes impoverished and everything takes place as if the plutonium were migrating on its own towards the blankets in which its reactivity value is less. What is more, fission products still play a role despite the weaker capture cross sections. Whatever be the case, the reactivity loss associated with the long term evolution of the fuel (§5.3.4) is small, so that the burnup rates are only limited by technological considerations and the high levels obtained reflect favorably on the costs (Tab. 5.36).

The control rods are made of boron carbide B_4C, most often enriched with boron $_5B^{10}$ to increase their effectiveness. A change in the power level is obtained by playing simultaneously on the insertion level of the control rods and on the flow rate of the primary pumps; in this way the temperatures can be maintained at their rated value (5.14). In Superphenix, regulating and control rely on the processing of a large amount of data (measurements of temperatures and of neutron flux), the goal of which is to obtain maximal performances and enhanced reliability.

Except for the high temperatures, the essential attraction of these reactors is the breeding. To measure this advantage, we must introduce a new notion.

5.4.6 Doubling Time

Let us take up the notations of subsec. 3.3.2 and consider the entire reactor (core and blankets). If A_1, A_2, S_{f1}, S_{f2} represent the absorption and fission rates in the fissile matter (subscript 1) and the fertile matter (subscript 2), the two relations can be written:

$$P_t = E_f(S_{f1} + S_{f2})$$

$$\frac{dM_1}{dt} = m_1 \left[(A_2 - S_{f2}) - A_1\right]$$

with the notations:

- m_1 mass of a fissile atom
- E_f energy produced by fission (~200 MeV)
- $M_1(t)$ mass of the fissile material contained in the reactor at time t
- P_t thermal power of the reactor.

The first equation is evident and the second represents the mass balance of the fissile isotopes since A_1 fissile atoms disappear per unit time, while $(A_2 - S_{f2})$ fertile atoms are transmuted into fissile atoms (it should be recalled that absorption includes fission, whereas only radiative capture leads to a conversion).

By dividing these equations one by the other, we get:

$$\frac{1}{P_t}\frac{dM_1}{dt} = \frac{m_1}{E_f}\frac{(A_2 - S_{f2}) - A_1}{S_{f1} + S_{f2}}$$

By noting that the conversion factor C can be written without loss of generality:

$$C = \frac{A_2 - S_{f2}}{A_1} \qquad \text{(cf. §3.3.2 with this time } S_{f2} \neq 0\text{)}$$

we arrive at the important relation:

$$\frac{dM_1}{dt} = \frac{m_1}{E_f} P_t \frac{A_1}{S_{f1}} \frac{C-1}{1+\delta} \tag{5.30}$$

where we have put $\delta = S_{f2}/S_{f1}$. This ratio, which represents the number of "fast" fissions in the fertile matter per fission in the fissile matter is essentially defined for a given type of reactor. It is small in thermal reactors (§8.4.4), but can exceed 0.2 in fast reactors. Since the quantities A_1 and S_{f1} are relative to the same isotopes (subjected to the same neutron flux), one has approximately:

$$\frac{A_1}{S_{f1}} \cong \frac{\bar{\sigma}_{a1}}{\bar{\sigma}_{f1}}$$

where $\bar{\sigma}_{a1}$ and $\bar{\sigma}_{f1}$ are the average values of the microscopic cross sections taken on a representative neutron spectrum of the reactor.

Let us consider one reactor, operating at a constant power P_{t0}. Equation (5.30) shows that the quantity of fissile matter M_1 increases linearly with time:

$$M_1(t) = M_1(0)\ (1 + Kt)$$

with

$$K = \frac{m_1}{E_f} \bar{\omega}_{s1} \frac{\bar{\sigma}_{a1}}{\bar{\sigma}_{f1}} \frac{C-1}{1+\delta} \tag{5.31}$$

where $\bar{\omega}_{s1} = P_{t0}/M_1(0)$ is the <u>mean specific power in the fissile matter</u>; this is a technological characteristic of the reactor (like $\bar{\omega}_{sp}$), whereas the parameters C, δ, $\bar{\sigma}_{a1}/\bar{\sigma}_{f1}$ follow from calculations or neutronic measurements (we have supposed them to be constant in time, whereas they vary somewhat with the composition of the fuel).

The mass $M_1(0)$ represents the quantity of fissile matter necessary to render the reactor critical at the beginning of operation. Hence, when $M_1(t)$ attains the value $2M_1(0)$, a new reactor can be put into operation relying on the fissile matter produced by the first. This takes place after a lapse of time T_d called the <u>linear doubling time</u> which, using (5.31) is given by:

$$T_d = \frac{1}{K} = \frac{E_f}{m_1} \cdot \frac{1 + \delta}{\frac{\bar{\sigma}_{a1}}{\bar{\sigma}_{f1}} (C - 1)\bar{\omega}_{s1}} \tag{5.32}$$

Let us consider a fleet of fast breeders of the same type, all of them using the fissile mass $M_1(t)$. The thermal power of this fleet is evidently:

$$P_t(t) = P_{t0} \frac{M_1(t)}{M_1(0)} = \bar{\omega}_{s1} M_1(t) \tag{5.33}$$

The increase of $P_t(t)$ and of $M_1(t)$ in the course of time results from the progressive launching of new reactors (each of them having the same characteristics). Applying the equation of material balance (5.30) to this set of reactors, and noting that the power P_t is now given by (5.33), we arrive at the desired law of growth:

$$\frac{dM_1}{dt} = K\, M_1\,(t) \qquad \text{or: } M_1\,(t) = M_1\,(0) \exp\,(Kt)$$

whence the exponential doubling time:

$$T_{de} = \frac{\ln 2}{K} = T_d \ln 2 \tag{5.34}$$

Taking $E_f = 200$ MeV, we find in the case of plutonium ($m_1 = 239/N_A$):

$$T_d \cong 2.56\ 10^3 \frac{1 + \delta}{\frac{\bar{\sigma}_{a1}}{\bar{\sigma}_{f1}} (C - 1)\bar{\omega}_{s1}} \tag{5.35}$$

where T_d and $\bar{\omega}_{s1}$ are expressed respectively in years and MW/ton of fissile material. The quantity $(C - 1)\bar{\sigma}_{a1}/\bar{\sigma}_{f1}$ is called the breeding gain and represents the net production of fissile isotopes for a fission of a fissile nucleus.

Let us consider the Superphenix reactor and the following data [9]:

$\delta = 0.2$ $\qquad$ $C = 1.19$ (cf. Tab. 5.36)

$\frac{\bar{\sigma}_{a1}}{\sigma_{f1}} = 1.3$ $\qquad$ $\bar{\omega}_{s1} = 625$ MW/t (cf. Tab. 5.36)

we obtain respectively for the doubling times:

$T_d \cong 20$ years

$T_{de} \cong 14$ years

The true values of the doubling times are obtained by multiplying the preceding results by $(1 + t_r/t_s)$ where t_s is the residence time of the fuel in the pile and t_r is the time necessary for reprocessing (including the cooling times in pools and transport). In addition, it is necessary to take account of the load factor of the plant and the plutonium losses in the course of reprocessing (Sec. 7.5), so that the true doubling times will be at least 50% higher than the values calculated with the help of formulae (5.32) and (5.34). It should be noted that these "corrected" values are fairly unknown, since they depend on the mastery of the fuel cycle. For a given assembly, the doubling times depend very little on δ and on $\bar{\sigma}_{a1}/\bar{\sigma}_{f1}$. In contrast, they are very sensitive to the values of the conversion factor C and specific power $\bar{\omega}_{s1}$ which vary greatly from one reactor to another.

Let us now consider molten salt thermal reactors (MSR, Tab. 5.3), which seem to be the only ones capable of breeding based on the $(U^{233} + Th^{232})$ cycle. For the principal parameters we only have available project values [23]: C = 1.07 and $\bar{\omega}_{s1}$ = 1500 MW/t. In spite of a much less favorable conversion factor, we expect doubling times of the same order ($T_d \cong 20$ years) as those of the Superphenix. The increase of the specific power has a compensating effect; this is the decrease of necessary investment in fissile matter, the essential advantage of thermal reactors. The difference between the true and the theoretical doubling times is here smaller, since fuel reprocessing is carried out continuously on the spot. This is the major argument in favor of molten salt reactors (mixture of uranium fluoride, thorium and lithium). On the other hand, a large uncertainty remains as to the value of the conversion factor. A decrease of 2 to 3% of the value given earlier would have dramatic consequences for the doubling times, and at present experimental data are not sufficient to be able to guarantee the calculated values.

From a practical viewpoint it is the doubling time and not the conversion factor which is relevant. It is this in particular which will determine the speed with which fast breeders can be introduced on the market in function of plutonium availabilities. Naturally, at first fast breeders can make use of plutonium formed in LWR reactors. Moreover, it is evident that the conversion factor of a fast breeder can always be diminished, and brought down to a value smaller than unity. There is thus no risk of seeing plutonium stocks develop beyond needs.

We will conclude by mentioning another concept of a fast breeder in which sodium is replaced by helium (GCFR). The conversion factors are now higher, but so also are the investments in fissile matter. This type of reactor combines the technology of HTGR reactors (gas, prestressed concrete vessel, etc.) with that of LMFBR reactors (fuel elements). These reactors are only at the planning stage. Let us mention in addition that in all cases the replacement of uranium oxide by its carbide should improve conversion factors and hence doubling times. Finally, at the cost of an increase of the critical fissile mass, one can substantially improve the conversion factors by alternating in the core the fissile and fertile zones; this path has been explored in the case of LMFBR reactors [24].

Chapter 6

ENVIRONMENT AND NUCLEAR SAFETY

6.1 GENERAL REMARKS

Nuclear power plants contain a large quantity of radioactive substances which represent a potential danger for the environment, not only in the event of a hypothetical accident, but also in the normal course of operation (inevitable leakage). In practice, we must distinguish between the two cases. In the first in particular, special devices, conceived and designed as a result of safety studies, permit the consequences of serious accidents to be held to a minimum. Based on such studies, a safety report is drawn up and submitted for the approval of the competent governmental authorities. No project, however modest, which is nuclear in character, can be exempted from this rule. We know that this is a constraint to which few other human activities can ever be submitted, and it is for this reason no doubt that the nuclear industry has achieved such a high degree of reliability, distinctly superior to that encountered in other domains.

One may object that the phenomena in question are new (radioactivity) and might thus lead to incalculable consequences, whence the high reliability requirement (a reliability still considered insufficient). To respond to this anxiety, whose source is probably found in the tragic events of Hiroshima and Nagasaki, as well as in the fact that none of our senses is capable of detecting nuclear radiation, an objective analysis must be made of the nature and effects of this radiation, and the aura of mystery often surrounding the subject must be dissipated.

We shall see in Section 6.2 that in spite of some remaining uncertainties, we can still draw the necessary conclusions for the establishment of norms. The following section draws up an inventory of radioactive materials and specifies the modes of confinement put into service to limit their release. The performances are such that practically all the radioisotopes (except in the case of accident) remain in the fuel, and so it is at the level of the reprocessing plant that the problems really arise (Sec. 7.5).

Safety problems are treated in Sec. 6.4, in which some typical accidents are analyzed. In addition we present the methodology on which evaluations of risk are currently based.

The last section has to do with thermal discharges in the environment. This "heat pollution" is not limited to nuclear power plants, but follows from the principles of thermodynamics.

Unless otherwise specified, all reactors considered in this chapter are of the LWR type.

6.2 NATURE AND EFFECTS OF RADIATION

6.2.1 Introduction

We know that an element is called radioactive when its nucleus disintegrates spontaneously. To each event there corresponds the emission of one or several particles, well defined in type and energy (α, β, γ), the identifying marks, so to speak, of the considered isotope. The detection of infinitesimal traces of certain elements is moreover based on this property; when the elements are stable, one begins by creating by activation (often neutronic) a radioactive isotope and it is this latter which in fact is detected (marking).

The first quantitative characteristic of a radioactive substance is evidently its activity A_c, that is, the number of decays per second; this is the magnitude which determines the intensity of the emission (Sec.1.4) In practice, two cases are seen:

- either the quantity of radioactive material is known at a given instant and shielded from all external influence, and thus its activity is inversely proportional to the half-life T of the radionuclide and subsequently decreases at a rate all the higher as the half-life is shorter (§1.4.1);

- or this quantity is not known, the radionuclide forming under neutron flux in a reactor, and thus the maximum activity attained at the end of irradiation depends on the ratio of the residence time in the pile to the half-life (§1.4.4).

In both cases, large values of T correspond to slow decreases (which is a drawback) but also to weak initial activities (which is an advantage). These first results show how mistaken it can be to claim that the isotopes of long half-life create the most problems; besides, at the limit, an element of infinite half-life is stable and thus devoid of radioactivity (1.5). Other factors are much more determining, as we shall see further on.

These considerations and those which follow apply as much to the natural radioactivity of uranium as to the artificial radioactivity of isotopes created by neutron flux in a reactor. At no stage is there a difference in kind between these two types of radioactivity, since the α, β, and γ emissions can appear in each case. The qualifying adjective "natural" in no way guarantees the harmlessness of a substance, any more than its artifical character indicates that it is particularly harmful. To appreciate correctly the hazards presented by nuclear radiation, it is first ncessary to study its mechanisms of interaction with matter, then to specify the physical amounts (doses) which play a primordial role in assessing the damage, and finally to define the inviolable limits (norms).

6.2.2 Interaction of Radiation with Matter

Every radiation absorbed by a material brings about an ionization, either directly (α or β rays) or indirectly (γ rays and neutrons). We speak of ionizing radiations when we wish to emphasize this property which is a true "common denominator". It is finally this ionization which determines the damage, and thus this is what should be calculated.

Let us first consider particles of the same family (α , β); due to their charge, they ionize matter very strongly, which means that they tear off the electrons from the atoms that they meet, each time creating a pair of ions. As we have already seen, this phenomenon is exploited in various types of detectors (§5.3.9). When the primary particles have been sufficiently slowed down, they lose their ionizing character (their energy is then lower than the ionization potential of atoms). This generally happens after a very small distance. In this way α particles of 10 MeV are stopped by 1/10 mm of water, electrons of 0.5 MeV by 1 mm of aluminum, etc.

These phenomena are totally different for neutrons and γ rays (photons). Firstly, they can have any stopping distance and only an average value can be defined (§4.2.1). This value can attain several centimeters in the densest materials.

Of the various types of interactions that γ rays can have with matter, we can by simplifying bring them down to three essential processes:

· The photo-electric effect: a photon γ is absorbed by an atom which causes the emission of an electron whose kinetic energy is equal to that of the photon reduced by the work of extraction (binding energy of the electron before its ejection); this is essentially a low-energy phenomenon (E_γ <0.5 MeV).

· Pair creation: in the vicinity of a heavy nucleus, where the electrostatic field is intense, a photon γ can materialize as an electron-positron pair; here it is a matter of a spectacular application of Einstein's law, since matter is created from electromagnetic energy. Since the rest energy of an electron ($m_e C^2$) is 0.51 MeV, this phenomenon can only be observed with photons whose energy is higher than 1.02 MeV. Finally, the positrons created are necessarily annihilated by interaction with electrons (negative) that they encounter, following a reaction inverse to the preceding, whence the emission of lower energy photons (0.51 MeV).

· The Compton effect: a γ photon can be scattered elastically by an atomic electron; after collision it will thus have a smaller energy (greater wavelength,cf. §1.1.3), the electron carrying off the difference in the form of recoil energy. This purely quantum phenomenon is preponderant in a large energy range (0.3 to 4 MeV).

The resemblance of these phenomena to those which we have encountered in neutron studies makes it possible to apply the methods developed in reactor physics to studies of γ ray penetration in matter (§9.1.6): the absorption terms correspond to the first two effects and the scattering terms to the third. What interests us here is that the energy of the photons is transferred to the atomic electrons, totally in the first two cases, and partially in the third. These more or less fast electrons in turn ionize matter over much shorter distances and we get back the case of the α and β particles analyzed above.

The phenomena associated with the propagation of neutrons are more complex. While in the previous cases the interactions were atomic in character, because only the electrons bound to atoms played a role, here they are of a nuclear type. As we have seen (Sec. 1.5), the collision of a neutron with a nucleus is either of the scattering type or else it gives rise to a veritable nuclear reaction. Depending on the case, for each event one obtains one or several totally ionized nuclei, of considerable kinetic energy with, as a consequence, a separation of charges, since the electronic cloud of the hit nucleus remains in place. The secondary radiations are here also charged particles, even more ionizing than the emissions of electrons induced by the γ rays. These γ rays are also of nuclear origin since they almost always accompany neutron absorption (fissions, captures).

We thus see that very different kinds of primary radiation finally act on matter in analogous ways.

6.2.3 Definition of Radiation Doses

Among the measurable quantities which have a meaning from the point of view of damage, we can define several types of doses.

Historically, the notion of exposure dose was introduced to calculate the ionizing power of X and γ rays in air. The unit of dose, the roentgen, corresponds to the creation of a set of ion pairs representing one electrostatic unit of charge per cm^3 of exposed air in normal conditions, that is $2.58\ 10^{-7}$ C/g.

It is very important to note that when one speaks as above of 1 cm^3 or of 1 g of air, it does not mean that the secondary electrons effectively created in this unit of volume or mass will there create the entire ionization of which they are capable. On the contrary, their energy will be deposited in a greater volume, and any apparatus for measuring doses thus defined will have to be of sufficient size. These apparatuses have already been described under the heading detection (§5.3.9). Since their response is proportional to the induced ionization in the space included between the electrodes, their calibration in roentgens is natural.

By definition, exposure doses only have meaning for γ and X rays in interaction with air. Since in general we are interested in damage done to various materials, the notion of absorbed dose is more significant. It is expressed in rads (radiation absorbed dose): 1 rad = 10^{-5} J/g.

It is now a matter of the energy transferred from the primary radiation to the unit of mass at a well-defined point of the considered material. Here too the energy carried off by the secondary particles can be "deposited" far from the point of emission. Nowadays the rad has displaced the roentgen, but the two notions are evidently related where air is concerned. Suppose we are given an ionization in air corresponding to 1 roentgen, namely, $1.61\ 10^{12}$ ions/g ($2.58\ 10^{-7}/1.6\ 10^{-19}$). To create it, we need

$8.77\ 10^{-6}$ J/g since 34 eV of energy is necessary on the average to tear off an atomic electron from an atom of oxygen or nitrogen. We thus see that 1 roentgen is equivalent to 0.877 rads in air.

Our task is now to relate the particle flux introduced in the preceding chapters to the doses defined above. Let us first consider a flux ϕ of γ photons. For photons of well defined energy E this flux is defined in the same way as for neutrons and a reaction rate can be written:

$$R\ (cm^{-3}\ s^{-1}) = \mu\phi$$

where $\mu(cm^{-1})$, the linear attenuation coefficient, has the same meaning as the macroscopic neutron cross sections. To conform with usage we have noted it μ and not Σ_t. It is obtained by summing the macroscopic cross sections of the three phenomena described in the previous subsection and evidently depends on the energy E of the photons. If $\langle\Delta E\rangle$ is the average energy loss per collision of the γ photons, and ρ the material density, then

$$\bar{\omega}_\gamma = R\frac{\langle\Delta E\rangle}{\rho} = \langle\Delta E\rangle\ \frac{\mu(E)}{\rho}\ \phi$$

represents the γ photon energy transmitted to the medium per unit mass and unit time. We note it $\bar{\omega}_\gamma$ by analogy with the specific powers introduced in reactor physics (4.9). If only the photoelectric effect and pair creation took place, since in these processes the photon disappears, the average energy loss $\langle\Delta E\rangle$ would be simply equal to the incident energy E of the photon (§6.2.2).

We can rewrite the preceding formula by introducing the intensity $\mathscr{I} = E\phi$ (energy flux) as one usually does for electromagnetic radiations:

$$\bar{\omega}_\gamma\ (MeV\ g^{-1}\ s^{-1}) = \frac{\mu_a(E)}{\rho}\ \cdot \mathscr{I}(MeV\ cm^{-2}\ s^{-1}) \tag{6.1}$$

where we have put:

$$\mu_a(E) = \frac{\langle\Delta E\rangle}{E}\ \mu(E) \tag{6.2}$$

The quantity μ_a, called the linear energy absorption coefficient, is known for most materials as a function of the photon energy. The expression (6.1) (after the choice of appropriate units) is the absorbed dose per unit time. This dose rate (in rad/s, mrad/hr, etc.) is simply proportional to the coefficient μ_a/ρ of the considered material. Knowing the absorbed dose in air for a fixed intensity $\mathscr{I}$, one can then predict the absorbed dose in other materials. We thus find that a dose of 0.877 rad in air, namely, as we have seen, 1 roentgen, is equivalent to an absorbed dose of about 1 rad in muscular tissue. For this reason exposure doses, which are easy to measure, remain of interest.

For neutrons, one can write an expression analogous to equation (6.1) by replacing μ by the scattering cross section Σ_s and the average energy loss per collision $\langle \Delta E \rangle$ by expression (4.34). We thus determine the energy corresponding to the recoil of nuclei during elastic collisions (§4.4.2) and subsequently convert it to rads. In fact, due to nuclear reactions, other components must intervene. As they may have different biological effects, it is not of interest to add the partial doses, to determine the total dose in rads.

Everything that we have said concerning absorbed doses applies to all materials and in particular to living organisms; all the same,the latter have special characteristics. Although all ionizing radiations are capable of producing qualitatively analogous biological effects, the same absorbed dose (measured in rads) may bring about quantitatively different damage depending on the type (and the energy) of the radiation considered. In general, the particles which created the highest specific ionization along their trajectory are those which (for the same absorbed dose) have the highest effectiveness. This is suggested moreover by certain radiochemical experiments which indicate that the effects of radiolysis are more marked for α rays than for γ rays. Whatever the case, one can define the relative biological effectiveness (RBE) as follows:

$$\text{RBE} = \frac{\text{dose of x rays of 250 keV (in rads)}}{\text{dose of the considered radiation (in rads)}} \tag{6.3}$$

for the same biological effect.

From the above coefficient one can calculate the biological dose in rems (roentgen equivalent man) with the help of the formula:

$$\text{biological dose (rem)} = \text{absorbed dose (rad)} \times \text{RBE} \tag{6.4}$$

We take RBE = 1 for X and γ rays as well as for electrons, which means that the notions of rems, rads, roentgens are the same for these radiations. In contrast, for ions the RBE may exceed 10. By virtue of the preceding we see that the RBE is not uniquely defined, since it depends on the biological effect considered, the organ irradiated, etc. For reasons of simplicity, it is customary to adopt a single value for each type of radiation, namely that which corresponds to the greatest damage.

Thus it is easy to define for photons the conversion factor $\chi_D(E)$ enabling us to pass from the intensities $\mathscr{I}(E)$ expressed in MeV cm^{-2} s^{-1} to the dose rate most often expressed in mrem h^{-1}. Using, for example, expressions (6.1) and (6.2) we find, starting from the known values of μ_a/ρ for muscular tissue, the desired conversion factors (Fig. 6.1)[25].

Biological doses associated to neutrons are indirectly evaluated. We consider a mono-energetic flux of neutrons penetrating a medium whose composition is representative of the human body. Transport calculations made once and for all have made it possible to determine the neutron distributions in such a medium, as well as the distribution of all the particles which result from their nuclear interaction with matter: recoil nuclei, secondary photons, ${}_2He^4$ and ${}_1H^1$ particles coming from threshhold reactions, etc. The absorbed dose (in rads) is calculated for each of these components and multiplied before summation by the corresponding RBE. We finally obtain the conversion factor neutron flux → biological dose $\chi'_D(E)$ for different incident neutron energies (Fig. 6.2)[26].

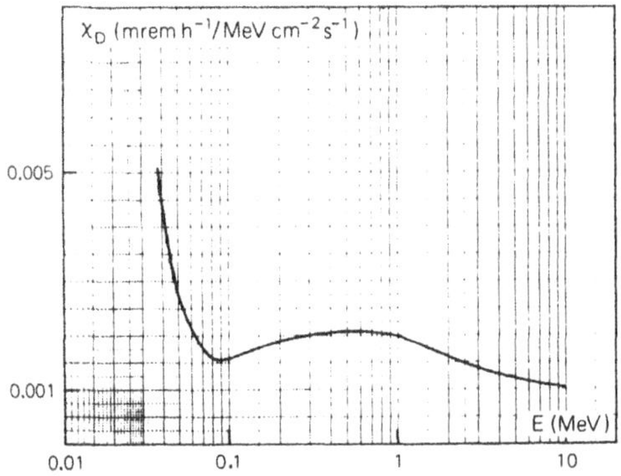

FIGURE 6.1 Conversion factor χ_D for γ photons.

From the preceding we can draw the following conclusions. The biological doses depend both on the nature of the radiations and on their spectral density at the considered point (§.4.4.3). In its turn, this density $\Phi(E)$ [or $\mathscr{I}(E)$] depends on the activity of the emitter (source intensity in curies), its proximity and on whatever protection screens may be interposed between it and the considered point. The calculation of spectral densities or, what amounts to the same, the flux in each energy group, calls for the methods of reactor physics to which we will not return (§9.1.6) and the passage to biological doses is done, as we have just seen, by introducing the conversion factors χ_D corresponding to each energy interval considered (Fig. 6.1 and 6.2). Thus a neutron dose at a point $\vec{r}$ can be written:

$$D_n(\vec{r}) = \sum_g \chi_D(g)\Phi_g^{(a)}(\vec{r}) \tag{6.5}$$

where $\Phi_g^{(a)}$ is the absolute flux for the group g while χ_D (g) is a given for the nuclear engineer (Fig. 6.2).

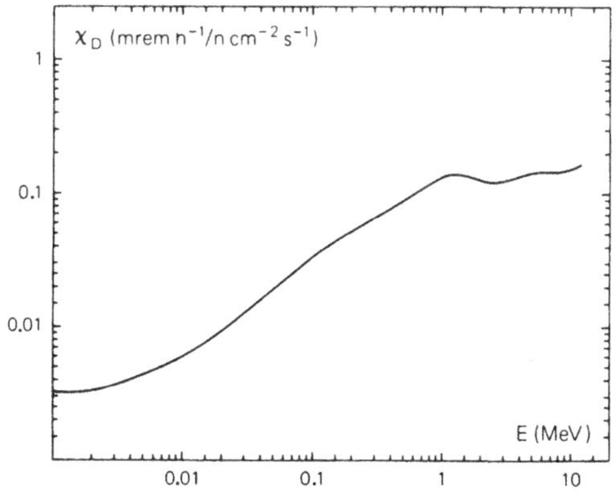

FIGURE 6.2. Conversion factor χ_D for neutrons.

Thus identical biological doses, that is, the same degree of damage, may correspond to very different activities. It is thus essential to distinguish rems from curies. The latter are of no interest (except as calculating agents) short of knowing precisely the type of emission which one is confronting (one could speak for example of a cobalt Co^{60} source of 1 kCurie) and the position of the irradiated person with respect to the radiation source.

Another important remark should be made. The most ionizing, and hence most dangerous, radiations are those which are the most easily stopped by thin screens, sometimes even by skin. Thus α or β emitters are only dangerous when they are ingested (for example, plutonium); we then speak of internal doses. γ emitters, on the other hand, play an important role in determining external doses; together with neutrons, they determine the thicknesses of biological shielding surrounding nuclear reactors.

The evaluation of internal doses brings in an additional parameter, the retention time of the considered radionuclide. Certain organs have the property of fixing to some extent certain elements: iodine is found in the thyroid, strontium in bones, etc. In this case the activities which were the point of departure for calculating external doses are unknown. Only metabolic considerations permit their determination; this being done, the biological doses are evaluated following the same methodology and are submitted to the same norms.

6.2.4 Biological Effects of Radiation

By definition biological effects depend essentially on doses (and dose rates). The questions is, how?

Important phenomena take place at the cellular level. A cell is an extremely complex system in which chemical reactions essential to life take place. Ionizing radiations may break organic molecules directly; or they may do so indirectly by creating free radicals which act on them. In both cases, one witnesses the appearance of new molecules which can perturb the workings of a cell. Biological effects of radiation are thus very similar to those of certain chemical agents and there is no new effect, irradiation being a means like any other of creating these substances. In this way we know a great number of carcinogenic chemical substances and it is not surprising that ionizing radiations also have the property of inducing cancers.

It is evident that the consequences of ionization will be all the more harmful the more vital the role of the concerned molecules in cellular functioning. The destruction of a DNA molecule, for example, may lead to a mutation. If this mutation takes place in a somatic cell there will be no macroscopic effect unless a very large number of cells have been affected. This is because a mutation entails in general the death of the corresponding cell and the multiplication of healthy cells compensates this disappearance. The case of sexual cells is much more serious since there is a possibility that they conserve their fertility, in which case the mutation is transmitted to the progeny. Much research is of course directed at this question. Let us note also that mutations are not caused exclusively by radiation.

From a practical point of view it is of interest to know what available statistics tell us about the stated effects on man. We must distinguish strong doses which have been abruptly administered (more than 20 rem) from small chronic doses spread out in time (a few rem/yr at the most). From the point of view of establishing norms, it is the latter which are of interest.

Much information is available about the immediate effects of instantaneous strong doses. We can schematically classify these effects in function of the biological doses defined in the preceding subsection (acute syndrome).

- From 600 to 1000 rem, high probability of death. Death takes place in less than a month, following vomiting, hemorrhages, etc.
- From 200 to 600 rem, we observe the same effects but in a less pronounced fashion. The lethal dose (50% of deaths) is situated in this zone.
- Below 200 rem, there is high probability of survival. Convalescence extends over a few weeks. As in the preceding cases, vomiting and extreme lassitude are symptomatic.
- Below 50 rem, no effect has been observed.

The doses listed above may have long-term effects. Cancer, particularly, is in question; it can only appear long after irradiation. Available data come from surveys of 80,000 survivors of the Hiroshima and Nagasaki bombings. Significant differences between persons irradiated 40 years ago and the rest of the Japanese population only appear above 100 rem. In this domain, the increase of the death rate would be equivalent to 100 cases annually per million inhabitants and per rem.

Let us now consider chronic doses (doses spread out in time). Doses of a few mrem/day, at most a few rem/yr of accumulated dose, are much more significant than the preceding for gauging the effects of the most widespread sources of radiation,natural or artificial.

Given the importance of the stakes, many studies have been made, and each time it was impossible to bring out the biological effects with such small doses. Besides, one observes that thousands of workers professionally exposed to doses of a few rem/yr have not suffered any significant damage.

Although the preceding seems to indicate the innocuousness of chronic doses, one must all the same admit that their effects exist, even if they have not yet been measured. To evaluate them, one can only extrapolate the known results for strong doses, and the two following hypotheses are usually made:

- the effects are proportional to the doses (linearity)
- for the same dose an irradiation of longer duration leads to the same damage (the dose rate is not a determining factor).

The first hypothesis neglects the existence of threshholds, which have moreover been proved in many cases (cataract, opaqueness of the crystalline lens which appears above 200 rem). The second hypothesis neglects the property of tissue regeneration. These two hypotheses are thus pessimistic but nevertheless serve as a basis for the establishment of norms.

Since 1930, the ICRP (International Commission on Radiation Protection) has been concerned with the definition of norms in the domain of ionizing radiations (at the start it was a question of X-rays and radium emissions). This independent commission was thus created well before the rise of the nuclear industry. Its latest recommendations fix limits on doses resulting from nuclear activities:

- 5 rem/yr for professionally exposed persons
- 0.5 rem/yr for others.

This difference is explained by the fact that persons in the first group are medically controlled (in particular, blood analysis). A third norm stipulates that the dose per generation must not exceed 5 rem, which corresponds to an <u>average annual dose</u> of 170 mrem/person. In the case of certain specific organs, the limits are higher. The International Atomic Energy Agency (IAEA) at Vienna has taken responsibility for establishing guidelines, based on the above figures, but in various countries the norms in vigor are often more stringent. These limits apply to external as well as internal doses. In the latter case, the maximum admissible dose can be given in terms of the quantity of ingested matter or activity which should not be exceded, for each radionuclide being considered. We speak of μCi (μCi = 10^{-6} Ci) or of μCi/ℓ in the case of isotopes diluted in ingested water or inhaled air. The IAEA has published very complete tables covering a large number of radio-isotopes [27].

It is of interest to situate a few typical radiations with respect to the preceding norms. Man has always been exposed to ionizing radiations. Natural radioactivity represents on the average a dose of 140 mrem/yr. The component corresponding to cosmic rays (on the average 30 mrem/yr) increases with altitude and may exceed 100 mrem/yr. The second component (γ rays) depends on the place considered and may go from 90 mrem/yr (average value) to 700 mrem/yr in certain regions. The last component (20 mrem/yr) corresponds to the radioactivity of the human body. Certain radio-isotopes (K^{40}, C^{14}) are in fact present in our organism. We see that the figure of 140 mrem/yr is of the same order of magnitude as the limiting average dose fixed at 170 mrem/yr by the IAEA.

If one considers the radioactivity coming from human activities, medicine heads the list with 70 mrem/yr whereas nuclear power plants will contribute less than 1 mrem/yr in the year 2000, taking anticipated programs into account. This is of course in terms of average values. We will come back to this figure which can be explained by the sophisticated processing to which the discharged waste of nuclear power plants is submitted (Sec. 6.3).

We will end by noting that in Switzerland, for example, the norms are much more stringent than those of the IAEA, since the populations living in the vicinity of a nuclear power plant must not receive from it a dose higher than 20 mrem/yr. This figure is well within the variations of doses induced by natural radioactivity.

6.3 WASTE DISCHARGE DURING NORMAL OPERATION

6.3.1 Introduction

Radionuclides present in a nuclear reactor constitute a source of extremely intense radiation even after shutdown. The thick shieldings around the core (steel, concrete, etc.) are such that no significant dose is induced at the external surface of the reactor block. In contrast, if a small quantity of radioactive matter succeeds in escaping, it constitutes a new source of radiation which although small presents a danger, since no protection screen now intervenes to attenuate the emitted radiation. This question will concern us in the following.

6.3.2 Inventory of Radioactive Matter [28]

More than 99.9% of the radioactivity induced by neutron flux in a nuclear reactor is localized in the fuel elements. The major part corresponds to isotopes created during uranium fission. There are a large variety of fission products, but the production rates are well known (§3.1.2). The corresponding activities are large, as is indicated by Table 6.3 relative to a 1100 MWe reactor which has functioned at full power for 300 days.

TABLE 6.3. Fuel radioactivity in MCi for a 1100 MWe reactor and irradiation of 300 days (actinides → Z ≥ 89).

Time following shutdown	Halogens (I, Br)	Rare gases (Xe, Kr, etc.)	Total FP	Actinides
0	1435	1240	13800	3450
1 day	265	221	2890	1330
1 month	6.74	4.77	947	9.35
1 year	2.10^{-6}	0.63	146	5.17

As we have already pointed out, the global activities are not of much interest. Rather, we must study the most dangerous emitters separately, taking particular account of their ability to diffuse through the fuel. The volatility as well as the possibility of ingestion by living beings must therefore be kept in mind. The properties of the most important isotopes are listed in Table 6.4. Short-lived isotopes, often of high activity (§6.2.1), pose few problems. It suffices to wait for them to decrease before discharging them into the environment (§6.3.4). It is a different story inside the plant itself, as these isotopes can diffuse toward the primary circuit, or an accident can take place. Gaseous fission products (noble gases, iodine) are evidently the most difficult to retain. Strontium Sr^{90} and cesium Cs^{137}, because of their half-life and biological effects, call without doubt for the greatest attention, essentially during fuel reprocesssing and definitive waste disposal (Sec. 7.5).

To the fission products we must add the actinides (Z ≥ 89) obtained by transmutation of fertile matter (§5.3.4). Their nuclear properties are analogous to those of the natural isotopes of the radioactive family of uranium U^{238} (Table 1.3). The most important, plutonium Pu^{239} (used in fast breeders) is a powerful α emitter of half-life 25,000 years. It is thus inoffensive in terms of external doses, but is dangerous when ingested, just like radium, the natural descendant of uranium (§7.5.5). The general norms for doses imply that the quantity of ingested plutonium must not exceed 1/3 μg/yr (in other words, 0.02 μCi/yr). Although small, these values are not easily reached, since plutonium is practically insoluble, and the only mode of ingestion is through breathing. In many respects its harmfulness is less than that of many chemical or radioactive substances. In conclusion, we will keep in mind that the plutonium problem essentially concerns people exposed professionally and that the places where it gets fixed are in the lungs and bones (§7.5.5).

TABLE 6.4. Estimate of the activity of the primary circuit of a 1000 MWe PWR reactor.
- (*) noble gases are excluded from this total.

Category	Isotope	Halflife	Activity ($\mu Ci/cm^3$)	Emission	Biological effects and critical organs
Fission products					
Metals – non volatile	Sr^{89}	53 d	2.5 10−3	β^-	Ingestion and fixing in the bones
	Sr^{90}	28 yr	4.4 10−5	β^-	
Metals – volatile	Cs^{134}	2.1 yr	7 10−2	β^-, γ	Throughout the body
	Cs^{137}	30 yr	0.43	β^-	
Halogens (volatile)	I^{129}	1.7 10^9 yr	—	β^-, γ	Inhalation and fixing in the thyroid
	I^{131}	8 d	1.5	β^-, γ	
	I^{133}	21 h	2.5	β^-, γ	
Total FP (*)			12.8		
Noble gases	Kr^{85}	10.6 yr	1.1	β^-, γ	External irradiation essentially
	Kr^{88}	2.8 h	2.6	β^-, γ	
	Xe^{133}	5.3d	174	β^-, γ	Inhalation
Total			187		
Corrosion products					
	Mn^{54}	300 d	4.2 10−3	β^+, γ	Ingestion of water contaminated by particles in suspension
	Mn^{56}	2.6 h	2.2 10−2	β^-, γ	
	Co^{58}	71 h	8.1 10−3	β^+, γ	
	Fe^{59}	45 d	1.8 10−3	β^-, γ	
	Co^{60}	5.3 yr	1.4 10−3	β^-, γ	Fixation throughout the body
	Zr^{95}	65 d	—	β^-, γ	
Total			3.7 10−2		

In considering the problem of discharge of radioactive wastes, it is the activity carried by the coolant that is the most significant. In the ideal case, the activity of the primary circuit is confined to the activation of the coolant. In water reactors, it is essentially a matter of nitrogen N^{16} of very short half-life (7.1 sec) formed during a reaction:

$$_0n^1 \text{ (fast)} + {}_8O^{16} \rightarrow {}_7N^{16} + {}_1H^1.$$

In practice, this intrinsic activity, though high, has no impact on the environment since the residence time in the decontamination circuits is such that the radionuclides will have disappeared before the waste is discharged (§6.3.4). On the other hand, just as for short-lived fission products, this activity puts out-of-bounds to operating personnel the zones of the power plant traversed by the primary circuit, at least during normal running.

The activities to be considered are thus of another kind:

- Corrosion products. Despite a very stringent selection of structural materials (zircalloy in the core, various steels outside), some amount of corrosion cannot be avoided. Thus the water conveys these products, certain isotopes of which will be activated in the course of passing through the core (generally (n,γ) reactions lead to an unstable nucleus). As Table 6.4 indicates, activated components of zircalloy and steels turn up.
- Fission products. A small portion of the fission products which have already been mentioned diffuse through the cladding (especially at the end of the cycle).
- Uranium traces. During fuel element manufacture, infinitesimal quantities of uranium make their way onto the outer surface of the clad, since absolute cleanliness cannot be guaranteed.

In contrast to the intrinsic activity of water, these new sources of radioactivity are difficult to calculate, since their intensity depends, according to the case, on the waterproofness of the clad or the condition of the surface of all the circuitry. The activities indicated in Table 6.4 only represent a pessimistic estimate based on the hypothesis that 1% of the fuel elements are faulty [29]; measured activities are in fact much lower. Whatever the case, the activity of the primary circuit is low compared to the global activity of the fuel. In fact, the primary circuit of a 1000 MWe PWR reactor contains about 300 m^3 of water; Table 6.4 would lead to a total fission product activity of 5.6 10^4 Ci. Comparing this with the corresponding fuel activity (Table 6.3), we see that the cladding (first barrier, §6.3.3) has served to reduce the activities by a factor of 2.5 10^5.

To finish off this list, we shall say something about tritium and carbon C^{14}, which play a special role. Tritium can be formed as the result of ternary fissions (rare) and, in water reactors, after neutron-deuterium reactions (preponderant reaction in CANDU reactors). We can estimate at 50 Ci/yr the corresponding activity of the primary circuit of a LWR reactor of 1000 MWe (transmission factor of the cladding, 0.1%). For PWR reactors, one must add to this figure 580 Ci/yr coming from neutron-boron reactions and neutron-lithium reactions:

$$_0n^1 \text{ (fast)} + {}_5B^{10} \rightarrow 2\ {}_2He^4 + {}_1H^3 \qquad (E_n > 1.5 \text{ MeV})$$

$$_0n^1 + {}_3Li^6 \rightarrow {}_2He^4 + {}_1H^3$$

We know that boron is used in soluble form in PWR reactors (§5.3.8 and 5.4.2), and that lithium allows the pH of the coolant to be adjusted. For this reason, PWR reactors have a tritium inventory about 10 times higher than that of BWR reactors.

Tritium, whatever its origin, mixes rapidly with water (liquid or steam) in the chemical form HTO. A pure β^- emitter, with a half-life of 12.3 yr, tritium presents a danger only if it is ingested (or inhaled). If this happens, the entire human body must be considered (and not one critical organ).

Finally, the radionuclide $_{12}C^{14}$ of half-life 5740 years comes from the activation of the carbon present in all reactors. HTGR reactors moderated with graphite are evidently the most concerned, but traces of carbon C^{14} are also found in LWR reactors because of the use of steel. A pure β^- emitter, it also can only create a biological dose if it is ingested (most often in the form of CO_2). It fixes itself most often in fatty tissue.

It is of interest to note that these last two radionuclides exist in nature in large quantities, but in very diluted form. They are created in the atmosphere through the action of cosmic rays. It is nitrogen N^{14} (the most abundant) which contributes in these two cases:

$$ {}_{0}n^{1}\ (\text{cosmic}) + {}_{7}N^{14} \rightarrow \begin{array}{l} {}_{6}C^{12} + \underline{{}_{1}H^{3}} \\ \underline{{}_{6}C^{14}} + {}_{1}H^{1} \end{array} $$

6.3.3 Containment of Radioactivity

Roughly, we can think of three major barriers (Fig. 6.5) which stand in the way of the migration of fission products into the environment.

The first barrier corresponds to the fuel element itself together with its cladding. Except in the case of a very serious accident (melting), only a fraction of the most volatile fission products arrives at the periphery of the rods and fills the space between the uranium oxide and the clad. If the latter is not absolutely leakproof a small quantity of radioactive substances penetrates into the primary circuit (§6.3.2). We thus see that the cladding is essential for safety, whereas it penalizes the reactor from the point of view of neutronics (parasitic captures, cf. §5.1.4) and thermohydraulics (thermal resistance of the clad-fuel contact, see §5.2.2). Strong irradiations may cause the cladding to crack, due in particular to the accumulation of gaseous fission products in the interstices and the deformation of the fuel. The limiting burnup rates are thus not fixed uniquely by the initial reactivity reserves (end of §5.3.7) and the measure of the activity of the primary circuit gives an indication as to the number of defaulting elements. One can tolerate a certain number of clad ruptures without stopping the reactor, provided that the primary fluid is continuously purified, as is the case. One might recall here that CANDU reactors are much better from this point of view, since the withdrawal of a fuel element is a routine operation.

The second barrier is constituted by the envelope of the primary circuit (Fig. 6.5): the reactor vessel, primary pipes, purification circuits and steam generators (PWR) or turbine-condenser (BWR). One sees immediately that the BWR reactors (direct cycle) are less favorable (Fig. 5.17). Any steam leak at the level of the turbine, for example, leads to an increase of the activity in the machine room (gaseous effluents), whereas in the PWR system the leaks are more limited (the steam generators act as a tampon) and the corresponding effluents are mostly liquid. This explains why soluble boronic poisons are excluded in BWR reactors because of the generation of tritium (§6.3.2), not to mention questions of

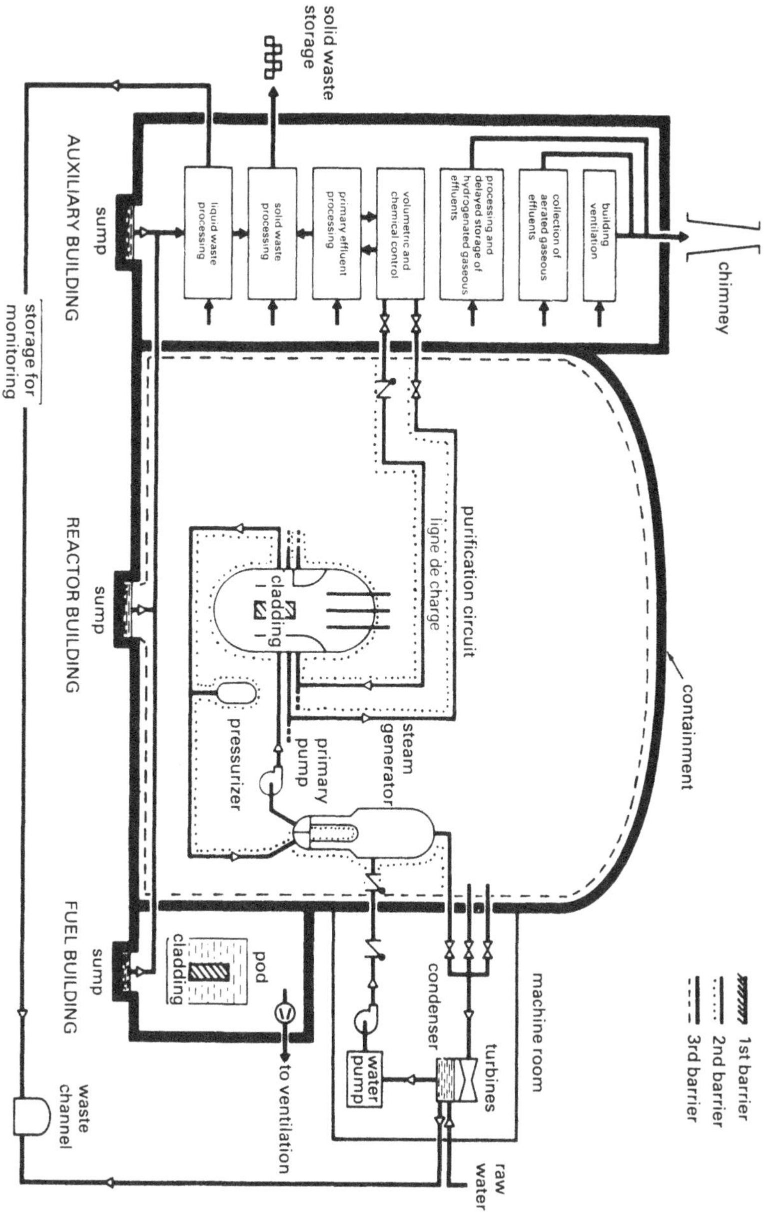

FIGURE 6.5. Sketch of the three principal barriers of a PWR reactor.

stability (§5.3.8). In the absence of special precautions, gaseous leaks could be a hundred times more than those of PWR reactors. The additional equipment required by BWR reactors counterbalances many of their advantages. We mention as an example the automatic valves which, in case of accident, cut off the reactor from the turbine.

The third barrier is what is called reactor containment (Fig. 6.5). In contrast to the preceding, this third barrier does not play much of a role during normal functioning, since an excellent global leakproofness has already been realized thanks to the first two barriers. The first generation graphite-gas reactors were not provided with a leakproof containment building. The goal of containment is thus to increase safety, especially in the case of accidental radioactive leaks. This last barrier also permits the collection of the effluents for reprocessing before definitive disposal into the biosphere (see below). In addition it protects the reactor against external dangers: hurricanes, airplane crashes, etc. Containment may be double, as is the case for BWR reactors, whose compactness allows for this. The thickness of the structures (concrete covered by a "leakproof skin") is such that the containment should be able to withstand the expected overpressures in the case of accident and resist external assaults (Fig. 6.6). Fast breeder reactors possess four barriers. We have seen that the sodium tank is surrounded by a safety vessel (§5.4.5). This, as well as the dome which covers it, constitutes the third barrier of primary containment, while the reactor building constitutes the secondary containment or fourth barrier (Fig. 5.34).

6.3.4 Purification and Wastes

The primary circuit's activity is small compared to that of the fuel (§6.3.2). All the same, it is evident that radioactive leakage will be considerably reduced if by a continuous process of decontamination the radio-isotope concentrations are maintained as low as possible in the primary circuit. Tiny holes made in this circuit permit the coolant to be purified. Purification systems are generally complex and depend on the type of reactor. In LWR reactors, the water circulates in circuits containing filters and especially ion-exchanging resins which retain a large amount of the active isotopes. This technology is not essentially new, since it is also found in some used-water purification stations. The solid wastes which result from this processing are disposed of later.

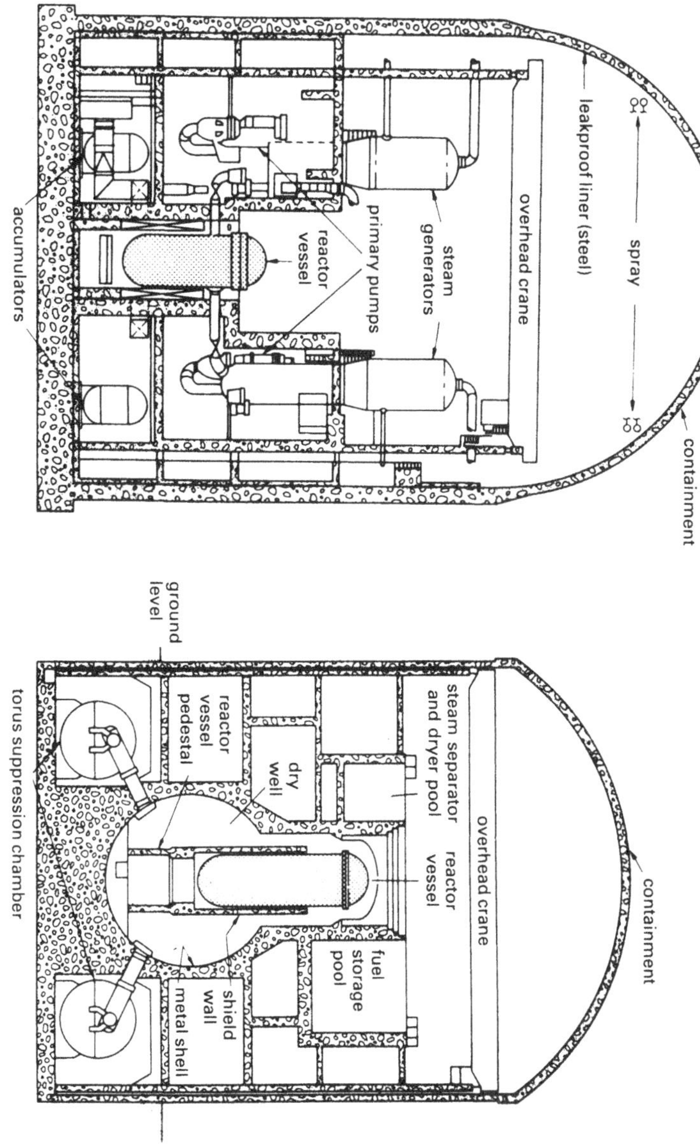

FIGURE 6.6. Containment of PWR reactors (left figure) and BWR reactors (right figure).

This example shows that decontamination does not suppress radioactivity but rather displaces and concentrates it, thus rendering easier the definitive disposal of radioactive wastes (§7.5.7). In an ideal system, all the waste would be found in solid form.

The second barrier (Fig. 6.5) is not absolutely leakproof so that weakly radioactive liquid and gaseous effluents will be found in the containment building. In the case of LWR reactors, the leaks most often take place at the level of the purification circuits and the latter are moreover incapable of retaining gaseous radio-isotopes (some iodine and noble gases). In addition, for BWR reactors (direct cycle), leaks from the steam circuit lead to a significant increase of the activity of the gaseous effluents. To these must be added those wastes which come (in smaller quantities, it is true) from various laboratories, laundries, etc. As can be seen in Fig. 6.5, various dump tanks permit the collection of contaminated water and ventilation takes care of the rest for the gaseous components.

For a long time it was thought that these wastes could be discharged into the environment if, after dilution, the most dangerous isotope concentrations did not exceed the permitted limits (§6.2.4 norms). In fact, for most working power plants this condition is satisfied (in other words, the major part of the activity of the primary circuit is retained in the form of solid wastes). In spite of that, the notion of maximum permissible concentration has been gradually replaced by that of weakest possible concentration: it is always necessary to seek to lower the radionuclide concentrations in the wastes wherever technology permits, even if the IAEA norms are amply satisfied. This new philosophy has led to a refinement from the point of view of environmental protection which far exceeds anything one meets in other industrial sectors. Thus the effluents are once again put through circuits somewhat like the preceding ones. Without entering into detail, we mention the following processing methods:

- liquid effluents: demineralization (resins), filtration, centrifugation, evaporation, electrodialysis, inverse osmosis, etc.
- gaseous effluents (wastes carried off by air): filtration (99.97% absolute filters for aerosols), activated charcoal (for iodine), recombination of radiolysis products, etc.

In both cases, decay tanks permit the radical elimination of short-lived radionuclides (residence times could attain several weeks). Resins, in this case, are much less called upon, because the impurity level of liquid effluents is much lower than that in the purification circuit.

After this last treatment, gaseous waste is expelled from the chimney stacks while liquid wastes are sent out through an evacuation channel (discharging into a river or a lake).

Naturally, the procedures used vary considerably from one installation to another, but one can state that at the present time, with the exception of tritium and the noble gases (see further on), the activities that are finally released into the environment are insignificant when compared, for example, with those of the radio-isotopes which are permanently manipulated in the nuclear medicine services of the major hospitals.

TABLE 6.7. Measured wastes of some nuclear power plants. A_c: Annually discharged activity in Ci, x: concentration expressed as a fraction (%) of the maximum permitted concentration (IAEA)

Name of installation	Electric power	*Liquid effluents*		*Gaseous effluents*	
		Fission and activation products	Tritium	Noble gases	Halogens
	[MWe]	A_c [x]	A_c [x]	A_c [x]	A_c [x]
BWR					
Dresden 2.3	800	22.1 [15]	$26\ [6 \cdot 10^{-3}]$	$4.3\ 10^5$ [1.51]	5.9 [3.6]
Monticello	540	$2.9\ 10^{-6}\ [2 \cdot 10^{-8}]$	$7.6 \cdot 10^{-5}\ [2.5\ 10^{-10}]$	$7.5\ 10^5$ [8.8]	0.59 [1.6]
Mühleberg	300	0.7 (équivalent Sr^{90})	12	3600	0.014
PWR					
Palisades	740	$6.8\ [5 \cdot 10^{-3}]$	208 [0.43]	500 [0.02]	$9.7\ 10^{-3}$ [0.3]
Point Beach 1.2	500	$1.53\ [5 \cdot 10^{-3}]$	563 [0.04]	$2.8\ 10^3$ [0.09]	$3\ 10^{-2}\ [1\ 10^{-4}]$
Beznau 1.2	350	11	590	$2.2\ 10^3$ [–]	$8\ 10^{-3}$

One can get an idea of the results obtained by analyzing Table 6.7, regarding some existing nuclear power stations. The figures presented come from an American study [30] of about twenty reactors. These are not the most modern of reactors. The data concerning the Swiss reactors of Mühlenberg and Beznau come from the 1979 report of the Swiss Federal Commission for the Monitoring of Radioactivity. We are first struck by the low amount of activity discharged annually as compared to the enormous activity contained in the core of a reactor (Table 6.3). Next, it appears that the Monticello reactor has very high performances, at least where liquid effluents are concerned. This is explained by the fact that this plant was one of the first to use a device for processing these wastes. The other reactors which did not benefit (or benefitted very little) from this technology nevertheless have acceptable wastes ($x < 100$) which means that the leakproofness of the second barrier is satisfactory. As foreseen, tritium wastes of PWR reactors are more significant (§.6.3.3), whereas other discharges are weaker than those of BWR reactors (direct cycle). Finally, we see that the activity of the noble gases remains large but permissible, even in the case of BWR reactors. These results permit us to verify the affirmations of subsec. 6.2.3, namely, that the strongest activities can correspond to the weakest doses (see the variations of A_c and of x). Thus, because of their biological effects (Table 6.4), the halogens, especially iodine I^{131}, must be taken into account even if their discharges are lower than 1 Ci/yr.

Although it is not necessary, one could reduce the quantity of noble gases by prolonging their residence time in the decay tanks of the processing device for gaseous effluents. At the end of one month, the activity could be reduced by a factor of at least 1000, because of the decrease of xenon Xe^{133}, the most abundant noble gas (Table 6.4). In the limit, there would only remain krypton Kr^{85} ($T = 10.6$ years). This radionuclide appears in large quantities only during fuel reprocessing (Sec. 7.5).

Tritium does not submit to the preceding processings, and one finds it in gaseous and liquid wastes. All the same, in the latter case there remains a possibility of sending the tritium-bearing water back into the primary circuit. This water is periodically renewed in order to limit its activity. Tritium thus appears finally in the form of "liquid waste" that must be stored. This procedure greatly reduces tritium discharges in the liquid phase (cf. the Monticello reactor, Table 6.7). In contrast, tritium contained in gaseous effluents is always released into the atmosphere. Happily, because of the low energy of the emitted β^- rays, the permissible concentrations are much higher than those induced by the discharges in the biosphere. Tritium of natural origin (end of §6.3.2) as well as that resulting from experimental nuclear explosions, are still preponderant at the present time. Taking anticipated programs into account, the share of tritium from nuclear power plants should not be felt before the year 2000.

In order to reduce the quantities of tritium one can give up boron as a means of control in PWR reactors, but ternary fissions will always remain (§6.3.2). As to the retrieval of tritium, which is a precious isotope (Ch. 2), it is difficult because of its dilution. One can nevertheless envisage various procedures, costly for the present, such as electrolysis, distillation, thermal diffusion, etc. Military programs (H-bombs) have led to numerous studies in this domain.

The last problem remaining to be analyzed is that of the dispersion of wastes. Whereas the discharge rates analyzed above depend exclusively on the nuclear power plant considered, the concentrations finally attained in the environment (and hence the doses) are in addition fixed by the dispersion modes envisaged and the characteristics of the chosen site. At this last stage, the impact on the environment can once again be minimized. Calculations of concentrations as a function of discharges involve complex phenomena which cannot be analyzed here. Laws which are more or less similar to that of neutron diffusion (§4.3.1) govern the "transport" of radionuclides. The flow characteristics of rivers in which liquid wastes are discharged as well as the meteorological conditions in the case of gaseous waste discharge play an important role. Numerous calculational programs have been perfected in recent years for the design of the chimney stacks and the choice of site.

Having determined the various concentrations in the vicinity of the plant, one can compare them with the maximum permissible concentrations (parameter x of Table 6.7) or deduce the doses (external and internal). Evidently it is necessary to take account of reconcentrations which may take place at certain points in the alimentary chain, a factor which works against dispersion.

Biological doses due to liquid wastes are related to water consumption. People who drink the water from a river downstream from the discharge point of a plant constitute the critical group. In the same way, the critical point corresponds to the maximum dose that one may encounter outside the plant. The results of measurements carried out in 1979 in the vicinity of three Swiss power plants are as follows [31]: the hypothetical dose associated to the residual water was everywhere less than 0.1 mrem/yr and the doses induced by gaseous wastes did not exceed 3 mrem/yr, doses which are hardly measurable. Such doses are in any case much lower than the norms, which are 20 mrems/yr (§6.2.4).

6.3.5 Control and Monitoring of Radioactivity

Just as dose evaluations are necessary at the project stage, dose measurement is indispensable from the moment a nuclear reactor becomes operational. A distinction is often made between controls effected within the plant and monitoring instructions applied outside. Any sudden increase of radioactivity is very important, since in general it means a failing in the plant: whence "nonstop" measurements.

Numerous detectors exist. Some, like Geiger-Muller counters, are close to the instrumentation already described (§5.3.9). They are characterized by much larger amplification factors (much larger applied voltages: 800 to 1500 V). The pulses are no longer proportional to the energies of the primary particles but one can detect β and γ radiations of weak intensity. For more precise measurements one appeals to high pressure ionization chambers whose sensitivity threshhold is about 1 μrem/hr. Scintillators are of similar sensitivity and are based on another principle. Nuclear rays induce an emission of light (phosphorescence) in certain solids, detectable by a photomultiplier.

All these apparatuses permit the global measurement of doses associated to the activity of the ambiant air. In fact, more detailed information is required. For that, various samples are taken from the environment: water, earth, milk, etc., and after concentration of the activity contained, analogous measurements are made. We point out that certain devices permit not only the identification of the primary radiation, but also measurement of the energies of the component particles (β, γ, etc.). This permits the identification of the most important radionuclides.

Persons who are professionally exposed (nuclear power plants, research centers, etc.), permanently carry dosimeters which give approximately the integrated doses they have received. The most currently used are veritable small "pocket" ionization chambers in the form of ballpoint pens, or badges which darken as a function of the received dose. Personnel working in "hot zones" in which accidental contamination is possible are submitted to stricter control.

6.4 SAFETY

6.4.1 Introduction

In the preceding section we considered the release of radioactivity and its impact on the environment, with reference to nuclear power plants in perfect working order. In the case of a serious accident, radioactive discharge can be much more significant. The goal of safety studies is not only to anticipate the consequences of an accident, but in particular to reduce the probability of its occurring. The measures already taken to reduce to a minimum the discharge of radioactive wastes during normal operation increase safety, and for that reason, sections 6.3 and 6.4 form a unit. Still, the most serious accidents require additional safety apparatus (§6.4.3 and 6.4.4), and further, an analysis of risks is indispensable for judging the global reliability of power plants (§6.4.5).

6.4.2 Safety Philosophy

Three levels of safety are generally considered.

The following requirements correspond to the first level.

- The reactivity coefficients (fuel and moderator) and the void coefficient (coolant) (§5.3.3) must be negative; for certain types of reactors (LMFBR) the void coefficient of the coolant can become positive but the fuel temperature coefficient, always negative, is dominant. In other words, certain physical mechanisms insure an intrinsic safety.
- The materials used must have well known properties consistent with the anticipated irradiation rate; this implies a very strict "factory control".
- Multiple barriers must be interposed between the fuel and the environment. These have already been discussed (§6.3.3).
- There must be a redundant number of measurement systems and methods of control (§5.3.9).
- The "nerve centers" of the plant must be such that they can be inspected and/or instrumented for continuous control of radioactivity.

To sum up, one might say that safety problems are essentially resolved at the time of conception of a reactor assembly, as well as at the preplanning stages. Any plant that would require major additional equipment for its safety would be an ill-conceived plant which would have little chance of being accepted by the competent authorities.

Let us now look at the second level of safety. In spite of the precautions taken at the first level, an accident is always possible (though not very probable). To increase safety, the following dispositions are generally made:

- All reactors are equipped with an emergency cooling system (ECCS) which takes over for the primary circuit in case this latter should fail.
- The emergency shutdown device (SCRAM) must be redundant. If the safety rods (§5.3.8) cannot be inserted, one must be able to use another source of anti-reactivity (injection of borated water in LWR reactors, rapid emptying in CANDU reactors, etc.).
- An independent electricity source (diesel-powered generators) is indispensable for the emergency cooling operation when the electricity is disconnected.

Finally, the third level of safety corresponds to ultimate measures which depend on the type of reactor. Supplementary safety devices are necessary when the preceding emergency systems are found to be inoperable. Their conception follows from the analysis of the most serious accidents resulting from a cascade of breakdowns.

Let us quickly review the accidents that can take place in a nuclear plant and list them in increasing order of seriousness [32] (p.102):

1. Trivial accidents.
2. Weak discharges into the environment (various leaks in the circuits).
3. Breakdown of the waste reprocessing machinery (§6.3.4).
4. Penetration of fission products into the primary circuit (faulty cladding in normal operation and unforeseen transients).
5. Situation similar to the preceding with in addition a primary → secondary leak (at the level of the steam generator).
6. Accidents during refuelling inside the containment (a fuel element falling, for example).
7. Accident of the same type but outside the containment.

8. Events leading to the reference accident considered in the safety report: rupture in the primary pipes, reactivity accident, etc.
9. A sequence of accidents more serious than the preceding.

Apart from the first type, all the accidents mentioned above lead to release of radioactivity in the environment.

In the following we shall analyse some reference accidents considered as the most serious ones which can take place (Type 8). Accidents of this type entail an imbalance between the energy produced in the fuel and the energy removed by the coolant. The first prevailing over the second, an increase of temperature occurs, at least at the start, which can seriously damage the reactor. In a reactivity accident, it is a prompt divergence which creates this imbalance (§6.4.3), while in other cases a decrease in the flow rate of the coolant is the culprit (§6.4.4). Thus each time one should study the behavior of the reactor in nonsteady state. From the neutronic point of view we know that this behavior is governed by the reactivity ρ (§4.6.4). This latter does not only depend on external actions (deliberate or accidental), but also on feedback phenomena which have already been enumerated in connection with control (§5.3.3). These effects are no longer compensated automatically (by the control rods) as they are during normal running, but contribute to accelerating or slowing down the unstable state triggered by the accident.

At any moment, the reactivity can thus be written (5.23):

$$\rho(t) = \rho_{ext}(t) + \alpha_c \delta T_c + \alpha_m \delta T_m + \alpha_v \delta v + \ldots \qquad (6.6)$$

an expression in which ρ_{ext} represents the contribution of external influences (withdrawal of a control rod, for example), while the ensuing terms stand for the response effects. We recall that the quantities δT_c, δT_m, etc., represent temperature variations counted starting from the rated value (critical state). Thus in the absence of an accident there is neither an insertion of reactivity ($\rho_{ext} = 0$), nor a thermohydraulic modification of the system ($\delta T_c = \delta T_m = \delta v = 0$), so that the global reactivity is zero and the reactor stable. In the opposite case, the reactivity coefficients α (§5.3.3) play a crucial role. The coefficient α_c is always negative, at least for power reactors; this is especially due to the Doppler effect (§9.4.1). The void coefficient α_v is negative for LWR reactors, and this expresses the fact that there is a reactivity loss when the moderation decreases (cf. Fig. 5.4 and §5.1.4).

According to the preceding, any increase of power in a LWR reactor (thus the increase of T_c and v after a certain lapse of time) is equal to an insertion of negative reactivity (antireactivity) which counteracts the external reactivity ρ_{ext} (first level of safety).

6.4.3 Reactivity Accidents

As long as the introduction of a reactivity ρ remains lower than the production rate of delayed neutrons β, the divergence of a reactor remains controllable, for its stable period is of the order of several seconds (§4.6.5). Reactivity accidents, on the other hand, correspond to the prompt supercritical state ($\rho > \beta$). The mechanisms that can lead to such a situation are essentially the following:

- abrupt withdrawal of control rods;
- lowering of coolant density with positive void coefficient (§5.3.3) following a halt of the primary pumps (LMFBR);
- rearrangement of the core as a result of melting;
- introduction of various materials.

The first mechanism concerns all reactors. Certain locking devices prevent the reactor operator from withdrawing control rods by a procedure contrary to the manufacturer's specifications. Still, in the wake of a failure of the neutron measurement apparatus, a withdrawal order could occur. Generally, it would lead to a weak reactivity ($\rho < \beta$), for the control rods individually have a low effectiveness. If in addition the manufacturer's procedure is not respected (locking mechanism breakdown), one can imagine prompt supercriticality ($\rho > \beta$) in the extreme case. Even though this accident is highly improbable and has never happened so far, it has been analyzed in great detail.

A simple theoretical study will enable us to understand better the effect of feedbacks. We know that the timescale is fixed in this case by the generation time Λ (§4.6.5) which attains at most 1 millisecond. Thus we cannot hope that the safety rods will fall in the requisite time to neutralize the accidental reactivity introduced. For the same reason, the precursor concentrations will not change appreciably in the duration of the phenomenon ($\Lambda \ll 1/\lambda_i$); therefore if P_0 is the initial value of the neutron population P(t), the second equation (4.110) can be written:

$$\lambda_i C_i(t) = \lambda_i C_i(0) = \beta_i P_0/\Lambda$$

and the first reduces to:

$$\frac{dP}{dt} = \frac{\rho(t) - \beta}{\Lambda} P + \frac{\beta}{\Lambda} P_0 \tag{6.7}$$

where Λ can be taken as a constant. In this equation P represents both the neutron population and the reactor power, since the two quantities are proportional. The phenomena take place so fast that one may assume that the heat liberated in the fuel is not transmitted to the coolant in this lapse of time (adiabatic hypothesis). We have thus:

$$M_c\, C_c \frac{dT_c}{dt} = P(t)$$

where $M_c C_c$ represents the heat capacity of the fuel. After integration we get:

$$\delta T_c = T_c(t) - T_c(0) = \frac{1}{M_c C_c} \int_0^t P(t')dt' \tag{6.8}$$

By only retaining temperature effects in the fuel the response term in equation (6.6) can be written simply:

$$\alpha_c \delta T_c = - \alpha_w \int_0^t P(t')dt'$$

where we have put $\alpha_w = - \alpha_c/(M_c C_c)$. This new parameter is called the <u>prompt reactivity coefficient</u>. It is positive (since $\alpha_c < 0$) and plays a fundamental role in the following.

We now consider at time t = 0 the sudden introduction of a constant reactivity: $\rho_{ext} = \rho_0$. The global reactivity can then be written (6.6):

$$\rho(t) = \rho_0 - \alpha_w W(t) \tag{6.9}$$

where W represents the energy liberated at time t:

$$W(t) = \int_0^t P(t')dt' \tag{6.10}$$

Since the function $\rho(t)$ is not known a priori, it is necessary to solve simultaneously (6.7), (6.9) and (6.10). After eliminating $\rho(t)$ and P(t) we are led to a second order differential equation in W(t):

$$\frac{d^2W}{dt^2} = \frac{\rho_0 - \beta - \alpha_w W}{\Lambda} \frac{dW}{dt} + \frac{\beta}{\Lambda} P_0$$

which is integrable only if we disregard the last term, which we will later do. This approximation is valid as soon as $P > P_0$, that is, during the critical phase of the accident.

We then obtain by integration:

$$\frac{dW}{dt} = P_0 + \frac{\rho_0 - \beta}{\Lambda} W - \frac{\alpha_w}{2\Lambda} W^2 \qquad (6.11)$$

and after having noted that $(dW/dt)_0 = P_0$ and that $W(0) = 0$, as shown by equation (6.10). This last nonlinear differential equation (with separated variables) is integrated in its turn by once again using the condition $W(0) = 0$:

$$W(t) = W^+ \frac{1 - \exp(-\omega t)}{1 + \left|\frac{W^+}{W^-}\right| \exp(-\omega t)} \qquad (6.12)$$

with

$$\left.\begin{aligned} \omega &= \sqrt{\left(\frac{\rho_0 - \beta}{\Lambda}\right)^2 + 2\frac{\alpha_w P_0}{\Lambda}} \\ W^{\pm} &= \frac{(\rho_0 - \beta) \pm \Lambda\omega}{\alpha_w} \end{aligned}\right\} \qquad (6.13)$$

where ω, $W^{\pm}$ are respectively the discriminant and the roots of the right-hand side of equation (6.11). Finally, the power is obtained by differentiating (6.12):

$$P(t) = \frac{dW}{dt} = \frac{2\Lambda\omega^2}{\alpha_w} \left|\frac{W^+}{W^-}\right| \frac{\exp(-\omega t)}{\left[1 + \left|\frac{W^+}{W^-}\right| \exp(-\omega t)\right]^2} \qquad (6.14)$$

This is one of the rare problems that can be treated analytically. Let us take for example the case of a thermal reactor ($\Lambda = 10^{-4}$) subjected to the introduction of a very significant reactivity ($\rho_0 - \beta = 2.32\ 10^{-3}$). We then obtain the curves of Fig. 6.8. In practice, the ratio $|W^+/W^-|$ is always large. During the first instants the term $|W^+/W^-| \exp(-\omega t)$ also remains important and expression (6.14) becomes:

$$P(t) \cong P_0 \exp\left[\frac{(\rho_0 - \beta)t}{\Lambda}\right]$$

We get back the expected very fast exponential growth in the absence of feedback (§4.6.5). Subsequently the accumulated thermal energy W(t) becomes such that the excursion is progressively braked until the moment when the power attains its maximum value at time

$$t_m = \frac{1}{\omega} \ln \left|\frac{W^+}{W^-}\right|$$

with

$$P_m = \frac{\Lambda\omega^2}{2\alpha_w} \cong \frac{(\rho_0 - \beta)^2}{2\Lambda\alpha_w} \qquad (6.15)$$

after which it tends to 0 like exp ($-\omega t$) as indicated by (6.14). The reactor stops by itself and the total liberated energy $W(\infty)$ has a finite value. Using (6.12) we obtain:

$$W(\infty) = W^+ \cong 2\frac{\rho_0 - \beta}{\alpha_w} \qquad (6.16)$$

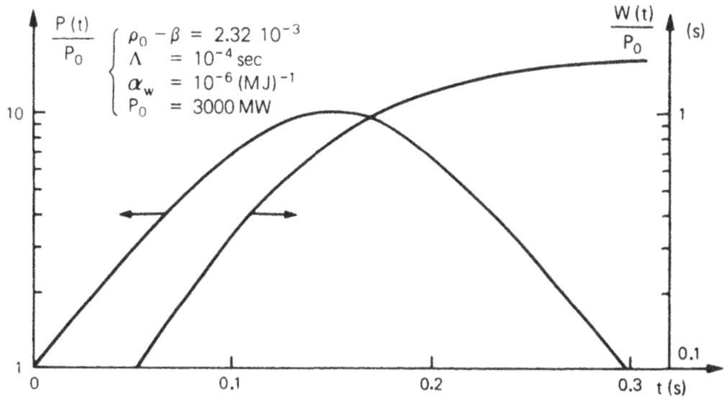

FIGURE 6.8

Before going further, we shall make a few comments about the preceding mathematical model. For large values of t (greater than one second) the influence of delayed neutrons ceases to be negligible and the decrease in power is much slower than expression (6.14) indicates. In addition, the power does not tend to zero but to a value slightly higher than the initial power, which corresponds to a new critical state. This second steady state, which is obtained so long as the core keeps its integrity, is such that the corresponding temperature increase compensates the introduction of the reactivity ρ_0 which initiated the accident. Due to the adiabatic approximation, the simple study just made does not permit us to get back this new equilibrium state, but this has no importance, for it is only reached well after the transient in question has died away and the results obtained above keep their sense.

In the numerical application which follows, we consider a PWR reactor of 1000 MWe, with (Table 5.22): M_c = 82.5 t and P_0 = 3000 MWt (initial power identical to rated power). For this reactor assembly we adopt the following values:

$$\alpha_c \text{ (Doppler)} \cong -2\ 10^{-5}\ °C^{-1}$$

$$C_c\ (UO_2) \cong 240\ J\ kg^{-1}\ °C^{-1}$$

whence the prompt reactivity coefficient:

$$\alpha_w = -\frac{\alpha_c}{M_c C_c} \cong 1.10^{-6}(MJ)^{-1}$$

power and energies being respectively expressed in MW and MJ. It is this latter value which was used in the preceding example. Two quantities present a particular interest, $W(\infty)/P_0$ and P_m/P_0. The first and most important represents the energy liberated during the accident with reference to the energy produced during one second of normal operation (P_0 x 1). The second, which defines the power peak, is more or less inversely proportional to Λ, which is why in Fig. 6.9 we represent the product $(\Lambda P_m)/P_0$. Lastly we will note that these quantities depend on α_w only through the product $\alpha_w P_0$ (6.13) which is virtually the same for reactors of the same type ($\alpha_w \cong 1/M_c$ and $P_0 \cong M_c$).

Examining the curves in Fig. 6.9 we note that even for large reactivities, the ratio $W(\infty)/P_0$ has unity as order of magnitude, the results depending hardly at all on Λ. The power peak on the other hand is very sensitive to the generation time. For the reactivity already considered $\rho_0 - \beta = 2.32\ 10^{-3}$, we obtain: $P_m/P_0 = 10$ for $\Lambda = 10^{-4}$s (thermal reactors) and $P_m/P_0 = 9000$ for $\Lambda = 10^{-7}$ (fast reactors), but in both cases the liberation of thermal energy remains reasonable: $W(\infty)/P_0 \cong 1.5$ (in fact, in order for the second case to be valid for fast reactors, α_w must in addition keep the preceding value of $1\cdot 10^{-6}$ $(MJ)^{-1}$).

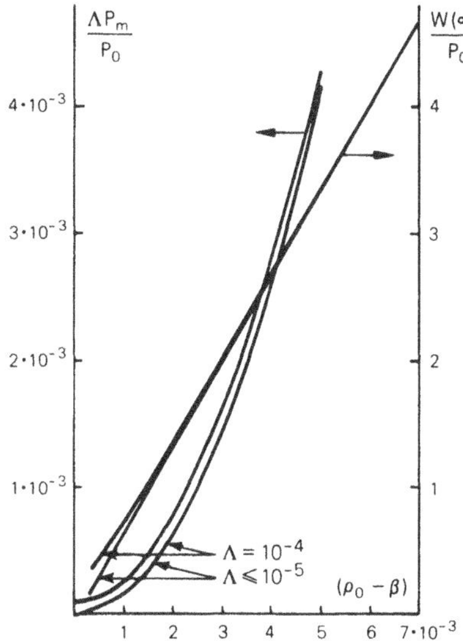

FIGURE 6.9.

The preceding results have been confirmed by numerical computer calculations which are free of the simplifying hypotheses adopted here. In addition, the instantaneous introduction of a reactivity ρ_0 is not very realistic, since all the envisageable mechanical time constants are far greater than the generation time Λ. Our conclusions are thus very pessimistic (in practice, for so rapid an introduction of reactivity to be achieved by withdrawal of the control rods, it would be necessary to use explosives!). We can moreover take up the preceding study considering this time an introduction of reactivity linear in time, that is to say, a reactivity ramp $\rho_{ext} = \dot{\rho}t$. We find then that the energy liberated during the accident is given by $W(\infty) \cong \sqrt{\dot{\rho}\Lambda}\,/\alpha_w$ [32](p.243): the low value of the generation time Λ of fast reactors is thus not necessarily a handicap as one often thinks. Moreover, the accidental introduction of reactivity in this type of reactor can only be fairly slow, even though capable of bringing about a prompt supercritical state, for the foreseeable sequence of initiating events is the following [33]: a general slowing down of the primary pumps followed by a complete failure of the emergency shutdown systems (no insertion of safety rods), a highly improbable accident which corresponds quite well to the insertion of a reactivity ramp resulting from the overheating of sodium (positive temperature coefficient).

The phenomenon which has just been described is called a nuclear excursion. The very rapid initial rise in power is neutronically something like that which happens in an atomic bomb, but once the feedback is taken into account, the phenomena are completely changed. We have seen that for the most serious accidents the liberated energy can correspond to what a power plant in normal operation produces in several seconds (Fig. 6.9). Even if the peak power can be more than 1000 times higher than its rated value for an extremely short time, the temperature increase is directly proportional to the liberated energy $W(\infty)$ (cf. equation (6.8)), which, as we have just seen, remains reasonable. Of course, for strong excursions (ρ_0 high, α_W low) meltdown and even vaporizing of part of the core could take place. In fast reactors this leads to a new increase in reactivity (positive void coefficient) while the prompt response coefficient α_W can be lower than that of LWR reactors. For this reason a reactivity accident is considered as the reference accident for fast breeders.

A number of experiments (EBR-II, 1957, FERMI-I, 1961) have supported the safety studies on fast reactors [32](p.256). LWR reactors, to which the theory outlined above applies well, have also been the subject of similar experimental studies. Simulations have been done on the small reactors SPERT and BORAX [32](p.459). In spite of a high enrichment and a less effective response, it was not possible to bring about an explosion. The most spectacular experiment was the deliberate destruction of a reactor (SL 1) following a particularly violent nuclear excursion. The pressure was such that the control rods were ejected and the tank rose by about three meters, shearing off the cooling circuit.

6.4.4 Loss of Coolant and Containment Integrity

The stopping of all pumps or primary circuit blockage leads to a flow loss and hence to cooling loss. This is a highly improbable accident, since several pumps and several circuits operate in parallel (§5.4.2). It thus belongs to the second type mentioned in subsec. 6.4.2: thermal disequilibrium is no longer caused by a nuclear excursion. We can imagine an accident which is even more serious, and more improbable, namely coolant loss following a rupture in the primary circuit (if this rupture took place, it would be at the joints of the primary pipes and the reactor vessel). This accident, which is known as LOCA (Loss of Coolant Accident), and which has never been observed, is taken as a reference accident for LWR reactors. In contrast, it is not easy to imagine this accident in an LMFBR plant, since the primary circuit which is immersed in the tank is not submitted to any significant pressure.

As for LWR reactors, mathematical models whose most questionable a priori aspects have been adjusted on the basis of experimental results obtained on mock-ups, have permitted a detailed description of the sequence of events [34]. This time, the safety rods fall quite quickly, so that the power associated to the fissions decreases right from the start. Moreover, the reactivity coefficients being negative, the global reactivity (6.6) becomes more and more negative, thus accelerating the decrease. In spite of this, this accident is more serious than the preceding as shown by Fig. 6.10. The coolant loss leads to a rapid increase in the cladding temperature accompanied by a drop in pressure (the observed fluctuations come from decompression sound waves). Subsequently the temperature diminishes, since the large power loss eventually makes itself felt. Unfortunately, as we know (§3.1.4), the residual power decreases very slowly, and the primary circuit is no longer capable even of evacuating this energy. Thus the temperature again begins to rise

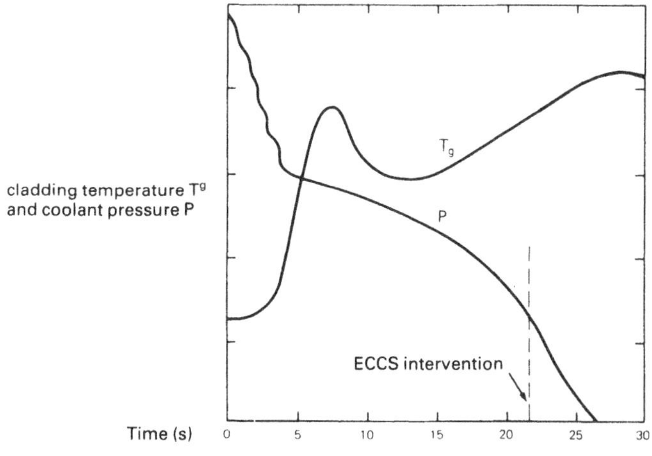

FIGURE 6.10. Behavior of a PWR reactor following a LOCA-type accident.

after 15 seconds and there no longer exist any physical phenomena capable of stopping it. If no precaution has been taken, the critical heat flux will rapidly be attained, entailing fuel meltdown (§5.2.4). It is here that emergency cooling, called ECCS (Emergency Core Cooling System) intervenes: this system permits the core to be flooded with water which must make up for the vaporization loss as well as leakages at the point of rupture. This must take place as quickly as possible (in less than 25 seconds in the example given in Fig. 6.10). For this, one uses last of all in PWR reactors pressurized water accumulators (passive system). Beforehand, and according to the existing pressure in the vessel, water which comes from the tank used during refuelling operations is injected in the core. One has recourse either to a low pressure system or to high pressure pumps used in auxiliary systems during normal operation. Cooling must continue until the moment when the reactor can be unloaded. There is no need to add that whatever the type of accident, the emergency shutdown of the reactor is accompanied by the halting of the turbine-alternator group. The steam is aimed directly on the condenser, which receives a part of the residual heat of the reactor (the other part is carried away by the coolant escaping from the primary circuit at the level of the break).

In BWR reactors one calls upon a low-pressure injection system as well as independent high or low pressure core spraying devices (Fig. 5.21).

For CANDU reactors, the philosophy is close to that for PWR reactors. The emergency shutdown system (safety rods) is doubled by an emergency system allowing for the injection of gadolinium nitrate in horizontal tubes made for this purpose (in the first reactors the moderator was rapidly drained, cf. Table 5.26). The emergency core cooling system is conceived and designed in function of the most serious cooling accident, here, too a LOCA. This system differs very little in conception from what we have just seen for PWRs.

Although a LOCA-type accident is not envisageable in a fast breeder, it is necessary to anticipate the possibility of cooling the core in case of stoppage of the primary pumps. The after-heat is then evacuated by a four-loop ECCS device (Superphenix), each loop possessing a sodium/sodium exchanger located in the reactor vessel and a sodium/air exchanger at the exterior [33]. This device is hardly necessary, since natural convection is very large (this is one of the reasons for the "pool" concept) and the enormous heat capacity of the sodium contained in the tank is such that it is not necessary to put these loops to work immediately after the accident (we note that the prototype Phenix lacked such a system since it was shown experimentally that natural convection sufficed). This scenario presupposes emergency shutdown; if this does not take place (two simultaneous failures), an insertion of positive reactivity will result in the overheating of the sodium and thus we will again have a reactivity accident (§6.4.3).

We shall now see how the containment enclosure behaves when the reactor has suffered one of the accidents described above. It is only at this stage that the third barrier will play a role (§6.3.3); for that, its integrity must be assured.

We consider afresh the coolant loss accident in a LWR reactor. Even if the ECCS functions, the primary fluid which escapes at the level of the break entails an increase of pressure in the enclosure which could damage the containment. To remedy this, decompression systems are used. By means of spraying, the temperature is reduced, and hence the atmospheric pressure of the containment (Fig. 6.6). The particular structure of BWR reactors permits the adoption of an original solution. The cavity (the first enclosure) which shields the vessel is connected to a condensation torus containing a large amount of cold water. When the pressure becomes too great, steam penetrates into the torus and condenses. The pressure then drops immediately in the first enclosure and tends to become identical to the saturated steam pressure in the cold torus (Fig. (Fig. 6.6).

After draining the reservoir, all the emergency cooling systems (reactor or containment) are finally fed via a heat exchanger with water which escaped from the primary circuit. For a PWR reactor, this water is collected in a sump at the bottom of the containment; for a BWR reactor, in the condensation torus. As for the auxiliary exchanger, it is cooled by river water, for example. The reference accident being the same for CANDU reactors, their containment is protected in the same way. In spite of all these precautions, a certain overpressure is to be expected, at least temporarily, and the containment must be able to withstand it. The escape rate of the contained atmosphere must be kept below 0.1% per day.

In the extreme case, we can imagine accidents which are more serious and even more improbable than those which we have just analyzed (type 9 of the classification of §6.4.2): they correspond to the destruction of the reactor core. Certain nuclear excursions may lead to this (see the analysis of the reactivity accident) as well as the rupture of the primary circuit (LOCA) followed by the nonfunctioning of the emergency cooling system (ECCS).

- In the first case, the energy generated leads to meltdown and partial vaporization of the core. After taking various latent heats into account, the available energy appears in mechanical form, in particular as a shock wave which can damage the containment. This accident, which is envisaged for LMFBR reactors, can come from a cooling arrest. As we have seen, this leads to a slow but large insertion of reactivity if one supposes in addition that the safety rods cannot penetrate the core. Detailed studies have shown that for the Superphenix the mechanical energy resulting from this type of accident would remain lower than 800 MJ [33]. This figure results from the very pessimistic hypothesis that all the molten fuel might interact with cold sodium penetrating unexpectedly into the core. The containment and the primary circuit are so conceived as to stand up to such conditions.

- In the second case it is the residual power which must be evacuated. Here it is a matter of a slow liberation of energy which poses serious problems from the moment that the primary and emergency circuits are inoperative. Here also a core meltdown can take place in spite of the absence of any nuclear excursion.

Whatever the cause of this accident, a large part of the molten fuel will collect at the bottom of the vessel. Let us imagine the following extremely pessimistic scenario: The temperatures are such that the steel melts in its turn and the magma spreads on the concrete floor of the containment. Because of lack of cooling, this molten mass goes through the floor and progresively sinks deeper into the ground until finally the heat is dissipated by spreading out in the earth. If we neglected this dispersion and violated somewhat the laws of physics, we would arrive at the conclusion that the molten fuel would sink through the entire planet, appearing at the antipodes. This is what in America is called the "China syndrome" (in addition a geographical error has slipped into this demonstration). The point of the witticism is to underline the seriousness of the accident.

Although certain accidents may have led to the melting of a few fuel elements (§6.4.6), a total core meltdown has never been observed, and much less a perforation of the vessel. This is due to the extreme improbability of this accident and also to some very complex physical phenomena ignored in safety studies, which are always pessimistic. Nevertheless, reactor design must take account of this possibility. It is thus that fast breeders have an"ash pit" which permits the recuperation of molten fuel in a subcritical geometry. Even if a fast reactor is not in its most critical configuration a secondary criticality might still take place due to core meltdown, since the fissile matter is now more concentrated. For LWR reactors, this re-criticality is absolutely impossible. It would be necessary to have available a highly enriched fuel. Low fuel enrichment (3%) demands the presence of a moderator to obtain the critical state. This moderator (water) cannot accompany uranium during its melting.

6.4.5 Evaluation of Nuclear Risks

Once all the precautions indicated above have been taken, one can still ask: "Is the reactor absolutely safe?" The answer has to be no, as for all human activities including the most inoffensive. Since safety can never be absolute, some means must be found to measure it. The most significant indicator is in the form of risk run by the general public, for example, the number of deaths per year. The risk of accident is currently defined as the probability of this accident multipled by the damage which it entails (release of radioactivity, number of deaths). Let us compare two accidents:

- The first very serious one takes place on the average every 10,000 years (probability 10^{-4}) and brings about the death of 10,000 persons.
- The second takes place on the average every 10 years, each time resulting in the death of 10 persons. In both cases the risk is the same since 1/10,000 x 10,000 = 1/10 x 10 = 1 death/yr (on the average). In order to know the global risk of a plant, one writes:

$$R = \sum_i P_i \cdot D_i \qquad (6.17)$$

where P_i and D_i represent respectively the probability and damage associated to an accident of type i.

The damage D_i depends on the hypotheses made with respect to release of radioactivity. It is a function of the gravity of the accident and of the volatility of the concerned radionuclides (Table 6.4). For simple cladding breaks, only the fission products accumulated in the cladding - fuel annular interstice need to be considered. In contrast, in the course of a rupture of the primary circuit followed by nonfunction of the emergency cooling system, resulting in core meltdown, all the noble gases and the greater part of the iodine would penetrate into the containment. The other radionuclides would in part be retained by the primary circuit in spite of its rupture (surface deposits). Provided that the containment is not destroyed, its atmosphere can have a very high activity without prejudice to the external environment. Naturally, pessimistic hypotheses are always made, since it is very difficult to determine with precision releases associated to accidents which are often complex.

Let us return to the preceding expression (6.17): it is surely the best definition of risk that one might choose, but the public more easily tolerates , even at higher risk, frequent but unspectacular accidents (for example, road accidents). In the past, nuclear engineers themselves had this unfortunate tendency: they spoke in terms of "maximum credible accident" which, during project studies, contributed to giving too little weight to other more plausible accidents. To some extent this tendency has remained to this day, since the reference accident (§6.4.4) plays a preponderant role in the conception of safety mechanisms; this role is somewhat excessive as has been indicated by the commission set up to investigate the Harrisburg accident [35]. In contrast, the conception of safety based on the preceding definition of risk does not give special status to any particular type of accident.

Psychological realities being what they are, it is preferable to give curves representing the frequency of accidents in function of their gravity, the most serious accidents being no longer "submerged" in the notion of risk, a notion too global for the public. This is exactly what was done by Rasmussen in his renowned report [36], where the annual frequencies of accidents are given in function of their damage, for 100 LWR-type nuclear power plants (Fig. 6.11). We note for example that the probability of an accident causing more than 100 deaths per year is 10^{-4} (one accident every 10,000 years). But what is this to be compared with?

What are the acceptable risks? It appears reasonable to base oneself on what one already knows statistically about other natural or manmade risks. This is exactly what was done when, from the point of view of biological doses, we compared power plant discharges with natural radioactivity.

We see that the risks stemming from nuclear plants are much smaller than those from other sources. One may object that these results are purely theoretical. It is thus necessary to say a few words about the method employed.

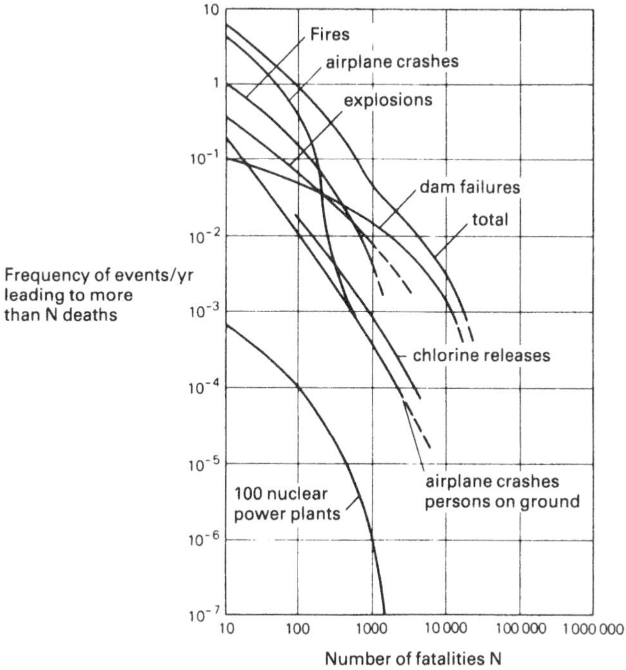

FIGURE 6.11a. Accidents associated to 100 LWR nuclear plants of 1000 MWe (forecasts) compared to accidents caused by other human activities.

We consider an event tree for each initiator accident. Let us suppose that the failure probabilities of various components of a safety system are known. We can then calculate the probability that this accident will lead to damage of a given type. As an example we have represented in Fig. 6.12 the tree diagram corresponding to the loss of coolant (§6.4.4). The results are subsequently summed for each class (one thus obtains curves analogous to those of Figs. 6.11) or are used in expression

(6.17) which gives the global risk.

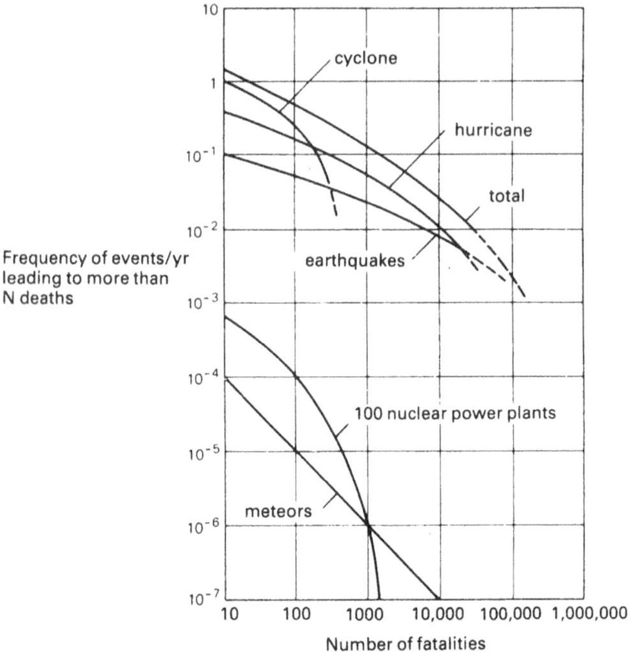

FIGURE 6.11b. Accidents associated to 100 LWR nuclear plants of 1000 MWe (forecasts) compared to accidents caused by various natural phenomena.

Insofar as the components are standard (pumps, electronic systems, etc.), we easily determine the corresponding failure probabilities. Let us consider a statistical experiment made on N_0 apparatuses which are in principal identical. After a certain time, only N(t) are still functioning; the failure probability is thus $P(t) = [N_0 - N(t)]/N_0$. This is the quantity which appears in Fig. 6.12 for each component type. Considered over one year of operation these probabilities are extremely small (high reliability) so that the probabilities of the complementary events are very close to unity. We see that the probability corresponding to the very serious case where all safety systems might fail is extremely small, since it is the product of five extremely small probabilities. Sometimes one gives the <u>annual failure rate</u> f (which should not be confused with P).

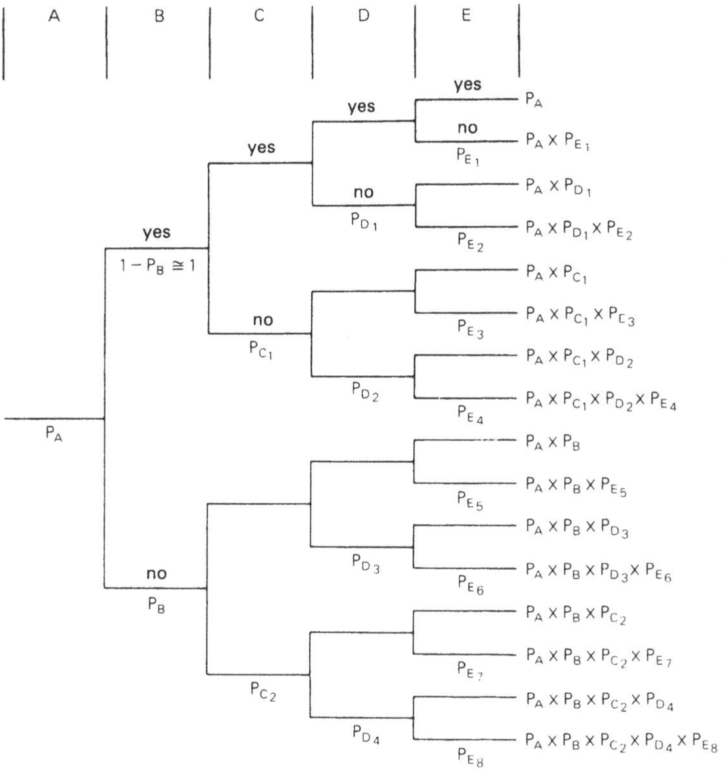

FIGURE 6.12. "Event - tree" for coolant loss. A: rupture of a primary pipe. B: availability of electric supply? C: emergency cooling operational? D: elimination of fission products possible? E: integrity of containment assured?

If at a given instant $N(t)$ apparatuses of the same type are in operation, at the end of time dt, which is small compared to $1/f$, we will observe dN failures with, by definition, $dN/N = -f\,dt$ (a law analogous to that of radioactivity). After integration of this equation we find: $N(t) = N_0 \exp(-ft)$ and: $P(t) = 1 - \exp(-ft)$. Taking account of the small values of f, we have approximately $P(t) \cong ft$ and f can be interpreted in this case as an annual failure probability to be used in a diagram such as that of Fig. 6.12.

In contrast, if we significantly vary the failure probabilities of the least known components (no experimental values), we can measure the uncertainty of the results. We believe that this uncertainty does not exceed a factor of 10, which does not modify in any way the conclusions that might be drawn from Fig. 6.11, namely that the risks associated with nuclear plants are lower than "classical" risks.

It is perhaps of more interest to compare nuclear plants to competitive plants burning heavy oils or coal. Quantitative comparisons are difficult. We know that significant emanations of sulphur dioxide and various nitrogen oxides result from the functioning of these thermal plants (for 1000 MWe plants burning coal, approximately : 500t/d of SO_2 and 75t/d of NO_x; for fuel-oil-burning plants, 170t/d of SO_2 and 74t/d of NO_x [28](p.624)). We also know that these substances are toxic, perhaps even carcinogenic. In the case of coal-burning plants, one must add radioactivity release which, though natural, is not less significant (in doses) than that of nuclear power plants.

It has been estimated [32](p.78) that in normal operation the risk associated to the running of a fuel-oil-burning plant is 10 to 100 times higher than that of a nuclear plant of the same power. These figures become 10,000 to 100,000 in case of accident and we get back the conclusions drawn from Figures 6.11. Figures are not available for coal-burning plants, but they are known as being much more polluting, and this is one reason why they have been partially abandoned.

In fact, all the technical information given in the preceding subsections, although concise, shows to what point nuclear reactor safety has been taken seriously. About 400 nuclear reactors were operating throughout the world in 1985 and not a single nuclear accident causing damage to the population was ever registered.* The same is true for prototype assemblies in the course of development, which in principle present a greater risk.

6.4.6 The Harrisburg Accident [35]

The analysis of this accident will enable us to illustrate the preceding subsections and to bring out certain specific points related to safety. The Harrisburg accident is in effect by its very nature the one closest to the reference accident described in subsection 6.4.4 (LOCA).

On the Three Mile Island site, one of the two PWR reactors (TMI-2) of 880 MWe power had the most serious accident in the entire history of nuclear energy.* On March 28, 1979, at 4 a.m. the steam generators stopped

*After the Chernobyl accident, this statement must, of course, be revised. Unfortunately, relevant information on this accident came too late to be included in this edition.

receiving the feedwater which normally came from the condenser (Fig. 5.17a); the decrease of steam production immediately led to the hydraulic disconnection of the turbine, which was the normal reaction of the installation. This classic initiator incident was not in itself serious, since an emergency feed circuit had been built in; nevertheless a cascade of failures (particularly human) led to a very critical situation. Here we resume very briefly the succession of events in chronological order (t = 0 corresponds to the stopping of the turbine):

- t ≅ 5s. The temperature and hence the pressure increase in the primary circuit; the pressure relief valve of the pressurizer opens and water is expelled towards the retrieval tank (not represented in Fig. 5.17a).
- t ≅ 8s. The pressure continues to increase, which triggers the emergency shutdown of the reactor by the fall of safety rods (§5.3.8); we note that in current plants, reactor shutdown would have followed that of the turbine.
- t ≅ 10s. Following the drop of the safety rods (SCRAM) the thermal power of the reactor rapidly decreases (§4.6.5) and in less than a second attains its value corresponding to the residual power, that is, around 7% of the rated power (§3.1.4). Prior to this the operators have noted that the auxiliary feed pumps of the steam generators have taken over.

Until this moment, the safety systems had responded correctly, but two failures were going to transform a simple incident into a serious accident because of the simple fact that the operating team realized too late what was really happening:

- first, the steam generators were not being fed, as they were thought to be, since two valves remained closed, rendering the emergency cooling system inoperative.
- subsequently (and more particularly) the pressurizer relief valve did not close when the pressure fell below its rated value as a consequence of the sudden drop of power resulting from the emergency shutdown of the reactor.

Let us pursue our chronological account of events:

- t ≅ 45s. The steam generators no longer being fed from the secondary progressively dry out; the afterheat of the core not being well evacuated, the temperature and the pressure of the primary circuit once again begin to rise.

- $t \cong 2$mn. The loss of water at the level of the pressurizer is such that the pressure in the reactor significantly decreases and the pumps (HP) of the emergency cooling system (ECCS) begin working (§6.4.4); this is exactly what is expected from such a system.
- $t \cong 4.5$ mn. Distressed by the level of water which keeps rising in the pressurizer, the operators decide to stop the emergency cooling system, which aggravates the situation.
- $t \cong 8$ mn. It is finally realized that the steam generators are suffering from a cooling failure. The two valves of the emergency secondary circuit mentioned earlier are then opened.
- $t \cong 15$ mn. The pressure becoming too strong, the membrane of the retrieval tank (into which the pressurizer discharges) breaks, which is a normal reaction of the equipment; a large quantity of radioactive water spreads into the containment enclosure.
- $t \cong 40$ mn. As it is evident at this stage that the containment is contaminated, the decision is made to stop the pumps which assure an outflow of the sump into the auxiliary building (Fig. 6.5).
- $t \cong 1$ hr. The principal pumps of the primary circuit begin to vibrate, no doubt because of the steam forming in the upper part of the core. Fearing a major cavitation, the operators stop the pumps. We recall that the steam generators are now operational, but the design of this plant is such that a natural convection loop cannot be established between them and the reactor. In addition the presence of steam does not help matters. The closing down of the principal pumps has thus created extremely unfavorable cooling conditions for the fuel.
- $t \cong 2$hr. It becomes evident that a few fuel elements are victims of cladding breaks, since gaseous fission products appear in the containment enclosure. The upper part of the core is no longer immersed and the temperatures are such that the zirconium of the cladding reacts chemically with the steam, whence the formation of hydrogen; a portion succeeds in getting into the enclosure and later ($t \cong 10$ hr) sets off a detonation.

· t ≅ 2hr.20mn. It is only at this moment that the authorities realize that the decompression valve of the pressurizer has remained open during the entire first phase. At this point, the stop valve situated just below the decompression valve is closed and the pressure begins to rise again, since the primary circuit has once again become leakproof. But the harm has been done: a part of the fuel is damaged and a large steam bubble prevents efficient cooling of the core. Let us add that for an unexplained reason, the emergency cooling has still not been put back into operation.

· t = 4hr. The pressure having slightly increased in the containment, the latter is isolated from the auxiliary building with which it normally communicates (cf. processing of effluents, §6.3.4). We note in passing that in current plants this automatic insulation would have taken place much sooner, triggered by the attained radiation levels. Nevertheless, in spite of the large amount of steam diffused into the containment, the pressure in the latter has remained low, since the dousing and ventilation systems functioned correctly (§6.4.4).

· t = 4hr.26mn. The operators once more put into operation the high pressure pumps of the emergency cooling system (ECCS) and two hours later the core is finally flooded.

We will not pursue further this incomplete account of the events, but will rather draw a few conclusions:

· the seriousness of this accident comes much more from errors of judgment than from equipment failures (non-closings of relief valves have been observed elsewhere);

· the emergency cooling systems functioned normally (vessel and containment); the draining of the accumulators took place as envisaged at low pressure (t ≅ 8 hr);

· the impact on the environment during the accident was negligible (the maximum dose in the neighborhood of the plant 70 mrem, and hence half of the natural dose , cf. §6.2.4); the third barrier thus fulfilled its role;

· the fuel was badly damaged; because of this there was a significant contamination of the containment and of the auxiliary building; even in 1981 there was no question of entering the containment compound;

- the cost of this accident was very high, due especially to the loss of electricity production.

6.5 WASTE HEAT

6.5.1 Introduction

Since waste heat is not specific to nuclear plants we shall limit ourselves to some general remarks. We know that the conversion of heat energy into mechanical or electrical energy takes place via a thermodynamic cycle whose gross output in the best of cases does not exceed 40% (fuel-oil plants and advanced HTGR and LMFBR nuclear plants, cf. Sec. 5.4). Because of various technological constraints (Sec. 5.2), the output of current nuclear plants (LWR) only attains 33% (a little more for BWR reactors which use a direct cycle). In other words, the quantity of heat to be evacuated at the level of the condenser represents 1.5 to 2 times the electrical energy produced. That is to say in every case waste heat is significant to the extent that this low-temperature heat is not used (§3.4.4).

6.5.2 Cooling by River Water

At present, most condensers of thermal and nuclear plants are cooled by the water of a river or nearby lake (Fig. 3.14). To obtain the thermodynamic outputs mentioned earlier, the water-steam mixture temperature in the condenser (cold source) must be as low as possible, in other words, close to that of the cooling water. This implies large exchange surfaces and high flow rates.

To make things clearer we will suppose that water is pumped at the rate of 50 m^3/s for a 1000 MWe plant and returned to the river (or lake) after having been submitted to a heating of about 10 °C.

The increase of the water temperature does not necessarily have a negative impact on the environment. One observes a decrease of viscosity which accelerates the sedimentation rate of suspended solid particles. Evaporation is also favored but in particular, the solubility of oxygen diminishes, and this has a direct impact on living beings. Certain fish species may be favored to the detriment of others. In addition, the temperature has a direct effect on the development of aquatic plants, whence the modification of the ecological balance.

One should note that if the water is returned at a temperature 10° higher than before, the actual increase in temperature of the river water, after mixing and following its flow, will be much smaller.

The norms in vigor in most industrialized countries fix the temperature of the condenser waste water at 30 °C at most and the temperature variation of the river or lake between the intake point and the point of return only 3 °C unless the chosen site benefits from very favorable conditions. These norms are very strict, since they ignore the fact that by heat exchange with the atmosphere the river in question can rapidly get back to its initial temperature if its flow rate is sufficiently high. If one restricted oneself to this last aspect of the question, one would nevertheless be led to fix a limit to the global power of the plants installed on a given hydrographic basin.

For all these reasons, other methods of heat evacuation must be put into service. For thermal plants, immense basins, veritable artificial lakes, have been used as a source of cooling water. This solution can only be adopted in countries where land price is low (US). The basin functions as a water-air exchanger, but the surfaces to be envisaged are truly immense (0.4 to 0.8 hectares/MW [28]). The only solution envisageable for Europe relies on the construction of cooling towers. These are of two types and have the well known form of hyperboloides of revolution.

6.5.3 Dry Towers

These are water-air exchangers which necessitate large exchange surfaces. The water is never in contact with air. If one restricts oneself to natural convection, the draught requires towers 200 m high and 250 m in diameter for plants of 800 MWe. Forced convection leads to smaller installations, but the pumping power is considerable and the global output of the plant diminishes. Dry towers are thus not envisaged beyond 300 MWe.

6.5.4 Wet Towers

Thermal exchanges are improved with wet or evaporation towers. Hot water coming from the condenser is dispersed in the form of drops falling from a height of about 10 m. One achieves a shower in some sense and the exchange surface is here defined by the number of drops. An ascending air current (natural draught) cools them. Water collected in the lower part of the tower is pumped back into the condenser. A significant reduction in size is obtained by this method: 130 m in height and 110 in diameter at the base. This is the most widely adopted solution at present. The emission of steam-saturated air can be a disadvantage for the environment as compared to dry towers, but the latter are unfortunately more expensive.

Chapter 7

THE NUCLEAR FUEL CYCLE

7.1 GENERAL REMARKS

No one today can question the importance of the problems that bear on the whole of the fuel cycle. But it must be admitted that this cycle was not subjected to very thorough study at the period when the choice of a commercially competitive nuclear reactor was being made. Today this approach seems unjustified, but it is not typical of nuclear energy alone, but characteristic of the entire history of technology. One explanation for it is that traditionally the economic agents who intervene at various points of a cycle have concerns and missions that are different. The energy crisis on the one hand and environmental problems on the other have since brought about an increased awareness, so that the general public as well as those in charge of the energy sector now have a more global view of the problems. To come back to the subject of nuclear energy, it is probable that if this change of attitude had taken place earlier, certain reactor concepts would have become imperative, all the more by being founded on fairly detailed studies. One thinks right away of molten salt reactors (§7.5.6) which conform to this new outlook. Since history cannot be rewritten, we shall present the fuel cycle as it is and not as it might have been. The purpose of these general considerations is simply to provide a partial response to questions which should rightly be raised regarding the complexity and the number of transformations which the fuel must undergo.

A general outline of the nuclear fuel cycle has already been given (§3.3.5), and the necessary industrial installations, from the mining of the ore to the ultimate disposal of wastes, have been schematized in Fig. 3.12. Now that we have seen by what means and in what form the fuel was "burned" in the nuclear reactors (Ch. 4 and 5), and with what impact on the environment (Ch. 6), the time has come to describe the transformations which the fuel undergoes from raw material (Sec. 7.2/4) to end product (Sec. 7.5).

In the following subsections, the fuel cycle is analyzed essentially from a technical angle, but it is of interest to add some information of an economic nature (Sec. 7.6). This is no doubt very open to question: on the one hand, figures available in the specialized literature vary substantially from one author to another; on the other hand, changes in the economic situation can modify predictions, even if these result from a concensus of experts (see the increase of petroleum prices in 1973).

Uranium enrichment being an important aspect of the fuel cycle, we shall take some time to look at the physical principles involved, all the more so because this question is generally treated in a summary fashion. Still, in order not to overburden the section concerned (7.3), certain theoretical problems have been relegated to the appendix (Ch. 10).

7.2 EXTRACTION AND CONVERSION OF ORES

7.2.1 Uranium and Thorium in Nature

Uranium is a heavy metal (in a pure state its specific density is 18.9 g/cm^3), relatively abundant, since it appears more frequently than such elements as tin, silver and lead. Its average concentration in the earth's crust is from 3 to 4 ppm (1 ppm = 1 part per million = 10^{-6} = 0.00001%). Like most metals, it is found in nature in the form of oxides or salts which are more or less complex. It is often associated with thorium. Contrary to other ores, uranium ore is relatively widely dispersed in the earth's crust, a fact that is of political interest. It is not likely that the situation which pertains to petroleum, that is, the major part of production concentrated in a few countries, could apply to uranium. The fact that the greater part of current production takes place in North America is due much more to intensive prospecting (§7.2.5) than to a freak of geology.

From the chemical point of view, uranium and thorium are found in the following forms:

- oxides of the type $[(UO_2)(UO_3)x]$
- mixed uranium and thorium silicates $[(Th,U)\ SiO_4]$
- mixed oxides $[(Th,U)\ O_2]$
- mixed vanadates of uranium and potassium $[K_2O\text{-}2UO_3\text{-}V_2O_5\text{-}2H_2O]$
- titanates $[(UO,\ TiO,\ UO_2)\ TiO_3]$ etc.

From the mineralogic point of view, these substances crystallize in varied and generally highly colored forms. One can distinguish:

- primary ores, formed while our planet cooled. They are found especially in granites (up to 200 ppm), in the Alps, for example, or in pitchblende, a mixed oxide of uranium and lead;
- secondary ores resulting from the action of water on the primary ores, whence the formation of more complex salts. These ores are richer and thus exploitable under current economic conditions (concentrations greater than 0.05% and capable of exceeding 2 to 3%);
- scattered ores. Uranium can be found in coal, in bituminous shale, in phosphates and in sea water (0.003 ppm). Even for these very low concentrations, uranium could be extracted if it appeared as a byproduct during the mining of another ore (in this case the costs, and especially the corresponding investments, would not be imputed to uranium). This is the case in South African gold mines, the silver and cobalt mines of Port Radium in Canada, etc.

Standard methods of mining are used, but the natural radioactivity of uranium can be put to good use for detecting it. The γ rays emitted by uranium descendants (see §1.4.2, Tab. 1.3) are detectable up to 1 km. A preliminary reconnaissance can be done by a low-flying aircraft, followed up by ground research. Once the deposit has been located, classical geophysical or geotechnical technology is used. Some amount of drilling then makes possible a more detailed analysis of the concentrations of ore thus discovered and a more precise idea of the extent of the deposit.

7.2.2 Mines

No doubt because of the fact that uranium mining is still in its early stages, most mines today are still open air. For the others, mining conditions are better than those of coal mines, for the galleries are generally holowed out of hard rock, reducing the risk of cave-in to a minimum. In addition, one works with much smaller quantities of extracted ore. Lastly, because these mines are new, they benefit from the most modern technology. For miners, the major dangers come from dust inhalation (silicosis), not a new problem. The use of water and especially sufficient ventilation helps limit these dangers.

Another risk, this time particular to uranium, can arise from its radioactivity. This is very weak compared to the activity of the fuel at its exit from a nuclear reactor (§7.5.2), and yet it can present a greater danger in the absence of specific precautions.

The effects on health of the inhalation of radium ${}_{88}Ra^{226}$ and its descendants (Tab. 1.3) have been studied in countries which have a stable population of miners. The probability of lung cancer developing in these miners has been evaluated and compared with the same probability observed in other miners working in analogous mines (hard rock) but without the presence of uranium. A certain correlation was established between lung cancer and radioactivity of the ore. When the same population of miners was sorted according to whether or not they used tobacco, it was shown that lung cancer appeared ten times more often in miners who smoked than in the others; this tended to obscure the sought-for correlation [37]. These statistics dating from 1968 were not very conclusive, for the risks to which the miners in the tunnels were exposed were no doubt higher than was thought. Because cancer only appears after a long latency period (§6.2.4) the conclusions had to be deferred. This has been confirmed by more recent studies, of which one, carried out on 5000 Czechoslovak miners, revealed a death rate due to lung cancer five times higher than the normal rate [38]. Given the preceding observations, these cancers resulted from working conditions in mines in the 1950's. For these reasons, tunnel ventilation has since been improved, at the same time reducing the risks of silicosis.

7.2.3 Processing of the Ore

The uranium extracted from the mines is weakly concentrated (0.1% to 2% by weight). The ore must thus be purified in a specialized factory. It is first crushed, then fine-ground and freed of its gangue, by decantation or flotation. It is then leached in sulfuric acid or sodium carbonate depending on the nature of the impurities to be eliminated. By chemical filtration followed by ion exchange, the oxide U_3O_8 is finally obtained. After precipitation and drying, the concentrated ore is sent out in the form of ammonium diuranate or sodium diuranate powder (yellow cake) which contains about 96% of U_3O_8 oxide by weight. The U_3O_8 oxide is thus composed of three isotopes: U^{238}, U^{235} (0.72%) and U^{234} (0.0057%). This latter, which belongs to the radioactive family of uranium U^{238} with which it is in equilibrium, can be left aside, so weak is its concentration.

The wastes consist of short-lived uranium descendants together with various chemical elements corresponding to the gangue (Tab. 1.3). Since these descendants have different chemical properties than those of uranium (different Z's), they will be automatically separated from the latter following the concentration procedure described above. The residue containing these wastes is piled up near the ore-processing factory (most often near the mines) and forms tightly packed heaps. They give off radon, the only gaseous product coming from uranium U^{238} (Tab. 1.3). This noble gas thus tends locally to increase the ambiant radioactivity rate. Lacking in chemical affinity, its retention by living organisms is negligible and like krypton Kr^{85} released by reprocessing plants (§7.5.5) it plays a role mainly in the evaluation of external doses (§6.2.4). In any case, this problem has been taken into consideration for many years and it is generally compulsory that the heaps be kept covered. In cold and wet climates (Canada), radon is not the most troublesome radionuclide. More disturbing are radium and other heavy radio-isotopes which may well be carried by the runoff into the groundwater [21].

Since ore processing only involves materials of low activity, the workers are submitted to extremely weak radiation doses, even in the case of accidental discharge. At the surface of the processing tanks the doses rarely exceed a few mrem/hr[28].

After this processing and right til the nuclear power plant, the fuel activity is particularly low (less than 1 Ci/t, cf. the example of §1.4.3), since the uranium U^{238} has been freed of all its descendants (with the exception of U^{234}).

7.2.4 Chemical Conversion

The U_3O_8 oxide obtained must be purified and especially transformed into a gaseous compound (UF_6) necessary for isotopic separation (§7.3.2). This conversion uses chemical procedures which are nowadays well established. Conversion plants exist in particular in the United States, France and Great Britain. Uranium oxide U_3O_8 is first reduced by hydrogen which results in uranium dioxide UO_2, the same as that used in reactors (up to an isotopic proportion if enrichment is necessary). In the second stage, hydrofluoric acid takes us to uranium tetrafluoride. Finally, in the presence of fluorine the tetrafluoride gets transformed into hexafluoride. The three contributing chemical reactions are thus:

$$U_3O_8 + 2\ H_2 \rightarrow 3\ UO_2 + 2\ H_2O$$

$$UO_2 + 4\ HF \rightarrow UF_4 + 2\ H_2O$$

$$UF_4 + F_2 \rightarrow UF_6$$

Based on this principle, two procedures are currently used:

- In the first, the U_3O_8 concentrate is submitted to a continuous succession of hydrofluoridations and fluoridations. Subsequently a fractionated distillation of hexafluoride UF_6 increases its purity (at the beginning the concentrate contains about 4% impurities).
- The second procedure, in contrast, consists of first purifying the U_3O_8 oxide before passing to fluoridation. This preliminary purification is done with the help of a solvent.

The result is the same in both cases. More or less pure uranium hexafluoride is obtained, but the effluents are different. In the first case, the impurities are rejected in solid form; in the second they are dissolved in the solvent.

From the environmental point of view, the only problem is that of accidental discharges of the fluorides in the gases or liquids. A conversion plant supplying about 50 LWR reactors of 1000 MWe (capacity dictated by economic criteria) discharges about 5 metric tons of fluoride products per year [39]. We know that the manufacture of aluminum also requires large quantities of fluorine; we point out by way of comparison that the aluminum factory of Steg (Switzerland) liberates 12t/yr of gaseous fluoride and 175 t/yr in the form of aerosols [40].

From the radiological point of view, the highest doses do not exceed 30 to 70 mrem/yr in the vicinity of the plants; they are essentially due to insoluble uranium aerosols and become insignificant beyond 1 km. An additional filtering could reduce these doses by a factor of 10 [28]. This confirms that the problems related to the chemical toxicity of fluorine and its derivatives are by far the most important.

Since CANDU reactors (§5.4.3) do not need enriched uranium, there is no need of passing through the intermediary of uranium hexafluoride. This eliminates the drawbacks mentioned above. The conversion is now of the simplest kind, since it is restricted to the reduction of uranium oxide U_3O_8 by hydrogen (cf. the first of the three chemical reactions given above). The uranium dioxide UO_2 thus obtained is sent directly to the manufacturing plant (Sec. 7.4). If the Canadian conversion plant also produces uranium hexafluoride, this is only for the export market [21]. This "short" cycle is also that of fast breeders which only need natural uranium (mixed later with plutonium in the fuel element manufacturing plant).

7.2.5 Estimates of Resources

Compared with coal- or petroleum-based industries, the history of the nuclear industry is short (less than 25 years) and its development irregular. The spectacular growth of the 1950's responded to a strong "military" demand, and was abruptly followed by a decline. The peaceful use of nuclear energy developed much more slowly than expected, and so for a number of years there was a surplus of equipment and capacity. The petroleum crisis (1973-74) set off a new rise in the demand for uranium. This brief historical recall sheds light not only on the structure of the nuclear industry, but also our limited knowledge of uranium resources.

Various factors have prevented an enumeration of resources: problems of classification, lack of information, search for a methodology for furnishing estimates, etc. Much remained to be done. Fairly recently the Nuclear Energy Agency of the OECD and the International Atomic Energy Agency (IAEA) have mounted a program of evaluation of world resources; the figures that follow are based on their 1982 estimates [41].

According to this reference, workable uranium resources (Tab. 7.1) are those for which the uranium price does not exceed $130/kg. Countries of the Communist bloc for which figures are not available are excluded from these data. So-called reasonably assured resources are those which correspond to ore deposits whose extent, grade and nature are well known. As for estimated additional resources (which should be added to the preceding), they are those for which the existence of the ore has not been entirely demonstrated; these estimates rest all the same on direct geological data about, for example, domains located in the extension of known deposits or belonging to geological formations which already include such deposits (it is thus a matter of relatively sure extrapolation). Finally, we add that the preceding cost limit applies to these two categories of resources and that the techniques of ore extraction and purification are the standard ones.

By examining Tab. 7.1 we see that North America and southern Africa (south of the Sahara) are the best endowed. Most of the European resources (72%) are to be found in Sweden (bituminous shale) but for cost reasons they are to a large extent excluded from the present census. As for estimated resources, North America is far at the head of the list with 68%; this is mainly the result of a much more intensive prospecting effort than that made elsewhere.

TABLE 7.1. Uranium resources (1982 evaluation).

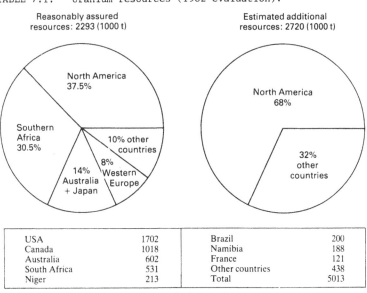

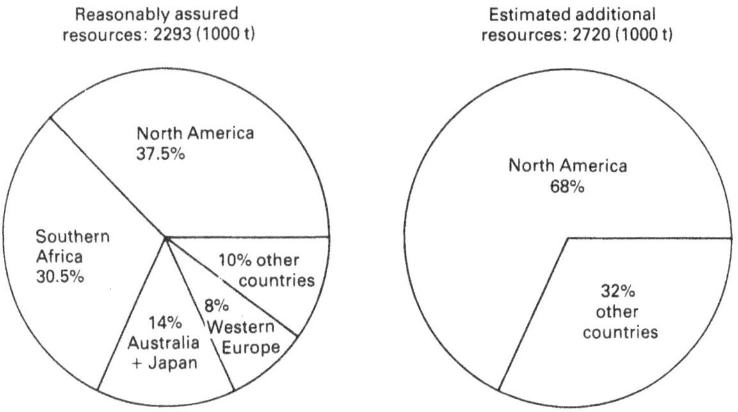

USA	1702	Brazil	200
Canada	1018	Namibia	188
Australia	602	France	121
South Africa	531	Other countries	438
Niger	213	Total	5013

Countries with the highest uranium supply.
Assured and estimated resources (1000 t).

For costs going from \$130/kgU to \$260/kgU other deposits can be considered. Moreover, uranium could be a byproduct of, for example, phosphoric acid production, purification of copper ores. Rocks containing phosphates, marine shale, granites and sea water can also be considered. All these nonconventional resources are limited. Except in the case of byproducts, their cost is often prohibitive. In order to render them usable, new extraction techniques are being developed. Some of them are particularly interesting from an environmental point of view since they only seek to extract uranium from the deposit (elimination of waste heaps). The solvents used for the retrieval of uranium oxide U_3O_8 in standard processing plants (§7.2.3) are now injected into the deposit and then pumped. Unfortunately this "on-site" laundering cannot be applied to all situations and an appreciable portion of uranium escapes extraction. The best conditions are obtained when the deposit is surrounded by impermeable layers. Finally, in spite of its very weak concentration, one can think of extracting uranium from seawater by filtration. Studies are in progress, especially in Japan.

Beyond the categories listed by IAEA/NEA (Tab. 7.1), nothing has been done on a large scale and one speaks in this case of speculative resources since the estimates are now based on indirect indications and geological extrapolations which are sometimes controversial. Figures going from 7 to 15 million tons have been advanced. In most countries the lack of basic information (geotechnical and geophysical) explains this degree of uncertainty. It should also be noted that theoretical models have suggested 80 to 280 million tons, but experts are quite skeptical about results which are so over-optimistic.

By examining the known resources in relation to the geological regions where they are located, we can nevertheless conclude that it is not logical that North America possess 54% of the estimated resources (Tab. 7.1), while it represents only 17% of the world landmass. In fact, apart from North America and western Europe, no other region of the earth has been truly and substantially explored, as was the case for fossil matter which has been the object of intense prospecting for more than a century. In any case the problem is not so much the existence of these resources, but rather their timely availability. To have an idea of the work that remains to be done in the matter of prospecting and resource charting, it suffices to remark that the OECD figures of 1977 concerning assured and estimated resources were lower by 20% than those shown in Table 7.1 (5 million tons). The rhythm of discoveries is thus very important and since no saturation phenomenon has yet appeared, the figures indicated for speculative resources do not appear unreasonable. It should also be noted that certain deposits may no longer be in the workable category if the price of extraction goes up; this was the case for Sweden, whose workable resources diminished considerably from 1979 to 1982, which at first sight might appear paradoxical. We finally note that prospecting is necessarily stimulated by the magnitude of nuclear programs. If this declines, the rhythm of discovery of new deposits will be affected, but one should not therefore conclude that all the uranium has been discovered.

7.2.6 Thorium Resources

For prices not exeeding $75/kg Th, the reserves are estimated at 630,000 tons of which 50% is in India (monazite sands). The remainder is located in Australia, Brazil, Malaysia and the United States. These ores are already being exploited, since they contain other interesting materials: titanium, zinc, zirconium, rare earths, etc. HTGR reactors are the only ones which use thorium (§5.4.4). As they are only at the prototype stage, thorium demand is very small, which explains why very little systematic prospecting has been done. Although the figure of 630,000 tons is smaller than the corresponding figure for uranium (Table 7.1), one estimates that thorium is about three times more abundant than uranium.

7.3 URANIUM ENRICHMENT

7.3.1 General Remarks

Apart from CANDU reactors burning natural uranium and fast breeders which only use plutonium as fissile matter, all other reactors need enriched uranium. We will not recapitulate the reasons responsible for this (§5.1.6); our purpose here is on the one hand to describe the principal enrichment methods and on the other hand to give information which will permit evaluation of the fuel cycle cost (Sec. 7.6). We will begin historically by going back several billion years in time.

The difference which exists between the half-lives of the two uranium isotopes (7.1 10^8 years for U^{235} as compared to 4.5 10^9 years for U^{238}) implies that in a very distant past, "natural" uranium corresponded to what we now call weakly enriched uranium. More precisely a simple calculation shows that 1.7 10^9 years ago, the isotopic fraction of uranium U^{235} attained 3%, in other words, that of current light water reactor fuel. Chain reaction possibilities existed at that epoch, since it sufficed for an ore rich in U_3O_8 oxide to be in the presence of water. This seems to be what happened in Oklo (Gabon) in a uranium oxide deposit [42]. Traces of fission products, abnormal isotopic compositions, etc., work in favor of this hypothesis, all the more so in that neutronic calculations have shown that a mixture of U_3O_8 oxide and silica (in equal amounts) which, because of its porosity can contain up to 50% water in volume, could give rise to a chain reaction. From the geological point of view, these conditions do not appear impossible. It does not seem that nature has had to suffer because of the existence of this "prehistoric pile," and the study of this exceptional natural phenomenon can furnish indications about the migratory power of fission products (§7.5.7).

Let us now see what sorts of enrichment procedures can be envisaged. Chemical procedures cannot be used to separate two isotopes since by definition their chemical properties are the same. This statement should in fact be slightly qualified since at the level of chemical kinetics, certain separation modes can be imagined.

The first idea that comes to mind is to use mass spectrography. This technique was developed for the purpose of measuring "exact" atomic masses of certain elements (§1.3.4) and also for isolating (for chemical studies) the rarest elements. The working of a spectrograph is simple. After ionization of the sample to be analyzed, the ions thus created are accelerated between two electrodes and deflected by a magnetic field. Excellent vacuum conditions are necessary, and one works with infinitesimal quantities. The lightest atoms are the most deflected. This method has the advantage of furnishing pure isotopes by a single operation but does not have an industrial character, given the small quantities of matter treated. In spite of this, this procedure was used in the US during the Second World War for the purpose of obtaining the first kilograms of more or less pure uranium U^{235} needed for the Manhattan Project (fabrication of the Hiroshima bomb). Present-day enrichment techniques had not been developed at the time, although their principals were known. Thus an adventure was launched which could not have been conceived of during peacetime. A large number of spectrographs were made, necessitating more than 10,000 tons of silver to fabricate several hundred electromagnets, copper at that time being reserved for military use. This silver came from the Federal Reserve!

After this historical recall, we will mention two present-day industrial processes: gaseous diffusion and centrifuging.

- Gaseous diffusion has been used on a large scale since 1944. The first plant was set up at Oak Ridge and other plants were later constructed in the US, USSR, Great Britain (Capenhurst) and France (Pierrelatte). The goals were evidently military (arms and submarines) but subsequently the same procedure was used for weakly enriched uranium needed by civilian programs. It should be recognized that this historical context was largely responsible for the development in the US of enriched uranium reactor assemblies, since isotopic separation plants were already available.

- The centrifuging process is more recent, at least at the level of industrial applications. It has however been under study in the US since the end of World War II, in competition with gaseous diffusion.

7.3.2 Gaseous Diffusion

Fluid mechanics teaches us that flows can be either turbulent or laminar. The number of molecules per unit volume is so large that in both cases fluids can be considered to be continuous media. Let us consider for example a gas in an ordinary state and a molecule which belongs to it. This molecule will enter into collision with other molecules a very large number of times before hitting the inner wall which assures the containment of the gas. This can be expressed by saying that its mean free path λ between two collisions is much smaller than the dimensions of the recipient considered. In these conditions, the study of a flow can be made directly at the macroscopic level, the boundary conditions being fixed by the walls. "Microscopic" theories are only useful in that they enable us to calculate the principal physical parameters: viscosity, conductivity, etc.

The situation is very different when the mean free paths are larger than the dimensions of the device under study. In this case one speaks of molecular flow, to emphasize the fact that it is no longer possible to ignore the discontinuous structure of the fluid. One thus appeals to the kinetic theory of gases for the description of the phenomena. This theory, which is related to neutron transport theory, gives, in its simplest form, the equations of gaseous diffusion (Sec. 10.1).

Let us consider a gas at temperature T which flows in a pipe of radius a and length ℓ. If this flow is molecular, the downstream pressure p_S being negligible compared to the upstream pressure p_E, one can show that the mass flow rate $\mathscr{W}$ can be simply written (10.14):

$$\mathscr{W} \cong \frac{\pi a^3}{\ell} \sqrt{\frac{\pi M}{2RT}}\, p_E \cong \frac{\pi a^3}{\ell} \sqrt{\frac{\pi RT}{2M}}\, \rho_E \tag{7.1}$$

where ρ_E is the mass density of the gas at the inlet and M its molecular mass. The particular interest of this type of flow appears when one considers a gas mixture. Since there is no collision between the molecules, the components of the fluid "ignore" each other, all the time obeying the law (7.1). For a binary mixture we thus have:

$$\frac{\mathcal{W}_1}{\mathcal{W}_2} = \sqrt{\frac{M_2}{M_1}\frac{\rho_{E1}}{\rho_{E2}}} \qquad (7.2)$$

This relation shows that a gas flows better the smaller the molecular mass, which is in accord with Darcy's empirical law. One can thus hope for a certain separation which would not have been possible with laminar or turbulent flows. But what are the conditions to be satisfied for a flow to be molecular? We have seen that by definition its dimensions, here the diameter 2a, must be much smaller than the mean free path of the molecules. As the latter is inversely proportional to the density of the gas, we arrive at the conclusion that the flow diameters must not exceed 0.1 μm under normal pressure conditions (§10.1.3). Only porous materials offer these possibilities, and in this case one speaks of gaseous diffusion.

To apply this procedure to the separation of uranium isotopes one must appeal to the only usable gaseous compound, UF_6 hexafluoride (§7.2.4). This compound, which sublimates at about 60 °C at atmospheric pressure, is stocked in solid state and subsequently preheated before its introduction in isotopic separation plants. The corresponding molecular masses are respectively:

$M_1 = 235 + 6 \times 19 = 349$ for the fissile isotope

$M_2 = 238 + 6 \times 19 = 352$ for the fertile isotope

We can thus already predict that isotopic separation will be difficult, since the mass ratio is close to unity (7.2).

In the separation plant the diffusion takes place through porous membranes also called barriers. The nature of their fabrication is often kept secret; in fact it is not easy to manufacture thin sheets penetrated by pores of diameters of the order of 200 A° (1 A° = 10^{-8} cm). Taking this last value and taking 60 °C for the temperature of the gas and 7 A° for the diameter of the molecules, the condition to be satisfied for a molecular flow can be written (10.9): $p \ll 6$ atm. We thus see that even pores this small need modest pressures, whence the need for colossal diffusing surfaces if one wishes to treat large quantities of matter (several million elementary barriers).

A separation stage consists of a diffuser comprising a large number of barriers, a compressor which assures gas circulation, and finally, an exchanger which brings the temperature of the gas at the compressor outlet back to the value it had at the inlet (§10.2.1) The toxicity of hexofluoride is similar to that of fluorine and hence precautions must be taken to assure the leakproofness of the entire circuitry (double enclosures, special compressor bearings, etc.).

The operating principle of a diffuser is simple, as shown in Fig. 7.2. The gas of isotopic fraction x penetrates upstream from the barrier with a flow rate $\mathscr{W}$. A depleted flow $\mathscr{W}_a$ of isotopic fraction x_a is extracted at the other end of the high-pressure compartment, while an enriched flow $\mathscr{W}_e$ of isotopic fraction x_e appears downstream from the barrier. The notations follow from what ensues. The dimensions are such that the extraction process has no separative power, so that the gas penetrates the pores with fraction x_a and exits with fraction x_e.

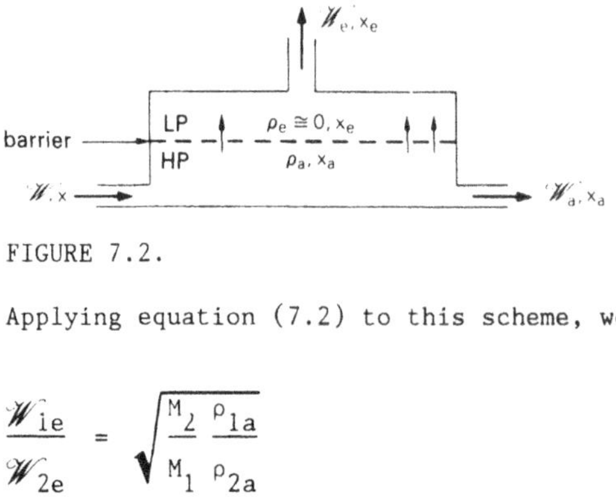

FIGURE 7.2.

Applying equation (7.2) to this scheme, we get:

$$\frac{\mathscr{W}_{1e}}{\mathscr{W}_{2e}} = \sqrt{\frac{M_2}{M_1}\frac{\rho_{1a}}{\rho_{2a}}}$$

the indices 1 and 2 corresponding respectively to the molecules of type $U^{235}F_6$ and $U^{238}F_6$. Introducing the mass fraction x, which can be defined as $\mathscr{W}_1/(\mathscr{W}_1 + \mathscr{W}_2)$ or $\rho_1/(\rho_1 + \rho_2)$, this expression becomes:

$$\frac{x_e}{1 - x_e} = \alpha \frac{x_a}{1 - x_a} \qquad (7.3)$$

with:

$$\alpha = \sqrt{\frac{M_2}{M_1}} \qquad (7.4)$$

Taking account of the preceding values of the molecular masses, we see that the mass fractions involved in (7.3) and the isotopic fractions of subsec. 3.3.3 are almost identical. Finally, the separation factor α is very close to unity (α = 1.0043). One generally puts $\varepsilon = \alpha - 1$, and this new quantity is called the enrichment factor (ε = 0.0043). Noting that ε is very small, equation (7.3) can be written (up to second order):

$$x_e - x_a \cong \varepsilon\, x_a(1 - x_a) \qquad (7.5)$$

In fact, in order to know the performances of one stage, we must refer to the inlet characteristics of the gas. For that, let us write the flow conservation equations:

$$\begin{aligned} \mathcal{W} &= \mathcal{W}_e + \mathcal{W}_a \\ x\,\mathcal{W} &= x_e\,\mathcal{W}_e + x_a\,\mathcal{W}_a \end{aligned} \qquad (7.6)$$

The first equality is relative to the mixture and the second to the molecules of the first type ($U^{235}F_6$), the conservation of the second component ($U^{238}F_6$) then being automatically assured.

From equations (7.5) and (7.6) we can deduce up to first order in ε the desired expressions:

$$\begin{aligned} x_e - x &= \frac{\mathcal{W}_a}{\mathcal{W}}\,\varepsilon\, x(1 - x) \\ x - x_a &= \frac{\mathcal{W}_e}{\mathcal{W}}\,\varepsilon\, x(1 - x) \end{aligned} \qquad (7.7)$$

We see that $x_e > x > x_a$: the downstream extraction is enriched but the upstream extraction is depleted. The variations of the isotopic fractions are thus extremely small for one stage since ε = 0.0043. If one puts $\mathcal{W}_a = 0$ in (7.7), $\mathcal{W}_e$ then attains its maximum value ($\mathcal{W}$) but there is no longer enrichment ($x_e = x$). We thus verify that in order to achieve isotopic separation in steady state a diffuser must have two outlets (Fig. 7.2). One can show (§10.2.3) that the optimum is achieved for values of $\mathcal{W}_e$ close to $\mathcal{W}/2$. One finds in these conditions and for very small fractions ($x \ll 1$): $x_e - x \cong \varepsilon\, x/2$. With the preceding value of ε

we find a relative increase of enrichment of only $2.15 \cdot 10^{-3}$. This gain is so small that a large number of diffusers must be mounted in series to arrive at the relatively modest enrichments of LWR reactors ($x \cong 3\%$). We can get an idea of the number of stages necessary to pass from a fraction $x_1 = 0.7\%$ to a fraction $x_2 = 3\%$. In this enrichment range, the average gain per stage is approximately: $< \Delta x > \cong \varepsilon/2 <x> \cong .\varepsilon(x_1 + x_2)/4 \cong 4 \cdot 10^{-5}$, whereas the desired global gain is $2.3 \cdot 10^{-2}$, and thus the number of stages necessary is of the order of 575. Especially in the last stages, the "depleted" extractions correspond to a gas whose enrichment is higher than the initial enrichment; this gas must thus be recirculated and this leads to a setup called a cascade: the diffusers are not only mounted in series but their depletion outlet is connected to the inlet of the preceding stage. This leads to the addition of a certain number of depletion stages, that is, stages traversed by a gas whose isotopic fraction is smaller than the preceding one. The enriched uranium produced by the cascade is obtained at the downstream exit of the last enrichment stage, whereas the upstream extraction from the first depletion stage represents waste (for the moment a noncommercializable byproduct corresponding to uranium of very small isotopic fraction (0.2% to 0.25%). As shown by the simple theory outlined in Sec. 10.2, a larger number of stages is in fact necessary (about 1300 in order to produce uranium enriched at 3% with wastes at 0.2%), and the flows which effectively traverse the barriers are much greater, because of recirculations, than the outlet outflow from the cascade. This is the price to pay for keeping the feed flow, and thus the consumption of natural uranium, to a minimum for a given production of enriched uranium.

Finally we note that the real value of the enrichment factor ε is lower than its theoretical value (0.0043 for uranium hexafluoride) for different reasons; in particular it is impossible to realize in each diffuser a downstream pressure sufficiently low for expression (7.1) to be rigorously valid.

7.3.3 Centrifuging

The principle of centrifuging is much simpler than that of gaseous diffusion. Let us consider (Fig. 7.3) a cylinder filled with gas rotating around its axis. The laws of mechanics (relative motion) tell us that everything takes place as if the cylinder were at rest and the molecules of gas were submitted to an "artificial gravity" directed from the axis toward the periphery (centrifugal force).

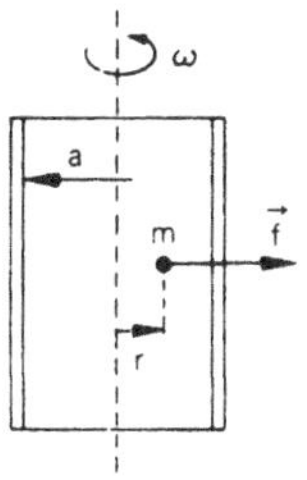

FIGURE 7.3.

The force acting on a molecule of gas of mass m can be written:

$$f(r) = m\,\omega^2\,r$$

where ω represents the angular velocity of the cylinder of radius a and r the distance to the axis of the molecule considered. To this field of force corresponds the potential energy:

$$U(r) = -\int_0^r f\,dr = -\,m\,\frac{\omega^2 r^2}{2}$$

Statistical physics shows that the molecular population is distributed according to the law [1]:

$$N(r) = K \exp\left[-\frac{U(r)}{2\,kT}\right] = K \exp\left(\frac{M\omega^2 r^2}{2RT}\right)$$

where M is the molecular mass and N(r) the number of molecules per unit volume at distance r (we recall the definitions: $k = R/N_A$ (§2.1.2) and $m = M/N_A$ (§1.2.3)). This fundamental law was already used in another form in our consideration of thermal spectra (Maxwell), and U = E then represented the kinetic energy of particles (§2.1.2).

The ratio of the molecular densities relative to points situated one at the periphery and the other on the axis of the cylinder is written simply:

$$\frac{N(a)}{N(0)} = \exp\left(\frac{M\omega^2 a^2}{2\,RT}\right)$$

Applying this result to a mixture of isotopes of molecular masses M_1 and $M_2 (M_2 > M_1)$, it then follows:

$$\frac{N_1(0)}{N_2(0)} = \alpha \frac{N_1(a)}{N_2(a)} \tag{7.8}$$

with:

$$\alpha = \exp\left[\frac{(M_2 - M_1)u^2}{2\ RT}\right] > 1 \tag{7.9}$$

$u = a \cdot \omega$ (peripheral velocity).

We observe that the mixture is richer in light molecules at the center than at the periphery; it is thus natural to note respectively x_e (enriched) and x_a (depleted) the isotopic fractions of the gas at $r = 0$ and at $r = a$, which leads us back to the fundamental equation (7.3) with an expression for the separation factor α (7.9) which is much more sensitive to the difference of masses.

It is of course necessary to extract the gas in one way or the other, in order to profit from this enrichment which appears at the level of molecular densities. To this end, one creates a temperature gradient along the axis of the cylinder which leads to the convection currents represented in Fig. 7.4. The lighter gas situated near the axis will have a tendency to rise, while the heavier gas which is found near the periphery will descend along the inner wall. Other methods exist, but whatever be the extraction mode, the real separation factor will be smaller than the theoretical value given by expression (7.9) which rests on the hypothesis of a gas in perfect thermodynamic equilibrium completely isolated from the external medium. With this reservation in mind, the enriched outflow $\mathscr{W}_e$ and the depleted outflow $\mathscr{W}_a$ correspond to gases whose isotopic fractions are respectively x_e and x_a and all that has been said in the context of cascades here remains valid; a stage corresponds to one or several centrifuges mounted in parallel.

The separation factor α depends strongly on the peripheral velocity u of the centrifuges (7.9). The latter cannot exceed a certain limit, which depends on the materials used. Certain special steels can tolerate up to 400 m/s. Limiting ourselves to the more conservative value $u = 300$ m/s, expression (7.9) leads, for a temperature of 60°C ($T = 333$°K) to the following result:

$\alpha = 1.05$ and $\varepsilon = 0.05$

The enrichment factor ε is 10 times higher than that obtained for gaseous diffusion (§7.3.2). Of course in both cases it is a matter of theoretical values, but one can expect a large reduction of the number of stages, which implies much smaller recirculation flows (§10.2.5).

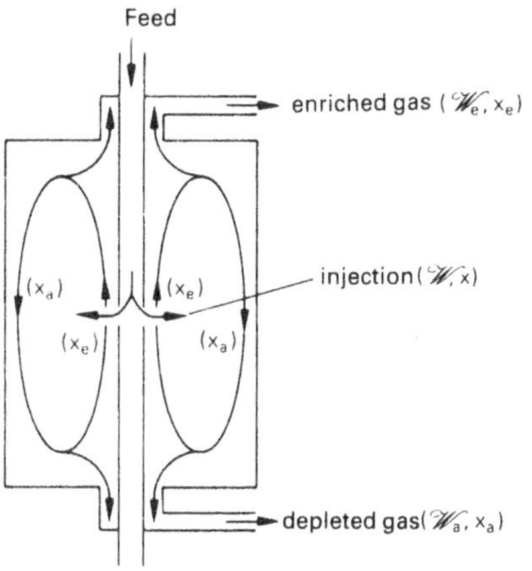

FIGURE 7.4.

7.3.4 Separative Work

The separative work which we note T_{sep} is a quantity which, without having the dimensions of work, is connected with the energy which must be expended in order to obtain a certain quantity of gas of the desired enrichment. This quantity is thus a function of the inlet and outlet flow rates as well as of the corresponding isotopic fractions. In contrast, it is independent of the enrichment procedure and therein lies its interest. Isotopic separation work plays an important role in the calculation of fuel costs. To obtain its expression, we will proceed by making an analogy with electrostatics [43].

Consider a charge q situated at a point $\vec{r}$ of space where there is an electric potential $V(\vec{r})$. We divide the initial charge q into two charges, q_1 and q_2, placed at two distinct points, $\vec{r}_1$ and $\vec{r}_2$. The energy variation corresponding to this displacement can be written as:

$$q_1\, V(\vec{r}_1) + q_2\, V(\vec{r}_2) - q\, V(\vec{r})$$

with:

$$q = q_1 + q_2$$

Let us now consider an isotopic separation apparatus (a plant or a simple stage) fed by an inflow $\mathscr{W}$ of hexafluoride to which correspond outflows $\mathscr{W}_e$ (enriched) and $\mathscr{W}_a$ (depleted) of respective isotopic fractions x_e and x_a. The feed inflow $\mathscr{W}$ is thus divided into two parts, $\mathscr{W}_e$ and $\mathscr{W}_a$ carried by two different "potentials", inasmuch as it is possible to define a potential V(x) depending only on the isotopic fraction x. By virtue of what we have seen earlier, it is natural to define:

$$T_{sep} = \mathscr{W}_e\, V\,(x_e) + \mathscr{W}_a\, V\,(x_a) - \mathscr{W}\, V(x) \tag{7.10}$$

the flows being always submitted to the conservation laws (7.6).

Just as T_{sep} is not work in the strict sense, the <u>isotopic potential</u> V(x) cannot be identified with a true potential. It must be recognized that this classical method of introducing separative work gives to this notion a certain mystery, and only a complete calculation of the energy effectively expended in a cascade permits us to verify that the expression (7.10) is the only valid definition (§10.2.4).

Whatever the case, we can determine V(x) by making a minimum number of hypotheses. To this end, we apply expression (7.10) to a <u>single stage</u> of diffusion or of centrifuging. We know that in this case the three isotopic fractions x, x_e and x_a are very close to each other (§7.3.2), so that Taylor expansions of $V(x_e)$ and of $V(x_a)$ up to second order around x are completely justified. We thus get for example:

$$V(x_e) = V(x) + (x_e - x)\,\dot{V}(x) + \frac{(x_e - x)^2}{2}\,\ddot{V}\,(x)$$

where $\dot{V}$ and $\ddot{V}$ are the first and second derivatives of V(x). Substituting these expansions into (7.10) we obtain:

$$T_{sep} = [\,\mathscr{W}_e (x_e - x)^2 + \mathscr{W}_a\,(x - x_a)^2]\,\frac{\ddot{V}\,(x)}{2}$$

the terms in V and $\dot{V}$ having disappeared because of the conditions (7.6). Finally, the fundamental equations (7.7) enable us to make a further simplification, thus obtaining:

$$T_{sep} = \frac{\mathscr{W}_e \mathscr{W}_a}{\mathscr{W}} \frac{\varepsilon^2}{2} x^2(1 - x)^2 \ddot{V}(x) \tag{7.11}$$

Be it diffusion barriers or centrifuges, the energy to be supplied at a stage does not depend on the enrichment of the gas which traverses it. Hence, in order for the separative work to have a sense from the energetic point of view, it is necessary that the quantity $x^2(1 - x)^2\ddot{V}(x)$ be identical to a constant and by definition one takes this constant to be 1. The function V(x) must thus satisfy the differential equation:

$$\ddot{V}(x) = \frac{1}{x^2(1 - x)^2} = \frac{1}{x^2} + \frac{1}{(1 - x)^2} + \frac{2}{x} + \frac{2}{1 - x} \tag{7.12}$$

which in its second form is easily integrated:

$$V(x) = (2x - 1) \ln \left(\frac{x}{1 - x} \right) + Ax + B \tag{7.13}$$

Knowing thus the function V(x) we can apply the expression (7.10) to the general case. To avoid any confusion with what has preceded, we will characterize by the index n the inflow into the installation (n = natural) and by the indices p and r the enriched and depleted outflows obtained (p - product, r - reject). With these notations the separative work can be written (7.10):

$$T_{sep} = \mathscr{W}_p V(x_p) + \mathscr{W}_r V(x_r) - \mathscr{W}_n V(x_n) \tag{7.14}$$

In the same conditions, the relations (7.6) permit the determination of the quantities of natural uranium necessary ($\mathscr{W}_n$) and the magnitude of the rejects ($\mathscr{W}_r$) as a function of the production of enriched uranium ($\mathscr{W}_p$):

$$\left. \begin{aligned} \mathscr{W}_n &= \frac{x_p - x_r}{x_n - x_r} \mathscr{W}_p \\ \mathscr{W}_r &= \frac{x_p - x_n}{x_n - x_r} \mathscr{W}_p \end{aligned} \right\} \tag{7.15}$$

Economic calculations (Sec. 7.6) only use the last two expressions, V(x) being obtained with the help of formula (7.13). Since the choice of the undetermined constants A and B has no influence on the results (this can be verified by using (7.15)), one generally puts A = B = 0 and the isotopic potential is then defined unambiguously.

The potential V(x) is shown in Fig. 7.5 as a function of the isotopic fraction x. It vanishes for x = 1/2 and the curve is symmetrical with respect to this point. For x = 1 or x = 0, V(x) becomes infinite; it follows that obtaining pure products ($x_p = 1$ or $x_r = 0$) also requires infinite separative work which is impossible (expected result). We can also say that pure uranium U^{235} as well as pure uranium U^{238} have an infinite "value" (not necessarily commercial); the name value is sometimes given to the function V(x).

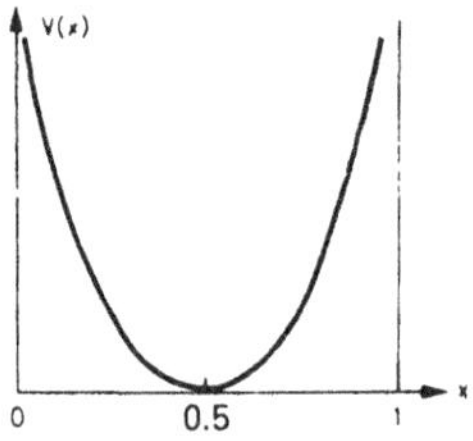

FIGURE 7.5.

7.3.5 Units and Numerical Examples

When the quantities $\mathcal{W}_p$, $\mathcal{W}_r$ and $\mathcal{W}_n$ represent quantities of matter expressed in kg, the isotopic separation work T_{sep} calculated with the help of (7.14) is expressed in separative work units (SWU). In order to be more precise, we sometimes write "kg SWU" to remind ourselves that the separative work has in fact in this case the dimensions of mass. If we consider flows (in kg/yr), the separative work will be expressed in kg SWU/yr. The consumption of a nuclear plant or the capacity of an enrichment plant call upon this latter unit.

In Tab. 7.6 we find several values of the isotopic potential V(x) corresponding to isotopic fractions x frequently met in economic calculations.

As an example, let us consider the fuel of an LWR reactor. The preparation of 1 kg of uranium ($\mathcal{W}_p = 1$) enriched at 3% ($x_p = 3\ 10^{-2}$) with the depletion rate fixed at 0.2% ($x_r = 2\ 10^{-3}$) requires $\mathscr{W}_n = 5.38$ kg of natural uranium ($x_n = 7.2\ 10^{-3}$) and entails a reject of $\mathscr{W}_r = 4.38$ kg of depleted uranium (7.15). The separative work needed for this production can be calculated with the help of (7.14), Tab. 7.6 furnishing the necessary values of the potentials:

$$T_{sep} = 1 \times 3.2675 + 4.38 \times 6.1877 - 5.38 \times 4.8555 = 4.25 \text{ kg SWU}$$

TABLE 7.6.

x (%)	V (x)	x (%)	V (x)	x (%)	V (x)
0.10	6.8929	2.5	3.4804	3.2	3.1913
0.15	6.4813	2.6	3.4349	3.3	3.1548
0.20	6.1877	2.7	3.3910	3.4	3.1192
0.25	5.9590	2.8	3.3485	3.5	3.0846
0.30	5.7713	2.9	3.3074	20.0	0.8317
		3.0	3.2675	50.0	0
0.72 (nat. U)	4.8555	3.1	3.2288	93.0	2.2245
0.9	4.6168				

Finally, if we were to apply the formalism of subsec. 10.2.2, we would find that the number of stages necessary is about 1273 for gaseous diffusion ($\varepsilon = 0.0043$) as compared to only 109 for centrifuging ($\varepsilon = 0.05$). The separative work is of course the same in both cases and it is only this which is of interest for buyers of enriched uranium.

Highly enriched uranium used in HTGR reactors (§5.4.4) furnishes a second interesting example. This time one finds that 178.5 kg of natural uranium are needed in order to produce one kg of 93% enriched uranium and the cost is 223.8 kg SWU, the isotopic fraction of the reject being always 0.2%. The number of stages is much greater: 4092 for gaseous diffusion and 352 for centrifuging. Because of this, certain isotopic separation plants specialize in the production of weakly enriched uranium ($x < 5\%$) and others in the production of highly enriched uranium (essentially for military applications).

7.3.6 Comparison of Various Processes

The electrical energy which must be expended to produce one unit of separative work evidently depends on the enrichment process. The costs are of the order of 2500 kWh/SWU for gaseous diffusion as compared to

250 kWh/SWU for centrifuging. The first of these two values can be theoretically estimated (§10.2.5). Centrifuging is clearly more advantageous if one considers this aspect only, but it is too soon to press these comparisons too far since this process has not fully attained its industrial maturity. It seems all the same that centrifuging does not look as good as gaseous diffusion where investments are concerned, so that its promoters only hope to achieve competitivity for plants of small capacity.

Other methods of enrichment exist, but are only at the experimental stage.

- Separation by laser. The emission and absorption spectra of two isotopes depend weakly on their mass. A highly monochromatic light source will thus selectively excite the two types of atoms. One expects an energy expense of the order of 100 kWh/SWU.
- Separation by aerodynamic effect takes place in a pipe. Although there is no movable piece, a centrifugal force appears due to the curvature of the molecular trajectories.

7.3.7 Environment

The problems which arise are analogous to those discussed with regard to the conversion of uranium oxide into hexafluoride (§7.2.4). Chemical pollution overshadows the radiological aspect. The release of fluoride is assessed at 0.7 t/yr for a production of enriched uranium (30 t) representing the annual consumption of a LWR reactor of 1000 MWe [39]. With regard to the operating personnel, the conclusions are the same; nevertheless, beyond an enrichment of 10% (thus higher than that required by LWR reactors), the radiotoxicity becomes more important; uranium U^{235} having a shorter half-life than uranium U^{238} (§7.3.1) its specific activity is in fact higher. In any case, very strict limits are imposed for the concentrations of fluoride compounds likely to contaminate the atmosphere of the factory (the same is true for uranium aerosols).

7.4 FUEL ELEMENT MANUFACTURE

7.4.1 General Remarks

In most reactors uranium is used in the form of UO_2 oxide. The oxide allows for higher specific powers than metallic uranium. Its melting temperature is much higher (≅ 2700 °C), which explains its performances despite a fairly poor thermal conductivity (§5.2.2). Uranium carbide has recently been proposed: being denser (density 13 - 14 as against 10.4 for the oxide) it would improve the performances of breeder reactors. This type of fuel, however, is still in the experimental stage, so we will limit ourselves in what follows to uranium oxide.

Since uranium leaves the enrichment plant in the form of hexafluoride UF_6, at least for LWR reactors, a last chemical transformation is necessary. In contrast to the enrichment phase, quite a large number of suppliers exist for the LWR fuel elements: the United States, West Germany, Belgium, France, Great Britain, Italy and Sweden. The techniques are quite conventional and any industrialized nation can easily master them. The fact that there are today no more than a dozen manufacturing plants is not due to lack of knowhow, but rather to economic considerations, which are such that below a certain size , a plant is not economically viable (this is equally true for conversion plants).

Fuel element manufacture takes place roughly in three phases:

- Chemical conversion of the enriched uranium hexafluoride UF_6 into UO_2 oxide powder
- Manufacture of pellets
- Manufacture and assembly of the fuel rods.

The fuel is always enclosed in a cladding whose role we have seen in the preceding chapter.

One characteristic of fuel element manufacture is the quality control which goes much further than that in other industries. Every rod is inspected and not only a randomly-chosen sample. For this, a large and qualified staff is necessary (first level of safety, §6.4.2). The inspection is essentially concerned with the leaktightness of the cladding, but also with the dimensions and the enrichment of the fuel rods, factors whose importance from the neutronic point of view is evident.

7.4.2 Manufacturing Process

The UO_2 oxide powder which is used for the manufacture of the pellets is obtained from the UF_6 by a wetway process making use of ammonia hydroxide. An intermediate compound (ammonia diuranate) is formed before the final conversion to UO_2. An analogous dryway process can also be envisaged.

The oxide powder is then compressed at high temperature (1700 °C) in the form of oxide pellets 10 mm long and 10 mm in diameter. For LWR reactors, these pellets are placed in tubes clad in zircalloy (a zirconium alloy which is a weak absorber of neutrons). Space is left to permit the longitudinal expansion of the rods thus formed. These rods, of an active length of about 4 m, are dried and their cladding is sealed. After this manufacturing process, the rods are put into assemblies. The description of these assemblies has been given (§5.4.2, Tab. 5.22).

Over the past ten years, the manufacture, and to some extent, the conception, of fuel elements has undergone constant improvement. We cite for example the BWR plant at Mühleberg (Switzerland) which, at the beginning of the 1970's, experienced a certain rate of cladding rupture during normal operation. Since 1974 there has been no occurence of this type of failure, after a change was made to slightly different fuel elements (smaller diameters) [40].

7.4.3 Environment

From the environmental point of view, the only problems come from the fluoride (gaseous) which is here a waste product which must be eliminated. It is first fixed by water, thanks to which procedure the discharges into the atmosphere are very small, of the order of 20% of the most restrictive norm (0.5 $\mu g/m^3$). As for fluoridated water, it is treated with lime, which results in solid calcium fluoride (CaF_2). On the other hand, the maximum radiation doses do not exceed 10 mrem/yr at a distance of 1 km from the plants [28]. This is of course true for the standard LWR fuel and not that which includes recycled plutonium (§7.4.5).

7.4.4 CANDU Reactors

There is little to say about the CANDU fuel, so simple is the cycle at this stage. We know that in this case the conversion plant directly produces the natural uranium oxide UO_2 needed by this type of reactor. Thus are avoided all the problems associated with fluoride products which appear at three stages of the LWR reactor cycle, namely, in the conversion plants, in the enrichment plants, and in the manufacture of fuel elements.

The UO_2 oxide is here also formed into pellets of 1.25 cm in diameter. They are placed in groups of 29 per fuel element into a zircalloy cladding 0.42 mm thick, and are sealed. The rods (or pins) thus made are in turn assembled in bundles as already shown (§5.4.3). We add only that the 28 or 37 rods which make up a bundle are soldered to two end-support plates, with spacers assuring a good separation between the rods (Fig. 5.28). At the present time, the CANDU fuel elements are manufactured by three Canadian firms [21].

7.4.5 Manufacture of Plutonium Fuel Elements

Fast breeder reactors use a mixed PuO_2-UO_2 fuel in which the proportion of plutonium oxide attains 15% (Tab. 5.36). This oxide which comes from the reprocessing plant (§7.5.4) is then mixed with natural uranium oxide UO_2 obtained directly, like that of CANDU reactors, from the conversion plant (§7.2.4). The U^{238}-Pu^{239} cycle requires no addition of enriched uranium, except perhaps at the startup if plutonium stocks are insufficient (§3.3.4). The reprocessing plant thus replaces the enrichment plant; what is more, the depleted uranium which accumulates on the site of the enrichment plant can be partially converted into plutonium in the breeder blankets, a fact which, from this point of view, offers almost unlimited possibilities. In this case the depleted uranium hexafluoride must first be transformed into an oxide and defluoridation operations can no longer be avoided (§7.4.2).

Plutonium can also be recycled in LWR reactors but its concentration in the mixed oxide is no more than about 3%. Even though some tests are going on currently, large-scale recycling of plutonium is not anticipated at the moment.

Even though based on the same principles, the manufacture of fuel elements containing plutonium is much more delicate than that of standard LWR elements. Because of the radiological problems posed by plutonium, all operations take place in airtight low pressure workshops and the complications which this entails necessarily reflect on manufacturing costs. Two types of special plants have thus been constructed, according to whether their production is destined for LWR reactors or for fast breeders (the amount of plutonium is larger in the second case). At present only a few pilot plants of limited capacity are in operation. We shall return to the problems posed by plutonium in connection with the reprocessing of irradiated fuel (§7.5.5).

7.4.6 Transport and Storage of Fresh Fuel

So far as the normal cycle of LWR or CANDU reactors is concerned, the fresh fuel (non-irradiated) poses no problems of handling, so weak is its activity; it is very much weaker than that of the ore from which it derives, since the processing of the ore has led to the elimination of the products of the descendants of uranium U^{238} (§7.2.3). The fuel elements are thus transported from the manufacturing plants to the nuclear power stations in special containers whose role is simply to protect them and not to stop the radiation, whose intensity is entirely negligible (we note that the α rays emitted by uranium U^{238} are stopped by the cladding and that one can thus manually handle a fresh fuel rod).

The same remarks apply to uranium hexafluoride, with, however, a reservation concerning its transport from the enrichment plant to the fuel element manufacturing plant: if the isotopic fraction is high the risk of criticality must be evaluated, which means that the quantity of hexafluoride per drum must be distinctly inferior to the critical mass of this enriched uranium compound.

After their arrival on the site of a nuclear power plant the fuel elements are stockpiled with care always being taken that they never attain a critical configuration (§4.5.3). In fact, there is no risk of criticality in the absence of water for so small an enrichment (at least 20% of uranium U^{235} would be necessary), but, since safety studies always presume the worst, each fuel element is placed at some distance from the next, to avoid an "unplanned reactor" in case of flood. If space is lacking, absorbant screens (borated materials) can be placed between the stocked elements.

Since a LWR reactor of 1000 MWe burns only 30 t of enriched uranium per year (Tab. 5.22), it is very easy to stock several refuellings, thus giving nuclear power stations an autonomy of 2 to 3 years. Thermal plants of the same power (fuel-oil or coal) only have an autonomy of a few months. This advantage evidently follows from the fundamental properties of nuclear fuel (§3.2.2) and is more or less valid for all reactor types.

7.5 REPROCESSING AND WASTE

7.5.1 Introduction

After having described the fuel cycle from the pre-power-plant stage, we shall here take up the problems that relate to the irradiated fuel from the reprocessing point of view. This "long" cycle corresponds to the policy adopted by most European countries, while such countries as the United States and Canada had not yet, in 1985, decided if they would follow this path or not. We will not reiterate what happens to the fuel during its stay in a reactor, but will simply base ourselves on the information given in the preceding chapters.

7.5.2 Intermediate Storage and Transport of Fuel Elements

In contrast to fresh fuel (§7.4.6), the fuel removed from a reactor can only be remote-handled and in the presence of protective screens. We know that β, γ, activities issue from the fission products of which only an infinitesimal portion is released by the nuclear power plant (§6.3.2). In LWR plants, unloading takes place once a year (§5.4.2) and the transfer of fuel elements to an intermediate storage site is made under a layer of water about 2 m deep. This insures a sufficient attenuation of the γ rays emitted by the fission products (this same principle is applied to experimental reactors of the "swimming pool" type). For CANDU reactors, the unloading machinery must also be protected against neutrons; in fact, the bundles extracted from a reactor in operation contain a certain quantity of fission product precursors of delayed neutrons (§3.1.3) whose half-lives can attain one minute (Tab. 3.4).

Once it has been removed from the core, the irradiated fuel is stored in a pool. On the one hand, the water provides an effective cooling by natural convection, and on the other, it acts as a shield against the γ emissions (the β rays are stopped by the cladding). Some circulation of the water is necessary for purification since the cladding is never absolutely leakproof (especially for high burnup rates). This flow also assures cooling by forced convection which is particularly required because of the high residual power densities of LWR fuel elements. Even though less pronounced here, due to the partial depletion of the fuel, the risk of criticality must be taken into account. The pools are so conceived as to be able to accept even new fuel elements, whence the storage methods already described (separation, absorbant screens, etc., cf. §7.4.6).

After a stay of about one year, the irradiated fuel is dispatched to the reprocessing plant. In the case of PWR reactors, the residual power is still of the order of 20 kW/t (cf. Tab. 5.22 and Fig. 3.5) and the activity from 3 to 4 MCi/t (see also Tab. 6.3). One should note that at this stage, short-lived fission products, like the halogens taken into consideration in plant safety studies (Tab. 6.3), have practically disappeared, with the exception of iodine I^{129} of long half-life (Tab. 6.4).

The irradiated fuel is transported from the storage tank to the reprocessing plant in special casks equipped with lead or steel protection. In some cases hydrogenated materials may be necessary as a result of the weak neutron emission of some transuranians (Cm, Am, Cf). By way of example we shall note that a 36t cask can receive 6 or 7 LWR elements. The IAEA has very strict norms for leaktightness. This must remain perfect

- in case of a free fall of the cask from a height of 9 m on a hard surface target
- in case of fire.

The first norm is equal to a speed of 47 km/h at the moment of impact. This scenario was simulated in the United States with the aid of a convoy launched at 100 km/h against a concrete wall. The casks which it transported resisted perfectly.

7.5.3 Reprocessing Objectives

The purpose is to recuperate what fissile matter is still usable, both residual uranium and formed plutonium. In addition, fission products must be eliminated. Some of these are neutron absorbers and cannot be recycled (at least not entirely) since they are partially responsible for the need to unload the reactor due to lack of reactivity (they act like ashes in a coal stove). Lastly, reprocessing allows for the isolation of certain interesting byproducts, but this normally requires additional operations.

The most widespread procedure is known by the name PUREX. One plays on the similarities of chemical properties which exist between uranium and plutonium with valences 6 and 4 respectively, which permits their being separated globally from their fission products. In a second stage, passing to valence 3, plutonium in its turn separates out from uranium.

An analogous procedure (UREX, which we will not describe), makes possible the separation of uranium U^{233} from thorium, and is thus applicable to HTGR reactor fuel (§5.4.4).

The fuel elements depend on the reactor type, as we have seen (Sec.

5.4), and this complicates the reprocessing operations. The tendency is thus to construct specialized plants (or sections of plants), it being understood that the chemical phase of reprocessing is always the same. Among the determining factors we can cite:

- the geometry of the fuel elements
- their physico-chemical state (metal, oxide)
- the initial enrichment
- the type of cladding
- the burnup rate
- the specific activity (Ci/t), etc.

In Tab. 7.7 the fuel element characteristics of several assemblies are resumed to help us understand why certain difficulties arose at the time of industrialization of processes known for more than twenty years. Even though the natural uranium-graphite-gas assembly has been abandoned, its fuel is still undergoing reprocessing and thus it will also be mentioned.

TABLE 7.7.

Assembly	Graphite-gas	PWR	LMFBR (Breeders)
Fuel element geometry	Hollow rods Ø 43 mm h = 60 cm	Square assemblies of rods Ø 9.5 mm h ≅ 4 m	Hexagonal assemblies Ø 8 mm h = 5 m
Nature of fuel	Natural uranium metal (0.72%)	Enriched UO^2 oxide (3.2%)	Mixed oxide UO^2 + PuO^2 (15%)
Cladding	Alloy of Mg and Zr (0.5%)	Zircalloy	Stainless steel
Burnup rate in MWd/t	5000	33,000	80,000
Residence time (yrs)	3	3	2 (core) 6 (blanket)
Unloaded tonnage t/yr	200	27.5	18.7
Residual uranium t/yr	198.3 (0.35% U^{235})	26.3 (0.9% U^{235})	16.1 (0.2% U^{235})
Plutonium t/yr	0.6	0.25	1.9
Fission products t/yr	1.1	0.95	0.7

In Tab. 7.7 we see the large variety of burnup rates which, as we know (§5.3.7), are mainly fixed by the initial reactivities that different reactors permit. In particular, natural uranium reactors have the lowest burnup rates, and thus their fuels pose the fewest problems since there are virtually no distant transuranians. These reactors having in addition quite low specific powers, their fuel has a specific activity very much lower than that of LWR fuel.

7.5.4 Reprocessing Plants

Unless otherwise specified, we shall henceforth consider the case of LWR fuel (there is little distinction to be made at this stage between PWR and BWR).

The fuel elements are first stocked in a pool in the order of their arrival. Here it is not a question of radioactivity but of regulating the ongoing operation of the plant. Here as elsewhere, risks of criticality are avoided by sufficiently separating the elements or putting absorbant screens between them (this is also true for the transport casks).

Next, one passes to the shearing operations which consist of separating the fuel from the structural materials. The rods thus obtained are from 2 to 3 cm long and still have their cladding (zircalloy). The rod is dissolved in nitric acid and the cladding fragments are recuperated. The solution is then transferred to the next stage of the process.

In the course of a first purification cycle, the liquid previously obtained is filtered and its acidity adjusted. An organic phase is obtained with the aid of diluted tributylic phosphate. This phase mixed with the preceding aqueous solution extracts the uranium and plutonium nitrates which, at this stage, behave in the same manner. The difference of density allows the two phases to be separated, with the fission products remaining for the most part in the aqueous phase. The uranium and plutonium are re-extracted by being washed in weakly acidulated water to prevent hydrolysis and plutonium precipitation. The solution of uranium and plutonium nitrates is concentrated by evaporation and sent to the following cycle.

In the second purification cycle the concentration of the solution is adjusted in such a way as to get back the original uranium content. An operation analogous to the preceding is done to eliminate in the aqueous phase the last traces of the fission products (the most recalcitrant are zirconium and ruthenium isotopes), as well as the neptunium (Np^{237})

remaining. The plutonium- and uranium-bearing solvent is now first mixed with a reducing solution which makes the plutonium pass to valence 3. In this state the plutonium is no longer extractible and thus returns to the aqueous phase (which in the second cycle admits of practically no more fission products). The uranium and the plutonium are thus separated. The uranium-bearing solvent is washed with slightly acidulated water (see first cycle). Various additional cycles permit an excellent separation to be made of the three components.

Thus one recuperates in the form of nitrates 98% to 99% of the uranium and plutonium present in the fuel. The rest is found in the waste products of the successive cycles, but all outputs of the chain are carefully accounted for.

Instead of sending the uranium out in the form of nitrates, one can directly prepare the fluorides necessary for the enrichment plants. The manufacture of mixed oxides PuO_2-UO_2, meant for plutonium recycling, can also be done on site. Thus the always delicate transportation of nitrates can be avoided.

We see that it is thus much easier to extract nearly pure plutonium than to separate the two uranium isotopes (Sec. 7.3). It is for this reason that military programs have always started off by manufacturing A bombs of plutonium; however, this plutonium as we have seen (§5.3.7), must be of "military" quality, that is, formed in plutonium or "experimental" reactors. The burnup rate being low in this case, reprocessing is easier. Such production evidently does not need the large-scale installations conceived for reprocessing the fuel from nuclear power plants -- quite the contrary.

The solutions of fission products issuing from the first and second purification cycles are concentrated by evaporation to reduce their volume before storage. Practically all the radioactive substances contained in a nuclear reactor (§6.3.2) can be found in these solutions. Their concentration must unfortunately be limited if certain precipitations are to be avoided. In addition, the solutions resulting from the second cycle contain 70% of neptunium ${}_{93}Np^{237}$. This element forms in reactors starting from uranium U^{235} or U^{238}, in accordance with the diagram of Fig. 7.8. It constitutes an interesting byproduct based upon which one can make plutonium Pu^{238} (not to be confused with the classic plutoniums Pu^{239}, Pu^{240}, etc.). This pure α emitter permits the realization of small "clean" energy sources used in particular in medicine (**pace-makers**).

The intermediate storage of the solutions of fission products takes place in double-bottomed stainless steel tanks placed in concrete vaults with a leakproof lining. The solutions are continuously stirred by pulsers to avoid precipitations and assure heat removal through a water circuit. Radiolysis as one would suspect is important because of the γ emission of the fission products. It is thus necessary to ventilate the free space to extract from it the hydrogen that forms. In this matter, one may recall that the oldest storage facility of this kind (1949) is that of Hanford (US) resulting from the American military program. At the start, the use of simple ordinary steel vats led to significant leakage provoked by corrosion. Fortunately, this was in a desert zone and these discharges ended with the installation of doubled stainless steel vats, which is the recommended solution for intermediate waste storage.

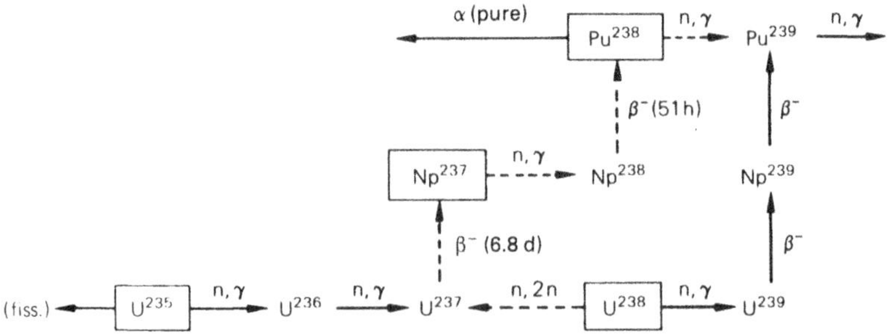

FIGURE 7.8.

Instead of keeping the fission products indefinitely in aqueous phase, it seems more advantageous to solidify them (reducing volume and increasing safety). The best known method is to vitrify the waste products (pilot plants and even industrial plants already exist). A revolving calcinator is continuously fed with the solution of fission products. The calcinate obtained is mixed with glass flakes in a melting pot heated by induction. The end product has good thermal conductivity which assures an excellent retention of the fission products. Both the radiochemical stability and the mechanical behavior are satisfactory.

Tests simulating a 1000-year storage (§7.5.7) have shown that the glass supported extremely well the radiation emitted by the radio-isotopes it contained (in a representative quantity). In particular the retention of these isotopes by the glass remained excellent even in the presence of water.

The vitrification of the wastes only takes place after a number of years, when the activity and the residual power of the mother solutions are weak anough to facilitate such a transformation. Questions of expediency can of course influence the timing.

We will conclude this subsection by a simplified matter balance sheet. For instance, a PWR fuel which contained 3.2% of uranium U^{235} and 96.8% of uranium U^{238} before irradiation is seen to have, after irradiation, the following composition: 0.9% of plutonium, 3.4% of fission products and 95.7% of uranium enriched at 0.9%. Reprocessing makes it possible to separate these three components. The uranium and the plutonium return to the fuel cycle in one form or another (§7.4.5) and the fission products, which represent the major part of the activity, constitute the highly-active wastes which we will consider further on. Since the process is not perfect, a fraction of plutonium and uranium (1 to 2%) is lost (some of it remains mixed with the fission products, some turns up in the effluents or as deposits on the pipework).

The preceding account is based on the perfectly justified hypothesis that the masses are conserved. In fact, the burnup rate of PWR reactors corresponds to 33,000 MWd/t (Tab. 5.22) or 2.85 10^{15} J/t; for its part, one fission liberates about 200 MeV (§3.1.4) or again, 3.2 10^{-11} J. One can thus conclude that, during irradiation (3 years), 8.9 10^{25} fissions/t have taken place in the fuel. Moreover, the mass defect associated with one fission is 200/931 = 0.214 a.m.u (§1.3.4), or $0.214/N_A$ = 3.55 10^{-25} g/fission (§1.3.3). From these last figures one deduces that the loss of mass associated with the energy production of the plant is 31 g/t only, that is, 0.0003%, which only affects the precentages at the third decimal place.

7.5.5 Operation and Environment

From the point of view of the environment as well as that of the protection of operating personnel, reprocessing is the phase of the fuel cycle which deserves the greatest attention. In contrast to what takes place in a nuclear reactor, the radioactive substances are no longer enclosed in a fuel cladding and the first barrier (§6.3.3) no longer exists at this stage. All manipulations are done remotely in a perfectly enclosed milieu (analogous conditions to those of subsec. 7.4.5).

For economic reasons the capacity of reprocessing plants must attain 1500 t/yr, which roughly corresponds to the annual production of 50 LWR plants of 1000 MWe (Tab. 5.22). Thus during normal operation a reprocessing plant represents in the aggregate a much greater source of radioactivity than the core of a 1000 MWe reactor.

At the moment of stripping and dissolving the fuel elements in nitric acid, gaseous fission products escape. These are especially krypton Kr^{85} ($1.12\ 10^4$ Ci/t), tritium (700 Ci/t) and residual iodine. The other noble gases considered in the context of nuclear plants have already disappeared (Tab. 6.4). Swept by the nitrogen which assures the ventilation, these gases are first cleared of the aerosols they contain (absolute filters), then, for krypton and tritium, released into the environment; as for iodine, it is trapped by being caustic-scrubbed. We have seen (§6.3.4) that tritium can be released without harm to the environment, at least up til the year 2000, going by current estimates of the nuclear program (§7.6.1). The same philosophy holds for krypton Kr^{85}, for this noble gas, which cannot be assimilated by living creatures, is only of interest in terms of external doses (§6.2.3). We should add that since this radionuclide is an almost pure β emitter, these doses are very small. Thus several million curies of krypton Kr^{85} are less noxious than a single curie of iodine. This is a striking illustration of the conclusions of subsec. 6.2.3 (see also Tab. 6.7). Nonetheless, just as for tritium, different processes are in the course of development so that future reprocessing plants will be able to trap the krypton Kr^{85} (by distillation) if that becomes necessary.

Liquid effluents are 99% recovered in the form of sludge stored in vaults on the site. They contain traces of radio-elements present in the fuel (strontium, cesium, plutonium, etc.) or in the cladding (zirconium Sr^{95}) which in principle should have been found in their entirety in one of the three nitrate solutions produced by the plant (§7.5.4). This sludge can also contain a certain quantity of tritiated water. Finally, the nonrecuperated part of the effluents is dispersed in the environment (in the sea at La Hague); these wastes are evidently submitted to the general norms concerning the biological doses they might induce.

The risks to which operating personnel are subject are evidently greater than in a nuclear power plant. The limited number of reprocessing plants makes it impossible to furnish valid statistics. The annual doses vary in certain plants from 0.3 to 1.9 rem [40], while the permitted dose, as we recall, is 5 rem/yr (§6.2.4). Since plutonium contamination cannot be entirely excluded, various medical techniques have been developed; one example is to wash the lungs with normal saline solution. Plutonium is insoluble in the human body and can thus be ingested only by inhalation. The technique cited comes down to eliminating by a mechanical procedure the solid particles of plutonium retained by the alveoli of the lungs [44].

There are two types of accident to consider. First, explosive chemical reactions might occur between the nitric acid and the solvent. They could destroy the tank containing the solution in which they develop, but the damage would not go beyond this destruction (no releases into the environment). It is thus wiser to work with fairly small quantities of material; at the same time one is reducing the risks of criticality. These risks correspond to the second type of envisageable accident and the reprocessing stage is without doubt the phase of the cycle most open to this type of problem. Because of the dilution of plutonium in a hydrogenated medium, the critical masses can be very small (compared with the quantities of plutonium processed by the plant). They can even be less than 1 kg of pure plutonium Pu^{239}, which is a record figure. The critical masses are related to the concentrations and the isotopic fraction of plutonium in a very complex way [45]. A critical configuration can nonetheless be avoided by limiting the concentrations and especially by giving the installations an appropriate form. In any case, a local divergence would be nothing at all like the reactivity accidents considered in reactor safety studies (§6.4.3), for the dispersion of the solution would lead very rapidly to a subcritical configuration.

7.5.6 Other Reprocessing Methods

Dryway reprocessing can be envisaged. The advantages are the following:

- a process easily adapted to different fuel types
- limited equipment required
- installations economically viable even for small units

- lower risk of criticality
- solid wastes only

Unfortunately the high temperatures required and the use of very aggressive chemical reagents complicate the implementation of such a process. So far, it has not been possible to pass from the laboratory to a successful industrial prototype.

We single out for mention:

- pyro-metallurgic and pyro-chemical processes: oxidation of molten uranium, extraction by molten salts, etc.
- volatilization of fluorides.

The molten salts cited above recall the reactor assemblies of the same name (MSR). Such reactors (a 5 MW prototype functioned at Oak Ridge for 5 years) use fuel in the form of liquid fluorides, a physico-chemical state which fits in perfectly with certain reprocessing procedures. One could imagine on the same site a molten salt reactor coupled with a reprocessing plant, the whole forming one compact installation. There would be no more fuel element manufacture, no more cladding and sectioning operations, no more transporting of irradiated fuel outside the site, fewer risks of proliferation, etc. In addition these reactors would perhaps permit breeding on the basis of the $U^{233}Th^{232}$ cycle [23].

7.5.7 Waste Disposal

Of all the problems posed by the nuclear industry, the ultimate disposal of radioactive waste is without doubt the one of greatest concern to the public. This is perfectly understandable if to evaluate the risks one sticks to over-general notions such as activities expressed in curies, or if only one aspect of the question is considered, namely, for example, the half-lives of radionuclides. We know what should be made of such an over-simplifying attitude (Sec. 6.2). Nonetheless, if the activities and the half-lives alone do not permit an evaluation of the harmfulness of a radionuclide, they do, on the contrary, play an important role in the choice of disposal method. Three categories of waste can thus be mentioned.

- Weakly radioactive waste (1 to 10 Ci/m^3) contains isotopes whose half-lives do not exceed several years (the actinides are absent). It comes essentially from hospitals, research centers, and from nuclear power plants and their decommissioning.

- Moderately radioactive waste (10 to 10,000 Ci/m^3) contains traces of actinides of long half-life (plutonium). It results from the reprocessing of effluents produced by nuclear power plants and plants manufacturing LMFBR fuel elements (UO_2 + PuO_2).
- Highly radioactive waste (several MCi/m^3) corresponds to vitrified fission products issuing from the aqueous solution obtained in the reprocessing plant in the course of the first purification cycle (§7.5.4). It represents 99.9% of the radioactivity produced in a reactor. It also contains small quantities of emitters of long half-life (Pu, Am,...).

The large mass of waste, that is to say 200 to 300 m^3/yr for a 1000 MWe reactor corresponds to the first two categories. (This is still nothing in comparison with the quantities of waste produced by the chemical industry). These figures are reduced, on the other hand, to only 2 to 3 m^3/yr when we consider the vitrified waste of the third category, by far the most important and the best defined.

Having classified these waste products, their definitive disposal complies with the following philosophy:

- No return of this waste into the biosphere should lead to doses exceding the standard norms (§6.2.4). Even though the search will always go on for ways to make containers as leaktight as possible for a sufficient length of time, the ultimate barriers will be those which nature opposes to the migration of radionuclides.
- The disposal must not create any new constraint for future generations. This excludes programs requiring permanent supervision but also those which could inhibit use of natural resources which seem unworkable to us today.

Let us first consider low and moderate activity waste. Historically, this has been disposed of in the ocean since 1946. Since 1960, the several dumpings that were done were carried out under OECD supervision. Assurance of safety is not based on the long term behavior of the containers, but on the diffusion speed of the radioactivity coming from the ocean depths to the surface. Taking into account the depths (more than 4500 m), the radioactive half-lives, biological chains, etc., one determines the amount of waste that can be dumped without risk. Even though the watertightness of the containers is not taken into account in these radio-ecological studies, their behavior is far from being bad. American technicians fished out containers after 20 years; they had perfectly well resisted the pressure and corrosion of sea water. In spite of this, the tendency is progressively to abandon this solution, for one does not wish to deprive future generations of the possibility of exploiting the ocean depths. Most countries have come to the point of burying the wastes not very deep in the earth. The essential aspect of security lies in the retention properties of the soil, but artifical barriers, the container and its covering (concrete or asphalt),are very effective.

Highly active waste containing isotopes of long half-life deserve particular attention since, as we know (§7.5.4), they account for nearly all the activity accumulated by a nuclear fuel during its irradiation in a reactor. After vitrification, the fission products have significant specific activities (1000 to 10,000 Ci/ℓ), but disappear after several hundred years. Particularly in question are strontium Sr^{90} and cesium Cs^{137} whose properties we have already seen. The confinement capacity of the blocks has not to be assured beyond 800 years. This is not a very long period on the scale of civilizations, and is negligible in terms of geological time.

We know that this waste contains some actinides whose decay is much slower (half-life of plutonium 25,000 years). Even though their radiotoxicity is much less than that of fission products at the moment of their storage (a factor of 10^4 at least), one must be able to count on natural barriers to avoid any return to the biosphere. It can, moreover, be shown that the radiotoxicity of the actinides produced in the reactor is lower than that of the radium ${}_{88}Ra^{226}$ liberated during the purification of the ore used by the same reactor (§7.2.3). This is indicated in Fig. 7.9 with regard to the time evolution of the toxicity indices of the most important radionuclides [46]. The toxicity index or contaminating power can be defined as the quantity of water in which it would be necessary to dilute the isotope in question to arrive at an activity per unit volume consistent with IAEA norms (§6.2.4). The curves of Fig. 7.9 have been normalized by taking 1 for the initial toxicity index of radium associated with the ore used, and the time origin (t = 10 yr) corresponds to the approximate date of definitive disposal. An examination of these curves confirms that strontium and cesium are indeed, as we have already mentioned, the most critical. For more than 500 years they prevail over radium and thus represent a contamination potential "added by nuclear plants" to the contaminating power of the ore. Beyond this, only the actinides are present, but their toxicity index is low. Without reprocessing, the amounts of plutonium would have been about a hundred times greater; this gives some measure of the benefit of the operation. This brief review shows that the figure of 800 years given above is entirely reasonable.

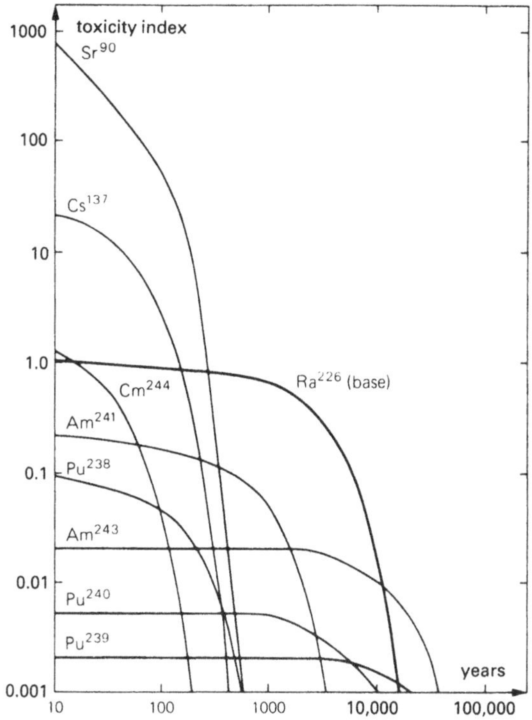

FIGURE 7.9. Contaminating power of waste.

The best solution contemplated at the present time consists in lodging these wastes in geologic formations without water circulation or in clayey formations.

In the first case, radiological security rests on the fact that there is no migration of radioactive isotopes insofar as the stability of the formations is assured. Saline formations fulfill this condition, as some of them have been stable for millions of years. In addition their plasticity allows them to adapt to certain movements of the earth. Anhydrite deposits possess the same properties. If, contrary to expectations, water should penetrate into these formations through cracks in the rock, annealing would take place by itself, which is obviously not true for salt which is soluble.

In the case of clayey formations, water can be present, but its circulation is made difficult by the very low permeability of clay. But the essential point is linked to the excellent retention shown by clays vis-a-vis radioactive ions. The Oklo phenomenon (§7.3.1) which took place in such a milieu is an example. The plutonium which was created in this "prehistoric pile" remained confined during its entire decay.

Not only clayey earths possess these properties. In France and Canada interest has been shown in granite rock formations and these have been adopted in Sweden. The granites have the advantages of abundance and stability and they cannot be considered as a possible resource even in the long term. In Switzerland one can find nearly all the geological formations listed above. Preliminary drilling will help determine the best formations [47].

Aside from the characteristics just indicated, the rocks in question must have a sufficient thermal conductivity to assure removal of the after-heat of fission products.

Studies of various types of geological storage are well underway, but the choice of definitive sites is still subject to discussion in most of the countries concerned with reprocessing. As large quantities of waste will not appear before 1995, there is ample time to prepare such storage sites. Research is currently going on sponsored by the European community.

Ultimately highly active wastes will, after verification (§7.5.4), be packed in stainless steel cylinders 10 mm thick (Ø 32 cm, h = 300 cm) and buried at depths of the order of 1000 to 2000 m in the geological layers described above. What makes this solution possible is that characteristic of nuclear energy which has been apparent throughout this work: for a given production of energy, nuclear plants make us of amounts of fuel which are insignificant compared with those required by thermal plants (a factor of at least 10^4 in weight), and it is not surprising that this reduction is reflected at the level of waste. It would be hard to imagine how geological disposal could be applied one day to wastes produced by other industrial activity, for the volumes involved would be prohibitive.

7.5.8 Radical Waste Disposal

Even though the disposal methods described above seem satisfactory, one might consider that the ideal solution would be the definitive elimination of the waste. Two possibilities have been proposed: transmutation and evacuation in outer space.

By transmutation we mean the recycling of waste (at least of the most troublesome isotopes) in reactors that may or may not be especially conceived for the purpose. This is in fact what is done when plutonium is recycled. In principle the other transuranians (americium, curium) could be recycled, and might constitute advantageous fuels (especially for fast reactors). Much work is being done on this question.

Thought has been given to isolating strontium Sr^{90} and cesium Cs^{137} which are without doubt the most troublesome fission products (Fig. 7.9). Their cross sections are unfortunately quite small, and transmuting the first of these elements in a thermal reactor would be at a certain cost. Thermonuclear fusion reactors or hybrid reactors will offer some possibilities. With the neutrons of 14 MeV which they emit, a large number of fission products can be transmuted. Accelerators might also be envisaged for very special cases.

The second method consists in launching the waste into space in solar orbits. Proposed about twenty years ago, this solution is coming back into fashion with the progress being made in the conquest of space. As in the previous case, a prior complete separation of emitters of long half-life would have to be made, since of course there is no question of sending the sum total of waste into space.

We note finally that certain isotopes can be of economic interest. From waste, they become byproducts. Outside of plutonium and krypton which have already been mentioned, there are palladium (1.4 kg/t), thorium (390 g/t), technetium (830 g/t) and ruthenium (2.2 kg/t). These isotopes once they are inactive can be recuperated.

Radio-isotopes such as strontium Sr^{90} (β emitter) and cesium Cs^{137} (γ emitter) have been extracted for possible experimental uses in industry, medicine and agronomy. Strontium is used as a heat source in small energy generators (satellites). Cesium is used as a radiation source for sterilization operations. The market is too limited, however, to have so far permitted an economic development sufficient to make an impact on the quantities of waste to be disposed of.

As we can see, a large number of possibilities open up in the long term. Are not most petroleum byproducts utilized today? It should be noted nonetheless that a more exacting, and thus more costly reprocessing is required in every case; but the overall cost of the fuel cycle is for the moment sufficiently low (§7.6.6) for studies in this direction to make sense.

7.6 ECONOMIC ASPECTS

7.6.1 Introduction

This section is concerned with the determination of needs implied by nuclear energy development, and with the evaluation of the costs of this energy (§7.6.6). With regard to the first point, everything depends of course on the hypotheses made about the evolution of electrical energy consumption and on the share which falls to nuclear energy. This share has not stopped increasing since 1970, the approximate date of commercial operation of the first reactors. In 1981 it reached 14% on the average in the OECD countries, exceeding 35% in France and Sweden.

Generally speaking, the increase of installed electrical power has turned out to be less than anticipated. In the past, it was of the order of 7% per year (doubling every 10 years), and experts thought in 1977 that it would stabilize around 4 to 5% per year, at least until the end of the century. In fact, demand has been lower (except in certain countries) because of the economic crisis. This has had repercussions on nuclear programs which, as we recall, are almost exclusively oriented to the production of electrical energy. In addition, opposition to nuclear energy from certain quarters strengthened this tendency, at least indirectly: delays in commissioning plants, delays in construction time (progressively from 6 years to 12 years in the United States), etc. For all these reasons, installed nuclear power has always been lower than predicted, even if its relative share has increased substantially as we have seen. In 1980, for example, installed power was 116 GWe (non-communist countries) while the 1975 and 1970 forecasts (for this date) were respectively 180 GWe and 260 GWe.

We shall use 1982 OECD forecasts as the basis for what follows [48]. Even though more modest than the preceding ones, they may still appear excessive if one believes that humanity as a whole is moving toward "zero growth". Without entering into a debate whose importance we recognize but which is beyond the scope of this book for it concerns the very long term, we shall simply note that it is dangerous to underestimate future energy consumption if we wish to know whether or not the needs for nuclear power plants will be covered.

In Fig. 7.10, the growth curve presented as the most likely is the result of a broad concensus of OECD member countries; installed nuclear power will be of the order of 500 GWe in the year 2000. For the period 1985-1990 there should be little uncertainty since the forecast corresponds to plants already under construction or at least decided upon. Nonetheless, even during this period some delays may take place; taking into account the uncertainty of national programs we arrive at the dotted-line curve of Fig. 7.10. Lastly, the high growth curve results much more from considerations related to the power plant construction rate that the nuclear industry could sustain than from any precise economic scenario. To be able to analyze certain aspects of the fuel cycle, such as the depletion of known uranium reserves (§7.2.5) or the introduction of advanced converters and fast breeders, the curves would have to be extended beyond the year 2000. At that point the forecasts become highly speculative [41].

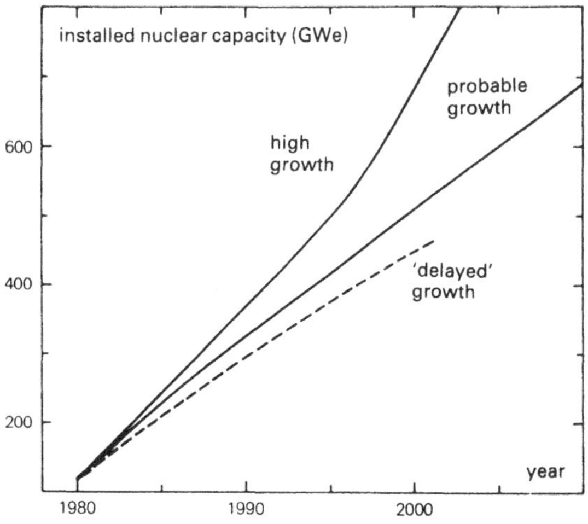

FIGURE 7.10.

The latest OECD forecasts (still anticipated in 1985), will lead, not surprisingly, to curves situated below the preceding ones. Still, until 1995, the changes should be slight, and the dotted-line curve of Fig. 7.10 should correspond fairly well to the new forecasts. Beyond that time, various experts predict installed capacities of 400 to 450 GWe in 2000 and 600-850 GWe in 2020. Since it would be a mistake to underestimate future uranium needs, the curves of Fig. 7.10 remain a good base for the subsections that follow.

7.6.2 Computation of Needs of LWR Reactors

The enrichment x_p, the mean specific power $\langle\bar{\omega}_{sp}\rangle$, the mean burnup rate $\langle W_{sp}\rangle$ and the amount of enriched fuel M_p contained in a reactor of 1 GWe (Tab. 5.22) will enable us to calculate these needs. Thus the irradiation time at full power, $T(a) = (1/365)\cdot(\langle W_{sp}\rangle/\langle\bar{\omega}_{sp}\rangle)$, leads to the annual consumption $\dot{M}_p = 0.7\ M_p/T$ when one considers a load factor of 70% (average value very often adopted in economic studies). On the other hand, the considerations of Sec. 7.3 enable us to calculate the quantity of natural uranium $\mathscr{W}_n/\mathscr{W}_p$ (7.15) as well as the separative work $T_{sep}/\mathscr{W}_p$ (7.14) necessary to produce 1 kg of uranium enriched at x_p. All these results are entered in Tab. 7.11, the isotopic fraction of depleted uranium rejected by the separation plant coming to 0.2%.

TABLE 7.11.

	PWR	BWR
x_p (%)	3.2	2.7
$\langle\bar{\omega}_{sp}\rangle$ (MW/t)	36.2	26
$\langle W_{sp}\rangle$ (MWd/t)	33,000	26,000
M_p (t/GWe)	82.5	111
T (yr)	2.50	2.74
$\dot{M}_p$ (t/GWe yr)	23.1	28.4
$\mathscr{W}_n/\mathscr{W}_p$	5.769	4.808
$T_{sep}/\mathscr{W}_p$ (SWU/kg)	4.684	3.606

Considering at a given instant a fleet of plants of the same type, of global electric power P, the annual consumption of enriched uranium comes to:

$$\dot{\mathscr{M}}_p = \dot{M}_p P + M_p \dot{P} \tag{7.16}$$

where $\dot{P}$ is the derivative with respect to the time of P (in GWe/yr). The first term corresponds to the consumption of existing reactors and the second to the commissioning of a number of new reactors, each one requiring a complete loading M_p.

One can easily deduce from the preceding the annual demand for natural uranium $\dot{\mathscr{M}}_n$ and the needs in separation work ℓ_{sep} by multiplying respectively (7.16) by $\mathscr{W}_n/\mathscr{W}_p$ and $T_{sep}/\mathscr{W}_p$. The results obtained for the two types of reactors are so close, despite their fairly different features (Tab. 7.11), that we can retain the following expressions:

$$\dot{\mathscr{M}}_n(\text{t/yr}) = 134\ P\ (\text{GWe}) + 500\ \dot{P}\ (\text{GWe/yr}) \tag{7.17}$$

$$\ell_{sep}\ (\text{SWU/yr}) = [106\ P\ (\text{GWe}) + 390\ \dot{P}\ (\text{GWe/yr})]\ 10^3 \tag{7.18}$$

valid in first approximation for all LWR reactors. We see in particular that a 1 GWe reactor annual requires (load factor 70%):

- <u>134 tons of natural uranium</u>
- <u>106,000 SWU.</u>

Naturally , if a different load factor is adopted these results must be changed in consequence (the coefficients $\dot{P}$ in equations (7.17) and (7.18) are not affected).

If we adopt the gaseous diffusion process to produce the 106,000 SWU, the energy cost will be 2.65 10^8 kWh (1 SWU = 2500 kWh, cf. §7.3.6), while during the same time the 1 GWe reactor will have produced 6.13 10^9 kWh (still keeping the load factor 70% to be consistent). We can then conclude from this that about <u>4.3% of the electric energy produced by LWR reactors must be allocated for the enrichment of the uranium which they burn.</u>

7.6.3 Covering Natural Uranium Needs

These needs are obtained by using in expression (7.17) the data from subsec. 7.6.1 (Fig. 7.10), and are shown by the curves in solid lines of Fig. 7.12. At the present time, the production rate of operating mines comes to 34,000 t/yr, while the demand is less than 30,000 t/yr, which might explain the tendency to a decline in uranium prices observed in recent years. The evolution in time of the maximum theoretical production of uranium, making use only of tested techniques and known resources, is represented in Fig. 7.12 by dotted lines. We see that the uranium needs of the OECD countries would, in the high-growth hypothesis, be covered until about the year 2000 by the production of these countries alone (there are of course local imbalances, Europe in particular is fairly poor). Evidently the production rates of the mines will adapt themselves to the real consumption which should correspond to the low projection of needs (lower solid curve of Fig. 7.12).

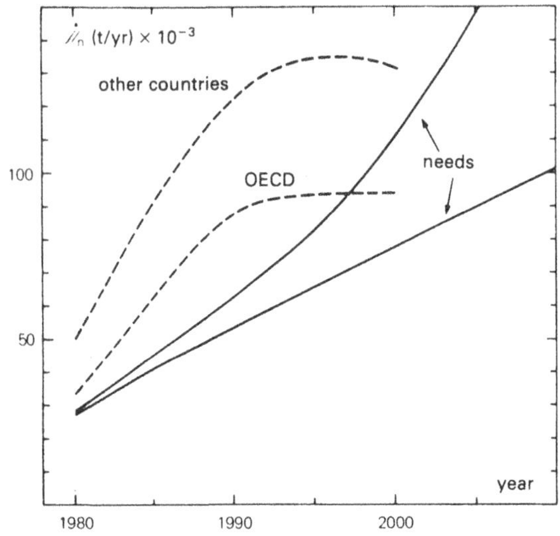

FIGURE 7.12.

The cumulated needs from 1980 to 2000 are obtained by integrating the curves $\dot{\mathscr{M}}_n(t)$. We find 1 or 1.3 million tons depending on whether we consider the most probable growth or high growth. In any case, the needs are distinctly less than the reasonably assured resources (Tab. 7.1).

Let us now see what improvements can be made to the fuel cycle. The uranium needs calculated above assume that the depleted uranium is rejected by the enrichment plants with an isotopic fraction of 0.2%. It is easy to show that the maximum theoretical reduction for a perfect isotopic separation would represent 30%. A reduction of this order could be obtained by recycling in existing reactors (LWR) the uranium and plutonium recuperated from the reprocessing plant (§7.5.4). Recycling plutonium in heavy water reactors would be even more advantageous (reduction of 50%).

The use of Th^{232}-U^{233} and U^{238}-Pu^{239} cycles in fast breeders would bring about even greater reductions, but the "penetration" of these cycles can only take place if the growth rate of nuclear energy is sufficient. Uranium is more than fifty times better used in fast breeder reactors (LMFBR) than in LWR reactors even when the plutonium is recycled in the latter. Centuries would pass before today's known resources would be exhausted, but this is only a potentiality. In a first period (2000-2025) the gradual introduction of breeders would make possible a decrease by half of natural uranium consumption [41], but all advanced fuel cycles, since they are based on the recycling of artificial fissile material, require reprocessing plants, manufacture of more active fuel elements and additional storage facilities.

We end this subsection by noting that if the high growth of Fig. 7.10 took place and continued beyond the year 2000, cumulated uranium consumption would reach 4 million tons in 2025, on the assumption that only LWR reactors were being used [41]. Added to the consumption for the years 1982-2000, this represents about 5 million tons, that is, about the entire assured and estimated resources (1982) (Tab. 7.1). This result, even though based on pessimistic hypotheses, should be an incitement to more intensive prospecting and encourage the marketing of advanced reactors.

7.6.4 Covering Enrichment Needs

The estimates of installed nuclear power (Fig. 7.10) together with the computation method of subsec. 7.6.2 (7.18), lead to the two curves (solid lines) of Fig. 7.13. In this figure, estimates of capacities are represented by the dotted curve [48]. They take into account three functioning American plants (Oak Ridge, Paducah, Portsmouth) whose initial capacity of 17.2 10^6 SWU/yr was brought up to 27.3 10^6 SWU/yr in 1982, as well as the European program. Until 1980, enrichment needs were essentially covered by the United States, and this for a long time was considered as an argument against enriched uranium reactors (§5.1.6). In fact, the situation is changing rapidly in Europe since, leaving aside military plants of small capacity (Capenhurst 0.4 10^6 SWU/yr and Pierrelatte 0.2 10^6 SWU/yr) a large installation financed by several countries (EURODIF) has entered into service at Tricastin (France). Based on gaseous diffusion, it has a capacity of 10.8 10^6 SWU/yr. This installation can supply 100 LWR reactors of 1000 MWe (§7.6.2).

A study of Fig. 7.13 shows that needs are well covered until 1995 if one considers the high estimates of installed nuclear power. Beyond

N

1995 we can say nothing about enrichment capacities. An isotopic separation plant in fact requires major investment, since it must reach a certain size (10 million SWU/yr) to be economically viable. Under these conditions, a decision to build can be made only if the demand for service is sufficient, and we fall back on the problem of the uncertainties linked with nuclear energy development.

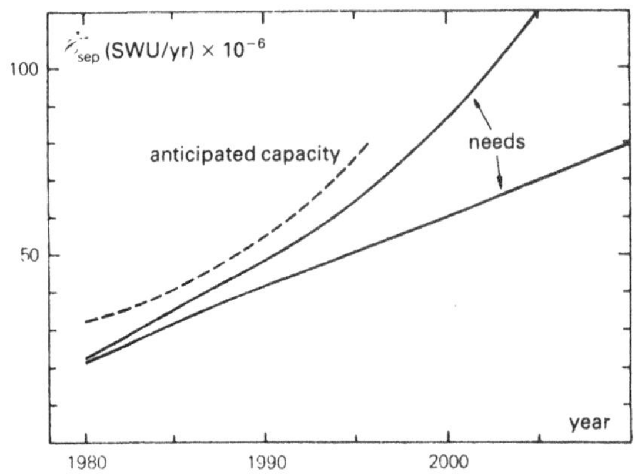

FIGURE 7.13.

The European enterprise URENCO which holds patents on the centrifuging process already operated in 1979 two pilot plants of 200,000 SWU/yr each. Despite doubts about the competitivity of the process, construction of two larger plants was begun in 1981; they should reach their full capacity (10^6 SWU/yr each) in 1988.

Very recently, the US government (DOE) made the decision to stop investment in gaseous diffusion and centrifuging and progressively to close down existing plants. In the coming century, only isotopic separation by laser will be done. In the AVLIS project, separation results from the selective excitation of the two uranium isotopes which are in a metallic vapor state. This decision shows that the process is no longer in the experimental stage; the low energy consumption involved obviously explains the interest of the process (a program also exists in France).

7.6.5 The Reprocessing Situation

The industrialized nations have a fairly well-defined policy regarding enrichment, but this is not the case for reprocessing. Even though the technical processes involved are well known, there is not much experience to draw from at the industrial level. The realization of facilities has not been neglected (a number of pilot plants exist), but postponed for the benefit of facilities situated earlier in the cycle: mines, enrichment plants and especially power plants. It was not until the plants were proved to be competitive and their reliability demonstrated that one became concerned about industrializing the reprocessing and packaging of wastes. For economic reasons,moreover, it would not have been possible to reverse the priorities. How could economic policy makers be convinced of the need to finance the construction of a reprocessing plant at a time (before 1970) when nuclear energy had not yet made its breakthrough and the choice of reactor assemblies had not yet been settled? We also see that premature construction in this domain would not have been viable because of the lack of fuel to reprocess.

All these considerations explain the present situation and the "delays" caused in the building of facilities which today seem indispensable. A certain amount of political equivocating has also contributed.

In the United States the first commercial plant (300 t/yr) was brought to a halt in 1972 for increase of capacity (750 t/yr), but administrative delays and the indecisiveness of federal policy led industrialists to withdraw from the deal. In 1976 the federal authorities simply put into question the whole principle of reprocessing as well as the fast breeder program for reasons of "non-proliferation". The Clinch River breeder project was also abandoned. Since that time, the new administration no longer expressly prohibits reprocessing, but industrialists need guarantees before commiting themselves (a change of policy is still to be feared, the form in which waste must be conditioned has not been defined, etc.). For different reasons, the uncertainties are still as great in 1985, to the extent that the crews responsible for launching the important Barnwell plant (1500 t/yr) have been dissolved.

In Great Britain the Windscale plant has been reprocessing the metallic fuel of the graphite - gas assembly since 1954. In 1972 a part of the plant was adapted for reprocessing UO_2 fuel with a planned capacity of 400 t/yr but a serious accident took place in 1973: zirconium residues caught fire causing an overpressure in a "cell" which led to a release of fission products in the building (the cell was not sufficiently leaktight) and 35 workers were contaminated [40]. Resumption of service in that unit was postponed, for in the meantime the decision was made to build a plant specializing in oxide reprocessing (1200 t/yr) rather than trying to convert older installations (the same philosophy holds for France). After a thorough debate of the question, a commission recommended that Parliament vote the authorization, which it did in April 1978. Despite the legal go-ahead, work on the new installation (THORP) did not begin until 1984. The authorities preferred to give priority to the reprocessing of metallic fuel (first generation MAGNOX reactors) and thus to concentrate on improving the older installations.

In France, the first plant at Marcoule (1000 t/yr), commissioned in 1958, was destined for metallic fuel, as was that of La Hague (800 t/yr), which went into operation in 1966. Here also the development of the LWR assembly led to adaptations. The new installations started up at La Hague in 1976. The UP2 plant made it possible to reprocess metallic fuels and oxides alternately. This is evidently not the best method from the point of view of performances. It was thus decided in 1985 that UP2 would henceforth only reprocess the UO_2 fuel. The current capacity of 400 t/yr will progressively be brought up to 800 t/yr. Metallic fuel from the last of the graphite-gas reactors will be reprocessed exclusively at Marcoule. Concurrently, a third plant (UP3), also meant for UO_2 fuel, should be put into service at La Hague in 1989. Of initial capacity 150 t/yr, it will eventually reach 800 t/yr. Thus at the end of the century, France should dispose of a reprocessing capacity (UO_2) of 1600 t/yr.

At the present time, the COGEMA company which runs the installations at La Hague is the only one to have demonstrated its knowhow on the industrial level. Other countries (West Germany, Japan, etc.) only have small demonstration units. West Germany has however recently decided to construct a 350 t/yr facility.

What can then be said about the extent to which reprocessing needs are being met? Aside from the La Hague facility in France, all the plants are either at a temporary or permanent halt due to changes in the nuclear policy of various countries, or only at the planning stage, or, at best, at the start of construction. <u>Reprocessing is thus the only point of the</u>

fuel cycle for which the demand for service could exceed the supply for several years. The situation is not alarming, however, since the major projects just cited (UP3 and THORP) allow hope of improvement in the near future. In any case, it is always possible to store the fuel elements in pools to await reprocessing. This does, however, hold back plutonium recycling, which as we know, permits a much better utilization of the fuel.

How did this situation come about?

First of all, it was logical in the development of the nuclear industry to give priority to power stations and enrichment plants, especially since fuel reprocessing did not seem to pose any serious technical problem (the processes were known due to military programs). Later, when it became necessary to adopt stricter norms, it was recognized that certain problems had been underestimated. But most of all, the change of assembly in Great Britain and France was fatal. These countries had put all their stakes on metallic uranium, and passing to UO_2 oxide led to substantial modifications of facilities. The technical reasons are roughly the following:

- LWR fuel elements are more complex than the elements of the first assembly, because less homogeneous. They dissolve less readily in nitric acid and the shearing operations become more complicated.
- The burnup rates as well as the specific powers being higher (MW/t), the amounts of plutonium and of fission products per unit mass are much greater for LWR reactors (about ten times more). From this it follows that radioactive fluxes are greater (cf. the first two columns of Tab. 7.7).

For these reasons, most countries, after attempting with more or less success to adapt their older installations to the new fuels, today prefer to envisage reprocessing plants specialized in one type of fuel, namely uranium oxide UO_2, which is used in nearly all reactor assemblies. But even here, it is necessary to make a distinction between LWR and LMFBR fuel, the latter containing much more plutonium.

7.6.6 The Cost of Nuclear Energy

The purpose of this section is to show the relative weights of the different stages (investment, enrichment, etc.) in the assessment of the overall cost per nuclear kWh. The unit prices (in $) are only indicative, and correspond to the situation prevailing on the 1981 market, so they should not be given too much importance. The essential for us is to show how they enter into the evaluation. Only LWR reactors are considered in what follows.

The cost of nuclear plants varies quite sharply from one country to another, for particular regulations can lead to the addition of expensive supplementary equipment. On the other hand, in recent years the evolution of the cost has more or less followed the rhythm of inflation: the price per installed electric kilowatt passed from \$1100/kWe in 1977 to \$1500/kWe in 1981. We shall adopt this latter figure, with the reservation made above.

We shall estimate the cost of fuel elements basing ourselves on the following unit prices:

- natural UF_6: \$95/kg of natural uranium
- enrichment: \$131/SWU
- manufacture: \$240/kg of enriched uranium

These prices have some meaning because a veritable market exists, even regarding enrichment, for the US and the USSR no longer have a monopoly in this domain. We note that the price of natural uranium has declined by 20% in four years, despite inflation, whereas manufacturing costs have risen more rapidly than inflation.

To go a bit further we will make a choice of reactor type, the 1000 MWe PWR whose characteristics appear in Tab. 7.11. Using the last two lines of this table as well as the preceding data, we find that the price of one kilogram of uranium enriched at 3.2% comes to:

$$95 \times 5.769 + 131 \times 4.684 + 240 \times 1 = \underline{\$1400/\text{kg (enriched U)}},$$

the uranium representing 39% and the enrichment 44%.

To start up the reactor one must buy a first (complete) loading of enriched uranium, which in our case represents (Tab. 7.11):

$$\$1400/\text{kg} \times 82.5 \times 10^3 \text{ kg} = 1.15 \cdot \$10^8 = \text{M\$ } 115.5$$

a sum which is added to the price of the plant (M\$ 1500/GWe) to constitute the necessary initial investment:

$$C = \text{M\$ } 1500 + \text{M\$ } 115.5 = \underline{\text{M\$ } 1615} \text{ (million dollars)}$$

This result shows that the first loading amounts to less than 10% of the capital invested.

We can now estimate the annual financial cost of this 1000 MWe PWR reactor. The part resulting from investments is obtained by a very simple reasoning. Let us consider a promoter who borrows the capital C ($) at time t = 0, and who makes staggered payments I(t) ($/yr) over a period T (liquidation time). If between instant t and instant t + dt he wants to repay the fraction dC of the borrowed capital, the mechanism of compound interest obliges him to pay out a larger sum, that is dC exp (αt) where α represents the interest rate (%/yr). This last value must be identical to I(t)dt where I(t) represents his rate of payment. One can thus write:

$$dC = I(t)\exp(-\alpha t)dt$$

whence we deduce by integrating over the liquidation time:

$$C = \int_0^T I(t)\exp(-\alpha t)dt$$

Since most often the owner of the installation will institute uniform annual payments, we arrive at the result:

$$I = \frac{\alpha}{1 - \exp(-\alpha T)} C$$

The coefficient which appears in this formula represents the annual installment rate. This very simple method of calculation can be applied to more complex problems (some fianciers who appear unaware of the exponential function involve themselves in much more clumsy calculations but arrive at very similar results).

Let us take for example: α = 6%/yr and T = 20 years. The annual installment rate comes to: 8.58%/yr and the annual financial cost to:

$$M\$\ 1615 \times 0.0856 \cong \underline{M\$138/yr}$$

For other fixed costs it is necessary to add at least the two following items:

· maintenance, salaries, etc.:	M$ 8/yr
· insurance and taxes:	M$ 39/yr
for a total of:	M$ 47/yr

These figures of course vary from one power plant to another and are only valid for industrialized countries.

Let us finally calculate the financial cost associated with the annual consumption of the reactor. The results depend evidently on the load factor which we maintain equal to 70%, which leads to a consumption of 23.1 t/yr (Tab. 7.11). We note first that the price of enriched uranium indicated above ($1400/kg) must be increased to take account of the fact that orders are generally placed two or three years in advance. This leads, through the expedient of compound interest, to a supplement of $320/kg. This figure is much more open to question than the preceding ones, for it depends on the policy followed by the owner of the installation, but its impact on the global cost of a kWh is finally fairly small. Whatever the case, we arrive at an expenditure of: $(1400 + 320) \times 23.1\ 10^3$, or:

M$ 39.7 /yr for the cost of the fuel before loading

It remains to figure the cost of the fuel cycle post-reactor. Here it is quite difficult to furnish data which have an economic sense because there is no real market. The tenders of the only supplier (the La Hague plant in France) are situated at around FF 4100/kg reprocessed in 1981, this price including the vitrification of the waste (§7.5.4). In addition, the expenses to anticipate for definitive waste disposal are difficult to figure in the current exploratory phase. In Switzerland they are evaluated at SFr 500/kg. From these two figures one can deduce that these operations should come out to $940/kg or to $940 \times 23.1\ 10^3$ M$/yr for a 1000 MWe reactor (Tab. 7.11), that is finally:

M$ 21.7/yr for reprocessing and disposal of waste.

We must finally take various credit items into account, for, in compensation for the expenditures, we recuperate on 1 kg of reprocessed uranium 0.957 kg of residual uranium (of isotopic fraction 0.9%) and 9 g of plutonium (§7.5.4). To produce this uranium, 1.288 kg of natural uranium would have been needed (7.15) and 0.212 SWU (7.14); this represents a credit of:

$$95 \times 1.2888 + 131 \times 0.212 = \$150/\text{kg reprocessed}$$

Even though a market hardly exists, the generally adopted price of plutonium is $10/g, which leads to $90/kg reprocessed. Thus the total uranium and plutonium recuperated are equal to a saving of

$$(150 + 90) \times 23.1\ 10^3 \text{ M\$}$$

or:

M$ 5.5/yr of annual credit.

This represents about a quarter of the expenditure occasioned by the reprocessing of the fuel. Nonetheless one should not therefore infer that the no-reprocessing policy is more advantageous, for in this case one would need to add the financial costs relative to definitive disposal of the spent fuel, henceforth treated as waste.

As final figures, one obtains:

- for the fixed costs: M$ 185/yr
- for the fuel cycle: M$ 56/yr
- for the total: M$ 241/yr

The fuel cycle represents only 23% of the annual financial cost and whatever the estimates, we always arrive at this order of magnitude (we willingly accept 25% [49]). More spectacular still are the portions represented by natural uranium, 5%, and the enrichment, 7%. This low sensitivity to the price of ore constitutes a definite advantage. Lastly, the reprocessing cost, whose future evolution is the big unknown, is placed at about 9% of the total costs.

The cost price of a nuclear kWh is found simply by dividing M$ 241/yr by the annual production of the 1000 MWe reactor considered in this study. The 70% load factor must of course be adopted for reasons of consistency. We find:

$$\frac{\$\ 2.41\ 10^{8}/\text{yr}}{0.7 \times 8760\ \text{h/yr} \times 10^{6}\ \text{kW}}$$

or about 3.9 cents/kWh. For a higher load factor this cost would of course be lower but the share of the cycle would increase (it would reach 32% for a load factor of 100%).

We reiterate that our goal in this subsection was not to arrive at a precise worth of the cost price of a nuclear kWh but rather to show the structure of this value. Nonetheless the last result obtained supports fairly well various recent studies [48], [49]. These studies also show that, in contrast to fuel-oil burning plants, nuclear plants lead to a considerable reduction in costs in all the OECD countries (a factor of 3.4 in France, 1.5 to 2 in the United States). The savings are however less perceptible when one takes coal-burning plants as a basis of comparison.

Chapter 8

FUNDAMENTAL PROBLEMS OF NEUTRONICS

8.1 MONO-ENERGETIC TRANSPORT THEORY

8.1.1 The Differential--Integral Transport Equation

The application of diffusion theory is subject to certain restrictions, as we have seen (§4.3.1). This is not surprising when we take account of the fact that this theory claims to furnish the scalar flux directly, whereas the only meaningful physical quantity is the angular flux, that is the neutron flux taken in a given direction $\vec{\Omega}$.

In contrast, the transport equation takes account (implicitly or explicitly) of the angular distributions of the particles under study and its field of application is thus much larger: kinetic theory of gases (Boltzmann), astrophysics (photon propagation in a star), reactor physics (neutron transport), plasma physics (transport of ions or of fast electrons in a plasma), etc.

In what follows, we will restrict ourselves to mono-energetic neutrons since the generalization to neutrons in the course of slowing down is evident if one takes account of the multigroup formalism (§9.1.6). Let us isolate at a point of space a direction characterized by the unit vector $\vec{\Omega}$ and let us effect a neutron balance analogous to that of subsec. 4.2.1. The neutrons which propagate in this direction are characterized at point M by the angular flux $\phi(s, \vec{\Omega})$, in accordance with the definitions of subsec. 4.2.2. As indicated in Fig. 8.1, point M is located on this trajectory by the abscissa s. Variations in this flux can only be caused by the neutrons which emerge in this direction and by those that leave it.

Let us give ourselves $\phi(s, \vec{\Omega})\,d\Omega$, $\Sigma_t(s)\phi(s, \vec{\Omega})d\Omega$ and $e(s, \vec{\Omega})d\Omega$, which correspond respectively to the flux ($cm^{-2}\ s^{-1}$), the collision rate ($cm^{-3}\ s^{-1}$) and the emission rate ($cm^{-3}s^{-1}$) for neutrons belonging to an infinitesimal solid angle $d\Omega$ surrounding the direction $\vec{\Omega}$. The balance for a thin slice of thickness ds perpendicular to $\vec{\Omega}$ can be written (Fig. 8.1):

$$[\phi(s, \vec{\Omega})d\Omega] - [\phi(s + ds, \vec{\Omega})d\Omega] = [\Sigma_t(s)\phi(s, \vec{\Omega})d\Omega]ds - [e(s, \vec{\Omega})d\Omega]ds$$

whence, making $ds \to 0$

$$\frac{d\phi(s, \vec{\Omega})}{ds} + \Sigma_t(s)\phi(s, \vec{\Omega}) = e(s, \vec{\Omega}) \qquad (8.1)$$

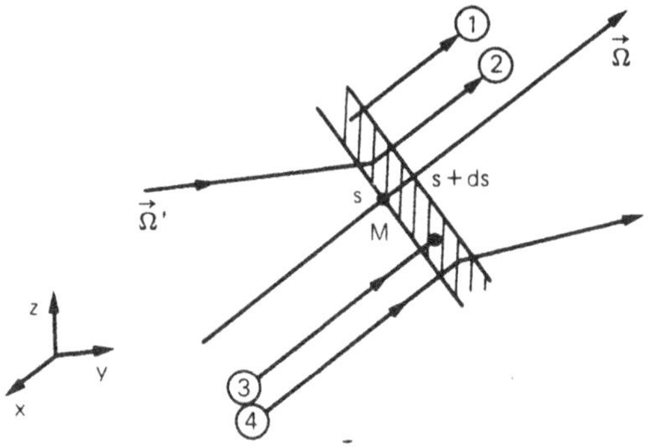

FIGURE 8.1. Neutron balance in a given direction: 1 creation, 2 useful diffusion, 3 absorption, 4 ill-fated diffusion.

Apart from the emission term $e(s, \vec{\Omega})$, this equation is identical to (4.2). We note that the total macroscopic cross section Σ_t depends in general on s, since in the course of its trajectory a neutron may traverse different media.

Equation (8.1) hardly seems complicated. However, this is not the case since, independently of the emission term $e(s, \vec{\Omega})$ the derivative $d\phi/ds$ has a certain complexity since the abscissa s is not defined on an axis fixed in space but on any direction $\vec{\Omega}$. It is only in the particular case of a collimated neutron beam interacting with a nondiffusing medium ($\Sigma_t = \Sigma_a$) that one gets back the simple problem treated in subsec. 4.2.1. In that case the neutrons keep their initial direction which one can take to be the axis Ox.

In the general case it is necessary to transform equation (8.1) by defining point M with respect to coordinates relative to a system of axes independent of $\vec{\Omega}$. Let us consider Cartesian coordinates and note Ω_x, Ω_y, Ω_z, the components of the unit vector $\vec{\Omega}$. By definition these <u>direction cosines</u> can be written:

$$\Omega_x = \frac{dx}{ds} \qquad \Omega_y = \frac{dy}{ds} \qquad \Omega_z = \frac{dz}{ds} \qquad (8.2)$$

Let us form the scalar product $\vec{\Omega} \cdot \vec{\text{grad}}\, \phi(\vec{r}, \vec{\Omega})$, where $\vec{r}$ represents the coordinates x, y, z of point M. We get:

$$\vec{\Omega} \cdot \vec{\text{grad}}\, \phi = \Omega_x \frac{\partial \phi}{\partial x} + \Omega_y \frac{\partial \phi}{\partial y} + \Omega_z \frac{\partial \phi}{\partial z}$$

$$= \frac{\partial \phi}{\partial x}\frac{dx}{ds} + \frac{\partial \phi}{\partial y}\frac{dy}{ds} + \frac{\partial \phi}{\partial z}\frac{dz}{ds} = \frac{d\phi}{ds}$$

which gives the total derivative of ϕ with respect to s taken in the direction $\vec{\Omega}$. Equation (8.1) thus becomes:

$$\vec{\Omega} \cdot \vec{\text{grad}}\, \phi(\vec{r}, \vec{\Omega}) + \Sigma_t(\vec{r})\phi(\vec{r}, \vec{\Omega}) = e(\vec{r}, \vec{\Omega}) \qquad (8.3)$$

In this form, the transport equation is valid irrespective of the coordinate system chosen for defining point $M(\vec{r})$.

It remains for us to calculate the righthand side of this equation. We have intentionally employed the term "emission" and not "source" to designate it. In effect, other than the sources $Q(\vec{r}, \vec{\Omega})$ corresponding to a true creation of neutrons, the emission $e(\vec{r}, \vec{\Omega})$ includes neutrons which after scattering at point M , happen to be going in the right direction $\vec{\Omega}$, whereas before they were moving in the direction $\vec{\Omega}'$ (Fig. 8.1). The elementary scattering rate for these neutrons can be written: $\Sigma_s(\vec{r})\, \phi(\vec{r}, \vec{\Omega}')d\vec{\Omega}'$, but only the fraction $f\,(\vec{\Omega}' \to \vec{\Omega})d\vec{\Omega}$ is in fact scattered in the direction $\vec{\Omega}$ which is of interest to us. The function $f(\vec{\Omega}' \to \vec{\Omega})$ is part of the nuclear data (in the same way as σ_s) and by its definition:

$$\int_{4\pi} f(\vec{\Omega}' \to \vec{\Omega})d\Omega = 1 \qquad (8.4)$$

The above integral represents the probability that a scattering, when it takes place, can occur in an arbitrary direction. Since it is a matter of certainty, this integral is equal to one.

If one considers all possible incident directions $\vec{\Omega}'$, the number of neutrons scattered in $d\Omega$ around $\vec{\Omega}$ will thus be:

$$\int_{4\pi} \Sigma_s(\vec{r})\phi(\vec{r}, \vec{\Omega}')d\Omega' \cdot f(\vec{\Omega}' \to \vec{\Omega})d\Omega \qquad (\text{in cm}^{-3}\ \text{s}^{-1}),$$

a quantity which must be added to the source $Q(\vec{r}, \vec{\Omega})d\Omega$ in order to obtain the global emission $e\,(\vec{r}, \vec{\Omega})d\Omega$. Introducing the latter result into (8.3), we are led to the transport equation in its integral-differential form.

$$\vec{\Omega} \cdot \vec{\text{grad}}\phi + \Sigma_t(\vec{r})\phi(\vec{r},\vec{\Omega}) = \Sigma_s(\vec{r}) \int_{4\pi} f(\vec{\Omega}' \cdot \vec{\Omega})\phi(\vec{r}, \vec{\Omega}')d\vec{\Omega}' + Q(\vec{r}, \vec{\Omega}) = e(\vec{r}, \vec{\Omega}) \qquad (8.5)$$

The function $f(\vec{\Omega}' \rightarrow \vec{\Omega})$ or angular distribution will henceforth be denoted $f(\vec{\Omega}' \cdot \vec{\Omega})$ to express the fact that a scattering is not characterized separately by $\vec{\Omega}$ and $\vec{\Omega}'$, but more simply by the cosine of the deflection angle (spherical symmetry of nuclei).

Whereas the diffusion equation (sec. 4.3) only involves the scalar flux which is a function of space variables alone, the transport equation (8.5) governs angular flux which depends on two additional variables (those which define $\vec{\Omega}$).

This equation has been established starting from the fundamental characteristics of the considered materials, which, in the case of passive media, are only Σ_t, Σ_s and $f(\vec{\Omega}' \cdot \vec{\Omega})$ whereas establishing the diffusion equation required an additional approximation (§4.3.1). Let us now see to what extent the diffusion equation is valid. To this end we multiply equation (8.5) by $d\Omega$ and then integrate it over $\vec{\Omega}$. Remarking that $\vec{\Omega} \cdot \vec{\text{grad}}\, \phi = \text{div}\,(\vec{\Omega}\phi)$, we obtain:

$$\text{div}\,\vec{J} + \Sigma_t \Phi = \Sigma_s \int_{4\pi} d\Omega \int_{4\pi} f(\vec{\Omega}' \cdot \vec{\Omega})\phi(\vec{r},\vec{\Omega}')d\Omega' + Q(\vec{r}) \qquad (8.6)$$

where the definitions of the scalar flux Φ (4.8) and of the net currents $\vec{J}$ (4.10) have been used and we have also put:

$$Q(\vec{r}) = \int_{4\pi} Q(\vec{r},\vec{\Omega})d\Omega \qquad (8.7)$$

the source density ($cm^{-3}\ s^{-1}$) in the usual sense (without consideration of the emission directions).

Permuting the order of integrations in (8.6) and using the normalization condition (8.4), we finally obtain:

$$\text{div}\,\vec{J} + (\Sigma_t - \Sigma_s)\Phi = Q \qquad (8.8)$$

an equation identical to the balance equation (4.12) since by definition $\Sigma_t = \Sigma_s + \Sigma_a$. This equation was thus exact, as stated (§4.2.3). There remains Fick's law (§4.3.1); in order to establish it we will place ourselves in the framework of a simpler geometry which will in no way restrict the range of our conclusions.

8.1.2 One-dimensional Plane Geometry

This case corresponds for example to a set of homogeneous plates of infinite transversal dimensions. It is natural to take the Ox axis perpendicular to all the plates. All the points M situated at the same distance x from the reference plate are submitted to the same flux. On the other hand, the directions $\vec{\Omega}$ belonging to the same cone of vertex angle θ are equivalent (Fig. 8.2). The angular flux thus depends only on a single spatial variable (x) and on a single angular variable (θ).

To express this, let us put:

$$\phi(\vec{r}, \vec{\Omega}) = \frac{\phi(x, \mu)}{2\pi}$$

$$Q(\vec{r}, \vec{\Omega}) = \frac{Q(x, \mu)}{2\pi} \qquad (8.9)$$

$$\mu = \cos\theta$$

Noting that $\vec{\Omega} \cdot \vec{\text{grad}}\phi$ reduces to $\mu(\partial\phi/\partial x)$ (since $\Omega_x = \cos\theta = \mu$ and $\partial\phi/\partial y = \partial\phi/\partial z = 0$), equation (8.5) becomes:

$$\mu\frac{\partial\phi}{\partial x} + \Sigma_t(x)\phi(x, \mu) = \Sigma_s(x)\int_{4\pi} f(\vec{\Omega}' \cdot \vec{\Omega})\phi(x, \mu')d\Omega' + Q(x,\mu) \qquad (8.10)$$

Let us make more explicit the double integral above by passing to spherical coordinates:

$$\mu = \Omega_x = \cos\theta;\ \Omega_y = \sin\theta\sin\alpha;\ \Omega_z = \sin\theta\cos\alpha \qquad (8.11)$$

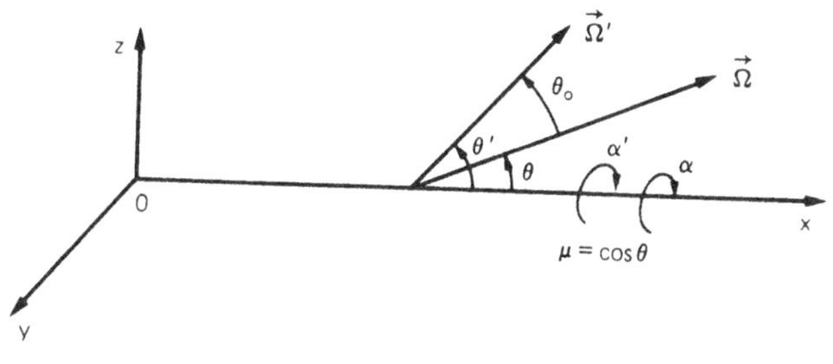

FIGURE 8.2

where θ and α are the polar and azimuthal angles which fix $\vec{\Omega}$ (Fig. 8.2). The components of $\vec{\Omega}'$ are expressed in the same fashion. Finally, since $d\Omega' = \sin\theta' d\theta' \, d\alpha'$ (α' going from 0 to 2π and θ' from 0 to π), equation 8.10 takes the form:

$$\mu\frac{\partial\phi}{\partial x} + \Sigma_t(x)\phi(x, \mu) = \Sigma_s(x)\int_{-1}^{1} g(\mu, \mu')\phi(x, \mu')d\mu' + Q(x, \mu) \qquad (8.12)$$

with:

$$g(\mu,\mu') = \int_0^{2\pi} f(\vec{\Omega} \cdot \vec{\Omega}')d\alpha' \qquad (8.13)$$

We have expressed the fact that the integration over α' is not over the flux. Since the scalar product $\vec{\Omega}\cdot\vec{\Omega}'$ can be written:

$$\mu_0 = \vec{\Omega}\cdot\vec{\Omega}' = \Omega_x\Omega'_x + \Omega_y\Omega'_y + \Omega_z\Omega'_z$$

or:

$$\mu_0 = \cos\theta\cos\theta' + \sin\theta\sin\theta'\cos(\alpha - \alpha') \qquad (8.14)$$

the quantity $g(\mu,\mu')$ is independent of α (one can show this by remarking that $f(\mu_0)$ like μ_0 is a periodic function of $(\alpha - \alpha')$ which can thus be developped in a Fourier series over the sin $m(\alpha - \alpha')$ and cos $m(\alpha - \alpha')$).

Let us place ourselves in the case very often met in practice where the anisotropy of the diffusion is linear, in other words:

$$f(\mu_0) = a + b\,\mu_0 \qquad (8.15)$$

Before substituting this expression into 8.13 we must calculate a and b. In what follows the vector $\vec{\Omega}'$ will be fixed, so that we can choose it as the common polar axis (it plays the role of Ox in the preceding) and $\vec{\Omega}$ will be defined with respect to it with the help of the polar angle θ_0 whose cosine is $\mu_0 = \vec{\Omega}\cdot\vec{\Omega}'$. Let us consider the normalization condition (8.4) which can be written with the new variables:

$$\int_{4\pi} f(\mu_0)d\Omega = 2\pi\int_{-1}^{1} f(\mu_0)d\mu_0 = 1$$

In the same way the <u>average cosine of the deflection angle</u> $\bar{\mu}_0$ can be written:

$$\int_{4\pi} \mu_0 f(\mu_0)d\Omega = 2\pi\int_{-1}^{1} \mu_0 f(\mu_0)d\mu_0 = \bar{\mu}_0$$

Expression (8.15) substituted in these two identities gives us the values of a and b, whence:

$$f(\mu_0) = \frac{1 + 3\,\bar{\mu}_0\mu_0}{4\pi} \qquad (8.16)$$

The parameter $\bar{\mu}_0$ alone measures the anisotropy of the process. Expressing μ_0 as a function of the coordinates θ, θ', α, α' (8.14) and substituting

$f(\mu_0)$ into (8.13) we get:

$$g(\mu,\mu') = \frac{1 + 3\bar{\mu}_0\mu\mu'}{2} \tag{8.17}$$

We can go further and introduce this latter expression into (8.12) in order to arrive at the desired transport equation:

$$\mu \frac{\partial\phi}{\partial x} + \Sigma_t(x)\phi(x,\mu) = \frac{\Sigma_s(x)}{2}\left(\Phi(x) + 3\bar{\mu}_0 J(x)\mu\right) + Q(x,\mu) \tag{8.18}$$

where the scalar flux Φ and the net current J appear naturally in the form:

$$\left.\begin{aligned} \Phi(x) &= \int_{-1}^{1} \phi(x,\mu)d\mu \\ J(x) &= \int_{-1}^{1} \mu\phi(x,\mu)d\mu \end{aligned}\right\} \tag{8.19}$$

These expressions follow from the definitions already given (4.8)(4.10) and the relations (8.9). The components of the current along Oy or Oz evidently vanish as one can ascertain by introducing the expression (8.9) and (8.11) in the general definition of the current (4.10).

Equation (8.18) has been the object of much mathematical research. It is the simplest equation that can be obtained in neutron transport theory.

8.1.3 Passage to Elementary Diffusion Theory

To effect this passage, it is necessary to deduce from (8.18) the equations connecting integral quantities like the scalar flux Φ and the net current J.

To do so, let us multiply (8.18) by $d\mu$ and integrate over μ from -1 to +1. We thus obtain as expected the balance equation (8.8) for this particular geometry:

$$\frac{dJ(x)}{dx} + \Sigma_a(x)\Phi(x) = Q(x) \tag{8.20}$$

where we have once again used expressions (8.19), the first being applied to the flux $\phi(x,\mu)$ as well as to the sources $Q(x, \mu)$. $Q(x)$, like $Q(\vec{r})$ (cf. equation (8.7)), represents the neutron source density ($cm^{-3}\ s^{-1}$) without reference to their direction.

As we have observed several times, this equation is exact, but does not enable us by itself to solve the problem in Φ. To obtain a second equation, let us multiply (8.18) by $\mu d\mu$ and integrate over the same interval (-1, +1), as in the preceding. We get:

$$\frac{d}{dx}\int_{-1}^{1} \mu^2 \phi(x,\mu)d\mu + \Sigma_t(x)J(x) = \Sigma_s(x)\bar{\mu}_0 J(x) \qquad (8.21)$$

The source Q(x,μ) has been supposed to be isotropic (independent of μ), which implies that

$$\int_{-1}^{1} \mu Q d\mu = 0.$$

In practice this hypothesis is not very restrictive. Equation (8.21) involves a new integral quantity.

The simplifying hypothesis which leads to Fick's law intervenes here, <u>and here only</u>. Let us suppose that the angular flux is linearly anisotropic. We will put:

$$\phi(x,\mu) \cong A(x) + B(x)\mu$$

as we did for the function $f(\mu_0)$ (8.15). The quantities A and B can be calculated as functions of Φ and J by substituting this expression into equations (8.19), whence finally:

$$\phi(x,\mu) \cong \frac{\Phi(x) + 3J(x)\mu}{2} \qquad (8.22)$$

By adopting this structure for the angular flux we can calculate the integral in μ which had not been eliminated from equation (8.21):

$$\int_{-1}^{1} \mu^2\phi(x,\mu)d\mu = \frac{\Phi(x)}{2}\int_{-1}^{1} \mu^2 d\mu + \frac{3\,J(x)}{2}\int_{-1}^{1} \mu^3 d\mu = \frac{\Phi(x)}{3}$$

and equation (8.21) can be written:

$$\frac{1}{3}\frac{d\Phi}{dx} + (\Sigma_t(x) - \bar{\mu}_0\Sigma_s(x))J(x) = 0$$

or:

$$\left.\begin{aligned} &J(x) = -D\frac{d\Phi}{dx} \\ &\text{with} \\ &D(x) = \frac{1}{3(\Sigma_t(x) - \bar{\mu}_0\Sigma_s(x))} \end{aligned}\right\} \qquad (8.23)$$

We get back Fick's law which was presented without proof in Sec. 4.3. Although our reasoning used a one-dimensional geometry, equations (8.23) are completely general. They suppose only that the angular flux is a linear function of $\vec{\Omega}$ and this hypothesis is represented here by equation (8.22). Assuming Fick's law thus amounts to admitting this restrictive property of the angular flux. If the diffusion is completely isotropic, then $\bar{\mu}_0 = 0$, and the diffusion coefficient D is given by equation (4.14). In the contrary case, we will put (8.23):

$$D = \frac{1}{3\,\Sigma_{tr}}$$

where Σ_{tr} is the macroscopic transport cross section defined as:

$$\Sigma_{tr} = \Sigma_t - \bar{\mu}_0 \Sigma_s = (1 - \bar{\mu}_0)\Sigma_s + \Sigma_a \qquad (8.24)$$

We should note that the hypothesis of a weak anisotropy of diffusion (8.16) is much less restrictive than the hypotheses of the same type made for the angular flux. The first characterizes a neutron-nucleus collision and is very often justified. But especially, one knows in advance if it is justified or not . As for the second, it depends on the problem treated and not only on the materials used. Let us consider for example the simple case of a collimated neutron beam falling on a plate of infinite lateral dimensions(§4.2.1). In the absence of scattering($\Sigma_s = 0$), the flux follows the exponential law (4.3) and conserves its initial angular distribution since no process intervenes which might deflect a neutron. The angular flux is thus non-vanishing only in the unique propagation direction ($\theta = 0$, $\mu = 1$). Such a distribution (in μ) is so singular that one cannot express it even approximately in the form (8.22) and diffusion theory is completely wrong in this limiting case; this is of no importance since the problem can be solved very simply in an entirely different way (§4.2.1).

Staying with the same case, let us consider scattering cross sections which are large compared to absorption cross sections ($\Sigma_t \gg \Sigma_a$). This means that before a neutron has been absorbed, it has been deflected such a large number of times that it has "forgotten" its initial direction. An angular distribution such as (8.22) thus tends to be obtained and diffusion theory should be valid. One can show this in the following way.

An angular flux will be almost isotropic if the current J is small compared to the scalar flux Φ (8.22). In other words, according to (8.23) if the inequality:

$$D \frac{d\Phi}{dx} << \Phi \tag{8.25}$$

is amply satisfied.

In this problem the source densities are absent (Q = 0) since the system is fed by neutrons through the entry face. The solution predicted by diffusion theory or deduced from equations (8.20) and (8.23) is in this case:

$$\Phi(x) = \Phi(0) \exp\left(-\frac{x}{L}\right) \tag{8.26}$$

where $L = \sqrt{D/\Sigma_a}$ is the diffusion length (§4.3.3).

The condition of validity (8.25) becomes: $D/L << 1$ or $\Sigma_a D << 1$, in other words $\Sigma_t >> \Sigma_a$ and one gets back the initial hypothesis.

Nevertheless even in this case, diffusion theory will not be exact near the entry surface. In effect, in this region the neutrons have not been subjected to many collisions with the nuclei, so that their angular distribution is not yet of type (8.22). The width of this transition zone is thus of the order of a few mean free paths λ_t and thus small compared to the diffusion length L, since we have assumed $\Sigma_t >> \Sigma_a$.

We can thus draw the following general conclusions: Elementary diffusion theory is valid if:

- the mean free paths are small compared to the diffusion lengths ($\lambda_t << L$ or $\Sigma_t >> \Sigma_a$),
- the points considered are situated at more than a few mean free paths from the boundaries separating the different media or from very localized sources.

For these reasons, the solution of a diffusion equation is called asymptotic in that it matches with the exact solution far from boundaries.

8.1.4 Milne's Problem

It is evident that the boundary effect mentioned above will be all the stronger the more different are the characteristics of the contiguous media. An important extreme case is that in which one of the two media is nondiffusing ($\Sigma_s = 0$) and lacking sources (Q = 0). The corresponding geometry is indicated in Fig. 8.3. The diffusing media (1) situated on the left (x < 0) is fed with neutrons from sources far away from the region which interests us. We observe immediately that at the boundary of the two media (x = 0), the angular flux vanishes for $\mu < 0$. In effect, medium (2) cannot send back any neutrons ($\mu < 0$). For it to be otherwise, it would have to possess sources or have a non-vanishing scattering cross section, which is contrary to the hypotheses. In contrast, for positive values of μ, the angular flux is non-vanishing and represents the leakage of neutrons from medium (1) towards medium (2) at different incident angles (Fig. 8.4).

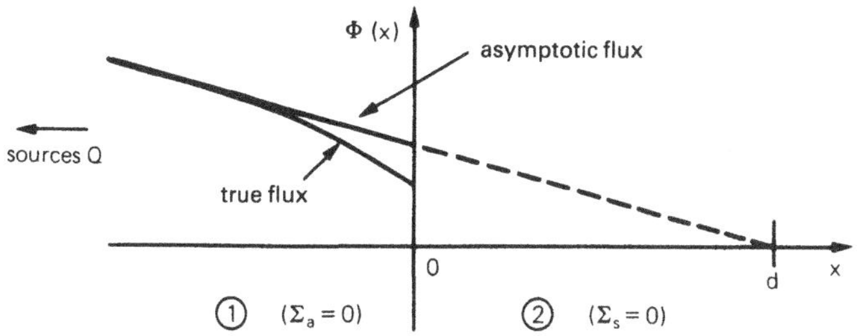

FIGURE 8.3

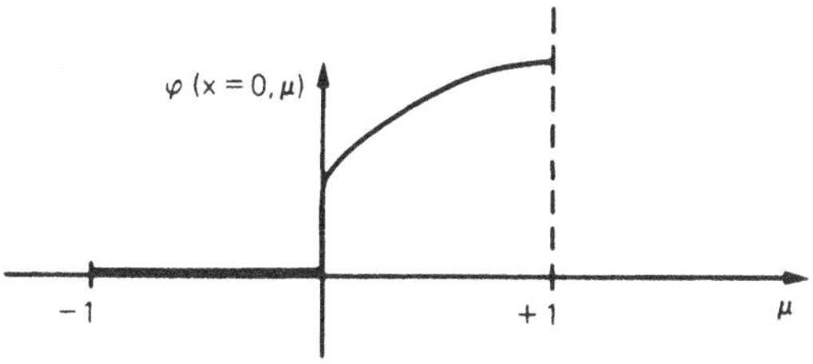

FIGURE 8.4

Such an angular distribution (over the interval $-1 < \mu < +1$) cannot be represented by (8.22) and diffusion theory is thus false, at least locally. Let us consider the case of vanishing absorption in the first medium ($\Sigma_a = 0$) and place ourselves outside the domain where the neutrons are emitted. Equation (8.20) which remains rigorous immediately gives:

$$J(x) = J(0) \qquad \text{for } x < 0 \tag{8.27}$$

The net current J(x) is thus constant and positive, its value being fixed by the sources Q situated on the left, very far from the boundary x = 0. This result is rigorous. On the other hand, the equation:

$$\Phi(x) = \Phi(0) - \frac{J(0)}{D} x \qquad (8.28)$$

obtained by integrating Fick's law (8.23) is only valid, like the latter, outside the transition zone of a few mean free paths situated at the left of x = 0. In particular, $\Phi(0)$ does not represent the true flux at x = 0 but is simply a parameter which enables us to adjust for large negative values of x the distribution (8.28) with respect to the exact distribution. The latter can only be obtained by solving the transport equation (8.18) in the case $\Sigma_a = 0$. Various more or less analytic methods have been proposed in the past, and this problem constitutes a stringent test for the numerical algorithms for solving such a problem.

Fortunately, a knowledge of the exact scalar flux in the vicinity of x = 0 is not indispensable. What is required is the boundary condition which must be imposed on the solution of the diffusion equation (8.28) so that it is asymptotic to the exact solution (Fig. 8.3). This amounts to finding a relation between the parameters J(0) and $\Phi(0)$ or to specifying the value that the logarithmic derivative of the flux must take at x = 0.

$$\left| \frac{1}{\Phi} \frac{d\Phi}{dx} \right|_{x = 0} = - \frac{1}{d} \qquad (8.29)$$

This condition can also be written:

$$\left| \Phi \right|_{x = d} = 0 \qquad (8.30)$$

The analytic continuation of the solution of the diffusion equation towards positive x must vanish at the extrapolation distance d. Naturally, $\Phi(x)$ has no meaning to the right of the boundary x = 0. For purely diffusive media, transport theory leads to:

$$d = 0.7104\ \lambda_t \qquad (8.31)$$

where $\lambda_t = 1/\Sigma_t$ is the mean free path already defined (§4.2.1).

Calculations show in addition that it is this quantity which determines the width of the transition zone (a few centimeters) in which elementary diffusion theory fails to be exact. The ratio of the approximate flux to the exact flux reaches its maximum value 1.2305 at $x = 0$ [50](p.265).

If the diffusive medium is in addition slightly absorbing, the asymptotic distribution (furnished by the diffusion equation) is no longer linear, but equation (8.29) always furnishes the condition to be satisfied with a slightly different value of d. As indicated in Fig. 8.5, the flux does not vanish at $x = d$ but at $x = x_0$. In practice, however, x_0 and d are very close.

If absorption becomes large compared to diffusion, elementary diffusion theory is everywhere false and condition (8.29) loses its utility.

The case which we have just treated is important in practice. The last region of an isolated material system is necessarily surrounded by vacuum. If the vacuum extends to infinity, it has the same effect on the considered system as the purely absorbing medium considered up til now: no neutron enters the system. This problem, known by the name of Milne's problem, was encountered for the first time by astrophysicists.

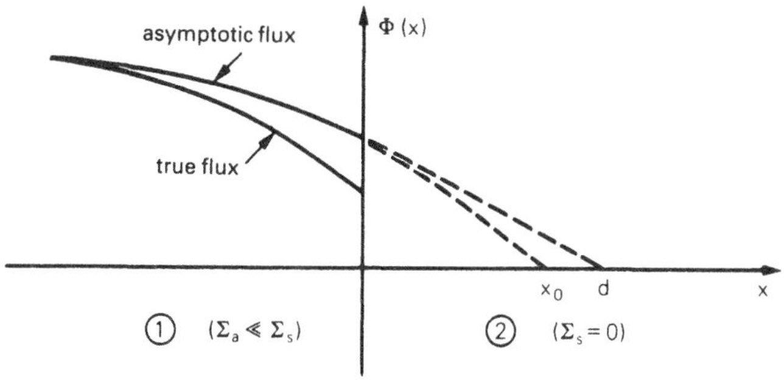

FIGURE 8.5

The transport of photons in a star appeals to the same formalism as does neutron transport. The sun, for example, can be considered as an isolated system in which photons are created far from the surface. The angular flux which emerges ($\mu > 0$) is not isotropic (Fig. 8.4). In particular the angular flux is weaker when the incidence is oblique ($\mu \cong 0$), which explains why the solar disc appears darker at its periphery.

Let us return to neutronic problems. If the empty region surrounding the considered material system does not extend to infinity, or if the separation surface is concave, then the preceding conclusions are no longer strictly valid, since neutrons may penetrate the system ($\mu < 0$) as one sees in Fig. 8.6. In contrast, at the boundary of a black body (infinitely absorbing medium) and a diffusive medium, the preceding considerations continue to make sense in every case provided that the axis Ox is replaced by the normal to the separation surface oriented from the diffusing medium to the absorbing medium. This is the case for control rods (§5.3.8) which can be considered as cylindrical black bodies immersed in a reactor and at the surface of which equation (8.29) must be satisfied. In this case, of course, d is no longer given by (8.31) but by a function of ($a\Sigma_t$) where a is the radius of the control rod. Here, too, transport calculations made once and for all enable us to know in advance the extrapolation distance d.

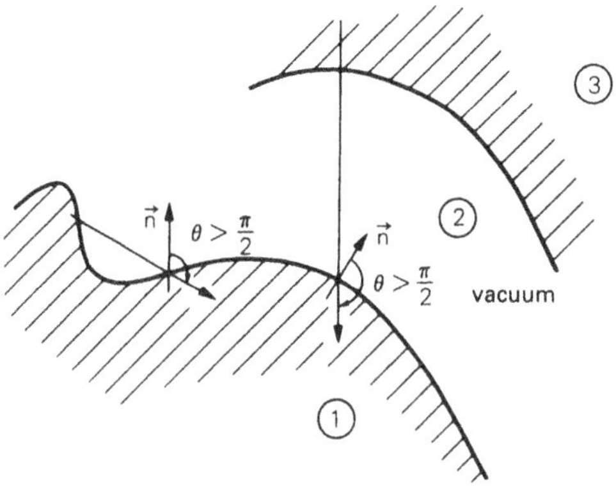

FIGURE 8.6.

The conditions of validity of the diffusion equation (§8.1.3) are almost always satisfied in nuclear reactors after the reactors have been made homogeneous. Only very small-sized reactors require a special treatment. Nevertheless the homogenization of the reactor core can necessitate transport calculations inasmuch as a very subtle knowledge of flux distributions in the interior of the fuel cells is required (Sec. 5.1). These calculations are thus limited to small regions of space (a few mean free paths) and often call upon the approach which will be described in the following section.

With regard more particularly to the external boundary of an isolated reactor, its dimensions are such that its radius of curvature is very large in comparison with mean free paths. Locally, the matter-vacuum separation surface can be likened to a plane and we can adopt the more restrictive condition (8.30) which can then be written in all generality:

$$\Phi(S_e) = 0$$

where S_e is the extrapolated surface obtained by displacing every point of the surface S limiting the system by an amount d going in the direction of the normal. The extrapolation distance d is then furnished by expression (8.31) with good accuracy since by hypothesis the absorption remains weak (otherwise diffusion theory would be inapplicable). All the same, if the diffusion is anisotropic, it would be more accurate to replace λ_t in (8.31) by $1/\Sigma_{tr}$ where the transport cross section is given by (8.24).

8.2 ANOTHER FORMULATION OF TRANSPORT THEORY

8.2.1 The Integral Transport Equation

There is another interesting form of the transport equation which, under certain not very restrictive conditions, only involves the scalar flux $\Phi(\vec{r})$. It is to be used when the considered media are small in size (a few mean free paths) or strongly absorbing, that is, in cases where elementary diffusion theory simply cannot be applied. A few examples of its application will be given in Sec. 8.4.

To obtain this equation, it is necessary to return to the differential equation (8.1) which as we have seen results from the neutron balance established in a given direction $\vec{\Omega}$. We will integrate this equation before going on to the usual spatial variables.

Let us consider an isolated medium of volume V, not necessarily homogeneous, and limited by a convex surface (S) (Fig. 8.7). We propose to calculate the angular flux $\phi(\vec{r},\vec{\Omega})$ at an interior point M of the system. Equation (8.1) implies that we must take the abscissa s in the considered direction $\vec{\Omega}$ and it is convenient to take as the origin (s = 0) the point M_0 where this direction intersects the surface S for the first time (Fig. 8.7).

Equation (8.1) is linear and of first order in s. We first look for a general solution of the equation without the righthand side, and then for a particular solution by the method of variation of constants. We are then led to the general expression:

$$\phi(s,\vec{\Omega}) = \left[K + \int_0^s ds' e(s',\vec{\Omega}) \exp[\int_0^{s'} \Sigma_t(s'')ds'']\right] \exp[-\int_0^s \Sigma_t(s'')ds'']$$

Since the system is isolated, the angular flux entering at M_0 must vanish, in other words, $\phi(s = 0,\vec{\Omega}) = 0$. At every point M_0 belonging to (S), Fig. 8.7 indicates that $\vec{\Omega}\cdot\vec{n} < 0$; we thus get back the property established in the preceding subsection ($\phi(0,\mu) = 0$ for $\mu < 0$).

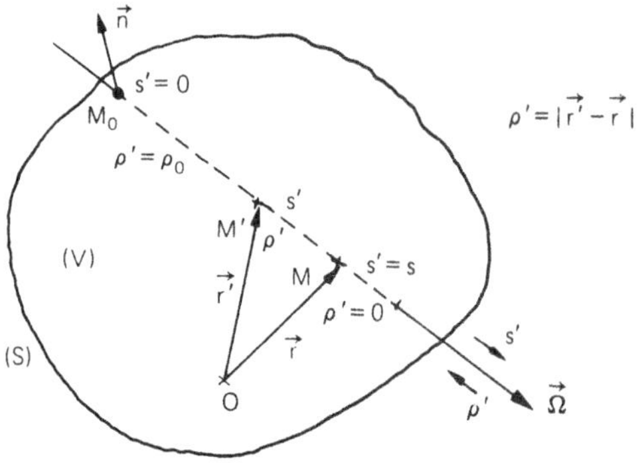

FIGURE 8.7.

Placing ourselves at the point M (Fig. 8.7) and expressing the preceding condition, we get:

$$\phi(\vec{r},\vec{\Omega}) = \int_0^s ds' e(\vec{r}', \vec{\Omega}) \exp(-\int_{s'}^s \Sigma_t(s'')ds'') \tag{8.32}$$

where $\vec{r}'$ corresponds to an arbitrary point M' situated between M_0 and M (Fig. 8.7). When $\vec{\Omega}$ is fixed, $\vec{r}'$ only depends on s':

$$\vec{r}' = \vec{r} + (s' - s)\vec{\Omega}$$

In what follows point M will remain fixed and the directions $\vec{\Omega}$ will vary. Since point M_0 moves on the surface (S), we are led to take M as the new origin, with the new abscissae (Fig 8.7):

$$\rho' = \rho_0 - s' \quad \text{and} \quad \rho'' = \rho_0 - s''$$

and equation (8.32) now becomes:

$$\phi(\vec{r},\vec{\Omega}) = \int_0^{\rho_0} d\rho' e(\vec{r}',\vec{\Omega}) \exp[-\tau(\vec{r}',\vec{r})] \tag{8.33}$$

where we have put:

$$\tau(\vec{r},\vec{r}') = \int_0^{\rho'} \Sigma_t(\rho'')d\rho'' \qquad (8.34)$$

This quantity is called the optical path by analogy with optics where integrals of this type over light rays also arise, Σ_t being replaced by the index of refraction.

In practice, τ can be calculated in the following way: the straight line passing through the points M and M' intersects the boundaries of the various media encountered at points M_i. On each of the segments (M_i, M_{i+1}) of length $\Delta\rho_i$, the total cross sections Σ_t are constant and equal to $\Sigma_{t,i}$. The optical path for this pair of points can be written:

$$\tau(\vec{r},\vec{r}') = \sum_i \Delta\rho_i \Sigma_{t,i}$$

which represents the distance which separates them measured in mean free paths ($\lambda_t = 1/\Sigma_t$). If M and M' belong to a homogeneous convex medium, we simply get

$$\tau(\vec{r},\vec{r}') = \Sigma_t \; |\vec{r} - \vec{r}'| \; = \Sigma_t \rho'$$

It is easy to interpret equation (8.33). The neutrons which arrive at M have necessarily been emitted along the trajectory M_0M, but each elmentary emission $e(\vec{r}', \vec{\Omega})d\rho'$ centered at M' of abscissa $0 < \rho' < \rho_0$ has its contribution multiplied by the attenuation factor $\exp(- \tau(\vec{r}',\vec{r}))$. This factor, which takes account of neutrons which have left $\vec{\Omega}$ following all sorts of collisions, is identical to that which was established for the simple case of a homogeneous material (4.3).

Equation (8.33) is completely rigorous, but in order to go further, we must introduce simplifying hypotheses concerning the emission rate. We have seen that the latter can be written (§8.1.1):

$$e(\vec{r},\vec{\Omega}) = Q(\vec{r},\vec{\Omega}) + \Sigma_s(\vec{r}) \int_{4\pi} f(\vec{\Omega} \cdot \vec{\Omega}')\phi(\vec{r},\vec{\Omega}') \, d\vec{\Omega}' \qquad (8.35)$$

Scattering is very often isotropic, the function f is thus independent of the scattering angle, and hence of $\vec{\Omega}\cdot\vec{\Omega}'$. Taking account of condition (8.4) we are led to put:

$$f(\vec{\Omega} \cdot \vec{\Omega}') = \frac{1}{4\pi}$$

We can admit, in an even less restrictive way, that the neutron sources (of fission, for example) are also isotropic. We can then put in the same way:

$$Q(\vec{r},\vec{\Omega}) = \frac{Q(\vec{r})}{4\pi}$$

These two hypotheses, combined with the definition of the scalar flux (4.8) enable us to rewrite (8.35) in the form:

$$e(\vec{r},\vec{\Omega}) = \frac{Q(\vec{r}) + \Sigma_s(\vec{r})\Phi(\vec{r})}{4\pi}$$

Substituting this expression of the emission rate into (8.33) and integrating the latter over 4π with respect to $\vec{\Omega}$, we obtain the scalar flux at point M:

$$\Phi(\vec{r}) = \int_{4\pi} d\Omega \int_0^{\rho_0} d\rho' \frac{Q(\vec{r}\,') + \Sigma_s(\vec{r}\,')\Phi(\vec{r}\,')}{4\pi} \exp[-\tau(\vec{r}\,',\vec{r})] \quad (8.36)$$

The preceding multiple integral corresponds to a complete sweep of the system considered (of volume V); moreover, introducing spherical coordinates associated to the fixed point M, the volume element dV' centered at M' can be written:

$$dV' = \rho'^2 d\rho' d\Omega \qquad \text{with } \rho' = |\vec{r}\,' - \vec{r}| \qquad \text{(cf. Fig. 8.7)}$$

whence the definitive form of the desired equation:

$$\Phi(\vec{r}) = \int_V [Q(\vec{r}\,') + \Sigma_s(\vec{r}\,')\Phi(\vec{r}\,')] \frac{\exp[-\tau(\vec{r},\vec{r}\,')]}{4\pi|\vec{r}\,' - \vec{r}|^2} dV' \quad (8.37)$$

This equation indicates that the neutrons emitted isotropically in volume dV' situated at M' induce at M a scalar flux $\Phi(\vec{r})$ equal to the emission intensity $[Q(\vec{r}\,') + \Sigma_s(\vec{r}\,')\Phi(\vec{r}\,')]dV'$ multiplied by the <u>transport kernel</u>:

$$\frac{\exp[-\tau(\vec{r},\vec{r}\,')]}{4\pi|\vec{r}\,' - \vec{r}|^2}$$

This kernel only involves the geometrical distance $|\vec{r}\,' - \vec{r}|$ and optical distance $\tau(\vec{r}\,',\vec{r})$ separating the <u>emitting</u> point (M') and the <u>receiving</u> point (M). It is thus perfectly symmetric.

This result was expected since it could have been deduced intuitively from equation (4.6). For this, it would have sufficed to take for the pointlike source S the emission rate associated to dV' and to replace $\Sigma_t \Delta\rho$ (optical path valid in a unique homogeneous medium of thickness $\Delta\rho$) by $\tau(\vec{r},\vec{r}\,')$, the optical path defined in the general case by (8.34).

The equation obtained by putting $\Sigma_s = 0$ in (8.37) explicitly gives the scalar flux in a purely absorbing system. This solution represents in the general case ($\Sigma_s \neq 0$) the flux of neutrons which have not suffered any collision. We thus find ourselves in the framework of subsection 4.2.1. It is interesting to note that taking account of scattering simply comes down to replacing the "true" sources Q by the emission rates $Q + \Sigma_s \Phi$, whence the integral equation (8.37), implicit in Φ.

This equation, like the diffusion equation, has the advantage of only involving the scalar flux $\Phi(\vec{r})$, the only interesting physical quantities (§4.2.2). It is much less restrictive since we have made no hypotheses on the angular flux (we have not appealed to (8.22)). On the other hand, it is much more complicated since it establishes a relation between the considered point $M(\vec{r})$ and <u>all the other points interior to the system $M'(\vec{r}\,')$</u>. Moreover, in the general case, the calculation of optical paths (8.34) becomes inextricably complicated, so that this approach is conceivable only for systems consisting of a small number of zones of simple geometrical shapes. This is the case, for example, for reactor cells (Sec. 5.1) which constitute material systems of small optical dimensions (a few mean free paths), consisting of only two or three materials of which one (the fuel) is strongly absorbing. Besides, these are just the characteristics which prevent us from using the diffusion equation (§8.1.3)

8.2.2 Collision Probabilities

In order to solve the type of problem indicated above, we try in practice to transform (8.37) into a system of linear algebraic equations. To this end the material medium of volume V is decomposed into I homogeneous zones of volume V_i numbered $i = 1,2, \ldots, I$. These zones are small enough so that at the heart of each of them the flux Φ and the sources Q vary very little. We thus replace these quantities by their average value in the zone, $\bar{\Phi}_i$ and $\bar{Q}_i$. Equation (8.37) becomes:

$$\Phi(\vec{r}) = \sum_{i=1}^{I} (\bar{Q}_i + \Sigma_{s,i}\, \bar{\Phi}_i) \int_{V_i} \frac{\exp[-\tau(\vec{r},\vec{r}\,')]}{4\pi|\vec{r}\,' - \vec{r}|^2}\, dV'$$

Integrating the above equation with respect to $\vec{r}$ in the zone j and noting that by definition $\int_{V_j} \Phi(\vec{r})dV = V_j \bar{\Phi}_j$, we are led to the desired linear system:

$$V_j \bar{\Phi}_j = \sum_{i=1}^{I} \left[\int_{V_j} \int_{V_i} dVdV' \frac{\exp[-\tau(\vec{r},\vec{r}')]}{4\pi|\vec{r}' - \vec{r}|^2} \right] (\bar{Q}_i + \Sigma_{s,i} \bar{\Phi}_i)$$

It is customary to write this system in the form:

$$V_j \Sigma_{t,j} \bar{\Phi}_j = \sum_{i=1}^{I} P_{i \to j} V_i (\bar{Q}_i + \Sigma_{s,i} \bar{\Phi}_i) \tag{8.38}$$

where we have put:

$$\int_{V_j} \int_{V_i} dVdV' \frac{\exp[-\tau(\vec{r}',\vec{r})]}{4\pi|\vec{r}' - \vec{r}|^2} = \frac{V_i}{\Sigma_{t,j}} P_{i \to j} \tag{8.39}$$

The quantities denoted $P_{i \to j}$ are called collision probabilities for the following reasons.

Let us first note that by definition $V_j \Sigma_{t,j} \bar{\Phi}_j$ and $V_i(\bar{Q}_i + \Sigma_{s,i} \bar{\Phi}_i)$ are respectively the collision rate in zone j and the emission rate in zone i. The matrix element $P_{i \to j}$ thus represents the probability that a neutron emitted uniformly and isotropically in zone i would have its first collision in zone j.

In practice, the calculation of $P_{i \rightleftarrows j}$ is much more complicated (8.39) than the solution of the system (8.38). As a consequence, the presence or absence of the scattering process has very little influence on the cost of these calculations. This is one peculiar feature of this approach. We also note that the collision probabilities depend on the fine geometry of the problem (zone shapes) and on the nuclear characteristics of the materials only through their total macroscopic cross section.

Equation (8.39) shows that in the general case it is very difficult to obtain the matrix elements $P_{i \to j}$, since it is necessary to calculate a sixfold integral! Nevertheless it is possible to obtain theorems which in practice considerably simplify the calculations. We see in particular that by permuting the indices i and j, the lefthand side of (8.39) remains unchanged (it suffices to permute also $\vec{r}'$ and $\vec{r}$, which does not affect the transport kernel). We thus establish the reciprocity theorem:

$$V_i \Sigma_{t,i} P_{i \to j} = V_j \Sigma_{t,j} P_{j \to i} \tag{8.40}$$

For a system of large dimensions, one can show, starting from (8.39) that:

$$\sum_{j=1}^{I} P_{i \to j} = 1 \qquad (8.41)$$

This result is obvious since every neutron emitted in zone i must necessarily suffer a collision somewhere in such a system. If the latter is not infinite, it is necessary to add to the lefthand side of (8.41) the term $P_{i \to S}$ which represents the probability that a neutron emitted in V_i leaks out of the considered system without undergoing any collision.

In one-dimensional plane geometry, the probabilities $P_{i \to j}$ (8.39) lead to double integrals. These can be calculated analytically. The expressions for the probabilities now only involve exponential integrals of the type $E_3(\tau)$ defined as [51]:

$$E_n(\tau) = \int_0^1 \exp\left(-\frac{\tau}{\mu}\right) \mu^{n-2} \, d\mu \qquad (8.42)$$

These functions well known to numerical analysts have been tabulated, but for computer calculations it is advisable to use their series expansions. The values of τ to be considered are all the "optical distances" $\tau_{i,j}$ which intervene in the problem (distances between zone boundaries).

For one-dimensional cylindrical geometry which is much more realistic since it corresponds to most reactor cells, the calculation of probabilities leads to a simple numerical integration which is quite acceptable. In this case one can go even further by considering that a scattering is no longer isotropic and the sources are no longer uniform [51].

Beyond this, for multidimensional geometries, it is impossible in practice to pursue this path without introducing a few additional approximations (on the angular fluxes at the interfaces for example). Fortunately the collision probabilities are not very sensitive to certain types of simplifying hypotheses. We note that once these probabilities are known, the numerical resolution of the system of equations (8.38) no longer depends on the geometrical complexity of the problem except for the number of zones [52].

Probabilities of the type $P_{i \to i}$ are generally easier to calculate and are very useful in the analysis of certain important phenomena (§8.4.1). As an example, we shall calculate the probability of collision inside a homogeneous plate of thickness h and of infinite lateral dimensions (Fig. 8.8).

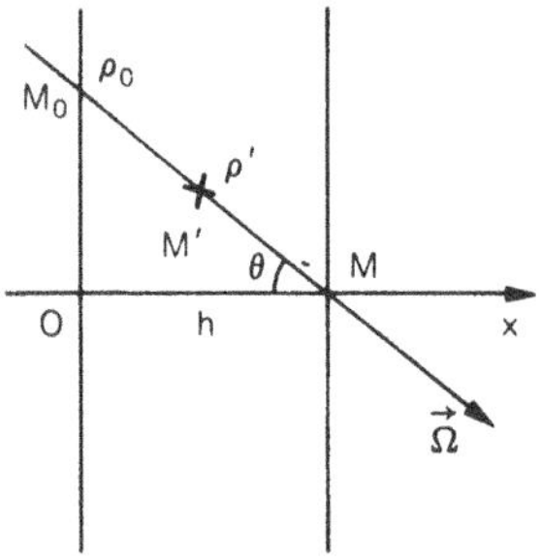

FIGURE 8.8.

Let us consider a uniform isotropic emission of neutrons in this plate. We can put:

$$e(\vec{r}',\vec{\Omega}) = \frac{e}{4\pi}$$

where e is the global emission rate ($cm^{-3}\ s^{-1}$) corresponding to all possible directions. The optical path between points M and M' is simply equal to $\Sigma_t\rho'$, since the plate is homogeneous (8.34). The angular flux at M (Fig. 8.8) can then be written (8.33):

$$\phi_M(\vec{\Omega}) = \frac{e}{4\pi}\int_0^{\rho_0} d\rho'\ \exp(-\Sigma_t\rho') = \frac{e}{4\pi\Sigma_t}\left[1-\exp\left(-\frac{\Sigma_t h}{\cos\theta}\right)\right]$$

since $\rho_0 = h/\cos\theta$. The preceding angular flux enables us to calculate neutron leakage at M per unit area and unit time, in other words the current J_M^+ (§4.2.2.):

$$J_M^+ = \int_{\Omega_x>0} \Omega_x\phi_M(\vec{\Omega})d\Omega = 2\pi\int_0^{\pi/2} \cos\theta\phi_M(\vec{\Omega})\sin\theta\ d\theta$$
$$= \frac{e}{2\Sigma_t}\left[\frac{1}{2} - \int_0^1 \mu\exp-\left(\frac{\Sigma_t h}{\mu}\right)d\mu\right]$$

where we have put $\mu = \cos\theta$. We recognize in the latter expression the exponential integral $E_3(\Sigma_t h)$ (8.42). These results can be expressed in the form:

$$\frac{2J_M^+}{h\ e} = \frac{1/2 - E_3(\Sigma_t h)}{\Sigma_t h} = P_s(\Sigma_t h) \qquad (8.43)$$

The first term is nothing but the probability that a neutron uniformly emitted in a plate exits without undergoing a collision. The desired collision probability is thus:

$$P_{cc} = 1 - P_s$$

The repetition of the subscript c in this expression simply recalls that the emissions and collisions have taken place in the same zone.

For an infinite cylindrical rod, the calculations are a little more complicated, but one can always express P_{cc} as a function of the single parameter $\Sigma_t \emptyset$ where $\emptyset$ is now the diameter of the rod. The function $P_{cc}(\Sigma_t \emptyset)$ has been tabulated and various approximate expressions have been proposed, for example [9](p.185):

$$P_{cc}(x) = \frac{x}{x + 1.08\left[1 + \dfrac{1}{0.3\,x^2 + 2.34}\right]} \qquad (8.44)$$

8.2.3 Application to Reactor Cells

The preceding theory is in principle only valid in the case of isolated systems whereas its domain of application is practically limited to cell calculation. There is no question of applying it to the complete reactor (which itself is isolated), for one would then be led to introduce thousands of zones. Taking account of the periodic structure of lattices, a cell can be viewed as a system without neutron leakage (it is necessary that the number of cells per multiplying zone be large, so that the lattices are practically infinite). The net current at the external surface of a cell thus vanishes, in other words, the neutron current J^- coming from contiguous cells compensates exactly the current J^+ corresponding to neutrons which leak out of the considered cell. Since these currents generally do not vanish, this means in particular that the angular flux at the external surface of the system no longer vanishes for $\vec{\Omega}\cdot\vec{n} < 0$ (Fig. 8.7).

Taking up again the demonstrations of subsec. 8.2.1 and attributing a certain angular distribution to the neutrons entering the cell (to which corresponds the current J^-), we are led to the system of equations:

$$\Sigma_{t,j}\, V_j \bar{\Phi}_j = \sum_{i=1} V_i \bar{e}_i P_{i\to j} + S\, \bar{J}^- P_{S\to j}$$

analogous to (8.38) in which:

- $P_{S \to j}$ is the probability that a neutron entering the cell through its external surface (S) will undergo its first collision in zone j of volume V_j;
- $\bar{J}^-$ is the average entering current defined on (S);
- $\bar{e}_i$ and $P_{j \to i}$ keep their previous meaning (§8.2.2).

In the same way, we can calculate the number of neutrons which leak out of the system without suffering collisions:

$$S\bar{J}^+ = \sum_{i=1}^{I} V_i \bar{e}_i P_{i \to S} + S\bar{J}^- P_{S \to S}$$

where $P_{i \to S}$ and $P_{S \to S}$ are respectively the probabilities that a neutron emitted in V_i or entering the cell will leave the system without suffering collisions. Since by definition J^- is equal to J^+ at the periphery of a cell, we can eliminate these currents from the two preceding equations in order to arrive exactly at the system of equations (8.38) in which it suffices to introduce the new probabilities $\tilde{P}_{i \to j}$:

$$\tilde{P}_{i \to j} = P_{i \to j} + \frac{P_{i \to S} \cdot P_{S \to j}}{1 - P_{S \to S}} \qquad (8.45)$$

with the identity :

$$P_{S \to S} = 1 - \sum_{j=1}^{I} P_{S \to j} \qquad (8.46)$$

These probabilities always satisfy (8.41) whatever be the size of the considered cell. This was not the case in general for the $P_{i \to j}$. The quantity $\tilde{P}_{i \to j}$ can be interpreted as the probability that a neutron emitted in zone i will have its first collision in zone j of an arbitrary cell. This difference from the preceding definition is due to the coupling of a large number of cells.

The preceding demonstration has a certain arbitrary aspect related to the choice of the angular distributions of the entering neutrons. Fortunately, the quantities $P_{S \to j}$ do not depend much on the hypotheses made and generally one supposes that the entering angular flux is isotropic, which considerably simplifies the calculations but leads to sufficiently accurate results. In these conditions, one can show that one has [9](p.183):

$$P_{S \to j} = \frac{4}{S} V_j \Sigma_{t,j} P_{j \to S} \tag{8.47}$$

whence one deduces that the reciprocity theory (8.40) applies also to the probabilities $\tilde{P}_{i \to j}$.

From all that has preceded, it follows that only the quantities $P_{i \to j}$ (for the isolated cell) must be calculated and even there we can restrict ourselves to $i \leqq j$ (8.40). As a consequence the probabilities $\check{P}_{i \to j}$ can be deduced from the preceding identities.

For a cell made up of two zones: the fuel (c) and the moderator (m), it suffices to calculate in the first place the three quantities P_{cc}, P_{cs} and P_{ms} which are the easiest to obtain. Next, we put j = c or m in (8.47), and we can deduce P_{sc} and P_{sm}, whence, with the help of (8.45):

$$\tilde{P}_{cc} = P_{cc} + \frac{P_{cs} \cdot P_{sc}}{1 - P_{ss}} = P_{cc} + (P_{cs})^2 \frac{V_c \Sigma_{t,c}}{V_c \Sigma_{t,c} P_{cs} + V_m \Sigma_{t,m} P_{ms}} \tag{8.48}$$

Finally, the identities (8.40) and (8.41) when applied to $\tilde{P}$ give us $\check{P}_{c,m}$, $\tilde{P}_{mc}$ and $\check{P}_{mm}$.

In numerous problems (§8.4.1) the quantity of moderators is such that the neutrons emitted by the fuel have little chance of leaving the cell ($P_{cs} \cong 0$). In these conditions $\check{P}_{cc} \cong P_{cc}$, and the latter quantity only depends, as we have seen, on the product $(\emptyset \cdot \Sigma_{t,c})$.

In contrast, for very closely spaced lattices, like those of light water reactors, one cannot avoid calculating the probabilities P_{cs} and P_{ms}. The quantities $\tilde{P}_{i \to j}$ (i,j = c or m) then depend on $\Sigma_{t,c}, \Sigma_{t,m}$ and on the cell geometry.

An interesting limiting case exists. If the lattice is so tightly spaced that the flux does not vary in the cell (its dimensions are small compared to the mean free path λ_t), the probabilities $\check{P}_{i \to j}$ must be equal to the number of collisions in zone j divided by the number of collisions in the entire cell, or:

$$\check{P}_{i \to j} = \frac{V_j \Sigma_{t,j} \bar{\Phi}_j}{\sum_i V_i \Sigma_{t,i} \bar{\Phi}_i} = \frac{V_j \Sigma_{t,j}}{\sum_i V_i \Sigma_{t,i}} \tag{8.49}$$

since $\bar{\Phi}_j = \bar{\Phi}_i$ by hypothesis.

This result is independent of i, since the place of emission is not important in such a system. Using these expressions, the system (8.38), first written out in terms of $\tilde{P}_{i \to j}$, gives us the value of the flux:

$$\bar{\Phi} = \bar{\Phi}_j = \left[\sum_i V_i \bar{e}_i\right] \cdot \left[\sum_i V_i \bar{\Sigma}_{t,i}\right]^{-1}$$

Let us call V the volume of the cell ($V = \sum_i V_i$) and let us put:

$$\bar{e} = \sum_i \frac{V_i}{V} \bar{e}_i \qquad \text{and} \qquad \bar{\Sigma}_t = \sum_i \frac{V_i}{V} \Sigma_{t,i}$$

we then get for this limiting case:

$$\bar{\Phi} = \frac{\bar{e}}{\bar{\Sigma}_t}$$

or since

$$\bar{e} = \bar{Q} + \bar{\Sigma}_s \bar{\Phi}$$

$$\bar{\Phi} = \frac{\bar{Q}}{\bar{\Sigma}_t - \bar{\Sigma}_s}$$

This is the expected result for infinite homogeneous media (4.26) and the homogenization procedure is that indicated in subsec. 5.1.4.

8.2.4 Fuel Utilization Factor

The preceding theory applies directly to the calculation of the thermal utilization factor f_t. We can assume that the thermal neutrons belong to an energy group for which the absorption and scattering cross sections are well defined for each of the materials belonging to the cell considered. We can thus obtain the average flux in each zone i of this cell by solving the system of equations (8.38). Considering for simplicity a cylindrical geometry (annular zones, cf. Fig. 8.9), the probabilities $P_{i \to j}$ can easily be obtained by numerical methods. Since the cells are not isolated, it is necessary to modify the probabilities $P_{i \to j}$ to take account of the fact that the net currents vanish at their periphery (not the entering currents)(§8.2.3).

The results depend of course on the source densities $\bar{Q}_i$ which must here be identified with the slowing down sources $q_i(E_t^*)$ taken at the upper limit $E = E_t^*$ of the thermal group (§4.5.4). We usually put $q_i = 0$ in the fuel since the latter has only a very weak moderating power ($\xi \cong 0$).

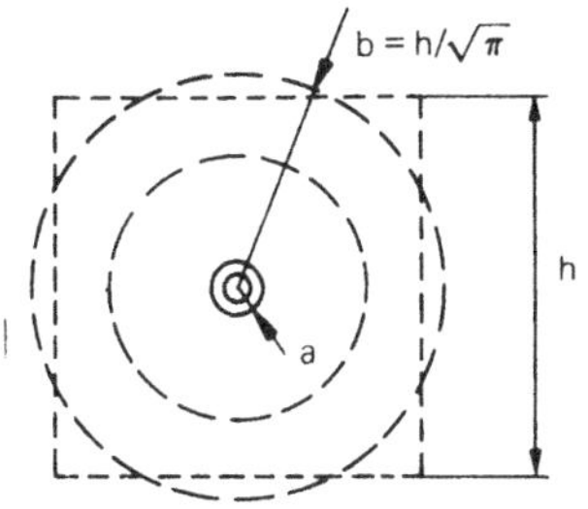

FIGURE 8.9. Sketch of a cylindrical cell.

Once the fluxes $\bar{\Phi}_i$ are known, we can deduce the absorption rates per zone ($V_i \, \Sigma_{a,i} \, \bar{\Phi}_i$) which enable us to calculate the average macroscopic absorption cross section $\bar{\Sigma}_a$ of the cell as well as the thermal utilization factor f_t:

$$\left.\begin{aligned} \bar{\Sigma}_a &= \sum_i \Sigma_{a,i} \, V_i \, \bar{\Phi}_i / V\bar{\Phi} = \sum_i \bar{N}_i \, \sigma_{a,i} \, \bar{\Phi}_i / \bar{\Phi} \\ f_t &= \frac{\Sigma_{a,c} \, V_c \, \bar{\Phi}_c}{\sum_i \Sigma_{a,i} \, V_i \, \bar{\Phi}_i} = \frac{\bar{N}_c \, \sigma_{a,c}}{\bar{N}_c \, \sigma_{a,c} + \sum_{i \neq c} \bar{N}_i \, \sigma_{a,i} \dfrac{\bar{\Phi}_i}{\bar{\Phi}_c}} \end{aligned}\right\} \quad (8.50)$$

where the index c corresponds to the fuel, the quantities $\bar{N}_i$ to the number of nuclei of type i per unit volume of the core (§5.1.4) and $\bar{\Phi}$ to the average flux in the cell.

For a system comprising three different kinds of zones: fuel (c), cladding (g) and moderator (m) (Fig. 8.9), we get back the homogenization rule (4.1) and expression (4.61) up to the factors $\bar{\Phi}_i/\bar{\Phi}_c$ and $\bar{\Phi}_i/\bar{\Phi}$. The latter (> 1) express the decrease of flux in the fuel due to the large absorption taking place. This diminution predicted by diffusion theory (§4.3.6) is obtained here with greater accuracy starting from equations (8.38), but the calculations can no longer be done "by hand." In order to obtain greater accuracy, we can subdivide the fuel and the moderator, the number of zones now being larger than the number of materials. We thus get rid of the hypothesis of uniform flux per zone which is at the base of equation (8.38). For light-water reactor cells this refinement is hardly necessary, so closely spaced are the lattices; but for heavy water reactors this procedure becomes indispensable, since the flux can increase by a factor of two , going from the fuel toward the periphery of the cell.

Numerous codes have been set up according to this principle. For more complex cells (two dimensions), the probabilities are obtained in an approximate fashion [52]. In a general way, the formalism (8.38) is often used in the preparation codes of multigroup cross sections relative to the reactor core, which must be made homogeneous in one way or another (§4.5.9) and the study of resonances in heterogeneous media gives another example of its application (Sec. 8.4).

8.3 SLOWING DOWN OF NEUTRONS IN A HOMOGENEOUS MEDIUM

8.3.1 Introduction

In this section as well as the following one, we will give some theoretical considerations to justify some of the demonstrations or conclusions presented in Sec. 4.4, whose bases were sometimes open to question. Subsections 8.3.4 and 8.4.1 lead in particular to results of great practical importance since they are used in preparation codes for multigroup cross sections (Sec. 9.1).

8.3.2 The Placzek Transient

Consider a homogeneous nonabsorbing medium fed by fission neutrons from a uniform source Q_f. The slowing down source q(E) is thus constant for every energy $E < E_s$ where E_s is the lower limit of the fission spectrum (§4.4.4). According to equation (4.39), we can write:

$$q(E) = \int_E^{E/\alpha} \frac{E-\alpha E'}{(1-\alpha)E'} \Sigma_s(E')\Phi(E')dE' = Q_f = \text{const.}$$

Putting:

$$\Sigma_s(E)\Phi(E) = \frac{Q_f}{\xi E} G(E) \tag{8.51}$$

the preceding equation becomes:

$$(1-\alpha)\xi = \int_{E}^{E/\alpha} \frac{E-\alpha E'}{E'^2} G(E')dE' \qquad (8.52)$$

where ξ and α are given by the expressions (4.31) and (4.35). In all problems of slowing down, it is convenient to introduce the notion of lethargy, defined as follows:

$$u = \ln\left(\frac{E_0}{E}\right) \qquad (8.53)$$

where E_0 is a reference energy higher than E_s. Introducing this new variable (8.52) becomes:

$$(1-\alpha)\xi = \int_{u-\gamma}^{u} [\exp(u'-u)-\alpha]\, G(u')du' \qquad (8.54)$$

with

$$\gamma = \ln\left(\frac{1}{\alpha}\right) = \frac{1-\alpha}{\alpha}(1-\xi) \qquad (8.55)$$

The solution already proposed for the spectra $\Phi(E)$ (§4.4.4) corresponds to $G = 1$ as can be seen by comparing expressions (8.51) and (4.46). In fact $G(u) = 1$ satisfies (8.54), but we cannot claim that we have the complete solution of the the problem.

Let us consider the case where the neutrons are all emitted at energy E_0 (the fission spectrum reduces to a single energy $E_0 = E_s \cong 2\text{MeV}$). The neutron flux and hence the function $G(E)$ thus vanish for $E > E_0$ or $u < 0$. The value $u = 0$ is thus going to play an important role, so it is natural to make it appear in (8.54) by writing:

$$(1-\alpha)\xi = \int_{0}^{u} [\exp(u'-u)-\alpha]\, G(u')du'$$

$$- \int_{0}^{u-\gamma} \alpha[\exp(u'-(u-\gamma))-1]\, G(u')du'$$

For the reasons which follow, we have made explicit in the second integral the variable $(u-\gamma)$ and put $\exp(-\gamma) = \alpha$ (8.55). In this form the last equation involves two convolution products, that is [16]:

$$(1-\alpha)\xi = \big|[\exp(-x)-\alpha] * G(x)\big|_{x=u} - \alpha\big|[\exp(-x)-1] * G(x)\big|_{x=u-\gamma} \qquad (8.56)$$

Let us apply a Laplace transform to (8.56). We get:

$$(1-\alpha)\frac{\xi}{s} = \left[\left(\frac{1}{s+1} - \frac{\alpha}{s}\right) - \alpha\left(\frac{1}{s+1} - \frac{1}{s}\right)\exp(-s\gamma)\right]\tilde{G}(s)$$

or finally:

$$\tilde{G}(s) = \frac{\xi(s+1)}{s + \frac{\alpha}{1-\alpha}\left[\exp(-s\gamma) - 1\right]} \tag{8.57}$$

The transform $\tilde{G}(s)$ of the desired function $G(u)$ is thus explicitly known. In the preceding we used the following "dictionary" [16]:

$$\left.\begin{array}{l} \tilde{F}_i(s)\cdot\tilde{F}_2(s) \;[\; f_1(u)*f_2(u) \\ \tilde{F}(s+a) \;[\; \exp(-au)f(u) \\ \tilde{F}(s)\exp(-\lambda s) \;[\; f(u-\lambda) \\ \frac{1}{s^{n+1}} \;[\; \frac{u^n}{n!} \end{array}\right\} \tag{8.58}$$

with the convention $f(x) = 0$ if $x < 0$.

Before going further, we can obtain from (8.57) an important result. In effect, expanding $\exp(-s\gamma)$ in s, we find that $|s\tilde{G}(s)|_{s\to 0} = 1$. However by a property of the Laplace transform [16], this limit is identical to $|G(u)|_{u\to\infty}$, whence we obtain the following conclusion:

For large values of u, and hence for energies E much smaller than E_0 (8.53), the function G(E) tends to unity and the results of subsec. 4.4.4 are correct.

Before inverting expression (8.57), we will make explicit $s - \alpha/(1-\alpha)$, which amounts to putting:

$$\tilde{G}(s) = \tilde{H}\left(s - \frac{\alpha}{1-\alpha}\right)$$

or using the second expression of the dictionary (8.58):

$$G(u) = \exp\left(\frac{\alpha}{1-\alpha}u\right)H(u) \tag{8.59}$$

Starting from (8.57), a simple calculation leads to:

$$\tilde{H}(s) = \xi\left(1 + \frac{1}{(1-\alpha)s}\right)\left(1 + \frac{B}{s}\exp(-\gamma s)\right)^{-1} \tag{8.60}$$

with:

$$B = \frac{\alpha}{1-\alpha} \exp\left(-\frac{\alpha\gamma}{1-\alpha}\right) = \frac{1}{1-\alpha}\,\alpha^{1/(1-\alpha)} \tag{8.61}$$

There only remains for us to pass from $\tilde{H}(s)$ to $H(u)$. To this end, we expand in series the second factor of (8.60) and after rearranging the terms in $1/s$, we obtain:

$$\tilde{H}(s) = \xi\left[1 + \frac{1}{(1-\alpha)s} + \sum_{n=1}^{\infty} (-1)^n B^n \left(\frac{1}{s^n} + \frac{1}{(1-\alpha)s^{n+1}}\right)\exp(-n\gamma s)\right]$$

The last two expressions of the dictionary (8.58) enable us to invert each of the terms of the preceding series:

$$H(u) = \xi\left[\delta(u) + \frac{1}{1-\alpha} + \sum_{n=1} (-1)^n B^n \left(1 + \frac{u-n\gamma}{(1-\alpha)n}\right)\frac{(u-n\gamma)^{n-1}}{(n-1)!}\right] \tag{8.62}$$

The translation formula implies that $(u - n\gamma)$ is positive, otherwise the function associated to this argument would vanish. The condition $u > n\gamma$ amounts to truncating the preceding series since for a given value of the energy and hence of u, n could not exceed a certain value. Let us suppose that we seek $H(u)$ in the interval $(r-1)\gamma \leq u \leq r\gamma$ where r is an integer. The preceding condition leads to $n < (r-1)$. In this interval the sum appearing in (8.62) stops at the term $n = r - 1$.

We thus have in the first few intervals:

$$\frac{H_1(u)}{\xi} = \delta(u) + \frac{1}{1-\alpha} \qquad u < \gamma$$

$$\frac{H_2(u)}{\xi} = \frac{1}{1-\alpha} - B\left(1 + \frac{u-\gamma}{1-\alpha}\right) \qquad \gamma < u \leq 2\gamma$$

$$\frac{H_3(u)}{\xi} = H_2(u) + B^2\left(1 + \frac{u-2\gamma}{2(1-\alpha)}\right)(u-2\gamma) \qquad 2\gamma \leq u \leq 3\gamma$$

We immediately obtain $G(u)$ with the help of (8.59) and we pass to the energy variable by using the definition of u (8.53).

In the past, the preceding expressions were obtained in a more direct fashion, at least for the first few lethargy intervals. The method presented here as the advantage of giving <u>explicitly</u> the solution for an arbitrary value of u (8.62).

For u = 0 the preceding solution shows a divergence because of the presence of the function $\delta(u)$. In fact, the first term of (8.62) corresponds to neutrons which have suffered no collision, that is to say, which emanate directly from the source. But the latter is confined in an infinitely narrow lethargy interval around u = 0. Since by hypothesis the neutrons are emitted at E_0, there corresponds a source density (§4.4.3) of the type $\delta(E - E_0)$ or $\delta(u)$. In the realistic case the delta function would be replaced by a fission spectrum.

The results obtained for various values of A are shown in Fig. 8.10. We see that for energies $E \ll E_0$, the function G(E) is unity. In addition, for $E = \alpha E_0$, a discontinuity appears (cf. equations (8.62) for $u = \gamma$) which is explained by the fact that just below αE_0 the neutrons have undergone at least two collisions, which is not the case just above. At $\alpha^2 E_0 (u = 2\gamma)$ a discontinuity in the derivatives remains, but starting from the third interval $(\alpha^3 E_0 < E < \alpha^2 E_0)$ or $(2\gamma < u < 3\gamma)$, G(E) attains its asymptotic value G = 1.

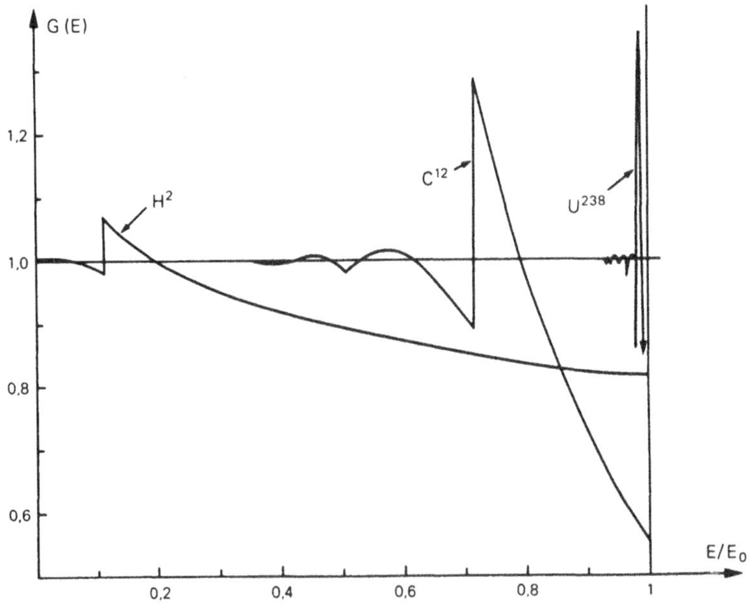

FIGURE 8.10. The Placzek transient.

This transient first shown by Placzek [53] is hardly important in practice and disappears totally for hydrogen ($A = 1$, $\alpha = 0$, $\gamma = \infty$). For deuterium($A = 2$), it persists over nearly a decade, but its amplitude is small. For heavy nuclei, on the other hand, the oscillations are larger, but confined to a region very close to the source. Finally, if we recall that the fission neutrons are not mono-energetic but distributed according to the fission spectrum, we see that the problem which we have just treated is both somewhat academic and very serious from the point of view of the extent of the transient.

8.3.3 The Case of Absorbing Hydrogenated Materials

We assume that only hydrogen is responsable for slowing down ($A = 1, \alpha = 0$), whereas absorption is due to heavy nuclei ($A >> 1$, $\alpha \cong 1$). Let us consider energies $E < E_s$ so that the source density $Q(E)$ vanishes. In accordance with (4.39) and (4.43):

$$q(E) = E \int_E^\infty \Sigma_s(E') \frac{\Phi(E')}{E'} dE'$$

$$\Sigma_a(E) \Phi(E) = \frac{dq}{dE}$$

The fact that the upper limit of the preceding integral is infinite (and not equal to E/α as in the general case) will enable us to solve this problem analytically without any restriction.

To this end, let us differentiate the first equation and eliminate dq/dE. We get:

$$(\Sigma_s(E) + \Sigma_a(E)) \Phi(E) = \int_E^\infty \Sigma_s(E') \Phi(E') \frac{dE'}{E'}$$

We introduce the collision rate density:

$$R_t(E) = \Sigma_t(E) \Phi(E) = [\Sigma_s(E) + \Sigma_a(E)] \Phi(E) \qquad (8.63)$$

The preceding integral equation becomes:

$$R_t(E) = \int_E^\infty \left[1 - \frac{\Sigma_a(E')}{\Sigma_t(E')}\right] R_t(E') \frac{dE'}{E'}$$

and after differentiating with respect to E:

$$\frac{dR_t}{dE} = \left[\frac{\Sigma_a(E)}{\Sigma_t(E)} - 1\right] \frac{R_t(E)}{E}$$

This equation with separated variables is easily integrated. We get:

$$\Sigma_t(E)\ \Phi(E) = R_t(E) = R_t(E_s)\ \frac{E_s}{E} \exp\left[-\int_E^{E_s} \frac{\Sigma_a(E')}{\Sigma_t(E')} \frac{dE'}{E'}\right]$$

In the absence of absorption($\Sigma_a = 0$), the exponential factor is unity. Hence

$$p(E) = \exp\left[-\int_E^{E_s} \frac{\Sigma_a(E')}{\Sigma_t(E')} \frac{dE'}{E'}\right] \tag{8.64}$$

represents the probability that a neutron escapes absorption during the course of slowing down. This expression is identical to the one (4.53) presented as being quite general in subsec. 4.4.4. In effect, since we are considering hydrogen, we are led to put $\xi = 1$ (Table 4.21) in equation (4.53). Let us note that here it has not been necessary to suppose that absorption was small in order to arrive at the expected result.

8.3.4 Resonances

Very locally, cross sections may depend strongly on energy. Thus, the functions $\sigma_a(E)$ and $\sigma_s(E)$ have very large values for the resonance energies E_R (§4.4.5).

Given a particular resonance (Fig. 8.11), the absorption cross sections almost vanish outside of the energy interval ($E_R - \Delta/2, E_R + \Delta/2$) and in this domain the flux is given by expression (4.46) in which the slowing down source q(E) is constant.

We propose here to determine the flux inside the resonance, in other words the place where the reasoning of subsec. 4.4.4 ceases to be valid. Since resonances are characteristic of fertile matter, we will first make explicit the two principal components of a reactor: the fuel and the moderator. Equation (4.49) can be written:

$$\Sigma_a(E)\ \Phi(E) = \frac{dq}{dE} = \frac{dq_c}{dE} + \frac{dq_m}{dE} \tag{8.65}$$

where q_c and q_m are the slowing down sources associated to the fuel and to the moderator (4.39). Differentiation of these quantities with respect to E leads for each of these materials to the identity (4.41) so that the preceding equation becomes:

$$\Sigma_t(E)\Phi(E) = \int_E^{E/\alpha_c} \frac{\Sigma_{s,c}(E')\Phi(E')}{(1-\alpha_c)E'}\, dE' + \int_E^{E/\alpha_m} \frac{\Sigma_m \Phi(E')}{(1-\alpha_m)E'}\, dE' \qquad (8.66)$$

where $\Sigma_t(E) = \Sigma_a(E) + \Sigma_{s,c}(E) + \Sigma_m$ represents the total macroscopic cross section of the fuel-moderator mixture. Since the moderator is not absorbing at these energies ($\Sigma_{a,m} = 0$), we can omit in its case the index s: ($\Sigma_{s,m} = \Sigma_{t,m} = \Sigma_m$).

Because of their very different atomic masses ($A_c >> A_m$) the parameters α (4.31) of the fuel and of the moderator are such that:

$$\alpha_c \ (\cong 1) > \alpha_m$$

whence the low efficiency of the fuel from the point of view of the moderation of neutrons.

Equation (8.66) can be solved numerically and many numerical codes exist [54] which give at each point the flux $\Phi(E)$ in each resonance (about thirty points in the band $E_R - \Delta/2 < E < E_R + \Delta/2$). If we recall that a fertile isotope such as uranium U^{238} has several hundred resonances, we see how much calculation is entailed in such an approach.

Luckily, in a large number of cases, one can calculate analytically by making the "narrow resonance" approximation. This approximation is based on the observation that the integration intervals (E, E/α) appearing in (8.66) are generally large compared to the width Δ of the resonances. This is always true for the moderator ($\alpha_m < 1$) but more questionable for the fuel, since $\alpha_c \cong 1$.

Leaving aside this last reservation, we do not make a great mistake in using in the integrals on the righthand side of (8.66) the expression for the flux $\Phi(E')$ given by (4.48), since the larger part of the integration interval corresponds to values of the energy E' for which absorption has not yet made itself felt (Fig. 8.11).

We thus put:

$$\Phi(E') = \frac{q(E_1)}{\bar{\xi}\Sigma_s(E')E'}$$

where

$$\Sigma_s(E') = \Sigma_{s,c}(E') + \Sigma_m$$

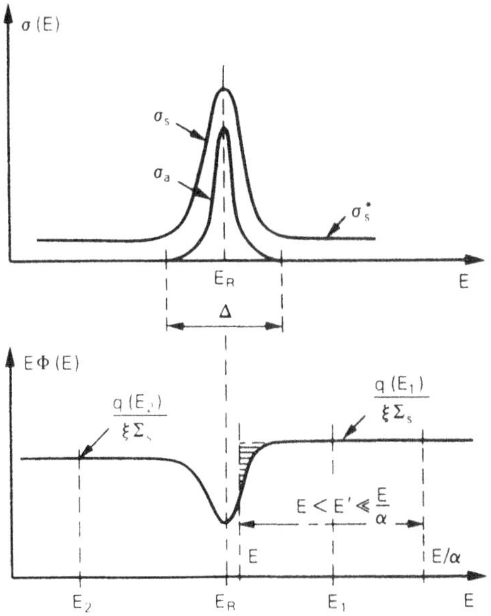

FIGURE 8.11.

Equation (8.66) thus becomes:

$$\Sigma_t(E)\Phi(E) = \frac{q(E_1)}{\bar{\xi}} \left(\int_E^{E/\alpha_c} \frac{\Sigma_{s,c}(E')}{\Sigma_s(E')} \frac{dE'}{(1-\alpha_c)E'^2} + \int_E^{E/\alpha_m} \frac{\Sigma_m}{\Sigma_s(E')(1-\alpha_m)E'^2} \right)$$

Finally noting that outside of the resonances the scattering cross sections vary little with the energy, we get:

$$\Phi(E) = \frac{q(E_1)}{\bar{\xi} E \Sigma_t(E)} \qquad (8.67)$$

The energy E_1 can be chosen arbitrarily above the resonance (Fig. 8.11) since in this zone the slowing down source q(E) is constant. Of course we should not go out too far, inasmuch as other resonances appear above the resonance being studied.

Formula (8.67) is used systematically in most of the codes which evaluate multigroup cross sections starting from fundamental nuclear data. This evaluation requires a knowledge of "fine spectra" $\Phi(E)$ in the interior of groups whose widths are much larger than those of the resonances (§9.1.3). If the resonances are absent ($\Sigma_t(E) \cong$ constant), equation (8.67) leads to a weighting in $1/E$ (4.90); in the opposite case the fluxes are very depressed at the level of the resonances, since $\Sigma_t(E)$ has a very large value for $E \cong E_R$ (Fig. 8.11).

Let us now go on to determine the escape probability p_R associated to the considered resonance. We shall integrate equation (8.65) from $E_2 \ll E_R - \Delta/2$ to $E_1 \gg E_R + \Delta/2$ (Fig. 8.11). We get:

$$q(E_1) - q(E_2) = \int_{E_2}^{E_1} \Sigma_a(E)\, \Phi\, (E)\, dE$$

This variation of the slowing down source is only due to absorptions which take place at the level of the resonance. In this energy domain the flux $\Phi(E)$ is given by (8.67), whence:

$$q(E_1) - q(E_2) = \frac{q(E_1)}{\bar{\xi}} \int_{E_2}^{E_1} \frac{\Sigma_a(E)}{\Sigma_t(E)} \frac{dE}{E}$$

By definition the desired probability p_R can be written:

$$p_R = \frac{q(E_2)}{q(E_1)} = 1 - \frac{1}{\bar{\xi}} \int_{E_2}^{E_1} \frac{\Sigma_a(E)}{\Sigma_t(E)} \frac{dE}{E}$$

or

$$p_R = \exp\left(- \frac{1}{\bar{\xi}} \int_{E_2}^{E_1} \frac{\Sigma_a(E)}{\Sigma_t(E)} \frac{dE}{E} \right) \qquad (8.68)$$

This quantity tends to unity when absorptions disappear ($\Sigma_a \to 0$).

The second expression results from the fact that the integral taken over energy is small. We have:

$$I = \int_{E_2}^{E_1} \frac{\Sigma_a(E)}{\Sigma_t(E)} \frac{dE}{E} = \int_{E_R-\frac{\Delta}{2}}^{E_R+\frac{\Delta}{2}} \frac{\Sigma_a(E)}{\Sigma_t(E)} \frac{dE}{E} < \int_{E_R+\frac{\Delta}{2}}^{E_R+\frac{\Delta}{2}} \frac{dE}{E}$$

since even when the energies are close to E_R, the ratio Σ_a/Σ_t is always smaller than one, whereas Σ_a and Σ_t can have very large values. We thus have

$$I < \ln \left(\frac{E_R + \frac{\Delta}{2}}{E_R - \frac{\Delta}{2}} \right) \cong \frac{\Delta}{E_R}$$

or

$$\frac{I}{\bar{\xi}} < \frac{\Delta}{\bar{\xi} E_R}$$

The resonances being narrow, this upper bound is always quite small, so that:

$$\exp\left(-\frac{I}{\bar{\xi}}\right) \cong 1 - \frac{I}{\bar{\xi}}$$

We finally obtain the resonance escape probability for the entire envisageable energy domain by multiplying all the probabilities defined by (8.68) for each resonance. We are again led to expression (4.53) in which E_s plays the role of E_1 for the first resonance encountered by a neutron in the course of slowing down and E_t^* corresponds to E_2 for the last resonance.

8.4 SLOWING DOWN OF NEUTRONS IN A HETEROGENEOUS MEDIUM

8.4.1 Resonances and an Equivalence Theorem

The core of a reactor is not homogeneous, but on the contrary is made up of fuel rods regularly spaced in a moderator (Sec. 5.1). Resonance absorption takes place exclusively in these rods, whereas the slowing down of neutrons comes essentially from the moderator outside. We have seen in subsec. 4.3.6 that a localized absorber brings about a decrease in flux (Fig. 4.14) which is all the greater as the absorption cross section is larger. Here the cross sections can be very large at the level of resonances, so that one can expect very strong depressions (a factor of 100 for example cannot be excluded). In these conditions, the results of the preceding subsection are not "a priori" applicable to this case.

In principle we must solve a problem which involves both space and energy, and thus must determine the flux distributions $\Phi(\vec{r}, E)$ which vary very rapidly for these two variables. The absorptions are large and the dimensions of the system small, since what we are studying is a reactor cell (Sec. 5.1), and thus diffusion theory is not applicable. In contrast, the formalism based on collision probabilities (§8.2.2) here has an application which will lead us to particularly simple results.

For a two-zone system, the first equation (8.38) can be written ($j = c$ and $i = c$ or m):

$$\left.\begin{aligned} V_c \Sigma_{t,c}(E)\bar{\Phi}_c(E) &= V_c \left(\bar{Q}_c(E) + \frac{d\bar{q}_c}{dE} + \Sigma_{s,c}(E)\ \bar{\Phi}_c(E) \right) P_{cc}(E) \\ &+ V_m \left(\bar{Q}_m(E) + \frac{d\bar{q}_m}{dE} + \Sigma_m\ \bar{\Phi}_m(E) \right) P_{mc}(E) \end{aligned}\right\} \quad (8.69)$$

where V_c and V_m represent respectively the volumes of the fuel and of the moderator. The preceding equation applies to neutrons of energies between E and E+dE. It is for this reason that the source densities must include terms in dq/dE as was shown during the demonstration of equation (4.40) (§4.4.3).

We could have written an analogous equation for the moderator ($j = m$). In what follows, such an equation would not be of much interest, given the approximations that will be made. Nevertheless, more elaborate theories would appeal to it or even to a certain number of equations of the type (8.69) if we wanted to know in detail the spatial distributions of the flux. Let us not forget that equations (8.39) assume that in each zone the flux and the sources are uniform, which implies a sufficient subdivision of the considered system.

For the resonance problem which interests us here, it suffices to know the average value of the flux $\bar{\Phi}_c(E)$ in the fuel.

The "true" sources vanish; in the moderator this is evident, since no neutrons can be created there, and in the fuel the fission neutrons are emitted above the energy E_s, the upper limit of the energy domain considered here. Finally, using the expression of dq/dE given by (4.41), we arrive at the relation:

$$V_c \Sigma_{t,c}(E)\bar{\Phi}_c(E) = P_{cc}(E)V_c \int_E^{E/\alpha_c} \frac{\Sigma_{s,c}(E')\bar{\Phi}_c(E')}{(1-\alpha_c)E'} dE' + P_{mc}(E)V_m \int_E^{E/\alpha_m} \frac{\Sigma_m \bar{\Phi}_m(E')}{(1-\alpha_m)E'} dE' \tag{8.70}$$

Equation (8.70) plays the same role for the fuel as equation (8.66) for a homogeneous mixture.

We note that the collision probabilities depend on the energy through the total cross sections $\Sigma_t(E)$ (8.39). Let us place ourselves in the framework of the narrow resonance approximation discussed in the preceding subsection. We are led to write (for $E' > E_R + \Delta/2$):

$$\bar{\Phi}_c(E') = \bar{\Phi}_m(E') = \frac{\bar{q}(E_1)}{\bar{\xi}\, \bar{\Sigma}_s(E_1)E'}$$

where E_1 is still an arbitrary energy (Fig. 8.11). Expression (4.48) is applicable since above the considered resonance the flux in the fuel is no longer depressed ($\bar{\Phi}_c = \bar{\Phi}_m$). Everything takes place as if one was in the presence of a homogeneous nonabsorbing medium in which the slowing down sources $\bar{q}$ and the macroscopic cross sections $\bar{\Sigma}_s$ were obtained by weighting in volume the quantities $\bar{q}_c$, $\bar{q}_m$ and $\Sigma_{s,c}$, $\Sigma_{s,m}$ (§5.1.4). Finally, as in the preceding, we will suppose that the scattering cross sections are independent of the energy outside of the resonance.

In these conditions, equation (8.70) becomes:

$$V_c E\Sigma_{t,c}(E)\bar{\Phi}_c(E) = \frac{\bar{q}(E_1)}{\bar{\xi}\, \bar{\Sigma}_s(E_1)} \left[V_c \Sigma_{s,c}(E_1)P_{cc}(E) + V_m \Sigma_m P_{mc}(E) \right] \tag{8.71}$$

where $\Sigma_{s,c}(E_1)$ is the non-resonant scattering cross section of the fuel (which remains beyond the resonance).

Since the moderator is nonabsorbing, Σ_m also represents its total cross section, whence, applying the reciprocity theorem of probabilities (8.40):

$$V_m \Sigma_m P_{mc}(E) = V_c \Sigma_{t,c}(E) P_{cm}(E)$$

Finally, if the dimensions of the moderator are such that a neutron emitted in the fuel has little chance of leaving the system, we can apply (8.41) which here reduces to:

$$P_{cc} + P_{cm} = 1$$

Employing these last two relations in (8.71) leads to the relation:

$$E\,\Sigma_{t,c}(E)\bar{\Phi}_c(E) = \frac{\bar{q}(E_1)}{\bar{\xi}\,\bar{\Sigma}_s(E_1)}\left[\Sigma_{s,c}(E_1)P_{cc}(E) + \Sigma_{t,c}(E)[1 - P_{cc}(E)]\right] \tag{8.72}$$

which only involves the probability $P_{c,c}(E)$ that a neutron emitted in the fuel undergoes its first collision in the fuel. For a cylindrical rod of diameter $\emptyset$, this probability only involves the "optical diameter" $x = \emptyset\Sigma_{t,c}(E)$ insofar as the cells have sufficiently large dimensions; otherwise it would be necessary to call upon the probabilities $\dot{P}_{cc}$ (§8.2.3).

We are now going to try to put (8.72) in a form close to that of expression (8.67) obtained in the case of homogeneous systems (§8.3.4).

By putting:

$$N_c\,\sigma_e(E) = \Sigma_e(E) = \Sigma_{t,c}(E)\,\frac{1 - P_{cc}(E)}{P_{cc}(E)} \tag{8.73}$$

we find that the neutron spectrum in the fuel is given by (cf. equation (8.72)):

$$\bar{\Phi}_c(E) = \frac{\bar{q}(E_1)}{\bar{\xi}\,\bar{\Sigma}_s(E_1)}\,\frac{\Sigma_{s,c}(E_1) + \Sigma_e(E)}{\Sigma_{t,c}(E) + \Sigma_e(E)}\,\frac{1}{E}$$

Taking up the reasoning of the preceding subsection, we calculate the resonance escape probability p, at first for a single resonance, and then for the totality of resonances, and we arrive without difficulty at the desired result:

$$p = \exp\left[-\frac{1}{\bar{\xi}\,\bar{\Sigma}_s(E_1)}\int_{E_t^*}^{E_s} \bar{\Sigma}_a(E)\,\frac{\Sigma_{s,c}(E_1) + \Sigma_e(E)}{\Sigma_{t,c}(E) + \Sigma_e(E)}\,\frac{dE}{E}\right] \tag{8.74}$$

where the absorption cross section $\bar{\Sigma}_a(E)$ is relative to the homogenized medium.

We shall introduce the microscopic cross sections:

$$\bar{\Sigma}_a(E) = \bar{N}_c \, \sigma_{a,c}(E)$$

$$\Sigma_{t,c}(E) = N_c(\sigma_{a,c}(E) + \sigma_{s,c}(E) + \sigma^*_{s,c})$$

$$\bar{\Sigma}_s(E_1) = \bar{N}_c \, \sigma^*_{s,c} + \bar{N}_m \, \sigma_m$$

We observe that expression (8.74) is formally identical to the pair of equations (4.55) and (4.56) obtained for homogeneous media. Still, the atomic densities $\bar{N}_i$ are here equal to the number of type i nuclei present in the cell divided by its volume (and not by the volume of the material i). In addition, the microscopic dilution cross section σ_e is "a priori" a function of energy (8.73). In fact, one can observe that this parameter is almost constant, whereas $\Sigma_t(E)$ varies strongly with energy.

Let us consider a fuel rod of diameter $\emptyset$ and rewrite (8.73) in the form:

$$\sigma_e(E) = \frac{1}{N_c \emptyset} \cdot b\,[\emptyset \Sigma_{t,c}(E)] \qquad (8.75)$$

with

$$b(x) = x \, \frac{1 - P_{cc}(x)}{P_{cc}(x)} \qquad (8.76)$$

For optical diameters going from zero to infinity, and thus for probabilities P_{cc} taking all possible values between zero and one, the quantity b(x) remains remarkably constant. If we consider sufficiently spaced out rods we observe that this quantity varies at most by 50% (cf. equation (8.44)), which is really very little in comparison with the variations of the cross sections of the fertile isotopes, $\sigma_{a,c}(E)$ and $\sigma_{s,c}(E)$ in the vicinity of a resonance. Thus there is no great mistake in replacing b in (8.75) by its average value $\bar{b}$. For uranium U^{238} and the totality of its resonances, $\bar{b} = 1.35$ is an excellent approximation [55]. The law $\sigma_e = \bar{b}/N_c\emptyset$ is identical to the expression (4.58) announced in subsec. 4.4.5. We see that $\sigma_e = \bar{b}/N_c\emptyset$ plays the same role for heterogeneous systems that $\sigma_e = \Sigma_m/N_c$ does for homogeneous systems.

If we calculate once and for all an effective integral (4.56) as a function of σ_e, we do not have to know in advance in what type of problem, homogeneous or heterogeneous, we expect to use it eventually.

We can interpret the preceding formulae by saying that the heterogeneity behaves like a fictitious diluting material of macroscopic cross section $\Sigma_e = \bar{b}/\emptyset$ (or $\bar{b}/\ell$ for other geometries). This very important result is known as the equivalence theorem and $\bar{b}$ is called the Bell factor. This theorem is frequently used in the preparation codes for multigroup cross sections in which the weightings are of the type $1/E\ \Sigma_t(E)$ (§9.1.3) with $\Sigma_t(E) = \Sigma_{t,c}(E) + \Sigma_e = \Sigma_{t,c}(E) + \bar{b}/\emptyset$.

8.4.2 Influence of the Lattice Pitch on the Bell Factor

The conclusions of the preceding subsection were based on the hypothesis that the probability $P_{cc}(x)$ only depends on the optical diameter x of the rod. For closely spaced lattices, this hypothesis is no longer justified and we must introduce the probability $\tilde{P}_{cc}$ which takes account of the finite dimensions of the cells (§8.2.3). Rather than use the "exact" expression (8.48) which necessitates the knowledge of three probabilities, we shall calculate $\tilde{P}_{cc}$ by somewhat simplifying the phenomena. It should be obvious that the effective integrals (4.56) are not very sensitive to errors that might be made in the evaluation of the dilution cross section σ_e.

We first introduce the Dancoff coefficient Γ, which represents the probability that a neutron leaving the considered rod penetrates any other rod without having undergone collisions in the interstitial moderator. In effect, the neutrons which cross from one rod to another after having suffered one or several collisions do not interest us, since there is little chance that they will conserve their initial energy, and thus that they would still be likely to be absorbed by the resonance under study.

The calculation of the coefficient Γ is complicated for it involves exponential attenuation factors relative to the passage of the neutrons in a straight line in the moderator. These calculations can nevertheless be done once and for all and the results tabulated as a function of $\emptyset\Sigma_{t,m}$ and $\emptyset/h$ where h is the lattice pitch and $\Sigma_{t,m}$ the total macroscopic cross section of the moderator. The Dancoff coefficient thus depends virtually not at all on the energy since $\Sigma_{t,m}$ has no resonances. Moreover, since all the rods play the same role, it comes to the same thing to say that Γ represents the reflection coefficient at the surface of a rod for neutrons which would like to escape from it (this coefficient as we have seen is unity at the external boundary of a cell).

We can consequently argue on the basis of a single rod. Let P_{cs} be the probability that a neutron emitted uniformly in a rod exits from it without undergoing collision; P_{sc} the collision probability for an entering neutron and P_{ss} the complementary probability of traversing the rod without collision. (We note that the index s is relative to the surface of the fuel and not to that of the cell, like the index S in subsec. 8.2.3)

We can write:

$$\left.\begin{aligned} &P_{cc} + P_{cs} = 1 \\ &P_{sc} + P_{ss} = 1 \\ &P_{sc} = x\, P_{cs} \end{aligned}\right\} \tag{8.77}$$

The first two relations result from the very definitions, while the third follows from the hypothesis of an isotropic entering angular flux, which leads us to put, following (8.47):

$$\frac{4V_c}{S_c}\,\Sigma_{t,c} = \emptyset\,\Sigma_{t,c} = x$$

We can now calculate $\check{P}_{cc}$ which comprises the following terms:

- P_{cc}: the probability that a neutron emitted in the rod has its first collision in the rod without leaving it.
- $P_{cs}\,\Gamma P_{sc}$: the probability that the neutron undergoes its first collision after being reflected by the surface S_c of the rod.
- $P_{cs}(\Gamma\, P_{ss})\Gamma P_{sc}$: the analogous probability in the case of two reflections.
- etc.

Summing all these terms we obtain:

$$\tilde{P}_{cc} = P_{cc} + \Gamma P_{cs} P_{sc}\,[\,1 + (\Gamma P_{ss}) + (\Gamma P_{ss})^2 + \ldots]$$

Whence, since the above series is convergent ($\Gamma P_{ss} < 1$), we get the expression for the desired probability:

$$\tilde{P}_{cc} = P_{cc} + \frac{\Gamma P_{cs} P_{sc}}{1 - \Gamma P_{ss}} \tag{8.78}$$

Finally, let us eliminate from (8.78) the quantities P_{cs}, P_{sc} and P_{ss}; using the relations (8.77) we get:

$$\tilde{P}_{cc}(x) = \frac{(1 - \Gamma)P_{cc}(x) + \Gamma x\,[1 - P_{cc}(x)]}{(1 - \Gamma) + \Gamma x\,[1 - P_{cc}(x)]}$$

The new probability only depends on the old one and on the Dancoff coefficient which is constant.

We must now calculate b(x) by using $\tilde{P}_{cc}$ and no longer P_{cc} (8.76). We get the new expression:

$$\tilde{b}(x) = x\left(\frac{1}{\tilde{P}_{cc}(x)} - 1\right) = b(x)\,\frac{1 - \Gamma}{1 - \Gamma + \Gamma b(x)}$$

where b(x) is the function $x\,[1 - P_{cc}(x)]/P_{cc}(x)$ analysed earlier. We have already emphasized that it is not very sensitive to large variations of the optical diameter $x = \emptyset\Sigma_{t,c}(E)$ in the region of a resonance. Taking a constant value for b(x) amounts to making the same approximation for $\tilde{b}(x)$. We will thus put:

$$\tilde{b} = \bar{b}\,\frac{1 - \Gamma}{1 + (\bar{b} - 1)\Gamma} \qquad (8.79)$$

with, for example $\bar{b} \cong 1.35$ for uranium U^{238} (§8.4.1).

The new Bell factor depends on the lattice pitch through the Dancoff coefficient and the equivalence theorem remains valid provided we put:

$$\sigma_e = \frac{\tilde{b}}{N_c\emptyset} = \frac{\bar{b}}{N_c\emptyset}\,\frac{1 - \Gamma}{1 + (\bar{b} - 1)\Gamma}$$

We thus see that for widely spaced rods ($\Gamma = 0$) the Bell factor is not modified. In contrast, in the absence of a moderator ($\Gamma = 1$), the dilution cross section σ_e vanishes and the self-shielding in the resonances is maximal (4.56).

As we have seen, the Dancoff factor can be tabulated, but approximate expressions exist which use the preparation codes of multigroup cross sections in which σ_e plays a fundamental role [14]. Let us call moderator opacity the quantity:

$$\gamma_m = \frac{\ell_m \Sigma_{t,m}}{\ell_m \Sigma_{t,m} + 1}$$

where the average string ℓ_m is expressed as a function of the volume of the moderator V_m and of the separation surface of the two media S_c according to the relation: $\ell_m = 4V_m/S_c$ (if the moderator is a liquid and acts as coolant (Sec. 5.1), ℓ_m is then nothing but the hydraulic diameter of the flow).

Taking account of these definitions, the following approximation has been proposed [55]:

$$\Gamma = (1 - \gamma_m)(1 - \gamma_m^4) \qquad (8.80)$$

8.4.3 Slowing Down of High Energy Neutrons

We now consider energies higher than E_s. In this energy domain there are no resonances, but the fuel gives rise to two new phenomena:

- inelastic scattering (§1.5.3)
- fast fissions in the fertile matter (§3.2.3)

As in the preceding subsections we are led to consider a reactor cell, thus a system of small size. If we wanted to know the neutron spectrum in the fuel, we would once again have to base ourselves on a formalism of the type (8.69) with different expressions for Q and dq/E. The corresponding multigroup formalism would lead to the desired solution provided we adopted a sufficiently large number of groups above the energy E_s. However, our purpose here is less ambitious.

We shall consider the simple case where all the neutrons of energy $E > E_s$ constitute a single group. This hypothesis amounts to supposing that the cross sections do not vary much in this energy band. Its validity depends of course on the choice of E_s. The fast fission cross sections being non-vanishing only above a certain threshhold (1.35 MeV for U^{238}), we can identify E_s with this latter (Fig. 8.12). We will make three additional hypotheses:

- the inelastic scattering of a neutron by a heavy nucleus (U^{238}) is accompanied by such a loss of energy that the scattered neutron is lost for the considered group;

- the elastic scattering in the fuel does not entail any slowing down, which does not mean that the corresponding cross section vanishes ($\alpha_c = 1$ but $\sigma_{s,e} \neq 0$);
- there is of course no creation of neutrons in the moderator (no fissile matter) and the only envisageable emissions correspond to elastically scattered neutrons below E_s.

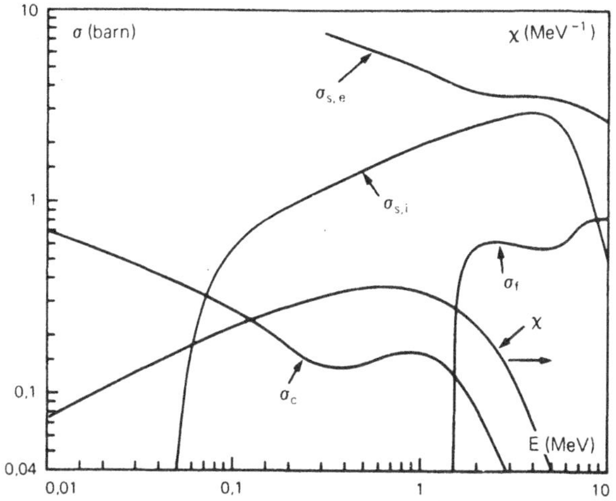

FIGURE 8.12. High energy neutron cross sections for uranium U^{238}.

Let us apply the first equation (8.38) to the fuel. We simply get ($j = c$, $i = c$):

$$V_c \Sigma_{t,c} \overline{\Phi}_c = V_c(\overline{Q}_c + \Sigma_{s,c}\overline{\Phi}_c)\, P_{c,c} \tag{8.81}$$

where the above quantities are independent of the energy (one-group theory). This equation is a particular case of (8.69) resulting from the absence of transfer of neutrons from the moderator to the fuel, at least at these energies (third hypothesis) and from the absence of any elastic slowing down ($q_c = 0$) in the fuel (second hypothesis).

This time $\overline{Q}_c$ does not vanish but is equal to the source of fission neutrons which can be decomposed into two terms:

$$\overline{Q}_c = \chi_s\, (\overline{Q}_{f,t} + \overline{\nu}\Sigma_{f,c}\, \overline{\Phi}_c)$$

The first term (which is preponderant) corresponds to fissions induced in the fissile matter by the slow neutrons ($E < E_s$), and the second to fissions induced by fast neutrons ($E > E_s$) in the fertile matter characterized by the fission cross section $\Sigma_{f,c}$. The first term is thus a datum, while the second involves the unknown fast flux $\bar{\Phi}_c$. The factor (§3.1.3)

$$\chi_s = \int_{E_s}^{\infty} \chi(E)dE$$

indicates finally that only a fraction of the fission neutrons is emitted above E_s (if the energy E_s is chosen sufficiently low, then $\chi_s = 1$).

Since only the fuel is involved, we will leave aside the index c and equation (8.81) can be explicitly written:

$$\Sigma_t \bar{\Phi} = [\chi_s Q_{f,t} + (\Sigma_{s,e} + \chi_s \bar{\nu}\Sigma_f)\bar{\Phi}]P_{cc}$$

that is:

$$\bar{\Phi} = \frac{P_{cc}}{\Sigma_t - (\Sigma_{s,e} + \chi_s \bar{\nu}\Sigma_f)P_{cc}} \chi_s \bar{Q}_{f,t} \qquad (8.82)$$

The index e affixed to Σ_s indicates that it is a matter of elastic scattering, the only kind which does not affect the energy of the neutrons (second hypothesis) and thus the only one which can appear in equation (8.82) in accordance with the theory of subsec. 8.2.2. We recall finally that a cylindrical fuel rod of diameter $\emptyset$, P_{cc} is a function of the single variable $(\emptyset \cdot \Sigma_t)$, at least for cells of sufficiently large dimensions (§8.2.3).

We can now make the following important remark. Suppose that for a certain value of $\emptyset$ the denominator of (8.82) vanishes, in other words:

$$P_{cc}(\emptyset\Sigma_t) = \frac{\Sigma_t}{\Sigma_{s,e} + \chi_s \bar{\nu}\Sigma_f} \qquad (8.83)$$

In order to achieve a steady state for Φ, equation (8.82) shows that the source of fission neutrons $\bar{Q}_{f,t}$ must vanish. Going back to the definitions, this would mean that a chain reaction could develop based only on fast fissions induced in the fertile matter. The relation (8.83) would then constitute the critical condition for such a scenario. Unfortunately, the nuclear data are such that the righthand side of (8.83) is always greater than unity (of the order of 1.6 for metallic uranium U^{238}), hence the impossibility of satisfying condition (8.83). As we have mentioned in subsec. 3.2.3, fertile matter alone does not permit a chain reaction to develop. It is essentially the inelastic scattering process which is responsible for this situation (the corresponding cross section appears in the numerator of (8.83)) and detailed calculations confirm this result. This situation is analogous to that which we have encountered in thermonuclear fusion(§1.5.4), the slowing down acting unfavorably when it is a matter of implementing threshhold reactions. While one can always reduce the slowing down due to elastic collisions by just using materials of high atomic weight ($A \gg 1, \xi \cong 0$), as is done in fast reactors, one is on the other hand totally powerless in regard to the inelastic scattering phenomenon. The latter is more pronounced, morever, for heavy nuclei, in particular for those of interest to us, such as uranium and thorium.

In spite of the preceding, fast fission, although insufficient, makes a non-negligible contribution to the establishment of a chain reaction, especially with regard to fast reactors. In thermal reactors, of course, the effect is quite small since the important processes take place at low energy. In the latter case one can restrict oneself to the calculation of the single parameter ε which approximately takes account of the phenomena analyzed above.

8.4.4 The ε and δ Factors

The factor ε introduced arbitrarily in subsec. 4.5.4 (4.80) can be defined as the ratio of the number of neutrons of energy greater than E_s to the number of neutrons produced by fission in the fissile matter ($\overline{Q}_{f,t}$). The product $\varepsilon\overline{Q}_{f,t}$ thus represents the source density of neutrons for the processes studied in the preceding subsections ($E < E_s$).

We thus have by definition:

$$\overline{Q}_{f,t} \cdot \varepsilon = (1 - \chi_s)[\overline{Q}_{f,t} + \overline{\nu\Sigma_f\Phi}] + \Sigma_{s,i}\overline{\Phi} + [\chi_s\overline{Q}_{f,t} + (\Sigma_{s,e} + \chi_s\overline{\nu\Sigma_f})\overline{\Phi}](1-P_{cc}) \tag{8.84}$$

The first term on the right is relative to neutrons emitted below E_s following fissions of all types which take place in the fuel.

The second term is identical to the inelastic scattering rate which, as we have seen, leads to the necessary energy loss (first hypothesis).

Finally, the last term consists of two factors: the first corresponds to all possible neutron emissions above E_s (fissions, elastic scattering) and the second to the probability that these neutrons leave the fuel without energy loss. The crossing of energy E_s takes place in the moderator (third hypothesis).

Using the value of the flux calculated earlier for neutrons of energy higher than E_s (8.82), we obtain the explicit form of ε:

$$\varepsilon = 1 + \chi_s \frac{[(\bar{\nu} - 1)\,\Sigma_f - \Sigma_c]P_{cc}}{\Sigma_t - (\Sigma_{s,e} + \chi_s \bar{\nu}\,\Sigma_f)P_{cc}}$$

All the macroscopic cross sections are relative to the fuel only. Dividing by the corresponding atomic density N_c we obtain:

$$\varepsilon = 1 + \chi_s \frac{[(\bar{\nu} - 1)\sigma_f - \sigma_c]P_{cc}}{\sigma_t - (\sigma_{s,e} + \chi_s \bar{\nu}\,\sigma_f)P_{cc}} \qquad (8.85)$$

The geometrical characteristics of the problem treated intervene only in P_{cc} since all other quantities are part of the fundamental nuclear data relative to the various isotopes present in the fuel. We confirm that in the absence of captures and of fast fissions ($\sigma_f = \sigma_c = 0$) the ε factor reduces to unity.

When the lattices are not too closely spaced, as is the case for graphite or heavy water moderated natural uranium reactors, the probability P_{cc} is relative to the fast neutrons emitted in the fuel rod and having their first collision in the same rod. P_{cc} is thus only a function of the product $x = \emptyset\Sigma_t$ and its approximate value can be obtained from (8.44).

In the general case, we must have recourse to the modified probabilities $\tilde{P}_{cc}$ (8.48); still, for closely spaced lattices we can assume that the ensemble moderator-fuel constitutes a homogeneous mixture. Applying formula (8.49) which can be written in this case:

$$\frac{1}{\tilde{P}_{cc}} = 1 + \frac{V_m\Sigma_{t,m}}{V_c\Sigma_{t,c}} = 1 + \frac{N_mV_m\sigma_{t,m}}{N_cV_c\sigma_{t,c}}$$

and reintroducing the index c in (8.85) in order to avoid any confusion, we find:

$$\varepsilon = 1 + \chi_s \frac{[(\bar{\nu} - 1)\,\sigma_f - \sigma_c)]_c}{\frac{N_m}{N_c}\frac{V_m}{V_c}\sigma_{t,m} + \sigma_{t,c} - [\sigma_{s,e} + \chi_s \bar{\nu}\sigma_f]_c} \qquad (8.86)$$

We see the appearance of the moderating ratio (5.3) which as we know plays a fundamental role in thermal reactor physics (§5.1.4). This result could have been obtained by supposing that the cell consisted of a single medium, the fuel, to which the external moderator would be added to form a homogeneous mixture. Expression (8.86) which corresponds to a limiting case applies quite well to light water reactors.

We can also deduce from this study devoted to high energy neutrons the ratio δ of the fission rate in fertile materials (fissions caused by fast neutrons) to the fission rate in fissile materials (fissions caused by slow neutrons). The latter rate being equal to $\bar{Q}_{f,t}/\bar{\nu}_1$ (by definition of $Q_{f,t}$), the ratio δ can be written:

$$\delta = \bar{\nu}_1 \frac{\Sigma_{f,2}\Phi}{Q_{f,t}}$$

where we henceforth distinguish fissile nuclei from fertile nuclei by using the indices 1 and 2. Denoting by ε^* the value of ε obtained by putting $\sigma_{c,2} = 0$ in the numerator of (8.85) [9] and eliminating the fast flux given by (8.82) we can put δ in the form:

$$\delta = \frac{\bar{\nu}_1}{\bar{\nu}_2 - 1}(\varepsilon^* - 1) = \frac{\bar{\nu}_1}{(\bar{\nu}_2 - 1) - \frac{\sigma_{c,2}}{\sigma_{f,2}}}(\varepsilon - 1) \qquad (8.87)$$

While ε plays an important role in determining multiplication factors (4.80), it is δ which enables us to know the additional energy that may be expected from fissions in fertile matter. In addition it is δ and not ε which can be experimentally obtained starting from measurements of the fission rates induced, in small samples of pure fissile or fertile matter, by the neutron flux of the reactor under study.

We will conclude this subsection with two examples. For neutrons of energies higher than the threshhold $E_s \cong 1.35$ MeV, we adopt the following nuclear data:

$$\left.\begin{aligned}&\sigma_{s,e} = 4.65\text{b},\ \sigma_{s,i} = 2.07\text{b},\ \sigma_f = 0.55\text{b},\ \sigma_c = 0.05\text{b}\\&\sigma_t = 7.32\text{b and } \bar{\nu} = 2.85 \text{ for uranium } U^{238}\ [9]\end{aligned}\right\}$$

as well as:

$$\left.\begin{aligned}&\sigma_t = \sigma_{s,e} = 1.6\text{b for oxygen}\\&\sigma_t = 2\text{b for hydrogen}\\&\chi_s = 0.561\end{aligned}\right\}$$

We consider a metallic uranium rod ($\rho_c = 19$ g cm^{-3}, $N_c = 4.8\ 10^{22}$ nuclei/cm^3) of diameter 4 cm belonging to a graphite or heavy water moderated lattice. In this case, the lattice spacing is important, and P_{cc} can be identified with the collision probability of a single rod ($\breve{P}_{cc} = P_{cc}$). With the preceding data we get: $\Sigma_{t,c} = 0.352$ cm^{-1} and $x = \emptyset\Sigma_{t,c} = 1.407$. For this last value, the desired probability is: $P_{cc} \cong 0.492$ and expression (8.85) leads to:

$$\varepsilon - 1 = \frac{0.543\ P_{cc}}{7.32 - 5.529\ P_{cc}} \cong 0.058$$

In the same way we would calculate:

$$\varepsilon^* - 1 \cong 0.061 \quad \text{and } \delta \cong 0.080$$

The latter result deduced from (8.87) is based on the value $\bar{\nu}_1 = 2.42$ (Tab.3.8). We may note in this connection that the fission of uranium U^{235} nuclei (due especially to slow neutrons) produces distinctly fewer neutrons than the fission of uranium U^{238} nuclei (2.42 as compared to 2.85).

The foregoing results only involve the nuclear and geometrical characteristics of the fuel rod. In contrast, for light water reactor lattices the results depend on the moderating ratio. In this case expression (8.86) gives a good order of magnitude for ε. Let us consider the usual fuel, enriched uranium oxide (UO_2). Here there is no need to distinguish between the two isotopes U^{238} and U^{235} since the latter is present in too small a quantity (the distinction appears only for slow neutrons).

Starting from the preceding data, we get: $\sigma_{s,e} = 7.85$b and $\sigma_t = 10.52$b per molecule of the oxide, the other cross sections remaining unchanged (oxygen contributes neither to capture nor to fission).

With regard to the external moderator (light water) we will only take account of the hydrogen, since it alone contributes to the slowing down of neutrons below the threshhold, in keeping with the hypotheses made at the beginning of this subsection. The total cross section of this isotope plays the same role as the inelastic cross section for a heavy nucleus and we will thus put $\sigma_{t,m} = 2\sigma_{tH} = 4b$. Taking 0.7 g cm^{-3} for the density of water at 300 °C and 10.4 g cm^{-3} for the density of the fuel UO_2 ($N_m = 2.34\ 10^{22}\ cm^{-3}$ and $N_c = 2.32\ 10^{22}\ cm^{-3}$), expression (8.86) becomes:

$$\varepsilon - 1 = \frac{0.543}{1.791 + 4.03\ \dfrac{V_m}{V_c}}$$

This result is very sensitive to the moderating volume ratio V_m/V_c. For present-day reactors this ratio is of the order of two, which leads to $\varepsilon \cong 1.055$.

The preceding simple theory generally underestimates the ε factor since, in spite of their efficiency, the moderators may diffuse some neutrons towards the fuel without slowing them down significantly (Fig. 4.17). The orders of magnitudes obtained show that the ε factor is not so important for thermal reactors. All the same, at present, reactor calculations are no longer made on the basis of the four factors formula (4.80) but in the framework of the multigroup theory applied first to the cells (a large number of groups of which several are above E_s) and secondly to the reactor by calling upon a system of diffusion equations (§4.5.9). The phenomena studied in this section (slowing down, resonances, fast fissions) are thus treated in a more consistent fashion over the whole range of the neutron spectrum.

APPENDICES

Q

Chapter 9

NEUTRON CALCULATIONS FOR REACTORS

9.1 MULTIGROUP FORMALISMS

9.1.1 Introduction

In this chapter we are going to generalize the somewhat simplified multigroup formalism presented in subsec. 4.5.8. The equations given in this section are at the heart of most of the numerical codes used today in reactor physics. These codes give not only the effective multiplication factor, but also the neutron flux in each group. This flux, which defines in greater or lesser detail the neutron spectra at each point, is not interesting in itself, but enables us to calculate all the useful quantities (§9.1.5). Finally, in the last section we will present some information about multigroup transport theory.

9.1.2 Scattering Matrices

Let us consider the equation of balance (4.87), which is the starting point of the multigroup theory. The slowing down source can be written in general for energy E_g (§4.4.3):

$$q(E_g) = \int_{E_g}^{E_0} P_2(E' \to E_g)\, \Sigma_s(E')\, \Phi(E')dE' \qquad (9.1)$$

where the variable $\vec{r}$ has been omitted for convenience, while E_0 represents the maximum energy of the neutrons in the problem considered. The probability P_2 has the same meaning as before (§4.4.2), except that it is no longer necessarily given by expression (4.33); inelastic scattering leads in effect to different expressions. By its very definition, this probability enjoys certain properties: $P_2(E' \to E') = 1$ and $P_2(E' \to 0) = 0$.

We can decompose the integral appearing in (9.1) into a sum of g partial integrals involving the energies E_h which define the groups (Fig. 9.1), whence we obtain:

$$q(E_g) = \sum_{h=1}^{g} \Sigma_{s,h} P_2(h \to E_g)\, \Phi_h \qquad (9.2)$$

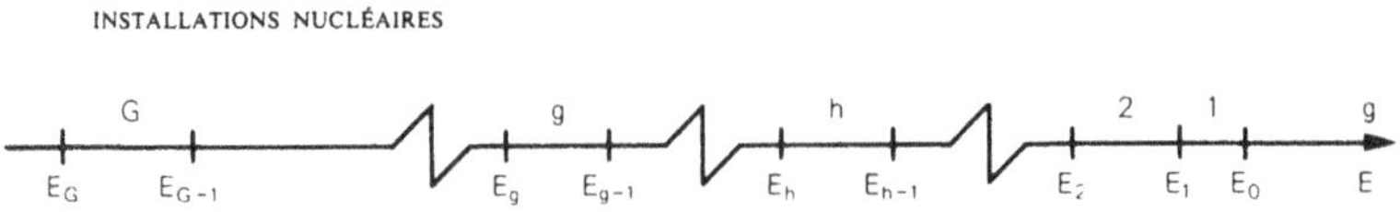

FIGURE 9.1.

with:

$$\Sigma_{s,h} = \left[\int_{E_h}^{E_{h-1}} \Sigma_s(E')\,\Phi\,(E')dE'\right] \Big/ \left[\int_{E_h}^{E_{h-1}} \Phi(E')dE'\right]$$

$$P_2(h \to E_g) = \frac{\int_{E_h}^{E_{h-1}} \Sigma_s(E')P_2(E' \to E_g)\Phi(E')dE'}{\int_{E_h}^{E_{h-1}} \Sigma_s(E')\,\Phi\,(E')dE'} \tag{9.3}$$

At this stage no approximation has been made, but the multigroup constants (9.3) depend on the desired solutions. Thus, the scattering cross section $\Sigma_{s,h}$ satisfies the average relation (4.89) already utilized. As has already been pointed out, if the groups are narrow enough, we can replace $\Phi(E')$ by an approximate expression flowing from qualitative physical considerations without any significant effect on the results. This is the key to any multigroup theory.

Replacing the slowing down sources in equation (4.87) by their new expression (9.2), we obtain:

$$\text{div}\,\vec{J}_g + (\Sigma_{a,g} + \Sigma_{R,g})\,\Phi_g = \sum_{h=1}^{g-1} \Sigma_s(h \to g)\Phi_h + Q_g \tag{9.4}$$

with:

$$\left.\begin{aligned} &\Sigma_s(h \to g) = \Sigma_{s,h}\,[P_2(h \to E_{g-1}) - P_2(h \to E_g)] \\ &\qquad\qquad\qquad\qquad\qquad\qquad \text{for } h \leq g - 1 \\ &\Sigma_{R,g} = \Sigma_{s,g}P_2(g \to E_g) \end{aligned}\right\} \tag{9.5}$$

Since the current $\vec{J}_g$ always satisfies Fick's law (4.95), we obtain a set of partial differential equations (in $\vec{r}$) which enjoys the same property as the system (4.96): when equation (9.4) is solved for Φ_g, the righthand side is known, since at this stage the flux Φ_h is known, the equations being solved successively according to increasing values of g(for g = 1 the sum over h disappears).

The scattering or transfer matrices satisfy an important relation which does not depend on the type of scattering. Observing that $P_2(h \to E_G) = 0$ when the last group corresponds to thermal neutrons (E_G=0), we obtain from the first equation (9.5) the identity:

$$\sum_{g=h+1}^{G} \Sigma_s(h \to g) = \Sigma_{s,h} P_2(h \to E_h)$$

which, because of the second equation (9.5), involves the removal cross section for group h; we thus have:

$$\sum_{g=h+1}^{G} \Sigma_s(h \to g) = \Sigma_{R,h} \qquad (9.6)$$

Every "removed" neutron which leaves group h by slowing down necessarily emerges in one of the groups g of lower energy ($g \geq h + 1$).

As a first example we consider the case of elastic scattering and we use a Fermi spectrum to calculate the scattering matrices (9.5): $E'\Sigma_s(E')\Phi(E') \cong$ const. (§4.4.4).

Taking for $P_2(E' \to E)$ the expression adapted to this case (4.33) we find:

$$(1-\alpha)\ln\left(\frac{E_{h-1}}{E_h}\right)P_2(h \to E_g) = \begin{cases} E_g\left(\dfrac{1}{E_h} - \dfrac{1}{E_{h-1}}\right) - \alpha\ln\left(\dfrac{E_{h-1}}{E_h}\right) & \text{if } \dfrac{E_g}{\alpha} \geq E_{h-1} \\[2ex] \dfrac{E_g}{E_h} - \alpha - \alpha\ln\left(\dfrac{E_g}{\alpha E_h}\right) & \text{if } E_{h-1} \geq \dfrac{E_g}{\alpha} \geq E_h \\[2ex] 0 & \text{if } E_h > \dfrac{E_g}{\alpha} \end{cases} \qquad (9.7)$$

and the scattering cross section for group h can be written in its turn:

$$\Sigma_{s,h} = \left[\ln\left(\frac{E_{h-1}}{E_h}\right)\right] \cdot \left[\int_{E_h}^{E_{h-1}} \frac{dE'}{E'\Sigma_s(E')}\right]^{-1} \cong \Sigma_s(E_{h-\frac{1}{2}}) \qquad (9.8)$$

The last approximation is based on the often-justified hypothesis that $\Sigma_s(E')$ does not vary much inside a group. The scattering matrices (9.5) can be deduced from expressions (9.7) and (9.8).

When the groups are large enough for $E_g/\alpha \leqq E_{g-1}$, the probabilities $P_2\ (h \rightarrow E_g)$ vanish, except for h = g; in the latter case they can be written:

$$P_2(g \rightarrow E_g) = \frac{\xi}{\ln\left(\frac{E_{g-1}}{E_g}\right)}$$

where ξ is the average logarithmic energy loss per shock (4.35). We thus get back the formalism of subsection 4.5.8, since equations (9.5) become:

$$\Sigma_s(h \rightarrow g) = 0 \qquad h < g - 1$$

$$\Sigma_s(g - 1 \rightarrow g) = \Sigma_{R,g-1}$$

$$\Sigma_{R,g} = \xi\, \Sigma_{s,g}/\ln\left(\frac{E_{g-1}}{E_g}\right)$$

In contrast, for hydrogen ($\alpha = 0$), the scattering matrix will be complete.

Let us now study the case of inelastic scattering and consider the excitation level Q_i of the target nucleus. If the latter has a high mass number (no recoil), the energy loss of a neutron in the course of a collision is equal to Q_i and the probabiity P_2 in this case has a very simple expression:

$$P_2(E' \rightarrow E_g) = \begin{cases} 1 \text{ if } E' < E_g + Q_i \\ 0 \text{ if } E' > E_g + Q_i \end{cases}$$

which expresses something evident: a neutron of too high an energy E' cannot cross E_g even after having lost the energy Q_i. Still taking a Fermi spectrum for $\Phi(E')$ (which can be debatable at high energy), we get (9.3):

$$P_2(h \rightarrow E_g) = \begin{cases} 1 & \text{if } E_g+Q_i>E_{h-1} \\ \left[\ln\left(\dfrac{E_g + Q_i}{E_h} \right) \right] \cdot \left[\ln\left(\dfrac{E_{h-1}}{E_h} \right) \right]^{-1} & \text{if } E_{h-1}>E_g+Q_i>E_h \\ 0 & \text{if } E_h>E_g+Q_i \end{cases} \quad (9.9)$$

The scattering cross section is always given by (9.8) but the datum $\Sigma_s(E')$ is relative to the inelastic collisions which lead to an excitation Q_i of the nucleus. For $E' < Q_i$ this cross section vanishes: inelastic scattering is a threshhold reaction. We finally find that the transfer matrix elements are other than zero only if the inequality: $E_{h-1} - E_g > Q_i > E_h - E_{g-1}$ is satisfied (Fig. 9.2); in this case they can be obtained by substituting the expressions (9.9) in (9.5). There is thus no neutron transfer between groups which are too close or too far away from each other.

For high energies, several levels can be excited. If they are resolved, that is to say if experiments can separately furnish $\Sigma_{s,i}(E')$ and Q_i for each level, then it suffices to sum the preceding results to obtain the multigroup constants $\Sigma_{s,h}$ and $\Sigma_s(h \rightarrow g)$ of the considered nucleus. At very high energy, the levels become indistinguishable, but the evaporation model well known in nuclear physics [56] leads us to put:

$$P_1(E' \rightarrow E) = A\,E \exp\left[- \frac{E}{T_N(E')} \right]$$

where $P_1(E' \rightarrow E)$ has the same meaning as in subsec. 4.4.2. A is a normalization constant and T_N is the "temperature" of the nucleus (statistical model). Writing (§4.4.2):

$$P_2(E' \rightarrow E_g) = \int_0^{E_g} P_1(E' \rightarrow E'')dE''$$

$$P_2(E' \rightarrow E') = 1$$

we get:

$$P_2(E' \rightarrow E_g) = \left[1 - \widetilde{\exp}\left(- \frac{E_g}{T_N} \right) \right] \Big/ \left[1 - \widetilde{\exp}\left(- \frac{E'}{T_N} \right) \right] \quad (9.10)$$

with the sole restriction: $E_g \leq E'$ and $\widetilde{\exp}(x) = (1 - x)\exp(x)$.

The other quantities can be determined as before, but we note that $P_2(h \rightarrow E_g)$ can no longer be obtained analytically (9.3) all the more so in that the temperature T_N depends on the energy of the incident neutrons ($T_N \cong K\sqrt{E'}$). Still, the preparation codes for multigroup cross sections always lead to a refined calculation of spectra (§9.3.3) and in this case the groups are so narrow that we can put (9.3):

$$P_2(h \to E_g) \cong P_2(E_{h-\frac{1}{2}} \to E_g)$$

where $E_{h-\frac{1}{2}}$ is the average energy of neutrons in group h.

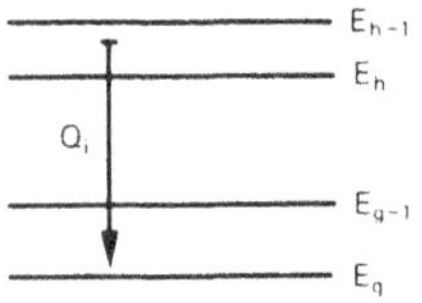

FIGURE 9.2.

9.1.3 Absorption and Neutron Balance

We start from the multigroup equations established in the preceding subsection (9.4), and put $Q_g(\vec{r}) = \chi_g Q_f^*(\vec{r})$, where χ_g represents the proportion of fission neutrons emitted in group g and $Q_f^*(\vec{r})$ the source density of fission neutrons ($cm^{-3}\ s^{-1}$) which is assumed to be known. The system of equations:

$$\operatorname{div}[\vec{J}_g(\vec{r})] + [\Sigma_{a,g}(\vec{r}) + \Sigma_{R,g}(\vec{r})]\,\Phi_g(\vec{r}) = \sum_{h=1}^{g-1} \Sigma_s(\vec{r}, h \to g)\,\Phi_h(\vec{r}) + \chi_g Q_f^*(\vec{r}) \qquad g = 1,2,\ldots G. \tag{9.11}$$

generalizes the formalism of subsec. 4.5.8, since the currents $\vec{J}_g$ always satisfy Fick's law (4.95).

Adding together the preceding G equations, we get:

$$\operatorname{div}\left(\sum_{g=1}^{G} \vec{J}_g\right) + \sum_{g=1}^{G} (\Sigma_{a,g} + \Sigma_{R,g})\Phi_g = \sum_{g=1}^{G}\sum_{h=1}^{g-1} \Sigma_s(h \to g)\Phi_h + Q_f^* \tag{9.12}$$

since $\sum_{g=1}^{G} \chi_g = 1$.

Inverting the order of the summations, we find that the double sum of the righthand side is equal to:

$$\sum_{h=1}^{G} \Sigma_{R,h}\Phi_h$$

which follows from the identity (9.6). The terms which include the removal cross sections cancel out, and equation (9.12) becomes:

$$\text{div}\, \vec{J}\,(\vec{r}) + R_a\,(\vec{r}) = Q_f^*\,(\vec{r}) \tag{9.13}$$

where:

$$\vec{J} = \sum_{g=1}^{G} \vec{J}_g$$
$$R_a = \sum_{g=1}^{G} \Sigma_{a,g}\,\Phi_g \tag{9.14}$$

represent respectively the net currents and the absorption rate for neutrons of arbitrary energy (see the definitions (4.88) and (4.89)).

Equation (9.13) could have been obtained directly from (4.87); it generalizes the mono-energetic equation of balance (4.12). The absorption rate here is no longer connected to the total flux Φ, but to the solution Φ_g of the system (9.11).

It is well to note that the scattering matrices never appear explicitly in an equation of balance such as (9.13). This is because the slowing down process does not affect the number of neutrons, but only their distribution among the various groups, whence an indirect influence on the absorption rate (9.14).

Since the absorption cross sections $\Sigma_{a,g}$ intervene directly in the neutron balance, they must be evaluated with great care. Thus in expression (4.89) we will adopt an approximate form of the spectrum $\Phi(E)$ inside group g which remains valid in extreme cases, in particular when resonances are present. Since resonances are always very narrow with respect to the width of the groups, the choice of a good spectrum is crucial. Nearly all preparation codes of multigroup data are based on the expression:

$$\Phi\,(E) \cong \frac{K}{E\,\Sigma_t(E)}$$

in accordance with the law established in subsec. 8.3.4 (8.67). This simple law is valid even for heterogeneous media, provided we use the equivalence theorem (§8.4.1). The microscopic absorption cross sections (4.89) can thus be calculated according to the recipe:

$$\sigma_{a,g} = \left[\int_{E_g}^{E_{g-1}} \sigma_a(E)\,\frac{dE}{E\,\Sigma_t(E)}\right] \cdot \left[\int_{E_g}^{E_{g-1}} \frac{dE}{E\,\Sigma_t(E)}\right]^{-1} \tag{9.15}$$

The denominator of this fraction can be simplified by observing that $\Sigma_t(E)$ has a large value only at the level of the resonances (Fig. 8.11) and thus only in a very small part of the interval (E_g, E_{g-1}). We can thus replace $\Sigma_t(E)$ by the scattering cross section $\Sigma_{s,g}$ which remains between the resonances. This simplification evidently does not apply to the numerator because of the presence of $\sigma_a(E)$. We thus get:

$$\sigma_{a,g} = \frac{\Sigma_{s,g}}{\ln\left(\frac{E_{g-1}}{E_g}\right)} \int_{E_g}^{E_{g-1}} \frac{\sigma_a(E)}{\Sigma_t(E)}\,\frac{dE}{E} \tag{9.16}$$

For a reactor core, we see by bringing out its different constituents (fuel and moderator) that the preceding expression is (up to a logarithm) none other than the effective resonance integral relative to the group considered (4.56) and in a certain sense the quantities $\sigma_{a,g}$ are no longer fundamental microscopic data, as they depend on the makeup of the considered medium through the dilution parameter σ_e. On the contrary, if the microscopic cross section $\sigma_a(E)$ has no resonance contribution but varies very little in the interval (E_g, E_{g-1}), then expression (9.15) gives the expected result: $\sigma_{a,g} \cong \sigma_a(E_{g-\frac{1}{2}})$. All standard cases are thus covered by the procedure indicated above with the exception of thermal neutrons which demand a special treatment as we will see in the following subsection.

We can disregard the preceding in the case of scattering cross sections which do not intervene directly in the balance. Very rough approximations are often admissible (§9.1.2) provided they respect the conservation law (9.6); otherwise an additional term would appear in equation (9.13) corresponding to neutrons created (or destroyed) by scattering, which would make no sense (certain numerical codes are such that the computer refuses to carry out the calculations if the law (9.6) is violated because of an error in the data).

Let us return to the balance equation (9.13) and integrate it over the volume V of the system under study. Using the Gauss theorem, we arrive at the relation:

$$S^* = A + F$$

with: (9.17)

$$S^* = \int_V Q_f^* (\vec{r})dV, \quad A = \int_V R_a (\vec{r})dV \quad \text{and } F = \int_S \vec{n}.\vec{J} (\vec{r})dS$$

where $\vec{n}$ is the normal exterior to the surface S which forms the boundary of the volume V. The quantities S^*, A and F represent respectively the production, the absorption and the leakage of neutrons. This evident relation, used since Chapter 3 for displaying the different materials involved in a reactor (3.3), characterizes stationary states. Here, we know how to evaluate the various terms of this balance.

To conclude, let us analyse the method of outer iterations applicable to multiplying media. Equation (4.99) can be written with our present notations:

$$k = \frac{S}{S^*}$$

where, because of (4.97):

$$S = \int_V Q_f (\vec{r})dV = \int_V \left[\sum_{g=1}^{G} (\bar{\nu} \Sigma_f)_g \Phi_g (\vec{r}) \right] dV \qquad (9.18)$$

Using equation (9.17) the preceding ratio becomes:

$$k = \frac{S}{A + F}$$

It is thus a matter of the effective multiplication factor k_e that we have already defined (4.62) or more exactly, of an approximate value for it, since the flux $\Phi_g(\vec{r})$, which enabled us to calculate S (9.18), A and F (9.17), has been obtained by solving equations (9.11) for an arbitrary distribution of source densities $Q_f^*(\vec{r})$. The calculations are then repeated, each time taking for $Q_f^*(\vec{r})$ the distribution Q_f (4.97) which results from the preceding calculation. This method converges, and generally about a dozen outer iterations suffice to obtain k_e up to 3 or 4 decimal places. Moreover, the quantities thus obtained before convergence have a physical meaning. Thus, for each iteration (q), the source $S_{(q)}$ given by (9.18) represents a new generation of fission neutrons and the ratio of the number of neutrons emitted in one generation to those of another can be simply written:

$$k_{(q)} = \frac{S_{(q)}}{S_{(q-1)}} \tag{9.19}$$

the above sequence tending to k_e.

For subcritical systems, the sum of all the generations is completely determined since, starting from a certain stage, we pass from one source $S_{(q)}$ to the following by multiplying it by $k_e < 1$ (convergent geometric series). The results depend on the initial choice of $Q_f^*(\vec{r})$, but not the factor k_e: for a stable state to be possible, though the reactor is subcritical, one needs to have an external source (neutrons emitted otherwise than by induced fission, cf. §5.3.9) whose intensity is correctly represented by the value of Q_f^* used in the course of the first iteration. Summing the fluxes obtained at each iteration, we obtain the total flux induced by the source and, although it is amplified by the induced fissions, it nevertheless remains proportional to this source: the flux level is thus no longer adjustable as it was in the case of a critical reactor.

On the contrary if the system is supercritical, the preceding series diverges as expected ($k_e > 1$), but the value of the multiplication factor k_e is perfectly defined as well as the distributions $\Phi_g(\vec{r})$ associated to it. When the reactor is not too supercritical, these quantities furnish useful information concerning the spatial distribution of the neutron flux which, in this case, increases with time (Sec. 4.6). In fact the problem belongs to the domain of space kinetics which we will not take up here, and it is quite clear that the preceding study based on steady state equations can only furnish fragmentary results. Rigorously speaking, these equations only apply to critical systems ($k_e = 1$); this important case poses particular problems (§9.1.5).

9.1.4 Neutron Thermalization

The cross section weighting method described in the preceding subsection (9.15) does not apply to the last group ($g = G$) when the latter corresponds to thermal neutrons. These neutrons are distributed over the interval ($E_G = 0$, $E_{G-1} = E_t^*$) according to a different law from that for neutrons in the course of slowing down. Let us suppose for example that perfect thermodynamic equilibrium has been achieved. In this case, we have the

Maxwell distribution (2.1) which is equivalent to a spectral flux density (§4.5.5):

$$vn(E) = \Phi(E) = C\ E \exp\left(-\frac{E}{kT}\right) \qquad (9.20)$$

With the help of expression (4.89) we can then determine the microscopic cross sections for thermal neutrons taken globally (t = G):

$$\sigma_{a,t} = \int_0^{E_t^*} \sigma_a(E)\ E \exp\left(-\frac{E}{kT}\right) dE \Bigg/ \int_0^{E_t^*} E \exp\left(-\frac{E}{kT}\right) dE \qquad (9.21)$$

Since generally the chosen cutoff energy E_t^* is much larger than kT (the maximum of $\Phi(E)$), we can replace the upper limit of these integrals by infinity.

Let us now suppose that $\sigma_a(E)$ behaves like $1/\sqrt{E}$, which is the case at low energy for most nuclides (§9.4.1). The preceding integrals can be analytically calculated (by putting $x^2 = E/kT$) and we thus arrive at an extremely simple result:

$$\sigma_{a,t} = \sigma_a(E_0)\sqrt{\frac{\pi}{4}\frac{T_0}{T}} \qquad (9.22)$$

where we have put $E_0 = kT_0$, E_0 being a reference energy.

One usually takes $E_0 = 0.025$ eV, in other words, $T_0 = 293$ °K; we thus see that it suffices to know the absorption cross sections for this particular energy, that is for neutrons of velocity $v_0 = 2200\ \mathrm{ms}^{-1}$.

The first cross section libraries consisted of these quantities and a few resonance integrals in the epithermal domain ($E > E_t^*$). In the case of cross sections no longer obeying the $1/\sqrt{E}$ law, one simply multiplied expression (9.22) by a function g(T) of the temperature obtained by numerical integration of (9.21) from experimental data $\sigma_a(E)$. Tables of g(T) for the most important isotopes U^{235}, Pu^{239}, etc., still exist [57].

This simple formalism is no longer used, unless our only interest is in orders of magnitude (cf. the tables of Ch. 3). The reason for this is that the spectra are never Maxwellian (except in the academic case of an infinite nonabsorbing medium) because of the strong neutron absorption at low energy. We can artificially save the preceding formalism by introducing a "neutron temperature" $T_n > T$ which reflects the deformation of the spectra due to absorption. Simple theories lead to the relation:

$$T_n - T = C \cdot \Sigma_a(E_0)/\ \xi\Sigma_s(E_0)$$

where $\Sigma_a(E_0)$ and $\xi\Sigma_s(E_0)$ are the usual parameters relative to the medium under study and to the reference energy E_0 (0.025 eV), the constant C resulting from experimental adjustments. In its turn this semi-empirical approach has been abandoned and nowadays one proceeds to a direct calculation of the thermal spectrum by having recourse once more to the multi-group formalism applied inside the energy interval $(0, E_t^*)$. The essential difference with respect to the multigroup theory developed so far lies in the fact that the matrices $\Sigma_s(h \to g)$ are now full ($h > g$ is no longer excluded), since a slow neutron can acquire energy in the course of a collision with a moving nucleus (the conclusions of subsec. 4.4.2 are no longer valid here). The calculation of the transfer matrices which depend on the temperature and structure of the materials being studied is outside the framework of this treatise [58]. Standard libraries contain these matrices for some important moderators (H_2), D_2O, C); as for the absorption cross sections $\sigma_{a,g}$, they are well defined, since the groups are sufficiently narrow (20 to 50 groups from 0 to E_t^*).

Quite often we simplify by considering a homogeneous infinite medium of the same composition as that of the cell being studied. Putting $\vec{J} = 0$, equations (9.4) lead to a system of algebraic equations in Φ_g that must be solved by iteration since the transfer matrices are now full. Finally, the sources Q_g are data which flow from the knowledge of neutron spectra above E_t^* (it is a question of the transfer of neutrons of energy $E' > E_t^*$ to $E < E_t^*$). To take account of the finite dimensions of the multiplying medium under study, one can improve this model by introducing the fundamental mode approximation (Sec. 9.3). Many thermalization codes are based on this latter approach [59].

For cells with large dimensions (heavy water reactors), their heterogeneity must be taken into account right from the calculation of spectra. These are in fact very different when one passes from the fuel to the moderator. We already know that we cannot use the diffusion equation in the fuel (§4.3.7), and it is here that formalisms based on collision probabilities (§8.2.2) are most often used. Equations (8.38) are written for each group of the thermal domain ($E < E_t^*$), the quantities $\Sigma_{t,j}$, $\Sigma_{s,i}$ and $P_{i \to j}$ depending on the index g, as do the flux $\overline{\Phi}_{i,g}$ and the sources

$\overline{Q}_{i,g}$. The latter include terms in $\Sigma_{s,i}$ $(h \rightarrow g)$ $\Phi_{i,h}$ which reflect energy transfers having to do with the "full" matrices referred to above. We must thus solve a system of rank $I \times G_t$ where I is the number of zones per cell and G_t the number of fine groups contained in the thermal group G. The calculation cost is especially due to the large number of probabilities $P_{i \rightarrow j}$ that must be considered in a standard problem [60].

Knowing thus the energy spectra inside the interval $(0,E_t^*)$, we can calculate with the help of expression (4.89) written for g = G all the cross sections relative to a single group of thermal neutrons, and we can do this for each isotope. These are the quantities which enable us finally to evaluate parameters $\Sigma_{a,G}$ and D_G of the last diffusion equation (4.96) or (9.4) by applying the homogenization rules (4.1) or (5.1) ultimately corrected for flux depressions inside the cells (8.50).

9.1.5 Flux Normalization and Auxiliary Calculations

In the case of critical reactors which interests us here, the sum of all neutron generations still remains a divergent series and a steady-state regime is only possible in the absence of additional sources. This means that if in spite of everything we continue to make outer iterations by applying without any precautions the procedure described at the end of subsec. 9.1.3, the flux will vary with the iteration, whereas the multiplication factors $k_{(q)}$ will have converged to the desired value (here $k_e = 1$). This amounts to saying in a different way that, as we already know, the solution $\Phi_g(\vec{r})$ is only defined up to a multiplicative factor.

To avoid the irksome appearance of numbers which are too large, numerical codes always normalize those results whose nature is not always apparent to users. Thus two different multigroup codes should not be expected necessarily to furnish the same results, except of course where the eigen value k_e is concerned and the flux distributions up to overall normalization. The normalization adopted results in general from the method chosen to accelerate the convergence, and thus it does not necessarily have a very clear physical sense. Still, very often the final values of the flux are relative to the emission of a fission neutron in the whole system ($S^* = 1$).

However it may be, in all practical cases, auxiliary calculations must complete the multigroup diffusion calculations. Most of the useful information does not, however, depend on the flux levels, for they only involve the ratios of reaction rates. For example, the form factor $f_p(\vec{r})$ of specific powers (§5.2.5) is given by expression (5.18) where the fission rate in the fuel is obtained by a formula analogous to (9.14):

$$R_f^{(c)}(\vec{r}) = \sum_{g=1}^{G} \Sigma_{f,g}^{(c)}(\vec{r})\,\Phi_g(\vec{r}) \tag{9.23}$$

in which the corresponding macroscopic fission cross sections $\Sigma_{f,g}^{(c)}$ may depend on the considered point through the fuel composition (cores with several zones). The quantity $R_f^{(c)}(\vec{r})$ is thus known at each point and the search for its maximum $R_f(\vec{r}_M)$ can be easily programmed.

The conversion factor can also be obtained without ambiguity in the general case by writing in accord with the considerations of subsec. 3.3.2:

$$C = \frac{A_2}{A_1} = \frac{\int_{\text{reactor}} R_c^{(2)}(\vec{r})\,dV}{\int_{\text{reactor}} R_a^{(1)}(\vec{r})\,dV} \tag{9.24}$$

The absorption rate $R_a^{(1)}$ and the capture rate $R_c^{(2)}$ now concern the unit volume of the different media (homogenized in each zone). They can be obtained easily in the same way as the fission rate by using the absorption or capture cross sections relative only to the fissile isotopes (1) or the fertile isotopes (2) (here it is no longer a matter of the cross sections $\Sigma_{a,g}(\vec{r})$ used in the multigroup equations which incorporate all the isotopes). In the case of fast breeder reactors, the numerator of (9.24) is sometimes decomposed into two integrals: one extending over the core, and the other over the blankets, whence two conversion factors (each one smaller than unity). We also note here that the results are independent of the normalization adopted in the codes used to produce the solution $\Phi_g(\vec{r})$ and more generally we note that the comparisons that can be made in reactor physics between theory and experiment most often have a bearing only on the ratios of measurable reaction rates.

Nevertheless circumstances exist in which knowledge of the absolute magnitude of the flux is indispensable. In such a case it is necessary to choose a flux normalization which corresponds to the mode of functioning of the power plant. If the maximum specific power $\bar{\omega}_M$ is imposed at the hot spot (§5.2.5), the absolute flux is then given by:

$$\phi_g^{(a)}(\vec{r}) = \frac{\bar{\omega}_M \rho_c}{E_f} \frac{\Phi_g(\vec{r})}{R_f^{(c)}(\vec{r}_M)} \tag{9.25}$$

where the quantities Φ_g and $R_f^{(c)}$ appeal to the raw results furnished by the multigroup codes, ρ_c and E_f representing respectively the mass density of the fuel and the energy associated to a fission. Such an expression enables us to get back the specific power distributions (5.17) by applying expression (9.23) to the absolute flux (9.25), the specific powers always being given by (4.9).

If on the contrary the reactor is operated at constant power (as is the case in practice), then all the results must be expressed as a function of the thermal power P_t of the reactor. The neutron flux in each group can then be written:

$$\phi_g^{(a)}(\vec{r}) = \frac{P_t}{E_f} \frac{\Phi_g(\vec{r})}{\int_{\text{reactor}} \left[\sum_{g=1}^{G} \Sigma_{f,g}(\vec{r})\, \Phi_g(\vec{r}) \right] dV} \tag{9.26}$$

where the macroscopic fission cross sections $\Sigma_{f,g}$ are relative to the unit volume of various homogenized media. As one can easily verify, the thermal power calculated starting from this flux is equal to P_t.

Fuel evolution calculations are generally based on this latter type of normalization and the one-group integrated flux θ (5.24) corresponds to a reactor operating at constant power. Having determined in advance the fuel composition as a function of θ on the basis of the simple formalism of subsec. 5.3.4, or better still, by taking account of the modifications of the spectra (§9.3.3), we can solve the system of multigroup equations at the beginning of each time interval (t_{n-1}, t_n) and auxiliary calculations give at each point the new value of the integrated flux:

$$\theta(\vec{r},t_n) = \theta(\vec{r},t_{n-1}) + (t_n - t_{n-1}) \sum_{g=1}^{G} \phi_g^{(a)}(\vec{r},t_{n-1}) \tag{9.27}$$

All this is of course for a steady state situation, and if the factors k_e obtained in the course of time differ from unity, it is tacitly assumed that the control rods or the soluble poison must intevene to maintain the criticality of the reactor. Generally in this type of study the burnable poison is brought into play, so that reactivity variations are small; moreover, if a soluble poison is present, one can iterate on its concentration in order to assure the condition $k_e = 1$ at each instant. One thus determines the time evolution of the reactor characteristics (hot point, flattening, etc.) following the flow chart of Fig. 9.3 (for thermal reactors we prefer to keep only the thermal neutrons in the definition of θ, the sum over g in (9.27) then being replaced by $\Phi_G^{(a)}$).

Of course in reality the power of a reactor is never constant, but that is shown simply by modifying the time scale. In effect we can establish a correspondance between the operation period t and the equivalent time t_e which, at nominal power $P_{t,n}$, would have led to the same energy production. This implies the relation:

$$P_{t,n} t_e = \int_0^t P_t(t')dt'$$

This time, often expressed in f.p.e.d. (full power equivalent days) is that which intervenes usually in evolution calculations, and naturally it is smaller than the real time t (if for nothing else than the annual reactor shutdown). The ratio t_e/t is called the load factor of the power plant, and it plays an important role in economic computations (Sec. 7.6). Of course, if the evolution calculations are not meant for predictions, but aim simply to retrace the history of a loading, the flux is then normalized at each instant with respect to the real power $P_t(t)$ of the reactor and then it is the real time which intervenes.

Determining reactor shielding also requires a knowledge of the true magnitude of the neutron flux, but the corresponding calculations are made independently, after those of the the reactor proper. There are several reasons for this:

- In the course of reactor calculations it is not necessary to introduce the various protection materials, for they are too far from the core (in mean free paths) to have an influence on its behavior; to avoid useless calculations one thus considers only the core and its reflectors (or blankets), this system being supposed to be isolated.
- The attenuation of the neutron flux during its passage through the protection screens represents several decades and an anisotropy

INSTALLATIONS NUCLÉAIRES

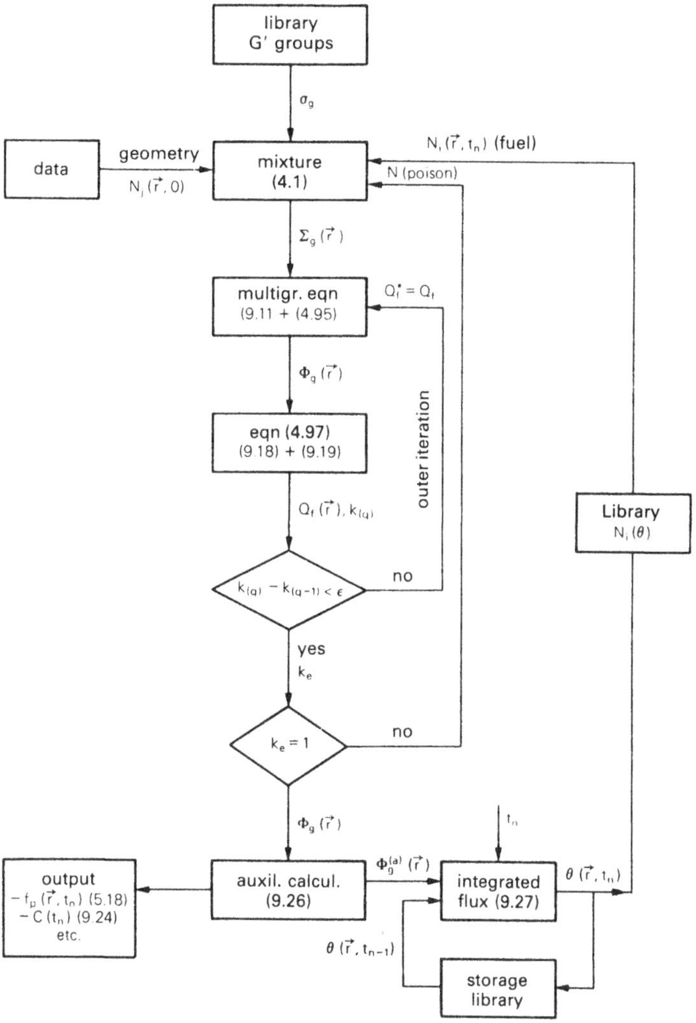

FIGURE 9.3. Reactor calculations in the course of reactor evolution. The equations to be solved are identified by their numbering in the text.

which results from it calls for a recourse to transport theory (§9.1.6). Further, it is the fastest neutrons (even in the case of thermal reactors) that play an essential role, since they are the most penetrating. At high energy, the processes are more complex and diffusion theory is hardly justified.

· Taking into account the primary photons γ coming from the core or the secondary ones engendered by neutron capture in the shields themselves requires special treatment. Here too, transport theory must be used, so that the neutrons and the γ photons are treated simultaneously.

The most consistent way of matching these two types of very different calculations (reactors and shields) is to determine the spatial distribution of the source densities $Q_f(\vec{r})$ of fission neutrons given by equation (4.97). To this end, we use the normalized results of multigroup diffusion calculations relative to the isolated reactor, the normalization having been done in accordance with one of the procedures indicated above. The shielding calculations must thus include the core as the first zone (the only one to possess neutron sources), but outer iterations are no longer necessary, since the quantities $Q_f(\vec{r})$ are already known. The whole system, including the core, can be considered as being passive, since the fission cross sections nowhere intervene (they are included in Q_f). This method enables us to treat shielding problems in an autonomous fashion without concerning ourselves with the methods used during core calculations, and the structure of the groups can be different so as to take better account of the nuclear characteristics of the shields.

9.1.6 Multigroup Transport Equations

These equations are to the preceding multigroup equations (9.11) what transport theory is to diffusion theory. Before deriving them, we must modify the mono-energetic transport equation (8.5) so as to include the slowing down process. The generalization is immediate: it suffices to introduce a new probability density $f(E' \rightarrow E, \vec{\Omega}' \cdot \vec{\Omega})$ such that $f dE d\Omega$ represents the fraction of neutrons of energy E' and of direction $\vec{\Omega}'$ diffused in the energy band $(E, E + dE)$ in the directions belonging to the solid angle $d\Omega$ around $\vec{\Omega}$. This function must evidently satisfy the identity:

$$\int_0^{\infty} dE \int_{4\pi} d\Omega \; f(E' \to E, \vec{\Omega}' \cdot \vec{\Omega}) = 1$$

and we note that:

$$P_1(E' \to E) = \int_{4\pi} d\Omega \; f(E' \to E, \vec{\Omega}' \cdot \vec{\Omega})$$

is nothing but the probability of energy transfer (without reference to directions) already encountered in subsec. 4.4.2 and which, for isotropic elastic scattering, is given by expression (4.32).

Reasoning again as in subsec. 8.1.1, we arrive at the equation (8.3):

$$\vec{\Omega} \cdot \vec{\text{grad}}\phi + \Sigma_t(E)\phi(\vec{r},E,\vec{\Omega}) = e(\vec{r},E,\vec{\Omega}) \tag{9.28}$$

but the emission rate is now given by:

$$e(\vec{r},E,\vec{\Omega}) = \int_0^{\infty} dE' \int_{4\pi} d\Omega' \Sigma_s(E') \; f(E' \to E,\vec{\Omega}' \cdot \vec{\Omega})\phi(\vec{r},E',\vec{\Omega}') + Q(\vec{r},E,\vec{\Omega}) \tag{9.29}$$

which generalizes equation (8.5). The desired quantity $\phi(E,\vec{\Omega})$ represents now the angular flux spectral density just as $\Phi(E)$ represented the scalar flux density (§4.4.3). The source density $Q(E,\vec{\Omega})$ (assumed known) is defined in an analogous fashion. The quantities Φ and Q multiplied by $dEd\Omega$ correspond in the strict sense to the flux ($cm^{-2}\ s^{-1}$) and to the source densities ($cm^{-3}\ s^{-1}$).

We have thus arrived at the most general transport equation among those utilized in reactor physics. The scattering process is alone responsible for the complexity of this equation (integral over E' and $\vec{\Omega}'$), while the absorptions are implicitly taken into account in the total cross section Σ_t (which includes Σ_a). Naturally, the macroscopic nuclear data Σ_t, Σ_s and f depend in general on the spatial variable $\vec{r}$ which has been omitted in this subsection in order to simplify the notation. Finally, as in the preceding, fission neutrons will eventually be taken into account in $Q(E,\vec{\Omega})$ which then ceases to be a datum and becomes a quantity on which one can iterate (outer iterations).

One usually puts:

$$\Sigma_s(E')f(E' \to E,\mu_0) = \Sigma_s(E' \to E,\mu_0) = \sum_{\ell=0}^{\infty} \frac{2\ell + 1}{4\pi} \Sigma_{s,\ell}(E' \to E)P_\ell(\mu_0) \tag{9.30}$$

with:

$$\mu_0 = \vec{\Omega}.\vec{\Omega}'.$$

The series expansion of the transfer cross section $\Sigma_s(E' \rightarrow E, \mu_0)$ in Legendre polynomials $P_\ell(\mu_0)$ enjoys an interesting property: for a finite number of terms (in practice this series is necessarily truncated) the mean square error is minimum in the interval $-1 < \mu_0 < 1$. Substituting this expansion in (9.29), and then expressing $P_\ell(\mu_0)$ as a function of the spherical harmonics $Y_{\ell,m}(\vec{\Omega})$, we obtain the emission rate in its most currently used form [50](p.227):

$$e(\vec{r},E,\vec{\Omega}) = \sum_{\ell=0}^{\infty} \frac{2\ell+1}{4\pi} \sum_{m=-\ell}^{\ell} \varepsilon_{\ell,m} Y_{\ell,m}(\vec{\Omega}) \int_0^{\infty} dE'\Sigma_{s,\ell}(E' \rightarrow E)\phi_{\ell,m}(E')$$
$$+ Q(\vec{r},E,\vec{\Omega}) \qquad (9.31)$$

where the angular moments of the flux are given by:

$$\phi_{\ell,m}(E) = \int_{4\pi} Y^*_{\ell,m}(\vec{\Omega})\phi(E,\vec{\Omega})d\Omega \qquad (9.32)$$

with

$$\varepsilon_{\ell,m} = \frac{(\ell - |m|)!}{(\ell + |m|)!}$$

If the directions $\vec{\Omega}$ are defined as indicated in Fig. 8.2, their components are always given by (8.11) and the spherical harmonics can be written:

$$Y_{\ell,m}(\vec{\Omega}) = P_\ell^m(\mu) \exp(i\ m\ \alpha) \qquad (9.33)$$

$P_\ell^m(\mu)$ being an associated Legendre polynomial, with $\mu = \cos\theta$ (Fig. 8.2).

The Legendre kernels, $\Sigma_{s,\ell}(E' \rightarrow E)$ are data of the problem in the same way as the usual macroscopic cross sections. They depend of course on the scattering cross section $\bar{\Sigma}_s(E')$, but also on properties that are revealed by the study of a collision. Thus, when the nucleus is at first at rest, it is necessary to take account of the correlation existing between the three variables E', E and μ_0 (see for example the case of elastic collision studied in §4.4.2).

Most transport codes are now based on the preceding formalism, and here too the energy variable is discretized by appealing to the notion of the group. Thus, the angular flux for the group g can be written:

$$\phi_g(\vec{r},\vec{\Omega}) = \int_{E_g}^{E_{g-1}} \phi(\vec{r},E,\vec{\Omega})dE$$

With analogous definitions for the other quantities, we obtain by integrating equations (9.28) and (9.31) over the energy from E_g to E_{g-1}:

$$\vec{\Omega}\cdot \vec{\text{grad}}\ \phi_g + \Sigma_{t,g}\phi_g(\vec{r},\vec{\Omega}) = e_g(\vec{r},\vec{\Omega})$$

$$e_g(\vec{r},\vec{\Omega}) = \sum_{\ell=0}^{\infty} \frac{2\ell+1}{4\pi} \sum_{m=-\ell}^{\ell} \varepsilon_{\ell,m} Y_{\ell,m}(\vec{\Omega}) \sum_{h=1}^{G} \Sigma_{s,\ell}(h \to g)\phi_{\ell,m;h} + Q_g(\vec{r},\vec{\Omega}) \tag{9.34}$$

To arrive at this result, it was necessary, as in subsec. 9.1.2, to decompose the integral over E' (9.31) into G partial integrals and to put:

$$\Sigma_{s,\ell}(h \to g) = \frac{\int_{E_g}^{E_{g-1}} dE \int_{E_h}^{E_{h-1}} dE'\Sigma_{s,\ell}(E' \to E)\phi_{\ell,m}(E')}{\int_{E_h}^{E_{h-1}} \phi_{\ell,m}(E')dE'} \tag{9.35}$$

These quantities represent the Legendre scattering matrices which for sufficiently narrow groups are not very sensitive to the choice of $\phi_{\ell,m}(E)$ just like the cross sections $\Sigma_{t,g}$ which, rigorously speaking, should be weighted by $\phi(E,\vec{\Omega})$. In practice, all these multigroup constants are obtained by taking a single weighting function, in other words, an approximate form of the scalar flux $\Phi(E)$ (§9.1.2), and the number of Legendre matrices to be considered does not generally exceed 5, since neutron scattering is almost isotropic (except if $E > 1$ MeV).

In slowing down problems, the energy can only decrease, so that in equations (9.34) we will necessarily have $h \leqq g$ and these equations will be successively solved with increasing values of g like the diffusion equations of the preceding subsections. Thus, here too, we are led to solve a succession of one-group problems.

It is of interest to get back the multigroup diffusion equations starting from (9.34) just as we did for mono-energetic neutrons (Sec. 8.1). To this end, let us integrate equations (9.34) over $\vec{\Omega}$ in 4π by noting that, except for $\ell = m = 0$, the integrals over the spherical harmonics vanish as a result of the orthogonality of these angular functions (9.33) ($Y_{\ell,m}(\vec{\Omega})$ is orthogonal to $Y_{0,0} = 1$). We are thus led to the equations:

$$\text{div } \vec{J}_g + \Sigma_{t,g}\, \Phi_g = \sum_{h=1}^{g} \Sigma_{s,0}(h \to g)\, \Phi_h + Q_g \tag{9.36}$$

in which the definitions of the scalar flux Φ_g (4.8) and of the net currents J_g (4.10) has been used as well as the identity $\phi_{0,0} = \Phi$ (9.32). Regrouping the terms in Φ_g, we get back equation (9.4) if we put:

$$\Sigma_{s,0}(h \to g) = \Sigma_s(h \to g) \qquad \text{if } h < g$$

$$\Sigma_{t,g} - \Sigma_{s,0}(g \to g) = \Sigma_{a,g} + \Sigma_{R,g}$$

We see that the first Legendre matrix ($\ell = 0$) plays a primordial role since it already intervenes in diffusion theory. The other matrices, on the contrary, only intervene in the transport equation itself (9.34). If, on the one hand, the collisions are very anisotropic (the Legendre matrices decreasing slowly with ℓ) and if the angular flux is similarly so -- which depends on the problem treated -- then diffusion theory may lead to very bad results (§8.1.3) and taking recourse to equations (9.34) becomes inevitable.

The preceding formalism is now systematically used in shielding studies for the reasons mentioned above. Still, a hybrid theory has been used in the past to solve this kind of problem. In the first groups ($E > 100$ keV), neutron propagation was treated by neglecting the scattering process (formalism identical to that of Sec. 4.1), but the total cross sections were replaced by the empirical removal cross sections. In contrast, diffusion theory was applied to the other groups, since it is much more justified at low energies. Finally, adjusting the results obtained for thermal neutrons on the basis of experiments allowed for the determination of the empirical cross sections of the first groups. The increasing power of calculational tools has enabled us to abandon this semi-empirical theory ("removal diffusion") which gave good distributions of thermal neutrons (and everything which stems from that: secondary γ, activation γ, etc.) but which became very questionable from the moment it was a matter of knowing rapid neutron fluxes, just those which contribute the most to biological doses (Sec. 6.2).

9.2 NUMERICAL METHODS

9.2.1 Introduction

In the preceding subsections we have seen that the multigroup formalism always leads us to solve successively mono-energetic equations (of diffusion or transport) whose source terms are known. These terms only depend in effect on the fluxes obtained by solving similar equations for lower indices g (here we of course assume that the fission neutron sources are known, cf. §4.5.8 and 9.1.3). Thus all mathematical developments in the framework of elementary diffusion theory lead us to an equation of the type:

$$\mathrm{div}\,(D\,(\vec{r})\,\vec{\mathrm{grad}}\,\Phi\,(\vec{r})) - \Sigma_a(\vec{r})\,\Phi\,(\vec{r}) + Q(\vec{r}) = 0 \qquad (9.37)$$

in which Σ_a eventually includes the removal cross section Σ_R and Q includes all neutron transfers from groups of lower indices to the considered group (9.4). This equation occupies a key position in reactor physics, and has thus been (and is still) the object of intense research involving numerical analysis. Except in particular cases (§4.5.7), the analytic approach rapidly becomes inextricable from the moment that one begins to consider realistic cases, so that in one way or another we always proceed to the discretization of the second order differential operator which appears in (9.37). We will limit ourselves in what follows to finite difference methods which are still at the base of most diffusion codes [15].

9.2.2 The Diffusion Equation with One Space Variable

A simple algorithm exists for this geometry. We will thus dwell on this case, all the more so because the proposed method can be generalized (§9.2.3). For plane geometry, equation (9.37) can be written:

$$\frac{d}{dx}\left(D\,(x)\,\frac{d\Phi}{dx} \right) - \Sigma_a(x)\,\Phi\,(x) + Q(x) = 0 \qquad (9.38)$$

Let x = 0 and x = H be the abscissae of the planar surfaces which bound the system to which equation (9.38) applies. Thus let us consider in the interval (0,H) the abscissae points x_i ($i = 1,2,\ldots I$), as well as the abscissae points $x_{i-\frac{1}{2}}$ situated at the middle of the intervals $(x_{i-1},\ x_i)$

and let us put (Fig. 9.4):

$$\Delta_i = x_i - x_{i-1} \quad \text{and} \quad \delta_i = x_{i+\frac{1}{2}} - x_{i-\frac{1}{2}} = \frac{\Delta_i + \Delta_{i+1}}{2}$$

Integrating (9.38) from $x_{i-\frac{1}{2}}$ to $x_{i+\frac{1}{2}}$ we obtain:

$$D_{i+\frac{1}{2}} \dot{\Phi}_{i+\frac{1}{2}} - D_{i-\frac{1}{2}} \dot{\Phi}_{i-\frac{1}{2}} - \bar{\Sigma}_{a,i} \bar{\Phi}_i \delta_i + \bar{Q}_i \delta_i = 0 \qquad (9.39)$$

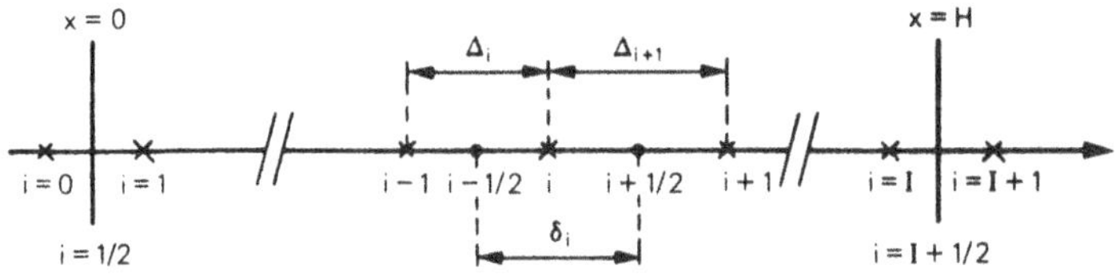

FIGURE 9.4.

with:

$$D(x_{i+\frac{1}{2}}) = D_{i+\frac{1}{2}}, \qquad \dot{\Phi}_{i+\frac{1}{2}} = \left|\frac{d\Phi}{dx}\right|_{x_{i+\frac{1}{2}}} \qquad \text{and} \quad \Phi(x_i) = \Phi_i$$

Equation (9.39) is rigorous provided we interpret $\bar{\Sigma}_{a,i}$ and $\bar{Q}_i$ as the average values of $\Sigma_a(x)$ and $Q(x)$ over the interval δ_i. However, this equation has too many unknowns. It is here that we make approximations:

$$\left.\begin{aligned} \bar{\Sigma}_{a,i} &\cong \Sigma_a(x_i) = \Sigma_{a,i} \\ \bar{Q}_i &\cong Q(x_i) = Q_i \\ \dot{\Phi}_{i+\frac{1}{2}} &\cong \frac{\Phi_{i+1} - \Phi_i}{\Delta_{i+1}} \quad \text{(finite difference)} \end{aligned}\right\}$$

These approximations become better the smaller are the quantities Δ_i and δ_i. Substituting these expressions in (9.39), we get:

$$-A_i \Phi_{i+1} + B_i \Phi_i - C_i \Phi_{i-1} = Q_i \qquad (9.40)$$

with

$$A_i = \frac{D_{i+\frac{1}{2}}}{\delta_i \Delta_{i+1}}, \qquad C_i = \frac{\delta_{i-1}}{\delta_i} A_{i-1} \qquad \text{and} \qquad B_i = A_i + C_i + \Sigma_{a,i} \qquad (9.41)$$

Before going further, we must note that a difficulty appears at the boundary of two zones. Since the value of the diffusion coefficient D(x) suddenly changes, the derivative of the flux is discontinuous (but not the current). Let $D^+_{i+\frac{1}{2}}$ and $D^-_{i+\frac{1}{2}}$ be the values of D(x) to the right and left of the boundary situated at $x = x_{i+\frac{1}{2}}$. We can express Fick's law at this point in two different ways, depending on which zone we place ourselves in (Fig. 9.4):

$$J_{i+\frac{1}{2}} = D^+_{i+\frac{1}{2}} \frac{\phi_{i+1} - \phi_{i+\frac{1}{2}}}{\frac{\Delta_{i+1}}{2}} = D^-_{i+\frac{1}{2}} \frac{\phi_{i+\frac{1}{2}} - \phi_i}{\frac{\Delta_{i+1}}{2}}$$

where $J_{i+\frac{1}{2}}$ is the net current.

Eliminating $\phi_{i+\frac{1}{2}}$ from these two equations, we succeed in putting the current in its usual form:

$$J_{i+\frac{1}{2}} = D_{i+\frac{1}{2}} \frac{\phi_{i+1} - \phi_i}{\Delta_{i+1}}$$

in spite of the discontinuity of D, provided we put:

$$\frac{1}{D_{i+\frac{1}{2}}} = \frac{1}{2} \left(\frac{1}{D^+_{i+\frac{1}{2}}} + \frac{1}{D^-_{i+\frac{1}{2}}} \right)$$

Provided we use this recipe, the preceding formalism (9.41) can be applied without restriction.

Writing (9.40) for i = 1,2 ...I, we obtain I equations with (I + 2) unknowns, whereas the boundary conditions enable us to eliminate the fluxes Φ_0 and Φ_{I+1} which have no sense, since they are relative to points situated outside the domain of application of the diffusion equation (9.38). To this end, let us arrange matters so that the discretization in x is such that the indices i = 1/2 and i = I + 1/2 correspond to the two faces x = 0 and x = H (Fig. 9.4). The boundary conditions can be generally written:

$$\dot{\Phi}_j = \pm \alpha_j \Phi_j \qquad (9.42)$$

the signs + and − corresponding respectively to j = 1/2 and j = I + 1/2. Thus for an isolated system, we simply have (8.29): $\alpha_j = 1/d_j$ where d_j is the extrapolation distance which is not necessarily the same for the two faces (8.31). Moreover, the condition of neutron autonomy implies that

$\alpha = 0$, since the vanishing of the net current entails through Fick's law the vanishing of $\dot{\Phi}$. Finally, in intermediate cases, the condition (9.42) can be interpreted as a reflection law (perfect reflection: $\alpha = 0$, nul reflection: $\alpha = 1/d$).

We shall discretize the derivative $\dot{\Phi}_j$ appearing in (9.42) as we have already done in (9.39). We then obtain the two desired additional equations:

$$\Phi_0 = \beta_1 \Phi_1 \quad \text{and} \quad \Phi_{I+1} = \beta_{I+1} \Phi_I \tag{9.43}$$

with

$$\beta_1 = \frac{2 - \alpha_{\frac{1}{2}} \Delta_1}{2 + \alpha_{\frac{1}{2}} \Delta_1} \quad \text{and} \quad \beta_{I+1} = \frac{2 - \alpha_{I+\frac{1}{2}} \Delta_{I+1}}{2 + \alpha_{I+\frac{1}{2}} \Delta_{I+1}} \tag{9.44}$$

where $\alpha_{\frac{1}{2}}$ and $\alpha_{I+\frac{1}{2}}$ are data whose physical meaning has been seen earlier. To arrive at these expressions it was necessary in addition to put:

$$\Phi_{\frac{1}{2}} \cong (\Phi_0 + \Phi_1)/2 \text{ and } \Phi_{I+\frac{1}{2}} \cong (\Phi_I + \Phi_{I+1})/2$$

approximations of the same order as the preceding, provided we define correctly Δ_1 and Δ_{I+1} ($\Delta_1 = 2x_1$ and $\Delta_{I+1} = 2(H - x_I)$).

The set of equations (9.40) and (9.43) constitutes a tridiagonal system and to profit from this particular feature we proceed as follows [61]:
We first look for a recurrence formula of the type:

$$\Phi_{i-1} = e_i \, \Phi_i + f_i \tag{9.45}$$

This relation written for i and i + 1 enables us to eliminate Φ_{i-1} and Φ_{i+1} from equation (9.40), which leads to an identity in Φ_i which must be satisfied whatever i may be. From these, one deduces the conditions:

$$\left. \begin{aligned} e_{i+1} &= \frac{A_i}{B_i - C_i e_i} \\ f_{i+1} &= \frac{Q_i + C_i f_i}{B_i - C_i e_i} \end{aligned} \right\} \tag{9.46}$$

These recurrence formulae enable us to calculate gradually all the parameters e_i and f_i from i = 2 to I + 1 starting from e_1 and f_1. The latter follow from the boundary condition on the left. Comparing (9.45) written for i = 1 with (9.43), we get:

$$e_1 = \beta_1 \text{ and } f_1 = 0$$

The fluxes can then be obtained with the help of the relation (9.45) written for i = I + 1, I,..., 3,2, the boundary condition on the right (9.43) enabling us to eliminate Φ_{I+1}. In sum, a sweep from left to right furnishes the auxiliary quantities e_i and f_i and a sweep from right to left the desired fluxes Φ_i (whence the expression "forward-backward substitution method").

When the system is composed of homogeneous zones, it is of interest to choose in each of them a regular subdivision (Δ_i = const.). In these conditions the error due to discretization is of the second order in Δ. Besides, the transition to one-dimensional cylindrical and spherical geometries can be made without difficulty. Considering the corresponding expressions of the divergence of a vector, equation (9.37) leads by a reasoning analogous to the preceding to the same discretized form (9.40), provided we put:

$$A_i = \frac{D_{i+\frac{1}{2}} S_{i+\frac{1}{2}}}{\Delta V_i \, \Delta_{i+1}} \quad \text{and} \quad C_i = \frac{\Delta V_{i-1}}{\Delta V_i} A_{i-1}$$

where $S_{i+\frac{1}{2}}$ is the right surface of the mesh i of volume ΔV_i.

Having thus calculated the flux in each group, we can easily deduce from it the reaction rates corresponding to the chosen discretization (x_i). As for the necessary integrals (9.18), (9.24), etc., they can only be obtained numerically, since the reaction rates are only known at certain points. We have for example in the case of plane geometry (9.18):

$$S = \int_0^H Q_f(x)dx \cong \sum_{i=1}^{I} Q_f(x_i)\delta_i$$

where $Q_f(x_i)$ is obtained from $\Phi_g(x_i)$ with the help of (4.97).

The discretization of an integral is generally a less delicate operation than that of a differential equation. In other words, a sufficiently fine subdivision such that (9.40) is a good approximation of (9.38) would be perfectly satisfactory for all envisageable quadratures.

9.2.3 Diffusion Equation with Several Variables

We restrict ourselves to two-dimensional geometries and adopt Cartesian coordinates (x, y). The mesh represented in Fig. 9.5 generalizes the subdivision discussed in the preceding subsection. Let us integrate equation (9.37) over the mesh labelled (i,j) of sides $x = x_{i\pm\frac{1}{2}}$ and $y = y_{j\pm\frac{1}{2}}$. Then Gauss' theorem leads to:

$$\delta_j \left[\overline{\left(D \frac{\partial \Phi}{\partial x} \right)}_{i+\frac{1}{2}} - \overline{\left(D \frac{\partial \Phi}{\partial x} \right)}_{i-\frac{1}{2}} \right] + \delta_i \left[\overline{\left(D \frac{\partial \Phi}{\partial y} \right)}_{j+\frac{1}{2}} - \overline{\left(D \frac{\partial \Phi}{\partial y} \right)}_{j-\frac{1}{2}} \right] +$$

$$\delta_j \delta_i \left[\overline{\overline{Q}}_{i,j} - \overline{\overline{(\Sigma_a \Phi)}}_{i,j} \right] = 0$$

where the quantities denoted $\overline{f}_{i\pm\frac{1}{2}}$, $\overline{f}_{j\pm\frac{1}{2}}$ and $\overline{\overline{f}}_{i,j}$ represent respectively the averages of a function f(x,y) taken over the sides i ± 1/2, j ± 1/2 and over the surface of the mesh (i,j). As in the preceding, these averages will be approximated by the values taken by this function at the center points of the considered domains, in other words, for example (Fig. 9.5):

$$\overline{f}_{i\pm\frac{1}{2}} \cong f(x_{i\pm\frac{1}{2}}, y_j) \quad , \quad \overline{\overline{f}}_{i,j} \cong f(x_i, y_i)$$

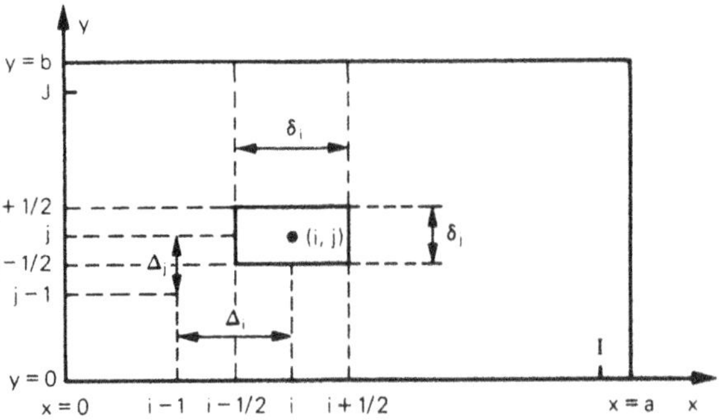

FIGURE 9.5.

Finally replacing the partial derivatives of the flux by finite differences, we obtain the system of algebraic equations:

$$- A^x_{i,j}\,\Phi_{i+1,j} + (A^x_{i,j} + C^x_{i,j})\,\Phi_{i,j} - C^x_{i,j}\,\Phi_{i-1,j} +$$
$$- A^y_{i,j}\,\Phi_{i,j+1} + (A^y_{i,j} + C^y_{i,j})\,\Phi_{i,j} - C^y_{i,j}\,\Phi_{i,j-1} + \qquad (9.47)$$
$$+ \Sigma_{a,i,j}\,\Phi_{i,j} = Q_{i,j}$$

We will not go into further details of this formalism; we simply note that the coefficients A and C only involve the diffusing properties of the medium through the diffusion coefficient D(x,y) evaluated over the four sides of the mesh ($D_{i+\frac{1}{2},j}$, $D_{i,j+\frac{1}{2}}$, etc.). As could be expected, a relation between five points appears in equation (9.47). If the diffusion vanishes in any of the directions Ox or Oy we get back (9.40). In the case of Oy for example, the flux must not depend on y, and thus we have necessarily $\Phi_{i,j+1} = \Phi_{i,j} = \Phi_{i,j-1}$ and the second line of (9.47) disappears. This remark suggests that we apply the following iterative method to the general case.

Suppose that at iteration (n) we approximately know the flux $\Phi_{i,j}$ so as to be able to evaluate the neutron leakage in the direction y (second line of (9.47)). Putting this term in the righthand side of equation (9.47) we are led to solve for each value of j a tridiagonal system in i analogous to that of the preceding subsection (9.40). The double sweep susbstitution method which makes use of the boundary conditions on the faces x = 0 and x = a can thus be applied. We thus arrive at a new set of values $\Phi_{i,j}$ which will now enable us to calculate the leakage in the direction x and thus to put the first line of (9.47) in the righthand side. The iteration (n + 1) thus consists of solving for each value of i a tridiagonal system in j. We repeat this procedure as many times as necessary, which amounts to sweeping the system sometimes horizontally, sometimes vertically. These iterations are called <u>inner iterations</u> for they concern the solution of each of the multigroup equations (4.96) or (9.4) and not the progressive readjustment of the fission neutron sources (§9.1.3)

Quite a few other methods for solving the diffusion equation exist. Especially for many dimensional geometries one more and more frequently calls upon the <u>finite element method</u> [62]. This permits us not only to consider meshes of varied shapes (often triangles which in cylindrical geometry permits a better fit with the curvature of the boundaries between zones), but also to go to higher order approximations (the fluxes are no longer assumed to vary linearly in each mesh). The relations between the meshes follow from a variational principle which is strictly equivalent to the original partial differential equations. Another method, of so-called "coarse meshes" consists in solving as correctly as possible the diffusion equation (or even the transport equation) inside each mesh (necessarily homogeneous). The connections between the meshes now take place through the currents traversing the faces of the meshes, and one generally arrives at algebraic equations of the type (9.47) with more exact values of the coefficients A and C. In this domain there is no unique method, but a large number of possible approaches.

9.2.4 The Transport Equation

Most of the multigroup transport codes are based on equations (9.34). In slowing down problems which are of interest to us here, the sum over h goes only from 1 to g, so that (9.34) can be seen as a mono-energetic equation when one solves it for $\phi_g(\vec{r},\vec{\Omega})$. Nevertheless an important difference exists with respect to multigroup diffusion equations (§9.1.2): the term h = g in the expression for the emission rate e_g is not known (in contrast to the others: h < g) since it depends on the desired solution $\phi_g(\vec{r},\vec{\Omega})$ through equation (9.32) which permits the calculation of $\phi_{\ell,m;g}(r)$. All codes based on this formalism [63] work in the following way: the emission rate e_g being supposed known, one solves the first equation (9.34) and, from the angular fluxes thus obtained, one deduces the moments $\phi_{\ell,m;g}$ (9.32) necessary for a new estimation of e_g. This type of inner iterations intervenes even in problems involving only a single space variable; this was not the case for the diffusion equation (§9.2.2). As for the outer iterations rendered necessary by the presence of fissile isotopes, they take place as in the preceding, noting that the angular source of fission neutrons is isotropic, that is:

$$Q_g(\vec{r},\vec{\Omega}) = \chi_g \; Q_f^*(\vec{r})/4\pi$$

where Q_f^* and χ_g have the same meaning as in subsec. 9.1.3. To solve the first equation (9.34) we consider a finite number of directions $\vec{\Omega}_k$(k = 1,2 ...K) on which we integrate numerically. This amounts to introducing the simple form (8.1) which leads to a relation between only two points when we pass to finite differences. At this level, the calculations are thus simpler than in diffusion theory, but this apparent simplicity is obtained at a price:

- The spatial sweeping must be done for each direction $\vec{\Omega}_k$ (in contrast to the diffusion equation which ignores this variable).
- The internal iterations relating to the emission rates converge very slowly if the diffusion in the group is large, that is, if $\Sigma_s(g \to g) \cong \Sigma_{t,g}$.
- Finally, the angular moments (9.32), and in particular the scalar flux can only be obtained by quadrature, whence the necessity for a large number of directions.

In summary, for the same number of groups, transport calculations are much more costly than diffusion calculations. Fortunately they are not necessary for the study of the behavior of power reactors, except where the fine distributions of the flux in the cells is concerned, and in this case, various justified approximations make these calculations feasible (§8.2.4). On the other hand, shielding studies, or studies of multiplying systems of small size (nuclear explosives) most often require transport calculations based on the general formalism of subsec. 9.1.6. The numerical solution method described above has been called the DSN method. In technical jargon, to speak of a calculation S16P5 means that the Legendre expansion has been cut off at the fifth order in the expression for the emission rate ($\ell \leqslant 5$) and that 16 polar angles θ are involved in the definition of the chosen directions $\vec{\Omega}_k$ (Fig. 8.2). For systems where the angular flux only depends on θ (§8.1.2), 16 will also represent the number of directions.

9.3 FUNDAMENTAL MODE

9.3.1 Introduction

It is often necessary to know neutron spectra in great detail. Thus one must often solve in principle the system of equations (9.11) for a large number of groups (at least 100). The volume of calculations that this could lead to could be prohibitive, especially for several-dimensional geometries. The most widely used procedure consists in treating approximately the spatial variations of the flux by initially writing in each homogeneous zone:

$$\Phi_g(\vec{r}) \cong \tilde{\Phi}_g\ (B^2)\ f\ (\vec{B},\vec{r}) \tag{9.48}$$

an expression in which the form function $f(\vec{B},\vec{r})$ is by definition a solution of the equation:

$$\nabla^2 f + B^2 f = 0 \tag{9.49}$$

and $\vec{B}$ is a unique parameter characterizing the zone under study.

Expression (9.48) represents the fundamental mode and the fluxes at all energies have identical spatial distributions. This factorization is evidently not rigorous, but it is very often justified in homogeneous multiplying zones of large dimensions (compared to diffusion lengths), except in the immediate vicinity of their boundaries. For example, in a homogeneous bare reactor, the parameter B^2 can be identified with the geometrical buckling as defined earlier (§4.5.3). Even when this parameter is not known a priori, a fundamental mode may apear during calculations and eventually negative values of B^2 can acquire meaning. Thus the flux distributions of Fig. 9.6 relative to a two zone cylindrical reactor show a fundamental mode in each zone. The central zone, which is the poorer, corresponds to a negative value of B^2 and the analytic continuation of $f(\vec{B},\vec{r})$, and hence of the flux $\Phi_g(\vec{r})$ can no longer vanish outside this zone (no extrapolation distance). Nevertheless, an expression like (9.48) constitutes a good approximation for the flux, except near the common boundary of the two zones. B^2 is no longer necessarily the geometrical buckling, but only a parameter of curvature.

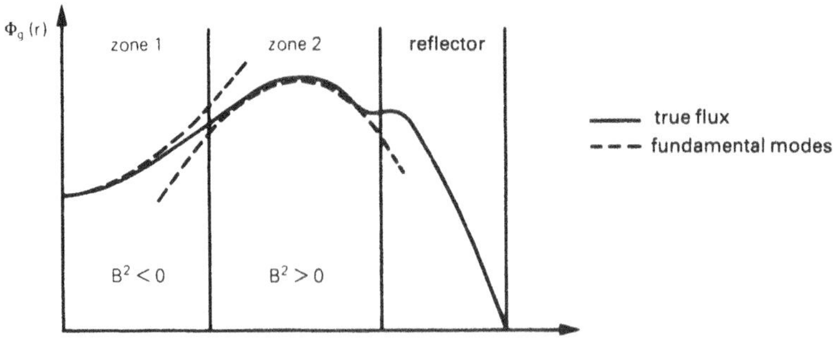

FIGURE 9.6.

9.3.2 Formalism

Whatever the case, if a fundamental mode exists, it must satisfy the original diffusion equations (9.11). Taking into consideration Fick's law and the defining relations (9.48) and (9.49), the leakage terms of these equations can be written:

$$\mathrm{div}\, \vec{J}_g(\vec{r}) = -D_g \nabla^2 \Phi_g(\vec{r}) = D_g B^2 \tilde{\Phi}_g f(\vec{B},\vec{r})$$

and the factorization of the other terms is evident since they are all linear combinations of the fluxes Φ_g, including the neutron sources Q_f^* (4.97). We finally note that all this implies the homogeneity of the considered zone (the macroscopic cross sections and the diffusion coefficients are independent of $\vec{r}$). In these conditions, the system of partial differential equations (9.11) leads to the system of algebraic equations:

$$(\Sigma_{R,g} + \Sigma_{a,g} + D_g B^2)\, \tilde{\Phi}_g = \sum_{h=1}^{g-1} \Sigma_S(h \rightarrow g)\, \tilde{\Phi}_h + \chi_g \tilde{Q}_f^* \qquad (9.50)$$

In this system, neutron leakage is represented by fictitious absorption cross sections $D_g B^2$ as already shown in one-group theory (§4.5.3). These equations, provided we solve them successively with increasing values of g, furnish the unknowns $\tilde{\Phi}_g$. The results of course depend on B^2 and the solution obtained is proportional to $\tilde{Q}_f^*$. This being done, the effective multiplication factor is obtained by the general procedure (§4.5.8). First we calculate the new source density of fission neutrons (4.97) making use of the factorization (9.48), that is:

$$Q_f(\vec{r}) = \tilde{Q}_f f(\vec{B},\vec{r})$$

with

$$\tilde{Q}_f = \sum_{g=1}^{G} (\bar{\nu}\,\Sigma_f)_g\, \tilde{\Phi}_g$$

substituting this latter result in (4.99), we obtain:

$$k = \sum_{g=1}^{G} (\bar{\nu}\,\Sigma_f)_g \frac{\tilde{\Phi}_g}{\tilde{Q}_f^*} \qquad (9.51)$$

We see that the integrations over space have disappeared and external iterations are no longer necessary. Expression (9.51) shows in effect that the fluxes $\tilde{\Phi}_g$ being proportional to $\tilde{Q}_f^*$, the factor k is independent of the choice of this latter quantity. It thus represents the effective multiplication factor k_e of the zone under study. Putting $Q_f^* = 1$, the unique solution of (9.50) thus furnishes all desired information as a function of B^2 and the composition of this zone. The basic libraries used in this type of calculation contain for each isotope (i) microscopic quantities such as: $\sigma_{s,h}^{(i)}$, $\sigma_s^{(i)}(h \rightarrow g)$, etc., which have been prepared once and for all using the recipes of subsec. 9.1.2 and 9.1.3. Starting from these data, the macroscopic cross sections and the diffusion coefficients necessary for equations (9.50) are obtained as usual by applying the mixture rule (4.1). Other than the parameter B^2, the only other data of the problem are thus the atomic densities N_i of the various constituents.

The explicit nature of the formalism described above leads to very fast computer calculations, even for several hundred groups. The variations of k_e with B^2 are schematically represented in Fig. 9.7. The value obtained for $B^2 = 0$ evidently corresponds to the infinite multiplication factor k_∞ (absence of neutron leakage) and the operating point of a homogeneous zone belonging to a critical system demands that $k_e = 1$.

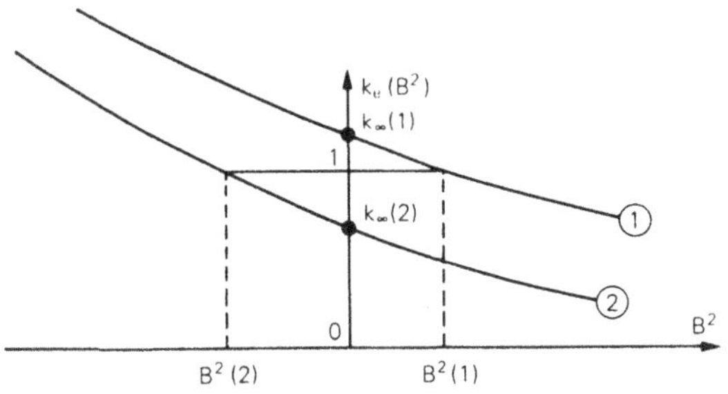

FIGURE 9.7.

Let us consider two multiplying zones, one rich (in fissile isotopes) with $k_\infty > 1$ and the other poor ($k_\infty < 1$). Figure 9.7 indicates that the first leads, in the critical state, to a positive value of B^2 (curve 1); it could thus function autonomously provided we gave it sufficiently large dimensions and in this case B^2 can be identified with the geometrical buckling (§4.5.3). In contrast, a homogeneous zone which is too poor (curve 2) cannot diverge by itself and the negative value of B^2 implies, to make sense, that a richer multiplying zone exists somewhere in the system (a reactor cannot go critical if all zones are characterized by negative values of B^2).

In a general way, values of B^2 which insure the equality $k_e = 1$ may be identified with material bucklings B_m^2, which may be introduced in one-group calculations in systems of several zones (§4.5.7). This does not mean that we can be satisfied with one-group theory when it is a matter of connecting the zones, but that, if one sticks to this model, the calculations of the fundamental mode furnish the best possible values of the material bucklings; the effects of the spectra are taken into consideration, whereas they were given a rather cavalier treatment in the course of the derivation of expression (4.83).

Except for special cases (§9.3.4), the calculations of the fundamental mode do not alone permit us to define the critical state of a reactor; they simply constitute the first phase of neutronic studies in which we take account of nuclear phenomena as precisely as possible, while at the same time not knowing how the zones will ultimately be connected. We will pursue this study with two important applications.

9.3.3 Practical Applications

Almost all cross section codes relative to a limited number of groups follow the procedure just described [14]. After having determined the "fine spectrum" in the fundamental mode approximation, that is, the quantities $\tilde{\Phi}_g$ for a large number of groups, these codes procede to the following condensation: the user of the code defines G' wide groups whose limits $E_g'(g' = 1,2,\ldots G')$ belong to the denser set of E_g and the cross sections for this new group structure can be easily obtained by imposing the invariance of the reaction rates. Thus the new absorption cross sections are given for each isotope by the expressions:

$$\left.\begin{aligned} \sigma_{a,g'}\,\tilde{\Phi}_{g'} &= \sum_{g\in g'} \sigma_{a,g}\,\tilde{\Phi}_g \\ \tilde{\Phi}_{g'} &= \sum_{g\in g'} \tilde{\Phi}_g \end{aligned}\right\} \qquad (9.52)$$

the second equation resulting from the very definition of the groups. In the same way one calculates the new scattering matrices:

$$\sigma_s(h' \rightarrow g')\ \tilde{\Phi}_{h'} = \sum_{g \in g'} \sum_{h \in h'} \sigma_s(h \rightarrow g)\ \tilde{\Phi}_h \qquad (9.53)$$

The new set of multigroup constants depends, in contrast to the preceding, on the parameter B^2. One can take the value of B^2 which renders the fundamental mode critical ($k_e = 1$) or, if there are to be no iterations in B^2, any plausible value based on simple theories (§4.5.4); the results are not very sensitive to the choice. Finally, having determined all the multigroup data for a limited number of wide groups, one can make the reactor calculation in all its geometric complexity by solving G' diffusion equations (9.11) with the help of the numerical methods of Sec. 9.2. Evidently at this stage one no longer uses the approximation (9.48).

The preceding model is often used in studies of the point evolution of a fuel (§5.3.4). If the integrated flux θ, the fundamental variable in this type of problem, includes neutrons of all energies, then it is the one-group cross sections which must be introduced in the evolution equations (5.27). These can be calculated with the help of (9.52) by putting $g' = 1$, since G fine groups are contained in the single wide group ($g' = G' = 1$). In thermal reactors one takes as reference the integrated flux relative to the thermal neutrons ($g = G$), since the latter are the most important. In this case, we have:

$$\sigma^*_{a,t}\ \tilde{\Phi}_G = \sum_{g=1}^{G} \sigma_{a,g}\ \tilde{\Phi}_g \qquad (9.54)$$

where $\sigma^*_{a,t}$ can be interpreted as an absorption cross section of thermal neutrons which has been corrected to take account of absorptions in the other groups. It reduces to the usual cross section $\sigma_{a,t}$ for a fuel which is sensitive to thermal neutrons only ($\sigma_{a,g} = 0$ for $g < G$).

In all practical cases, a few useful cross sections ($\sigma^*_{a,8}, \sigma^*_{a,5}$, etc.) depend on the composition of the zone concerned through $\tilde{\Phi}_g$ (§9.3.2). Now the composition evolves with the integrated flux, and this evolution is regulated by the cross sections. The evolution equations (5.27) and the fundamental mode (9.50) are thus coupled, which leads to the sequence of calculations displayed in Fig. 9.8. In fact, calculations of the spectra $\tilde{\Phi}_g$ are only repeated insofar as the composition of the fuel has substantially changed;the quantities $\sigma^*_{a,i}$ vary slowly with the integrated flux θ and a short loop involving only equations (5.27) can be envisaged.

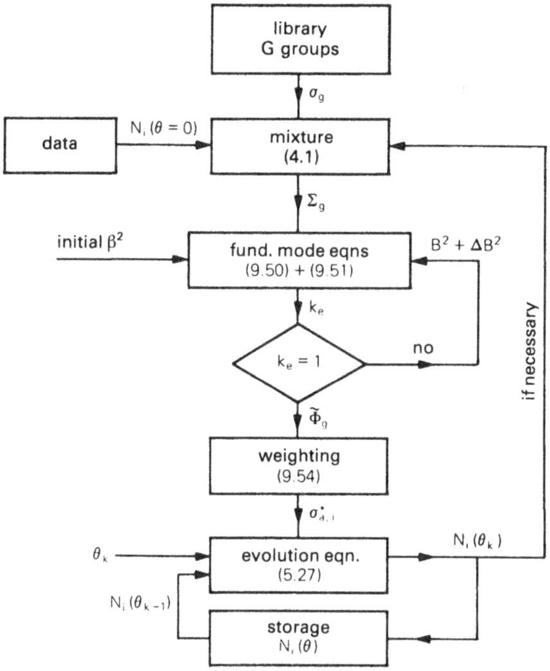

FIGURE 9.8. Point evolution of the fuel. The equations to be solved are identified by their numbering in the text.

9.3.4 Homogeneous Bare Reactor

Since such a system is isolated, the fluxes at all energies must vanish on its extrapolated surface. Rigorously speaking, this surface is not completely defined, since the extrapolation distances (§4.3.2) depend a little on the energy through the total cross section Σ_t of the medium (4.20). However, the extrapolation distances are very small compared to the dimensions of the reactors (if that isn't the case, diffusion theory itself is false), so that we can conclude that the fluxes $\Phi_g(\vec{r})$ must all virtually vanish on the s..ne surface (S) whatever g may be. We see immediately that the fundamental mode (9.48) enjoys this property if the form function also satisfies the condition:

$$|f(\vec{B},\vec{r})|_{\vec{r}\in S} = 0$$

In this case equations (9.49) and (4.71) have strictly the same meaning and B^2 is nothing but the geometrical buckling, known in advance of any calculation of $\tilde{\Phi}_g$. Its value only depends on the form of the reactor and we recall that for a spherical reactor we had obtained the value $B^2 = \pi^2/(R + d)^2$ (cf. §4.5.3). It is quite remarkable that this result remains valid in multigroup theory. All the same, the multiplication factor k_e and other reactor parameters, which are calculated starting from $\tilde{\Phi}_g$ for the preceding value of B^2, will be different from what was indicated in subsec. 4.5.4, and it is interesting to see under what conditions these differences disappear.

To this end, let us consider the G groups of subsec. 9.3.2 with the following restrictions:

- inelastic scattering only takes place in the first group (E_1 corresponds to the threshhold E_s of subsec. 8.4.3)
- the fission neutron spectrum only covers the first two groups ($\chi_1 = \chi_s$; $\chi_2 = 1 - \chi_s$; $\chi_g = 0$ for $g > 2$)
- the groups are of such a width that each of them is only fed by the one before.

In these conditions, equations (9.50) can be written:

$$\left.\begin{aligned}
&(\Sigma_{R,1} + \Sigma_{a,1} + D_1 B^2)\,\tilde{\Phi}_1 = \chi_s\,\tilde{Q}_f^* \\
&(\Sigma_{R,2} + \Sigma_{a,2} + D_2 B^2)\,\tilde{\Phi}_2 = \Sigma_{R,1}\,\tilde{\Phi}_1 + (1-\chi_s)\,\tilde{Q}_f^* \\
&(\Sigma_{R,g} + \Sigma_{a,g} + D_g B^2)\,\tilde{\Phi}_g = \Sigma_{R,g-1}\,\tilde{\Phi}_{g-1} \qquad (2 < g < G) \\
&(\Sigma_{a,t} + D_t B^2)\,\tilde{\Phi}_t = \Sigma_{R,G-1}\,\tilde{\Phi}_{G-1}
\end{aligned}\right\} \quad (9.55)$$

Because of the third hypothesis the matrices $\Sigma_s(h \to g)$ reduce to the terms $h = g - 1$ and we can put: $\Sigma_s(h \to h + 1) = \Sigma_{R,h}$ (9.6). Finally, we recall that the last group corresponds to thermal neutrons, whence the change of indices $G \to t$ and $\Sigma_{R,G} = 0$.

Solving equations (9.55) and keeping only the values of $\tilde{\Phi}_1$ and $\tilde{\Phi}_t$, we get:

$$\tilde{\Phi}_1 = \frac{\chi_s \tilde{Q}_f^*}{\Sigma_{R,1} + \Sigma_{a,1} + D_1 B^2} \tag{9.56}$$

$$\tilde{\Phi}_t = \frac{\Sigma_{R,1}\tilde{\Phi}_1 + (1 - \chi_s)\tilde{Q}_f^*}{(\Sigma_{a,t} + D_t B^2) \prod_{g=2}^{G-1} \left(1 + \frac{\Sigma_{a,g} + D_g B^2}{\Sigma_{R,g}}\right)} \tag{9.57}$$

The second expression can be obtained without difficulty by multiplying the lefthand side and the righthand side of equations (9.55), excluding the first expression.

According to our hypotheses, the removal cross sections $\Sigma_{R,g}$ reflect the elastic slowing down of neutrons except for the first group. We thus have in this case (4.94):

$$\Sigma_{R,g} = \xi\Sigma_{s,g} / \ln \left(\frac{E_{g-1}}{E_g} \right)$$

and according to (9.16):

$$\frac{\Sigma_{a,g}}{\Sigma_{R,g}} = \int_{E_g}^{E_{g-1}} \frac{\Sigma_a(E)}{\xi\Sigma_t(E)} \frac{dE}{E}$$

In the same way we can make explicit the leakage terms:

$$\frac{D_g B^2}{\Sigma_{R,g}} = \frac{D_g B^2}{\xi\Sigma_{s,g}} \ln \left(\frac{E_{g-1}}{E_g} \right) \cong B^2 \int_{E_g}^{E_{g-1}} \frac{D(E)}{\xi\Sigma_s(E)} \frac{dE}{E}$$

The last two quantities being generally small, we can replace each factor of the product Π appearing in (9.57) by an exponential ($1 + x \cong \exp x$), whence the result:

$$\tilde{\Phi}_t = p \exp(-B^2\tau) \frac{\Sigma_{R,1}\tilde{\Phi}_1 + (1 - \chi_s)\tilde{Q}_f^*}{\Sigma_{a,t} + D_t B^2} \tag{9.58}$$

where p, the resonance escape probability (4.53) and τ, the slowing down area (4.78) have the same meaning as in subsec. 4.5.4 (it suffices to identify E_1 with E_s and E_{G-1} with E_t^*).

We pursue our analysis, and make explicit the critical condition obtained for the fundamental mode by supposing that fissions only take place in the first group (fertile isotopes) and especially in the last group (fissile isotopes). This fourth restriction enables us to write (9.51) in the form (k = 1):

$$\tilde{Q}_f^* = (\bar{\nu}\Sigma_f)_1 \tilde{\Phi}_1 + (\bar{\nu}\Sigma_f)_t \tilde{\Phi}_t \qquad (9.59)$$

in other words, because of (9.56) and (9.58), the critical condition:

$$1 = (\eta_c f)_t \, p \, \varepsilon \frac{\exp(-B^2 \tau)}{1 + L_t^2 B^2}$$

is identical to the pair of equations (4.80) and (4.81).

To get this result, it was necessary to put:

$$\left.\begin{aligned} (\eta_c f)_t &= \left(\frac{\bar{\nu}\Sigma_f}{\Sigma_a}\right)_t \\ L_t^2 &= D_t/\Sigma_{a,t} \\ \varepsilon &= 1 + \chi_s \frac{(\bar{\nu}\Sigma_f)_1 - (\Sigma_{a,1} + D_1 B^2)}{\Sigma_{R,1} + \Sigma_{a,1} + D_1 B^2 - \chi_s(\bar{\nu}\Sigma_f)_1} \end{aligned}\right\} \qquad (9.60)$$

The first two expressions, already introduced in subsec. 4.5.4, are relative to thermal neutrons (fuel multiplication factor η_c, thermal utilization factor f and the diffusion area L^2). As for the expression for the fast fission factor ε, it is close to that which was already proposed for homogeneous media (§8.4.4) when the leakage of very fast neutrons ($D_1 B^2 << \Sigma_{a,1}$) is disregarded. It becomes identical to (8.86) if one supposes the slowing down in the first group to be due to inelastic collisions in the fuel and elastic collisions in the moderator, with in both cases $P_2(1 \rightarrow E_1) = 1$ (every neutron scattered in the first group necessarily leaves it).

With the same hypotheses one can also calculate the conversion factor, starting from the general expression (9.24) and considering the fundamental mode:

$$C = \frac{\tilde{R}_c^{(2)}}{\tilde{R}_a^{(1)}} = \frac{\sum_g \Sigma_{c,g}^{(2)} \tilde{\Phi}_g}{\sum_g \Sigma_{a,g}^{(1)} \tilde{\Phi}_g} \quad \frac{\sum_g \Sigma_{c,g}^{(2)} \tilde{\Phi}_g}{\Sigma_{a,t}^{(1)} \tilde{\Phi}_t}$$

where the indices (1) and (2) are relative to fissile and fertile isotopes.

For the first, only the thermal neutrons are efficient and for the second the capture and absorption cross sections are indistinguishable, except in the first group where fast fission intervenes. We thus get, using the preceding results:

$$C = \left(\frac{\eta}{\eta_c}\right)_t - 1 + \eta_t \left[\varepsilon (1 - p) \exp(-B^2\tau) + \varepsilon^* - \varepsilon\right] \qquad (9.61)$$

an expression very close to (5.4). The additional term $\eta_t(\varepsilon^* - \varepsilon)$, in which ε^* is the value of ε when one puts $\Sigma^{(2)}_{c,1} = 0$, reflects the conversion in the first group (this term is very small for thermal reactors).

In a similar way the absorption cross section of the fertile isotope adapted to the thermal group can be written (9.54):

$$\left.\begin{aligned} \sigma^{*(2)}_{a,t} &= \sigma^{(2)}_{a,t} + \frac{(\nu\Sigma_f)^{(1)}_t}{N^{(2)}} f(N^{(2)}) \\ \text{with:}& \\ f(N^{(2)}) &\cong \varepsilon(1 - p) \exp(-B^2\tau) + \varepsilon^* - \varepsilon + \frac{\varepsilon^* - 1}{\nu_1 - 1} \end{aligned}\right\} \qquad (9.62)$$

Let us disregard the index t and apply this result to uranium U^{238} (the index 8 replaces (2) henceforth). The second evolution equation (5.27) can be written:

$$\frac{dN_9}{d\theta} = \sigma^*_{a,8} N_8 - \sigma_{a,9} N_9$$

in which $\sigma^*_{a,8}$ includes resonance absorptions (whence the asterisk) while $\sigma_{a,9}$ is the thermal cross section for plutonium (no resonances). Substituting (9.62) into this last equation and noting that $(\nu\Sigma_f)^{(1)}_t$ corresponds to a mixture of fissile isotopes, we get:

$$\frac{dN_9}{d\theta} = \sigma_{a,8}N_8 - \sigma_{a,9}N_9 + \left[(\nu\sigma_f)_5 N_5 + (\nu\sigma_f)_9 N_9 + \ldots\right] f(N_8) \qquad (9.63)$$

In this equation all the coefficients are microscopic cross sections in the strict sense, that is, they correspond to thermal energy neutrons and are thus assumed to be known. With respect to the initial equation (5.27) for which $\sigma^*_{a,8} = \sigma_{a,8}$ the additional term reflects the spectrum effect mentioned in subsecs. 5.3.5 and 9.3.3. If, in addition, we assume that

$f(N_8)$ is slowly varying, which in fact is true since p and ε vary little with consumption, the new equation (9.63) becomes linear in its turn, and the system (5.27) can again be solved analytically. This simplified formalism has very often been used in the past.

In conclusion, we see on the basis of this very particular example (homogeneous bare reactor) to what extent the multigroup theory represents progress with respect to the simple models of subsections 4.5.4 and 5.1.4. In effect, it was necessary to make three or four simplifying hypotheses in order to get back these models starting from the multigroup equations. The latter (9.50) can be solved so easily on the computer that they have beaten all previous formalisms which were too restrictive, even in cases as simple as the one treated in this subsection.

9.3.5 Fundamental Mode in Transport Theory

The existence of a fundamental mode is evidently independent of the formalism used, so that the preceding approach must be applicable to the transport equation. To simplify, we will place ourselves in the framework of one-dimensional plane geometry. We know that in this case the angular flux is independent of the azimuthal angle α (Fig. 8.2). Let us suppose in addition that the source densities and the diffusions are isotropic, so that equation (9.34) reduces to ($\ell = m = 0$):

$$\mu\frac{\partial\phi}{\partial x} + \Sigma_t\ \phi(x,\mu) = \frac{\Sigma_s\Phi + Q(x)}{2} \tag{9.64}$$

an expression in which the index g is omitted after one has put:

$$\Sigma_s = \Sigma_{s,0}(g \to g) \quad \text{and} \quad Q(x) = \sum_{h=1}^{g-1}\Sigma_{s,0}\ (h \to g)\ \Phi_h + Q_g$$

This equation relative to a particular group is identical to (8.18) when we make the same hypotheses ($\bar{u}_0 = 0$ and $Q(x,\mu) = Q(x)/2$) and the entire formalism of subsec. 8.1.2 can be kept. The same problem treated by diffusion theory leads us to write in each group (9.4):

$$-D\frac{d^2\Phi}{dx^2} + \Sigma_a\ \Phi(x) = Q(x) \tag{9.65}$$

where Q has the same meaning as above, whereas $\Sigma_a = \Sigma_t - \Sigma_s$ is an absorption cross section in a loose sense which includes the removal cross section of the group.

Let us consider a homogeneous zone of large dimensions and look for solutions of the form:

$$\left.\begin{aligned} Q(x) &= \tilde{Q} \cos Bx \\ \Phi(x) &= \tilde{\Phi} \cos Bx \end{aligned}\right\} \qquad (9.66)$$

in accordance with the definition of a fundamental mode since cos Bx is a solution of (9.49) for plane geometry ($\nabla^2 = d^2/dx^2$).

Substituting (9.66) into (9.65) we get:

$$\tilde{\Phi} = \frac{\tilde{Q}}{\Sigma_a + DB^2} \qquad (9.67)$$

Keeping the preceding factorizations in the case of the transport equation (9.64), we are led to write the angular flux in the form:

$$\phi(x,\mu) = \tilde{\phi}_1(\mu) \cos Bx + \tilde{\phi}_2(\mu) \sin Bx \qquad (9.68)$$

an expression which will be justified in the following. Let us integrate the latter over μ from −1 to +1. The lefthand side then shows the scalar flux Φ (8.19) which when factorized in accord with (9.66) leads to the constraints:

$$\left.\begin{aligned} \int_{-1}^{1} \tilde{\phi}_1(\mu)\, d\mu &= \tilde{\Phi} \\ \int_{-1}^{1} \tilde{\phi}_2(\mu)\, d\mu &= 0 \end{aligned}\right. \qquad (9.69)$$

The expansion (9.68) must be the solution of the transport equation (9.64) and we find by substitution and equating terms in cos Bx and sin Bx:

$$\left.\begin{aligned} \tilde{\phi}_2(\mu) &= \frac{\mu B}{\Sigma_t} \tilde{\phi}_1(\mu) \\ \tilde{\phi}_1(\mu) &= \frac{\Sigma_s \tilde{\Phi} + \tilde{Q}}{2\Sigma_t} \; \frac{1}{1 + \left(\frac{\mu B}{\Sigma_t}\right)^2} \end{aligned}\right\} \qquad (9.70)$$

Finally, substituting the expression for $\tilde{\phi}_1(\mu)$ into the first relation (9.69), we deduce from it the scalar flux $\tilde{\Phi}$ in an explicit form:

$$\tilde{\Phi} = \frac{\tilde{Q}}{\dfrac{B}{\mathrm{Arctg}\left(\dfrac{B}{\Sigma_t}\right)} - \Sigma_s} \qquad (9.71)$$

As to the second relation (9.69), it is automatically satisfied since $\phi_2(\mu)$ is an odd function (9.70).

If we try to put this latter result into the form (9.67) we are led to define a corrected diffusion coefficient D^* such that:

$$\left.\begin{aligned} D^* &= \frac{1}{3\,\Sigma_t \gamma\left(\frac{B}{\Sigma_t}\right)} \\ \text{with:} \\ \gamma(x) &= \frac{x^2}{3}\,\frac{1}{\frac{x}{\text{Arctg}x} - 1} \end{aligned}\right\} \quad (9.72)$$

This quantity thus depends on B but tends to the classical diffusion coefficient (4.14) when B/Σ_t tends to zero ($\gamma(x) \to 1$ if $x \to 0$). We can thus keep the entire formalism of subsec. 9.3.2 provided we introduce in each group D^*_g in place of D_g, and thus take account of transport effects. All the same we may wonder if this refinement is necessary, since a fundamental mode can appear in a homogeneous zone only if the dimensions of the latter are large compared to the mean free paths $(1/\Sigma_t)$, in other words if B/Σ_t is small, since B varies like the inverse of the dimensions. Recourse to transport theory is more justified if one wants to take account of the anisotropy of the diffusion ($\ell \neq 0$ in (9.34)), but the formalism becomes more complicated. The method used in this case, called the Bethe method [64] can nevertheless be simplified. We can show that the preceding function $\gamma(x)$ still plays a preponderant role [65].

Most numerical condensation codes based on spectrum calculations in the fundamental mode (§9.3.3) use the correction introduced in this section. The presence of the function Arctgx in the formalism significantly increases calculation times, since it is evaluated a great many times (for each group); it is thus important to know in advance if this correction must be made or not, and the option $\gamma(x) = 1$ is generally reserved in the codes.

9.4 REACTIVITY FEEDBACKS

9.4.1 Doppler Effect

This effect affects microscopic cross sections at the level of resonances if the widths Δ of the latter have as order of magnitude the thermal agitation energy of the nuclei. Contrary to the hypotheses made in the course of slowing down studies (§4.4.2), we can no longer assume that the nuclei are at rest before undergoing a collision; in particular the capture rate in fertile materials will depend on the temperatures.

We can qualitatively explain this phenomenon in the following way. The neutron-nucleus interaction cross section depends strongly on the relative energy E_r of two particles. As shown in Fig. 9.9, the curve $\sigma(E_r)$ shows a very marked maximum for $E_r = E_R$. Such a curve is characteristic of the interaction under study, independently of the temperature T of the medium. For T = 0, we clearly have $E = E_r$, since the nuclei are at rest, and only neutrons of energy E such that $E_R - \Delta/2 < E < E_R + \Delta/2$ can be absorbed (Fig. 9.9). For temperatures $T \neq 0$ the conclusions are different: a neutron of energy $E < E_R - \Delta/2$ is capable of being absorbed by a nucleus moving in its direction, since its relative energy E_r, higher than E, can very well belong to the energy band $(E_R - \Delta/2, E_R + \Delta/2)$. An analogous reasoning for neutrons of energy $E > E_R + \Delta/2$ moving in the same direction as the nucleus, leads to the same conclusion.

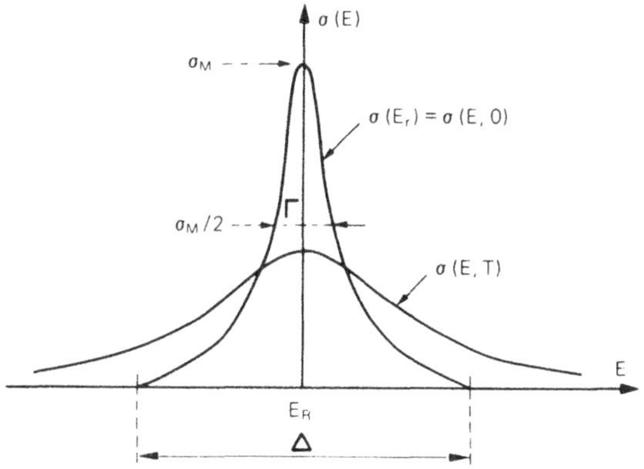

FIGURE 9.9. Doppler broadening of a resonance.

We deduce from the preceding that temperature brings about a broadening of the resonances when takes as a variable the absolute energy of the neutrons (Fig. 9.9). This does not yet explain the effect on the reactivity mentioned in subsec. 5.3.3 since, if the resonances broaden, their amplitude diminishes. Only a quantitative method will enable us to approach this problem correctly.

Among the models proposed by nuclear physics, the simplest is that of Breit and Wigner [66]. It leads to the following expressions for cross sections:

$$\left.\begin{aligned} \sigma_s(E) &= \sigma_M \frac{\Gamma_n}{\Gamma} \frac{1}{1 + 4\left(\dfrac{E - E_R}{\Gamma}\right)^2} \\ \sigma_a(E) &= \frac{\Gamma_\gamma}{\Gamma_n} \sqrt{\frac{E_R}{E}}\ \sigma_s(E) \end{aligned}\right\} \qquad (9.73)$$

in which σ_M is the maximum total cross section $(\sigma_s(E_R) + \sigma_a(E_R))$, Γ the <u>width of the reaction</u> (width of the peak at mid-height), while Γ_n and Γ_γ are the partial widths relative to two processes in competition: elastic scattering and radiative capture. The widths are expressed in the same units as the energies and we have by definition: $\Gamma = \Gamma_n + \Gamma_\gamma$.

Each resonance is thus characterized by four parameters: E_R, σ_M, Γ_n and Γ_γ, and in practice one is led to sum expressions such as (9.73) in order to obtain the cross sections of heavy nuclei which comprise a large number of resonances. At low energies ($E < E_R$, where E_R characterizes the first resonance), the preceding formulae show that $\sigma_s(E)$ is approximately constant and small, while $\sigma_a(E)$ varies like $1/\sqrt{E}$. These properties have often been invoked in preceding chapters. For completeness, we should point out that a second term should be introduced in $\sigma_s(E)$ to take account of a quantum effect: the interference between the resonating waves which have led to expressions (9.73) and the <u>potential</u> waves responsible for the existence of a non-vanishing cross section σ_s^* between the resonances (§4.4.5).

Other more complicated models are sometimes used, but expressions (9.73) suffice for understanding, if not for calculating, the Doppler effect. We will henceforth consider <u>a particular resonance</u> and replace E by E_r in order to take account of the thermal agitation of the nuclei. In the neighborhood of this resonance, the cross sections can thus be written (9.73):

$$\sigma_a(E_r) \cong \sigma_M \frac{\Gamma_\gamma}{\Gamma} \frac{1}{1 + 4\left(\frac{E_r - E_R}{\Gamma}\right)^2} = \frac{\Gamma_\gamma}{\Gamma_n} \sigma_s(E_r) \tag{9.74}$$

Since the widths Γ are very small compared to the resonance energies E_R, these expressions rapidly tend to zero as soon as E_r differs slightly from E_R. Let us now consider the density of nuclei N characterizing a solid medium. The temperatures to be anticipated in the fuel are higher than the Debye temperature, and thus we can identify this population of nuclei with a gas governed by the Maxwell distribution [1]. This means that among N nuclei of mass M, those which propagate with velocities between $\vec{V}$ and $\vec{V} + d\vec{V}$ are in number:

$$dN = N\ P\ (\vec{V})\ dV_x\ dV_y\ dV_z \tag{9.75}$$

with:

$$P\ (\vec{V}) = \left(\frac{M}{2\pi kT} \right)^{3/2} \exp\left(- \frac{MV^2}{2kT}\right) \tag{9.76}$$

We have already used this law in another form in the context of plasmas (§2.1.2); moreover, it is in accord with (2.1) when one passes from the variable $\vec{V}$ to the kinetic energy of the nuclei.

If a beam of neutrons of density n, of direction $\vec{\Omega}$, and of fixed energy E, enters into collision with the preceding dN nuclei, the reaction rate will be (1.15):

$$dR = dN \cdot n\ v_r\ \sigma(E_r)$$

or, if one considers all the nuclei (9.75):

$$R(E) = N\ n \int_{-\infty}^{\infty} dV_x \int_{-\infty}^{\infty} dV_y \int_{-\infty}^{\infty} dV_z\ v_r\ P(\vec{V})\ \sigma(E_r) \tag{9.77}$$

The variables E, E_r (or v_r) and $\vec{V}$ are related; we have in effect:

$$v_r^2 = |\vec{v} - \vec{V}|^2 = v^2 - 2\vec{v}.\vec{V} + V^2$$

Noting that the velocities of the nuclei $\vec{V}$ are considerably smaller than those of the neutrons $\vec{v}$, we can neglect the term in second order V^2, in other words: $v_r^2 \cong v^2 - 2vV_z$ by taking the direction $\vec{\Omega}$ of the neutrons as the z axis of the vector space $\vec{V}$. As for the relative energy, it can be written (§4.4.2):

$$E_r = \frac{1}{2} \frac{mM}{m + M} v_r^2 \cong \frac{m}{2} v_r^2$$

since the mass of a neutron m is always small compared with that of a resonant nucleus. The desired correlation can now be put in the form:

$$E_r \cong E - m\, v\, V_z \tag{9.78}$$

Returning to expression (9.77), the integrations in V_x and V_y can be done analytically, since $\sigma(E_r)$ only depends on V_z. Using (9.76) and the remarkable property:

$$\int_{-\infty}^{\infty} \exp(-u^2)\, du = \sqrt{\pi}$$

we finally get:

$$R(E) = N\, n \sqrt{\frac{M}{2\pi kT}} \int_{-\infty}^{\infty} v_r\, \sigma(E_r) \exp\left(-\frac{MV_z^2}{2kT}\right) dV_z \tag{9.79}$$

In all the preceding chapters, we have written the reaction rates in the form:

$$R(E) = \Sigma(E)\, \Phi = N\, n\, v\, \sigma(E)$$

which is strictly valid for nuclei at rest. Nevertheless, this expression can be kept in the general case by defining $\sigma(E)$ in such a way as to get back the correct reaction rate (9.79), whence the final result:

$$\sigma(E,T) = \sqrt{\frac{M}{2\pi kT}} \int_{-\infty}^{\infty} \sqrt{\frac{E_r}{E}}\, \sigma(E_r) \exp\left(-\frac{MV_z^2}{2kT}\right) dV_z \tag{9.80}$$

in which E_r and V_z are connected by the relation (9.78).

The quantity $\sigma(E,T)$ is not properly speaking a microscopic quantity, since it depends on the temperature T, but it enables us to keep the entire formalism which was developed in Sec. 4.4.

To obtain $\sigma(E,T)$ in the neighborhood of a particular resonance, we must introduce the analytic expression for $\sigma(E_r)$ (9.74). As is customary, we put:

$$x = 2\,\frac{E - E_R}{\Gamma}, \qquad y = 2\,\frac{E_r - E_R}{\Gamma}, \qquad \text{and } \zeta = \Gamma\sqrt{\frac{A}{4E_R kT}} \tag{9.81}$$

with

$$A = \frac{M}{m}$$

We can then put the cross sections in the form:

$$\sigma_a(E,T) = \sigma_M \frac{\Gamma_\gamma}{\Gamma} \psi(\zeta,x) = \frac{\Gamma_\gamma}{\Gamma_n} \sigma_s(E,T) \tag{9.82}$$

where $\psi(\zeta,x)$ is a universal function [67]:

$$\psi(\zeta,x) = \frac{\zeta}{\sqrt{4\pi}} \int_{-\infty}^{\infty} \exp\left[- \frac{\zeta^2}{4} (x - y)^2 \right] \frac{dy}{1 + y^2} \tag{9.83}$$

This function enjoys the following properties:

$$\begin{aligned} &\cdot\ \psi(\zeta,x) = \psi(\zeta, -x) \\ &\cdot\ \psi(\infty,x) = \frac{1}{1 + x^2} \\ &\cdot\ \int_{-\infty}^{\infty} \psi(\zeta,x)dx = \pi \end{aligned} \tag{9.84}$$

The first identity expresses the symmetry with respect to the resonance energy and the second the fact that at zero temperature the Doppler broadening disappears, which amounts to replacing E_r by E in (9.74). The last property implies that the resonance integral for infinite dilution is insensitive to the Doppler effect, as we will see further on.

If we limit ourselves to a single resonance, equation (4.56) can be written:

$$I_{eff}(\sigma_e) = \int_{E_2}^{E_1} \frac{\sigma_a(E)}{1 + \dfrac{\sigma_a(E) + \sigma_s(E)}{\sigma_s^* + \sigma_e}} \frac{dE}{E}$$

where E_1 and E_2 are two energies which generously encompass the resonance being studied (§8.3.4). Introducing expressions (9.82) as well as the variable x (9.81), we get, since $2(E_{1,2} - E_R)/\Gamma$ is very large:

$$\left.\begin{aligned} &I_{eff}(\sigma_e) = \sigma_M \frac{\Gamma_\gamma}{E_R} \beta J(\zeta,\beta) \\ &\text{with} \\ &J(\zeta,\beta) \cong \int_0^{\infty} \frac{\psi(\zeta,x)}{\beta + \psi(\zeta,x)} dx \\ &\text{and} \\ &\beta = \frac{\sigma_e + \sigma_s^*}{\sigma_M} \end{aligned}\right\} \tag{9.85}$$

This new universal function is very important, since it only involves two useful parameters: ζ linked to the temperature (9.81) and β to the dilution cross section σ_e (4.57).

When the dilution is infinite ($\beta >> \psi$ irrespective of the value of x) we have (9.84):

$$J(\zeta,\infty) \cong \frac{1}{\beta} \int_0^\infty \psi(\zeta,x)dx = \frac{\pi}{2\beta}$$

whence:

$$I_{eff}(\infty) = \frac{\pi}{2} \sigma_M \frac{\Gamma_\gamma}{E_R}$$

and the results are independent of ζ, and hence of the temperature.

For an arbitrary dilution, but zero temperature ($\zeta = \infty$), we get on the contrary (9.81):

$$J(\infty,\beta) = \int_0^\infty \frac{dx}{1 + \beta(1 + x^2)} = \frac{\pi}{2\sqrt{\beta(1 + \beta)}}$$

whence:

$$I_{eff}(\sigma_e) = \frac{\pi}{2} \sigma_M \frac{\Gamma_\gamma}{E_R} \sqrt{\frac{\beta}{1 + \beta}}$$

and the results are now very sensitive to the dilution.

The function $J(\zeta,\beta)$ has been tabulated [68]. For a fixed value of β, and thus of the dilution, it increases with the temperature ($\zeta \searrow$) and the same is true of the effective integral I_{eff} (9.85).

If we want to know the resonance escape probability of a thermal reactor, we must add the contributions of all the resonances to cover the entire energy interval from E_t^* for E_s (§4.4.5). The preceding results are thus transposable to the total effective integral and the increase of the latter with the temperature entails a diminution of p (4.55) and of the reactivity (4.109) in keeping with the assertions of subsec. 5.3.3. In the same way, multigroup absorption cross sections are affected by the Doppler effect, so that program libraries are generally supplied for several temperatures and dilutions, at least where the most important fertile isotopes are concerned.

In summary, a rise in temperature favors resonant nuclear reactions through the combined effect of Doppler broadening and limited dilution.

9.4.2 Xenon Poisoning

Xenon Xe^{135} is essentially formed by β^- disintegration of an abundant fission product, iodine I^{135}, but the true primary fission product is in fact tellerium Te^{135}, whose half-life is so small that this intermediate stage can be disregarded. Xenon may also appear as a primary fission product, but that is a very infrequent process. We can make a diagram of the preceding as follows:

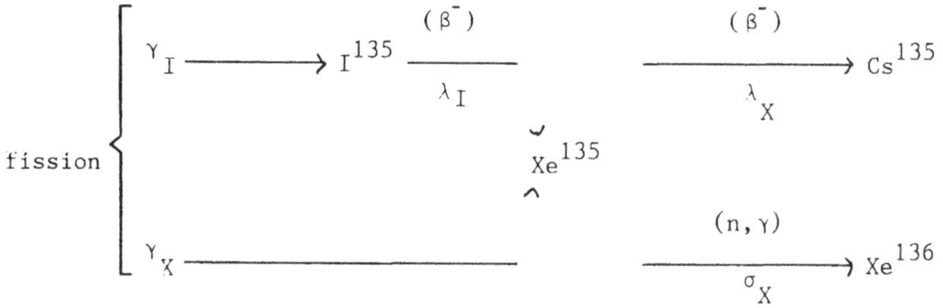

with the notations:

- γ_I and γ_X: the fission production rates of iodine and xenon which up to a factor have the same meaning as y(A) in §3.1.2.
- λ_I and λ_X: β^- disintegration constants of iodine and xenon.
- σ_X: the microscopic cross section for neutron capture by xenon and for thermal neutrons.

For thermal reactors burning uranium U^{235}, we can assume the following numbers:

- $\gamma_I = 0.061$ and $\gamma_X = 0.003$
- $\lambda_X = 2.1 \cdot 10^{-5}\ s^{-1} (T = 9.17\ h)$ and $\lambda_I = 2.87 \cdot 10^{-5}\ s^{-1} (T = 6.7h)$
- $\sigma_X = 3\ 10^6$ b (thermal neutrons)

The last figure shows how powerful an absorber xenon Xe^{135} is, even when compared to the most absorbing isotopes used in nuclear reactors (σ_a attains 680 b for uranium U^{235} and 3840 b for boron B^{10}). Thus, even when present in a very small quantity, it can have a large influence on the reactivity, and it is thus important to know its concentration in the fuel.

Let N_I and N_X be the atomic densities (in cm^{-3}) of iodine and xenon. The evolution equations can be written:

$$\left.\begin{aligned} \frac{dN_I}{dt} &= \gamma_I \Sigma_{f,c}\Phi - \lambda_I N_I \\ \frac{dN_X}{dt} &= \gamma_X \Sigma_{f,c}\Phi + \lambda_I N_I - (\lambda_X + \sigma_X\Phi)N_X \end{aligned}\right\} \quad (9.86)$$

The fission rate in the fuel $\Sigma_{f,c}\Phi$ multiplied by γ_I or γ_X leads to the primary production rates of iodine and xenon nuclei (in $cm^{-3}\ s^{-1}$), whereas the coupling between the two equations (9.86) results from the β^- disintegration of iodine (see the radioactivity chains of subsec. 1.4.2). Finally, xenon Xe^{135} disappears in two ways: by β^- disintegration or by neutron capture as indicated by the above diagram.

Since in the simplest cases the flux depends on the spatial variables, the same will be true of the atomic densities N_I and N_X via equations (9.86). Moreover, since xenon evolution is slow compared to the phenomena considered in kinetics (Sec. 4.6), the reactor will always remain critical, the control mechanisms doing whatever is necessary. The fluxes thus obey steady state diffusion equations and are fixed by the power level (§9.1.5). For each value of $N_X(\vec{r},t)$, we can correct at each point of the system the macroscopic absorption cross section of thermal neutrons by adding the term $N_X\sigma_X$ to the parameter $\Sigma_{a,G}$ which figures in the last multigroup equation (4.96). This equation is thus coupled to the evolution equations (9.86) which must be simultaneously solved following a scheme analogous to that envisaged for the slow evolution of the fuel (§9.1.5).

It is nevertheless possible to obtain a good order of magnitude of the effect on xenon reactivity by relying on the simple formalism of subsec. 4.5.4. This implies a uniform distribution of the poison so that the homogeneity of the multiplying medium is preserved. In effect, xenon can be considered as an additional structural material which will only modify the thermal utilization factor f_t, its influence on the diffusion area L^2_t not being important. Let us rewrite expression (4.61) in the form:

$$\frac{1}{f} - 1 = \frac{\Sigma_{a,m} + \Sigma_{a,g}}{\Sigma_{a,c}}$$

where $\Sigma_{a,c}$, $\Sigma_{a,m}$ and $\Sigma_{a,g}$ are the macroscopic absorption cross sections relative to the usual reactor components (fuel, moderator, structural materials). This is for thermal neutrons although the index t has been omitted.

By virtue of the preceding, we can calculate in the same way the new thermal utilization factor f' in the presence of xenon; for this it suffices to add to the numerator of the preceding expression the quantity $N_X\sigma_X$, whence:

$$\frac{1}{f'} - 1 = \frac{1}{f} - 1 + \frac{N_X\sigma_X}{\Sigma_{a,c}}$$

in other words, because of (4.82) and (4.80):

$$\frac{k'_e - k_e}{k_e} = \frac{k'_\infty - k_\infty}{k_\infty} = \frac{f' - f}{f} = - f' \frac{N_X\sigma_X}{\Sigma_{a,c}}$$

or, finally, in terms of reactivities (4.109):

$$\Delta\rho = \rho' - \rho \cong -f \frac{N_X\sigma_X}{\Sigma_{a,c}} \tag{9.87}$$

Let us consider for a moment a reactor functioning at constant power. In this case the fluxes are independent of the time. Putting $dN_I/dt = dN_X/dt = 0$, equations (9.86) lead to the equilibrium concentrations:

$$\left.\begin{aligned} \tilde{N}_I &= \gamma_I\Sigma_{f,c}\,\tilde{\Phi}/\lambda_I \\ \tilde{N}_X &= (\gamma_X + \gamma_I)\Sigma_{f,c}\tilde{\Phi}/[\lambda_X + \sigma_X\tilde{\Phi}] \end{aligned}\right\} \tag{9.88}$$

attained after a transient of about two days (§9.4.3).

Moreover, since this simple theory assumes a uniform distribution of atomic densities, $\tilde{\Phi}$ represents a certain average value of the neutron flux $\Phi_t(\vec{r})$ which is called the <u>effective flux</u>. For one-zone reactors we have roughly $\tilde{\Phi} = 0.5\ \Phi_M$ where Φ_M is the maximum flux. For more flattened distributions (§5.2.5), this coefficient tends to unity and the value of $\tilde{\Phi}$ is subject to less uncertainty.

We can deduce from expressions (9.87) and (9.88) the desired reactivity variation:

$$\Delta\rho \cong - f \frac{\Sigma_{f,c}}{\Sigma_{a,c}} (\gamma_X + \gamma_I) \frac{\sigma_X\tilde{\Phi}}{\lambda_X + \sigma_X\tilde{\Phi}} \tag{9.89}$$

We can evaluate the order of magnitude of this effect by considering two extreme cases:

- natural uranium: $\Sigma_{f,c}/\Sigma_{a,c} = 0.55$
- pure uranium U^{235}: $\Sigma_{f,c}/\Sigma_{a,c} = 0.85$

These values can be obtained by observing first that $\Sigma_{f,c}/\Sigma_{a,c} = \eta_c/\bar{\nu}$ (3.6) and using tables (3.8) and (3.10). In these conditions we obtain for a value of f equal to 0.9 and for infinite flux $\tilde{\Phi}$, reactivity losses of the order of 3.2% in the first case and 4.9% in the second. Enriched uranium reactors are thus more sensitive to the xenon effect. Reactivity variations as a function of the effective flux $\tilde{\Phi}$ are represented in Fig. 9.10. A flux of the order of $2 \cdot 10^{14}$ cm^{-2} s^{-1} can be considered as infinite, but in power reactors this value is not attained, since the average flux in the fuel rarely surpasses 10^{14}n cm^{-2} s^{-1}. Whatever the case, reactivity losses are of the order of 2% to 4% depending on the type of reactor, and this is not negligible. Thus right from the start we must have at our disposal an equivalent reactivity margin which can be covered during the power rise by control rods or the soluble poison (Sec. 5.3). Of all the short- and middle-term effects, the xenon effect is the most important. Contrary to previous assertions (§4.5.1), criticality depends on the absolute level of the flux; in fact, there is no contradiction, for the composition of the multiplying medium is no longer a datum, the quantity of xenon present in the fuel depending on the power, that is to say, on the flux.

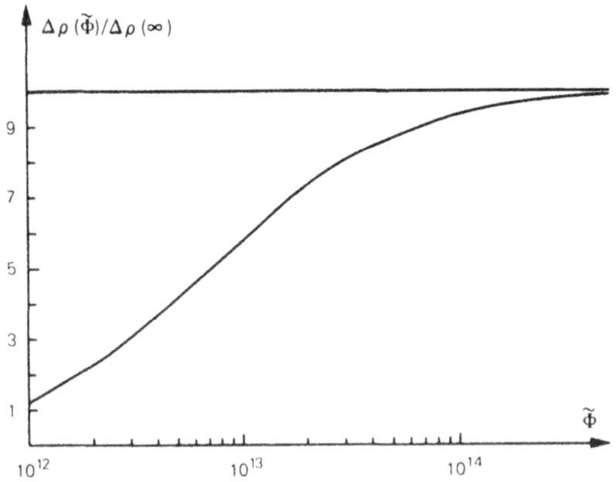

FIGURE 9.10.

9.4.3 Xenon-Related Transients

In the preceding example, we considered a steady state situation. Now let us see what happens when the reactor passes from one power level to another. This passage takes place by rendering the reactor slightly supercritical or slightly subcritical (Sec. 4.6) for a time lapse which is very short compared with the times considered here (several hours). Once this has taken place, criticality will subsequently be assured by intervention of the control methods responsible for compensating the xenon effect. We shall thus assume in what follows that the reactor remains critical, but that the flux passes instantaneously from a value $\tilde{\Phi}_0$ to a value $\tilde{\Phi}_1$. In contrast, the new equilibrium concentrations of iodine and xenon will only be reached after a certain time which is linked to the half-lives of these two radio-isotopes. By supposing, as in the preceding subsection, that the atomic densities are uniform, and thus that $\tilde{\Phi}_0$ and $\tilde{\Phi}_1$ are effective fluxes, we can analytically integrate the equations (9.86) for times $t > 0$ corresponding to the new state ($\Phi = \tilde{\Phi}_1$). The initial concentrations $N_I(0)$ and $N_X(0)$ relative to the preceding level are furnished by the expressions (9.88) by putting $\Phi = \tilde{\Phi}_0$.

In these conditions, a simple calculation leads to:

$$\left.\begin{aligned} N_I(t) &= \frac{\gamma_I \Sigma_{f,c}\tilde{\Phi}_1}{\lambda_I}\left[1 + \frac{\tilde{\Phi}_0 - \tilde{\Phi}_1}{\tilde{\Phi}_1}\exp(-\lambda_I t)\right] \\ N_X(t) &= (\gamma_X + \gamma_I)\frac{\Sigma_{f,c}\tilde{\Phi}_1}{\alpha_1}\left\{1 + \frac{\tilde{\Phi}_0 - \tilde{\Phi}_1}{\tilde{\Phi}_1}\left[\frac{\lambda_X}{\alpha_0}\exp(-\alpha_1 t) + \right.\right. \\ &\left.\left. + \frac{\gamma_I}{\gamma_X + \gamma_I}\frac{\alpha_1}{\alpha_1 - \lambda_I}[\exp(-\lambda_I t) - \exp(-\alpha_1 t)]\right]\right\} \end{aligned}\right\} \quad (9.90)$$

where we have put: $\alpha_0 = \lambda_X + \sigma_X\tilde{\Phi}_0$ and $\alpha_1 = \lambda_X + \sigma_X\tilde{\Phi}_1$.

For large values of t, these densities tend towards the expected values ($\Phi = \tilde{\Phi}_1$ in (9.88)).

Henceforth we will only be interested in xenon whose effect on reactivity is always given by (9.87). It is of interest to study the sign of the derivative of $N_X(t)$ at the origin. The latter can be written:

$$\left.\frac{dN_X}{dt}\right|_{t=0} = \Sigma_{f,c}(\tilde{\Phi}_1 - \tilde{\Phi}_0)\frac{\gamma_X\lambda_X - \gamma_I\sigma_X\tilde{\Phi}_0}{\alpha_0}$$

Two cases must be considered:

- If $\tilde{\Phi}_0 < \gamma_X\lambda_X/\gamma_I\sigma_X$, this derivative has the same sign as $(\tilde{\Phi}_1 - \tilde{\Phi}_0)$, and thus the same as $(N_X(\infty) - N_X(0))$ and the function $N_X(t)$ is monotonous.
- If $\tilde{\Phi}_0 > \gamma_X\lambda_X/\gamma_I\sigma_X$, this derivative has on the contrary a sign opposite to that of $(N_X(\infty) - N_X(0))$ and the new equilibrium state will only be attained after passing through an extremum.

Since the quantity $\gamma_X\lambda_X/\gamma_I\sigma_X$ is of the order of $5 \cdot 10^{11}$ n cm^{-2} s^{-1}, whereas the nominal flux exceeds 10^{13} n cm^{-2} s^{-1} in power reactors, it is the second case which is the more realistic (except during a complete start-up since then, $\tilde{\Phi}_0 = 0$).

We have shown in Fig. 9.11 (lefthand side) the evolution of the reactivity loss which follows the first power rise of a reactor or its re-start after a prolonged shutdown, so that xenon is initially absent. The saturation values (9.89) are attained after about forty hours. After operating for an undetermined duration at nominal power, the reactor can be expected to have various power levels, and the reactivity losses appear in the righthand side of this figure. All these results follow from expressions (9.87) and (9.90), and are based on the data of the preceding subsection. The value of $2 \cdot 10^{13}$ cm^{-2} s^{-1} adopted for the effective nominal flux $\tilde{\Phi}_n$ is somewhat small if one considers enriched light water reactors, but too large in the case of natural uranium reactors.

We observe that any reduction of power leads first to an increase of the reactivity loss in accord with the preceding analysis. The "xenon hump" is maximum for a complete shutdown of the reactor and this is the case to be considered during the dimensioning of the means of control. Still, for high fluxes, the antireactivity peak is such that it is not possible to cover it (it represents five times the reactivity loss at equilibrium for $\tilde{\Phi}_n = 10^{14}$ cm^{-2} s^{-1}). In this case, short of restarting almost immediately, the reactor operator will have to wait a day or two before being able to increase the power. This dead time corresponds to that part of the "xenon hump" which exceeds the reactivity reserve. For power reactors, the fluxes being smaller, this problem does not appear in practice until towards the end of the cycle, when the reactivity margins have practically disappeared.

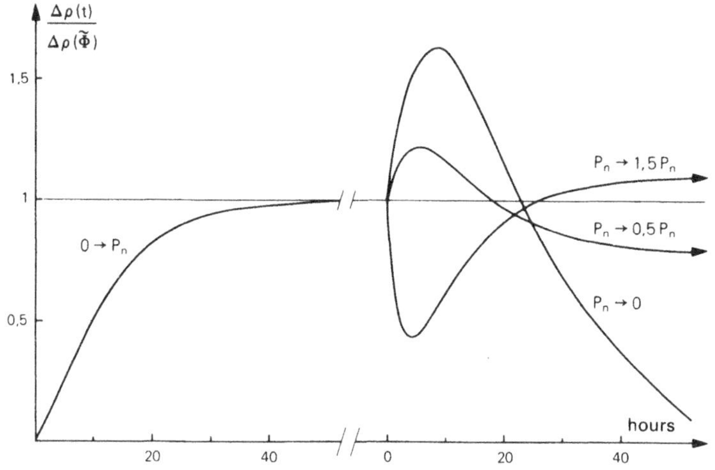

FIGURE 9.11. Variation of the xenon effect after an abrupt change of power in a reactor.

9.4.4 Spatial Instabilities

These instabilities which involve both space and time are due to the presence of xenon Xe^{135}. Let us imagine that in a certain zone of the reactor the neutron flux increases while it diminishes elsewhere. Without external intervention, this tendency could grow. Indeed, an increase of the flux causes an increased consumption of xenon (by neutron capture), which leads to an improvement of the thermal utilization factor f (§9.4.2) and hence of the material buckling B_m^2 (4.65). Inversely, in zones where the flux diminishes, the bucklings get worse. However, we know (§5.2.5) that flux peaks appear in places where the bucklings are the highest (Fig. 5.10, curve 3): this initial distorsion will thus get amplified until the disintegration of iodine, which is regulated by the flux, ends up by producing a xenon excess in places where the flux had a tendency to increase indefinitely. The spatial distributions will then progressively begin to tip.

In order for these oscillations to maintain themselves, the reactor parameters must fulfill certain conditions. The quantitative study of this phenomenon appeals to the numerical method outlined in subsec. 9.4.2.

The evolution equations (9.86) furnish at each instant t_n the concentrations N_I and N_X at every point of the system starting from the values of N_I, N_X and Φ assumed known at the previous instant t_{n-1}. Subsequently, for this new fuel composition, the diffusion calculations are redone and, after normalizing (9.26), one has available the flux at time t_n, which enables one to make the following step (t_{n+1}). To display any eventual instability, it suffices to start from a representative flux distribution of the reactor (without xenon) to which one adds a local perturbation.

One can avoid the preceding numerical approach if one is only interested in the stability criterion. Various approximations are then legitimate, in particular one may consider only small variations of the quantities N_X, N_I and Φ and base oneself on the one-group formalism (thermal neutrons). In these conditions equation (4.84), which is rigorously speaking nonlinear, since B_m^2 depends on N_X, can be linearized. The same is true of equations (9.86) in spite of the presence of the term $\sigma_X \Phi N_X$. Naturally, if the obtained fluctuations get amplified with time, this model no longer correctly describes the flux distributions, but that is not the object of this approach. The approach is analogous to that used in plasma physics in studies of the stability of magnetic confinement. Here it permits in addition a purely analytical treatment [69] that we will not describe, since it has been left aside in favor of the more rigorous numerical method referred to earlier. We will simply present the principal results which follow from the approximate expression of the thermal neutron flux:

$$\Phi(\vec{r},t) = \Phi_0(\vec{r}) + \sum_{k=0}^{\infty} a_k \exp(\gamma_k t) \sin(\omega_k t + \delta_k) g_k(\vec{r}) \qquad (9.91)$$

in which $\Phi_0(\vec{r})$ is the unperturbed flux, $g_k(\vec{r})$ one of the eigen functions of the equation:

$$\nabla^2 g_k(\vec{r}) + B_m^2(\vec{r})\, g_k(\vec{r}) = -\mu_k^2\, g_k(\vec{r}) \qquad (9.92)$$

and μ_k^2 the corresponding eigen value.

The time constants γ_k and ω_k only depend on the characteristics of the reactor through μ_k^2 and on the characteristics of the poisons (iodine and xenon). Finally, a_k and δ_k are integration constants whose values are fixed by the initial conditions.

The first eigen value (k = 0) vanishes since equation (9.92) can then be identified with (4.84) and the function $g_0(\vec{r})$ is proportional to $\Phi_0(\vec{r})$, hence positive throughout. The other eigen values increase with the index $k: 0 < \mu_1^2 < \mu_2^2 \ldots$ and the eigen functions change sign in the interior of the reactor all the more often as k is higher. Thus, in a homogeneous bare reactor (B_m^2 = const.), equation (9.92) reduces to (4.71) with $B_k^2 = B_m^2 + \mu_k^2$ since we are now interested in all the eigen values. For spherical geometry, we get, by restricting ourselves to radial functions only (beginning of §4.5.3):

$$\mu_k^2 = \left(\frac{\pi}{R + d}\right)^2 [(k + 1)^2 - 1] \quad \text{and} \quad g_k(\rho) = \frac{1}{\rho} \sin \left[\pi(k + 1)\frac{\rho}{R + d}\right] \tag{9.93}$$

the material buckling B_m^2 having been replaced by its critical value (4.69). As the spatial oscillations of the flux have no reason to respect spherical symmetry, the preceding functions (9.93) only constitute a subset of the complete set of eigen functions.

Let us return to equation (9.91). We see that the reactor will be stable if all the γ_k are negative. Taking account of the expression of these parameters, we are led to the stability criterion [70]:

$$\mu_k^2 M^2 + [-\alpha_c(T_c - T_e) - \alpha_m(T_m - T_e)] > \frac{|\Delta\rho|}{\gamma_X + \gamma_I} \cdot \frac{\gamma_I \sigma_X \tilde{\Phi}_0 - \gamma_X \lambda_X}{\lambda_X + \lambda_I + \sigma_X \Phi_0} \tag{9.94}$$

in which M^2 denotes the migration area (§4.5.4) and $|\Delta\rho|$ the reactivity loss due to xenon in steady state (9.89). The second term of this inequality comes from taking into account the temperature effects, and T_c, T_m and T_e represent respectively the nominal temperatures of the fuel, the moderator and the coolant at the core inlet. Since power reactors are generally stable vis-a-vis these effects, this term is positive [70], which, in the case of LWR reactors is evident, since α_m and α_c are negative (§5.3.3). For fluxes $\tilde{\Phi}_0$ smaller than $\gamma_X\lambda_X/\gamma_I\sigma_X$, the righthand side of (9.94) is negative and stability assured whatever be the characteristics of the reactor. We have already encountered this flux in the previous subsection and seen that beyond this limit, a xenon hump appears subsequent to a power change. As its value is small ($5 \cdot 10^{11}$ cm^{-2}s^{-1}), compared to the usual fluxes (more than 10^{13} cm^{-2} s^{-1}), the righthand side of (9.94) is positive in all practical cases.

Let us first study the fundamental mode for which $\mu_0^2 = 0$. The term involving the temperatures, although positive, is too small for condition (9.94) to be satisfied. This means that in expression (9.91) γ_0 is positive and hence that oscillations in time but not in space ($g_0(\vec{r})$ is positive) are going to develop. This instability does not pose any problem, since the oscillation periods are of the order of several hours and regulating rods (§5.3.8) have enough time to intervene. It is for this reason that the instability of the fundamental mode is never mentioned, though it is real enough.

We now consider the subsequent modes ($k \neq 0$); the first term of the inequality (9.94) now contributes to stability ($\mu_k^2 \neq 0$). We must note that the eigen values μ_k^2 vary like the inverse of the square of the dimensions of the reactor under study (see for example the spherical reactor (9.93)), and hence for small-size systems, condition (9.94) will be satisfied. In the opposite case, spatio-temporal oscillations will appear ($\gamma_k > 0$), resulting from the fact that the functions $g_k(\vec{r})$ change sign at the interior of the reactor. If we examine, for example, the behavior of a homogeneous spherical reactor, the flux distributions have the shape indicated in Fig. 9.12 if one adheres to the instability of the first radial harmonic, the fundamental being supposed stabilized by classical means of control (this example is based on expressions (9.93) taken with $k = 1$).

This type of phenomenon is what one has in mind when one speaks of xenon instability, for it requires a particular type of control. Let us consider the more realistic case of a cylindrical reactor. Other than radial oscillations of the previous type, we must take account of azimuthal oscillations which are much more likely. More precisely, the eigen values can most often be classified as follows [70]:

$$(\mu_1^2)_{az} < (\mu_2^2)_{az} < (\mu_1^2)_r < \ldots$$

and the corresponding first eigen function is of the type:

$$g_1(\vec{r}) \cong \sin\left(\frac{\pi z}{H}\right) g_1(r) \cos(\theta + \delta)$$

as one can see by solving the eigen value equation (9.92) expressed in cylindrical coordinates (r, θ, z) for a material buckling depending only on r (radial flattening of the flux, cf. §5.2.5). In the expression for

$g_1(\vec{r})$, the functions of r and of z are everywhere positive, but this is not the case for the function of θ. An azimuthal oscillation of the flux will thus be produced if $(\mu_1^2)_{az}$ is small enough for condition (9.94) not to be satisfied. The first sketch in Fig. 9.13 corresponds to this case, the signs + and − indicating the position of the maxima and the minima at a given instant (half a period later the signs will be reversed). If the succeeding modes are instable in their turn, the modes which preceed them (on the scale of k) will be so, "a fortiori" (Fig. 9.13).

INSTALLATIONS NUCLÉAIRES

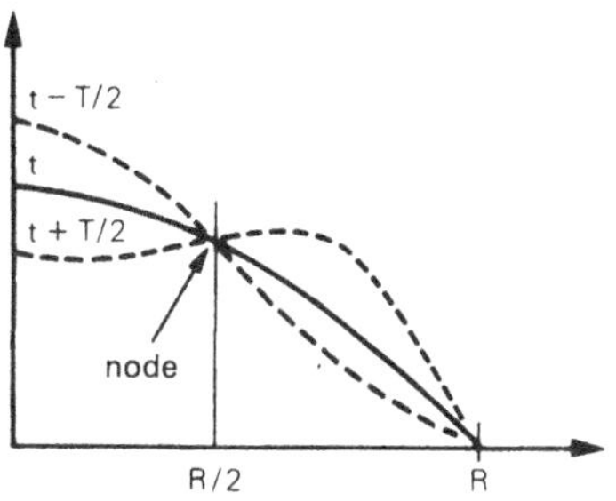

FIGURE 9.12.

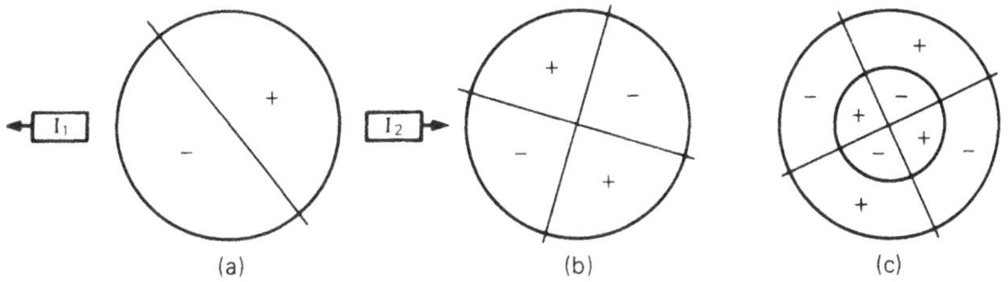

FIGURE 9.13. Spatial oscillations of the flux, instability: a) of the first azimuthal mode, b) of the first two azimuthal modes, c) of the two preceding modes and of the first radial mode.

Unlike the fundamental mode, the spatial harmonics cannot be controlled by the general regulating mechanisms of the reactor. The "curtain" movements of the regulating rods or the readjustments of the quantity of soluble poison (water reactors) only act in a global fashion. They modify the reactivity and stabilize the fundamental mode but they have no influence on spatial oscillations. To control the first azimuthal harmonic, one must have at hand at least two detectors (§5.3.9) placed as indicated in Fig. 9.13. Of course, the position of the neutral plane (the place of the oscillation nodes) is not known in advance since it depends on the initiating perturbation, but in all practical cases the information difference $(I_1 - I_2)$ makes it possible to detect this type of oscillation and to know at every instant where the extrema of the flux are located. The signal thus obtained commands the selective introduction of regulating rods in places where the fluxes are too high and their withdrawal elsewhere. On the other hand, the information sum $(I_1 + I_2)$ is transmitted to the normal regulating systems (§5.3.9), for it gives a good picture of the general level of the flux, and thus of the power. In practice, when a reactor is subject to this type of instability, as was certainly the case for the first generation of graphite moderated natural uranium reactors, the spatial control takes place by quarters. We should also note that this type of control does not necessarily imply a greater number of regulating rods; they are simply used in a more selective way.

At the project level, one evidently tries to make a reactor intrinsically stable with regard to xenon instabilities, but this is not imperative, since in any case reactor control is at present much more sophisticated than it was in the past. One tries in fact to optimize the flux distributions permanently for economic reasons, and the equipment required for this makes it possible at the same time to neutralize spatial oscillations if these have a tendency to develop.

Summarizing, we retain the following points:

- large-size reactors (with reference to the migration length) are particularly subject to spatial instabilities;
- temperature effects are generally stabilizing, especially in the case of LWR reactors;
- xenon instability grows with the flux level;
- specific power flattening (§5.2.5) is destabilizing.

We note finally that this type of instability results from the fact that xenon is not formed directly, as shown by the qualitative reasoning at the beginning of this subsection, and as also shown by the stability condition (9.94) when we put $\gamma_I = 0$.

9.4.5 Samarium Poisoning

This effect is analogous to the preceding one, since the chain to consider can be written:

$$\text{fission: } \gamma_P \longrightarrow Pm^{149} \xrightarrow[\lambda_P]{\beta^-} Sm^{149} \xrightarrow[\sigma_S]{(n,\gamma)} Sm^{150}$$

Samarium Sm^{149} plays the role of xenon Xe^{135} and promethium Pm^{149} that of iodine I^{135}. Still, there are two differences:

- samarium Sm^{149} is stable and can only disappear by neutron capture;
- samarium is not a primary fission product ($\gamma_S = 0$).

On the other hand, as in the case of iodine, we disregard one stage, that of neodymium Nd^{149}, since this radionuclide has a half-life much smaller than that of promethium.

The characteristics of this chain are the following:

- $\gamma_P = 0.011$
- $\lambda_P = 3.6\ 10^{-6}\ s^{-1}$ (T = 53.5h)
- $\sigma_S = 6.5\ 10^4 b$ (thermal neutrons)

and the evolution equations can be written:

$$\left.\begin{aligned} \frac{dN_P}{dt} &= \gamma_P \Sigma_{f,c} \Phi - \lambda_P N_P \\ \frac{dN_S}{dt} &= \lambda_P N_P - \sigma_S \Phi N_S \end{aligned}\right\} \qquad (9.95)$$

in which N_P and N_S are the atomic densities corresponding to the Pm^{149} and Sm^{149} nuclei.

For a reactor operating at constant power (flux $\tilde{\Phi}$ in steady state) we have the corresponding saturation values:

$$\Delta\rho \cong -f \frac{\Sigma_{f,c}}{\Sigma_{a,c}} \gamma_P \qquad (9.96)$$

This result is independent of the neutron flux and of the absorption cross section of samarium. The two extreme cases envisaged in the preceding lead to reactivity losses of the order of 0.54% (natural uranium) and

0.84% (pure uranium U^{235}). The samarium effect is distinctly smaller than the xenon effect and the time constant relative to the power rise is of the order of a month.

The transients can be studied with the help of expression (9.90) by putting $\lambda_X = 0$, $\gamma_X = 0$, $\gamma_I = \gamma_P$ and $\lambda_I = \lambda_P$. At reactor shutdown, the reactivity loss is found to increase regularly (no maximum) and attains its limiting value:

$$\Delta\rho(\infty) = \Delta\rho(1 + \sigma_S\, \tilde{\Phi}/\lambda_P) \tag{9.97}$$

This result is due to the fact that samarium Sm^{149} being stable, it cannot disappear in the absence of neutrons. For high flux reactors, samarium can thus be more troublesome than xenon, because if the necessary reactivity reserve is not available, it is not enough simply to wait; on the contrary, refuelling is necessary. Fortunately, for standard reactors this extra poisoning is acceptable; it represents 18% of the nominal reactivity loss for a flux of 10^{13} cm^{-2} s^{-1} (9.97).

Chapter 10

SUPPLEMENT ON ISOTOPIC SEPARATION

10.1 MOLECULAR FLOW

10.1.1 Kinetic Theory of Gases

Every flow is characterized by certain macroscopic quantities: the velocity $\vec{u}$, the pressure p and the molecular density N, or what amounts to the same, the mass density $\rho = Nm$ (the mass of a molecule denoted m).

The classical equations of hydrodynamics [71] give the relations between these quantities. In addition, these equations contain dissipative terms. If these terms also can be expressed as functions of these same quantities and of some other empirical parameters (such as viscosity and conductivity), then the preceding system of equations is complete (cf. for example the Navier-Stoke equations) and the macroscopic point of view can be kept throughout. In the opposite case, resorting to a microscopic theory is inevitable. The kinetic theory of gases that we will now briefly describe corresponds to this approach.

Let $\vec{V}$ be the velocity of a molecule and $P(\vec{r},t,\vec{V})$ be the probability density such that:

$$dN = N(\vec{r},t)P(\vec{r},t,\vec{V})d^3V \tag{10.1}$$

represents the number of molecules per unit volume at the point $\vec{r}$ and at instant t, with velocities between $\vec{V}$ and $\vec{V} + d\vec{V}$. N retains its earlier meaning and d^3V designates the volume element in velocity space ($d^3V = dV_x dV_y dV_z$). We have by the very definition of P:

$$\left.\begin{aligned} &\int\int\int_{-\infty}^{\infty} P(\vec{r},t,\vec{V})d^3V = 1 \\ &\int\int\int_{-\infty}^{\infty} \vec{V}\, P(\vec{r},t,\vec{V})d^3V = \langle\vec{V}\rangle = \vec{u} \end{aligned}\right\} \tag{10.2}$$

where the average value of $\vec{V}$ is nothing other than the flow velocity $\vec{u}$, also called the drift velocity, the only quantity which appears at the macroscopic level. If the molecular distribution is isotropic, P then

s•

depends only on the absolute value of $\vec{V}$ as one can see by passing to polar coordinates ($d^3V = V^2 dV d\Omega$). The second equation (10.2) then shows that $\vec{u} = 0$ and the gas is necessarily at rest (only thermal agitation remains, since $\vec{u} = 0$ does not imply $\vec{V} = 0$).

In the kinetic theory of gases, the product N.P, also called the distribution function, plays the same role as the angular flux density introduced in neutronics (§9.1.6). The fundamental variable $\vec{V}$ simply replaces the couple $(E,\vec{\Omega})$. Moreover, the distribution function of the gas satisfies a kinetic equation analogous to the most general neutron transport equation (§9.1.6), the latter being only a adaptation of the kinetic equation established a century ago by L. Boltzmann. Once this equation has been solved, the quantity $P(\vec{r},t,\vec{V})$ enables us to obtain all useful quantities such as $\vec{u}$ (10.2) or the pressure tensor whose components are the mean values of $(V_i - u_i)(V_j - u_j)$ with respect to the probability P [72].

Fortunately, in order to understand what follows a complete account of the kinetic theory of gases is not necessary. It suffices to know that this theory only applies to sufficiently dilute gases and that an approximate expression for P is of the form:

$$P(\vec{V}) = \left(\frac{m}{2\pi kT} \right)^{3/2} \exp \left[- \frac{m|\vec{V} - \vec{u}|^2}{2kT} \right] \qquad (10.3)$$

in which we have omitted the variables $\vec{r}$ and t on which $\vec{u}$ and T (the gas temperature) generally depend. This expression is rigorously valid when the gas is at rest ($\vec{u} = 0$) and uniform (T constant). We have used it several times either in this form (§9.4.1) or in a different form by introducing energy as a variable (2.1). We say then that the gas is in perfect thermodynamic equilibrium and $P(\vec{V})$ is a Maxwell distribution. In the general case ($\vec{u} \neq 0$) if the distribution (10.3) obtains, we say on the contrary that the thermodynamic equilibrium is local; in some sense the Maxwell spectrum remains "attached" to the flow. In these conditions one shows that the flow is governed by the Euler equations since the pressure tensor can be diagonalized [72]. The microscopic and macroscopic formalisms are then to a large extent decoupled.

10.1.2 The Gas - Wall Interaction

Let us consider a flow parallel to the axis Ox (Fig. 10.1) bounded by a horizontal wall. The probability density (10.3) becomes:

$$P(\vec{V}) = \frac{1}{\pi^{3/2}\, V_t^3} \exp\left[-\left(\frac{V_x - u}{V_t}\right)^2\right] \exp\left(-\frac{V_y^2}{V_t^2}\right) \exp\left(-\frac{V_z^2}{V_t^2}\right) \tag{10.4}$$

where we have put:

$$V_t = \sqrt{\frac{2kT}{m}} = \sqrt{\frac{2RT}{M}} \tag{10.5}$$

the second expression of the thermal velocity V_t involving the perfect gas constant as well as the mass of a gram molecule ($k = R/N_A$ and $M = mN_A$).

Noting that (§9.4.1):

$$\int_{-\infty}^{\infty} \exp\,(-x^2)dx = \sqrt{\pi}$$

we check that the identities (10.2) are satisfied.

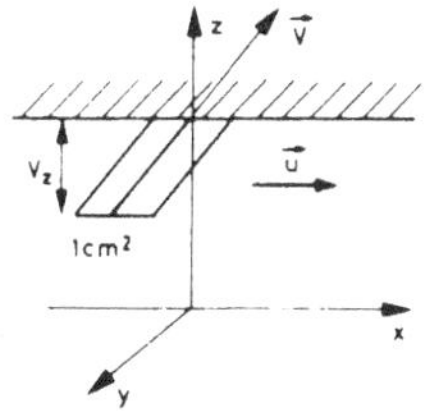

FIGURE 10.1

Let us now calculate the number of molecules dJ_z with velocities between $\vec{V}$ and $\vec{V} + d\vec{V}$ which penetrate the solid wall per unit area and unit time. They are contained in an oblique cylinder of cross section 1 cm^2 and of height V_z (Fig. 10.1), whence:

$$dJ_z = V_z dN = N\, V_z P\, (\vec{V})\, d^3V \tag{10.6}$$

since dN is the molecular density for this class of molecules (10.1). The total number of molecules entering the wall is thus:

$$J_z^+ = N \int_{-\infty}^{\infty} dV_x \int_{-\infty}^{\infty} dV_y \int_0^{\infty} dV_z\, V_z\, P(\vec{V})$$

which is a generalization of the notion of current introduced in the case of mono-energetic neutrons (§4.2.2). Taking account of expression (10.4), we finally obtain:

$$J_z^+ = \frac{NV_t}{2\sqrt{\pi}} = N\sqrt{\frac{RT}{2\pi M}} \qquad (10.7)$$

If we took $-\infty$ as the lower limit of the integral in V_z, the net current J_z would vanish (no flow perpendicular to the wall).

The molecules which enter the wall at the rate fixed by (10.7) rapidly come into thermodynamic equilibrium with the solid material, in spite of the fact that they penetrate it very little. This means that they are distributed according to a Maxwell spectrum without drift; in other words, the molecules which return towards the gas are characterized by expression (10.4) in which we simply put $\vec{u} = 0$, since the gas and the wall have the same temperature. Thus to the incident molecules of velocity (V_x, V_y, V_z) correspond an equal number of scattered molecules of velocity $(V_x - u, V_y, - V_z)$. Everything takes place as if after a reflection a molecule "forgot" that it was part of a flow; it thus suffers a momentum loss with components: $mu, 0, 2mV_z$. Thus for all the molecules hitting a unit area of the wall, we have the loss per unit time (10.6):

$$\left.\begin{aligned} p_{x,z} &= N \int_{-\infty}^{\infty} dV_x \int_{-\infty}^{\infty} dV_y \int_0^{\infty} dV_z (mu) V_z P(\vec{V}) \\ p_{y,z} &= 0 \\ p_{z,z} &= N \int_{-\infty}^{\infty} dV_x \int_{-\infty}^{\infty} dV_y \int_0^{\infty} dV_z (2mV_z)\, V_z\, P(\vec{V}) \end{aligned}\right\}$$

These three components represent the pressure that the gas exerts on the wall. In fact, an increase per unit time of the gas momentum must be equal to the external force acting on it (fundamental law of mechanics), and thus inversely a loss must be equivalent to an action on the external medium (in this case, the wall).

We can make the preceding expressions more explicit by replacing $P(\vec{V})$ by its expression (10.4). We get:

$$\left.\begin{aligned} p_{x,z} &= m\,u\,J_z^+ = \frac{NV_t}{2\sqrt{\pi}}\,m\,u = \sqrt{\frac{RT}{2\pi M}}\,\rho\,u \\ p_{z,z} &= \frac{Nm}{2}\,V_t^2 = NkT = \frac{RT}{M}\,.\,\rho \end{aligned}\right\} \qquad (10.8)$$

The second expression gives the expected result; the pressure normal to the wall is independent of the flow and conforms to the perfect gas law (it is one of the proofs of the validity of the kinetic theory of gases). As for the first, it constitutes the basis of any theory of molecular flow.

10.1.3 Molecular Flow Characteristics

In a molecular flow the mean free path of the molecules is by definition much larger than the diameter of the conduit under consideration. The interactions with the wall thus play a crucial role. This type of flow was first studied by Knudsen and it is known by his name.

Let σ be the microscopic collision cross section of the molecules (approximately their apparent cross section). The mean free path λ is given by the relation: $\lambda = 1/N\sigma$ where N represents the molecular density introduced earlier (in cm^{-3}). Here too we note the analogy with the mean free path of neutrons (§4.2.1).

The flow will thus be molecular if $\lambda \gg 2a$, where a is the radius of the conduit. Taking $\sigma = \pi d^2/4$, d being the diameter of a molecule, we get the inequality:

$$N \ll \frac{2}{\pi a d^2}$$

or,using the perfect gas law ($p = NRT/N_A$), the condition on the pressure:

$$p \ll \frac{2RT}{\pi a d^2 N_A} \qquad (10.9)$$

For usual conduit diameters (at least a few centimeters), the limiting pressures are extremely low. The Knudsen flow thus belongs to vacuum technique. In contrast, flows through porous matter can be molecular at atmospheric pressure since the values of a to be considered are relative to pores of extremely small diameter (less than a tenth of a micron). We thus understand the importance of this type of flow for gaseous diffusion.

10.1.4 Molecular Flow in a Cylindrical Conduit

Let us consider a conduit of diameter 2a and of length ℓ (Fig. 10.2). Since the tangential pressure p_t of the gas is directed along the axis Ox (cf. $p_{x,z}$ in subsec. 10.1.2), the wall exerts on the fluid slice dx a braking force $df = -2\pi a\, p_t\, dx$, at a point situated on the axis. We can thus disregard the wall provided we introduce a longitudinal force distribution of intensity X per unit mass, such that the resulting force associated to dx is exactly equal to df:

$$\rho X \pi a^2 dx = df = -2\pi a\, p_t\, dx$$

and using the first equation (10.8) we get:

$$X = -\frac{2}{a\rho} p_t = -\frac{1}{a}\sqrt{\frac{2RT}{\pi M}}\, u \qquad (10.10)$$

For unidimensional steady flows, the equations of fluid mechanics can be written [71]:

$$\left.\begin{aligned} &\rho\, u = G \\ &u \frac{du}{dx} = -\frac{1}{\rho}\frac{dp}{dx} + X \end{aligned}\right\} \qquad (10.11)$$

where G, the mass flow rate per unit area (g $cm^{-2}s^{-1}$), is a constant of the motion, the cross section of the canal being independent of x. This formalism governs molecular flows, since the only dissipative mechanism considered results from the gas - wall interaction (the term X); this mechanism is completely masked in the usual flows (laminar or turbulent) by internal energy dissipations.

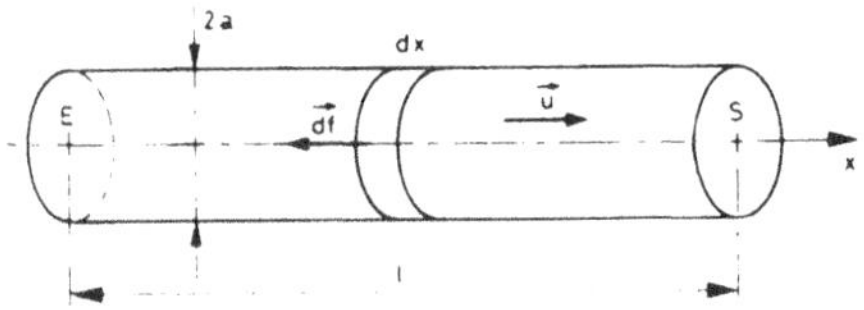

FIGURE 10.2

Let us multiply the second equation (10.11) by ρ and replace X by its value (10.10). We get:

$$G \frac{du}{dx} + \frac{dp}{dx} + \frac{1}{a} \sqrt{\frac{2RT}{\pi M}}\, G = 0$$

If we assume that the flow is isothermal (T independent of x), the integration of this equation is immediate since G is a constant. We get:

$$G(U_S - U_E) + p_S - p_E + \frac{\ell}{a}\sqrt{\frac{2RT}{\pi M}}\, G = 0$$

where the indices E and S refer to the inlet and the outlet of the conduit. Finally noting that:

$$U_E = \frac{G}{\rho_E} = \frac{RT}{M}\frac{G}{p_E} \qquad \text{and } U_S = \frac{RT}{M}\frac{G}{p_S}$$

we are led to a quadratic equation in G whose solution is:

$$G = \frac{B}{2A}\left[- 1 + \sqrt{1 + \frac{4A\Delta p}{B^2}} \right] \tag{10.12}$$

with:

$$\left.\begin{aligned} A &= \frac{RT}{M}\frac{\Delta p}{p_E p_S} \\ B &= \frac{\ell}{a}\sqrt{\frac{2RT}{\pi M}} \\ \Delta p &= p_E - p_S \end{aligned}\right\} \tag{10.13}$$

The flow rate G only depends, as it must, on the upstream and downstream pressures. The formalism gets considerably simplified if we note that $4A\Delta p$ is much smaller than B^2, since this implies the inequality (10.13):

$$2\pi \left(\frac{a}{\ell} \right)^2 << \left(\frac{p_E p_S}{(p_E - p_S)}\right)^2 \cong \frac{p_S}{p_E}$$

which is amply satisfied in practice (a/ℓ is extremely small when one considers the pores of diffusion barriers). In these conditions, expression (10.12) leads to the following simple result:

$$\mathscr{W} = \pi a^2 G = \pi \frac{a^3}{\ell} \sqrt{\frac{\pi M}{2RT}}\, (p_E - p_S) \tag{10.14}$$

The pressure loss is thus proportional to the flow rate as is the case for a laminar flow, but the analogy stops there, since the viscosity coefficient nowhere intervenes. It is rather the geometry of the problem which is involved. Expression (10.14) is at the base of the theory of isotopic separation by gaseous diffusion (§7.3.2).

10.2 STUDY OF CASCADES

10.2.1 Realization of a Cascade

Let us consider a set of diffusers (§7.3.2) or of centrifuges (§7.3.3) connected in series. Each stage is fed on the one hand by the "enriched outlet" of the preceding stage and on the other hand by the "depleted outlet" of the succeeding stage, as indicated in Fig. 10.3.

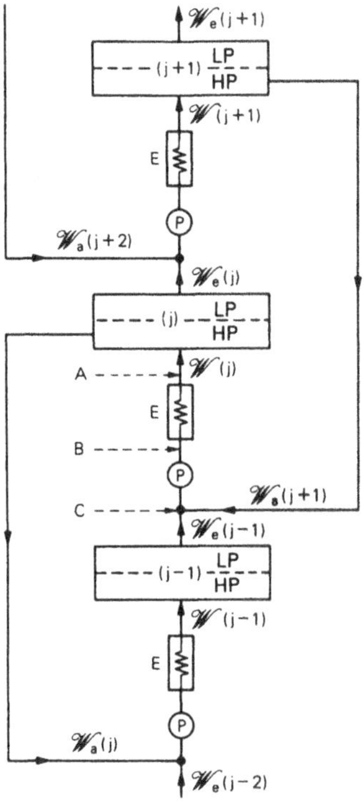

FIGURE 10.3.

In the case of gaseous diffusion, the pressure loss in the course of traversing each barrier (§10.1.4) must be compensated by a pressure increase at the inlet of each stage, which necessitates a compressor. Besides, since the compression is more or less adiabatic, the heating of the gas which results from it requires in its turn the presence of a heat exchanger. Let us consider, for example, the pressures p and temperatures T at points A,B,C (Fig. 10.3). We have:

$$p_A \cong p_B > p_C \quad \text{and} \quad T_A \cong T_C < T_B$$

so that all the stages are submitted to the same temperature and pressure conditions.

The preceding setup is known as a cascade. It is traversed by two currents: one, ascending, which gets progressively enriched, the other, descending, which gets depleted.

Cascade calculations are in general very complicated. Nevertheless they are greatly simplified if one insures that the gases that mingle at the inlet of each stage have the same composition, whence the condition (Fig. 10.3):

$$x_e\,(j-1) = x(j) = x_a(j+1) \tag{10.15}$$

in which the isotopic fractions have the same meaning as before (§7.3.2), while j is the serial number of the stage in the cascade (x grows with j).

If this condition is satisfied (and later we will see how) the recirculation flow rates are minimum. Thermodynamic considerations lead to the same result. Let us consider two gases of isotopic fractions x_1, x_2 and flow rates $\mathscr{W}_1, \mathscr{W}_2$ which mix to form a single gas characterized by x and $\mathscr{W}$. In a very general way, flow conservation leads to the equations:

$$\left.\begin{aligned} \mathscr{W} &= \mathscr{W}_1 + \mathscr{W}_2 \\ x\mathscr{W} &= x_1\mathscr{W}_1 + x_2\mathscr{W}_2 \end{aligned}\right\} \tag{10.16}$$

In addition, the entropy (per unit mass) of a gas consisting of two isotopes can be written [73] (p.352):

$$S(x) = A\,[x \ln x + (1-x)\ln(1-x)] + B \tag{10.17}$$

where A and B are two constants which only depend on the global properties of the gas. When the mixing indicated above takes place, the entropy variation (per unit time) is given by the expression:

$$\Delta S = \mathscr{W} S(x) - \mathscr{W}_1 S(x_1) - \mathscr{W}_2 S(x_2)$$

Taking account of (10.16), we may suppose that ΔS only depends on the initial characteristics x_1 and x_2. Differentiating ΔS with respect to x_1, we get:

$$\frac{\partial}{\partial x_1} \Delta S (x_1,x_2) = \mathscr{W} \frac{dS(x)}{dx} \frac{\partial x}{\partial x_1} - \mathscr{W}_1 \frac{dS(x_1)}{dx_1}$$

or, using equations (10.16) and (10.17):

$$\frac{\partial}{\partial x_1} \Delta S(x_1,x_2) = A\mathscr{W}_1 \left[\ln \left(\frac{x}{x_1} \right) - \ln \left(\frac{1-x}{1-x_1} \right) \right] \tag{10.18}$$

For every value of x_2, the preceding derivative vanishes if $x = x_1$, which also implies, because of (10.16) that $x = x_2$. We know that the most advantageous transformations from the energetic point of view are those which are accompanied by the least entropy variation (here, null variation); condition (10.15) is then justified and in this case the cascade is said to be ideal.

10.2.2 Number of Stages in an Ideal Cascade

Let us apply the fundamental equations (7.7) to a particular stage (j). Noting that the cascade is ideal (10.15), we get:

$$\left. \begin{aligned} x(j+1) - x(j) &= \frac{\mathscr{W}_a}{\mathscr{W}} (j) \varepsilon\, x(j) \, [1 - x(j)] \\ x(j) - x(j-1) &= \frac{\mathscr{W}_e}{\mathscr{W}} (j) \varepsilon\, x(j) \, [1 - x(j)] \end{aligned} \right\} \tag{10.19}$$

These expressions only involve homologous quantities, that is to say, the enrichments of the gas at the inlet of three successive stages: $j-1$, j, $j+1$. Adding up the lefthand and righthand sides of these equations, we eliminate the flow rates (7.6), which are still unknown at this stage, whence the fundamental relation:

$$x(j+1) - x(j-1) \cong \varepsilon\, x(j) \, [1 - x(j)] \tag{10.20}$$

Let $N(x)$ be the number of stages necessary for the isotopic fraction to go from a value x_0 to a distinctly different value x. Given the weak performances of a stage, this number will be large. The difference

$N[x(j+1)] - N[x(j-1)]$ represents exactly two stages (by definition of j). Since according to (10.20) the difference $[x(j+1) - x(j-1)]$ is of the order of ε, and thus very small (§7.3.2), a truncated expansion of N(x) around x(j) is justified. We thus get:

$$2 = N[x(j+1)] - N[x(j-1)] = [x(j+1) - x(j-1)]\,\dot{N}[x(j)] + O(\varepsilon^3)$$

where $\dot{N}(x)$ is the derivative of N(x). Disregarding the higher order terms and using (10.20), we obtain the differential equation:

$$\frac{dN}{dx} = \frac{2}{\varepsilon\, x(1-x)} \tag{10.21}$$

whence, after integration:

$$N(x) = \frac{2}{\varepsilon} \ln \left(\frac{x(1-x_0)}{x_0(1-x)} \right) \tag{10.22}$$

10.2.3 Evaluation of Flow Rates

It is now possible to determine the enrichment gain per stage. In effect, replacing x by $x(j+1)$ and x_0 by $x(j)$, expression (10.22) leads by the definition of j to $N(x) = 1$, and hence:

$$x(j+1)\,[1 - x(j)] = x(j)\,[1 - x(j+1)] \exp\left(\frac{\varepsilon}{2}\right)$$

whence, restricting ourselves to terms of the second order in ε:

$$x(j+1) - x(j) = \frac{\varepsilon}{2} x(j)\,[1 - x(j)]\,[1 + \frac{\varepsilon}{4}(1 - 2x(j))] \tag{10.23}$$

In the same way, playing with the indices j and j − 1, we obtain:

$$x(j) - x(j-1) = \frac{\varepsilon}{2} x(j)\,[1 - x(j)]\,[1 - \frac{\varepsilon}{4}(1 - 2x(j))] \tag{10.24}$$

The last two relations combined with the stage equations (10.19) lead to the partition of the flows:

$$\left.\begin{aligned} \frac{\mathscr{W}_a}{\mathscr{W}}(j) &= \frac{1}{2}\left[1 + \frac{\varepsilon}{4}(1 - 2x(j))\right] \\ \frac{\mathscr{W}_e}{\mathscr{W}}(j) &= \frac{1}{2}\left[1 - \frac{\varepsilon}{4}(1 - 2x(j))\right] \end{aligned}\right\} \tag{10.25}$$

As stated in subsec. 7.3.2, the flow admitted at each stage is approximately equally divided between the enriched and depleted outlets. All the same, the ideal cascade requires a flow rate $\mathscr{W}_e$ somewhat lower than $\mathscr{W}/2$ so long as x remains smaller than 50%, and in the opposite case, a little higher. Regulating flow rates is very delicate in practice; the barriers (or the centrifuges) having fixed characteristics, the simplest thing is to adjust the amount withdrawn $\mathscr{W}_a(j)$ by modifying the pressure drops in the recycling circuits (Fig. 10.3).

Until now we have based our argument on only one stage (or one pair of stages). Henceforth we will consider the cascade in its totality (Fig. 10.4), the stages being numbered: $j = 1,2,\ldots N$ and the feeding taking place at the level $j = f$.

Let us consider the subsystem which comprises all the enrichment stages whose serial number is higher than j, with $j \geq f$. This subsystem receives the flow $\mathscr{W}_e(j)$ and experiences two sorts of losses: the first corresponds to the enriched outlet of the last stage, of flow rate $\mathscr{W}_e(N) = \mathscr{W}_p$ (it is a matter of a gas having the desired isotopic fraction x_p), and the second to the depleted outlet of the stage $(j + 1)$ of flow rate $\mathscr{W}_a(j + 1)$ (cf. Fig. 10.3). These is no need here to consider other losses, for the withdrawn amounts $\mathscr{W}_a(j + 2)$, $\mathscr{W}_a(j + 3)$, etc. are re-injected downstream from the stage j under consideration. In these conditions the material balance of this subsystem can be written:

$$\left.\begin{aligned} &\mathscr{W}_e(j) = \mathscr{W}_a(j + 1) + \mathscr{W}_p \\ &x_e(j)\mathscr{W}_e(j) = x_a(j + 1)\mathscr{W}_a(j + 1) + x_p\mathscr{W}_p \end{aligned}\right\}$$

where, as always, the second relation characterizes the first component of the gaseous mixture ($U^{235}F_6$). Assuming that the cascade is ideal (10.15), the preceding equations lead to:

$$\mathscr{W}_e(j) = \frac{x_p - x(j)}{x(j + 1) - x(j)}\mathscr{W}_p$$

or using equation (10.23) and restricting ourselves to first order in ε:

$$\mathscr{W}_e(x) = \frac{2\mathscr{W}_p}{\varepsilon}\frac{x_p - x}{x(1 - x)} \quad \text{for } x \geq x(f) \qquad (10.26)$$

We should note that putting $j = N$ and $x = x(N)$, $\mathscr{W}_e(N)$ is effectively equal to the enriched flow rate $\mathscr{W}_p$ of the cascade, since $x_p = x(N + 1)$.

Taking up the same argument for the depletion stages $(j \leq f - 1)$, we are led to write:

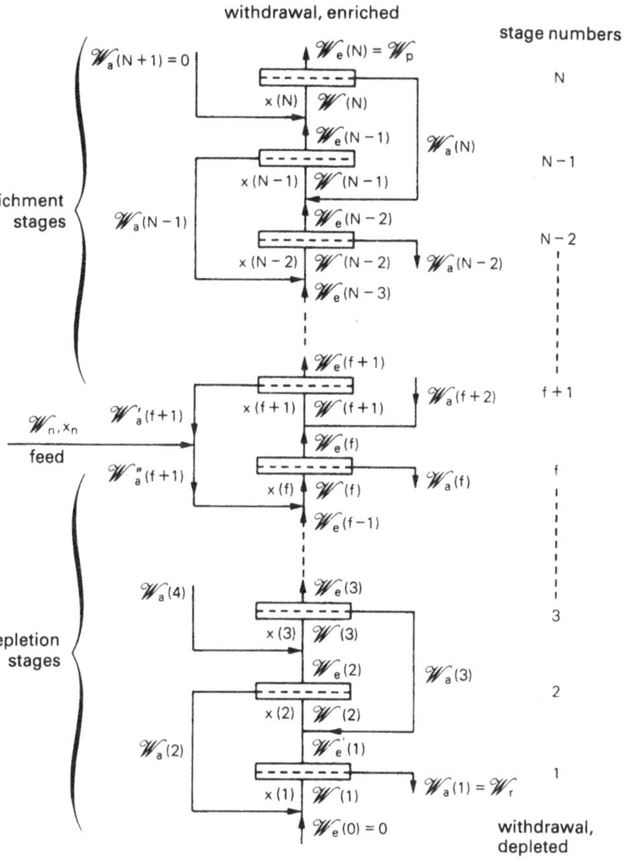

FIGURE 10.4. Flow diagram of an ideal cascade.

$$\mathscr{W}_a(j+1) = \mathscr{W}_e(j) + \mathscr{W}_r$$

$$x_a(j+1)\,\mathscr{W}_a(j+1) = x_e(j)\,\mathscr{W}_e(j) + x_r\mathscr{W}_r$$

where $\mathscr{W}_r$ represents the flow rate of the depleted outlet of the first stage, that is $\mathscr{W}_r = \mathscr{W}_a(1)$; thus it is a case of a byproduct of isotopic fraction x_r (r = reject). These equations lead to the solution:

$$\mathscr{W}_e(x) = \frac{2\mathscr{W}_r}{\varepsilon}\,\frac{x - x_r}{x(1-x)} \qquad \text{for } x \leqq x(f-1) \qquad (10.27)$$

For $x = x(1)$, we find that $\mathscr{W}_e(1) \cong \mathscr{W}_a(1) \cong \mathscr{W}_r$ since $x(0) = x_r$ (Fig.10.4).

Finally, at the general feed level, we must verify that:

$$\mathcal{W}_n = \mathcal{W}_a''(f + 1) - \mathcal{W}_a'(f + 1)$$

as clearly indicated in Fig. 10.4 ($x_n = x(f)$).

Flow conservation at the inlet of stage f and the hypothesis of a half-and-half sharing of the flows at each stage enable us to write the preceding relation in the form:

$$\mathcal{W}_n = 2\mathcal{W}_e(f) - \mathcal{W}_e(f + 1) - \mathcal{W}_e(f - 1)$$

Applying equation (10.26) to the first two terms and equation (10.27) to the last term and in addition expressing x(f + 1) and x(f − 1) as functions of x(f) with the help of relations (10.23) and (10.24), we get: $\mathcal{W}_n = \mathcal{W}_p + \mathcal{W}_r$ to first order in ε. This is the expected verification.

10.2.4 Separative Work

The preceding results enable us to introduce this notion in a much more natural fashion than we did in subsec. 7.3.4. To this end it suffices to calculate the mechanical energy required by the installation.

Let $\mathcal{W}(x)$ be the feed flow rate of a stage. In the case of gaseous diffusion the work of compression per stage can be written $\tau = \mathcal{W}(x)\Delta\mathcal{H}$ where the enthalpy variation $\Delta\mathcal{H}$ of the gas is independent of the stage being considered. In the case of centrifuging, the energy expenditure is of a different nature (weak compression). The power q of each centrifuge is fixed by its mechanical characteristics (various frictions). Thus the power expended in each stage is $\tau = n_c q$ where n_c represents the number of centrifuges operating in parallel. This number is equal to the total flow rate $\mathcal{W}(x)$ divided by the rated flow rate of a centrifuge i_c. We thus get back the same expression as for gaseous diffusion by putting $\Delta\mathcal{H} = q/i_c$; this "pseudo-enthalpy" is also independent of the stage being considered.

In order for the isotopic fraction of the gas to increase from x to x + dx, the number of necessary stages is dN and the corresponding power is:

$$dW = \tau\ dN = \Delta\mathcal{H}\ \mathcal{W}(x)dN = 2\Delta\mathcal{H}\ \mathcal{W}_e(x)\dot{N}(x)dx$$

where the functions $N(x)$ and $\mathscr{W}_e(x)$ have been calculated previously (cf. equations (10.21) (10.26) and (10.27)).

The total energy to be supplied at the enrichment stages can thus be written:

$$W_1 = 2\Delta\mathscr{H}\int_{x_n}^{x_p} \mathscr{W}_e(x)\dot{N}(x)dx = \Delta\mathscr{H}\frac{8\mathscr{W}_p}{\varepsilon^2}\int_{x_n}^{x_p} (x_p - x)\frac{dx}{x^2(1-x)^2}$$

and for the depletion stages (Fig. 10.4)

$$W_2 = 2\Delta\mathscr{H}\int_{x_r}^{x_n} \mathscr{W}_e(x)\dot{N}(x)dx = \Delta\mathscr{H}\frac{8\mathscr{W}_r}{\varepsilon^2}\int_{x_r}^{x_n} (x - x_r)\frac{dx}{x^2(1-x)^2}$$

We see the appearance in the preceding integrals of the second derivative of the isotopic potential $V(x)$ as it was defined in subsec. 7.3.4 (cf. equation (7.12)).

Introducing this "potential", the total energy to be spent takes the form:

$$W = W_1 + W_2 = \Delta\mathscr{H}\left\{\frac{8\mathscr{W}_p}{\varepsilon^2}\int_{x_n}^{x_p} (x_p - x)\frac{d^2V}{dx^2}dx + \frac{8\mathscr{W}_r}{\varepsilon^2}\int_{x_r}^{x_n} (x - x_r)\frac{d^2V}{dx^2}dx\right\}$$

or integrating by parts:

$$W = \frac{8\Delta\mathscr{H}}{\varepsilon^2}\left\{\mathscr{W}_p\,[-(x_p - x_n)\dot{V}(x_n) + V(x_p) - V(x_n)]\right.$$
$$\left. + \mathscr{W}_r\,[(x_n - x_r)\,\dot{V}\,(x_n) + V\,(x_r) - V\,(x_n)]\right\}$$

The flow conservation laws (7.15) show that the terms containing the derivatives $\dot{V}\,(x_n)$ disappear.

We finally obtain:

$$\left.\begin{aligned} W &= \frac{8\Delta\mathscr{H}}{\varepsilon^2}\,T_{sep} \\ T_{sep} &= \mathscr{W}_p V(x_p) + \mathscr{W}_r V(x_r) - \mathscr{W}_n V(x_n) \end{aligned}\right\} \qquad (10.28)$$

The energy which really must be spent is proportional to the separative work introduced in subsec. 7.3.4 starting from an expression of the potential $V(x)$ given by (7.13). This way of presenting things enables us to calculate in certain cases the cost of the separative work unit (S.W.U). This cost expressed in energy units is nothing but the coefficient of the first equation expressed in kWh/kg (§10.2.5); in contrast to the separative work it depends on the enrichment process proposed.

10.2.5 Numerical Applications

Let us consider the preparation of a kg of uranium ($\mathscr{W}_p = 1$) enriched at 3% ($x_p = 3\ 10^{-2}$), for a depleted uranium waste at 0.2% ($x_r = 2\ 10^{-3}$). As we have seen (§7.3.5), this requires that $\mathscr{W}_n = 5.38$ kg of natural uranium and leads to a depleted uranium waste $\mathscr{W}_r = 4.38$ kg. The parameter ε being $4.3\ 10^{-3}$ for gaseous diffusion and uranium hexafluoride, the number of enrichment stages can be easily calculated with the help of formula (10.22) by putting $x = x_p$ and $x_0 = x_n$:

$$N_1 = \frac{2}{\varepsilon} \ln \left[\frac{x_p(1 - x_n)}{x_n(1 - x_p)} \right] \cong 675$$

The number of depletion stages can be obtained in the same way:

$$N_2 = \frac{2}{\varepsilon} \ln \left[\frac{x_n(1 - x_r)}{x_r(1 - x_n)} \right] \cong 598$$

The total number of stages in series necessary to obtain uranium enriched at 3%, the depleted uranium waste being at 0.2%, is thus 1273. This already gives an idea of the size of a cascade.

We can also calculate the flow rate $\mathscr{W}(x)$ of the circulation in the cascade with the help of (10.26) and (10.27). It is at a maximum for $x = x_n$ and takes the value:

$$\mathscr{W}_M = 2\mathscr{W}_e(x_n) \cong \frac{4\mathscr{W}_p}{\varepsilon} \frac{x_p - x_n}{x_n(1 - x_n)} \cong 2967 \text{ kg!}$$

which shows the disproportion between the quantities of processed matter and the quantities which effectively traverse the inlet stage of the cascade. The flow rates and the number of stages are represented in Fig. 10.5 as functions of the isotopic fraction x attained in the stage being considered.

The above results are quite realistic. In any case, they explain the gigantic sizes of separation plants based on gaseous diffusion.

Let us now rapidly see what the preceding values give for centrifuging. The separation factor per stage is much better since $\varepsilon \cong 0.05$; we thus find that 109 stages and a maximum flow rate of 255 kg are necessary for producing 1 kg of uranium enriched at 3%. The quantities of natural uranium consumed ($\mathscr{W}_n'$), the extent of the waste ($\mathscr{W}_r'$) and the separative work (T_{sep}) are evidently the same in both cases (§7.3.5).

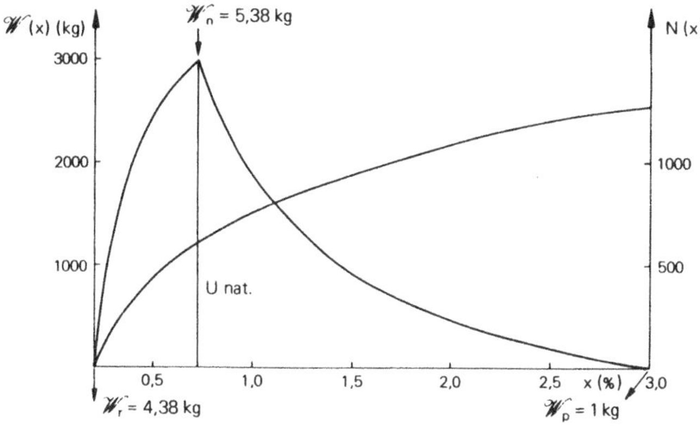

FIGURE 10.5. Flow rates and number of stages in an ideal cascade: $x_p = 3\%$, $x_r = 0.2\%$.

We will conclude this subsection with a theoretical calculation of the energy cost of isotopic separation by gaseous diffusion. In this case we can calculate the enthalpy jump $\Delta\mathscr{H}$ that a compressor gives to a gas. Let us assume that the compression is isentropic, which implies that $d\mathscr{H} = dp/\rho$ and the constancy of the product: $p\rho^{-\gamma}$, where γ is the ratio of specific heats [73](p.150). In these conditions $\Delta\mathscr{H}$ can be written:

$$\Delta\mathscr{H} = \int_0^{p_S} \frac{dp}{\rho} = \frac{p_S}{\rho_S}\frac{\gamma}{\gamma - 1} = \frac{RT}{M}\frac{\gamma}{\gamma - 1}$$

the pressure p_E of a compressor at the inlet being negligible compared to the pressure p_S at the outlet. We know that for a mono-atomic gas, γ is is equal to 5/3, and hence for uranium hexafluoride, whose molecules have several internal degrees of freedom, γ will be lower than this limiting value. Hence we deduce the inequality:

$$\Delta\mathscr{H} > \frac{5}{2}\,\frac{RT}{M}$$

in other words for a temperature of 60°C (T = 333°K and M = 0.352 kg)

$$\Delta\mathscr{H} > 2.10^4 \text{ J/kg}$$

Finally, expression (10.28) written for $T_{sep} = 1$ SWU and $\varepsilon = 4.3\ 10^{-3}$ leads to:

$$W > 2360 \text{ kWh}$$

which is a value very close to what one expected (§7.3.6) in spite of the uncertainty concerning the enthalpy variation. In the case of centrifuging, it is more difficult to calculate $\Delta\mathscr{H}$, but the fact that ε is ten times larger explains why the cost of the SWU is much lower (§7.3.6).

10.2.6 Choice of Depletion Rate

In economic studies, one generally takes $x_r = 0.2\%$ as the depletion rate and this is what we have done in the numerical examples of subsec. 7.3.5. In fact this value is not arbitrary, since it depends on the respective costs of natural uranium and of enrichment services. If uranium becomes more expensive, it is clear that it will be advantageous to diminish the isotopic fraction of depleted uranium, and if need be, to increase the separative work. A very simple calculation will enable us to determine the optimum depletion rate.

If C_n is the price of a kilogram of natural uranium and C_s that of a SWU (§7.3.5), then the cost of a kilogram of enriched uranium (at x_p) can be written:

$$C = \mathscr{W}_n C_n + T_{sep}\, C_s$$

or, using expressions (7.14) and (7.15) for $\mathscr{W}_p = 1$:

$$C = \frac{x_p - x_r}{x_n - x_r}\, C_n + [\ V(x_p) - V(x_n) + \frac{x_p - x_n}{x_n - x_r}\,(V(x_r) - V(x_n))\ ]C_s \qquad (10.29)$$

For a given enrichment x_p, the global cost of enriched uranium only depends on the isotopic fraction of the wastes. Differentiating the preceding expression with respect to x_r, we get the condition to be satisfied in order for the cost to be the minimum:

$$\frac{C_n}{C_s} = (x_r - x_n)\, \dot{V}(x_r) + V(x_n) - V(x_r) \qquad (10.30)$$

where the potential V(x) is defined by (7.13). We note that the results do not depend on the enrichment x_p. Figure 10.6 shows how the optimum isotopic fraction of depleted uranium varies as a function of the ratio C_n/C_s. Expression (10.30) shows that an isotopic fraction of 0.2% for the waste can be considered as optimum when $C_n/C_s \cong 1.2$, this value corresponding more or less to the market conditions in 1977. The fall of uranium prices observed since then would rather lead to $C_n/C_s \cong 0.73$ (§7.6.6) and hence to $x_r = 0.26\%$ (Fig. 10.6).

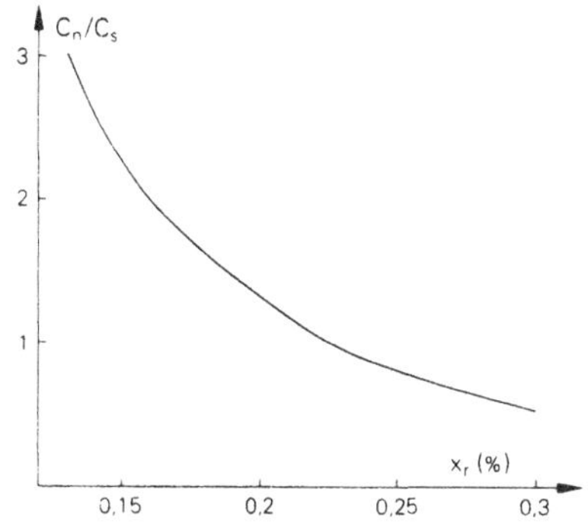

FIGURE 10.6.

BIBLIOGRAPHY

1. M. ALONSO, E.J. FINN, Fundamental University Physics, Vol. III Quantum and Statistical Physics (Addison-Wesley Publishing Company, Reading, Massachusetts, 1972), pp. 448-455.

2. D. L. BOOK, Revised and Enlarged Collection of Plasma Physics Formulas and Data (Naval Research Laboratory Memorandum Report 3322, 1977) p. 76.

3. T. KAMMASH, Fusion Reactor Physics (Principles and Technology) (Ann Arbor Science Publishers Inc., Ann Arbor, Michigan, 1977).

4. S. GLASSTONE, R. H. LOVBERG, Controlled Thermonuclear Reactors (Robert E. Krieger Publishing Company, Huntington, New York, 1975), pp. 33-36.

5. M. HUGUET, P. LALLIA, Confinement magnétique par Tokamak: les grandes réalisations en cours. Revue Générale Nucléaire, No. 6, November-December 1980, pp. 522-534.

6. G. H. CANAVAN, The Status of the US ICF Program. Proceedings of IAEA Technical Committee Meeting on Advances in Inertial Confinement Systems, Osaka, 29 Octobre 1979, pp. 128-140.

7. R. CARRUTHERS, P. A. DAVENPORT, J. T. D. MITCHELL, Culham Laboratory Report CLM-R85, 1967.

8. G. ARFKEN, Mathematical Methods for Physicists (Academic Press, New York, 1970).

9. J. BUSSAC, P. REUSS, Traité de Neutronique (Physique et calcul des réacteurs nucléaires) (Hermann, Paris, 1978).

10. E. HELLSTRAND, G. LUNDGREN, The Resonance Integral of Uranium Metal and Oxide, Nucl. Sci. Eng. 12, 435 (1962).

11. A. KOLMOGOROV, S. FOMINE, Eléments de la Théorie des Fonctions et de l'Analyse Fonctionnelle, Editions MIR, Moscow, 1974, pp. 212-242 (see also: [8] (pp. 425-449).

12. B. MILLS, Nuclear Applications 5, 1968, p. 211 (see also G. I. Bell [58] (p. 247) and note that the critical radii being inversely proportional to the densities, it is easy to modify the experimental value corresponding to 15.7 g cm^{-3} to adapt it to the example of §4.5.6).

13. H. C. HONECK, Specifications for an Evaluated Nuclear Data File for Reactor Applications, BNL-50066, ENDF/B, Brookhaven National Laboratory, 1972.

14. J. ADIR et al., User's and Programmer's Manual for the GGC3 Multigroup Cross Section Code, Part 1, GA-7157 (General Atomic, 1967).

B. J. TOPPEL et al., A Code to Calculate Multigroup Cross Sections, ANL-7318 (Argonne National Laboratory, 1967).

15. R. G. STEINKE, A Review of Direct and Iterative Strategies of Solving Multidimensional Finite Difference Problems, University of Michigan Nuclear Engineering Report, 1971.

D. L. DELP et al., "FLARE" A Three-Dimensional Boiling Water Reactor Simulator, GEAP-4598, General Electric Company Report, 1964.

16. R. BOITE, J. NEIRYNCK, Théorie des Réseaux de Kirchhoff (Ecole Polytechnique Federale de Lausanne, 1978), pp. 273-297.

17. J. WEISMAN, Elements of Nuclear Reactor Design (Elsevier Scientific Publishing Company, New York, 1977), p. 232.

18. L. S. TONG, Boiling Heat Transfer and Two-Phase Flow (John Wiley & Sons, Inc., New York, 1967).

19. M. BENEDICT, Nucl. Sci. Engl. 11, 377 (1961).

20. P. DOZINEL, Industrialisation des centrales à eau légère, Proceedings: Les Centrales Nucléaires et leur Sécurité (Association Suisse pour l'Energie Atomique, Geneva, 1976), p. 3.

21. W. PASKIEVICI, Le programme Nucléaire Canadien et les Réacteurs CANDU, IGN-457/459/460 (Inst. de Gén. Nucl., Ecole Polyt., Montreal, 1982).

22. Bulletins d'informations sur Superphénix N°1 à 5 (Société Novatome, Le Plessis Robinson, France, 1978-1980).

23. M. W. ROSENTHAL et al., The Development Status of Molten-Salt Breeder Reactors, ORNL-4812 (Oak Ridge National Laboratory, 1972).

24. J. C. MOUGNIOT et al., Gains de régénération des réacteurs rapides à combustible oxyde et à réfrigérant sodium, Conf. maturité de l'énergie nucléaire, D1 II N° 11, Paris, 1975 (see also: Nuclear News, May 1982, p. 43).

25. H. GOLDSTEIN, Fundamental Aspects of Reactor Shielding (Pergamon Press, New York, 1959), p. 17.

26. Normes fondamentales de radioprotection -- "Safety" Series of the International Atomic Energy Agency, N° 38, Vienna 1973.

27. Safe Handling of Radionuclides -- IAEA (see [26]).

28. G. G. EICHHOLZ, Environmental Aspects of Nuclear Power (Ann Arbor Science Publishers, Inc., Ann Arbor, Michigan, 1976).

29. H. R. DENTON, Statement on the Sources of Radioactive Material in Effluents for Light Water Cooled Nuclear Power Reactors and State of

Technology of Waste Treatment Equipment to Minimize Releases (U.S. Atomic Energy Commission, Washington, D.C., 1973).

30. Report on Releases of Radioactivity in Effluents and Solid Waste from Nuclear Power Plants for 1972 (U.S. Atomic Energy Commission, Washington, D.C., 1973).

31. O. HUBER, 23e Rapport de la Commission Fédérale Suisse de la Surveillance de la Radioactivité pour l'Année 1979.

32. E.E. LEWIS, Nuclear Power Reactor Safety (John Wiley & Sons, New York, 1977).

33. H. NOEL, H. FRESLON, G. LUCENET, Les Dispositions de Sûreté Relatives à la Centrale de Creys-Malville, B.I.S.T. Commissariat à l'Energie Atomique, N° 227, Jan.-Feb. 1978.

34. C.K. KEEPER, How Safe are Reactor Emergency Cooling Systems? Physics Today, August 1973.

35. Report of the President's Commission on the Accident at Three Mile Island, Washington, D.C., Oct. 1979.

36. Reactor Safety Study, U.S. Nuclear Regulatory Commission Report WASH-1400, Appendix VI, 1975.

37. Radiation Exposure of Uranium Mines, Hearings Joint Committee on Atomic Energy, 90th U.S. Congress, Washington, D.C., 1968.

38. J. SEVC, E. KUNZ, V. PLACEK, Lung Cancer in Uranium Mines and Long-term Exposure to Radon Daughter Products, Health Physics, 30, 433 (1976).

39. T. H. PIGFORD, Annual Rev. Nucl. Sc., 24515 (1974).

40. Report N° 4 of the Société Helvétique des Sciences Naturelles sur l'Energie Nucléaire: Le Cycle du Combustible des Réacteurs à Eau Légère, 1981.

41. Uranium: Resources, Production and Demand. Joint report of the Nuclear Energy Agency of the OECD and the IAEA, "Livre rouge," Paris, Feb. 1982.

42. "Le phénomène d'Oklo," IAEA Colloquium, Libreville (Gabon), June 1975.

43. R. BARJON, Physique des Réacteurs de Puissance, Inst. des Sci. Nucléaires, Grenoble, 1975, p. 501.

44. J. LAFUMA, Comportement Biologique du Plutonium et des Transplutoniens, Proceedings: Les Centrales Nucléaires et leur Sécurité, Association Suisse pour l'Energie Atomique, Geneva, 1976, p. 140.

45. E. D. CLAYTON, Anomalies of Criticality, Battelle Pacific North West Laboratories, 1976.

46. J.-P. BUCLIN, "Le problème de l'élimination des déchets radioactifs" Document Centrales Nucléaires of the Association Suisse pour l'Energie Atomique, 1977, p.45.

47. "Elimination des déchets radioactifs en Suisse", Société Coopérative Nationale pour l'Entreposage des Déchets Radioactifs (CEDRA), 1978.

48. "Perspectives de l'Energie Nucléaire dans les Pays de l'OCDE", Comité de direction de l'Energie Nucléaire de l'OCDE, April 1982 (private communication).

49. Untersuchung über die Kosten der Elektrizitätsversorgung Studie Nr 13, 1980, document prepared by the "Union des Centrales Suisses d'Electricité"(private communication).

50. A. M. WEINBERG, E. P. WIGNER, The Physical Theory of Neutron Chain Reactors (The University of Chicago Press, Chicago, 1958).

51. J. LIGOU, J. STEPANEK, P. A. THOMI, Forme Intégrale de l'Equation du Transport, Approximations Polynomiales et Diffusion Anisotrope, Proceedings: Numerical Reactor Calculations, IAEA, Jan. 1972, pp. 231-265.

52. J. R. ASKEW, Review of the Status of Collision Probability Methods, see [51], pp. 185-196.

53. G. PLACZEK, Phys. Rev. 69, 423 (1946) (see also: [50] p. 290).

54. L. W. NORDHEIM, G. F. KUNCIR, A Program of Research and Calculations of Resonance Absorption, G.A.-2527, General Atomic, 1961.

L. W. NORDHEIM, Nucl. Sci. Eng. 12, 457 (1962).

55. H. H. HUMMEL, ANL-7110, Argonne National Laboratory, 1965, p. 321.

56. J. M. BLATT, V. F. WEISSKOPF, Theoretical Nuclear Physics (John Wiley & Sons, New York, 1966), pp. 365-374.

57. C. H. WESTCOTT, Effective Cross Section Values for Well-Moderated Thermal Reactor Spectra, AECL-1101, Atomic Energy of Canada Lt, 1962.

58. A. J. GOODJOHN, G. C. POMRANING, Reactor Physics in the Resonance and Thermal Regions, Vol. I (M.I.T. Press, Cambridge, MA, 1966).

G. I. BELL, S. GLASSTONE, Nuclear Reactor Theory (Van Nostrand Reinhold Co., New York, 1970), pp. 315-362.

59. G. C. POMRANING, A Method of Solution for Particle Transport Problems, NASA Report GA-6497, 1965.

60. H. C. HONECK, "THERMOS" a Thermalization Transport Code for Reactor Lattice Calculations, BNL-5826, Brookhaven National Laboratory, 1961; see also Nucl. Sci. Eng. 8, 1960, p. 193.

61. R. D. RICHTMYER, K. W. MORTON, Difference Methods for Initial-Value Problems (John Wiley & Sons, New York, 1967), pp. 198-201.

62. D. M. DAVIERWALLA, C. MAEDER, F. SCHMIDT, Final Elements and Nodal Methods in Neutron Diffusion, from: Transport Theory and Advanced Reactor Calculations, Ch. V, IAEA-TECDOC-254, International Atomic Energy Agency, 1981, pp. 253-272.

63. W. W. ENGLE, Jr., A User's Manual for ANISN K-1693, Oak Ridge Gaseous Diffusion Plant, 1967.

64. H. A. BETHE, L. TONKS, H. HURWITZ, Phys. Rev. 80, 11 (1950) (see also: [50], pp. 370-371).

65. J. LIGOU, J. STEPANEK, Nucl. Sci. Eng. 53, 255-256 (1974).

66. G. BREIT, E. P. WIGNER, Phys. Rev. 49, 519 (1936) (see also: [50], pp. 39-54).

67. H. A. BETHE, G. PLACZEK, Phys. Rev. 51, 450 (1937).

J. J. DUDERSTADT, L. J. HAMILTON, Nuclear Reactor Analysis (John Wiley & Sons, New York, 1976), pp. 48-51.

68. L. DRESSNER, Resonance Absorption in Nuclear Reactors (Pergamon Press, New York, 1960), p. 100.

69. D. RANDALL, D. St. JOHN, Nucleonics 16, 82-87 (1958).

70. J. G. TYROR, R.I. VAUGHAN, An Introduction to the Neutron Kinetics of Nuclear Power Reactors (Pergamon Press, New York, 1970), 58-73.

71. L. LANDAU, E. LIFCHITZ, Physique Théorique, Tome VI: Méchanique des Fluides (Editions MIR, Moscow, 1971).

72. K. HUANG, Statistical Mechanics (John Wiley & Sons, New York, 1963), 95-103.

73. L. LANDAU, E. LIFCHITZ, Physique Théorique, Tome V: Physique Statistique (Editions MIR, Moscow, 1971).

ANALYTIC INDEX

With very few exceptions, the only technical terms cited here are those connected with nuclear engineering. Most of these are borrowed from the common language, but have taken on a specific meaning in this discipline which warrants consideration. The references are to the pages where the terms are defined.

For Product Safety Concerns and Information please contact our EU representative GPSR@taylorandfrancis.com Taylor & Francis Verlag GmbH, Kaufingerstraße 24, 80331 München, Germany

Printed and bound by CPI Group (UK) Ltd, Croydon, CR0 4YY
08/05/2025
01864500-0002